ENCYCLOPEDIA OF GLOBAL STUDIES

ENCYCLOPEDIA OF GLOBAL STUDIES

EDITORS

Helmut K. Anheier
Hertie School of Governance and University of Heidelberg

Mark Juergensmeyer
University of California, Santa Barbara

MANAGING EDITOR

Victor Faessel
University of California, Santa Barbara

⑤SAGE reference

Los Angeles | London | New Delhi
Singapore | Washington DC

Los Angeles | London | New Delhi
Singapore | Washington DC

FOR INFORMATION:

SAGE Publications, Inc.
2455 Teller Road
Thousand Oaks, California 91320
E-mail: order@sagepub.com

SAGE Publications Ltd.
1 Oliver's Yard
55 City Road
London EC1Y 1SP
United Kingdom

SAGE Publications India Pvt. Ltd.
B 1/I 1 Mohan Cooperative Industrial Area
Mathura Road, New Delhi 110 044
India

SAGE Publications Asia-Pacific Pte. Ltd.
3 Church Street
#10-04 Samsung Hub
Singapore 049483

Publisher: Rolf A. Janke
Acquisitions Editor: Jim Brace-Thompson
Editorial Assistant: Michele Thompson
Developmental Editor: Carole Maurer
Reference Systems Manager: Leticia Gutierrez
Reference Systems Coordinator: Laura Notton
Production Editor: Jane Haenel
Copy Editors: Colleen Brennan,
              Sheree Van Vreede
Typesetter: C&M Digitals (P) Ltd.
Proofreaders: Caryne Brown, Pam Suwinsky,
              Tracy Villano
Indexer: Virgil Diodato
Cover Designer: Gail Buschman
Marketing Manager: Kristi Ward

Printed in the United States of America.

Library of Congress Cataloging-in-Publication Data

Encyclopedia of global studies / editors, Helmut K. Anheier, Mark Juergensmeyer.

v. cm.
Includes bibliographical references and index.

ISBN 978-1-4129-6429-6 (cloth)

1. Globalization—Encyclopedias. 2. Globalization—Social aspects—Encyclopedias. I. Anheier, Helmut K., 1954–
II. Juergensmeyer, Mark.

JZ1318.E62 2012
303.48′203—dc23   2011045608

12 13 14 15 16 10 9 8 7 6 5 4 3 2 1

Contents

Volume 4

List of Entries

Reader's Guide

The Reader's Guide is provided to assist readers in locating articles on related topics. It classifies articles into 14 general topical categories: Global Civil Society; Global Communications, Transportation, Technology; Global Conflict and Security; Global Culture, Media; Global Demographic Change; Global Economic Issues; Global Environmental and Energy Issues; Global Governance and World Order; Global Health and Nutrition; Global Historical Antecedents; Global Justice and Legal Issues; Global Religions, Beliefs, Ideologies; Global Studies; Identities in Global Society. Entries may be listed under more than one topic.

Global Civil Society

Activism, Transnational
Amnesty International
Anti-Apartheid Movement
Antiglobalization Movements and Critics
Antislavery Movements
Associations
Charities, Charity
Civil Society, Global
Civility
Connectedness, Global
Elites
Foundations
Foundations, Asian: International Activities
Foundations, European: International Activities
Foundations, U.S.: International Activities
Gay and Lesbian Movement
Humanitarian Intervention
Humanitarianism
Humanity, Concepts of
Indigenous Peoples' Rights
International Nongovernment Organizations (INGOs)
International Nongovernment Organizations, Quasi-Forms
Open Society Institute
Opinion, World
Philanthropy
Publics and Polis, Global

Red Cross
Social Capital
Social Entrepreneurship
Social Movements
Social Networking
Solidarity Movements
State–Civil Society Relations
Uncivil Society
UN–Civil Society Relations
Waqfs
Women's Movement
World Economic Forum
World Social Forum

Global Communications, Transportation, Technology

Air Travel
Airlines
Civil Aviation
Communicative Power
Computing
Computing, Personal
Containerization
Cybernetics
Email
Global Communications and Technology
Handheld Devices
Information Age
International Air Transportation Association

Journalism
Knowledge Management Systems
Knowledge Production Systems
Leisure
Lifestyles
Literature
McDonaldization, McWorld
Maps and Map-Making
Memory
Memory Wars
Music
Myths
News
Nobel Prize
Olympic Movement
Postmodernity
Prizes and Awards, International
Scripts and Writing Systems
Sites, Global
Soccer
Sports, Recreation
Standards and Standard Setting, Global
Theater
Think Tanks
United Nations Educational, Scientific and
    Cultural Organization (UNESCO)
Universities and Higher Learning
Virtual Worlds
Wikipedia
Work
World Cultures
World's Fairs

Global Demographic Change

Acculturation
Aging Societies
Assimilation
Baby Boomers
Beirut
Cities
Communities, Transnational
Contraception
Demographic Change
Demographic Transition
Deterritorialization and Reterritorialization
Diasporas
Dubai
Family Policies
Family Systems, Kinship

Fertility
Hong Kong
Immigration
Immigration and Transnationalism
Intergenerational Relations
Johannesburg
Landless Persons
London
Los Angeles
Malthusian Idea
Migrant Shopping Patterns
Migration
Migration, Illegal
Migration Policies, Types of
Mortality
Mumbai
New York City
Overpopulation
Paris
Population and Demographic Change
Population Control Policies
Population Growth and Population Explosion
Retirement Systems
Rio de Janeiro
Rurality
Shanghai
Shelter and Housing
Singapore
68 Generation
Tokyo
Undocumented Persons
Urban Diseconomies
Urbanization

Global Economic Issues

Accounting Systems
Agriculture Sector
Asian Tiger Phenomenon
Banking, Offshore
Banks
Capitalism
Consumer Protest
Consumerism
Corporations, Transnational
Currencies
Data Systems and Reporting, Global
Dependency
Dependency Theory
Depression, Great

Global Environmental and Energy Issues

Greenhouse Gases
International Maritime Organization
Kyoto Protocol
Land Use
Natural Gas
Nature, Concepts of
Nuclear Power
Oceans
Oil
Organization of Petroleum Exporting
   Countries (OPEC)
Parks, Reserves, and Refuges
Petroleum Geopolitics
Polar Regions
Remediation
Sustainability
United Nations Environment Programme (UNEP)
Waste Management
Water

Global Governance and World Order

Accountability
Arab League
Association of Southeast Asian Nations (ASEAN)
Borders
Bretton Woods Agreements/System
Caliphate
Charismatic Leaders
Civilization
Colonialism
Democracy
Dynasties
Empires
Empires, Modern
European Union
Failed States
Global Governance and World Order
Global Order
Global South
Governance Networks, Transnational
Hegemonic Power
Hollow State
Independence Movements
International Relations
Leadership
League of Nations
Legitimacy
Methodological Nationalism
Nation-State

Neocolonialism
Non-Aligned Movement
North Atlantic Treaty Organization (NATO)
Organization of American States (OAS)
Pan African Union
Petroleum Geopolitics
Political Parties, Transnational
Power, Global Contexts of
Regional Governance
Regionalism
Republics
Social Democracy
Sovereignty
Subsidiarity
Summits, Summitry
Transparency
Treaty of Rome
United Nations
Utopia, Dystopia
Vatican
Welfare State
Westphalia, Treaty of, and the
   Post-Westphalian World
World Federalist Movement
World Government
World Order, Visions of

Global Health and Nutrition

Abortion
Birth Control
Burial and Crematory Practices
Diseases
Drugs and Pharmaceuticals
Food
Food and Agriculture Organization
   of the United Nations
Global Health and Nutrition
Health Care Access
Health Care Systems
HIV/AIDS
Hygiene
Infant Mortality
Malnutrition
Medical Systems
Public Health
Sexually Transmitted Diseases
Tuberculosis
Viruses, Killer
Viruses and Diseases, Emerging

World Food Program
World Health Organization

Global Historical Antecedents

Global Historical Antecedents
Global History, Studies in

Global Justice and Legal Issues

Animal Rights
Arbitration
Asylum
Citizenship
Civil Rights
Constitutionalism
Crime, Transnational
Dharma
Free Speech
Gay Rights
Global Justice and Legal Issues
Human Rights, International
Indigenous Peoples' Rights
Intellectual Property Rights
International Court of Justice
International Criminal Tribunals
Interpol
Justice, Transitional
Justice Movements, Transnational
Labor Rights
Law, International
Law, Regional
Law, Transnational
Law, World
Law of Arctic Regions
Law of the Sea
Legal Systems
Lex Mercatoria
Natural Law
Nuremburg Precedent
Penal Systems
Policing Systems
Prisoners' Rights
Shari'a (Islamic Law)
Truth Commission
Universal Jurisdiction
Women's Rights

Global Religions, Beliefs, Ideologies

African Diaspora Religions
African Religions
Baha'i
Battle of Badr
Buddhism
Capitalism
Christianity
Christianity-Related Movements
Communism, as International Movement
Communist International
Communitarianism
Confucianism
Cosmopolitanism
Crusades
Darwinism and Social Darwinism
Enlightenment, The
Ethics, Global
Fascism
Feminism
Freemasons
Global Religions, Beliefs, Ideologies
Hare Krishna (International
    Society for Krishna Consciousness)
Hinduism
Hindu-Related Movements
Humanism
Idealism
Ideologies, Global
Imperialism
Indigenous Religions, Globalization of
Individualism
Islam
Islam-Related Movements
Jainism
Judaism
Liberalism, Neoliberalism
Marxism and Neo-Marxism
Modernization
Mormonism
Myths
Nationalism, Neo-Nationalism
Neoconservatism
Populism
Postmodernism
Protestant Reformation

To the memory of S. N. Eisenstadt

About the Editors

Editors

Helmut K. Anheier (PhD, Yale University, 1986) is dean of the Hertie School of Governance in Berlin, Germany, and professor of sociology, Heidelberg University, where he also serves as academic director of the Center for Social Investment. He is a leading figure in the global study of civil society and a pioneer in developing the field of global studies. From 2001 to 2011, Dr. Anheier was professor of public policy and social welfare at the University of California, Los Angeles (UCLA), and, from 2001 to 2009, centennial professor at the London School of Economics and Political Science. He founded and directed the Centre for Civil Society at the London School of Economics (1998–2002), the UCLA Center for Civil Society (2001–2010), and the UCLA Center for Globalization and Policy Research (2004–2009). Prior to this, he was a senior research associate and project codirector at the Johns Hopkins University Institute for Policy Studies and associate professor of sociology at Rutgers University. Before embarking on an academic career, Dr. Anheier served as social affairs officer to the United Nations.

Dr. Anheier's work has focused on civil society, policy analysis, philanthropy, organizational studies, and comparative methodology. He is the author of over 350 publications, including over 30 authored and edited books. He is founding editor of two academic journals, *VOLUNTAS* and the *Journal of Civil Society*. He issued the *International Encyclopedia of Civil Society* (2010) and edited several monograph series. His articles have appeared in journals such as the *American Journal of Sociology, Social Forces, Annual Review of Sociology, Contemporary Sociology, Sociological Forum, British Journal of Sociology, International Sociology*, and *World Development*. Dr. Anheier has won several national and international awards, including the 2006 PNP Best Book Award of the American Academy of Management, as well as research prizes. He is currently researching the role of philanthropy internationally, issues of cultural policy, and methodological questions at the intersection of globalization, civil society, and culture. Dr. Anheier serves on the board of several scholarly and philanthropic organizations.

Mark Juergensmeyer is professor of sociology and global studies, affiliate professor of religious studies, and director of the Orfalea Center for Global and International Studies at the University of California, Santa Barbara. He is regarded as a pioneer in the study of global religion and one of the founders of the academic field of global studies. Since the 9/11 attacks, he has been a frequent commentator in the news media on topics of religion and politics in global affairs, including BBC, CNN, PBS, the *New York Times*, the *San Francisco Chronicle*, and the *Huffington Post*. Prior to his positions at Santa Barbara, he served as coordinator of the religious studies program at the University of California, Berkeley; director of the Office of Programs in Comparative Religion at the Graduate Theological Union; and founding dean of the School of Hawaiian, Asian, and Pacific Studies at the University of Hawai'i. He has been a visiting professor at Punjab University and Guru Nanak Dev University in India and is past president of the American Academy of Religion. He is the recipient of honorary doctorates from Lehigh University in Pennsylvania and Roskilde University in Denmark. He received the Grawemeyer Award for his book *Terror in the Mind of God: The Global Rise of Religious Violence*, which is based on interviews with activists around the world—including individuals convicted of the 1993 World Trade Center bombing, leaders of

Hamas, and abortion clinic bombers in the United States. It was listed by the *Washington Post* and *Los Angeles Times* as one of the best nonfiction books of the year. A previous book, *The New Cold War: Religious Nationalism Confronts the Secular State*, was listed by the *New York Times* as a notable book of the year. He is author or editor of 20 other volumes, including *Global Rebellion: Religious Challenges to the Secular State, Sikh Studies: Comparative Perspectives on a Changing Tradition, Gandhi's Way: A Handbook of Conflict Resolution, The Oxford Handbook of Global Religion, Global Religion: An Introduction, Rethinking Secularism,* and *Religion in Global Civil Society*. He has also coedited the *Encyclopedia of Global Religion,* also published by SAGE.

Managing Editor

Victor Faessel is program director of the Orfalea Center for Global and International Studies at the University of California, Santa Barbara. He has worked as a senior editor for several online and print publications, as an assistant editor of English-language publications for the Center for Interdisciplinary Study of Monotheistic Religions (CISMOR) at Doshisha University (Kyoto, Japan), and as a managing editor of the online global studies journal *global-e*. Dr. Faessel studied at universities in Chicago and Vienna, Austria, before completing a PhD in mythological studies at Pacifica Graduate Institute, and he continues to pursue his interest in the contemporary global setting of myth at the (and as the) intersection of imagination, ideology, and cultural memory.

Contributors

Jan-Frederik Abbeloos
Ghent University

Donald E. Abelson
University of Western Ontario

David Abernathy
Warren Wilson College

Francis Adams
Old Dominion University

Randall Adams
Alice Lloyd College

Afe Adogame
University of Edinburgh

John Agnew
University of California, Los Angeles

Dieter Ahlert
Westfaelische Wilhelms-University

Habib Ahmed
Durham University

Tjitske Akkerman
Universiteit van Amsterdam

Martin Albrow
*London School of Economics and Political
   Science*

Matthew Allen
Curtin University of Technology

Ricky Lee Allen
University of New Mexico

Ahmed H. al-Rahim
University of Virginia

Paul Amar
University of California, Santa Barbara

David Anderson
*International Tribunal for the Law of the Sea,
   Germany*

David M. Andrews
Scripps College

Helmut K. Anheier
*Hertie School of Governance and University of
   Heidelberg*

Robert J. Antonio
University of Kansas

Richard Appelbaum
University of California, Santa Barbara

Daniel Araya
*University of Illinois at
   Urbana-Champaign*

Clive Archer
Manchester Metropolitan University

Matthew Arentz
University of Washington

Deborah Avant
University of California, Irvine

Salvatore J. Babones
University of Sydney

Holger Backhaus-Maul
*Martin-Luther-University
   Halle-Wittenberg*

Vida Bajc
Queen's University

John M. T. Balmer
Brunel University London

Steven Barrie-Anthony
University of California, Santa Barbara

Gad Barzilai
University of Washington

Paul Arthur Battersby
*Royal Melbourne Institute of Technology
(RMIT) University*

Bernhard H. Bayerlein
University of Mannheim

Bart Beaty
University of Calgary

Martin Beck
Konrad Adenauer Stiftung

Betsi Beem
University of Sydney

Ebru Bekaslan
University of Massachusetts

Roland Benedikter
*University of California, Santa Barbara, and
Stanford University*

Lehn M. Benjamin
George Mason University

Neil G. Bennett
City University of New York

Janet Benshoof
Global Justice Center

Yael Berda
Princeton University

Peter Berglez
Örebro University

Nitza Berkovitch
Ben Gurion University

Ivan Bernier
Laval University, Quebéc City

John W. Berry
Queen's University

Rajeev Bhargava
*Centre for the Study of Developing
Societies, Delhi*

Amita Bhide
Tata Institute of Social Sciences

Katarzyna Bieszke
University of Gdansk

Volodymyr Bilotkach
University of California, Irvine

Cyrus Bina
University of Minnesota, Morris Campus

John P. Blair
Wright State University

Robin Bloch
University of Wolverhampton

David E. Bloom
Harvard School of Public Health

Ingrid Boas
Institute for Environmental Studies

Tom Boellstorff
University of California, Irvine

Alessandro Bonanno
Sam Houston State University

József Böröcz
Rutgers, State University of New Jersey

Saturnino M. Borras Jr.
International Institute of Social Studies (ISS)

Elizabeth R. Boskey
State University of New York

Daniella E. Bove-LaMonica
Truman National Security Project

Hans Günter Brauch
Free University of Berlin

John Breen
*International Research Center for Japanese
Studies (Nichibunken)*

Jonathan R. Brestoff
University of Pennsylvania

Susan Brownell
University of Missouri, St. Louis

M. Lane Bruner
Georgia State University

William I. Brustein
University of Illinois at Urbana-Champaign

Alison Brysk
University of California, Santa Barbara

Nicola Bullard
Focus on the Global South

Colin D. Butler
Australian National University

Thomas J. Butler
Cary Institute of Ecosystem Studies

Luis Cabrera
University of Birmingham

Craig Calhoun
London School of Economics

Gralf-Peter Calliess
University of Bremen

Robert M. Campbell
Mount Allison University

Marita Carballo
Kantar Group

Curtis L. Carter
Marquette University

Thorkil Casse
Roskilde University

Danielle Celermajer
University of Sydney

Miguel Centeno
Princeton University

Kin-man Chan
Chinese University of Hong Kong

Nayan Chanda
Yale Center for the Study of Globalization

Christopher Chase-Dunn
University of California, Riverside

Jamsheed K. Choksy
Indiana University

Jonathan Chow
University of California, Berkeley

Karen K. Clark
Western Oregon University

Elaine Coburn
American University of Paris and Ecole des Hautes Etudes en Sciences Sociales, Paris

William Coleman
Balsillie School of International Affairs

Philip Cooke
Cardiff University

Timothy J. Cooley
University of California, Santa Barbara

Scarlett Cornelissen
University of Stellenbosch

Sarah E. Cornell
University of Bristol

Marie Cornwall
Brigham Young University

Thomas Olaf Corry
University of Cambridge

Robert Costanza
Portland State University

Michael Cottrell
University of Saskatchewan

Sheleyah A. Courtney
University of Sydney

Anne Cova
Institute of Social Sciences, University of Lisbon

Beverly Crawford
University of California, Berkeley

Paul R. Croll
Augustana College

Stuart Cunningham
Queensland University of Technology

Sara R. Curran
University of Washington, Seattle

Michael Curtin
University of California, Santa Barbara

Catherine Dauvergne
University of British Columbia Faculty of Law

Gareth Davey
Hong Kong Shue Yan University

James Dawes
Macalester College

Martin Dawidowicz
United Nations

Bastiaan de Gaay Fortman
Utrecht University

Jason Dedrick
University of California, Irvine

Mathieu Deflem
University of South Carolina

Donatella della Porta
European University Institute

Katrina Demulling
Boston University

Jane C. Desmond
University of Illinois at Urbana-Champaign

Alan Detheridge
Thunderbird School of Global Management

Pradeep Ajit Dhillon
University of Illinois at Urbana-Champaign

Mario Diani
University of Trento

Ibrahim Dincer
University of Ontario

Laurent Dubois
Duke University

Hai Van Duong Dinh
Westfälische Wilhelms-University Münster

Torben Bech Dyrberg
Roskilde University

Adam C. Earnheardt
Youngstown State University

S. N. Eisenstadt
Van Leer Jerusalem Institute

Caleb Elfenbein
New York University Gallatin School

Rose Elfman
University of California, Santa Barbara

Hilal Elver
University of California, Santa Barbara

Henrik Enderlein
Hertie School of Governance

Thomas R. Engel
University of Bayreuth

Ulf Engel
University of Leipzig and Stellenbosch University

Dieter Ernst
East-West Center, Honolulu

Leobardo F. Estrada
University of California, Los Angeles

Amitai Etzioni
Institute for Communitarian Policy Studies

Victor Faessel
University of California, Santa Barbara

Richard Falk
University of California, Santa Barbara

Martin F. Farrell
Ripon College

James Farrera
Sophia University

Mark Featherstone
Keele University

Richard Feinberg
University of California, San Diego

Patricia Fernández-Kelly
Princeton University

Steve Ferzacca
University of Lethbridge

Lorenzo Fioramonti
Centre for Social Investment

Johan Fischer
Roskilde University

Mark Fliegauf
University of Cambridge

Peter Flügel
School of Oriental and African Studies, University of London

John Foran
University of California, Santa Barbara

Jennifer C. Franco
Transnational Institute

Bruno S. Frey
University of Zurich

Brian Frizzelle
University of North Carolina, Chapel Hill

Marc D. Froese
Canadian University College

Haruhiro Fukui
University of California, Santa Barbara

Elaine Fulton
University of Birmingham

Alan Gamlen
University of Oxford

Adèle Garnier
Universität Leipzig/Macquarie University

Catherine Gautier
University of California, Santa Barbara

Olya Gayazova
DePauw University

Katherina Gehrmann
Westfaelische Wilhelms-University

Gilbert Geis
University of California, Irvine

Alexander C. T. Geppert
Freie Universität Berlin

Karin Geuijen
Utrecht University

Shannon Gibson
University of Miami

Fiona Gill
University of Sydney

Angus Kress Gillespie
Rutgers University

James Giordano
University of Oxford

Dru C. Gladney
Pomona College

Marlies Glasius
University of Amsterdam

Georg Glasze
University of Erlangen-Nuremberg

Andrew R. Goetz
University of Denver

James Goldgeier
George Washington University

Bernard K. Gordon
University of New Hampshire

John L. Graham
University of California, Irvine

Matthew Green
College of DuPage

Liah Greenfeld
Institute for the Advancement of Social Sciences

Anni Greve
Roskilde University

Bent Greve
Roskilde University

Thomas Greven
Freie Universität Berlin

Mohinder S. Grewal
Institute of Electrical and Electronics Engineers

Giles Gunn
University of California, Santa Barbara

Dina Hadad
University of Birmingham

Aviva Halamish
Open University of Israel

David Halle
University of California, Los Angeles

David C. Hammack
Case Western Reserve University

Michael Hammer
One World Trust

István Hargittai
Budapest University of Technology and Economics

Faye V. Harrison
University of Florida

Jonas Peter Hartelius
EastWest Institute

Tsuyoshi Hasegawa
University of California, Santa Barbara

Akiko Hashimoto
University of Pittsburgh

Robert Hassan
University of Melbourne

John Haworth
Manchester Metropolitan University

Jeffrey Haynes
London Metropolitan University

Tracey Heatherington
University of Wisconsin, Milwaukee

Alexandre Babak Hedjazi
University of Geneva

Ludger Helms
University of Innsbruck

Mark Herkenrath
University of Zurich

John Hickman
Berry College

Herkko Hietanen
Helsinki Institute for Information Technology

Matthew Hilton
University of Birmingham

Dilip Hiro
Independent Scholar

Michael Hoelscher
University of Heidelberg

Kirsten L. Hokeness
Bryant University

Steven A. Hokeness
WellOne Medical Center

Siobhan Holohan
Keele University

Martin Hölz
Heidelberg University

Natasha Howard
University of New Mexico

Yu-ling Huang
State University of New York, Binghamton

Andrew Hurrell
Oxford University

Johan Hvenmark
Ersta Sköndal University College

Joy Hylton
Chapman/Brandman University

Ramona Cristina Ilea
Pacific University

Michael D. Intriligator
University of California, Los Angeles

Yudhishthir Raj Isar
American University of Paris

William A. Jackson
University of York

Estelle James
State University of New York, Stony Brook

Paul James
Royal Melbourne Institute of Technology (RMIT) University

Marie-Louise Janssen
University of Amsterdam

Mark M. Jarzombek
Massachusetts Institute of Technology

Bruno Jetin
Université Paris Nord

David T. Johnson
University of Hawaii at Manoa

David Martin Jones
University of Queensland

Erik Jones
Johns Hopkins University

Mark Juergensmeyer
University of California, Santa Barbara

Tobias Jung
UK Research Centre on Charitable Giving and Philanthropy

Howard Kainz
Marquette University

Mary Kaldor
London School of Economics

Sebnem Kalemli-Ozcan
University of Houston

Stephanie C. Kane
Indiana University, Bloomington

Athina Karatzogianni
University of Hull

Lamia Karim
University of Oregon

Inge Kaul
Hertie School of Governance

Hiroko Kawanami
Lancaster University

Roger Keil
York University

Christopher C. Kissling
Lincoln University

Peter J. Kivisto
Augustana College

Hans Köchler
University of Innsbruck

Edward A. Kolodziej
University of Illinois at Urbana-Champaign

Markus Kotzur
University of Leipzig

Kenneth L. Kraemer
University of California, Irvine

Sebastian Kubitschko
Goldsmiths, University of London

Robert Thomas Kudrle
University of Minnesota

Jenny Kuhlmann
University of Leipzig

Ashwani Kumar
Tata Institute of Social Sciences

Martin Kunze
Martin-Luther-University Halle-Wittenberg

Ferhan Kuyucak
Anadolu University

Edmund Siu-Tong Kwok
BNU-HKBU United International College

Anael Labigne
Berlin Graduate School for Transnational Studies

Jackie Larm
University of Edinburgh

Henry Laurence
Bowdoin College

Pasi Lautala
Michigan Technological University

William Lazonick
University of Massachusetts

Pierrick Le Goff
Allstom

Diana Leat
CASS Business School London

Kelley Lee
London School of Hygiene and Tropical Medicine

Nikki J. Y. Lee
Yonsei University

Bronwyn Leebaw
University of California, Riverside

Peter T. Leeson
George Mason University

Walter Leimgruber
University of Fribourg

Athena S. Leoussi
University of Reading

Philipp Lepenies
KfW Development Bank

Robert Lepenies
Hertie School of Governance, Berlin Graduate School for Transnational Studies

Daniel Levy
Stony Brook University

Emanuel Levy
Independent Film Critic

Jonathan Lewis
Hitotsubashi University

Gene E. Likens
Cary Institute of Ecosystem Studies

Jie-Hyun Lim
Hanyang University

Benjamin Linkow
Miami University

Björn-Ola Linnér
Linköping University

Regina A. List
Hertie School of Governance

Robert Lloyd
One World Trust

Antony Loewenstein
Freelance Journalist

Maria Lorca-Susino
University of Miami

Thomas E. Lovejoy
The Heinz Center

Eriberto Lozada
Davidson College

Cecelia Lynch
University of California, Irvine

Malcolm MacLachlan
Trinity College Dublin

André Magnan
University of Regina

John Mandalios
Griffith University

Peter Mandaville
George Mason University

Hasheem Mannan
Centre for Global Health

Henrik Secher Marcussen
Roskilde University

Katherine Marshall
Georgetown University

Joseph Masciulli
St. Thomas University

Gordon Mathews
Chinese University of Hong Kong

Michel Mathien
University of Strasbourg

Robert J. McCalla
Saint Mary's University

John A. McCarthy
Vanderbilt University

Linda McCarthy
University of Wisconsin, Milwaukee

Marie C. McCormick
Harvard School of Public Health

Mary E. McCoy
University of Wisconsin, Madison

Pamela McElwee
Arizona State University

Myles McGregor-Lowndes
Queensland University of Technology

Doris McIlwain
Macquarie University

Dan L. McNally
Bryant University

Anne McNevin
*Royal Melbourne Institute of Technology
   (RMIT) University*

Frédéric Mérand
University of Montreal

Erica Mesker
University of California, Santa Barbara

Matthias Middell
University of Leipzig

Eric Mielants
Fairfield University

Walter Mignolo
Duke University

John Mikler
University of Sydney

Toby Miller
University of California, Riverside

Melinda Mills
University of Groningen

H. Brinton Milward
University of Arizona

Manoranjan Mohanty
Council for Social Development, New Delhi

Mikhail A. Molchanov
St. Thomas University

Bjørn Møller
Danish Institute for International Studies

Leila Monaghan
University of Wyoming

Christine Monnier
College of DuPage

Patrick M. Morgan
University of California, Irvine

Klaus Müller-Hohenstein
University of Bayreuth

D. E. Mungello
Baylor University

Stephen Murphy-Shigematsu
Stanford University

Vasudha Narayanan
University of Florida

Joseph Natoli
Michigan State University

Susanne Neckermann
University of Zurich

Jan Nederveen Pieterse
University of California, Santa Barbara

Helen E. S. Nesadurai
Monash University, Malaysia

Alex Nicholls
University of Oxford

Mark Nuttall
University of Alberta

Thomas Oatley
University of North Carolina, Chapel Hill

Holly Oberle
Freie Universität Berlin

Julia O'Connell Davidson
University of Nottingham

Thomas Olesen
Aarhus University

Andreas Önnerfors
Leiden University

Stephen P. Osborne
University of Edinburgh

J. S. Oxford
Barts and the London School of Medicine and Dentistry

Anssi Paasi
University of Oulu

John S. W. Park
University of California, Santa Barbara

Joseph Sung-Yul Park
National University of Singapore

Saadia M. Pekkanen
University of Washington, Seattle

Samuel Peleg
Netanya College and Inter-Disciplinary Center (IDC) Herzliya

Michael A. Peters
University of Illinois

Lynne Phillips
University of Windsor

Peter Phipps
Royal Melbourne Institute of Technology (RMIT) University

Brent L. Pickett
University of Wyoming

Geoffrey Allen Pigman
Bennington College

Detlef Pollack
Westfälische Wilhelms-Universität Münster

Susanne Popp
Augsburg University

Jason Potts
ARC Centre of Excellence for Creative Industries and Innovation

José A. Prades
Université du Québecà Montréal

Vikramāditya Prakāsh
University of Washington

Christopher Priestman
Staffordshire University

Luca Prono
Independent Scholar

Stephen D. Reese
University of Texas

Wolfgang Reinhard
University of Erfurt

Ruth Reitan
University of Miami

Emiliano Reyes
Independent Scholar

James F. Reynolds
Duke University

Lisa Ann Richey
Roskilde University

Sasho Ripiloski
Royal Melbourne Institute of Technology (RMIT) University

Isaias R. Rivera
Tecnologico de Monterrey (ITESM)

Roland Robertson
University of Aberdeen

Laura Robinson
Santa Clara University

Tom Rockmore
Duquesne University

Andrea Römmele
Hertie School of Governance

Marc A. Rosen
University of Ontario

Jörg Rössel
University of Zurich

Dietmar Rothermund
Heidelberg University

Bo Rothstein
University of Gothenburg

Victor Roudometof
University of Cyprus

Ravi K. Roy
California State University, Northridge

Beth A. Rubin
University of North Carolina, Charlotte

Galya Benarieh Ruffer
Northwestern University

Leila J. Rupp
University of California, Santa Barbara

Melissa A. Rury
U.S. Environmental Protection Agency

Michael Ruse
Florida State University

Jörn Rüsen
Kulturwissenschaftliches Institut

Alexander Ruser
University of Heidelberg

Dominic Sachsenmaier
Jacobs University, Bremen

Abdullah Saeed
University of Melbourne

Amandeep Sandhu
Temple University

Bhaskar Sarkar
University of California, Santa Barbara

Mahua Sarkar
State University of New York, Binghamton

Saskia Sassen
Columbia University

Joachim J. Savelsberg
University of Minnesota

Stephen W. Sawyer
American University of Paris

Stephanie Schacht
Princeton University

Jens Schröder-Hinrichs
World Maritime University

Andreas Schröer
Portland State University

Hagen Schulz-Forberg
Aarhus University

James Schwoch
Northwestern University

Hakan Seckinelgin
London School of Economics

Philip Seib
University of Southern California

Rebecca Sheff
Macalester College

Mona Kanwal Sheikh
University of Copenhagen

Susumu Shimazono
University of Tokyo

Megan Shore
King's University College

Meenal Shrivastava
Athabasca University

Merril Silverstein
University of Southern California

Lívia Mathias Simão
University of São Paulo

Ian Simmons
University of Durham

Pashaura Singh
University of California, Riverside

Joseph M. Siracusa
Royal Melbourne Institute of Technology (RMIT) University

David H. Slater
Sophia University, Tokyo

Peter Smith
Mahidol University

Tomasz Snarski
University of Gdansk

Rodrigo R. Soares
Pontifical Catholic University of Rio de Janeiro

S. Wojciech Sokolowski
Johns Hopkins University

Hugh Somerville
University of Surrey

Norman Spengler
University of Heidelberg

Graham Spinardi
University of Edinburgh

Amy E. Stambach
University of Wisconsin, Madison

Peter N. Stearns
George Mason University

Manfred B. Steger
Royal Melbourne Institute of Technology (RMIT) University

Matthew Stephen
Social Science Research Center, Berlin

Michael Strange
Malmö University

Christoph Stückelberger
University of Basel

Erin B. Taylor
University of Sydney

Ruti Teitel
New York Law School

Teivo Teivainen
University of Helsinki

Nuno S. Themudo
University of Pittsburgh

Steve Thomas
Trinity College Dublin

Håkan Thörn
Gothenburg University

Bassam Tibi
University of Goettingen

John Tiffin
Victoria University of Wellington

Madina Tlostanova
Peoples' Friendship University of Russia

Stefan Toepler
George Mason University

Marcella Bush Trevino
Barry University

Alli Mari Tripp
University of Wisconsin, Madison

Michael Louis Troilo
University of Tulsa

Belgi Turan
University of Houston

Annette Van den Bosch
Monash Asia Institute

Jan Van den Broeck
University of Bergen

Martha C. E. Van Der Bly
London School of Economics and Political Science

Bijan Vasigh
Embry-Riddle

Manuel A. Vásquez
University of Florida

Jean-Baptiste Velut
Sorbonne Nouvelle University of Paris

Anthony J. Venables
University of Oxford

Dacia Viejo Rose
University of Cambridge

Vincent Virga
Independent Scholar

Hendrik Vollmer
University of Bielefeld

Ernst Ulrich von Weizsäcker
*International Panel for Sustainable
　Resource Management*

James Raymond Vreeland
Georgetown University

Robert H. Wade
London School of Economics

Ole Wæver
University of Copenhagen

Roger Waldinger
University of California, Los Angeles

Judd Walson
University of Washington

Veda E. Ward
*California State University,
　Northridge*

Patrick Webb
Tufts University

Tony Weis
University of Western Ontario

Tracy A. Weitz
University of California, San Francisco

Christopher Joseph Westgate
Texas A&M

Richard Widick
University of California, Santa Barbara

Antje Wiener
University of Hamburg

Filip Wijkström
Stockholm School of Economics

Colin C. Williams
University of Sheffield

Erin K. Wilson
*Royal Melbourne Institute of Technology
　(RMIT) University*

Bronwyn Winter
University of Sydney

Scott Wisor
Australian National University

Ron Witt
United Nations Environment Programme (UNEP)

Wendy H. Wong
University of Toronto

Michael Woods
Aberystwyth University

Sirpa Wrede
University of Helsinki

Xiaoqing Eleanor Xu
Seton Hall University

Yunxiang Yan
University of California, Los Angeles

Na Yin
*City University of New York Institute for
　Demographic Research*

Alexandra Young
University of Sydney

Yelena Nikolayevna Zabortseva
University of Sydney

Malgorzata Zachara
Jagiellonian University

Eleanor Zelliot
Carleton College

Jürgen Zimmerer
University of Sheffield

Michael Zürn
Wissenschaftszentrum Berlin

Gentian Zyberi
Utrecht University

Introduction

The *Encyclopedia of Global Studies* has been created to be the standard reference work for the emerging field of global studies. It covers the entire range of transnational topics and the diverse intellectual approaches that have been marshaled by scholars in order to analyze all aspects of the global and globalizing world—including the globalization of economies, societies, cultures and polities; the diasporas of ethnicities and religious groups and the dispersions and migrations of peoples; the transnational aspects of social and political change; the global impact of environmental, technological, and health changes; and the organizations and issues related to global civil society.

This publication is the first encyclopedia of and for global studies and, indeed, the first attempt to map this emerging field in its entirety. Its objective is to take stock of the concepts, approaches, theories, and methodologies that make up global studies. It also tries to cover the entire scope of events, activities, ideas, processes, and flows that are transnational or that could affect most regions of the Earth. Although scholars have analyzed these phenomena for many decades, as an academic field, global studies blossomed largely after the turn of the 21st century. It has expanded rapidly since the first programs in global studies were founded in Asian, European, and American universities in the 1990s. Since then, new undergraduate and graduate degree programs and new centers of research have been created every year.

What, then, is this field called "global studies"? Some scholars argue that it is unique, that the phenomena are new, and that therefore new scholarly approaches must be created that are distinctly appropriate to studying transnational subject matter. But most scholars accept the notion that, although the current age is more global than ever before, transnational and global phenomena have always been a feature of the world's physical, social, and cultural life. For this reason, they analyze transnational phenomena utilizing established approaches in the social sciences and humanities. In that sense, the field of global studies is interdisciplinary. It includes the work of disparate scholars over the decades who have attempted to understand the interconnected relationships among societies, polities, economies, and cultural systems on a global scale. The results of their inquiries are found in this encyclopedia. Most of the entries herein are by topic—global religion, economic development, pandemics, or the Internet, for instance. Some focus on analytic approaches to global studies, and a few spotlight significant ideas such as Marxism, capitalism, and world-systems theory. Others address events such as September 11, 2001, or the Nuremberg trials, places like London or Tokyo, or organizations like the United Nations or the North Atlantic Treaty Organization. All these entry titles are grouped under broad headings, a dozen or so areas that define the field of global studies. This listing of entry titles by topic area can be found in the Reader's Guide, located immediately after the alphabetic listing of entries in the front matter.

How were these major headings determined? In the initial planning stages for this project, a series of workshops with scholars was held in London, Tokyo, and Santa Barbara, California, to help frame the central themes that are shaping the field of global studies. The editors established an editorial board of some of the world's most significant scholars in the field and formed an advisory committee representing most of the leading academic centers of global studies in the world. Members of the editorial board and advisory committee helped suggest both topics and appropriate authors and played an important role in crafting the encyclopedia.

These workshops and advisory committees established the following major areas covered by the entries in this *Encyclopedia of Global Studies*. These areas are diverse—from the more obvious aspects of globalization, such as economic and demographic transformations, to the more subtle cultural and ideological aspects—but they are also interrelated. Thus, entries under one heading could also be listed under others. The major areas we identified cover problematic aspects of global change, such as environmental and health issues and transnational inequalities, but they also include the movements and organizations that have been mobilized to confront and mitigate these problems on a global scale.

Global Studies. One important set of topics the encyclopedia considers are the very terms and concepts scholars use to conceptualize and study global themes. Entries under this heading include global concepts, globalization, hyperglobalism, proto-globalization, as well as entries on the academic field of global studies. Also included are entries about the history of the field, its organizational development, and some of the leading intellectual issues and ideas current within it.

Global Economic Issues. Perhaps the most apparent aspect of contemporary globalization is economic and financial, including the transnational ownership, production, and distribution of goods and services, and especially financial flows. The entries related to this area also include global recessions, consumerism, labor issues, the illegal economy of sex and drugs, and global economic actors from Google and Walmart to the World Trade Organization.

Global Demographic Change. The dynamics of a global era are shaped by demography. Some regions of the world have rapidly growing populations, whereas others are aging and even shrinking. In some regions like Europe, almost everyone can live anywhere, and it seems that increasingly they do. Many countries in the world today have become multicultural and have to deal with immigrant communities from around the world. In other regions, migration is either restricted or involuntary, with millions of displaced persons in refugee camps. The entries in this category cover diaspora communities, refugees, overpopulation, migration, the effect of Baby Boomers, and the emergence of global cities such as Los Angeles and Dubai.

Global Communications, Transportation, Technology. The emergence of global communities and, indeed, the massive globalization phase in recent decades have been made possible by new and more efficient forms of transportation and by new communication technologies. The entries related to this area cover automotive and air transport, global positioning systems, computers, email, and the Internet. They include an entry on handheld devices including iphones and androids and an entry on new developments in communications such as Twitter and Facebook.

Global Culture, Media. New Internet social networking, as well as television, video, and more traditional forms of communication and interaction, have given rise to a global culture—common artistic forms of literature and the visual arts and shared values and sensitivities. Entries in this area include the Academy Awards, blogs, and transnational television networks such as the Cable News Network (CNN), the British Broadcasting Corporation (BBC), and Al Jazeera. It also includes entries on global cuisine, soccer and other transnational sports, and the concept of global art and architecture.

Global Religions, Beliefs, Ideologies. Religious traditions and ideologies have always been global in that they move beyond state boundaries, but as cultural groups and individuals are dispersed around the world, so are the ideas and beliefs of their communities. The entries related to this area include the global aspects of major religious traditions like Islam, Christianity, and Buddhism; smaller traditions such as Sikhism and Baha'i; new sects such as Hare Krishna; an entry on religious movements that includes organizations such as Scientology, Falun Gong, and others; and secular ideologies, including Marxism and nationalism. It also includes the emergence of new global ideas such as cosmopolitanism and the concept of global ethics.

Identities in Global Society. As the global community becomes more tightly knit, old social identities such as nationality and religious affiliation are being modified, however slowly, and recombined.

Importantly, new ones emerge; these are based less on nationality and ethnicity and are more related to regional, racial, sexual, and multicultural associations. Entries in this section include ethnic identities such as Hispanic and Asian American and multicultural, cosmopolitan, and gender identities.

Global Civil Society. Since the mid-1970s, a plethora of new movements, groups, and organizations have emerged that cross traditional national boundaries. Human rights movements and nongovernmental organizations of many kinds have created a global civil society. Entries in this area include movements for women's rights, indigenous peoples' rights, and gay and lesbian rights, as well as antiglobalization movements and transnational activism such as the democratic movements of the Arab Spring.

Global Environmental and Energy Issues. The future of life on the planet depends on developing adequate energy needs and controlling a host of new global environmental problems, from global warming to the pollution of the air, water, and seas. Often issues of energy and environment are linked, that is, in the efforts to develop environmentally sound forms of energy production. Entries in this area include climate change and global warming, acid rain, biofuels, tsunamis, sustainability, oil and natural gas production, and the Kyoto Protocol.

Global Health and Nutrition. Associated with environmental issues are matters of global health and nutrition. The availability of healthy food is the most basic global health issue; on the more extreme side are the problems of malnutrition and pandemics. The entries in this area include HIV/ AIDS, abortion, birth control, food, and drugs.

Global Conflict and Security. Since the end of the Cold War, a host of new conflicts have emerged, both within national borders and, more frequently, transnationally. The rise of transnational terrorism organizations creates a set of new security concerns for individual nations and for collaborative intelligence and security networks on a global scale. This area deals with issues of global security and new forms of global conflict and includes entries such as terrorism, 9/11, civil war, genocide, failed states, conflict resolution, military alliances, and peace activism.

Global Governance and World Order. The future of world order is tied to forms of transnational cooperation and global governance. Although a single world government is unlikely to emerge in the foreseeable future, there are a variety of institutions and movements that help adjudicate differences, resolve tensions, and enable the continuation of the global community. The entries in this area include the United Nations, the European Union, the Arab League, and the global South. It also includes concepts of democracy and legitimacy and the ideals of world government.

Global Justice and Legal Issues. One of the central features of the emerging world order is the protection of human rights and the provision of legal and regulatory infrastructures for transnational cooperation. The entries under this heading explore a variety of movements for rights, from animal rights to labor rights, and from gay rights to free speech. It also includes Interpol, international tribunals, systems of law relating to the seas and transnational crimes, and concepts of law from dharma to shari'a, as well as legal systems designed to be applicable as world law.

Global Historical Antecedents. Finally, the encyclopedia includes entries that recognize that globalization and the transnational forces shaping the present age have historical precedents. Entries related to historical periods of globalization and incidents with a global impact are scattered throughout the major areas covered in the encyclopedia, from colonialism, the slave trade, and Malthusian ideas to the great empires and caliphates of history. There are also entries specifically on the historical antecedents to globalization and on the growth of the field of global history as opposed to regional history and world history.

In sum, the *Encyclopedia of Global Studies* covers new ground in two ways: No other encyclopedia covers all of these topics in a systematic and comprehensive fashion, and no other covers them from the specifically global perspective reflected in the way each of the entries is written and presented. Thus, this encyclopedia is different from other reference sources available online or in print. Also, unlike publically accessible online resources, this work is authoritative—the entries were written or supervised by the most learned and competent scholars in the field. The major entries were written by these scholars; other entries were written by younger scholars under the guidance of senior colleagues to gain the participation of the future generation of scholars in global studies. When invited to write the entries for this encyclopedia, the authors were instructed to be specific—that is, the essays are written specifically *for* the field of global studies. Each essay has undergone a rigorous editorial process, and some were re-written several times to make sure they accurately covered the essential features of the global studies field. Every article illuminates some aspect of global studies or a subject related to it, such as globalization, transnational activity and themes, and elements of global society.

The creation of an encyclopedia of this magnitude is an enormous undertaking involving hundreds of colleagues over several years and across all continents. The editors and managing editor worked together as a team, meeting in person in Berlin, London, Los Angeles, and Santa Barbara, and in audio and video conference calls frequently in between meetings. The staff of graduate assistants who worked diligently over the years—and frantically in the final several months—were based in Santa Barbara, Heidelberg, and Berlin, and at times worked from locations as remote as Buenos Aires, Rio de Janeiro, London, and Cambridge, England. The process of the encyclopedia's creation, therefore, was as global as its subject matter. The Orfalea Center for Global and International Studies at the University of California, Santa Barbara, served as the project's home base, and the Orfalea Center's program director, Victor Faessel, served as the managing editor.

We wish to acknowledge the enormous contributions of those who supported and labored on this publishing venture, beginning with our colleagues at the University of California, Santa Barbara, the University of Heidelberg, and the Hertie School of Governance in Berlin. Our diligent editorial support staff at Santa Barbara included graduate students Barbara Morra, Erica Mesker, John Soboslai, and Cecilie Fenger and, at an early stage in the development of the project, undergraduate student Meredith Bailey. Our colleagues at Santa Barbara went out of their way to assist with the project; we appreciate especially the support of Giles Gunn, Richard Appelbaum, Richard Falk, Oran Young, Dean Ernst von Weizsäcker, and Dean Melvin Oliver. At Heidelberg, we wish to thank Michael Hoelscher and Martin Hölz in the Sociology Department, as well as the Centre for Social Investment staff, in particular Georg Mildenberger and Norman Spengler. At the Hertie School of Governance, thanks go to Regina A. List, Markus Fliegauf, Zora Chan, and Saskia Kyas. The editors and staff of SAGE Publications were consistently supportive and encouraging. We thank especially Rolf Janke, James Brace-Thompson, Jane Haenel, and Carole Maurer and, at a critical moment late in the project's development, Geoff Golson. Perhaps most of all we thank the many colleagues who contributed entries to this project, knowing that their primary reward would be the satisfaction of having helped create an enduring fountain of information about an emerging field of studies to which they and we are deeply committed.

Finally, we want to honor the memory of S. N. Eisenstadt, one of the world's great sociologists, who has pioneered the study of multiple modernities and whose intellectual vision has always had a global dimension. His essay on modern identities written for this encyclopedia is likely one of his last publications. In tribute to his formidable intellectual legacy and in recognition of the high standard of scholarship and insight that he has set for us all, we gratefully dedicate this project to his memory.

Helmut Anheier, Mark Juergensmeyer,
and Victor Faessel

ABORTION

Although it is an intimately personal medical procedure, abortion is also a complex and contentious social issue on both national and global levels. As a health procedure, abortion is the voluntary disruption of a pregnancy. The larger social meaning of abortion is best understood within the larger social, political, and economic context where geography, nation, social position, and law intersect in ways that matter to women's lives.

Abortion can be performed with the use of instruments or by taking drugs. Worldwide there are an estimated 42 million pregnancies (about 1 in 5) that end in abortion each year. The most common technique for abortion is uterine aspiration (with either manual or electric suction), but medication abortion with mifepristone (aka the abortion pill) and misoprostol is growing in popularity. Use of misoprostol alone to induce abortion occurs in places where abortion is highly restricted, but the medication is available in the clandestine marketplace. Regardless of the legal status of abortion, women terminate their pregnancies under both safe and unsafe and legal and illegal conditions. Worldwide, an estimated 68,000 women die annually as a result of unsafe abortion, although the risk of dying from abortion where it is legal and safe is very low.

Women of all ages, races, nations, and religious backgrounds have abortions. Most abortions take place before the 12th week of pregnancy, but women continue to need access to later abortion services even where earlier services are readily available. There are many reasons women decide to have abortions. The most common reasons include inability to afford a(nother) child, relationship instability, and work/school obligations. Newer research in this field exposes how women understand these reasons within the larger context of wanting to be a good mother to current and/or future children. Unwanted pregnancies also result from acts of sexual coercion and violence, especially where women have less social power or in conflict areas. Women with wanted pregnancies may also have abortions when their own health or the health of the fetus is compromised. Work within the larger field of reproductive health has measured the significant unmet need for family planning across the globe as it contributes to high rates of abortion, even in countries where abortion is highly restricted. Low access to contraception and social disapproval of premarital sex also contribute to the higher abortion rate in the United States as compared to its western European counterparts.

The legal status of abortion differs across the world. The most liberal abortion laws can be found in South Africa, which recognizes abortion as a human right, and Canada, which has no abortion law and thus leaves the entire matter to the health care system. Some countries, such as the United States and most of western Europe, limit abortion based on the gestational age of the pregnancy. In the United States, this limit is the point of potential viability when it is believed that the fetus has a reasonable chance of survival outside the womb. Both Mexico City and Cambodia allow abortion for any reason through the 12th week of pregnancy. In contrast, many other developing countries limit access to abortion based on the circumstances of the pregnancy itself, for example, when the pregnancy threatens the life or health of the pregnant woman or when it is the result of rape or incest. Some countries, like Ethiopia and Israel, interpret these exceptions broadly, allowing many women to access abortion. Other countries limit legal abortion to only a small number of cases, as does Colombia. A few countries, including Nicaragua and Iraq, prohibit abortion in all circumstances.

Social debates over abortion take many forms. One debate surrounds the moral status of the fetus in which the woman's right to bodily autonomy is positioned against the fetus's right to life. The argument for fetal rights is usually predicated on a belief that life begins at conception and is often grounded in conservative religious beliefs. Pro-life feminism rejects the patriarchal position against abortion and sees abortion as reflecting the failure of society to provide the structural supports for motherhood. In contrast, the reproductive justice approach locates a woman's right to abortion within a larger framework of human rights, including the right to have a child, to not have a child, and to parent the children one has. Where women have a legal right to abortion, abortion rights supporters understand this right as contributing to women's equal participation in society. However, that capacity is limited by racial/ethnic and economic social inequalities.

A new argument against abortion has emerged in the American debate that draws on empirical research rather than morality claims. It contends that abortion hurts the woman as well as the fetus. To prove this point, abortion rights opponents have conducted a series of studies that found a significant association between having an abortion and higher rates of poor mental health, including depression, suicide, and substance use. Their conclusions have been challenged by the American Psychological Association, whose Task Force on Abortion, after reviewing these studies, found no evidence of harm from abortion and numerous methodological flaws in studies making those conclusions.

Research on abortion social movements has explored the uniquely contentious American experience as well as provided some cross-cultural comparisons. The U.S. story of abortion dates to the early days of the republic when abortion was a common and unproblematic experience for women. The first opponents to abortion were physicians who sought to distinguish themselves from midwives who routinely provided this service. Scholars argue that the early physician anti-abortion movement was part of a larger professionalizing project within organized medicine, which succeeded in making abortion illegal at the end of the 19th century. Abortion did not reappear on the larger public agenda until the 1960s, when both the medical community and women's rights supporters began to advocate for abortion law reform, resulting in the 1973 U.S. Supreme Court *Roe v. Wade* decision legalizing abortion.

The *Roe* decision served as a catalyst for two new umbrella social movements, most commonly referred to as the "pro-life movement" and the "pro-choice movement." In addition to studying the political histories of the movements, sociologists have studied the people who comprise the movements. Scholars have found that differing views of motherhood or women's position in society explained women's engagement in abortion social movements. Research on pro-life activists has found that many view their efforts as fulfilling a personal obligation to God, serving as a form of religious practice or as a way to repent for their own abortion experience. Social movement theorists have also examined the ways in which the persistence of the abortion debate in the United States has led to the professionalization of the pro-choice movement, substituting permanent advocates for grassroots activists. These scholars also pay significant attention to the highly violent nature of the U.S. abortion debate, in which abortion providers have been murdered and property destroyed through arson and acid attacks. International scholars discuss the direct link between abortion rights advocacy and the transnational feminist movement as well as the international exportation of tactics of the U.S. pro-life movement.

The intersection of law and society is a point of investigation for scholars of abortion in the United States. Researchers have found that abortion regulations, including mandatory waiting periods, funding restrictions, and facilities requirements, have led to a significant decline in overall access to care. Additionally, the requirement that adolescents involve their parents in the abortion decision creates significant impediments for young people's access to care and serves as a form of social shaming for unapproved sexuality. Perhaps the highest profile debate over the regulation of abortion care in the United States involved the fight over restricting a procedure abortion rights opponents call "partial birth abortion." Despite the lack of medical accuracy in the naming of the technique, the law's vagueness about what was actually restricted, and medical evidence that the technique is safest for women with certain medical presentations, the U.S. Supreme Court found in favor of a federal ban on the technique.

Comparing the U.S. experience with abortion to that of Germany, scholars locate the differences in disagreements over abortion within the larger question of the role of the welfare state and the differing role of the media in each society. Researchers argue that the ongoing requirement that a woman's abortion decision be approved by two physicians rather than be solely at the discretion of the pregnant woman may diffuse some of the tension over abortion in the United Kingdom. In contrast, abortion in Japan is seen through the lens of a cultural practice called *mizuko*, which provides a ceremonial ritual for the spirit of the aborted fetus. Other work explores the role of organized religion in the outlier status of countries where abortion is illegal despite the neighboring countries allowing abortion, for example, the Republic of Ireland and Thailand. Also, in the international context, scholarship addresses the unique role of sex selection abortion in countries where son preference intersects with small family size, as in China and India. Finally, new research is exploring abortion migration and the Internet market for abortion technologies.

Within the scholarly literature, there is new attention to the role of stigma in the abortion context. Stigma is experienced at all levels of society (micro, meso, and macro), and research has found it to have negative impacts on the emotional health of women undergoing abortion. Scholars also contend that stigma contributes to the unwillingness of health care professionals to engage in abortion work. Culturally, stigma silences broader social conversations about the abortion issue.

Because abortion is a medical service, the role of the health care provider features heavily in writings about abortion. In the United States, scholars have been interested in the ways in which abortion remains marginalized from mainstream medicine and how feminism and medical authority are balanced in abortion provision. Health care workers who provide abortion care often tell their own stories to both humanize the abortion providers and explain their rationale for engaging in this work.

The right of health care institutions and providers to refuse involvement in abortion care—what are often called "conscience refusals"—plays an increasing role in reduced access to abortion across the globe. For example, in Poland, conscience refusals led to both legal restrictions on abortion and reduced access to care in the clandestine market. In the United States, these health care refusals have been shown to have a significant negative effect on the standard of care for women's health. Research also exposes the constraints on physicians who are willing but unable to provide abortion care because of institutional prohibitions. Finally, in places where abortion was recently liberalized, such as Colombia, exercise of personal conscience has limited the development of abortion services to meet women's demand for care.

Women have abortions for many reasons and under legal/illegal and safe/unsafe conditions. Abortion remains a highly contested social issue with active social movement organizations and actors. The legal status of abortion differs across the globe, as does the provision of that care.

Tracy A. Weitz

See also Birth Control; Feminism; Fertility; Religious Politics; Social Movements; Women's Movement; Women's Rights

Further Readings

Cahn, N. R., & Carbone, J. (2010). *Red families v. blue families: Legal polarization and the creation of culture*. Oxford, UK: Oxford University Press.

Ferree, M. M., Gamson, W. A., Gerhards, J., & Rucht, D. (2002). *Shaping abortion discourse:*

Democracy and the public sphere in Germany and the United States. Cambridge, UK: Cambridge University Press.

Freedman, L. (2010). *Willing and unable: Doctors' constraints in abortion care.* Nashville, TN: Vanderbilt University Press.

Joffe, C. (2009). *Dispatches from the abortion wars: The costs of fanaticism to doctors, patients, and the rest of us.* Boston: Beacon Press.

Luker, K. (1984). *Abortion and the politics of motherhood.* Berkeley: University of California Press.

Mohr, J. C. (1978). *Abortion in America: The origins and evolution of national policy, 1800–1900.* New York: Oxford University Press.

Petchesky, R. P., Judd, K., & International Reproductive Rights Research Action Group. (1998). *Negotiating reproductive rights: Women's perspectives across countries and cultures.* London: Zed Books.

Tooley, M. (2009). *Abortion: Three perspectives.* New York: Oxford University Press.

ACADEMY AWARDS

The Academy Awards, nicknamed the Oscars, given for film achievements by the Academy of Motion Picture Arts and Sciences (AMPAS), is an American event but has been universally embraced as the ultimate symbol of success and accomplishment in the world of global cinematic entertainment. Indeed, the importance of the Oscar Awards goes way beyond the film world and the American locale.

For awards to bear motivational significance, they have to fulfill at least three functions: They have to be visible and known to every artist, they have to carry a high degree of prestige, and they have to be within reach of success by any aspiring artist or production company. The Oscars meet all of these conditions: They are visible, they are prestigious, and they are within reach.

There are several reasons for the institutionalization and extraordinary preeminence of the Oscars. First and foremost is the longevity of the award. Conferred for the first time in May 1929 (for achievements in 1927–1928), the Oscar is the oldest film prize in history. A tradition of 82 years (and still going strong) has made the Oscar a respectable symbol with a solid heritage.

The other entertainment awards are like the children and grandchildren of the Oscars. The Antoinette Perry Awards (Tonys), by the League of New York Theaters and Producers and the American Theater Wing, were first presented in 1947. The Emmys, awarded by the National Academy of Television Arts and Sciences, were presented for the first time in 1949. The Grammys, the youngest showbiz awards, were first bestowed by the National Academy of Recording Arts and Sciences in 1959.

Scope and Prestige

The Tony is essentially a local award, given for achievements in the Broadway theater and largely limited to the New York City arena. Movies, by contrast, speak a universal language and have the potential of reaching everyone. Even people who don't live in the United States and don't speak English are aware of the Oscars and their significance.

The Oscar's prestige stems from the status of the Academy within the film industry. The Academy has always been elitist, with membership that constitutes a very small percentage of the film industry. Yet, despite elitism, the Academy's procedures are quite democratic: The Academy, with its various branches, gives equal representation to all artists, regardless of specialty (writers, directors, players). The nomination process is based on peer evaluation: The Acting branch selects nominees in acting, the Directors branch for directing, and so on. However, each Academy member proposes nominees for the Best Picture, and the entire membership votes for the winners in all the categories.

Film artists, like other professionals, attribute the utmost importance to recognition from their peers because they consider them the only experts with the necessary knowledge to make competent evaluation of their work. For most filmmakers, the significant reference group, which sets standards to be emulated and also serves as a frame for judging merits, consists of fellow workers.

Scarcity of Awards

The scarce number of awards also contributes to the Oscar's prestige. In the entire Academy history, about 700 players have been nominated for an Oscar and only 220 have actually won. Every year, only 20 actors are nominated in four categories— Actor in a Leading Role, Actress in a Leading Role, Actor in a Supporting Role, and Actress in a Supporting Role—and only four win, one winner for each category. These 20 performances are selected out of thousands of eligible performances.

Similarly, the 5 films (enlarged in 2009 to 10) competing for Best Picture are chosen from a large pool of over 300 eligible films. Hollywood film production has declined, though: In the 1940s, over 500 films were released on an average year. Even so, the Oscar is more competitive than most awards, due to the large number of films, performances, and achievements every year.

The Academy has refused to divide the categories by genre (e.g., drama and comedy). The Tonys and the Golden Globes share separate sets of categories for dramatic plays and musicals/comedies. Those in favor of one prize claim that increasing the number of awards decreases their prestige; too many categories belittle the award. The Grammys are awarded in over 70 categories, and singers can be nominated in multiple categories for the same song.

The Oscar is awarded to artists of all nationalities: One fourth of the nominees have been foreign, non-American artists. This international dimension extends the visibility of the Oscar and contributes to its prestige. And the Oscar's prestige, in turn, makes for intense international competition. The scarcity of awards and the intense international competition have made the Oscar all the more desirable.

The Oscar as Politically Correct Entertainment

Most Academy members tend to judge a film by the importance of its subject and relevance of its issue; this was clear in 1982, when the film *Gandhi* swept most of the Oscars. Cinematically, according to many critics, it was a rather conventional, solemn biography of the noble political figure, lacking epic scope and visual imagination. *Gandhi* may have been a better movie had it been directed by a more subtle and inventive filmmaker. However, Gandhi's figure was so inspirational and his preaching for nonviolence so timely a message in the context of the 1980s that Academy voters favored the movie over Steven Spielberg's *E.T.*,

Sidney Lumet's *The Verdict*, and Sydney Pollack's comedy, *Tootsie*.

Pollack's *Tootsie*, for example, was accomplished on every level, but it lacked the noble intent and "important" theme that *Gandhi* possessed. It was praised by the *New York Times* critic Vincent Canby, who described the film as having the quality of an important news event. Although he also faulted it for its earnestness, Canby thought that the film succeeded in reminding the audience about the existence of exceptional people, people who were able to rise above the profit motive that paradoxically motivated many of the moviemakers themselves.

It is worth noting that the Academy's taste didn't differ much from that of the critics. *Gandhi* opened to almost unanimously favorable review; the only dissenting voices among the major critics were Andrew Sarris and Pauline Kael. And it won the New York Film Critics, the National Board of Review, and the Golden Globe awards. However, there was no consensus among critics that year: the Los Angeles Film Critics cited *E.T.* as Best Picture, and National Society of Film Critics cited *Tootsie*.

With its more conservative membership, which is about a generation older than many of Hollywood's most active innovators and two generations older than most American moviegoers, the Academy has traditionally favored earnest, noble, and inspirational fare that propagated political correctness even before the concept existed.

The Academy's tendency to choose earnest movies that deal with "important" or "noble" issues over audacious movies that are more artistically innovative or politically charged is easily documented. The Academy's preference is for safe, mainstream, noncontroversial film fare that is imbued with a widely acceptable message:

Noble Theme Over Artistic Quality

In 1937, *The Life of Emile Zola* over *The Awful Truth* and *Lost Horizon*

In 1941, *How Green Was My Valley* over *Citizen Kane*

In 1942, *Mrs. Miniver* over *The Magnificent Ambersons*

In 1944, *Going My Way* over *Double Indemnity*

In 1951, *An American in Paris* over *A Place in the Sun*

In 1952, *The Greatest Show on Earth* over *High Noon*

In 1956, *Around the World in 80 Days* over *Giant*

In 1964, *My Fair Lady* over *Dr. Strangelove*

In 1966, *A Man for All Seasons* over *Alfie* and *Who's Afraid of Virginia Woolf?*

In 1967, *In the Heat of the Night* over *Bonnie and Clyde*

In 1971, *The French Connection* over *A Clockwork Orange*

In 1976, *Rocky* over *Network* and *All the President's Men*

In 1980, *Ordinary People* over *Raging Bull*

In 1981, *Chariots of Fire* over *Reds*

In 1982, *Gandhi* over *Tootsie* and *E.T.*

In 1983, *Terms of Endearment* over *The Right Stuff*

In 1989, *Driving Miss Daisy* over *My Left Foot*

In 1990, *Dances With Wolves* over *GoodFellas*

In 1994, *Forrest Gump* over *Pulp Fiction*

In 1997, *Titanic* over *L.A. Confidential*

In 1998, *Shakespeare in Love* over *Saving Private Ryan*

In 1999, *American Beauty* over *The Insider*

In 2000, *Gladiator* over *Traffic*

In 2001, *A Beautiful Mind* over *The Lord of the Ring: The Fellowship of the Ring*

In 2009, *Slumdog Millionaire* over *Benjamin Button* and *Milk*

In 2011, *The King's Speech* over *Inception* and *The Social Network*

Huge Impact

The immense effect, both symbolic and pragmatic, of winning the Oscar is another unique feature. Unlike the prestigious Nobel Prize, there is no financial honorarium, although the Oscar's economic worth is extraordinary: The winners' salaries often skyrocket overnight. Winning an Oscar means hard cash at the box office; the Best Picture award can add $20 to $30 million in theater ticket (or DVD) sales.

The Oscars are influential in both domestic and global markets. In the 21st century, foreign box office receipts amount to more than half of movies' overall gross sales. Along with prestige and money, the Oscar-winning actors gain negotiating power for better roles with better directors, and they also enjoy increased popularity outside the Hollywood film industry. Winners in other categories enjoy increased reputation within the motion picture industry, even if they do not become better known among the general public. No other entertainment award has such comparable effects. The Oscar's preeminence in the entertainment world is enhanced through extensive coverage in all media: print and radio in the first two decades and TV over the past 50 years. This media blitz is not confined to the United States: The Oscar show is a popular TV program, watched live or on tape by over 1 billion people in over 170 countries.

Every profession is stratified, although some more sharply than others. In acting, the inequality in rewards (money, prestige, popularity, power) between the elite and the rank and file is particularly sharp. There are three relevant audiences and three corresponding evaluations in the film world: evaluation by peers, evaluation by critics, and evaluation by the public. The first evaluation is internal to the film world, whereas the other two are external or outside the industry. However, all three evaluations are important because they operate at the same time, and each exerts some impact on the film world.

What makes the Oscar such an influential award is its combination of all three evaluations. Through the Oscar, the Academy voters function as peers, as critics, and as tastemakers. No other award combines so well the usually disparate critical and popular judgment. The Oscar is the only award to exert such a direct and pervasive influence on every element of the industry: the movies, the filmmakers, and the audiences.

Emanuel Levy

See also Cinema; Cultural Industries; Film Festivals; Global Culture, Media; Hollywood; Prizes and Awards, International

Further Readings

Biskind, P. (1998). *Easy riders, raging bulls.* New York: Simon & Schuster.

Biskind, P. (2005). *Down and dirty pictures.* New York: Simon & Schuster.

Hillier, J. (Ed.). (2001). *American independent cinema.* London: British Film Institute.

Levy, E. (1987). *John Wayne: Prophet of the American way of life.* Lanham, MD: Scarecrow Press.

Levy, E. (1990). *Small-town America in film.* New York: Continuum.

Levy, E. (2000). *Cinema of outsiders: The rise of American independent film.* New York: New York University Press.

Levy, E. (2003). *All about Oscar: The history and politics of the Academy Awards.* New York: Continuum.

Lewis, J. (Ed.). (1998). *The new American cinema.* Durham, NC: Duke University Press.

Neale, S., & Smith, M. (Eds.). (1998). *Contemporary Hollywood cinema.* New York: Routledge.

Waxman, S. (2005). *Rebels on the backlot: Six maverick directors and how they conquered the Hollywood studio system.* New York: HarperCollins.

ACCOUNTABILITY

The processes of globalization create a demand for accountability by generating a growing complexity in everyday life, as well as in professional life, with fundamental changes related to both the targets and recipients of accountability efforts and to the methods and procedures within the organizations that are expected to render an account. The complex issue of accountability attracts interest in the global age, as there is a growing sense of entitlement to "good governance" and a demand for improved performance across all sectors of society and at the local, national, international, and transnational levels. The topic figures to be one of the major future challenges to global governance, as it affects and involves actions and actors across all sorts of organizations. Especially within the nonprofit sector, there has been a growing accountability movement; nevertheless, there are also contested perspectives on these processes of evaluation.

Definitions

Depending on the chosen approach and perspective, there are several possible definitions of accountability as well as a variety of dimensions and characteristics one can take into account. Helmut Anheier and Amber Hawkes refer to accountability from the actor's perspective simply as answering for one's behavior. Similarly, One World Trust, a leading U.K.-based think tank, which publishes the Global Accountability Report, considers it to be a process through which an organization makes a commitment to respond to and balance the needs of stakeholders in its decision-making processes and activities and delivers against this commitment. In other words, accountability is seen as a responsibility taken on proactively by the actor or organization.

By contrast, in one of the more commonly used definitions, Jonathan A. Fox and L. David Brown see it more as a process—coming from outside—of holding actors responsible for their actions. Similarly, Anne Marie Goetz and Rob Jenkins think of accountability as the capacity held by the actor affected by an action to demand that someone provide reasons to justify his or her behavior or to impose a penalty for poor performance. Along these lines, Valerie Sperling considers the accountability relationship to be a power relationship that consists of two core components: answerability and enforcement. Building on the concept of a power relationship, Richard Mulgan identifies a set of key features, including the existence of an external authority to which the "account" is given, social interaction between those seeking answers and those providing the answers, and the assertion of a right of authority or superiority of those demanding the account over those who are being held accountable.

Researchers have identified various dimensions of accountability. Some, including O. P. Dwivedi and Joseph G. Jabbra, have distinguished administrative, legal, political, professional, and moral dimensions. Another perspective separates internal from external accountability. Internal accountability refers to responsibility for one's own actions, whereas external accountability refers to answering to others and encompasses the various dimensions listed earlier. Finally, some identify dimensions that enable an organization to be accountable. One World Trust lists four such dimensions—transparency, participation, evaluation, and complaint and response mechanisms—all of which must be integrated to ensure accountability.

Alnoor Ebrahim and Edward Weisband note that most discussions about the concept pose two further questions: Accountability to whom and accountability for what? The "to whom" question refers ideally to the multiple actors affected by the decisions or actions of the person or organization to be held accountable, that is, stakeholders. For governments, they could include taxpayers, voters, service recipients, and other nations; for private corporations, the shareholders, customers, members of the community in which they operate, and even employees; for nonprofit organizations, funders, members, service recipients, and government regulators; and for international organizations, member nations, funders, and so forth. The answer to the "for what" question ranges from finance (i.e., responsible use of resources), to governance (i.e., decision-making processes), to performance (i.e., the effectiveness and quality of the service or product provided), all the way—especially for nonprofit organizations—to mission (i.e., the extent to which the actions lead to mission fulfillment). The most comprehensive approach to accountability has been provided by Jonathan Koppell (2005), which separates several dimensions that may involve different actors and levels, making it especially useful for analyzing global issues:

- Transparency: "*Did the organization reveal the facts of its performance?*" Transparency is an extremely important tool for assessing organizational performance. A transparent organization gives access to the press, the public, and other interested parties.
- Liability: "*Did the organization face consequences for its performance?*" This dimension attaches consequences to an organization's performance. Liability can come in the form of setbacks (such as diminished budget authority, increased monitoring, etc.) or positive reinforcement (such as cash bonuses to employees and other rewards).
- Controllability: "*Did the organization do what the principal desired?*" Many analyses of accountability focus on how much the stakeholder has control over the organization or principal. For example, government bureaucracies should reach consensus on public

policy issues and "carry out the will of the public."
- Responsibility: "*Did the organization follow the rules?*" This means being lawful, adhering to professional or industry standards and behavioral norms, and being morally sound.
- Responsiveness: "*Did the organization fulfill the substantive expectation?*" Responsiveness works more horizontally, and refers to the levels of attention organizations give to their clients and stakeholders' *needs* and *demands*. It implies accountability outward rather than upward.

The multiple approaches and definitions testify to the complexity of this important issue. As alluded to earlier, the actual forms of accountability differ depending on which kind of organization is being held accountable. Civil society organizations are called on to increase their accountability efforts in terms of financial disclosure, transparency in governance, and measurement of performance. In the corporate sector, especially following the collapse of Enron in 2001, accountability has become a fundamental element of corporate governance, including transparency, internal and external checks and balance, and performance reports. Furthermore, public service accountability is a core element of democratic societies because it is a fundamental condition for preventing the abuse of delegated power and for ensuring that power is directed toward the achievement of broadly accepted national goals with the greatest possible degree of efficiency, effectiveness, and prudence. Finally, at the international level, especially, the question of accountability "to whom" has come to the forefront.

Theories and Research Results

One of the basic theories applied to the complex issue of accountability is the economic principal-agent theory. Here it is suggested that actors or organizations and their stakeholders have different goals and interests, so that, for example, in the case of nonprofit organizations, the organizations might well misrepresent their abilities to funders in order to obtain a grant or contract. As a result, and to promote greater levels of trust, both parties must ensure transparency and invest in disclosing their activities, mainly via monitoring and oversight systems.

The stewardship theory takes as its point of departure the collective—rather than competing—goals of the two engaging parties. According to this theory, information on performance provided through accountability mechanisms helps improve overall performance and efficiency and helps to create trust and ensure goal alignment. Institutional theory is another way of explaining why there are performance-based accountability systems. Isomorphic developments across the sectors are taking place, as it became more and more important to unveil the activities of organizations to improve procedures. For nonprofit organizations, for example, this can be an incentive "to be perceived as successful and legitimate by outside organizations" (Carman, 2010, p. 258).

Not only the manner according to which organizations fulfill accountability requirements but also the surroundings in which it takes place is part of theoretical and empirical research. From a global perspective, changes such as privatization or deterritorialization have a huge impact on the mechanism of accountability, as transnational institutions (companies, civil society organizations, as well as legal or UN organizations) have the power now to hold states accountable and can claim that these processes apply to citizens in particular countries (see Sperling, 2009).

Scope and Growth

There seems to be an increasing trend toward demanding and publicizing accountability efforts for all sectors and at many different levels. At the global level, in particular, several initiatives have been launched to encourage and evaluate accountability. For example, since 2006, the U.K.-based One World Trust has published the Global Accountability Report (GAR), which offers selected data and trends on the accountability undertakings of international governmental organizations (IGOs), international nongovernmental organizations (INGOs), and transnational corporations (TNCs). The report, which is updated generally on an annual basis, creates indexes based on the degrees of transparency, participation, evaluation, and complaints and response handling. According to the 2008 GAR, even the highest performers among the three groups of entities have only basic accountability policies and systems in place.

Since 1995, the nonprofit partnership Account-Ability has worked, especially with the corporate sector, to promote social and ethical accountability and to develop a set of standards for reporting. Hundreds of corporations and other organizations in some 30 countries have implemented the AA1000 series of standards. In addition, Account-Ability teamed up with csrnetwork, a consultancy now known as Two Tomorrows, to produce an annual Accountability Rating, based on the AA1000 standard and other frameworks, which was prominently published in *Forbes* magazine. By 2009, the partners agreed that because the practices they promoted and assessed either already had been sufficiently adopted by companies or were being measured by other ratings, such as the Dow Jones Sustainability Index and the FTSE-4Good Index, their mission had been accomplished and the Accountability Rating was no longer necessary.

Among civil society organizations, 11 of the largest INGOs joined to launch in 2006 the INGO Accountability Charter, which lays out a number of basic principles and commits signees to annual reporting using the Global Reporting Initiative's guidelines. By the latter part of 2010, the number of INGOs adopting the Charter had increased to 17. At about the same time, the European Foundation Centre, the members of which are among the leading philanthropies in Europe, and the U.S.-based Council on Foundations formed a joint working group, which ultimately agreed on Seven Principles of Accountability for International Philanthropy, which are integrity, understanding, respect, responsiveness, fairness, cooperation and collaboration, and effectiveness, and developed a set of good-practice options for implementing the principles. Similar initiatives have emerged among internationally oriented civil society organizations in a variety of fields, including humanitarian assistance.

Current Issues and Development

It is clear that globalization is altering all forms of accountability relationships—within and between states, at the level of international institutions, transnational corporations, and nongovernmental organizations, and between those institutions and the people they affect. The challenge for researchers and practitioners then will be to identify these changes and to develop new forms and mechanisms of accountability. An additional task will be the further development and expanded application of international accountability principles and standards, like those promoted by AccountAbility and the INGO Accountability Charter for the corporate and civil society sectors, as well as assessment of their impact on accountability relationships and, ultimately, performance.

Helmut K. Anheier and Martin Hölz

See also Corporations, Transnational; Foundations, European: International Activities; Foundations, U.S.: International Activities; Transparency

Further Readings

Anheier, H. K., & Hawkes, A. (2008). Accountability in a globalising world: International non-governmental organizations and foundations. In M. Albrow, H. K. Anheier, M. Glasius, M. E. Price, & M. Kaldor (Eds.), *Global civil society 2007/8. Communicative power and democracy* (pp. 124–143). Thousand Oaks, CA: Sage.

Carman, J. G. (2010). The accountability movement: What's wrong with this theory of change? *Nonprofit and Voluntary Sector Quarterly, 39*(2), 256–274.

Dwivedi, O. P., & Jabbra, J. G. (1988). Public service responsibility and accountability. In O. P. Dwivedi & J. G. Jabbra (Eds.), *Public service accountability. A comparative perspective* (pp. 1–16). West Hartford, CT: Kumarian Press.

Ebrahim, A., & Weisband, E. (Eds.). (2007). *Global accountabilities: Participation, pluralism, and public ethics.* Cambridge, UK: Cambridge University Press.

Fox, J. A., & Brown, L. D. (Eds.). (1998). *The struggle for accountability: The World Bank, NGOs, and grassroots movements.* Cambridge: MIT Press.

Goetz, A. M., & Jenkins, R. (2002). *Voice, accountability and human development: The emergence of a new agenda* (Background paper for the Human Development Report 2002). New York: United Nations Development Programme.

Koppell, J. (2005). Pathologies of accountability: ICANN and the challenge of multiple accountabilities disorder. *Public Administration Review, 65*(1), 94–108.

Lloyd, R. (2008). Promoting global accountability: The experiences of the Global Accountability Project. *Global Governance, 14,* 273–281.

Mulgan, R. (2000). "Accountability": An ever-expanding concept? *Public Administration, 78*(3), 555–573.

Solomon, J., & Solomon, A. (2004). *Corporate governance and accountability.* Chichester, UK: Wiley.

Sperling, V. (2009). *Altered states. The globalization of accountability.* Cambridge, UK: Cambridge University Press.

ACCOUNTING SYSTEMS

Globalization has made the role of accounting systems for extending economic and, more generally, organizational activities across space and time more salient to both organizational agents and their stakeholders. Accounting systems are arrays of artifacts and practices organized for generating, circulating, and accumulating numerical records. Accounting systems exist in a variety of organizational settings, and they are subject to different degrees of standardization within and across organizations. Numerical records of various kinds referring to diverse sets of events and entities are produced and circulated within accounting systems, although usually financial information is preeminent. Establishing and perpetuating accounting within a regular system of records is always an achievement of particular forms of social organization regulating how accounting information is produced and circulated. Across organizations, the emergence of regional, national, and international organizational fields has resulted in a gradual standardization of accounting systems.

Since the 1970s, academic discourse within the social sciences has reflected this salience. The interdisciplinary journal *Accounting, Organizations and Society* is representative of the expanding academic engagement with accounting. In discussions of the historical origins and development of accounting systems, the gradual emergence of isomorphic and standardized forms, and the way in which accounting systems extend organization across space and time, central interdisciplinary issues relating to accounting systems are subsequently addressed.

Historical Origins and Development

Rudimentary accounting systems were among the earliest forms of writing in human civilization. Use of clay tokens in accounting for cattle and agricultural production, for example, is documented for the Sumerian civilization from the 9th millennium BCE onward. Archaic forms of accounting did not necessarily utilize numerical representations of volume or value, as clay tokens representing specific goods could simply be stowed away to be later retrieved.

Some authors have claimed that even the practice of double-entry bookkeeping, the hallmark of contemporary accounting systems, can be traced back to very early historical precedents. The significance of the double-entry innovation is that it allows one to trace both the sources (original ownership, transfer of rights) and utilizations (investments, transactions) of goods over time. Although one may imagine instances of double-entry accounting systems that do not employ numerical representations (e.g., a cattle trader keeping separate debit and credit boxes for cow tokens), more complex exercises in reckoning with debits and credits (of producing balances and ratios, of timing and differentiating accounts, and so on) only became possible once numerical abstractions of goods were used. Because the use of double-entry methodologies is suggestive of systematic reflections on the acquisition, refinement, and sale of goods in terms of volume and value, the double-entry system tends to be considered as a prerequisite for capitalist forms of economic organization to emerge.

Regardless of earlier historical precedents to both the capitalist mode of production and the double-entry accounting system associated with it, there is little doubt that the diffusion of double-entry bookkeeping after the advent of the printing press (accounting textbooks constituted a large share of the early books that were printed and distributed in mass circulation) supported the subsequent unfolding of economic organization within capitalist modes of production and trade.

The double-entry system has remained the unchallenged paradigm of accounting in business organizations throughout the industrial and informational stages of capitalism. Yet, the relationship within accounting systems in business firms between the keeping of records for purposes of organizing and managing production and trade on the one hand, and the preparation of reports for stakeholders in organizational capital on the other, has frequently been a matter of dispute among practitioners and accounting scholars. Respective structural tensions within accounting systems have been reflected in the differentiation between *management accounting* for internal and *financial accounting* for external purposes. Fears that critical functions of management accounting—which may be as concerned with money and cash flow as with the control of time and the evaluation of quality—are being displaced by interests in financial bottom lines have repeatedly been articulated by both scholars and practitioners.

Alongside educational and scholarly discourse about proper forms of bookkeeping, the development of accounting systems in business organizations has coevolved with production and information technologies and efforts to rationalize production and managerial control, and it simultaneously has responded to the demands of financial reporting articulated by tax and regulatory agencies, by private stakeholders, and by financial markets. The influence of various professions—for example, of the legal profession on financial reporting or of engineering professions on management accounting—has also been notable throughout the diffusion of accounting discourses and technologies. Genuine accounting professions specializing exclusively in jurisdiction over accounting practices and systems (rather than diverse kinds of accounting expertise being incorporated into various professions) have become institutionalized in some countries (as, early on, in the United Kingdom, then, more gradually, in the United States), although not in others (e.g., in most continental European and Asian countries). *Auditing*, as the inspection of accounts for internal or external stakeholders, has in most countries been incorporated into accountants' professional jurisdictions, although sometimes with a focus on legal rather than financial expertise.

Double-entry bookkeeping was generally *not* a paradigmatic accounting system in public sector and nonprofit organizations in most countries until the last few decades of the 20th century. In most state bureaucracies around the globe, forms of *cameralistic* bookkeeping focused on the successful implementation of budgets rather than on the tracking of capital investments. State bureaucracies have been keeping various other numerical records of nonfinancial character as well, and censuses, for example, may also be considered accounting systems put in place for purposes of measuring and governing territories and populations. The notion of "statistics" emerged from such forms of bureaucratic accounting systems within nation-states. With the wave of public sector reforms focused on privatization and "new public management" starting regionally in the late 1970s and diffusing globally through the course of the 1990s, private sector accounting, double-entry bookkeeping, and various forms of management and financial accounting have increasingly been institutionalized within public and nonprofit sector bureaucracies around the globe. Management consultants trained in accounting and globally operating accounting firms providing consultancy to national governments, international governmental organizations, and nongovernmental organizations have been driving and influencing this process of diffusion. Diffusion has been reinforced through restrictions within the international provision of credit and the funding of development projects.

The extending scope of accounting systems both within organizations (spanning across advanced management information and resource planning systems) and for purposes of financial reporting (toward reporting on so-called intangible assets) has drawn criticisms that, with the diffusion of accounting systems, organizational activities across sectors have increasingly been "financialized." Traditional forms of financial accounting and managerial control are nowadays coupled with more recent techniques, like benchmarking or the balanced score card, which include nonfinancial indicators and qualitative elements, but whether this qualifies or amplifies managerial orientations to financial bottom lines rather than other outcomes is a matter of contention. Although accounting systems have historically emerged from practices of writing that were not necessarily numerical and then unfolded into numerical systems that are not exclusively financially oriented, the diffusion and growth of accounting systems definitely correlate with attempts to economize in organizations and organizational fields in terms of return on monetary investments.

Isomorphism and Standardization

The diffusion of accounting systems illustrates that organizations rarely, if ever, set up accounting systems that are completely of their own making. In setting up accounting systems, organizations draw on various resources from their environments, like information technologies and personnel trained in accounting by other organizations. Organizations imitate other organizations and hire consultants, and, in doing so, they respond to expectations and norms among their members, stakeholders, and regulators about proper forms of keeping and circulating numerical records.

Expectations about what kind of accounting system is appropriate for any given organization tend to converge within distinct organizational fields, as is evidenced by the historical divergence of accounting systems between private and public sectors. Drivers of convergence and the resulting isomorphism of accounting systems across organizations are educational organizations, accounting professions, financial markets, regulatory agencies, and nation-states. Sometimes the term *accounting system*, rather than referring to concrete accounting practices in specific organizations, is used to refer to typical forms of accounting practices prevailing within specific organizational fields and to sets of standards regulating these practices.

The process of globalization has brought about a gradual convergence and standardization of accounting practices and systems across diverse organizational fields, most notably in the domain of financial accounting. In financial reporting, International Accounting Standards and U.S. Generally Accepted Accounting Principles have been challenging and gradually displacing national traditions of financial accounting, auditing, and reporting. The will to attract capital in global financial markets has fueled this trend across all types of business organizations, and interests of firms, investors, and market regulators have been steadily increasing the demand for standardized forms of financial reporting since the 1970s. The emerging global accounting profession, largely oriented toward the British blueprint for defining a combined accounting and auditing jurisdiction, has mediated this demand, and big international accounting firms acting as consultants to firms, banks, nation-states, and private and public regulators have been the dominant actors in this process. Questions of regulatory effectiveness—usually starting from observations that regulatory roles have been conflated with consultancy services and the fact that the overall process of private self-regulation is hardly transparent to outsiders or to democratically elected governments—have been posed in the wake of spectacular corporate collapses (Enron, WorldCom, Parmalat, etc.). Corporate collapses have also contributed to a reduction in the number of big accounting firms from the "Big 8" to the "Big 4" during the last quarter of the 20th century.

Nevertheless, particularly with further globalization of capital investing, the demand for standardized forms of financial reporting is not expected to wane in the near future, and similar dynamics of expanding and standardizing financial reporting may ultimately start to play out in public sector organizations—driven by the interests of international governmental organizations like the United Nations, the Organisation for Economic Co-operation and Development, the International Monetary Fund, and the World Bank, and by attempts of national governments to comply with expectations of "good governance" informed by popularized forms of accounting discourse. Standardization with respect to management accounting has, in comparison, been quite limited.

Convergence of management accounting systems has been the result of institutionalizing regular forms of accounting education in management and business schools, and in colleges and universities from which organizations have recruited their personnel. The prominence of accounting skills in MBA (master's of business administration) curricula, and their respective inclusion in the training of managers around the globe, has provided a backdrop for the diffusion of innovations in management accounting, which, to a considerable extent, have been subject to the fashions and fads in management discourse. In a longer historical perspective, the current packaging of accounting expertise completes the marginalization of nonfinancial experts (particularly those trained in engineering) in the design and operation of management accounting systems and the yielding of managerial control over all aspects of production processes to finance specialists.

Another increasingly important aspect of convergence across management accounting systems is the use of information technology, management information systems, and SAP R/3–type software by organizations across organizational fields and sectors. Although installing these systems in organizations requires a good deal of customization, it also renders organizational operations of different kinds, across different organizations and diverse organizational fields, gradually comparable. Isomorphism in the use of information technology has clearly been reinforcing the diffusion of accounting-related expertise and of respective innovations across different organizations, organizational fields, sectors, and political segments of world society.

Accounting Systems as Extending Organizations Across Time and Space

The diffusion and extension of accounting systems affects balances of power within and across organizations, favoring those with access to numerical records, those competent in interpreting them, and those able to systematically employ numbers in acting on organizational contexts about which numerical information is produced and circulated. Being embedded in the circulation of numbers, these organizational contexts become accessible to *action at a distance* (a concept from actor-network theory, which has become very prominent in interdisciplinary accounting discourse).

Management accounting systems produce numbers on operations, products, and individual outputs that are inspected by production managers who, in turn, adapt controls and a reward system, to see the numbers change subsequently, to further calibrate the reward system, and so on; companies' annual reports are analyzed by investors, and inserted into investment portfolio calculations, and capital is shifted as a result; tax authorities inspect income statements and a variety of cash-flow documentations to calculate taxes due; governmental agencies use all kinds of statistics in calibrating regulatory schemes. In any one of these examples, certain settings of organizational action turn into centers of calculation that accumulate numbers and employ them in acting at a distance on other settings, like factory floors, households and families, corporations, and, not least, other accounting systems. With respect to centers of calculation, these latter settings may appear to define peripheries, but participants facing action at a distance by others may adapt to being inspected and manipulated by the numbers, particularly once they are competent in utilizing numbers themselves and have an appropriate idea of how numbers will be interpreted and utilized in centers of calculation. The emergence and continuous adaptation of various forms of creative accounting demonstrate such accommodations, which, alongside problems of surveillance and control associated with them, historically have been accompanying the diffusion and extension of accounting systems from the start.

Problems of standardizing, regulating, and policing the production and circulation of numerical records are inevitable for organizations attempting to extend their ability to organize across space and time through the use of accounting systems. Accounting records make present what is past and distant, and those basing their decisions and actions on numerical information often have no other means of checking on what is otherwise away and gone. With the globalization of organizing activities, the distance-spanning abilities of accounting systems have been embedding organizational units spread around the globe in overarching flows of information.

The historical mushrooming of accounting systems from local representations of the past to informational architectures in which organizing is made subject to potentially endless evaluations and projections through space and time has two programmatic aspects—one technological, the other discursive. On the one hand, it has been driven by discourses of government and management defining spheres of interest and potential intervention. On the other hand, such discourse has been supported by numerical records defining certain spheres of intervention to start with (e.g., census figures defining demographic problems, sales figures defining market shares). In the extension of accounting systems, discourses and technologies combine in escalating the need for numerical information.

As evidenced by the diversity of creative accounting, there are also social aspects of the growth of accounting systems that cannot altogether be programmed very well by either discursive or technological means. There is a tendency of accounting systems to establish playing fields in which different organizational interests compete by drawing on numbers to support positions and status. Once decisions of superordinate organizational levels are based on forms of intraorganizational competition, the outcome of which is expressed numerically (e.g., in return on investment ratios), competitors are drawn into procuring requisite numbers regardless of the regulatory intentions with which the accounting system might originally have been invested. Participants at the level of intervention may seek to use accounting systems to extend their influence upward through forms of numerical impression management. In this way, accounting systems extend organizations across time and space not only on a formal and programmatic level, but also in disseminating social conflict and informal rivalries across networks of circulating numbers.

Social scientists interested in accounting have pointed out that once decision makers shift attention almost exclusively to numerical representations, and once regulatory struggles devolve into reiterated trials of strength between increasingly complex informational architectures while forms of creative accounting try to resist these systems through their own devices, organizational activities at regulatory and executive levels are likely to drift away from other involvements in organizational domains. Especially in those areas of global business activity in which the objects of financial accounting, financial-market regulations, and reporting standards have become entangled in complex webs of financial products, options, and derivatives, there has been speculation of an emergent hyperreality supported by accounting systems running exclusively under their own steam of financial information. Similar observations may suggest themselves with respect to the circulation of indicators (of trade balances, social welfare, climate changes, etc.) among governmental organizations in transnational political arenas, although the respective accounting systems largely remain to be explored.

Hendrik Vollmer

See also Banks; Capitalism; Finance, Financial Systems; Homogenization; Information Age; International Monetary Fund (IMF); International Nongovernmental Organizations (INGOs); Liberalism, Neoliberalism; Organisation for Economic Co-operation and Development (OECD); Population and Demographic Change; Professions; Standards and Standard-Setting, Global; World Bank

Further Readings

Armstrong, P. (1987). The rise of accounting controls in British capitalist enterprises. *Accounting, Organizations and Society, 12,* 415–436.

Fligstein, N. (1987). The intraorganizational power struggle: Rise of finance personnel to top leadership in large corporations, 1919–1979. *American Sociological Review, 52,* 44–58.

Johnson, H. T., & Kaplan, R. S. (1987). *Relevance lost: The rise and fall of management accounting.* Boston: Harvard Business School Press.

Macintosh, N. B., Shearer, T., Thornton, D. B., & Welker, M. (2000). Accounting as simulacrum and hyperreality: Perspectives on income and capital. *Accounting, Organizations and Society, 25,* 13–50.

McBarnet, D., Weston, S., & Whelan, C. J. (1993). Adversary accounting: Strategic uses of financial information by capital and labour. *Accounting, Organizations and Society, 18,* 81–100.

Miller, P. (1990). On the interrelations between accounting and the state. *Accounting, Organizations and Society, 15,* 315–338.

Napier, C. J. (2006). Accounts of change: 30 years of accounting history. *Accounting, Organizations and Society, 31,* 445–507.

Quattrone, P., & Hopper, T. (2005). A "time-space odyssey": Management control systems in two multinational organisations. *Accounting, Organizations and Society, 30,* 735–764.

Robson, K. (1992). Accounting numbers as "inscription": Action at a distance and the development of accounting. *Accounting, Organizations and Society, 17,* 685–708.

Thompson, G. F. (1991). Is accounting rhetorical? Methodology, Luca Pacioli and printing. *Accounting, Organizations and Society, 16,* 572–599.

Vollmer, H. (2007). How to do more with numbers: Elementary stakes, framing, keying, and the three-dimensional character of numerical signs. *Accounting, Organizations and Society, 32,* 577–600.

ACCULTURATION

Acculturation is a common feature of the global era. It is the process of cultural and psychological change that takes place as a result of contact between cultural groups and their individual members. Such contact and change occur for many reasons (such as colonization and migration); it continues after initial contact in culturally plural societies, where ethnocultural communities maintain features of their heritage cultures over generations, and it takes place in both groups in contact. Adaptation to acculturation takes place over time; occasionally it is stressful, but often it results in some form of mutual accommodation.

The initial interest in acculturation examined the effects of European domination of colonial and indigenous peoples. Later, it focused on how immigrants (both voluntary and involuntary) changed following their entry and settlement into receiving societies. More recently, much of the work has been involved with how ethnocultural groups and individuals relate to each other, and how they change, as a result of their attempts to live together in culturally plural societies. Nowadays, all three foci are important areas of research, as globalization results in ever-larger trading and political relations.

The concept of psychological acculturation was introduced by Theodore D. Graves in 1967; it refers to changes in an individual who is a participant in a culture contact situation, being influenced both directly by the external (usually dominant) culture and by the changing culture (usually nondominant) of which the individual is a member. There are two reasons for keeping the cultural and psychological levels distinct. The first is that in cross-cultural psychology, individual human behavior is viewed as interacting with the cultural context within which it occurs; hence, separate conceptions and measurements are required at the two levels. The second reason is that not every group or individual enters into, participates in, or changes in the same way; there are vast group and individual differences in psychological acculturation, even among people who live in the same acculturative arena.

At the cultural level, there is a need to understand key features of the two original cultural groups prior to their major contact. It is also important to understand the nature of their contact relationships and the resulting cultural changes in both the original groups and in the ethnocultural groups that emerge following contact during the process of acculturation. These changes can be minor or substantial and range from being easily accomplished to being a source of major cultural disruption.

At the individual level, there is a need to consider the psychological changes that individuals in all groups undergo and to examine their eventual adaptation to their new situations. These changes can be a set of rather easily accomplished behavioral shifts (e.g., in ways of speaking, dressing, and eating), or they can be more problematic, producing acculturative stress as manifested by uncertainty, anxiety, and depression. Adaptations can be primarily internal or psychological (e.g., sense of well-being or self-esteem) or sociocultural (e.g., as manifested in competence in the activities of daily intercultural living).

As noted earlier, not every group or individual engages the acculturation process in the same way. The concept of *acculturation strategies* refers to the various ways that groups and individuals seek to acculturate. These variations have challenged the assumption that everyone would assimilate and become absorbed into the dominant group. At the cultural level, the two groups in contact (whether dominant or nondominant) usually have some notion about what they are attempting to do (e.g., colonial policies). At the individual level, persons will vary within their cultural group (e.g., on the basis of their educational or occupational background).

Four acculturation strategies have been derived from two basic issues facing all acculturating peoples. These issues are based on the distinction between orientations toward one's own group and those toward other groups in the larger society. This distinction is rendered as a relative preference for maintaining one's heritage culture and identity and a relative preference for having contact with, and participating in, the larger society along with other ethnocultural groups. It has now been well demonstrated that these two dimensions are independent of each other. These two issues can be responded to on attitudinal dimensions, varying along bipolar dimensions ranging from positive to negative preferences. Orientations to these issues intersect to define four acculturation strategies. When individuals do not wish to maintain their cultural identity and seek daily interaction with other cultures, the *assimilation* strategy is defined. In contrast, when individuals place a value on holding on to their original culture, and at the same time wish to avoid interaction with others, then the *separation* alternative is defined. When

there is an interest in maintaining one's original culture while in daily interactions with other groups, *integration* is the option. In this case, there is some degree of cultural integrity maintained, while at the same time the person seeks, as a member of an ethnocultural group, to participate as an integral part of the larger social network. Finally, when there is little possibility or interest in cultural maintenance (often for reasons of enforced cultural loss), and little interest in having relations with others (often for reasons of exclusion or discrimination), then *marginalization* is defined.

The original definition clearly established that both groups in contact would change and become acculturated. The four terms defined in the previous paragraph describe the acculturation strategies of nondominant peoples. Different terms are needed to describe the strategies of the dominant, larger society. Assimilation when sought by the dominant group is termed the *melting pot*. When separation is forced by the dominant group, it is *segregation*. Marginalization, when imposed by the dominant group, is *exclusion*. Finally, for integration, when diversity is a widely accepted feature of the society as a whole, it is called *multiculturalism*. With the use of these concepts and measures, comparisons can be made between individuals and their groups, and between nondominant peoples and the larger society within which they are acculturating. The acculturation ideologies and policies of the dominant group constitute an important element of intercultural research, while the preferences of nondominant peoples are a core feature in acculturation research. Inconsistencies and conflicts between these various acculturation preferences are common sources of difficulty for those experiencing acculturation. This can occur when individuals do not accept the main ideology of their society (e.g., when individuals oppose immigrant cultural maintenance in a society where multiculturalism is official policy or when immigrant children challenge the way of acculturating set out by their parents). Generally, when acculturation experiences cause problems for acculturating individuals, we observe the phenomenon of acculturative stress, with variations in levels of adaptation. Much research has shown that those seeking to integrate (i.e., a double cultural involvement) achieve the best psychological and sociocultural adaptations, while those who are marginalized have the poorest outcomes. Assimilation and separation strategies are typically associated with intermediate levels of adaptation.

John W. Berry

See also Assimilation; Colonialism; Cosmopolitan Identity; Cultural Hybridity; Diasporas; Ethnic Identity; Identities in Global Society; Immigration; Migration; Multiculturalism; National Identities

Further Readings

Berry, J. W. (2005). Acculturation: Living successfully in two cultures. *International Journal of Intercultural Relations, 29,* 697–712.

Berry, J. W. (2008). Globalization and acculturation. *International Journal of Intercultural Relations, 32,* 328–336.

Berry, J. W., Phinney, J. S., Sam, D. L., & Vedder, P. (Eds.). (2006). *Immigrant youth in cultural transition: Acculturation, identity, and adaptation across national contexts.* Mahwah, NJ: Erlbaum.

Liebkind, K. (2001). Acculturation. In R. Brown & S. Gaertner (Eds.), *Blackwell handbook of social psychology* (Vol. 4, pp. 386–406). Oxford, UK: Blackwell.

Redfield, R., Linton, R., & Herskovits, M. J. (1936). Memorandum on the study of acculturation. *American Anthropologist, 38,* 149–152.

Sam, D. L., & Berry, J. W. (Eds.). (2006). *The Cambridge handbook of acculturation psychology.* Cambridge, UK: Cambridge University Press.

Ward, C. (2001). The A, B, Cs of acculturation. In D. Matsumoto (Ed.), *The handbook of culture and psychology* (pp. 411–445). Oxford, UK: Oxford University Press.

ACID RAIN

The critical issue of acid rain is a good example of a transnational environmental problem. An increase in acidic gases and particles in the atmosphere produced in one country can impact other countries further downwind of these acidifying emissions.

The acidic nature of rain was first observed near industrial cities in England and Scotland by an English chemist, Robert Angus Smith, in 1832. However, it was not until the late 1960s and early 1970s that acid rain was recognized as a widespread environmental problem in Europe and eastern North America. According to Gene Likens, F. Herbert Bormann, and Noye Johnson (1972), *acid rain* is a general or popular term, now known to include not only wet deposition from rain, snow, sleet, hail, cloud, and fog water but also dry deposition from acidifying particles and gases. *Acid deposition* is the more scientific term for this phenomenon.

The sources of most acid deposition are anthropogenic, mainly the burning of fossil fuels for power generation, industrial activity and transportation, and the smelting of metal ores. These activities produce SO_2 and/or NO_x ($NO + NO_2$) gases, which are oxidized and converted to sulfuric and nitric acid, respectively. In their simplest forms, the reactions are:

$$SO_2 + H_2O \rightarrow H_2SO_4 \leftrightarrow H^+ + HSO_4^- \leftrightarrow 2H^+ + SO_4 =$$
$$NO_2 + H_2O \rightarrow HNO_3 \leftrightarrow H^+ + NO_3^-$$

pH is a measure of hydrogen ion (H^+) concentration, and the scale is logarithmic (pH = $-\log H^+$ concentration), so precipitation with a pH of 4.0 has 10 times more H^+ ions (100 µeq/l) than precipitation with a pH of 5.0 (10 µeq/l). The pH of rain in industrialized regions is mainly the result of sulfuric and nitric acid. Precipitation is naturally somewhat acidic because of the carbonic acid from CO_2 and organic acids from biological activity. Volcanic activity can increase atmospheric acidity by producing hydrochloric acid (HCl), as well as sulfuric acid. Lightning and forest fires can convert molecular nitrogen (N_2), the main component of the atmosphere, to nitrogen oxides, which then can form nitric acid. These natural sources of acidity are generally small and reduce the pH of precipitation from 5.6 or higher to about 5.2. However, in many industrialized areas of the world, the average pH of precipitation is 4.0 to 4.5, with individual events often much lower. Organic acids can contribute to acidity (Likens, Keene, Miller, & Galloway, 1987), but their contribution is usually less than 20% of the total acidity in industrial areas.

The largest amounts of acid deposition occur in eastern North America, central and northwestern Europe, and more recently in Southeast Asia (see

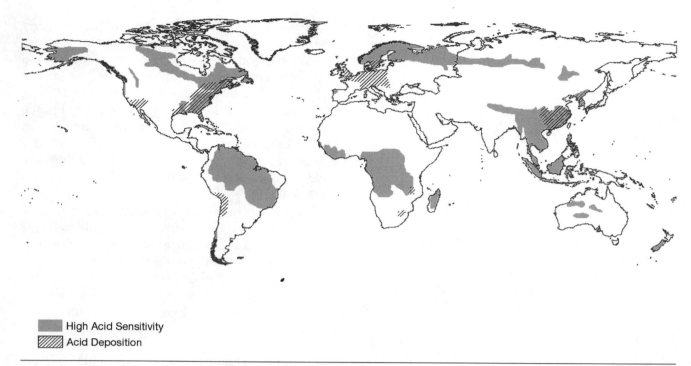

High Acid Sensitivity
Acid Deposition

Figure 1   Areas sensitive to acid deposition (shaded) and areas receiving acid deposition (hatched areas show pH of rain < 4.5).

Source: Based on Kuylenstierna, Rhode, Cinderby, & Hicks (2001); Rhode, Dentener, & Schulz (2002).

Figure 1). These are all areas downwind of large emissions of SO_2 and NO_x resulting mainly from fossil fuel–based power production and industrial activities. China is the leading producer of SO_2, having produced 33.2 million metric tons in 2006 (Lu et al., 2010), and the United States produces the most NO_x, 16.6 million metric tons in 2005 (U.S. Environmental Protection Agency, 2010).

Acid rain can occur hundreds to thousands of kilometers downwind from the original emission sources, often crossing international boundaries and complicating relations with neighboring countries. Acidity of precipitation has decreased in the past few decades in Europe and eastern North America, mainly due to SO_2 emission controls and also switching to low-sulfur coal. There has been less of a reduction in NO_x emissions in Europe and North America, and global nitrogen emissions are expected to increase in the future.

Southeast Asia, and China in particular, has seen an increase in acid deposition because of large increases in fossil fuel combustion and a lack of significant pollution controls on SO_2 and NO_x emissions. India has also had a large increase in fossil fuel combustion. However, the influence of acid-neutralizing alkaline dust in the atmosphere has limited acid deposition in these areas, according to Zhifang Xu and Guilan Han (2009).

Effects of Acid Deposition

The impacts of acid deposition were documented in aquatic ecosystems of Europe and North America in the 1970s and continue today. Tens of thousands of lakes and streams are more acidic than they were in the 1950s. These waters are chemically altered, usually to the detriment of fish, invertebrate, and phytoplankton abundance and diversity. High acidity can mobilize monomeric aluminum, which is toxic to most forms of life. High aluminum concentrations from increased acidity damages fish gills, impairs respiration, and results in increased mortality. Higher acidity, especially from sulfur deposition, also enhances methyl mercury accumulation in fish. Mercury is a neurological toxin to organisms that eat fish, including humans. Acid depositions in areas with significant winter snowfall have "episodic acidification." The first thaws leach acidity from the entire snowpack, resulting in very acidic runoff. Often this runoff does not have sufficient time to be neutralized by base cations in soil, and therefore a pulse of acidity enters streams and lakes, resulting in fish mortality and damage to other aquatic organisms.

Acid deposition alters the chemistry of soils with low buffering or acid-neutralizing capacity and, in turn, impacts forest ecosystems. Acid deposition leaches important plant nutrients such as Ca^{++} and Mg^{++} and other base cations from soils. When this depletion occurs faster than the production of base cations through weathering or through atmospheric deposition of base cations, then increased soil acidification occurs. In addition, lower soil pH mobilizes soil aluminum, which negatively impacts terrestrial vegetation as well as aquatic organisms. At a pH of 4.6, aluminum can be 1,000 times more soluble than at a pH of 5.6 (Weathers, Likens, & Butler, 2007).

Soil acidification from atmospheric inputs can also occur from deposition of reduced nitrogen compounds such as ammonia (NH_3) and ammonium (NH_4^+). Ammonium is biologically active and, if not taken up by vegetation, is nitrified in the soil by bacteria; in the process, H^+ ions are released, increasing soil water acidity and mobilizing soil aluminum.

Forest damage has been well documented in many regions of central Europe, eastern North America, and southern China. It is difficult to attribute this damage entirely to acid deposition because other stresses may also be impacting many of these sites (high summertime ozone, stress from disease and pests, climate effects, etc.) in interacting ways. However, forest decline often occurs where there are high levels of acid deposition and acid-sensitive soils with low buffering capacity (see Figure 1). The intersection of these two conditions leads to both forest decline and acidification of streams and lakes.

Recovery

It was expected that due to legislation in Europe and North America, which has reduced emissions of SO_2 and to a lesser extent NO_x, aquatic ecosystems would recover and the acid rain problem would be "solved." However recovery, even with a reduction in acid inputs, has been slow and more complex than expected in acid-sensitive regions. In eastern North America, it was found that after

decades of acid deposition, sensitive soils lost much of their acid-neutralizing capacity (i.e., loss of base cations). Indeed, acid deposition is still occurring, and soils with low buffering capacity are now even more sensitive because of loss of these base cations. An environmental problem that has been decades in the making will most likely take decades for recovery.

Gene E. Likens, Thomas J. Butler,
and Melissa A. Rury

See also Climate Change; Deforestation; Environmental Change; Extractive Industries Sector; Forests; Global Environmental and Energy Issues; Petroleum Economy

Further Readings

Kuylenstierna, J. C. I., Rhode, H., Cinderby, S., & Hicks, K. (2001). Acidification in developing countries: Ecosystem sensitivity and the critical load approach on a global scale. *Ambio, 30,* 20–28.

Likens, G. E., Bormann, F. H., & Johnson, N. M. (1972). Acid rain. *Environment, 14,* 33–40.

Likens, G. E., Driscoll, C. T., & Buso, D. C. (1996). Long-term effects of acid rain: Response and recovery of a forest ecosystem. *Science, 272,* 244–246.

Likens, G. E., Keene, W. C., Miller, J. M., & Galloway, J. N. (1987). Chemistry of precipitation at a remote, terrestrial site in Australia. *Journal of Geophysical Research, 92,* 13299–13314.

Lu, Z., Streets, D. G., Zhang, Q., Wang, S., Carmichael, G. R., Cheng, Y. F., et al. (2010). Sulfur dioxide emissions in China and sulfur trends in East Asia since 2000. *Atmospheric Chemistry and Physics, 10,* 6311–6331.

Rhode, H., Dentener, F., & Schulz, M. (2002). The global distribution of acidifying wet deposition. *Environmental Science & Technology, 36,* 4382–4388.

U.S. Environmental Protection Agency. (2010). *Our nation's air: Status and trends through 2008* (Report No. EPA-454/R-09-002). Research Triangle Park, NC: Office of Air Quality Planning and Standards. Retrieved August 31, 2011, from http://www.epa.gov/airtrends/2010/index.html

Weathers, K. C., Likens, G. E., & Butler, T. J. (2007). Acid rain. In W. N. Rom (Ed.), *Environmental and occupational medicine* (4th ed., pp. 1507–1520). Philadelphia: Lippincott, Williams & Wilkins.

Xu, Z., & Han, G. (2009). Chemical and strontium isotope characterization of rainwater in Beijing, China. *Atmospheric Environment, 43,* 1954–1961.

ACTIVISM, TRANSNATIONAL

Transnational activism can be defined as the mobilization of collective claims by actors located in more than one country and/or addressing more than one national government and/or international governmental organization or another international actor. An example is the Occupy Wall Street movement that began in the United States in 2011 in protest against global corporate capitalism and then became a feature of anti-corporate protest in London, Rome, Berlin, and other cities around the world. While forms of transnational activism have been present since a distant past, economic and political globalization has apparently increased their frequency, as well as attention to them.

Social movement studies, like other areas of the social sciences, have been late to acknowledge phenomena of transnationalization and are still in search of adequate theories, concepts, and methods to address them. In fact, most research in the social sciences has time and again confirmed the important role that national political opportunities play in influencing social movement mobilizations, their scope, duration, and forms. The modern repertoire of contention has emerged with the creation of the nation-state, and social movements have played an important role in the establishment of (national) citizenship rights. Thus, it was at the national level that movements fought for access to the public sphere and to decision makers, forged alliances, and suffered from state repression. Case studies as well as cross-national comparisons have addressed these issues in depth, remaining (like most political sociology and political science) anchored in the nation-state. In this regard, social movement studies were not exceptional: Research on political parties or interest groups showed the same pattern. On the other hand, for a long time, international relations have considered states as the main, or even only, actor. This situation started to change in the first decade of the 21st century when research in the social sciences addressed transnational activism via different concepts. In what follows, these concepts are reviewed by distinguishing the actors, forms, and identities in transnational activism.

The Actors of Transnational Activism

Transnational activism requires transnational actors. Global civic society, international governmental organizations, transnational social movement organizations, and global justice movements are concepts developed for naming these actors.

In social theory, *global civic society* is a much used and much debated term to indicate a civil society that represents itself as a global actor, networking across national borders and challenging international institutions. Stimulated by the "velvet," peaceful revolutions in Central and Eastern Europe and prior oppositional movements there, the concept of civil society stressed the potential role of a third, autonomous sphere between the state and the market. The organization of a global civil society has been linked to globalization processes in economy, culture, and politics.

Similarly, empirical research in international relations has addressed the birth of *international nongovernmental organizations* (INGOs), pointing at the recent increase in their numbers, membership, and availability of material resources, as well as their influence on policy choices. The related concept of *transnational social movement organizations* (TSMOs) was coined to define the INGOs active within networks of social movements. While nongovernmental organizations and social movements developed as national politics grew, the formation of INGOs and TSMOs has been seen as a response to the growing institutionalization of international politics.

Focusing on the interactions between these actors and international governmental organizations, or IGOs (initially especially the United Nations, later on the European Union), the first studies emphasized their capacity to adapt to the IGOs' rules of the game, preferring a diplomatic search for agreement over democratic accountability, discretion over transparency, and persuasion over mobilization in the street. Some of these actors have been highlighted as having not only increased in number but also strengthened their influence in various stages of international policy making. Their assets include an increasing credibility in public opinion and consequent availability of private funding, a specific knowledge base, rootedness at the local level, and independence from governments. Finally, they are said to enhance pluralism within international institutions by representing groups that would otherwise be excluded and by turning attention to transnational processes, making the governance process more transparent. Some of these claims have been challenged, however. Research indicated that, in contrast to business organizations and other economic actors, the actors of the global civil society are usually loosely organized and poorly staffed, consisting mainly of transnational alliances of various national groups. Their inclusion in international politics has also been selective: Only those organizations that adapt to the rules of the game obtain some access, although usually of an informal nature, to some IGOs. Finally, rootedness at the local level and independence from governments are variable.

The *global justice movement* has emerged at the turn of the millennium, involving some of the mentioned transnational types of organization, but also national and local ones. In the research carried out by Donatella della Porta, it has been defined as formed by the loose network of organizations and individuals, engaged in collective action of various kinds, on the basis of the shared goal of advancing the cause of justice (economic, social, political, and environmental) among and between peoples across the globe. At local, national, and transnational levels, organizations from different social movements have converged in a series of roundtables, networks, and coalitions that are very often not limited to one national state. *Netzwerke, reti, redes, coordinadoras, tavoli, nets,* and *forums* are frequent terms in the names of new organizations that allow not only for overlapping memberships in different organizations by individual activists but also for the convergence of organized actors.

The Forms of Transnational Activism

Studies on INGOs and TSMOs highlighted that many of them had become increasingly institutionalized, both in terms of acquired professionalism and in the forms of action they employ, devoting more time to lobbying or informing the public than to marching in the street. Nevertheless, in more recent times, specific forms of transnational protests (e.g., counter-summits, global days of action, and social forums) have been invented and have spread.

Protest event analysis has repeatedly concluded that concerns about transnational decisions have been mainly expressed at the national level, where elected political institutions are considered more accountable to the citizen-electors. Using data on protest collected mainly from newspaper sources, researchers stress the paucity of protests directly targeting IGOs. Relying on Reuters World News Service and the Reuters Textline, Doug Imig and Sidney Tarrow found a very limited number of protests addressing European Union (EU) institutions. Protest events addressing international institutions emerged as constantly marginal (or even of declining relevance) in research projects on single countries (e.g., in Germany), as well as specific issues such as migrant rights or environmental protection.

If previous research had stressed, as mentioned, the taming of social movements with a shift from the street to the lobbies, recent studies, addressing especially the global justice movement, pointed instead at a growth of disruptive transnational forms of protest. Especially since the protest against the third World Trade Organization (WTO) conference in Seattle in November 1999, countersummits, global days of action, and transnational social forums have contributed to building awareness of, and interest in, transnational activism. These protests developed from a number of campaigns that networked various organizations against the North American Free Trade Agreement (NAFTA); against the Multilateral Agreement on Investment; for the cancellation of poor countries' foreign debt (among others, in the Jubilee 2000 campaign); or for a more socially responsible Europe (e.g., in the European Marches Against Unemployment, Insecurity and Exclusion). Within these campaigns, new frames of action developed, symbolically constructing a global self but also producing structural effects in the form of new movement networks.

One main new form of transnational protest is the *counter-summit*, defined as the gathering of transnational activists in parallel to official summits of international institutions. In the 1990s, the end of the Cold War opened opportunities for movement in the form of UN-sponsored conferences but also autonomous networking, especially against the war in Iraq and former Yugoslavia, and in solidarity with the Zapatista movement. In the early 2000s, confrontational counter-summits developed with the contestation of IGOs such as the World Bank, the International Monetary Fund (IMF), the World Trade Organization (WTO), the G-8, and even the European Union. Prominent counter-summits included marches as well as direct action against the IMF and World Bank meetings in Washington, D.C., and Prague in 2000 and 2001; against the EU summits in Amsterdam in 1997, Nice in 2000, and Gothenburg in 2001; against the World Economic Forum in yearly demonstrations in Davos; and against the G-8 summit in Genoa in 2001. After the Seattle protests in 1999, there was an escalation of conflicts between protestors and police during the contestation of international summits.

Together with counter-summits, *global days of action* brought activists to march, on the same day, in many countries. In what was defined as the hugest mass protest ever in the world history, millions of people joined the international day of protest against the Iraq war on February 15, 2003, marching in thousands of cities around the world.

Since 2001, transnational networking intensified in the *world social forums*, as well as its many macro-regional and national versions. In general, social forums have been an innovative experiment promoted by the global justice movement. Distinct from a counter-summit, which is mainly oriented toward protest, the social forum is a public space of debate among activists. In yearly editions, world social forums as well as European social forums provided arenas for encounters and debates to thousands of organizations and tens of thousands of activists from different countries. The 2011 global protests against transnational corporate capitalism began with Occupy Wall Street sit-ins in New York City and spread around the world.

Not only have supranational events increased in frequency, they have also constituted founding events for a new cycle of protest that has developed at the national and subnational levels on the issue of global justice. Even though they remained a rare occurrence, transnational protests (in the forms of global days of action, counter-summits, or social forums) emerged as particularly "eventful" in their capacity to produce relational, cognitive, and affective effects on social movement activists and social movement organizations.

Global Claims

Researchers looking at the cross-national diffusion of movement frames, as well as of strategies of public order control, have pointed out how frames spread from one country to another. Geographical proximity, but also the process of identification, facilitates reciprocal cross-fertilization. Intensifying exchanges among social movement organizations, cultural globalization increased communication across countries and across movements. Additionally, with the development of transnational campaigns, calls for international norms on issues such as human rights and environmental protection have been put forward.

In particular, the global justice movement has contributed to the definition of certain global issues, such as global justice or global democracy. If the symbolic reference to the globe is considered by some scholars as nothing really new—referencing the traditional internationalism of the workers' movement or the transnational campaigns against slavery—others have instead stressed the centrality of the global dimension today.

Transnational communication helped solidify not only a definition of problems as global but also the cognitive linkages between different themes in broad transnational campaigns. If in the 1980s social movements had undergone a process of specialization on single issues, with "new social movements" developing specific knowledge and competences on particular subissues, the global justice movement has bridged together a multiplicity of themes related to class, gender, generation, race, and religion as different movements met in a lengthy, although not very visible, process of mobilization. In fact, the global justice movement developed from protest campaigns around "broker issues" that tied together concerns of different movements and organizations. In all these campaigns, to different degrees, elements of diverse cultures—secular and religious, radical and reformist, younger and older generations—have been linked to a broader discourse with social (and global) injustice as the cohering theme, while still leaving broad margins for separate developments. At the transnational level, local and global concerns were linked around values such as equality, justice, human rights, and environmental protection. In this sense, the global justice movement has been said to contribute to, and reflect, the spread of composite and tolerant identities. While the discourse of the movement emphasized pluralism and diversity, a common master frame developed around a definition of the self that opened toward a global dimension.

In parallel, the enemy is singled out in neoliberal globalization, which activists perceive as characterizing not only the policies of the international financial organizations (the World Bank, IMF, and WTO), but also the free-market and deregulation policies by national governments. These policies are considered to be responsible for growing social injustice, with especially negative effects on the environment, the global South, and on women and other groups. Alongside social justice, the search for a global democracy has emerged as a central concern. If the development of a global form of governance with the increasing influence of (private) global economic actors challenges the traditional legitimation of democracy through electoral accountability, the most widespread request has been for the development of democratic global institutions.

Although still deeply rooted in the national political systems and corresponding movement families, cosmopolitan activists tended to bridge the local with the global and vice versa. In doing so, they are contributing to the development of a transnational political system as well as transnational collective identities.

Multilevel Opportunity Structures

Regarding transnational activism as in other areas, phenomena of transnationalization were, not by chance, first addressed in the context of studies of international relations and international sociology. Research on human rights or conflict resolution also stressed the emergence of international norms that challenged the vision of international politics as an anarchic or exclusively power-oriented system of states. Bringing "transnational relations back in," Thomas Risse, Stephen Ropp, Kathryn Sikkink, and others have stressed the role of environmental transnational and human rights campaigns in developing normatively grounded international policy regimes. Global civil society actors, INGOs, and TSMOs emerge as important agents in these processes and are, in fact, more and

more recognized by global institutions, such as the United Nations.

In addition, research on European integration and Europeanization has increasingly addressed the role of civil society. Some changes in European institutions have been said to facilitate access by movement organizations. First, if the building of the European institutions in a manner oriented to the creation of a common market explains the dominance of producers' interests, with the progression of market-making legislation (from the European Commission, the European Council, but also the European Court of Justice) there was also an increase in demand for market-correcting policies (with mobilizations of consumers, environmentalists, and so on). Moreover, in recent times, the debate about good governance and the democratic deficit induced the European Commission to reflect on the involvement of civil society and, especially after Maastricht, to look for broader social acceptance of EU policies (e.g., the White Paper on Governance) as well as for allies in the power play with the European Council. In fact, some social movement organizations have recently been granted increased participation in return for expertise and legitimacy. The European Commission has meetings with nongovernmental organizations involved in the social platform and environmental groups. The support of the European Union for the European Trade Union Confederation also has been significant. The European Parliament has worked as a main channel of access to various organizations, especially in areas where parliamentary committees are more active (e.g., environmental issues) and movement organizations' relations with the European Commission more difficult. Feminists, environmentalists, and union members have also been able to obtain favorable decisions from the Court of Justice, especially with the increasing competence of the European Union with respect to environmental and social policies. Although access remained unequal, some formal and informal opportunities for influencing the EU institutions have been opening up and tested by social movement organizations. Beyond their varying degrees of success, initiatives at the EU level have facilitated networking among social movement organizations of different countries, focusing their attention on the European dimension of multilevel governance.

There is increasing reflection on multilevel opportunity structures for multilevel social movements. In one of the first volumes on transnational activism from a social movement perspective, Donatella della Porta, Hanspeter Kriesi, and Dieter Rucht pointed at the specificities of IGOs as offering political opportunities (and constraints) for social movements addressing domestic as well as global problems. In this sense, two main paths of transnationalization were identified: (1) social movements with domestic political concerns (especially in authoritarian regimes) searching for external, international allies to put pressure on their domestic political elites; and (2) social movements directly addressing their own governments, in order to influence political decisions at the international level.

The development of campaigns targeting diverse IGOs stimulated further reflections on the range of opportunities that various international institutions offered to social movements. Such elements as a consensual culture and a reciprocal search for recognition were available for the United Nations but not for the much more closed and hostile international finance and trade institutions (WTO, IMF, and World Bank, G-7/G-8) that became the target of lively protest during campaigns such as "50 Years Is Enough" and "Our World Is Not for Sale." Social movements that target international institutions looked for the specific leverage offered, for example, by the unanimity rules of the WTO, which make alliances with some states particularly relevant, and by access to the international experts and formal channels of consultation granted by the International Labour Organization. Additionally, in recent research, IGOs emerged as complex and fragmented institutions, composed of different bodies that provide external actors with differentiated opportunities. The European Council, the European Commission, the European Parliament, and the European Court of Justice are all targeted by social movements, but protest strategies vary according to the characteristics of these specific bodies. Even when considering only the European Commission, it appears that different movements find it more or less difficult to get access to or to oppose a specific (sympathetic) General Directorate in the European Commission.

In sum, if economic, neoliberal globalization offered the target for much transnational activism, INGOs acted, to use Sidney Tarrow's metaphor, as a coral reef for the formation of transnational protest actors.

Donatella della Porta

See also Antiglobalization Movements and Critics; Civil Society, Global; Globalization, Phenomenon of; Justice Movements, Transnational; Social Movements; World Social Forum

Further Readings

Boli, J., & Thomas, G. M. (1999). *Constructing the world culture: International nongovernmental organizations since 1875.* Stanford, CA: Stanford University Press.

Della Porta, D. (Ed.). (2007). *The global justice movement: Cross-national and transnational perspectives.* Boulder, CO: Paradigm.

Della Porta, D., Andretta, M., Mosca, L., & Reiter, H. (2006). *Globalization from below.* Minneapolis: University of Minnesota Press.

Della Porta, D., & Caiani, M. (2009). *Social movements and Europe.* Oxford, UK: Oxford University Press.

Della Porta, D., Kriesi, H., & Rucht, D. (Eds.). (1999). *Social movements in a globalizing world.* New York: Macmillan.

Della Porta, D., Peterson, A., & Reiter, H. (Eds.). (2006). *The policing of transnational protest.* Aldershot, UK: Ashgate.

Della Porta, D., & Tarrow, S. (Eds.). (2005). *Transnational protest and global activism.* New York: Rowman & Littlefield.

Imig, D., & Tarrow, S. (Eds.). (2001). *Contentious Europeans: Protest and politics in an emerging polity.* Lanham, MD: Rowman & Littlefield.

Keck, M., & Sikkink, K. (1998). *Activists beyond borders.* Ithaca, NY: Cornell University Press.

Risse, T., Ropp, S., & Sikkink, K. (Eds.). (1999). *The power of human rights international norms and domestic change.* New York: Cambridge University Press.

Smith, J. (2008). *Social movements for global democracy.* Baltimore: Johns Hopkins University Press.

Tarrow, S. (2005). *The new transnational activism.* New York: Cambridge University Press.

AESTHETICS

Global aesthetics refers to the theories and practices of visual arts in the context of a transnational art world, integrated through the multinational art market. It also includes the relationships between artists, curators, dealers, and art writers across the world. The concept of global aesthetics that emerged through the transnational movements of people and artworks challenges the hegemony of traditional aesthetic theories but is still linked with global financial centers and corporate power. The professional artist and other key art world players are educated in fine art faculties that emulate the best international models and that produce shared practices, themes, and ways of making sense of art. They may have different traditions and histories, but they share a sense of modernity and contemporaneity that creates an intercultural and cross-cultural art world.

Art Market

Global aesthetics developed as part of the institutionalization of art and the globalization of the art market. The global city required branding that was provided by a destination museum built, or renovated and extended, by a globally recognized architect. The network of relationships between a global art market center and the museum facilitated the establishment of aesthetic values and financial values, or price, through the art world relationships in the city. The links between the art market and other financial markets, and the process for price formation that developed as a result of the use of art as an investment commodity, also changed the activities and relationships that determine changes in aesthetic value.

Since changes were made in the U.S. Revenue Code in 1954—allowing art donations to public galleries, nonprofit foundations, and educational institutions to be tax deductible for up to 30% of the donor's tax liability—tax legislation and museum donation in developed economies has been inextricably linked to the art market. The most direct effects of record-breaking auction sales in the second half of the 20th century were on the prices for particular artists and the social status that collectors acquired, but record prices also affected public art collections and the aesthetic values that audiences experienced. In the market that developed in the late 20th century, the exhibition value of the work of art became more important to collectors and museums than ever before and often determined its price.

Most works of art take a physical form as an object or the documentation of a concept, performance, or event. However, the status of the work of art is not determined by its physicality, or even the art that it represents, but rather by its exhibition and exchange value. The art worlds of the postwar period analyzed by Diana Crane, Howard S. Becker, and Raymonde Moulin were not the same as the art worlds of the 1980s and 1990s. There was a change in the relationships between national art worlds and the global market. All art worlds and markets became part of the same system for artists' reputation and price formation. The multinational auction houses Christie's and Sotheby's integrated national markets with global centers in New York and London through their competitive practices and the public prices they established for art. After the Scull collection of Pop Art was sold in New York in 1977, contemporary art was offered at auction, creating increasingly speculative markets. The sale of contemporary art at auction, rather than through dealers who had created the 20th-century market for contemporary art, changed the situation for living artists as well as for their estates.

New Global Aesthetics

Beginning in the 1980s, corporate art collections were established and expanded on both sides of the Atlantic. Using their economic power, global corporations with their own curators emulated the public art museum and gallery by organizing and touring their own collections at home and abroad. Corporate sponsorship, donations, and exhibitions successfully used the public museum and gallery as public relations venues for corporate business. Business influence was successfully integrated into every phase of contemporary art, through commissions for production, in exhibition, sales and distribution, and finally through its reception by audiences. The imposition of corporate taste was made possible by the economic power of the global corporation. New connections made between creativity and capital through concepts such as the creative class and creative industries and a new nexus between information technology, the Internet, and global financial services displaced older aesthetic concepts of fine arts and crafts. These new connections also undercut the social critique immanent in art historical discourse and contemporary art criticism.

Contemporary art forms, video, film, photography, installations, and conceptual and performance art are based on the technologies that are transforming communication and all interactions across the world. At the end of the first decade of the 21st century, more than 50 international *biennales* had been held that aimed to attract international tourism to a city. The biennale assembles a large number of artists from different geographical regions and cultures in order to exhibit work that, in turn, is taken up by curators and dealers to show in an expanding multinational gallery system and the global museum. Curators who travel widely and are commissioned to produce new exhibitions are in the forefront of creating new global aesthetic tendencies. They have become star curators whose decisions to select or exclude make or break artists' reputations and careers.

The biennale is not just a distribution network; it has its own language of forms. The dominant forms are video, film, and photography; installations that are often multimedia; and conceptual and performance art recorded digitally. William Kentridge is a draftsman but is best known for his drawings for film projection installations, such as *Johannesburg, 2nd Greatest City After Paris*. Film, video, and photography collapse time and space in that they can be shown simultaneously in different biennales. These media are also economical to produce and to transport. Even site-specific installations or conceptual art activities can be reproduced in photography or language. These forms also express the phenomenology of communication density and the focus on global cities as sites of meaning construction.

If the media is the message, shared themes come from urban contexts in which most professional artists work. The inheritance of Duchamp and Dada took the form of institutional critique, and the current use of tactical media as a tool kit is borrowed from the antiglobalization movement.

Artists and viewers share an understanding of formal devices such as pastiche, radical juxtaposition, defamiliarization, and the decontextualization of objects and images from their known environments. In the discursive framework that is established, the local and regional are made intelligible through commonly shared strategies for making meaning that go beyond traditional aesthetics and cultural histories. The postmodern idea that the individual completes the work in the act of defining the spaces of viewing, reading, and consumption for his or her own use underlies the success of the global museum and the international biennale.

Impact of Globalization

Globalization affects the ways in which cultural narratives are created and used by audiences. Communication by means of new and complex systems and the global spread of mass-mediated imagery changes the expectations of people in all areas of culture, including the museum. Globalization accelerated the mass movement of people as refugees, as migrants, and as cultural tourists. The relationships between culture, tourism, and development resulted from the rapid growth in museums and tourism in the 1990s and the competition for funding and audiences. The art museum that emerged in the modern nation-building era is experiencing dramatic discontinuities in the global era.

The process of becoming global results in notions of citizenship and national identity being renegotiated, in response to contemporary patterns of global migration and cultural globalization. In many cases, the trajectory of such negotiations is far from clear. The shared understanding that may have been assumed between artists, curators, and audiences in the past can no longer be assumed. The art museum stands between two contradictory perspectives: One is the dominant art-historical narrative, and the other is the new sense of cultural diversity. The quality of the permanent collection is no longer sufficient to attract the masses to museums. Like a shopping mall, museums are seeking to attract a broad range of visitors who will stay as long as possible and who are less interested in originality, or in art itself, than the additional opportunities for consumption and interaction.

The professional museum world and its critics in academe have conceptualized this debate as one between the "universal" museum and the "glocalized" museum. The challenges of globalization identified by top museum directors were the imperative to preserve before presenting collections, the ethics of lending works of art for fees, and the neglect of permanent collections by the emphasis on temporary exhibitions. For example, a study of 100 international museums built in the first decade of the 21st century showed that more space (15%–20%) was reserved for temporary exhibits than at any previous time. Permanent collections accounted for 20% to 25%, with the remaining space taken up with offices, storage, and education areas. The directors of the Guggenheim, the Hermitage, and the Tate museums support the branch museum system made possible through their strong museum brand, which they argue offers the global public accessibility to support their status as global players and universal museums.

Other writers on museums argue that museums that retain their awareness of local identity and needs can still adapt to the global market and may preserve their local or regional character, resisting homogenization and unequal competition. Museums in former Eastern Bloc countries in Asia, Africa, and the Pacific have shown that this is possible. Te Papa in New Zealand is one example. In these areas, museum development is a consequence of global forces but also a protection against outside cultural forces and illicit smuggling of art and artifacts across national borders. The opposing argument to the universal museum is that aesthetics and the museum can offer access to alternative ideas, values, objects, skills, and other aspects of culture.

Perpetual reinvention is one of the markers of globalization, creating ever new products, styles, and markets while basic relations of power remain unchanged. A cultural globalization that loses locality, identity, and cultural context in a world culture that lays claim to the universal does not constitute a complete break with the past. The means of transmitting the model and the reach of the model are global, yet the model has a local First World, Euro-American identity. Other national, regional, and cultural identities do not vanish; they become subordinated. The question of discrepant temporalities and differently paced modernities in Asia, in particular, provide a key to new understandings of the long-term processes of globalization, which supplant rather than merely adjust the paradigms of Western modernization.

The opening of the Musée du Quai Branly in Paris in 2007, for example, was promoted as a response to the challenge to create cultural dialogue in a globalizing world. However, the permanent collection, with its largely colonial origins, and the exhibition of contemporary cross-cultural and intercultural artists' work did not convince audiences or prevent criticisms that indigenous peoples to whom the collection materials belong should be reconnected to their heritage. All artists create art within the structures that seek to exploit the exchange value of art as commodity. Third World and indigenous artists face the challenge of making works that allow them to be themselves as artists while resisting the imposed signification of tradition, typicality, and authenticity. They have the task of making work that can communicate, or in some way be habitable across the world, while refusing the global assimilation of otherness, or neoliberal inclusiveness. The shared visual language of global aesthetics enables artists to exploit cultural difference and to critique the institution while retaining aesthetic appeal.

Annette Van den Bosch

See also Architecture; Art; Artists; Cultural Hybridity; Cultural Industries; Global Culture, Media; Identities in Global Society; Postmodernism

Further Readings

Carroll, N. (2007). Art and globalisation: Then and now. *Journal of Aesthetics and Art Criticism*, 65(1), 131–143.

Gunther, C., Pioch, A., & Sahnwald, V. (2005). The challenge of globalization. *Curator*, 4(4), 364–368.

Müller, K. (2005). The concept of universal museums. *Curator*, 48(1), 10–12.

Van den Bosch, A. (2005). *The Australian art world: Aesthetics in a global market*. Sydney: Allen & Unwin.

Wu, C.-T. (2002). *Privatising culture: Corporate art intervention since the 1980s*. London: Verso.

African Diaspora Religions

As many as 10 million Africans were transported from West and Central Africa to the Americas and the islands of the Caribbean between the 16th and 19th centuries, creating one of the largest and most jarring events of forced population change in global history. This Atlantic slave trade involved their removal from familiar customs and practices, and separation from families and communities. As a result of this diaspora, Africans were scattered and dispersed around the world. Yet they often managed to retain both traditions and identities in their new environments. As a result, important elements of African cultures—including religions, languages, and folklore—survived the traumatic dislocation, serving as crucial links to their past lives.

In this entry, the term *African diaspora religions (ADRs)* refers to various African-based religions relocated to the Americas as a consequence of Africans' enslavement. ADRs highlight religious traditions originally from Africa which not only were able to survive cultural and ideological assault but also proved to be robust enough to provide spiritual resources for people whose identities were rooted in African cosmologies. ADRs are both urban and rural phenomena, emerging and developing as a direct result of the existential impacts of slavery and the associated belittling of African spirituality in the Americas.

ADRs can be grouped into various types. First, there are the neo-African religions—including Candomblé in Brazil; Santería in Cuba, the Dominican Republic, and Puerto Rico; and Vodun (Voodoo) in Haiti. Despite differences, they draw on similar ideas and concepts, often borrowing practices from Catholicism that reminded adherents of religious themes already encountered in Africa. The second type is ADRs influenced by Protestant missionary activity. Examples include Cumina and the Convince cult in Jamaica, the Big Drum Dance of Carriacou (Grenada), and St. Lucia's Kele. Third, there are ADRs influenced by Pentecostal groups from the United States, especially found in Jamaica. A fourth type of ADR includes religions that emphasize divination, healing, and spirit mediumship. Examples include Umbanda in Brazil, the Maria Lionza cult in Venezuela, and Puerto Rico's Espiritismo. The final type of ADR examined here is Rastafarianism, found primarily in Jamaica, a religion with a pronounced sociopolitical agenda.

Neo-African Religions

Three representative examples are briefly discussed here: Candomblé (Brazil), Santería (Cuba), and Vodun (Voodoo; Haiti, Dominican Republic). Candomblé is practiced mainly in Brazil. Transported from Africa by indigenous priests and adherents, it developed in Brazil, during the era of slavery (1549–1888). The religion was originally confined to the slave population and, as a result, persecuted both by the dominant Catholic Church and the state. After slavery was ended, Candomblé grew to become a major, established religion. Now, about 2 million Brazilians (1.5% of the total population) are followers of Candomblé. Adherents come from all social classes. There are tens of thousands of temples in Brazil.

Candomblé is a religion of the body, focusing on emotions and expressions. Undertaken with blood sacrifice, trance, music, and dance, it does not have a clear code of ascetic conduct. These characteristics differentiate Candomblé from another fast-growing religion in Brazil: Pentecostalism. In short, Candomblé is a festive religion, where notions central to Western theology—including, sin, guilt, and expiation—play little or no role.

Santería, also called Regla de Ocha or Regla Lucumi, is practiced widely in Cuba. It is also found among people of Cuban extraction in the United States. Emanating from the Yoruba tradition of West Africa, Santería is, like Candomblé, a complex of divination, spirit possession, and sacrifice. To become a member of the Santería religion, one must undertake initiation, where the principal ceremony is the *asiento* (placing of the divinity in the initiate). The focal point of Santería is the god Babalawo, regarded by adherents as the diviner of the future. He also seeks causes of sicknesses, in both the past and the present, and is the officiating priest at initiations.

Vodun (or Voodoo) is traceable to an African word for "spirit." The term can be traced back to the West African Yoruba people, who lived in what is now Benin (historically, Dahomey). Slaves brought their religion with them when they were forcibly shipped to Haiti and other islands in the Caribbean.

Religions Influenced by Protestant Missionary Activity

All such ADRs derive from West Africa. Cumina, for example, has its traditions in those of the Ashanti-Fanti people of the Gold Coast (now, Ghana), transported in millions to the Americas during the slave trade. It was in the Ashanti-Fanti religious cult of ancestral reverence that many slaves in Jamaica discovered a medium through which to express their religious and political sentiments.

Cumina is a purely African religious cult, and elements of it remain in the rural communities of Jamaica. In times of rebellion, and there were many such times in Jamaica during colonial rule, Cumina was thought to protect followers from colonialists' bullets. An adherent possessed by the spirit of the ancestors would be swept up in dynamic dancing and would not recover from an altered state of consciousness until awakened later from the trance. The individual would be entirely ignorant of anything that had transpired. This possession trance is still found in all the ADRs of the Caribbean.

Groups Influenced by Pentecostal Groups From the United States

Jamaica has many Pentecostal churches, including the Jamaica Pentecostal Church of God Trinity and the United Pentecostal Church. Such churches reflect both an intersection and a lack of fit between Western and West African religiously grounded "moral orders," which surfaced during recent Jamaican acceptance and transformation of North American Pentecostalism. Today, Jamaica's many Pentecostal churches highlight the current social/political significance of religious morality into the context of local/global transnational interconnections. Such Jamaican churches are bolstered by organizational and economic links to the transnational—mainly North American—Pentecostal movement, which not only informs and helps amend beliefs and practices of many ordinary Jamaicans followers but also helps insulate them from pressures toward secularization.

Jamaica's Pentecostal churches were built on syncretistic ingredients of Jamaica's "moral inheritance." This was informed by various factors, including British missionary revivalism and Calvinist moralizing, introduced to enslaved peoples in Jamaica, who primarily emanated from West Africa's Gold Coast. The European moral order centered on acceptance of a single, transcendent God, with personal sin to be overcome by rigorous self-discipline. Death would lead to salvation. Such beliefs dovetailed with a suspicion of expressive ritual practice, bolstered by the missionary practice of stressing the desirability of ordered domesticity, hard work, and sexual morality as indicative of social worth. This could be contrasted with the perceived moral order of the slaves, which rested on a belief in an immanent world populated by multiple spirits, where both good and evil reside. So-called tricksters (exemplified by Anansi, the clever spider, hero of West African folktales) could make evil become good, and good turn into evil, through mediation of moral practices centering on rites of spirit possession linked to healing.

In Jamaica, acceptance of North American Pentecostalism converged with elements of the African-derived moral order. Central among these were glossolalia (speaking in tongues) and the doctrine of perfectionism leading toward individuals becoming saints. These ritually embodied signs of transformation by the holy ghost were interpreted by Jamaican converts as "tricks." The Pentecostal advent was seen as a swift, unsuspected (rather like an unpredictable turn of events in an Anansi story) transformation. It was not understood as the product of systematic and "ethical rationalism," which characterized pre-Pentecostal missionization.

Religions That Emphasize Divination, Healing, and Spirit Mediumship

Examples include the Afro-Brazilian religion Umbanda. It is characterized not only by African religious elements but also by its affinities with Catholicism and Kardecist Spiritualism. Although it has its own identity, Umbanda is similar in some respects to other Afro-Brazilian religions, including Candomblé, Macumba, Batuque, and Quimbanda. Umbanda emerged in Rio de Janeiro in the 1920s, a time of significant industrialization, before spreading to São Paulo and southern Brazil. It is also found in Argentina and Uruguay. Its emergence and development is linked with the name of Zélio Fernandino de Moraes, a psychic, who worked among the poor. Leaders of the religion are known as *pai-de-santo* and *mãe-de-santo*. For many adherents, one of the purposes of belonging to the religion is to seek upward mobility.

While followers of Umbanda are linked by certain beliefs, it is also the case that there are various branches of the religion, each with their own beliefs and practices. Adherents have the following in common: belief in a One Supreme Creator God (known as the Orixá Olorum) and in lesser deities called Orixás. The latter are believed to act as the Orixá Olorum's helpers. They are the spirits of the deceased believed to counsel and guide the living through their lives on earth. They are also believed to be psychics who can channel messages from the spirit world having to do with reincarnation and spiritual evolution through successive lives. Adherents of Umbanda are under a religious obligation to practice charity, to aid the less fortunate.

Rastafarianism

In Jamaica, where economic downturn and political polarization are well-established phenomena, a syncretistic religious cult emerged, known as Rastafarianism. For decades, Rastafarianism has epitomized the desire of many Jamaicans for redemption from, initially, colonial rule and now a poor postcolonial socioeconomic situation.

Jamaica's 2.8 million people, mostly descendants of West African slaves, are predominantly Christian, although about 100,000 describe themselves as Rastafarians. The emergence of Rastafarianism in the 1930s was fueled by the unacceptability for many Jamaicans of the image of a white-skinned God promulgated by the British Christian colonists. Rastafarians regard the last Ethiopian emperor, Haile Selassie ("Ras Tafari"), who ruled from 1932 until his overthrow and death in 1974, as God. Rastafarians recognize the Black American Marcus Garvey (1887–1940) as the religion's greatest prophet. Garvey's militant message of liberation, which he preached until his death, was highly influential in helping to spread Rastafarianism as the route to spiritual and political emancipation from British rule.

Following Jamaica's independence in 1962, serious riots occurred in 1965 and again in 1968, reflecting the polarization of society between a small, rich elite and the mass of poor people. At this time, the Rastafarians' idea of a new type of society based on equality and communitarian ideals offered a radical alternative to the status quo. Rastafarianism enjoyed a period of growing popularity, underpinned by the popularity of the great reggae artist Bob Marley, a member of the Rastafarian faith. Following the death of Marley in 1980, however, the influence of the Rastafarian movement declined precipitously. It lost much of its direct political influence and is currently of only marginal significance in Jamaica.

Conclusion

ADRs are variable and various. What they have in common is that they emerged and developed during the long period during which Africans were taken against their will from Africa to Europe and the Americas, between the 16th and 19th centuries. ADRs were persecuted in the African diaspora, regarded with suspicion by authorities as having the potential to serve as vehicles of political challenge. Conventional expressions of Christianity condemned ADR practices as both heathen and demonic. During colonial times, ADR followers faced legal challenges in many countries, including Jamaica. Laws were passed restricting Africans' right to preach and teach their religions. In Haiti, Catholic priests taught that Vodun was not a religion from God. Instead, it was said to come from the Devil.

Today, many ADRs still face problems as a consequence of their practice of sacrifice. In a recent case in the United States, however, the U.S. Supreme Court made the judgment that preventing them from undertaking sacrifices in the context of religious ceremonies violated their religious freedoms. Undeterred by both historical and contemporary setbacks, ADRs collectively continue to exhibit growth. One of their main attractions is that they evoke a world where the gods' power and strength helps to forge human destiny. Moreover, they typically celebrate family, community, and life's blessings, and offer adherents ways to understand the world and to deal with its trials and tribulations.

Jeffrey Haynes

See also Global Religions, Beliefs, and Ideologies; Religious Conversion; Religious Identities; Religious Movements, New and Syncretic; Religious Politics

Further Readings

Fernández Olmos, M., & Paravisini-Gebert, E. (2003). *Creole religion of the Caribbean: An introduction from Vodou and Santería to Obeah and Espiritismo.* New York: New York University Press.

Hopkins, D. N. (2005). *Being human: Race, culture, and religion.* Minneapolis, MN: Fortress Press.

McCarthy Brown, K. (2001). *Mama Lola: A vodou priestess in Brooklyn.* Berkeley: University of California Press.

AFRICAN RELIGIONS

African religions have been global in their impact around the world on diaspora African communities, and in the effect of global religions on the characteristics of the religious traditions of Africa. Africa is home to more than 6,000 different ethnic and cultural groups. Many traditionally have their own religious beliefs and customs. Despite this variety, many indigenous religious traditions share a belief in a Supreme Being, a close interconnection between the sacred and the non-sacred, and rich oral traditions that pass both religious and ethical teachings down from generation to generation. For long periods of time, it looked as though many African indigenous religions would eventually become extinct. This was mainly due to the development of importance of two of the world religions: Christianity and Islam, which together threatened to overwhelm many if not all African traditional religions. In the 21st century, however, there is a vibrant resurgence of African religions throughout much of the continent. Leaders of African religions can often organize and render spiritual and healing services without hindrance from the state or rival religions. Yet, most Africans today are followers of either Christianity or Islam, while a minority belongs to various expressions of African religion. Although many such religions share a belief in a Supreme Being, they are also in many cases syncretistic systems of belief, sometimes practiced alongside Christianity or Islam.

The term *African religion* refers to two particular attributes. First, it is a label conventionally applied to religious groups in Africa that may have roots in, inter alia, Islam or Christianity, yet additionally adopt characteristics derived from specific African cultures and belief systems. Many of today's African religions are syncretistic, although this is not necessarily their defining characteristic. In fact, it might be argued that the very use of the term *syncretistic* merely reflects an ethnocentric certainty that one interpretation of a faith—whether Christianity or Islam—is merely that of the dominant orthodoxy, which derives from, for example, Rome, Canterbury, Saudi Arabia, or Iran.

Second, many African religions have emerged and developed relatively recently, a result in part of the destabilizing effects of colonially induced modernization, including the socioeconomic consequences of state centralization and rural-to-urban migrations so characteristic of recent African development. In other words, the recent advance of many African religions is reflective of the efforts of ordinary people to come to terms with changing socioeconomic environments, which changed massively within one or two generations in the 20th century. It is also consequential to the effects of the centralization of power, typical of the overwhelming majority of African states, which led to many people feeling both marginal and impotent in relation to state domination.

Development

The development of African religions should be seen in both global and local historical contexts. Their emergence and development in many different African geographical, cultural, and religious contexts follows the significant impact of modernization, which enveloped all parts of Africa, especially from the late 19th century, consequential to the swift colonial subjugation of 90% of the continent from the third quarter of the 19th century. One important form of African religion that emerged at this time was the various expressions of "African Christianity," especially during and following the colonial period, which practically ended in Africa by the 1970s. Such expressions of African Christianity were an indigenous response to a number of developments associated with the impact of colonialism and postcolonial African independent governments. Such African religions were often linked to expressions of nationalist aspiration, becoming sometimes significant vehicles of community aspiration, which sought to deal with threats to the community by increasing the solidarity groups felt by invoking traditional religious symbolisms and concerns and molding them for use in the modern era. Sometimes, in addition, the development of African religions has been linked to Islam, which also served as an exemplar of group solidarity, highlighting followers' material interests in the context of Muslim marginality in many African societies, especially away from North Africa.

Between World War I (1914–1918) and World War II (1939–1945), various manifestations of mission Christianity tended to appeal, more or less exclusively, to certain distinct African status constituencies: Pentecostalism to the lower classes and mainstream mission Christianity to the emerging middle classes. Social status differences were also shown among African religions that emerged from Christian foundations, including African Independent churches and syncretistic Christianized bodies, such as the Zionist churches of South Africa and the syncretist Aladura churches of West Africa. Each recruited members largely from among those of low social standing. Others, such as the Harris(t) church of West Africa, were self-consciously modernist in their thrust; they focused explicitly on the ending of worshipping of traditional deities and the adoption of a single God. In effect, the Harris(t) movement was a response to the ineffectuality of the plethora of separate religious cults extant at the time. The adoption of the Harris(t) faith was a more or less conscious move toward modernization by Africans who joined the church, in the same way that conversion to the controversial Ahmadiyya Muslim sect was for the Africans who joined that religious entity.

In Africa, religious beliefs began to change in response to developments in society, often catalyzed by Western penetration and colonization. The result was that, for followers of, for example, Harris(t) and Ahmadiyya, religion became an autonomous or discrete part of life rather than something that was indistinguishable from other social aspects. Such religious developments not only were a response to colonialism in a spiritual sense but also often represented opportunities for wealth accumulation for their leaders. Like their mainstream counterparts, these African religions often generated power and status for those who led them.

The emergence of African religions in the late 19th and 20th centuries reflects a continued popular adherence to traditional religious ideas, symbols, and rituals, often juxtaposed with modernist accretions from outside the region. The resulting religions were recognizably "African" yet at the same time (in most cases) hybrid faiths that may or may not have become routinized into formal organizational structures. The development of such hybrid religions in Africa is indicative of how, over the course of the 20th century in the region, religious beliefs continually formed and reformed, melding religious and cultural resources in response to changing sociopolitical and economic conditions. Of particular importance in the appeal of any religion in Africa is its dual attraction as both a materialist and a spiritual-healing force. As a result, the most tenacious elements of "traditional" religion, the most likely to survive migration to towns, were those that touched common bedrock of African traditional religions: the individual's concern for divinatory and magico-medical assistance.

Despite the clear connection of the development of religious vehicles with both spiritual and material concerns, the emergence of African religions in the pre-independence period—especially during the 1940s and 1950s—has often been explained in terms of the unique pressures and transformations associated with colonialism. Once often regarded as forerunners of nationalist political parties, the continued existence of such African religions and their continued development after colonialism had ended was then explained as a result of the cultural and psychological tensions that supposedly deepened with the state-led attempts to modernize in postcolonial Africa.

Classification and Categorization

The very diversity of Africa's thousands of indigenous religions makes attempts at classification both difficult and ultimately unrewarding. Attempts to categorize them in relation to their origins—such as local and externally derived traditions and psychological roots—tend to be of little general analytical use because such classifications provide only restricted or partial enlightenment as to the nature of their organizational structures and sources of support.

It is impossible to pinpoint a convenient handful of factors that African religions share. An imprecise, but common, way to categorize them is to relate their religious beliefs to those of the world religions. Five types of African religion are typically noted: (1) *traditionalist*, involving a return to spirit-mediumship, for example, among the Zezeru of Zimbabwe; (2) *neo-primal/revitalization*, which is close to traditionalist but which adopts some characteristics of imported faiths, for example, Godianism of eastern Nigeria, Bori cults among Hausa women in Nigeria, and spirit-possession movement among Lebu females in Senegal; (3) *syncretist/synthetist*, including spiritual and prophet-healing churches, for example, Aladura and Musama Disco Christo churches (the Aladura churches are syncretic churches that combine elements of traditional African belief with conventional Christian dogma); (4) *messianist*, for example, L'Église de Notre Seigneur Jesus-Christ sur terre of Simao Toko in Angola and the Kimbanguist church in Democratic Republic of Congo; and (5) *millenarian*, for example, the Maitatsine movement in northern Nigeria, which evolved from mainstream Islam.

The chief problem with such a typology is that it seeks to pigeonhole disparate religious entities into a self-consciously neat framework that relates their originality to Christianity and/or Islam but fails to delve sufficiently into relevant political, economic, and social factors that affected their emergence and development. Looked at from a more general social perspective, eight factors are of importance in their founding, although not all will be relevant to the emergence and development of every African religion: (1) racial, political, or class discrimination (leading to the establishment of Ethiopian churches and the Maitatsine maverick-Muslim group); (2) social and cultural upheaval; (3) historical background (e.g., land grabbing by European colonists in southern and eastern Africa; (4) denominational rivalries between mainstream sects; (5) religious concerns (e.g., traditional religious desire for followers to have a religion with which they "feel comfortable"); (6) ethnic exclusiveness (African religions may be vehicles for ethnicity, e.g., conflict between Xhosa and Fingo in South Africa, or between Digo and Kikuyu against Kalenjin in Kenya, was reflective, in part, of different religious beliefs held collectively by each distinct ethnic group); (7) ecclesiastical shortages (few religious professionals on the ground); and (8) for leaders, economic imperatives, as some people establish religious entities partly in order to collect money, which they use mainly for themselves and their families.

Conclusion

African religions usually evolve in response to some kind of social crisis and are often founded by someone who claims to have had a mystical experience and is henceforward regarded as an authentic prophet. Reflecting this, African religions often have millenarian hopes, where the divinity is thought to help adherents. As with the development of Christianity and Islam in Africa, African religions typically go through stages of development over time, often reflective of changes in wider political, economic, and social contexts. For example, in various African Independent churches in southwestern Nigeria, the status position of women followers increased relative to females adhering to other religions in the local society. There are a number of other examples among both Islam-oriented and Christian-related African religions showing a similar enhancement of women's status. For example, recent female prophets, such as Gaudencia Aoko (Legio Maria in Kenya), Alice Lenshina (Lumpa Church of Zambia), and Alice Lakwena (Holy Spirit Movement in Uganda), all used the vehicle of religion to enhance their own personal—and by extension, their gender's—social position in one of the only ways available in traditionally male-dominated societies. However, the use of religion as a means of social enhancement for women is not a recent development in Africa: Dona Beatrice, allegedly the incarnation of Saint Antony, was burned to death as a heretic at Mbanza Congo (present-day Angola) at the beginning of the 18th century by Portuguese colonialists. Her crime was to preach an Africanized Christianity, which later led to her proclaimed status as national heroine during the anticolonial war against the Portuguese, which lasted from 1961 to 1974.

There is no doubt that social change plays a significant role in the formation of African religions. With the declining ability of the postcolonial African state to adequately provide social services, current African religions typically offer both spiritual and material benefits (perhaps including health care delivery systems and employment opportunities). It would be wrong, however, to assume that it is only poor, disoriented people who join African religions. In fact, in many cases, these religions attract followers from all walks of society, including the middle classes and the politico-economic elite, although the latter may be secret members, not wishing to appear to be "traditional."

Jeffrey Haynes

See also Identities, Traditional; Religious Conversion; Religious Identities; Religious Movements, New and Syncretic; Religious Politics

Further Readings

Lugira, A. M. (2009). *African traditional religion* (3rd ed.). New York: Chelsea House.

Mbiti, J. S. (1991). *Introduction to African religion* (2nd ed.). London: Heinemann.

Shaw, R. (Ed.). (2009). *Readings in new African religions*. Oxford, UK: James Currey.

AGING SOCIETIES

The global diversity of patterns related to population aging is a significant feature of the changing character of global society. Population aging refers to a process in which the proportion above an identified threshold age in a population is increasing. Although many developing countries are experiencing this sort of demographic change, this process is more common, and has begun earlier, among more developed nations. Currently, a diverse array of populations are aging, and the degree of aging and the speed with which it is occurring vary considerably across countries and regions.

Population aging will continue to be an important feature of a great number of nations for decades to come. The shift of age structure toward older ages has socioeconomic consequences, some of which are discussed in this entry, such as those for economic growth and pension systems, among others. First, however, this entry addresses the ways in which population aging is measured and the trends and differentials in aging seen around the world.

Dynamics of Population Aging

Indicators of aging—such as the proportion of a population that is age 60 or over, or age 80 or over, and a population's median age—are commonly used to evaluate the population aging process.

By 2010, the population age 60 or over accounted for 11% of the world population, 3 percentage points higher than in the middle of the 20th century. This proportion is projected to double by 2050, a level that has already been achieved in the more developed regions (as classified by the United Nations). Such a high figure stands in stark contrast to the 5% level found among the least developed countries and 9% in the other less developed countries. As much as 33% of the population will be at least 60 years old in the more developed regions by 2050. The proportion age 60 or older in the less developed regions had not grown much since 1950 until entering the 21st century, and it is projected to more than double in next 40 years (United Nations, 2008).

As the more developed regions continue to age, the pace of aging has quickened. A single percentage point increase in the proportion of the population age 80 or over, otherwise known as the "oldest old," from 1% to 2%, took 30 years to accomplish, between 1950 and 1980. Subsequently, it took only 15 years to surpass 3% in 1995 and another 15 years to reach 4.3% in 2010. It is now projected to take only 10 years to increase an additional percentage point for each decade until 2030, after which the time required to increase 1 percentage point will decline to only 5 years (Figure 1).

The eight most populous countries have distinct aging patterns. Japan saw its population age dramatically in the 20th century and will continue to see an aging trend, albeit at a reduced speed. The U.S. population rapidly grew older in the latter half of the 20th century, but that speed was tempered as it approached the 21st century. The pace of aging has increased in recent years but will likely decrease once again as we approach mid-century. Some countries, such as China, Brazil,

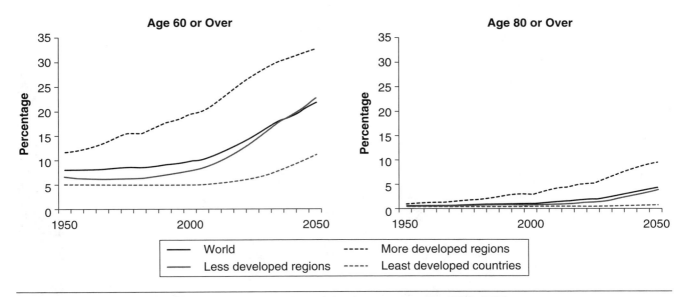

Figure 1   Percentage of older population, world and development regions, 1950–2050.

Source: Data from United Nations, Department of Economic and Social Affairs, Population Division (2009).

Indonesia, and India, were quite "young" in the 20th century but have now begun to age much faster. Pakistan's population had been getting considerably younger in the 20th century, but the proportion age 60 or older has been rising and will eventually attain and then surpass the level witnessed in 1950. Nigeria is also expected to experience population aging in the next couple of decades.

Growth patterns of the "oldest old" population in the eight most populous countries differ greatly. Currently, the age of 1 out of every 26 Americans is 80 years or older, but by 2050 that proportion will likely double. Today in Japan, 1 out of 16 people is age 80 or over and, strikingly, in 40 years that figure will rise to 1 in every 6. One out of 70 people in China or Brazil is now age 80 or over, and in 40 years that proportion will closely approach that in the United States. In India, Indonesia, Pakistan, and Nigeria today, not even 1 in 100 people are classified among the oldest old, and by 2050 that group will still not exceed 1 in 25 of their respective populations (Figure 2).

The median age of the world's population is currently 29 years, an increase of 5 years since 1950. By 2050, half of the world's population will be more than 38 years old. In the more developed regions, the median will exceed 46 years of age, compared with 39 in the less developed regions

and 29 among the least developed countries. The future increase in median age is expected to be slower in the more developed regions than in the less developed regions.

Rather than rely solely on chronological age to measure aging, Warren Sanderson and Sergei Scherbov offer alternatives that adjust age for life expectancy and disability. The alternative measures suggest slower population aging than traditional ones.

Demographic Components of Population Aging

The demographic transition, which refers to long-term reductions in fertility and mortality, results in a population age structure shifting substantially toward older ages.

Lower Fertility

When fertility is high—that is, well above "replacement level," which is the number of children a woman must have, on average, to replace herself with a daughter who will in turn bear children (that number is somewhat greater than two, depending on the level of mortality)—the population age structure will be broad-based. This is due to the fact that recent birth cohorts, in this

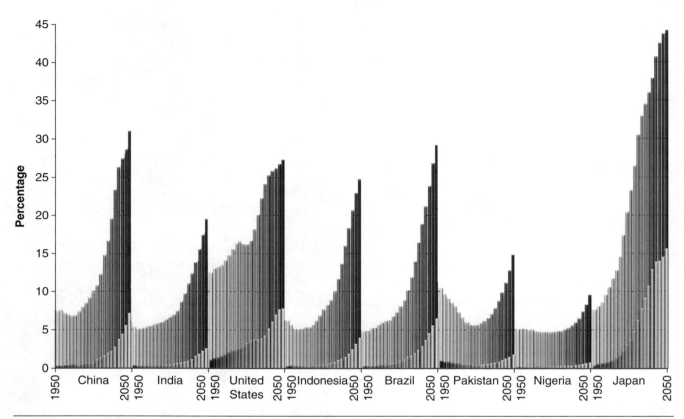

Figure 2   Percentage of population age 60+ versus age 80+, most populous countries, 1950–2050.

Source: Data from United Nations, Department of Economic and Social Affairs, Population Division (2009).

scenario, would be much larger than cohorts now in old age, who were born long ago. As fertility declines, that broad base narrows, eventually—in the context of exceptionally low fertility, experienced by several countries today—to the extent that the base of the age structure (i.e., those in the younger years) is smaller than the upper part of the age distribution.

World total fertility stands at 2.6 children per woman in 2005–2010, compared with 4.9 in 1950–1955. It is projected to drop further to 2.0 children per woman in 2045–2050. Replacement-level fertility is about 2.1 children for a more developed country and somewhat greater for a country whose population is subject to higher mortality. Less developed regions have experienced a dramatic decline of total fertility since 1950 (6.0 children per woman in 1950–1955 to 2.7 in 2005–2010) and will likely keep declining. Total fertility in the more developed regions has dropped from 2.8 to 1.6 children per woman over that same 55-year time span. Although this level is projected

to rise very slightly in the following decades, at 1.7 or 1.8 children per woman, fertility will remain well below the level needed to replace older generations (Figure 3a). Among the eight most populous nations, all but Pakistan and Nigeria are projected to achieve below replacement fertility by 2045–2050.

Babies were born in unprecedented numbers in many countries during the two decades or so after World War II. The high fertility rates were remarkable but transitory; however, their effect was lasting. Sometimes referred to as a "pig in a python," these large birth cohorts initially resulted in a disproportionately young population. At this time, however, these "Baby Boomers" are attaining older ages and accelerating the population aging process, especially in the more developed world.

Lower Mortality

As time passes, mortality improvements tend to be concentrated in the older ages, evidenced in the

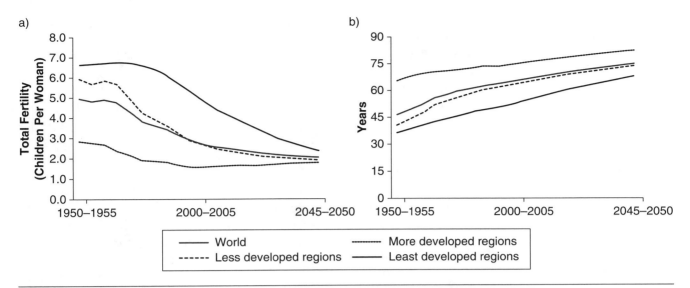

Figure 3   (a) Total fertility rate, world and development regions, 1950–2050; (b) Life expectancy at birth, world and development regions, 1950–2050.

Source: Data from United Nations, Department of Economic and Social Affairs, Population Division (2009).

additional years of life one may expect to live, given one has already survived to, say, age 60. Such improvements will raise the proportion of the population found in the upper reaches of the age distribution.

Global life expectancy is currently 67.6 years, 21 years higher than that in 1950–1955, and is projected to rise another 8 years by 2045–2050. From 1950–1955 to 2005–2010, the gain in life expectancy for people born in the more developed regions was 11.1 years, compared to 24.6 years for those born in the less developed regions and 19.5 years in the least developed countries (Figure 3b).

Socioeconomic Consequences of Population Aging

The consequences of fertility reduction and mortality improvement extend well beyond the purely demographic. Changes in population age structure may have profound socioeconomic ramifications.

Dependency Ratio

The dependency ratio is used to measure the burden of support for children and the aged to which the working-age population is subject. The total dependency ratio can be decomposed into the youth dependency ratio and the old-age dependency ratio. The former is defined as the number of children (ages 0–14) per 100 working-age individuals (ages 15–64). The old-age dependency ratio substitutes in the numerator the number of individuals age 65 or over for the number of children. The dependency ratio is based on a notion that older people and children are supported in large part by the working-age population, either directly, for example, through family transfers, or indirectly, for example, through government transfers.

In the more developed regions today, the old-age dependency ratio is double the 12% level of 1950 and quite similar to the youth dependency ratio. Over the next 40 years, as Baby Boomers climb toward the top of the age distribution, the old-age dependency ratio is projected to grow even more rapidly, to 45% in 2050, far exceeding the expected youth dependency ratio of 26% that year.

Among the least developed countries, the vast majority of the "dependent" population today is accounted for by their youth, 71% versus only 6% by those age 65 or over. The old-age dependency ratio is projected to nearly double its current level to about 11% in 2050, but the youth dependency ratio will remain much higher, at 41%.

Although no notable trend in the world total dependency ratio is expected over the next four decades or so, its composition will likely change: As a consequence of lower fertility and greater longevity, the youth dependency ratio is projected to keep declining, while the old-age dependency ratio will likely continue its growth, indeed at a faster pace. By 2050, the old-age dependency ratio (25%) will likely be close to the youth dependency ratio (31%), whereas today the former is only slightly over one quarter of the latter (Figure 4).

The Demographic Dividend

Important implications for economic growth arise as a nation undergoes its demographic transition. At first, fertility declines decrease youth dependency, and the working-age population grows faster than its "dependents." Rapid growth in the working-age population that is not accompanied by similar growth of the more youthful population could potentially have positive effects on economic growth, such as increases in income per capita and tax revenues. This process may be termed the *demographic dividend*, as put forward by David E. Bloom and his colleagues. Whereas the more developed regions and parts of East Asia may have reaped this benefit, the process in most developing countries started later and has been less dramatic. Its fruits, if they are to be realized, will appear in the coming decades.

A second process is at work here as well. Working-age people save more than dependents, including elderly dependents. Obviously, working-age people have the ability to save more than others. But in an environment of increasing life expectancy and longer periods of retirement, they also have incentives to save more than did earlier generations. When the share of working-age people is high, savings will tend to be high. Savings are channeled into investments, which, if they are chosen carefully and projects executed successfully, translate into more rapid economic growth and higher income per capita. With the long-term prospect of continued long life expectancy in sight, the benefit of higher savings rates may allow the demographic dividend to continue indefinitely.

Although older people often need social supports and are defined as "dependents" by virtue of their age, it is worth noting that the human capital accumulated by the older population is of considerable value as populations age. Older people can and do often still work and earn money, provide important guidance to younger workers and family members, and serve as an important source of daily logistical support in families.

Public Pensions

By comparing the earliest pensionable age and life expectancy in a given country and by approximating the number of beneficiaries and the pension cost for an average beneficiary, we could roughly estimate the financial burden on the system. An individual who claims pension benefits at the earliest eligible age and who dies at the age indicated by his or her country's life expectancy at birth will enjoy such benefits for 23.0 years in China, 22.7 years in Japan, 19.0 years in Brazil, 17.2 years in the United States, 15.7 years in Indonesia, 13.5 years in India, and 11.3 years in Pakistan. A Nigerian with his or her country's life expectancy will not have a chance to collect pension benefits in his or her life because life expectancy at birth is currently lower than the earliest pensionable age in Nigeria. By 2050, if the age at pension eligibility is not modified, then due to universal improvements in life expectancy we would expect the duration that an individual with his or her country's life expectancy spends on the pension roll will be substantially longer than is the case today (Figure 5).

In countries such as the United States, where the pension system is of the pay-as-you-go variety, population aging can present significant problems. According to the U.S. Social Security Administration, between 2015 and 2035, the number of beneficiaries is expected to rise rapidly as Baby Boomers claim Social Security benefits. The Baby Boom generation had fertility rates that were low relative to those of their parents. That, in conjunction with the fact that old-age mortality continues to improve, implies that the ratio of beneficiaries to workers who contribute to the system will rise quickly.

A shifting demographic landscape may also require individuals to rethink social and financial decisions, such as labor force participation, saving and investment, marriage, education, childbearing, and living arrangements, in the context of smaller families and longer lifetimes. The socioeconomic consequences caused by changing age structure have drawn much attention from policymakers in recent years. Challenges for future policy will

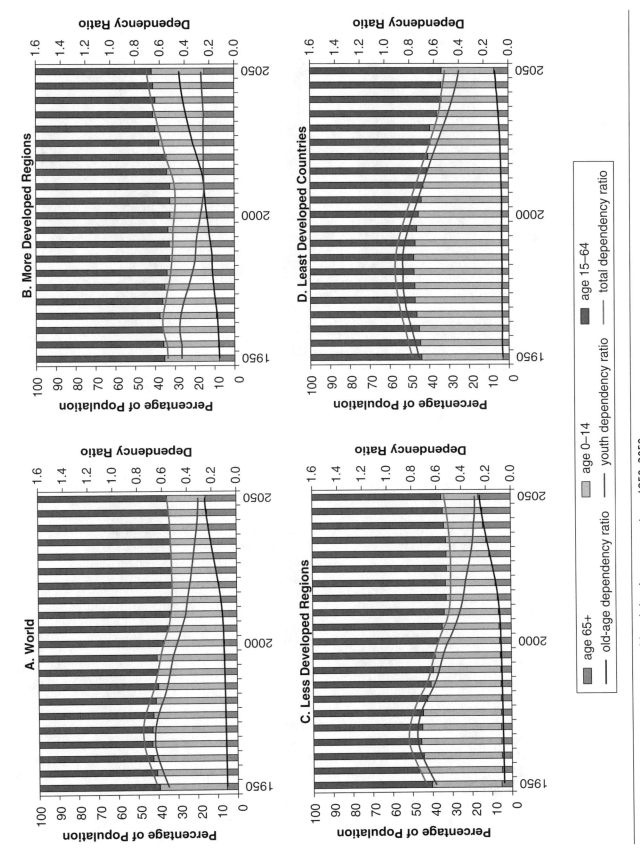

Figure 4   Dependency ratio, world and development regions, 1950–2050.

Source: Data from United Nations, Department of Economic and Social Affairs, Population Division (2009).

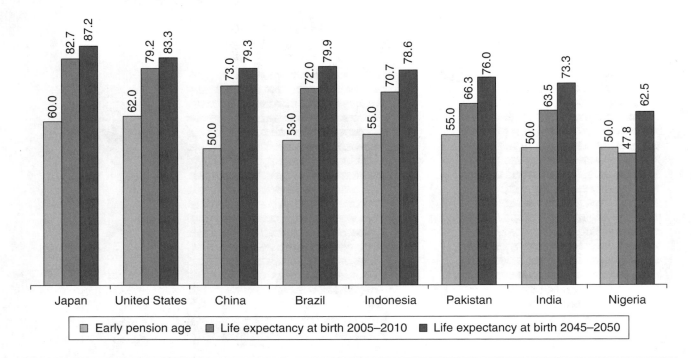

Figure 5   Early pension age versus life expectancy.

Source: Data from the U.S. Social Security Administration (2008–2009) and United Nations, Department of Economic and Social Affairs, Population Division (2009).

Note: Earliest pensionable age is 50 for men and 45 for women in China, 53 for men and 48 for women in Brazil, and 55 for men and 50 for women in Pakistan.

surely include maximizing social and economic well-being in the face of profound demographic transformation.

Na Yin and Neil G. Bennett

See also Baby Boomers; Demographic Change; Demographic Transition; Family; Family Policies; Fertility; Population and Demographic Change; Retirement Systems

Further Readings

Bennett, N. G., & Olshansky, S. J. (1996). Forecasting US age structure and the future of Social Security: The impact of adjustments to official mortality schedules. *Population and Development Review*, *22*(4), 703–727.

Bloom, D. E., & Canning, D. (2008). Global demographic change: Dimensions and economic significance. *Population and Development Review*, *34*(Suppl.), 17–51.

Bloom, D. E., & Williamson, J. G. (1998). Demographic transitions and economic miracles in emerging Asia. *World Bank Economic Review*, *12*(3), 419–455.

Bongaarts, J. (2006). How long will we live? *Population and Development Review*, *32*(4), 605–628.

Gruber, J., & Wise, D. (1998). Social Security and retirement: An international comparison. *American Economic Review*, *88*(2), 158–163.

Kinsella, K., & He, W. (2009). *An aging world: 2008*. U.S. Census Bureau, International Population Reports, P95/09-1. Washington, DC: U.S. Government Printing Office.

Lee, R. D. (2003, Fall). The demographic transition: Three centuries of fundamental change. *Journal of Economic Perspectives*, *17*(4), 167–190.

Lee, R. D., & Tuljapurkar, S. (1997). Death and taxes: Longer life, consumption, and Social Security. *Demography*, *34*(1), 67–81.

Martin, L. G., & Preston, S. (Eds.). (1994). *Demography of aging*. Washington, DC: National Academy Press.

National Institute on Aging and National Institutes of Health. (2007, March). *Why population aging matters: A global perspective* (DHHS Publication No. 07–6134). Bethesda, MD: Author.

Panel on a Research Agenda and New Data for an Aging World, Committee on Population, Committee on National Statistics, and National Research Council. (2001). *Preparing for an aging world: The case for cross-national research*. Washington, DC: National Academy Press.

Sanderson, W., & Scherbov, S. (2010). Remeasuring aging. *Science, 329*(10), 1287–1288.

United Nations, Department of Economic and Social Affairs, Population Division. (2009). *World population prospects: The 2008 revision* (Working Paper No. ESA/P/WP.210). Retrieved August 31, 2011, from www.un.org/esa/population/publications/wpp2008/wpp2008_highlights.pdf

U.S. Social Security Administration. (2008–2009). *Social Security programs throughout the world, 2008–2009*. Washington, DC: Author.

AGRICULTURE SECTOR

Despite being tied to the land and drawing on centuries, if not millennia, of tradition and cumulative experience, agriculture has not been spared the effects of globalization. As an economic activity, it is losing its exceptionality and becoming one sector among others contributing to economic growth. Globalizing processes have accelerated changes in the countryside in most countries, changes already in motion due to mechanization and chemical farming. More food is being produced on less land by fewer farmers than a half-century ago. Old patterns of relationships between farmers, the suppliers of their inputs. and the buyers of their crops are shifting as a result of corporate restructuring. Politically, the long-standing protective mantle of the nation-state is yielding to new forces, new rules, and new constraints defined at regional and global levels. Culturally, farming practices and the consumption of foods have been shifting significantly in many parts of the world.

Globalization

Globalization is a disputed concept, one used in both academic analysis and popular debates outside the academy. Despite these disputes, some consensus has emerged about the processes involved. The word *global* is a reference to scale and points to phenomena that are somehow "transplanetary," to use Jan Aart Scholte's phrase. The spread of such transplanetary phenomena is not confined to the economic (as is often assumed in popular discourse), but includes political, cultural, military, legal, and nonhuman aspects as well. Most scholars acknowledge that the growth of transplanetary relationships has been uneven, with their density and speed of growth being more pronounced in wealthier countries than in poorer ones and differentially articulated spatially within all countries. There is nothing inevitable about globalizing processes; global historians have noted the growth and retraction of transplanetary phenomena over several centuries. If anything, doubts about claims to inevitability or unidirectionality in transplanetary integration have been renewed by the financial and economic crisis that intensified in 2008 and 2009.

Most scholars recognize that these transnational connections have accelerated in number, intensity, and extensity since the late 1970s. There are varying explanations for this apparent acceleration. At the heart of most explanations is dynamism in the transformation of capitalism propelled in substantial measure by the rapid growth of international financial markets and financial integration. The explosion of international finance and the financialization of capitalism have shaped the global order in ways not seen before. Capitalism is "global," Manuel Castells writes, in that for the first time in history, it shapes social relationships across the whole planet.

The particularly global form of contemporary capitalism is linked in complex ways with innovations in information and communication technologies that have permitted some transplanetary connections to become "supraterritorial." These connections are less strictly bound by physical location or nation-state boundaries than at any time since the collapse of an earlier highly integrated international economic order in 1914. Indeed, technology has likely made connections less restricted by the traditional territorial powers of states than ever before. These technologies have permitted more connections to become planet wide, and these global connections have intruded into the daily lives of more people than ever before (taking into account the caveats about inequalities in distribution noted earlier).

Based on this thinking, globalization might be described as the growth of transplanetary connections among people. In the contemporary era, many of these connections take a supraterritorial form. In participating and acting in these connections, individuals and communities see the world increasingly as one place and imagine new activities and roles for themselves in this world.

Economic Globalization

The production of agricultural commodities has gradually become enmeshed in linkages that are more globally extensive today than they were a half-century ago, whether through suppliers of inputs to agricultural production or through the processing, distribution, and sale of agri-food products. Trade in agricultural commodities and in processed food products has risen over the same period. These more intense regional and economic relationships have developed through the greater presence of multinational firms in the sector and through important changes in technology used in the transportation and distribution of commodities and processed food products. Consequently, global economic relations are a more important factor in the lives of farmers and of food consumers than they were a half-century ago.

Since the end of World War II, agriculture has continued the movement from subsistence, peasant polyculture toward commercial farming and expanded international trade. Accordingly, processing companies buying from farmers have demanded more evenness in quality and standardization in size, and the markets for these more specialized and standardized products are extending, gradually, further away from the locality in which crops or animals are grown. Inputs to farmers' activity have added to the global linkages enmeshing agricultural production. Companies developing seeds for field crops have taken on a multinational structure. The boundaries between seed companies and the biotechnology sector have lowered as such prominent firms as Monsanto and Bayer Life Science have used biotechnology to instill various properties in plants. Where genetically manipulated seeds are sold to farmers, these corporations also tend to set out particular conditions for the planting of crops and the use of herbicides and pesticides. Similar patterns of multinational corporate firms and increased industrial concentration can be found in the animal feed, agricultural equipment, agricultural chemicals, and fertilizer industries. The exploitation of regional and global economies of scale by companies in these sectors integrates agricultural producers into relationships that transcend not only the specific locality in which crops are grown and animals raised but also the territorial borders of the nation-state in which they live and work.

Advances in transportation technologies, management strategies using information technology, and storage and handling facilities have facilitated growth in regional and global trade of food products. Whether we are speaking of oranges, bananas, green beans, or table grapes, these are now available virtually all year in the supermarkets of the Organisation for Economic Co-operation and Development (OECD) countries and increasingly in many "emerging" countries as well. This availability is the result of counter-seasonal production in the Northern and Southern hemispheres, the growth of greenhouse production, advances in refrigeration that permit the chilling of commodities within hours of harvest, the maintenance of cool temperatures from the place of harvest through the final delivery to supermarket shelves, the use of huge container ships that permit the transportation of commodities across oceans onto trains and then back onto ships, and the availability of information technology that ensures coordination of shipping from original point of harvest through rail, trucking, and shipping firms. Such "cool chains" are important not only for fresh produce but for beef, lamb, pork, and poultry products as well.

Political Globalization

Agriculture has long been involved in trade and exchange, with trading in spices, grains, sugar, and cotton forging many of the economic circuits that provided the basis for contemporary globalization. Often taking place under the auspices of empires, these arrangements involved political globalization only to the extent to which empires themselves extended global political connections. With the end of these European empires in the early part of the 20th century, political arrangements for agriculture became much more the responsibility of nation-states. Although the immediate postwar period saw the creation of a rules-based, multilateral system to liberalize trade, this system included agriculture in only a limited way.

This situation changed significantly with the founding of the World Trade Organization (WTO) in 1995 at the conclusion of the Uruguay Round of trade negotiations. With the Agreement on Agriculture and a companion Agreement on Sanitary and Phytosanitary Measures, political globalization increased significantly. These agreements introduced a policy framework for liberalizing trade, took some small liberalizing steps in implementing that framework, and, most importantly, set up a process for continuing to implement the framework. These steps were institutionalized further at the WTO with the creation of the Committee on Agriculture and the Committee on Sanitary and Phytosanitary measures. Since their founding in 1995, both of these committees have evolved into important policy discussion forums and have provided the institutional capacity for managing continuing attempts to liberalize trade further.

The introduction of genetic engineering into agriculture and the subsequent growing and production of genetically modified commodities and processed foods with genetically modified ingredients added to the sites of authority where agriculture is subject to decision making at the global level. These sites deal with food security and food safety (the Food and Agriculture Organization of the United Nations, the Codex Alimentarius, the International Plant Protection Convention, the World Health Organization), biological diversity (the Convention on Biological Diversity, the Cartagena Protocol on Biosafety), and intellectual property (the Trade-Related Aspects of Intellectual Property Rights Agreement of the WTO, and the World Intellectual Property Organization). Along with the WTO and its two committees dealing with agricultural issues, these various sites might be seen, according to William Coleman, as constituting a transnational policy space in agriculture. The form of governance has shifted from being state-centric to what Scholte calls "polycentric."

These globalizing processes in agriculture have given rise to significant political resistance. Groups such as Via Campesina, which represents peasants and small farmers across the world, and the Slow Food movement, oppose the disappearance of traditional country landscapes and local village life and the establishment of larger, heavily mechanized farms occupying increasingly depopulated rural areas. Globalization is seen as sweeping aside these very particular and prized components of local culture in favor of an industrial "countryscape" that is the same the world over. These "global civil society" movements articulate alternatives when it comes to the safety and quality of food, the protection of the environment, or the preservation of centuries of tradition in the growing, preservation, and preparation of food. For such groups, there often can be no compromise with the new production-centered, liberalized order in farming.

Cultural Globalization

The buying and selling of agricultural commodities and food products are also cultural decisions. The choices of what foods to eat and how they are prepared are actions integral to the cultures of communities everywhere. More generally, how countrysides are sculpted for the growing of food affects the images that national and more local communities construct of themselves. Cultural globalization also includes the circulation of ideas, including ideas about how agriculture should fit into a market economy and the place of agriculture in the nation-state.

The choice of foods that individuals and communities make, the combinations of foods that they prepare for meals, and the ways in which these foods are prepared are integral parts of culture. In thinking about increased globalization of culture, including foods and food preparation, theorists speculate whether this development is likely to lead to fewer differences between cultures around the world and thus a decline in cultural diversity. Others make reference to the capacity of communities to indigenize cultural products (i.e., incorporate selected parts into their own cultures) or to hybridize them (i.e., to combine them with their established cultural products and practices to produce a new cultural combination).

These issues arise in the cultural realm in part because of changes in the composition of population movements over the postwar period. For example, in looking at migration to North America or to western Europe, one can see that immigrants had tended to be drawn from the region or from contiguous regions in the early postwar period. In Canada and the United States, immigrants were still more likely to be European in the 1950s and 1960s, and in western Europe, migration tended to come from southern Europe or northern Africa to the north in the same period. Gradually, however, these patterns have changed, and migrants come from farther afield. Emigration from East and South Asia has become the dominant source in North America while increasing numbers come to Europe from sub-Saharan Africa and the Middle East. Moreover, within other regions, such as Southeast Asia and the Middle East, there have been first intraregional, followed by later interregional, population flows.

As cultural differences become higher between migrant communities and domestic populations in many areas of the globe, the migrant communities feel a stronger need to protect and retain their own traditional cultures. Fulfilling this need becomes easier as globalization has intensified. As discussed earlier, advances in transportation and communications technologies have facilitated the shipment of foods from one part of the world to another. Transnational communities thus have more access to their familiar foods than did similar communities in earlier periods. Increasingly extensive population migration brings with it more trade and movement of various objects important to diasporas' cultures, including foods, than in the past.

As these diaspora communities become established in new nation-states and develop the networks they need to import and to consume traditional foods, their food cultures, in turn, have an impact on the broader population of their new political homes. Beginning first with the setting up of restaurants and then the introduction of the new foods into supermarkets, exposure and consumption of a more diverse range of foods becomes common in many nation-states. This exposure and incorporation of foods from transnational communities into the mainstream cultures of the new host nation-states add to economic demand and fuel further the economic globalization of the agri-food sector.

Entertainment migrants or tourists have also increased significantly in numbers over the postwar period. When figures on tourism first began to be kept in 1950, there were 25.3 million international tourists. In 2009, the World Tourism Organization estimates that there were 880 million international tourists spending US$850 billion. Over the same period, international tourism also became less an opportunity restricted to the wealthy in the developed countries and more accessible to large numbers of their respective populations. As a tourist "industry" builds up in popular destinations, some in the developed countries and others in developing countries, efforts are made to provide tourists with familiar foods. Many do not wish to consume exclusively the standard foods of their host destinations; they prefer to stay in hotels built in ways similar to those in their home countries and to consume foods from home that they like. These demands prompt both a process of reverse trade, where agricultural and food products from the developed countries are imported into developing countries for tourists, or changes in local agriculture as the growing of these familiar commodities is contracted out to local farmers.

Global food corporations intensify these processes further by promoting broader consumption of foods familiar in the developed countries. Whether we speak of McDonald's or Coca-Cola, increased consumption of beef, the substitution of wheat-based breads for other grains, or the distribution of baby formula, these developments add to the diversity of products available in many countries. They may also threaten the longer-time viability of some traditional foods and cultural practices, thereby raising the question of a decline in cultural diversity.

The Globalization of Policy Ideas

Global flows of culture also include the movement of ideas. Within the policy realm, when particular sets of ideas coalesce around a number of principles, theoretical bases of research, and some clear views on causes and effects, they are often termed *policy paradigms*. In the immediate postwar period, a policy paradigm of this kind was common across the OECD countries. It emphasized the fragility of agricultural markets, the need for state financial support to sustain farmers' incomes, the value of protecting many commodity markets from foreign competition, and the importance for any nation-state to be self-sufficient in food. This set of ideas can be referred to as the *dependent paradigm*.

The principles and policy ideas in this paradigm were, of course, largely incompatible with the neoliberal thinking that lay behind the economic globalization promoted by the United States and European countries in the 1970s and 1980s. Gradually, some of the core ideas of neoliberalism were adapted to the specifics and particularities of agricultural markets. These provided the basis for a new competitive policy paradigm that became an anchor for a political challenge to the dependent paradigm. The *competitive paradigm* became globalized, with its thinking coming to influence the core points of the policy framework found in the WTO's Agreement on Agriculture. Some farmers and governments in several EU countries regretted the global triumph of the competitive paradigm and articulated a new challenge around a set of ideas that emphasized the potential contributions of agriculture to environmental stewardship, rural development, and employment, as well as to food production. These policy ideas, in turn, have coalesced into a new *multifunctional policy paradigm* enjoying increasing influence in the European Union and subsequently promoted on a global scale as an alternative to the competitive paradigm.

Finally, with the increased levels of economic globalization in the input, processing, and distribution components of the agri-food sector, a still different set of ideas about agriculture, markets, and the role of governments has come to influence policy making. These ideas form the core of a *globalized production paradigm*. Rather than keeping the production of food at the center of policy, as is common to the competitive and dependent paradigms, or at the near-center, as occurs with the multifunctional paradigm, these ideas emphasize the notion of food production as part of a supply chain. Given the transnational character of many of the corporations dominating the key links of the supply chain, the paradigm stresses the potential economic gains to be realized from reducing the obstacles to extending the global reach of these supply chains. Its objectives extend to policy areas, including intellectual property protection, food safety, meeting the needs of the food consumer, and liberalizing trade in services as well as goods.

In summary, through the mechanism of policy paradigms and in conjunction with economic and political globalization, a series of competing ideas about the place of agriculture in society and the role of governments have become themselves globalized over the past three decades. Debates about the role of agriculture in both wealthy and poorer countries have taken place increasingly in transnational policy spaces than in states alone.

William Coleman

See also Corporations, Transnational; Cuisine; Culture, Notions of; Food; Food and Agriculture Organization of the United Nations; Global Health and Nutrition; Globalization, Phenomenon of; Peasant Economies; Protectionism; Rurality; Trade Agreements; World Trade Organization (WTO)

Further Readings

Barton, J. H., Goldstein, J. L., Josling, T. E., & Steinberg, R. (2006). *The evolution of the trade regime: Politics, law, and economics of the GATT and the WTO.* Princeton, NJ: Princeton University Press.

Castells, M. (1999). *The rise of the network society* (2nd ed.). Oxford, UK: Blackwell.

Clapp, J., & Fuchs, D. (Eds.). (2009). *Corporate power in global agrifood governance.* Cambridge: MIT Press.

Coleman, W. D. (2005). Globality and transnational policy-making in agriculture: Complexity, contradiction, and conflict. In E. Grande & L. Pauly (Eds.), *Complex sovereignty: Reconstituting political authority in the twenty-first century* (pp. 93–119). Toronto, ON: University of Toronto Press.

Coleman, W. D. (2008). Agricultural trade and the WTO. In L. Pauly & W. D. Coleman (Eds.), *Global ordering: Institutions and autonomy in a changing world* (pp. 64–84). Vancouver: University of British Columbia Press.

Coleman, W. D., Grant, W. G., & Josling, T. E. (2004). *Agriculture in the new global economy.* Cheltenham, UK: Edward Elgar.

O'Brien, S. (2010). Anti-fascist gluttons of the world unite! The cultural politics of slow food. In P. Rethmann, I. Szeman, & W. D. Coleman (Eds.), *Cultural autonomy: Frictions and connections* (pp. 219–239). Vancouver: University of British Columbia Press.

Scholte, J. A. (2005). *Globalization: A critical introduction* (2nd ed.). London: Palgrave Macmillan.

AIR TRAVEL

The history of aviation is at the heart of the ever-expanding global communications network. The technology developed from kite flying and the use of hot air military balloons in China in the third century CE, through the designs of Leonardo da Vinci, to balloons used in the 19th century in the American Civil War, to the current scale of global activity. At the time of the first powered flights of airships toward the end of the 19th century, it was not clear whether the major route of development would be through powered airships or by heavier-than-air machines. It was probably the dramatic impact of the disasters that befell hydrogen airships that determined the virtual elimination of airships from long-term development, although there are some who still see an important role for them in the future.

It is doubtful whether early pioneers foresaw the huge social and economic impact that would result from bringing global horizons within reach through air transport. From the earliest stages, there was enormous determination to push back the geographical boundaries, prompted by the legendary efforts of the Wright brothers and others around the early 1900s, with international flight pioneered by Louis Blériot in 1909 across the English Channel. The New Year's Day flight by Tony Jannus on January, 1, 1914, was the first scheduled airline flight with a passenger, using a Benoist seaplane in the flight from St. Petersburg to Tampa in Florida, reportedly at a height of 15 feet. Deutsche Luftschiffahrts-Aktiengesellschaft was the world's first airline, founded in November 1909, with government assistance, operating airships manufactured by the Zeppelin company.

Commercial Services Develop

World War I stimulated rapid development of flying technology. The postwar period saw a golden age of flying, with air shows touring cities and towns across the United States and other countries and air races driving forward airframe design and engine performance. The first air mail flights in the United States, between New York and Washington, D.C., with a stopover in Philadelphia, took place in 1918. The requirements for such services contributed directly toward developing larger aircraft with longer ranges.

The flights of John Alcock and Arthur Whitten Brown in 1919, Charles Lindbergh in 1927, and the trans-Pacific crossing by Kingsford Smith in 1928 signaled the potential for commercial passenger and freight traffic. Early commercial flights between Florida and Cuba were offered in 1920 using flying boats. This was also the great age of dreamers, and many enterprises failed, but, after Lindbergh's flight, commercial aviation became a serious business with large-scale investment. It was a period of rapid growth: For example, in the United States, there were fewer than 10,000 commercial travelers in 1926, but by the end of the decade, there were approximately 170,000 per year. At this time most of the traffic was business, with leisure being confined to the wealthy.

Development in the United States was paralleled elsewhere. By August 1919, a daily service operated between Paris and London for as many as 14 passengers. This proved not to be financially viable because of high operating costs, high fares, and low passenger turnout. One of the early international collaborations was Franco-Roumaine in 1920, a joint project between Romania and France. Worldwide, individual nations rushed to establish their own flag carriers. In the Netherlands, KLM was formed on October 7, 1919. The Russian company Aeroflot was founded as Droboflovlot in 1928. Air France was formed in 1933 through the merger of several smaller companies with extensive routes across Europe, French colonies in northern Africa, and elsewhere. In Britain, European and intercontinental flights remained largely separate until 1974.

During the early 1920s, development was sporadic: Most airlines at the time were focused on mail. The all-metal 12-passenger Ford Trimotor became the first successful American airliner. Around that time, Pan American World Airways ("Pan Am") began to create a network with flying boats that linked Los Angeles to Shanghai and Boston to London. Pan Am and Northwest Airways were the leading U.S. airlines to go international before the 1940s. Around the early 1930s, aircraft such as the Ford Trimotor and the Boeing Model 80 still could not avoid turbulence, and air travel was almost inevitably accompanied by air sickness. Pan Am introduced male stewards, and Boeing Air Transport was the first to introduce stewardesses. The Douglas air company entered the fray, notably with the DC3 (see Figure 1), of which over 17,000 were built, with some still flying, carrying around

75% of internal U.S. traffic by the beginning of World War II, eliminating much of the discomfort by flying at around 20,000 feet.

Countries rushed to protect their airline's rights, an aspect that has continued to plague attempts to rationalize the global aviation industry in recent years. In November 1944, at an international conference in Chicago, 32 nations signed the Chicago Convention, which led to the establishment of the International Civil Aviation Organization (ICAO) in 1947. The conference laid the foundation for a set of regulations that has made safety a paramount consideration and paved the way for the application of a common air navigation system throughout the world.

Aviation After World War II

Traditional piston-engine, propeller-driven aircraft technology reached its height during World War II. More revolutionary was the turbojet engine, which opened the way to much higher speeds through jet engines, coinvented by Hans von Ohain in Germany and Frank Whittle in Britain. After the war, tension between the United States and the Soviet Union led to a drive for supremacy in aerospace technology, including the first faster-than-sound flight by the Bell X-1 in 1947.

The real impact of the airplane came in commercial transportation. By 1950, the airliner was well on the way to replacing the railroad and the ocean liner as the primary means of long-distance travel. The entry of the first turbojet airliners into scheduled service in 1952 accelerated the pace of this revolution. These three decades after World War II were good years for the American airframe and engine industry, with the jet-engined products of Boeing, McDonnell-Douglas, Lockheed, and other U.S. firms dominating the international air routes. Most of these new aircraft were based on American bombers, which had spearheaded new technologies such as pressurization. In Europe, the 1950s saw the De Havilland Comet emerge as the forerunner of the jet age, with other leaders including the Sud Aviation Caravelle and the Soviet Tupolev Tu-104 and -124. Concorde first flew in 1969 and operated until 2003 (see Figure 2). The Boeing 727 and, subsequently 737, were leaders in the narrow bodied jet category with over 6,000 of the various models of the 737 having been produced to date.

Figure 1   The DC-3, one of the most influential aircraft in the history of commercial aviation, revolutionized the aviation industry.

Source: http://en.wikipedia.org/wiki/File:TWA_1940.jpg

Figure 2   Concorde.

The postwar air transport boom was nothing short of a social revolution. With regional and local airlines and air freight operations linking to international air carriers, aviation became the circulation system for globalization of economies, communication, migration, and tourism. The economic, social, and political consequences included the creation of global markets and opportunities for global travel undreamed of a generation before, thus opening up a global tourism industry and

Figure 3   Pan Am Boeing 747 in 1985. The deregulation of the American airline industry increased the financial troubles of the iconic airline, which ultimately filed for bankruptcy in 1991.

Source: http://en.wikipedia.org/wiki/File:Pan_Am_Boeing_747_at_Zurich_Airport_in_May_1985.jpg. Reprinted with permission of Eduard Marmet.

increasing cultural interchange. While in-depth analysis of the benefits and costs of globalization does not belong here, it is pointed out that aviation-based tourism is one of the few sources of wealth for many developing countries.

The widebody age began in 1970 with the entry into service of the four-engined, double-deck Boeing 747 (see Figure 3). Three-engined aircraft followed, including the McDonnell Douglas DC-10 and the Lockheed Tristar. The first widebody twin jet, the Airbus 300, entered service in 1974. Several successors have arrived since then, including the Airbus A330-A340 series and the Boeing 767 and 777, with the "Superjumbo" Airbus A380 starting commercial services in 2007.

For U.S. carriers, however, the era of growth and optimism stuttered in the 1970s, as the industry became plagued by a stream of problems, including labor unrest, congestion, increased fuel costs, and public concern over issues ranging from safety and service to air and noise pollution. The Airline Deregulation Act of 1978 initially attracted new competitors to the field and led to lower ticket prices. But deregulation brought with it difficulties, such as opaque fare structures and longer working hours for flight crews. It also brought opportunities for new business models for airlines, led by Southwest Airlines. The challenge to established airlines by low-cost carriers

such as Southwest was to be repeated in Europe, initially through airlines such as Laker Airways and subsequently through others such as easyJet and Ryanair.

The Modern Industry

There are four key components of the industry: manufacturing, airports, airlines, and air navigation service providers (ANSPs). The public generally sees airlines as the face of the industry as they are the consumer-facing element. Competition between airlines is a mixture of fierce commercial pricing and subsidies from governments, often simultaneous and leading to calls for a "level playing field." It is not difficult to start an airline but just as easy to go bust. Warren Buffet is often quoted as saying that if a farsighted capitalist had been present at Kitty Hawk, he would have done his successors a huge favor by shooting Orville down.

Manufacturers have consolidated globally to a handful of airframe and engine companies that face considerable challenges in bringing new products to the market—not least being that the working life of a commercial aircraft is generally about 30 years. As environmental pressures increase, manufacturers, airlines, and aviation regulators are faced with addressing the interdependencies, often conflicting, between noise and gaseous emissions. One dilemma currently facing the industry is the replacement for the narrow-bodied Boeing 737 and similar types; will it be a similar looking aircraft or a more radical "open rotor" type?

Airlines interface with the consumer and have to provide a safe and reliable service that meets the expectation of the customer in terms of schedule, comfort, and price. And one should not forget air freight, some carried by dedicated aircraft and some in the holds of passenger airliners (e.g., British Airways cargo accounted for some 25% of total revenue ton kilometers in 2008). With a typical working life of 30 years, it is not surprising that the airline fleet replacement rate varies, depending on the business model and the regulatory environment. Some observers have suggested that scrappage schemes, such as those used recently in Europe and the United States for cars, could be used to provide incentives for the introduction of more modern aircraft.

Figure 4   Aircraft of the future? Subscale model of the NASA Blended Wing Body (BWB) technology.

Source: Photo by Tony Landis, NASA Dryden Flight Research Center photo collection.

Airports, often locally owned and managed, have to serve the interests of the communities they serve. They are in the front line over environmental issues such as noise and ground traffic congestion. Capacity is limited in some areas, leading to high landing charges and contributing to use of airports that are further "out of town" and less expensive by some low-cost airlines such as Ryanair. Examples of major current capacity issues include the rejection of an application to build a third runway at London's Heathrow Airport. The ANSPs have the challenge of routing the aircraft safely and efficiently sometimes through skies that carry a huge amount of air traffic, particularly in Europe, the eastern seaboard of the United States, and over the North Atlantic. Globally there are moves to improve routing and to fly direct routes; however, routes are still typically 3% to 10% longer than the "great circle" direct line. One example is the wider application of continuous descent approaches, which bring both noise and fuel-burn benefits.

Aviation and the Climate Challenge

The greatest problem facing the aviation industry today is the growing contribution to humans'

impact on climate. Globally, aviation accounts for some 2.4% of the total man-made emissions of carbon dioxide (CO_2), with some countries contributing disproportionately; for example, internal flights in the United States account for some 25% of the total man-made emissions of CO_2, and all flights departing from U.K. airports account for about 6% of the total. Aircraft are known to have other impacts on the climate associated with the formation of cirrus cloud and condensation trails and through emissions of nitrogen oxides (NO_x). These are not as well understood, and, for the time being, the attention of the industry is focused on reducing CO_2.

Local and global regulators face a challenge to give clear guidance on whether to optimize gains in fuel efficiency and CO_2 emissions, on noise, which continues to be a major nuisance to communities living under airport flight paths, or on emissions of NO_x, with its impacts on both climate and local air quality.

Advances in engine and airframe technology alone are unlikely to be sufficient to allow aviation to achieve broad targets such as the EU objective to reduce CO_2 emissions by 80% to 95% by 2050, compared to 1990. A key area for the future growth of flying could be access to sustainably produced biofuels and the extent to which these can be produced. Long-term CO_2 targets will probably be achieved only by use of market mechanisms such as emissions trading, where aviation buys reductions from sectors where the cost of reducing CO_2 is lower than for aviation. If humans are to reduce emissions of greenhouse gases to levels deemed acceptable by organizations such as the International Panel on Climate Change, then aviation faces a particularly tough challenge; failure to reach targets through technology, trading, and other methods could result in demand control with access to flying rationed in some as yet undetermined way. And, of course, one consequence is that the real cost of flying is likely to increase.

The Global Future of Air Travel

The subsectors of the aviation industry in the United Kingdom have suggested that the U.K. industry is capable of reducing its CO_2 emissions to 2005 levels by 2050. This has been challenged by the U.K. Committee on Climate Change but is supported by the position of the International Air Transport Association, which has indicated that global aircraft emissions of CO_2, including trading, can be halved by 2050 compared to 2005.

Although the pattern of change in the aviation industry varies from country to country, aviation continues to grow. In 2004, the total scheduled traffic carried by the airlines of the 188 contracting states of the International Civil Aviation Organization amounted to almost 1,890 million passengers and some 38 million tons of freight. The overall passenger/freight/mail ton kilometers performed showed an increase of some 13% over 2003. Meanwhile, the aerospace industry has been driving technological advances in a wide variety of fields. The great breakthroughs in materials science and technology, electronics, and computer sciences are inextricably reflected in the possibilities of air travel. No one can accurately predict the future, but it seems that air travel will be around for a long time, even if the cost goes up and the aircraft looks different.

The development of commercial aviation has made the world a smaller place. After World War II, the development of international networks brought access within the grasp of a wider range of people. But it was deregulation and the rapid development of low-cost carriers in the last decades of the 20th century, coupled with growing prosperity, that really made a difference in access, such that today it is estimated that some 50% of people in the United Kingdom fly at least once per year and a growing proportion are leisure travelers. One reputable estimate for March 2009 was a global total of 2.38 million flights for the month, offering 289.8 million seats. This, of course, still means that a significant proportion of people in developed countries, and the vast majority in less developed economies, do not have access to aviation.

Aviation has promoted international trade through bringing producers and purchasers together across the globe. Videoconferencing and better telecommunications may substitute for a lot of air travel, but there is a strong conviction that, if you wish to "cut a deal" politically or in business, then eyeball-to-eyeball contact is necessary. Indeed, it may be that there is a rebound effect from communication technology that sparks the need for direct contact. It can be argued that better face-to-face communication between government representatives has brought benefits in political understanding. One undoubted benefit to people has been the opening up of the world of tourism and the possibility to visit friends and relatives, many of these visits resulting from migration of individuals and families to take up new opportunities, a process that will continue creating ongoing demand for air transport.

Hugh Somerville

See also Airlines; Biofuels; Civil Aviation; Climate Change; Energy Efficiency; Global Communications and Technology; Global Environmental and Energy Issues; Global Warming; Sustainability; Tourism Sector

Further Readings

Calder, S. (2002). *No frills: The truth behind the low-cost revolution in the skies*. London: Virgin Books.

Committee on Climate Change. (2009). *Meeting the UK aviation target—options for reducing emissions to 2050*. London: Author.

Gittell, J. H. (2003). *The Southwest Airlines way*. New York: McGraw-Hill.

Heppenheimer, T. A. (1995). *Turbulent skies: The history of commercial aviation*. New York: Wiley.

Intergovernmental Panel on Climate Change. (1999). *Aviation and the global atmosphere*. Cambridge, UK: Cambridge University Press.

Millbrooke, A. (1999). *Aviation history*. Englewood, CO: Jeppesen Sanders.

Muse, L. (2002). *Southwest passage: The inside story of Southwest Airlines' formative years*. Austin, TX: Eakin Press.

Sutter, J., & Spenser, J. (2006). *Creating the world's first jumbo jet and other adventures from a life in aviation*. Washington, DC: Smithsonian Books.

Websites

International Air Transport Association: http://www.iata.org/index.htm

International Civil Aviation Organization: http://www.icao.int/icao/en/adb/wla/libinfo.htm

Smithsonian National Air and Space Museum: http://www.nasm.si.edu

Sustainable Aviation: www.sustainableaviation.co.uk

U.S. Centennial of Flight Commission. History of Flight: http://www.centennialofflight.gov/essay_cat/8.htm

AIRLINES

Airlines provide crucial services in the globalizing world, as they facilitate international business, trade, and tourism. In many countries, governments have traditionally protected their national airlines from competition in international markets. Regulatory barriers in the global aviation industry remain substantial, despite progress toward liberalization.

Airlines are businesses engaged in air transportation of passengers and/or cargo for profit. The airline business is very competitive. The first known airline was formed in Germany in 1909. Its name was DELAG, and it used Zeppelin airships to transport passengers between German cities. In June 2010, Delta Air Lines became the world's biggest airline. The oldest airline of those currently operating is KLM Royal Dutch Airlines, which celebrated its 90th anniversary in 2009.

Airlines differ in size, from carriers owning or leasing a single aircraft to the airline companies owning hundreds of airplanes and offering scheduled transportation to a multitude of destinations in dozens of countries. Some airlines operate solely on the domestic market (e.g., Southwest Airlines in the United States); others (e.g., KLM) perform only international services. Many airlines operate the so-called hub-and-spoke networks, whereby passengers are channeled via one or several airports in the carrier's network, called hubs. Some of the so-called low-cost airlines focus on point-to-point services, selling tickets for nonstop flights only (Ryanair is a vivid example). A number of airlines (e.g., FedEx, Kalita Air) carry only cargo.

The airline business is considered very competitive, with thin profit margins, and airlines often lose considerable amounts of money. Airlines derive revenue by charging their customers fees (known as *airfare* in case of passenger transportation and *cargo charges* in case of freight transport). Recently, some airlines have been working to diversify their revenue sources, introducing checked luggage fees, emphasizing on-board sales, and selling advertising. The most important technique used by the airlines to enhance the revenue potential is called yield management, which amounts to using available information about passengers' or freight carriers' demand to practice price discrimination and ensure high load factors to achieve lower average costs.

Airlines' main capital costs relate to purchase or lease of the aircraft. The operating costs include aircraft maintenance, fuel, labor, aircraft and luggage handling, airport charges (takeoff, landing, parking, etc.), navigation charges, and catering. Exact breakdown and relative importance of these costs depend a lot on the airline's business model; however, aircraft maintenance, fuel, and labor costs are typically the most important items.

Oftentimes, the airlines are viewed as countries' symbols and are considered to play an important role in ensuring national security. For example, the U.S. Department of Defense has the authority to request any U.S.-based airlines to provide aircraft for the department's operations. Noncompliance results in the airline losing its operating certificate. Consequently, governments have historically been heavily involved with the airline industry; regulatory barriers in international airline business remain generally high, even though some progress toward liberalization has recently been made.

International airline business still largely operates around a network of bilateral and (a recent phenomenon) multilateral air service agreements. These agreements place varying restrictions on the airlines' operations. The most restrictive ones include very specific constraints, from the number of airlines that can be designated by each party to fly between the countries, to the number of end points to be served, to frequency of service and aircraft capacity, to airfares the airlines are allowed to charge. Until recently, the majority of international airfares have been determined by the airlines at the International Air Transport Association (IATA) semi-annual conferences. Many bilateral air service agreements include provisions requiring the airlines to use IATA-approved airfares.

The most important developments in liberalization of the international airline business include gradual creation of the common market within the European Union (completed by 1995) and the recently signed Open Aviation Area agreement between the United States, Canada, and the European Union. The former has removed all barriers to competition within the European

Union, creating a union-wide airline market and triggering rapid development of the so-called low-cost no frills carriers, such as Ryanair and easyJet. The Open Aviation Area agreement's main advance is removal of the nationality clause on the transatlantic airline market, or allowing EU airlines to operate services to the United States and Canada from EU countries other than their home base.

Liberalization of the international airline markets has been shown to bring substantial benefits to customers in terms of lower airfares, more flight options, and generally lower barriers to conducting business between the respective countries. Despite recent developments, many important international airline markets (such as the transpacific market and markets within Asia) remain heavily regulated.

Volodymyr Bilotkach

See also Air Travel; Civil Aviation; Frequent Flier Miles; International Air Transport Association; Markets; Transportation Systems

Further Readings

Creaton, S. (2005). *Ryanair: How a small Irish airline conquered Europe*. London: Aurum Press.

Doganis, R. (2005). *The airline business*. Oxford, UK: Routledge.

Jones, L. (2005). *easyJet: The story of Britain's biggest low-cost airline*. London: Aurum Press.

Lauer, C. (2010). *Southwest Airlines*. Santa Barbara, CA: Greenwood.

Merian, D. (2007). *Flying high: A memoir about Howard Hughes, TWA, and crew*. Bloomington, IN: Authorhouse.

Williams, G. (2002). *Airline competition: Deregulation's mixed legacy*. Burlington, VT: Ashgate.

AL JAZEERA

Al Jazeera, a Qatar-based satellite television news network, exemplifies the global expansion of information flow and illustrates the political impact that global media possess. Since its creation in 1996, Al Jazeera's Arabic channel has shown news consumers in the Arab world that they need not rely exclusively on Western media organizations, such as the BBC and CNN, particularly for news about themselves.

Although some critics challenge the channel's commitment to Western-style journalistic objectivity, others believe that misses the point about Al Jazeera's popularity. Its greatest asset among its viewers is its *credibility*; it lets the Arab public see events that affect them through their own eyes, and it provides the rest of the world with a different perspective on news. Its English-language channel, begun in 2006, gives Al Jazeera even greater global influence, delivering reports from places that many Western television news organizations overlook.

By offering a mix of innovative programming, high production values, and persistent marketing, Al Jazeera has established itself as the go-to information resource in much of the Middle East. In many of the cafes from Morocco to Kuwait, the televisions in the corner are tuned to Al Jazeera. A 2004–2005 survey of television viewers in Cairo found that 46% of households watched satellite television, and, of these, 88% watched Al Jazeera.

The channel's iconoclastic approach to news includes criticism of government corruption, discussions about women's rights, and other topics that staid state-run news organizations tend to ignore. Al Jazeera's coverage of the 2005 Egyptian elections, for example, included reports about charges of vote rigging and police interference, matters that many of Egypt's own news organizations did not dare to cover. Al Jazeera's coverage of the January 2011 protests in Tahrir Square was so inflammatory that the Egyptian government attempted—unsuccessfully—to shut down the network's Egyptian coverage in the midst of the protests. On a daily basis, Al Jazeera's talk shows often feature fiery debates about political and social issues. The substance and tone of Al Jazeera's programming have altered the public sphere in the Arab world and beyond, establishing new boundaries for discourse and changing the public's expectations of media and government.

Despite having an Arab audience estimated at 35 million, affection for the channel is by no means universal, even within the Middle East.

There are those who dislike the fractiousness of its talk shows, some who see a religious slant in its news coverage, and others who simply don't care for its rock-the-boat journalism.

Nevertheless, Al Jazeera is a political force within the Middle East and globally. It is a descendant of Voice of the Arabs, an Egyptian radio station launched in 1953 that was designed to foster pan-Arab unity. Al Jazeera made its mark as a pan-Arab force with its coverage of the Palestinian intifada in 2000 and further established itself with its reporting from Afghanistan, Iraq, and other scenes of conflict. This kind of coverage has periodically led to harsh criticism of the channel from the U.S. government, which has alleged that Al Jazeera encourages anti-American sentiment. Some American public diplomacy efforts in the Middle East have been designed to counter Al Jazeera's influence.

The channel is known for providing graphic images of civilian casualties: During the 2008–2009 conflict in Gaza, its coverage of Palestinians under fire implicitly encouraged street demonstrations and anger not only toward Israel but also toward Arab regimes perceived as being inadequately supportive of the Palestinians. At the same time, Al Jazeera English was the only English-language channel with correspondents on the ground in Gaza, and its coverage—which brought reports about the conflict to a worldwide audience—underscored Al Jazeera's significance as a global player.

Al Jazeera also has considerable credibility among non-Arab Muslim audiences and various diasporic populations. Pakistanis in London, Arab Americans in Detroit, and others elsewhere in the world have turned to Al Jazeera as a news provider that is, like themselves, representative of "the other" in the eyes of many. As Al Jazeera's reach continues to grow, it may bring a new degree of cohesion to such scattered populations, including the *ummah*, the global Islamic community.

In terms of globalized communication as a connecting mechanism, an "Al Jazeera effect" has taken hold, extending beyond traditional media and into online sources. This phenomenon expands the possibility of underrepresented publics having news sources that they trust. It may encourage them to become participants in, not merely consumers of, the news process. During the Arab Spring in 2011, for instance, participants in protest relied on Al Jazeera to keep them informed and, subsequently, involved. New media allow people to make their own voices heard on interactive websites, text and video blogs, and other such platforms. This participatory process has expanded rapidly as the "digital divide" has narrowed and people throughout the world have accessed information by using cell phones and other easily acquired communications technology.

Al Jazeera complements this process. With its Arabic and English satellite channels and its own web-based content, it fosters unprecedented global interconnectivity, encourages democratization, and increases the dynamism of global communication and politics. Despite these developments in the politics-media linkage, political institutions remain the key to substantive change. Even an Al Jazeera can do only so much.

Al Jazeera is a model for the evolving global news community. Venezuela's Telesur television channel patterned itself somewhat on Al Jazeera, and other regional news organizations are likely to appear. This may enhance regional and other kinds of political identities and increase parity in the international political structure. Given this trend, Al Jazeera may be regarded as a pioneer in ensuring a more diverse news universe and a more populist information society.

Philip Seib

See also Global Communications and Technology; Global Culture, Media; Media, Global; News; Television

Further Readings

Eickelman, D. F., & Anderson, J. W. (Eds.). (2003). *New media in the Muslim world* (2nd ed.). Bloomington: Indiana University.

El-Nawawy, M., & Iskander, A. (2002). *Al Jazeera.* Boulder, CO: Westview Press.

Lynch, M. (2006). *Voices of the new Arab public.* New York: Columbia.

Rugh, W. A. (2004). *Arab mass media.* Westport, CT: Praeger.

Seib, P. (2008). *The Al Jazeera effect.* Washington, DC: Potomac.

Zayani, M. (Ed.). (2005). *The Al Jazeera phenomenon.* Boulder, CO: Paradigm.

ALTERNATIVE ENERGY SOURCES

The utilization of alternative energy sources is an important step toward abating many of the world's global environmental problems. Energy resources are important for all countries: They are required for achieving good standards of living and wealth, and they foster social, cultural, technical, and economic development. Conventional energy sources, especially fossil fuels, have been the dominant energy resources used by societies. But conventional energy sources have recently led to numerous challenges, including environmental harm, uncertain future supplies, economic disparities among regions that have and do not have such resources, and global instability. In recent decades, alternative energy sources have begun to be used, particularly those that are renewable. Renewable energy sources can contribute beneficially to the economic and social development of the country, while protecting the environment and enhancing global stability and sustainability. As alternative resources become more affordable and other pressures like environmental damage increase, it is expected that alternative energy resources will play an increasing role in the energy systems of countries.

Population growth is expected to make alternative energy sources even more necessary, as the global population by 2050 is predicted by some to reach between 7 and 12 billion people. Simultaneously, global demand for energy services is expected to increase by as much as an order of magnitude by 2050, while primary-energy demands are expected to increase by 1.5 times. The supply and utilization of alternative energy sources will likely be critical components of industrial and technological development around the world.

In this entry, alternative energy sources are described, and the ramifications of their use in areas such as environmental stewardship, sustainability, and global stability are discussed. Environmental impacts of energy use, such as climate change, stratospheric ozone depletion, and acid precipitation, are examined. Predictions for future energy use are considered. Also, potential benefits of alternative energy sources to current problems are identified, and the solutions that they offer are explored. This entry is intended to provide an explanation of alternative energy sources and their role in development, environmental protection, sustainability, security, and global stability.

Energy

Energy can exist in many forms and can be converted from one form to another with energy-conversion technologies. Energy technologies also allow energy to be utilized to provide energy services. Energy carriers are produced from energy sources and are used in all aspects of life.

Energy is characterized by the laws of thermodynamics. The first law embodies the principle of conservation of energy, while the second law relates to the quality of energy and often includes the concepts of entropy and exergy.

It is important to distinguish between energy forms, sources, and carriers. *Energy* comes in a variety of forms, including fossil fuels and related fuels (e.g., gasoline, diesel fuel), uranium, electricity, work, thermal energy (e.g., steam), and solar energy. *Energy resources* (sometimes called primary energy forms) are found in the environment. Some are available in finite quantities (e.g., fossil fuels, oil sands, peat, uranium), whereas others are relatively renewable, including solar energy, falling water, wind, tides, geothermal heat, and biomass fuels. Energy resources are often processed from their raw forms prior to use. *Energy carriers* (sometimes called energy currencies) are the energy forms that we transport and utilize; these include some energy resources (e.g., fossil fuels) and processed energy forms (e.g., gasoline, electricity, work, and heat). Most processed energy forms are not found in the environment. The range of energy carriers is diverse, including work, electricity, and heat, as well as secondary chemical fuels like oil and coal products, synthetic gaseous fuels, hydrogen, methanol, and ammonia.

The distinction between energy sources and carriers can be confusing. Energy sources are the original resource from which an energy carrier is produced. Some energy carriers are also energy sources, but many energy carriers are not energy sources. For instance, electricity is only an energy carrier, as it is not a resource found in nature. Similarly, hydrogen is an energy carrier but is not an energy source. Rather, hydrogen can be produced from various energy sources using energy-conversion processes (e.g., natural gas reforming, coal gasification, water electrolysis,

Table 1   Energy Sources

Nonrenewable	Renewable

Fossil fuels
  Coal
  Oil
  Natural gas
  Alternative fossil fuels (oil sands, peat)
 	
Others
  Biomass (if use rate > replenishment rate)
  Uranium
  Fusion material (e.g., deuterium)
  Wastes (usable as energy forms or convertible
  to more useful energy forms)
	Solar radiation
	
	Solar-related energy sources
	  Hydraulic energy
	  Wind energy
	  Wave energy
	  Biomass (if use rate < replenishment rate)
	  Ocean thermal energy (from temperature
	  difference between surface and deep waters)
	
	Non-solar-related energy sources
	  Geothermal energy (internal heat of earth and
	  ground-source energy)
	  Tidal energy (from gravitational forces of sun
	  and moon and rotation of earth)

thermochemical water decomposition). Nevertheless, discussions of a "hydrogen economy," in which hydrogen becomes a primary chemical energy carrier and replaces fossil fuels, often erroneously refer to hydrogen as an energy source.

Energy Sources

Many types of energy sources exist (see Table 1). Fossil fuels are dominant in society today, but numerous non-fossil-fuel energy sources exist.

Nonrenewable energy sources include energy resources that are available in finite quantities. These include conventional and alternative fossil fuels, as well as nonrenewable energy resources such as uranium and fusion material (e.g., deuterium). Nuclear energy is not a renewable resource, but research is ongoing to determine the degree to which nuclear fuel lifetimes can be lengthened via breeder reactors and other advanced nuclear technologies.

Renewable energy is often characterized as "green energy" and includes the following:

- *Solar radiation.* This is the main type of renewable energy; it reaches the earth at a rate of 1.75×10^{17} W, which is about 20,000 times greater than the global energy-use rate. Solar energy can be can be converted directly to electricity in photovoltaic devices; collected as heat for thermal processes, such as space and water heating; or concentrated for high-temperature heating and thermal electricity generation.

- *Solar-radiation-related energy forms.* Several other renewable energy types stem from solar radiation. These include hydraulic energy, which is derived from falling and running water in rivers, waterfalls, and so forth; wind energy, which is increasingly used for electricity generation; wave energy, which utilizes the motion of waves; ocean thermal energy, which exists because of the temperature difference between surface and deep waters of the ocean; and biomass energy. Biomass energy, which includes wood, plants, and other forms of organic matter, can be used directly as a fuel or converted into more desirable fuels. Several fast-growing trees have been identified as good candidates for biomass energy production. But biomass is a renewable energy resource only when the rate at which it is used does not exceed the rate at which it is replenished.

- *Nonsolar-radiation-related energy forms.* Some renewable energy types stem from other phenomena. These include tidal energy, which exploits the motion of tides and which is caused by gravitational forces of the sun and moon and the rotation of the earth; and geothermal energy. The latter term applies to both (1) the natural temperatures of the ground, which can be used in conjunction with heat pumps; and (2) thermal energy derived as a consequence of the internal heat of the earth in such forms as hot wells and geysers, which can be used directly for heating.

Several important points related to the energy sources listed in Table 1 are worth noting:

- Renewable energy resources do not normally lead to greenhouse gas emissions. However, biomass can lead to such emissions if not managed carefully.
- Although not a renewable energy source, nuclear energy does not contribute to climate change as it emits no greenhouse gases.
- Waste materials and waste energy that would otherwise be discarded are sometimes considered renewable energy. Wastes can be used directly as energy; for example, heat from hot materials like stack gases and cooling-water discharges can be recovered to provide heating. Wastes can also be converted to more useful forms; for example, material wastes can be fed to waste-to-energy incineration to provide useful heat and/or generate electricity.

Alternative Energy Sources

Conventional energy sources are commonly considered at present to include conventional fossil fuels, large-scale hydraulic energy, and nuclear energy.

Alternative energy sources are usually taken to include the renewable energy sources listed in Table 1. In addition, alternative energy sources are considered to include alternative fossil fuels (e.g., oil sands, oil shales, tar sands, peat), fusion energy sources, micro-hydro, and wastes. The oil crises of the early 1970s fostered research and development into alternative energy sources and related technologies worldwide, although environmental and economic concerns have also prompted much research in recent years. Several alternative energy sources are shown in Figure 1.

Energy systems based on renewable energy have increased in attractiveness as a result of projected high costs of oil and other fossil fuels combined with expected advances and cost reductions in renewable energy technologies. Converting natural phenomena into useful energy forms, renewable energy technologies have become increasingly important. These technologies use sunlight and its indirect impacts on the earth (wind, falling water, heating, plant growth), gravitational forces, and the heat of the earth's core as resources. These energy resources represent a large potential, much greater

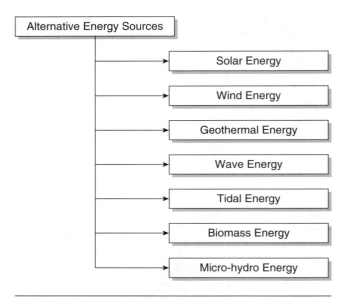

Figure I   Several alternative energy sources.

than equivalent fossil resources. But renewable energy sources are generally diffuse and not fully accessible; some are intermittent, and all have distinct regional variations. Such characteristics yield technical, institutional, and economic challenges regarding utilization. Significant progress has been reported in recent years on improving efficiencies, reducing initial and operating costs, and enhancing the reliability and applicability of renewable energy technologies. The attributes of renewable energy technologies, which include modularity, flexibility, and low operating costs, are different from those for traditional, fossil-based technologies, whose attributes include large capital investments, long implementation lead times, and future fuel cost uncertainties. The overall benefits of renewable energy technologies are often not well understood; consequently, they are often evaluated to be not as cost-effective as traditional technologies.

The following efforts have been expended to help improve the commercial potential of alternative energy sources:

- *Education and awareness*: Understanding of alternative energy sources needs to be enhanced via education and increased public awareness of options.
- *Research and development (R&D)*: R&D is needed and has been carried out, often in cooperation with industry, to develop and commercialize renewable energy technologies.

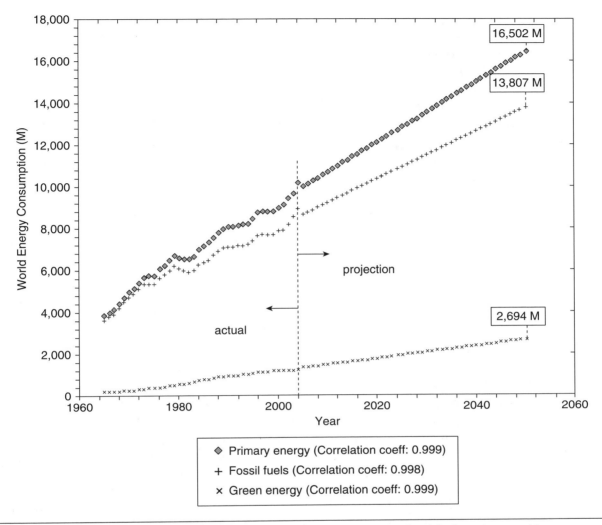

Figure 2   Actual and predicted global consumption of primary energy, fossil fuels, and renewable energy sources. M denotes million tons of oil equivalent (MTOE).

Source: Ermis, K., Midilli, A., Dincer, I., & Rosen, M. A. (2007). Artificial neural network analysis of world green energy consumption, *Energy Policy, 35*(3), 1731–1743. Copyright © 2007, Elsevier. Reprinted with permission.

R&D partners can also include other stakeholders in the energy industry, such as universities and research organizations, energy utilities, and governments.

- *Technology assessment and transfer*: To assist commercialization efforts, alternative energy sources and related technologies need to be assessed thoroughly in terms of factors such as performance, efficiency, cost, reliability, environmental impact, and safety, through demonstrations and field trials. Further, R&D results need to be transferred to potential users, in urban and remote areas of all countries, to support the development of markets.

- *Standards development*: The development of standards, through combined efforts of national and international standards organizations and regulatory bodies, is necessary to promote adoption of alternative energy sources and related technologies in the marketplace.

Energy Utilization

World primary energy consumption of fossil fuels and renewable energy from 1965 and 2005 and predicted to 2050 is shown in Figure 2, which was developed using data provided by such institutions as the Organisation for Economic Co-operation and Development, the International Energy Agency, and BP. World primary energy consumption is seen to be expected to reach 16,502 million tons of oil equivalent (MTOE) by 2050. It has been suggested that reserves are less than 40 years for petroleum, 60 years for natural gas, and 250 years for coal, although these time frames change with new developments.

Alternative energy sources are often advantageous in developing countries. For instance, the market demand for renewable energy technologies in developing nations will likely grow as developing countries seek a better standard of living.

Environment, Efficiency, and Sustainability

A critical energy-related concern is climate change, mainly due to emissions of CO_2 and other greenhouse gases from fossil fuel combustion. Climate change has a significant impact on food chains, weather events, flooding, and other geosystemic phenomena. Other energy-related environmental concerns include air pollution emissions (e.g., CO_2, CO, NO_x, SO_x, non-methane hydrocarbons, particulates), acid precipitation, ozone depletion, forest and arable land destruction, and radioactive emissions. Fossil fuels have also caused some major problems regarding human health and welfare and global unrest.

In numerous jurisdictions, the idea that consumers share responsibility for environmental impact and its costs has been increasingly accepted, and energy prices have been increased, in part to account for environmental costs.

Several definitions of sustainable development have been put forth, including the following common one: "development that meets the needs of the present without compromising the ability of future generations to meet their own needs" (World Commission on Environment and Development, 1987). Although a secure supply of energy is not sufficient for development within a society, a sustainable supply of energy resources is generally agreed to be necessary for achieving sustainable development. Alternative energy sources can contribute to energy sustainability by helping meet society's need for a sustainable supply of energy sources, especially when used in conjunction with effective and efficient technologies. Clearly, energy resources such as fossil fuels are finite and thus lack the

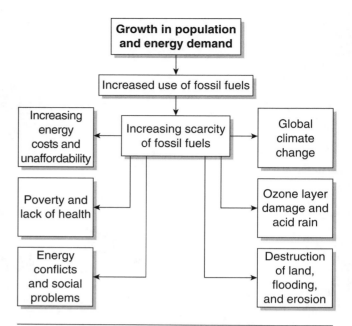

Figure 3   Global challenges associated with conventional energy, particularly related to increasing population and growth in energy use.

characteristics needed for sustainability, while many alternative energy sources are sustainable over the relatively long term.

Environmental concerns are significantly linked to sustainable development. Activities that continually degrade the environment are not sustainable and lead to health, ecological, and other problems. Improved efficiency leads to reduced energy losses and to environmental benefits by reducing outputs of pollutants, usually over the entire life cycle. Techniques like exergy analysis, which provides more meaningful measures of efficiency and loss than the more conventional energy analysis, allow efficiency to be better understood and improved.

Some of the global problems affecting world stability that impact significantly the achievement of sustainability are presented in Figure 3, wherein the main problems are observed to be linked to fossil fuel utilization on local, regional, and global bases.

In both developing and industrialized countries, alternative energy sources—particularly those that are renewable—are a key component of sustainable development because they generally cannot be depleted; cause less environmental impact than other energy sources; provide a flexible array of options for their use; favor system decentralization and are somewhat independent of national networks, enhancing the system flexibility and providing economic benefits to isolated populations; and are of a small scale, which reduces the time from design to commissioning and improves adaptability to unpredictable growth and/or changes in energy demand.

Alternative energy sources, especially those that are renewable, are needed to reduce the environmental impact of energy use, improve standards of living and health, provide economic and cultural development, produce global stability, and lead to sustainable development.

Ibrahim Dincer and Marc A. Rosen

See also Climate Change; Electricity; Environmental Movement; Environmental Security; Extractive Industries Sector; Global Environmental and Energy Issues; Global Warming; Petroleum Economy; Sustainability

Further Readings

BP. (2009, June). *BP statistical review of world energy.* Retrieved August 31, 2011, from http://www.bp.com/liveassets/bp_internet/globalbp/globalbp_uk_english/reports_and_publications/statistical_energy_review_2008/STAGING/local_assets/2009_downloads/statistical_review_of_world_energy_full_report_2009.pdf

Dincer, I., & Rosen, M. A. (2004). Exergy as a driver for achieving sustainability. *International Journal of Green Energy, 1*(1), 1–19.

Dincer, I., & Rosen, M. A. (2005). Thermodynamic aspects of renewables and sustainable development. *Renewable and Sustainable Energy Reviews, 9,* 169–189.

Dincer, I., & Rosen, M. A. (2007). *Exergy: Energy, environment and sustainable development.* Oxford, UK: Elsevier.

Ermis, K., Midilli, A., Dincer, I., & Rosen, M. A. (2007). Artificial neural network analysis of world green energy consumption. *Energy Policy 35*(3), 1731–1743.

Goldemberg, J., Johansson, T. B., Reddy, A. K. N., & Williams, R. H. (1988). *Energy for a sustainable world.* New York: Wiley.

Haberl, H. (2006). The global socioeconomic energetic metabolism as a sustainability problem. *Energy, 31,* 87–99.

Lior, N. (2008). Energy resources and use: The present situation and possible paths to the future. *Energy, 33,* 842–857.

Organisation for Economic Co-operation and Development and International Energy Agency, International Energy Agency. (2008). *World energy outlook 2008.* Retrieved August 6, 2011, from http://www.iea.org/textbase/nppdf/free/2008/weo2008.pdf

Rosen, M. A. (2009). Combating global warming via non-fossil fuel energy options. *International Journal of Global Warming, 1*(1–3), 2–28.

Rosen, M. A., Dincer, I., & Kanoglu, M. (2008). Role of exergy in increasing efficiency and sustainability and reducing environmental impact. *Energy Policy, 36*(1), 128–137.

World Commission on Environment and Development. (1987). *Our common future.* Oxford, UK: Oxford University Press.

AMERICAN REVOLUTION

Even at its time, the American Revolution was a global event, and its impact on world history has been significant. With the conclusion of the Seven Years' War in 1763, Great Britain commanded the greatest empire since the fall of Rome. Victory, however, brought with it the necessity of reorganizing the vast North American territories wrested from France and Spain. In an effort to prevent further warfare with the Indian peoples, the Proclamation of 1763 closed the vast trans-Appalachian area to White settlement. With a view to defending and policing these new territories, the British government maintained an unprecedented standing army in mainland America. To meet the costs of this commitment, as well as to relieve the massive financial burden left by the war, London sought to impose new taxes and enforce imperial trade laws that had long been ignored by the colonists. The end of the French and Indian War—as the Seven Years' War was known in America—thus marked the end of the period of "salutary neglect."

British measures were designed not only to bring peace and stability to North America but also to require the colonies to share the cost of imperial defense and administration. The colonies, however, had come to think of themselves as self-governing entities, as having "dominion status," to use a term of later origin, and they refused to have their duties prescribed for them by Parliament and King. Parliament and King were unwilling to accept such a novel theory of empire. Great Britain, consequently, became involved in a war not only with the New World colonies but eventually with most of Europe. The war, although not wholly disastrous to the British army, deprived Great Britain of the most valuable of its colonial possessions and removed it from the pinnacle of power that the country had attained by the Peace of Paris of 1763.

The initial aim of armed revolt was not independence but rather a restoration and recognition of what the colonials held to be their rights as British subjects. They professed to have been content with their status under British policy prior to 1763. That the colonies turned to independence in the second year of the struggle was partly the consequence of the British government's rejection of compromise and its adoption, instead, of severe repressive measures. It was also the consequence of a dawning realization of the advantages that might accrue from independence. No one set forth the arguments for independence so persuasively as an immigrant from England named Thomas Paine. Paine had arrived in America in late 1774, leaving behind a number of failed careers. Less than 2 years later, in January 1776, he published the pamphlet *Common Sense*. This pamphlet sold some 120,000 copies in the first three months and was the single most effective articulation of the case for independence. Among Paine's arguments, two were significant for the future foreign policy of the United States. Independence, argued Paine, would free the former colonies from being entangled in European wars in which they had no concern, and a declaration of independence would improve their chances of securing foreign aid.

Greatly inferior to the mother country in numbers, wealth, industry, and military and naval power, the colonies could hardly hope for decisive military success unless aided by one of the major European powers. Months before deciding on independence, Congress had set up a secret committee to make contact with friends abroad. This committee had sent to Paris a secret agent in the guise of a merchant to seek supplies and credit. The agent, Silas Deane of Connecticut, arriving in Paris in July 1776, soon found that the French government was disposed to giving secret assistance to England's rebelling colonies. French ministers, in fact, had been on the lookout since 1763 for an opportunity to weaken and humiliate France's victorious rival,

Great Britain. The celebrated French playwright and amateur diplomat Caron de Beaumarchais, who had already been in contact with another colonial agent, Arthur Lee, in London, believed that such an opportunity had now arrived. So, too, believed the Comte de Vergennes (French foreign minister), and Vergennes and Beaumarchais were able to persuade King Louis XVI that aid to the colonies was in the French interest.

As yet, however, France was not willing to openly avow friendship for the colonies and offered material aid only in secret. This was managed through the creation by Beaumarchais of a fictitious commercial firm, Rodrigue Hortalez et Compagnie, through which gunpowder and other essential supplies from the French arsenals were channeled to the armies of George Washington. Spain, too, was persuaded by France to give aid through this and other means. All in all, measured in contemporary U.S. dollars, France contributed to the American cause nearly $2,000,000 in subsidies and over $6,350,000 in loans; Spain supplied approximately $400,000 and $250,000 in subsidies and loans, respectively.

These arrangements for secret "lend-lease" had been instituted before Deane's arrival in Paris. After the Declaration of Independence had been drafted, Congress sent to France the most widely known, most admired, and most persuasive American of his day, Benjamin Franklin. The principal purpose of Franklin's mission was to secure, from the French government, official recognition of the United States as an independent nation. Recognition could be accomplished by the signing of a treaty between France and the United States. Franklin brought with him to Paris a draft of a proposed treaty of amity and commerce, which had been prepared by a committee of Congress and which embodied the liberal commercial principles that Congress hoped to see adopted not only by France but by the entire trading world as well. The Plan of Treaties of 1776 was the first major state paper dealing with American foreign policy and would guide the makers of such policy far beyond the exigencies of the revolution. John Adams, the principal author of the model treaty, repeatedly asserted that any Franco-American treaty should take the form of a commercial connection with no military or political ties. Adams said of France: "We ought not to enter into any

Alliance with her, which should entangle Us in any future Wars in Europe. . . . We ought to lay it down as a first principle and a Maxim never to be forgotten, to maintain an entire Neutrality in all future European Wars" (Butterfield, 1961, pp. 337–338).

Though friendly to the United States, Vergennes was unwilling to grant formal recognition, thus risking war with England, until the Americans could offer some evidence of their ability to do their share in winning the war. He did not wish to involve France in a war for a losing cause. Such evidence was not forthcoming until December 1777, when news arrived that General Burgoyne's British army, thrusting down from Montreal into New York, had been forced to surrender to General Gates at Saratoga. This was what Vergennes had been waiting for; he tried to enlist Spain in the cause, and when Spain procrastinated, he resolved that France should proceed without Spain. On December 17, the American commissioners were informed that France would grant recognition and make a treaty with the United States. On February 6, 1778, a Treaty of Amity and Commerce and a Treaty of Alliance were signed in Paris, the latter to take effect if Great Britain went to war with France because of the former. The Treaty of Amity and Commerce clearly reflected the principles set down by Adams in the Plan of Treaties of 1776. The Treaty of Alliance, however, ran contrary to his calls to avoid an alliance with France, "which might embarrass Us in after times and involve Us in future European Wars" (Butterfield, 1961, pp. 337–338).

The Treaty of Amity and Commerce placed each nation on a most-favored-nation basis with reference to the other and embodied, practically unaltered, the liberal principles of the "Plan of 1776"—principles that would protect the interest of either signatory that might chance to be neutral when the other was at war. The Treaty of Alliance was to go into effect if France should become embroiled in the existing war against Great Britain. Its object was "to maintain effectually the liberty, sovereignty, and independence absolute and unlimited" of the United States. France renounced forever any designs on Bermuda or on any parts of the continent of North America that, before the Treaty of Paris of 1763 or by virtue of that treaty, had belonged to Great Britain or to the former British colonies. France reserved the right to possess any of the British West Indian colonies. The United States, on the other hand, was free to conquer and hold Bermuda or any of Great Britain's mainland possessions. Neither party was to make a separate peace with Great Britain or lay down its arms until American independence had been won. Both parties mutually guaranteed "from the present time and forever against all other powers" the American possessions that they then held and with which they might emerge from the war. France, in addition, undertook to guarantee the liberty, sovereignty, and independence of the United States.

The treaty just described constituted the only "entangling alliance" in which the United States participated until the mid-20th century. It was to cause serious embarrassment before it was set aside in 1800, but in the winning of independence, it was indispensable. A French army under General Rochambeau was sent to America, and French fleets under Admiral d'Estaing and Admiral de Grasse operated off the American coast. The importance of French aid is illustrated by the fact that in the final scene of the revolution, at Yorktown, Cornwallis's British army was caught between a French fleet and an allied army, of which two thirds were French.

To win independence, the United States had found it necessary to involve itself in the international rivalries and politics of Europe. Those same rivalries and politics, however, threatened to terminate the war with American independence still unwon. Spain, having entered the war reluctantly, soon grew tired of it. In 1780, the Spanish government received a British mission to come to discuss peace terms. For America, the Spanish ministers proposed a long truce between Great Britain and its "colonies," without specific recognition of independence and with a division of territory on the basis of *uti possidetis*, or retention by each party of the areas then occupied. This would have left the British in control of Maine, the northern frontier, New York City, Long Island, and the principal seaports south of Virginia.

The surrender of Cornwallis to Washington and Rochambeau at Yorktown, October 19, 1781, was the climax of Great Britain's misfortunes. Great Britain was now at war, or on the verge of war, with most of the Western world. The Netherlands was added to the list of Britain's open enemies, forcing the Dutch into war rather than permitting continuance of their neutral trade with France. The Baltic countries, Russia, Denmark, and Sweden had in 1780 organized themselves into a League of Armed Neutrality for the purpose of protecting their commerce against what they considered the illegitimate exactions of the British Navy; and they had been joined by Prussia, the Emperor (of the Holy Roman Empire), the Kingdom of the Two Sicilies, and even Portugal, Great Britain's traditional ally. There was little that the British could hope to gain by prolonging the war.

In February 1782, following receipt of the news of the disaster at Yorktown, the British House of Commons resolved that the war ought to be terminated. In March, the ministry of Lord North, whose policies had precipitated the American conflict, resigned, and a new ministry headed by the Marquis of Rockingham took office. The Earl of Shelburne, as secretary of state for the Southern Department, initiated peace talks by sending Richard Oswald, a Scot, to confer with the American representatives in Paris. After Rockingham's death in July 1782, Shelburne became prime minister but continued to guide negotiations with the United States. This was fortunate, for Shelburne was an advocate of a generous peace, which might result in recapturing for Great Britain the bulk of American trade and at some future date, perhaps, tempt the United States back into some sort of imperial federation.

Great Britain eventually acknowledged the independence and sovereignty of the 13 states individually; promised to withdraw all its armies, garrisons, and fleets from their soil and waters "with all convenient speed"; and conceded to American fishermen the "liberty" to ply their trade much as before in the territorial waters of British North America. The United States, on its part, made certain promises in the interest of Loyalists and British creditors. The parties agreed that creditors on either side should "meet with no lawful impediment" in the recovery of the full value of bona fide debts previously contracted. The United States agreed that there should be no further prosecutions or confiscations of property against any persons for the parts they had taken in the war, and promised that it would "earnestly recommend" to the legislatures of the states that, with certain exceptions, rights and properties of Loyalists be restored.

This preliminary treaty, minus the secret article, became the definitive treaty, signed September 3, 1783, at the same time that Great Britain made peace with other enemies. Great Britain ceded the Floridas, with limits undefined, to Spain, which was not a party to the treaty between Great Britain and the United States, and hence did not consider itself bound by its provisions with respect to the navigation of the Mississippi River and the southern boundary of the United States. With both Spain and Great Britain, the United States still had many difficulties to overcome before the paper stipulations of the treaty could be converted into reality.

Joseph M. Siracusa

See also Colonialism; Empires, Modern; Hegemonic Power; Independence Movements; Revolutions; War

Further Readings

Bemis, S. (1935). *The diplomacy of the American Revolution*. Bloomington: Indiana University Press.

Butterfield, L. H. (Ed.). (1961). *Diary and autobiography of John Adams* (4 vols.). Cambridge, MA: Belknap Press.

Dull, J. (1985). *A diplomatic history of the American Revolution*. New Haven, CT: Yale University Press.

Graebner, N., Burns, R., & Siracusa, J. (2011). *Foreign affairs and the Founding Fathers: From Confederation to Constitution, 1776–1787*. Santa Barbara, CA: Praeger.

Mackesy, P. (1964). *The War for America, 1775–1783*. Cambridge, MA: Harvard University Press.

Schlesinger, A. (1918). *The colonial merchants and the American Revolution*. New York: Longmans.

Stinchcombe, W. (1969). *The American Revolution and the French Alliance*. Syracuse, NY: Syracuse University Press.

AMERICANIZATION

Americanization is often conflated with globalization, although it is a multifaceted term applied to both domestic and international contexts, and encompasses political, linguistic, cultural, and economic dimensions. Historically, it has had both positive and negative connotations, depending on the time, place, context, and positionality of the speaker. *Americanization* refers to both a process and a result, the merits of which have been passionately supported, advocated, rejected, and resisted by governmental, nongovernmental, community, industry, and individual actors in the United States and abroad for more than the past two centuries.

In a domestic context, Americanization has referred to the process of becoming American or the making into an American of an individual or group of people. (In this context, the term *American* refers to "of the United States" and not the Americas more generally.) The blending of ideas of citizenship and cultural identity that accrue to this concept take on meaning because of national ideologies asserting that the United States is, above all, a nation of immigrants. Such a commitment to pluralism brings with it tensions of how to create a national identity out of such diverse cultural, linguistic, religious, and ethnic origins of those immigrants.

A specifically problematic aspect of this national ideology is that it implicitly dismisses the presence of indigenous Native American peoples, masks the histories of enslaved African peoples who migrated against their will, and ignores the history of residents of Mexico who were forced to become part of the U.S. territories in 1848 with the signing of the Treaty of Guadalupe Hidalgo.

Americanization has its limits, though, and those have shifted during specific historical periods as beliefs about who was considered "assimilable" changed. For example, there was a "Nativist" backlash against increasing numbers of southern and eastern European and Asian immigrants who arrived in the mid to late 19th and early 20th centuries. Northern European Protestant settlers from earlier eras were now joined by Irish Catholics, central European and Russian Jews, Germans, Italians, Hungarians, and Polish immigrants, among others. From mid-1800s to 1920, approximately 25 million new immigrants entered the country. Philosophies of social Darwinism, eugenics, and scientific racism provided apparent intellectual justification for discriminatory treatment of many of these groups. At the same time, violence against African Americans and Asian immigrants rose, culminating for the latter in the 1882 Chinese Exclusion Act. Native Americans were taken from their homes and sent to government boarding schools where speaking their own language was forbidden as part of the effort to "Americanize" them.

Among those immigrants deemed assimilable, special schools and public pageants helped promote the transition from foreigner to American. This symbolic Americanization, often involving a literal marching in and out of a giant cauldron, or "melting pot," on stage, applied only to those who could conceivably be understood as "White," linking the ideas of racialization, eugenics, and normativity with Americanization.

At the same time, the United States was expanding its reach beyond the territories of the continental United States. During the 1898 imperial expansion of the Spanish-American War, debates about who could become "American" were extended to overseas territories like Cuba, Puerto Rico, and the Philippines. Publications linked current racialist thinking to populations outside the United States, assessing their potential for Americanization.

In the late 20th century, another metaphor for cultural pluralism, "the salad bowl," came to signify a form of Americanization different from assimilation, one that held cultural difference as a positive value. Multiculturalism emerged as a concept in public discourse, but it often merely mapped former "racial" categories onto "cultural" ones, not guaranteeing true equality. In the 21st century, debates about Americanization continued and often took the form of arguments about whether or not there should be a national language policy in the face of large numbers of Spanish-speaking immigrants.

The other use of the term *Americanization* refers to the influence of the United States abroad. The term usually indexes a process of change in patterns of social organization, political structures, or consumption seen as a result of contact with ideas, goods, or practices originating in, or strongly associated with, the United States.

Almost anything can be termed *Americanized*: a change in India from British-accented English to American-accented English, a growing appetite for hip-hop music in Japan, or the expansion of McDonald's restaurants in China. Two things are important here: that the practice or product may or may not actually come from the United States but is perceived to do so and that such changes are usually more accurately described as adoptions and adaptations. McDonald's restaurants in China, for example, serve a different menu and are used differently by patrons than in the United States. Yet, the presence of McDonald's is sometimes pointed to as evidence of Americanization. Perceptions of

Americanization are often accompanied by feelings of anti-Americanism, that is, a rejection of things, ideas, and practices associated with the United States.

A final issue is the conflation of Americanization with globalization. If globalization refers to a perceived increase in the flow of people, goods, finance, and ideas across national borders, then the substitution of Americanization for that concept supposes that a majority of those goods and ideas are coming from the United States. Such an assumption, while emphasizing the power of the United States, can also ignore multiple sites of economic and political power in the world as well as the active process of selection and adaptation that accompanies cultural change.

Jane C. Desmond

See also Assimilation; Colonialism; Darwinism and Social Darwinism; Empires, Modern; Global Economic Issues; Globalization, Phenomenon of; Hegemonic Power; McDonaldization, McWorld; Migration; Modernization; Myths; Power, Global Contexts of

Further Readings

U.S. Department of Homeland Security, Task on New Americans. (2008, December 18). *Fact Sheet: Building an Americanization movement for the 21st century: A report to the President of the United States from the Task Force on New Americans.* Retrieved August 4, 2011, from http://www.uscis.gov/files/article/taskforcerecomm_18dec2008.pdf

Van Elteren, M. (2006, September). Rethinking Americanization abroad: Toward a critical alternative to prevailing paradigms. *Journal of American Culture, 29*(3), 345–367.

Watson, J. L. (Ed.). (1997). *Golden Arches East: McDonald's in East Asia* (2nd ed.). Palo Alto, CA: Stanford University Press.

AMNESTY INTERNATIONAL

Amnesty International (AI) is an international nongovernmental organization (NGO) committed to protecting human rights worldwide. It is widely recognized for its accomplishments, such as winning the Nobel Peace Prize in 1977. Among human rights NGOs, it is notably a membership organization, claiming 2.2 million members in 2010. This distinguishes it from its competitors and is an important factor in determining the organizational structure of the NGO, how it operates, and the types of human rights it advocates. Throughout most of its history, its primary focus has been on civil and political rights, but since 2001, it has integrated social, economic, and cultural rights into its agenda. AI's International Secretariat (IS) is located in London, United Kingdom, and it has national sections in 80 countries. Some of its most important campaigns have been against torture, the death penalty, and nondiscrimination based on sexual orientation.

On Sunday, May 28, 1961, an opinion piece titled "The Forgotten Prisoners" appeared in the London *Observer*. Written by barrister Peter Benenson, it detailed the stories of individuals who were jailed for their "conscience": nonviolent political and religious dissent from their respective governments. The response to Benenson's article was larger than expected; it not only created support for a yearlong campaign to help so-called prisoners of conscience (POCs), but it opened the way for an international movement and a new human rights concept. POCs served as a rallying point for mobilizing volunteers to form groups in order to "adopt" these victims of human rights abuse. Prisoner adoption meant persistently penning letters on their behalf to local and higher level officials until a definitive outcome, whether positive or negative, was achieved.

AI, from the beginning, espoused a number of principles. First, the organization was to take no funding from governments but instead rely on private, and preferably individual, donations from members. This helped reinforce the notion of political impartiality. Second, membership was truly meaningful in the sense that, organized as groups under national sections, individual members not only contributed to the coffers of AI but also actively contributed to the advocacy work of freeing POCs. Policymaking also comes from the membership at International Council meetings, currently biennial. Third, the need to generate support from the membership in support of its advocacy agenda meant that, for 40 years, AI's scope of human rights advocacy was extremely limited under its mandate. This self-imposed mandate constricted the IS from expanding the scope of the NGO's activities. This was both the strength of the organization, focusing international attention to a subset of civil and political rights, and a source of criticism. Eventually the NGO moved to support a broader range of rights in its advocacy.

Many have tried to explain why AI has been successful. Its involvement in high-level international discussions about torture and extrajudicial executions resulted in UN-led initiatives such as the Convention Against Torture. The accuracy of its reporting has always helped AI in gaining legitimacy vis-à-vis states. This attribute of AI's research has been recognized by scholars and policymakers alike. The desire to maintain high-quality reporting pushed AI to centralize research tasks at its administrative core, the IS. Although others contributed to the information on the treatment of individuals, it was the IS that compiled the research and disseminated casework among the adoption groups, in addition to producing publicly distributed reports on human rights violations. In recent years, research functions have been delegated to some of the larger national sections, such as AIUSA, after a period of negotiation between the IS and more powerful national sections in the 1980s and 1990s. Finally, it is often noted that AI's unique organizational structure contributed to its success. By centralizing research functions but distributing such information widely to a broad network of activists, AI is able to extend its influence over human rights in a way that has, to date, been unprecedented.

In spite of AI's successes, it is hard to measure its impact, or the impact of any human rights NGO for that matter. Scholars have assessed, for example, the impact of AI on media coverage of human rights abuses, or whether press releases and country reports improve human rights conditions in abusive states. The evidence, at best, is mixed. Scholars find that although AI affects state behavior, it is not always in a positive way. Moreover, NGOs like AI do not always report on the most pressing issues, as their efforts are also dependent on a host of other factors, such as state power and how salient that state is in the media's eye.

Since the 1980s, AI has also changed internally. Until the 1970s, the organization was dominated by European national sections—the Germans, Dutch, and British were particularly active. But in the 1980s, and more acutely since the end of the Cold War, AI has become much more international, branching out into developing and non-Western countries as part of a conscious effort to be more globally representative. The rise of AIUSA in the mid-1980s as the economic powerhouse of NGOs also shifted the balance from Europe to North America. Since the 1990s, the three secretaries-general have been from developing countries: Pierre Sané, who served in the 1990s, is from Senegal, and Irene Khan, who served in the 2000s, is from Bangladesh. The new secretary-general, Salil Shetty, whose term began in 2010, is from India. With the changes in composition of the members and the distribution of influence among national sections also comes a change in focus. AI has worked, since the early 2000s, on issues of global justice, moving away from its traditional strength in prisoners' rights, death penalty, and torture. Thus, AI has evolved from a prisoners' rights NGO to one that has moved to encompass a much wider human rights agenda, one that pushes beyond civil and political rights into much bigger questions on development, as well as economic, social, and cultural rights.

Wendy H. Wong

See also Civil Rights; Civil Society, Global; Human Rights, International; Humanity, Concepts of; International Nongovernmental Organizations (INGOs); Prisoners' Rights

Further Readings

Baehr, P. R. (1994). AI and its self-imposed limited mandate. *Netherlands Quarterly of Human Rights, 1,* 5–21.

Cingranelli, D. L., & Richards, D. L. (2001). Measuring the impact of human rights organizations. In C. Welch (Ed.), *NGOs and human rights: Promise and performance* (pp. 225–237). Philadelphia: University of Pennsylvania Press.

Clark, A. M. (2001). *Diplomacy of conscience: Amnesty International and changing human rights norms.* Princeton, NJ: Princeton University Press.

Hafner-Burton, E. M. (2008). Sticks and stones: Naming and shaming the human rights enforcement problem. *International Organization, 62,* 689–716.

Hopgood, S. (2006). *Keepers of the flame: Understanding Amnesty International.* Ithaca, NY: Cornell University Press.

Kaufman, E. (1991). Prisoners of conscience: The shaping of a new human rights concept. *Human Rights Quarterly, 13,* 339–367.

Lake, D. A., & Wong, W. H. (2009). The politics of networks: Interests, power, and human rights norms. In M. Kahler (Ed.), *Networked politics: Agency, power, and governance* (pp. 127–150). Ithaca, NY: Cornell University Press.

Larsen, E. (1979). *A flame in barbed wire: The story of Amnesty International.* New York: Norton.

Ramos, H., Ron, J., & Thoms, O. N. T. (2007). Shaping the northern media's human rights coverage, 1986–2000. *Journal of Peace Research, 44,* 385–406.

Ron, J., Ramos, H., & Rodgers, K. (2005). Transnational information politics: NGO human rights reporting, 1986–2000. *International Studies Quarterly, 49,* 557–588.

Winston, M. E. (2001). Assessing the effectiveness of international human rights NGOs. In C. Welch (Ed.), *NGOs and human rights: Promise and performance* (pp. 25–54). Philadelphia: University of Pennsylvania Press.

ANIMAL RIGHTS

The animal rights movement operates on a global scale and frequently confronts the effects of economic globalization. *Animal rights* can be understood narrowly to mean that animals are entitled to moral or legal rights, but the term is more commonly used to refer to a variety of views that require that the interests of nonhuman animals deserve substantial recognition and protection. Although the number of people committed to animal rights has increased over time, the idea that animals' welfare should be protected has been voiced for the past 3,000 years. Arguments put forth throughout history have informed the work of contemporary activists and led to the modern animal rights movement. This movement grew considerably in the last decades of the 20th century, leading to the formation of grassroots and national animal rights organizations in many countries across the world as well as a number of international animal rights groups. Although they often focus on particular campaigns and practices, animal rights groups generally advocate vegetarian and vegan diets and denounce practices and industries that harm nonhuman animals for the benefit of human beings.

Historical Perspectives

Despite many people's assumptions that it is a modern idea, the concern for the rights and interests of animals goes back to ancient times. Greek philosophers, such as Pythagoras, argued more than 2,500 years ago that we should not harm animals because they could be the souls of dead relatives who have reincarnated as animals. Pythagoras and his followers counseled against eating animal flesh on these grounds as well. Pythagoreans thus became some of the earliest known vegetarians, and the term *Pythagorean* continued to refer to vegetarians until the 19th century.

Although Pythogoras's belief in reincarnation fell out of favor in the West, the view that animals' interests deserved protection persisted. Many influential thinkers—Percy Shelley, Voltaire, Jeremy Bentham, Gandhi, and Tolstoy, to name just a few—advocated that animals are entitled to much better treatment; some of these thinkers proposed that animals had rights, including the right not to be eaten by humans.

Western thinkers were not alone in articulating the view that humans have obligations toward nonhuman animals. In 1000 BCE, the Hindu Upanishads also claimed that people can be reincarnated as animals, a view that led some Hindus to oppose meat eating. Likewise, some Buddhist traditions have counseled against killing animals for meat, advocating instead compassion toward animals. Also in India, since ancient times, Jains have thought that animals possess souls, and because all souls are divine, one should not harm animals in any way. Due to their nonhierarchical, antiviolence beliefs, Jains have refrained from harming even the smallest of creatures. Jains continue to work toward minimizing all harm to animals, operating many animal shelters in India and abstaining from the consumption of meat and eggs.

Historical Opposition to Animal Protection

Among the most influential thinkers who argued that humans do not have any obligations to animals were Aristotle and René Descartes. Aristotle believed that a natural hierarchy of living beings exists: Animals were naturally inferior to humans, and their function was to serve humans' needs. Whereas Aristotle based his arguments in nature, the Enlightenment thinker René Descartes compared animals to automatons or machines, without sensate experiences such as pain and without consciousness. Variations of the arguments made by Aristotle and Descartes continue to be seen in current attitudes toward animals and inform many opponents of animal rights.

Immanuel Kant advocated the more middle ground position that we have duties toward animals, but only indirect ones. This view, which is still very popular today, holds that people should not be cruel to an animal because of the harm it indirectly causes people rather than the direct harm done to the animal. Most animals are owned by either individuals or the state, and harming such animals, without the permission of the owner, would violate our duties to the owner. Furthermore, Kant believed that acting cruelly toward animals would change the way we treat other human beings; recent research supports this belief by demonstrating that many serial killers started out by torturing and killing animals.

Some Christians oppose animal rights, as they believe that animals do not have souls, that they were not created in God's image, or that God gave people dominion over animals; thus we should be able to do anything we want to animals. These views date back to at least medieval times, when they were articulated by Thomas Aquinas and other Christian philosophers, and they continue to have many adherents. However, some modern Christians claim that these are misinterpretations, arguing that dominion requires respect for God's creation. Modern factory farms and hunting for sport, for example, violate our duty to treat animals with the respect that God does in his dominion over us. Debates over the moral status of animals are not confined to Christianity; adherents of all the major religions are also struggling to understand how their religion requires humans to treat nonhumans.

The Philosophical Beginnings of the Modern Animal Rights Movement

Academic philosophers have played a pivotal role in creating and sustaining the contemporary animal rights movement. Foremost among them are Peter Singer and Tom Regan, who are widely regarded as setting up the intellectual foundations for the modern movement. Peter Singer's book *Animal Liberation*, published in 1975, provided the impetus for the creation of many modern animal rights groups, including People for the Ethical Treatment of Animals (PETA). *Animal Liberation* has been translated into numerous languages and has had an enormous influence among contemporary thinkers and activists. In *Animal Liberation*, Singer picks up on Jeremy Bentham's conviction that the criterion for moral considerability is not intelligence or the ability to speak; rather, it is the ability to suffer. Singer presents an extensive argument to support the idea that the interests of all sentient animals—including humans, dogs, cats, pigs, cows, chickens, and rats—deserve equal moral consideration. After laying out his theoretical argument, he exposes the harsh reality of factory farms and laboratories, showing that animals are not given equal moral consideration; on the contrary, they are treated with little regard for their basic interests. Singer thus argues that our treatment of animals is morally unjustified and we need to abstain from purchasing animal products produced in such deplorable conditions. Aware that this idea is very controversial, Singer dedicates a considerable amount of the book to considering common objections and responding to them.

Philosophers distinguish between the idea of equal moral consideration and moral rights. Although others, in the 19th century, had put forth the idea that animals have moral rights, Tom Regan's book *The Case for Animal Rights* was the first to present this idea in a detailed and philosophically rigorous fashion. In short, Regan argues that animals are entitled to negative rights: the right not to be killed and the right not to have one's bodily integrity violated. Both Regan and Singer oppose speciesism, which refers to an attitude of prejudice and bias in favor of one's own species and against other species.

Since Singer's and Regan's seminal works appeared, academic scholarship on animals has exploded, engendering extremely informative empirical studies on animal minds, behavior, and emotional lives. Likewise, scholars of cultural studies, history, law, religion, philosophy, sociology, and many other fields have proposed new ways of thinking about our relationships with nonhuman animals. Armed with both theoretical arguments and empirical data about the existence of love, fear, empathy, and memory among animals, activists around the world have been successful in making the case for animal rights and drawing people into the animal rights movement.

Animal Rights Groups

Animal rights groups have appeared in countries across the globe, and membership in these groups has increased dramatically over the past three decades. Animal rights groups generally object to the use of animals for entertainment (e.g., circuses, zoos, rodeos, movies, cockfighting, dogfighting), sport (e.g., fishing, hunting, rodeos), clothing (e.g., fur, leather, wool), and animal testing. Even though the goals of some groups are quite expansive, many groups focus more narrowly on one issue or a set of issues. The methods and tactics of animal rights groups differ too. Some groups, such as the Animal Liberation Front, condone property damage, whereas most groups adhere to strict principles of nonviolent action. The latter often focus on educational events, community building, awareness raising, legislative campaigns, negotiation with businesses, or cooperation with the media. While PETA is perhaps the best known organization, with offices in many countries, there are many other local and international groups, ranging in membership from a handful of people to millions of members. The Humane Society of United States, for example, has over 10 million members and is the largest animal protection organization in the world.

While animal protection groups historically focused on anti-vivisection and anti-fur campaigns, since the mid-1990s, they have increasingly focused on the use of animals for food. This happened in part because of the very large number of animals raised and killed for food (56 billion land animals per year, according to the Food and Agriculture Organization of the United Nations) and because of the extreme suffering they endure for their entire lives. Factory farms—also called concentrated animal feeding operations or intensive livestock farms—employ particularly cruel practices, including severe confinement, castration without anesthesia, debeaking, and separation of mother and young. Some groups, such as Vegan Outreach, focus exclusively on animals used for food, whereas others, such as PETA and the Humane Society, address other issues as well.

Some collaboration exists between those advocating for animal rights and those working on other social justice issues such as feminism and environmentalism. Academics have worked extensively to highlight the intersections between these movements. For example, in recent years, there has been increasing awareness among scientists, environmentalists, activists, and the popular media of the negative environmental effects of livestock, drawing more attention to the implications of raising animals for food and increasing the appeal of vegetarian and vegan diets.

Legal Changes

Although animal rights is not a concept that is widely accepted worldwide, animal advocates have brought about significant legal changes. Many countries have adopted legislation protecting animals from unnecessary harm or suffering. Some countries, such as Austria, have passed legislation outlawing the use of wild animals in circuses and the cropping of ears and tails of pigs. In 2008, Spain outlawed the ownership of apes for use in circuses and filming. Germany amended its constitution to protect the rights and dignity of animals. The European Union is currently phasing out veal crates for calves, battery cages for laying hens, and the prolonged use of sow stalls and tethers for breeding pigs. Following the European Union's lead, a number of states in the United States recently voted to ban gestation crates for pigs, battery cages for chickens, and/or veal crates, and all states have outlawed cockfighting.

Ramona Cristina Ilea

See also Activism, Transnational; Fisheries; Food and Agriculture Organization of the United Nations; Jainism; Solidarity Movements

Further Readings

Armstrong, S., & Botzler, R. (Eds.). (2008). *The animal ethics reader* (2nd ed.). New York: Routledge.

Linzey, A., & Regan, T. (Eds.). (2007). *Animals and Christianity: A book of readings*. Eugene, OR: Wipf & Stock.

Regan, T. (1983). *The case for animal rights*. Philadelphia: Temple University Press.

Singer, P. (1975). *Animal liberation*. New York: HarperCollins.

Singer, P. (Ed.). (2005). *In defense of animals: The second wave*. Malden, MA: Wiley-Blackwell.

Sunstein, C., & Nussbaum, M. (Eds.). (2004). *Animal rights: Current debates and new directions*. New York: Oxford University Press.

Walters, K., & Portmess, L. (1999). *Ethical vegetarianism: From Pythagoras to Peter Singer*. New York: State University of New York Press.

ANTI-APARTHEID MOVEMENT

From a global perspective, the anti-apartheid movement was one of the most significant social movements during the postwar era. In addition to the South African liberation movements, the transnational anti-apartheid network connected thousands of groups and organizations, including solidarity organizations; unions; women's, youth, and student organizations; and radical churches on all continents. This "movement of movements" lasted for more than three decades, from the late 1950s to 1994, when the first democratic elections in South Africa were held. In this sense, the anti-apartheid movement took part in the construction of a global civil society during the Cold War.

The broader global civil society campaign against apartheid was initiated in December 1958 at the All-African People's Conference in Accra, when the South African Congress Alliance made a call for an international boycott of South African goods. The International Confederation of Trade Unions responded to the call in 1959, encouraging all its member organizations to appeal to its members to boycott South African goods, as did the anticolonial Committee of African Organizations in London. At a meeting in Holborn Hall in London in 1959, organized by the Committee of African Organizations and addressed by, among others, Julius Nyerere, then president of the Tanganyika Africa National Union, a boycott committee was formed, and soon it evolved into the independent Boycott Movement, which in 1960 changed its name to the Anti-Apartheid Movement (AAM). In March 1960, the campaign was fueled by the shots in Sharpeville (where South African police killed 69 people at a peaceful demonstration), which was reported globally by the media and caused a moral outrage all over the world. In various countries, anti-apartheid protests occurred, demanding that governments and the United Nations put pressure on the South African government to end apartheid. As a "postcolonial capital," London became a crucial node in the emerging transnational network of South African exile activists, organizations, and activities. Further, two of the most important organizations in the transnational solidarity network had their base in London: the International Defence and Aid Fund and the AAM, the latter becoming a key organization in the context of British new social movements. This early history of the anti-apartheid movement points to the significant role of anticolonial movements in the global South in the construction of transnational and global political cultures emerging with the new social movements from the 1960s onward.

In retrospect, transnational support for the struggle against apartheid in South Africa might appear to have been something uncontroversial in most parts of the world, but it was not an easy affair to sustain such support through the decades. The movement's key issue, to support the liberation movement's call for sanctions, was especially controversial.

In the process of its transnational campaigns, the anti-apartheid movement targeted supranational organizations, like the United Nations, the Commonwealth, and the European Union. In the United Nations and the Commonwealth, apartheid presented a dilemma to the leading nations of the Western bloc: On the one hand apartheid, in a profound way, contradicted the values that were the cornerstones of the liberal hegemony of the Western world after World War II. On the other hand, South Africa was regarded as an ally in the Cold War struggle. This led the United States, Britain, and France to publicly condemn apartheid while at the same time blocking sanctions against South Africa in the UN Security Council. As the movement operated simultaneously in the context of different national civil societies *and* in the context of global civil society, it also made democratic claims that were related both to national and to global publics. The most important strategy in this respect was the consumer boycott. For example, the leading solidarity organization, the British AAM, defined the boycott act as "voting for sanctions" and referred to opinion polls showing an overwhelming popular support for boycotts. In this process, the movement claimed that there was also global popular support for its cause, referring to successful transnational boycott campaigns and petitions. For example, at the Commonwealth meeting in Bahamas in 1985, Abdul Minty of AAM presented a declaration urging for sanctions that was signed by organizations that represented 18 million people.

The anti-apartheid movement was also involved in conflicts *within* global civil society. As consumer boycotts extended to corporations with subsidiaries in South Africa, the anti-apartheid movement was challenged by a coalition of actors (including business corporations, churches, and leading Western labor unions) presenting a counterstrategy to sanctions—*constructive engagement*, part and parcel of the emerging "code of conduct" approach. In 1977, Leon Sullivan, Baptist reverend, successfully launched principles for U.S. firms with affiliates in South Africa; these were called the Sullivan Principles. It was argued that the presence of corporations that subscribed to these principles would support democratization in South Africa. Key anti-apartheid organizations regarded this strategy as a cover for doing "business as usual" in South Africa. In the mid-1980s, constructive engagement was abandoned even by many of its influential Republican supporters in the United States because of lack of any visible results, according to Robert K. Massie, while the sanctions campaign won ground and in the end also made a difference. It was, for example, considered as a hard blow to South Africa when Chase Manhattan Bank, which had been targeted by a divestment campaign, in 1985 announced that it would not grant South Africa any further loans. In the same year, the European Union finally decided to go for (limited) sanctions.

The influence of the transnational movement, which existed for more than four decades, was not limited to the South African context, as it created transnational networks, organizations, and collective action forms that made—and still make—an impact on national as well as global political culture.

Håkan Thörn

See also Civil Rights; Civil Society, Global; Colonialism; Global Justice and Legal Issues; Human Rights, International; Justice Movements, Transnational; Social Movements; Solidarity Movements

Further Readings

Crawford, N. C., & Klotz, A. (Eds.). (1999). *How sanctions work. Lessons from South Africa.* London: Macmillan.

Fieldhouse, R. (2005). *Anti-apartheid: A history of the movement in Britain. A study in pressure group politics.* London: Merlin Press.

Massie, R. K. (1997). *Loosing the bonds: The United States and South Africa in the apartheid years.* New York: Doubleday.

Seekings, J. (2000). *The UDF: A history of the United Democratic Front in South Africa 1983–1991.* Cape Town, South Africa: David Philip.

Thörn, H. (2006). *Anti-apartheid and the emergence of a global civil society.* Basingstoke, UK: Palgrave Macmillan.

ANTIGLOBALIZATION MOVEMENTS AND CRITICS

Antiglobalization movements are transnational social movements that challenge what they perceive as a monolithic global laissez-faire economic regime. From the 1990s, these movements have accused global political and economic networks of delivering too much power to dominant elites at the expense of disenfranchised poor populations and countries. The term *antiglobalization* is rejected by some supporters who, although espousing grassroots resistance to global liberalization and greater local control over resources and decision making, point out that they are themselves global: They draw attention to global inequity, organize transnationally, and maintain a critical stance toward significant aspects of the state system. For this reason, many supporters favor other terms such as *alterglobalization movement*, *global justice movement*, or simply *the movement of movements*.

Critics accuse the movements of ideological incoherence, self-interested protectionism, and illiberal and undemocratic political methods, and point to Western liberal elite dominance within the movements. The debate has raised many central questions in global studies: how social movements may (or may not) herald a new era of global politics or global civil society, the possible transformation of democracy, normative issues of global justice, policy debates concerning development and trade, the environment, and the design of international institutions. The following charts the origins of the movements, discusses the critics of antiglobalization, and assesses the impact of the debate on global studies as an academic field.

The Origins of Antiglobalization Movements

Popular opposition to free trade has a long pedigree going back to mercantilist opposition to its invention and heated political struggles over tariffs and trade not least in the 19th and 20th centuries. However, antiglobalization refers specifically to opposition to neoliberalism and can be traced back to the 1980s in South America, where the so-called Washington Consensus program of economic reform developed. The revolutions of Eastern Europe in 1989 and the Zapatista uprising pressing for land reform and autonomy in Chiapas, Mexico, which began January 1, 1994, the day the North Atlantic Trade Association came into force, are also considered significant sources of inspiration for antiglobalization movements. However, only during the late 1990s did the antiglobalization movement form as a transnational network of organizations staging high-profile events. Major landmarks for antiglobalization movements include the attempt to disrupt the 50th anniversary of the World Bank in Madrid in 1994 ("50 Years Is Enough"); the so-called Global Street Party that encircled the site of the 1998 G-8 summit held in Birmingham, United Kingdom, with the motto "Our Resistance Is as Transnational as Capital"; the Global Action Day on July 18, 1999, planned by a diverse collection of civil society groups to take place simultaneously in 43 countries; and the so-called Battle of Seattle in 1999, demonstrations surrounding the World Trade Organization Ministerial Conference. The World Social Forum was held annually under the motto "Another World Is Possible."

Eventually this series of events matured in the discourse of supporters as well as opponents into a self-consciously global movement around the turn of the millennium. The network that organized many of the biggest events during this period, Peoples' Global Action, defined itself later as "one of the principal instigators of the new global, radical, anticapitalist movement, which

today is challenging the legitimacy of the global governance institutions." The global protests in 2011 following the Occupy Wall Street demonstrations in New York City are examples of the continuing expansion of antiglobalization movements in the 21st century. These massive protests in cities around the world were aimed at the economic control of transnational corporate capitalism.

Critics of Antiglobalization

Antiglobalization as a term originates from its critics—mostly neoliberal defenders of free trade, the liberal state order, and the Bretton Woods architecture of global economic governance and its main policies of free trade, liberalization, and monetarist economics. *New York Times* columnist Thomas L. Friedman used the then little-known term in 1997 to label such dissidents as Dick Gephardt and Pat Buchanan, who were concerned for domestic U.S. industries. Gephardt was labeled "the leader of the anti-globalization movement." Later Friedman portrayed antiglobals as "flat-Earthers" who denied the reality of globalization and worked against the interests of the underdeveloped Third World poor. Other major critics were associated with economically neoliberal think tanks such as the Cato Institute or neoliberal media such as the British *Financial Times* (especially its chief economics commentator, Martin Wolf) or *The Economist*. Another cluster had backgrounds in development economics, such as Jagdish Bhagwati, or were high-ranking officials in Bretton Woods institutions, such as former director of the World Trade Organization, Mike Moore. Their common argument is that globalization is on balance generating wealth, development, and even democracy for the world's poor and oppressed. For them, antiglobalization is a dangerous mix of single-issue idealism and old-style economic special interests. They refuse to distinguish sharply between protectionist, nationalist, and even racist opposition to free trade and globalization, on the one hand, and left-wing pluralist parts of the movement, on the other hand. Extraparliamentary political action is seen as undemocratic, and self-appointed civil society organizations are contrasted with what they see as legitimate multilateral institutions set up and run in large part by democracies. Criticism of the World Trade Organization and neoliberal policies of the Washington Consensus is interpreted as an unsophisticated denial of the virtues of markets rooted in nostalgia or unrealistic hopes in socialist regulation. Moreover, globalization is not a top-down political project of an elite but a bottom-up technology and market-driven evolutionary process that has such deep roots that it cannot be rolled back indefinitely, barring catastrophe (some worry that antiglobalization risks bringing on the latter).

Implications for Global Studies

For global studies, antiglobalization movements provide an important case for exploration of the globalization of political and social relations as a distinct field as well as for central policy fields such as the politics of trade.

For social movement scholars, antiglobalization protests provide an opportunity to study a social and political movement outside the confines of the state, involving the construction of global identity, nonconventional action repertoires, and transnational organizational networks. Some prefer to focus on the organizational ties between groups organizing events to show how networks are built and effectively deployed. This particularly drew attention to the implications for politics and protest of new media and the Internet connecting people on the ground and across vast distances. Others maintain that unity is largely a fiction, as there were incompatible groupings within the movement (something implicitly accepted by some activists who refer to a "movement of movements"). One faction of statists was eager to defend national welfare systems and regulation, while "alternatives" (or anarchists) campaigned in favor of participatory democracy and localism and "reformists" looked to modify global governance. The category of "social movement" also came under scrutiny. Constructivist scholars such as Catherine Eschle have focused on how, given the diversity, the idea of such a movement could be socially constructed through discursive practices. It is worth noting that the idea of there being a global movement arrived relatively late. Early "manifestos" of the movements—such as journalist Naomi Klein's book on global corporations, *No Logo*, and campaigner George Monbiot's *Captive State* —identify "pockets of anti-corporate resistance" (Klein) and "a ragged band of protesters"

(Monbiot) rather than a global antiglobalization movement.

In terms of social theory, the antiglobalization debate has questioned whether the radical distinction between ordered politics and society inside and warlike relations between states is breaking down. According to R. B. J. Walker, social movements are becoming more visible as they move first out of the shadow of being social to becoming also political and transgressing the borders of domestic politics pointing toward new but as yet largely invisible social forms beyond the simplified idea of sovereignty. For others, antiglobalization movements are an expression of an emerging global civil society challenging, but also informing and cooperating with, the largely state-run international system: civilizing globalization. Like-minded groups and individuals linked through means, ends, and identity are now operating transnationally and focusing on global objects of governance such as global health, trade, development, environment, and even security in a grand dialogue with global governance institutions and states in an evolving global political architecture.

Realist skeptics, on the other hand, view antiglobalization movements as incidental to the continued power over states that still command hard power and remain superior even in terms of legitimacy and soft power, whereas theoretical schools that focus more on norms, institutions, and nonstate actors cast doubt on the transformatory power of such movements, pointing to the low level of institutionalization and loose network structure of the movements and the inherent weaknesses of such things. Antiglobalization movements will be short-lived or have their causes co-opted by establishment nongovernmental organizations or international organizations, although continued functional integration may also, according to this view, provide grounds for more social movement advocacy in the future.

Approaches inspired by historical materialism have devoted more attention to antiglobalization, tending to view it as an expression of deeper running contradictions in the global economic system that are likely to become more acute as global economic and political integration continues through continued globalization. Those inspired by the writing of Italian Marxist Antonio Gramsci, for instance, have advanced the idea of antiglobalization as a counter-hegemonic force in a different way. For them, it heralds the emergence of an alliance of social forces opposed to the elite project of globalization—"globalization from below" to counteract hegemonic "globalization from above." In this light, antiglobalization represents an ideological struggle to forge alliances across social groups and national boundaries presenting a globalized version of counter-hegemonic bid for power known from domestic politics. Mass demonstrations are here seen to perform a mythology of resistance similar to the idea of the general strike earlier. André Drainville regards antiglobalization as evidence of an emerging global social space, previously populated only by soldiers, diplomats, and tradesmen—a globalization of globalization, so to speak, which challenges not just policy but fundamental categories of the old system such as territory and hierarchy.

In terms of global public policy, the antiglobalization movement became the occasion for a heated debate concerning development strategies and particularly the role of trade. The liberalization of trade and capital was defended vehemently by development economists and neoliberals who pointed to evidence of market-led poverty alleviation. Critics countered that more focus should be given to individual cases, the wider societal costs of restructuring and the social construction of markets—that is, the ways in which markets were institutionalized. The conditions under which trade would lead to human development also received much attention, notably from writers such as Harvard professor of economics Dani Rodrik. Reviews and adjustments to the wider Washington Consensus were also made in the wake of the debate, including new measures to include civil society in decision making, leading some to identify a post–Washington Consensus focused more on local ownership of policies, notions of human development, and a move away from one-size-fits-all policy models.

Thomas Olaf Corry

See also Civil Society, Global; Global Economic Issues; Global Governance and World Order; Global South; Globalization, Approaches to; Justice Movements, Transnational; Liberalism, Neoliberalism; Power, Global Contexts of; Social Movements; Solidarity Movements; World Social Forum

Further Readings

Cavanaugh, J., & Mander, J. (Eds.). (2002). *Alternatives to economic globalization. A better world is possible.* San Francisco: Berrett-Koehler.

Della Porta, D. (2006). *Globalization from below: Transnational activists and protest networks.* Minneapolis: University of Minnesota Press.

Eschle, C. (2004). Constructing "the anti-globalisation movement." *International Journal of Peace Studies, 9*(1), 61–84.

Kaldor, M. (2000). Civilising globalisation? The implications of the "Battle in Seattle." *Millennium: Journal of International Relations, 29,* 105–114.

Kingsnorth, P. (2003). *One no, many yesses: A journey to the heart of the global resistance movement.* London: Free Press.

Micklethwait, J., & Wooldridge, A. (2000). *A future perfect: The challenge and hidden promise of globalization.* London: Heinemann.

Peoples' Global Action. (2001). *Manifesto.* Retrieved January 30, 2009, from http://www.nadir.org/nadir/initiativ/agp/en/pgainfos/manifest.htm

Walker, R. B. J. (1994). Social movements/world politics. *Millennium: Journal of International Studies, 23*(3), 669–700.

Wolf, M. (2004). *Why globalization works. The case for the global market economy.* London: Yale University Press.

ANTISLAVERY MOVEMENTS

Although enslaved conditions persist even in the global era, the terms *slavery* and *antislavery movements* usually refer to the historical slave trade of earlier centuries. Antislavery movements, also known as abolitionist movements, aimed to abolish trade in African slaves and slavery in western Europe and the Western Hemisphere.

Abolitionists were driven by the rationalist ideology rooted in the Enlightenment with its belief in the inherent rights of a human being, or liberal humanism, or by the doctrine of the Society of Friends (Quakers) that, because there is something of God in everybody, all persons must be valued equally. Quakers became the pioneering abolitionists in Protestant-majority countries such as Britain, British America, and the United States. Their campaign was complemented by some liberal individuals in England who took the cases of recaptured Black slaves to the courts. Slaves' repeated rebellions also advanced abolitionism.

The German and Dutch Quakers in Germantown, Pennsylvania, were the first to protest against the enslavement of Africans in 1688. Eight years later, Pennsylvanian Quakers officially declared their opposition to the importing of African slaves into North America. As the 18th century unrolled, sentiment against the slave trade grew steadily in North America and western Europe. So, too, did the number of slave rebellions, organized or spontaneous. During the 17th and 18th centuries, there were over 250 slave uprisings or attempted uprisings in North America. In the British West Indies, slaves revolted 73 times in the 18th century.

The slave rebellion in France's Caribbean colony of Santo Domingo (later renamed Haiti) in 1791—2 years after the French Revolution—led to the abolition of slavery by Paris in order to retain the local population's loyalty to revolutionary France. The popularly elected Assembly of the First Republic (1792–1794) abolished slavery in France and its colonies in 1794. Although Napoleon I reestablished slavery and slave trade in 1802, the founding of the Black Republic of Haiti gave impetus to the abolitionist movements in the Caribbean and South America.

Whether they worked as plantation laborers or house servants, slaves were treated as property in law. In 1720 and 1749, English courts ruled that a runaway slave in England could be recovered. In 1772, Lord Chief Justice Mansfield considered the case of James Somersett, an escaped slave who had been recaptured and put aboard a Jamaica-bound ship. He concluded his verdict thus: "The state of slavery is . . . so odious that nothing can support it but positive law. . . . I cannot say that this case is allowed or approved by the law of England and therefore the black must be discharged" (Hiro, 1991, p. 3). This judgment is wrongly construed to mean that, thereafter, slavery in England became illegal. Nothing of the sort happened. Mansfield's verdict merely said that, until Parliament enacted specific legislation covering slavery, the power in dispute—to transport a slave from England to the colonies—could not be exercised legally.

Because of the tireless campaigning by Quakers and other citizens through speeches, sermons, and pamphlets—combined with the founding of the Society for the Relief of Free Negroes Unlawfully Held in Bondage in Philadelphia in 1775—Pennsylvania became the first American state to pass a law for the Gradual Abolition of Slavery in 1780. In contrast, slavery and slave trade were entrenched in the 11 southern colonies of British America and the West Indies colonies of the British Empire, where they were inextricably linked with the plantation economy based on slave labor.

In 1783, nearly 300 British Quakers submitted to Parliament a petition against the slave trade, the first ever. They helped establish the Committee of the Abolition of the Slave Trade in 1787. Of the 12 founders, 9 were Quakers, and the rest were evangelical Christians—Thomas Clarkson, Granville Sharp, and William Wilberforce, who was a member of Parliament. Quakers were barred from Parliament until the early 19th century.

Although Wilberforce received much of the kudos for the antislavery movement in Britain, Clarkson did much of the groundwork. By gathering evidence to support the case for banning the slave trade, Clarkson earned the wrath of rich, influential slave traders. During his research visit to Liverpool, he was injured so severely by a paid gang of sailors that he nearly died. His pamphlet "A Summary View of the Slave Trade and of the Probable Consequences of Its Abolition" was a powerful document.

Wilberforce's strength lay in his friendship with Prime Minister William Pitt the Younger, who encouraged Wilberforce to focus on the issue. The British Parliament passed the Slave Trade Act in 1807, banning this trade throughout the British Empire. Thereafter, British abolitionists lobbied other countries to follow suit. As a result, the Netherlands outlawed the slave trade in 1814.

At America's Constitutional Convention of 1787, delegates agreed to authorize the federal government to abolish the importing of slaves into the United States gradually over the next 20 years. Thus, December 31, 1807, became the last day slaves could be imported into the United States, but the slave trade within the country continued.

The abolitionists' next target was the institution of slavery. They achieved their objective with the adoption of the Slavery Abolition Act of 1833 by Britain's Parliament, and this act applied to all of its empire. Wilberforce lived to see this happen.

Three years earlier, William Lloyd Garrison—along with Ted Weld, an evangelical minister, and Robert Purvis, a free Black American—had established the American Anti-Slavery Society in the United States. The AAS demanded the immediate abolition of slavery. Garrison argued that slavery was antithetical to freedom and equality, the founding principles of America. His newspaper, *The Liberator*, played a crucial role in mobilizing public opinion against slavery chiefly in the American North. Along with the AAS, the Church Anti-Slavery Society, the American and Foreign Anti-Slavery Society, and the American Missionary Association lobbied for an end to the practice of slavery.

They faced stiff opposition in the agrarian American South because slavery was an integral part of the economic system there. The prospect of slavery extending to the western United States became a crucial factor in the slavery debate during the 1850s. The victory of Abraham Lincoln in the 1860 presidential election boosted the abolitionist movement. The Southern states seceded from the Union and formed a confederation. A civil war ensued the following year. Lincoln issued the Emancipation Proclamation in 1863, freeing the slaves held in the Confederate States. (It was in that year that the Netherlands abolished slave labor, becoming the last European country to do so.) In 1865, the Thirteenth Amendment to the U.S. Constitution, which prohibited slavery throughout the Union, was adopted.

In most of Spanish-speaking Latin America, slavery was abolished during the Wars of Independence, from 1810 to 1822. But slavery persisted in Portuguese-speaking Brazil until 1888 and also in Spain's Caribbean colonies of Cuba and Puerto Rico because of the fierce resistance by the plantation owners.

Dilip Hiro

See also Enlightenment, The; Human Rights, International; Humanism; Humanity, Concepts of; Independence Movements; Slavery

Further Readings

Blackburn, R. (1998). *The making of New World slavery: From the baroque to the modern, 1492–1800*. London: Verso Books.

Blackburn, R. (1998). *The overthrow of colonial slavery, 1776–1848*. London: Verso Books.

Buxton, T. F. (2011). *The African slave trade*. Cambridge, UK: Cambridge University Press.

Hiro, D. (1991). *Black British, White British: A history of race relations in Britain*. London: HarperCollins.

Morgan, K. (2001). *Slavery, Atlantic trade and the British economy, 1660–1800*. Cambridge, UK: Cambridge University Press.

Ransom, R. L. (1989). *Conflict and compromise: The political economy of slavery, emancipation, and the American Civil War*. Cambridge, UK: Cambridge University Press.

Reddie, R. (2007). *Abolition! The struggle to abolish slavery in the British Empire*. Oxford, UK: Lion Hudson.

Russell-Wood, A. J. R. (2002). *Slavery and freedom in colonial Brazil*. London: Oneworld.

Thomas, H. (2006). *The slave trade: History of the Atlantic slave trade, 1440–1870*. London: Phoenix.

Walvin, J. (2007). *Short history of slavery*. London: Penguin.

Williams, E. E. (1994). *Capitalism & slavery*. Chapel Hill: University of North Carolina Press.

APARTHEID

The term *apartheid* comes from a period of racial separation in South Africa which, at the time, received global attention and which continues to be used as an epithet for similar situations in other parts of the world. *Apartheid* in Afrikaans means "separateness" and refers to a specific political project implemented in South Africa during the 20th century. Over time, it has come to describe any policy of separation and exclusion, from the segregation of Black communities in the United States to the isolation of the Palestinian people caused by the security barrier, or "wall," built by the Israeli government between Israel and the West Bank.

Although several policies aimed at separating South Africa's race groups had been adopted in the early 1900s, the official commencement of the apartheid "project" was marked by the 1948 electoral victory of the Afrikaans-dominated National Party. Influenced by theories of White supremacy and closely linked to Germany's Nazi movements, the National Party's leadership set out to institutionalize the most systematic system of racial segregation in history. Initially, policies were concentrated on the so-called "grand apartheid," that is, a general restructuring of the country's social landscape, which compelled people to live in separate places defined by race, stripped non-Whites of political rights, formalized racial classification by introducing an identity card reporting each citizen's racial group, and turned the "reserves" created by the British colonizers into fully fledged "homelands" for the Black majority, to which it allotted only 13% of the national territory.

Since the mid-1950s, under the charismatic influence of Hendrik Verwoerd, the White-led government also embarked on a series of social reforms known as "petty apartheid." Separate beaches, buses, hospitals, schools, and universities were created. Signboards that bore the message "Whites only" mushroomed in public areas, labeling park benches, shops, parking areas, and restaurants. Specific laws were introduced to prohibit marriage between people of different races, and having sexual relations with a person of another race became a criminal offense (the so-called Immorality Act). All non-White South Africans (i.e., those classified as Black, coloured, or Indian) became second-class citizens, most of their settlements were demolished, and entire townships were forcibly removed to give way to White-only neighborhoods.

Internally, apartheid was opposed by a number of political and civic movements. The African National Congress, a political party led by Nelson Mandela and Oliver Tambo, led the struggle against racial segregation along with the Pan Africanist Congress and the South African Communist Party. Thousands of local organizations, civic groups, and nongovernmental organizations also joined in the resistance movement, thereby constituting one of the most widespread nonviolent civic struggles of the century. At first, international solidarity was lukewarm. While civil society organizations, trade unions, and left-leaning social movements in most Western countries opposed apartheid from its early days, their governments and international institutions shied away from an outright condemnation of the South African system of racial segregation. It was only after the Sharpeville Massacre in 1960, when the South African police killed 69 Black protesters at a political rally, that the United Nations officially condemned apartheid. In the coming decades, the international community slowly woke up to the atrocities committed in South Africa and agreed on a comprehensive set of sanctions against the apartheid regime. Most countries, also in Europe, started adopting targeted sanctions only in response to the state of emergency declared by the South African government in 1985.

Formally, apartheid ended on February 2, 1990, when the then president F. W. de Klerk gave a historic speech in Parliament announcing the release of Nelson Mandela and calling on public institutions to abrogate racial segregation. Yet, the transition to democratic rule dragged on for over 4 years, amid contestation, White-led terrorist attacks, and infighting among the main Black political movements, thereby revealing the deep-seated divisive effects that apartheid had exerted on the South African society.

Since the 1994 democratic elections, the apartheid architecture and its rule have been dismantled. The rights to vote, own property, and move freely across the country (and abroad) were extended to all citizens. The main political forces and official parties (whether right-wing or left-leaning) have accepted the democratic dispensation enshrined in the new Constitution, which is heralded as one of the most progressive in the world. Nevertheless, although all South Africans are formally equal before the law, differences and injustices remain, especially at the social and economic levels. Land ownership is still concentrated in White hands, and the bulk of the economy is controlled by traditional companies, especially in the mining sector, which thrived during apartheid.

More recently, the term *global apartheid* has gained currency in the political debate surrounding the reform of global institutions. Coined by former South African president Thabo Mbeki, the expression describes a world system divided between powerful (mostly Western) countries, which control intergovernmental bodies (e.g., the United Nations, World Bank, International Monetary Fund) and pull the strings of the global economy, and the majority of poor and developing nations, which are relegated to the periphery and factually disenfranchised from global governance. Nowadays, the term *apartheid* is commonly used in the international debate (particularly by human rights groups) to denounce any form of institutional separation aimed at dividing people on the basis of race, ethnicity, gender, religion, or wealth. The former U.S. president Jimmy Carter created a lively public discussion when he suggested that the Israeli occupation of Palestine amounted to a kind of apartheid.

Lorenzo Fioramonti

See also Anti-Apartheid Movement; Civil Rights; Civil Society, Global; Colonialism; Global Justice and Legal Issues; Human Rights, International; Justice Movements, Transnational; Pan African Union; Social Movements; Solidarity Movements

Further Readings

Bond, P. (2003). *Against global apartheid*. Cape Town, South Africa: University of Cape Town Press.

Bond, P. (2005). *Elite transition: From apartheid to neoliberalism in South Africa* (2nd ed.). London: Pluto Press.

Coombes, A. E. (2003). *History after apartheid*. London: Duke University Press.

Kozol, J. (2005). *The shame of the nation: The restoration of apartheid schooling in America*. New York: Crown.

Massey, D. S., & Denton, N. A. (1993). *American apartheid: Segregation and the making of the underclass*. Cambridge, MA: Harvard University Press.

Terreblanche, S. (2002). *A history of inequality in South Africa, 1652–2002*. Pietermaritzburg, South Africa: University of Natal Press.

ARAB LEAGUE

The Arab League represents one of the most significant regional organizations in the time of globalization. The League of Arab States, as it is formally called, reflects the historical, cultural, economic, and political reality of the Arab world in which the Arabic language forms a unifying feature separating the Arab states from other regions and wider Islamic contexts. The league presents a region of complexities where long-standing conflicts and challenges hinder a regional operation within a global system. This essay provides a brief account of the history, aims, development, and reality of the Arab League and highlights the league's stand with regard to the main political events and changes within the Arab world.

The Arab League (al-Jāmi'at al-'Arabiyya) is a regional organization of Arab states formed on March 22, 1945, in Cairo. The founding member-states were Egypt, Iraq, Lebanon, Saudi Arabia, Syria, Transjordan (Jordan, as of 1950), and Yemen. Countries that later joined are Algeria (1962), Bahrain (1971), Comoros (1993), Djibouti (1977), Kuwait (1961), Libya (1953), Mauritania (1973), Morocco (1958), Oman (1971), Qatar (1971), Somalia (1974), Southern Yemen (1967), Sudan (1956), Tunisia (1958), and the United Arab Emirates (1971). The Palestine Liberation Organization was admitted in 1976 to regard Palestine as an independent member. The league is organized into council, special committees, and a permanent secretariat; the secretariat has its headquarters in Cairo.

The idea of the Arab League had been advocated since 1942 by the British, who wanted to rally Arab countries against the Axis powers. While the idea of Arab unity was one of the main aims and patriotic dreams in the Arab region, Egypt and other Arab countries wanted cooperation without the loss of independent state sovereignty. Thus, with an Egyptian initiative in 1943, the league was established in March 1945, just before the end of World War II. The pact of the league promoted a regional organization of sovereign states that was neither a union nor a federation (Articles 1 and 3).

The purpose of the league, as defined by Article 2 of its pact, is to "to draw closer the relations between member-states and coordinate their political activities with the aim of realizing a close collaboration between them, to safeguard their independence and sovereignty, and to consider in a general way the affairs and interests of the Arab countries." The pact also identified a number of categories in which the cooperation is deemed essential and required organized committees and individual representations (Article 4). These categories are economic and financial matters; communications, including railways, posts, and telegraphs; cultural matters; matters concerned with nationality and passports; social welfare; and health matters.

The pact also forbids the use of force to settle disputes among members (Article 5) and requires mediation to resolve disputes among members or between them and third parties. The signing on April 13, 1950, of an agreement on joint defense cooperation also committed the members to coordination on military defense measures.

Since its early days, the league has encouraged liberation movements and the independence of Arab states, regarding them as essential steps to achieving the ultimate goal of Arab unity. In 1945, the league supported Syria and Lebanon in gaining their independence from the French mandate and also called for an independent Libya; also, in 1961, the league supported Tunisia in its conflict with France. The league early announced opposition to the formation of a Jewish state in Palestine and demanded that Palestine as a whole be made independent, with the majority of its population Arab. Following the establishment of the state of Israel in 1948, the league continued to maintain a boycott of Israel and of companies trading with Israel.

The league did not succeed in fulfilling its aim of promoting an Arab unity; this was due to a number of reasons, including the long-standing conflicts between its members (such as Syria and Iraq) and also the Arab-Israeli conflict.

After Egypt and Israel signed a peace treaty (Camp David Accords) in 1979, other members of the Arab League voted to suspend Egypt's membership and to transfer the league's headquarters from Cairo to Tunis. Nonetheless, Egypt was reinstated as a member of the Arab League in 1989, and the league's headquarters returned to Cairo in 1990. In 1988, the league endorsed the Palestine Liberation Organization's plan for a negotiated settlement with Israel, and in 2002 the league for the first time offered Israel normal relations with Arab countries if it met certain conditions; however, many of those conditions were not acceptable to Israel.

The league has been more effective in activities fostering economic, social, and cultural cooperation among Arab states. In its early years, the league concentrated on these activities. As a result of the league's efforts to cooperate on these issues, a number of important initiatives and programs were launched, for example, the Arab Telecommunications Union (1953), the Arab Postal Union (1954), and the Arab Development Bank (1959,

later known as the Arab Financial Organization). The Arab Common Market was established in 1965 and is open to all Arab League members. The common market agreement provides for the eventual abolition of customs duties on natural resources and agricultural products, free movement of capital and labor among member countries, and coordination of economic development. Thus, the league has been instrumental in creating an Arab postal union and a union for wireless communication and telecommunication.

The Arab League has played an important role in shaping school curricula, preserving Arabic manuscripts, advancing the role of women in the Arab societies, promoting child welfare, encouraging youth and sports programs, preserving Arab cultural heritage, and fostering cultural exchanges between the member-states. The league has promoted translations into Arabic and reproduction of foreign works. Literacy campaigns have been launched, intellectual works have been reproduced, and modern technical terminology has been translated for use within member-states. The league encourages measures against crime and drug abuse and deals with labor issues, particularly among the emigrant Arab workforce.

Members of the Arab League share common positions on such issues as supporting Palestinians under occupation, liberating the occupied territories, supporting democracy, and meeting international standards of human rights. The interpretation of this agreement in real measure has been hampered by a number of practicalities, however, including the fact that decisions made by the league are binding only on the members who voted for them.

Dina Hadad

See also Colonialism; Ethnic Identity; Heritage; Human Rights, International; Neocolonialism; Petroleum Geopolitics; Regional Governance; Regional Identities; Regionalism; Sovereignty

Further Readings

al-Jāmi'a al-'Arabiyya (Pact of the League of Arab States), March 22, 1945. Retrieved October 18, 2011, from http://avalon.law.yale.edu/20th_century/arableag.asp

Camp David Accords (1978–1979). Retrieved October 18, 2011, from http://www.jimmycarterlibrary.gov/documents/campdavid/index.phtml

Hitti, P. (1970). *History of the Arabs*. New York: Palgrave Macmillan.

Hourani, A. (1983). *Arabic thought in the liberal age*. Cambridge, UK: Cambridge University Press.

Hourani, A. (1992). *The history of Arab peoples*. New York: Warner Books.

Website

League of Arab States: http://www.arableagueonline.org/wps/portal/las_en

ARBITRATION

Arbitration is a key feature of doing business in a globalizing economy and is a main contributor to the development of transnational law. To fully understand why arbitration has reached this status, it is important to explain the main differences between arbitration and court proceedings and to underline the ways in which arbitration is an integral part of the process of globalization.

Arbitration can generally be defined as a mechanism for resolving disputes through one or more arbitrators empowered by the parties to decide on the matter in dispute by rendering an arbitral award. Over the years, arbitration has developed substantially in domestic and international commercial relations and is traditionally considered the preferred procedural way to settle disputes in cross-border transactions.

Unlike judges who are appointed by the state, arbitrators are appointed through contractual agreement between the parties in dispute. Arbitration thus allows the parties to have a say in the profile, nationality, and qualifications of the selected arbitrators. In cross-border transactions, this flexibility in the constitution of the arbitral tribunal gives the opportunity to establish a truly international and multi-jurisdictional arbitral panel detached from the respective national affiliations of the parties. Another feature of arbitration is the final and binding nature of the arbitral award, which is exposed to judicial challenge only on limited procedural grounds such as violation of public policy. In particular, arbitral awards are not meant to be subject to review of their merits and contents by national courts, thereby fostering security and speed in the dispute resolution mechanism. Finally, although court decisions are often accessible to the public at large via official reporting of court cases, arbitral awards are protected by confidentiality restrictions. This gives to the parties in dispute the assurance that their conflict situation will not be advertised to a wide audience.

In recent years, arbitration has been the subject of a certain level of criticism, mainly on the ground that it would be a costly method of resolving disputes or the time frame to obtain an enforceable arbitral award would be too long. As a result, substitutes to arbitration proceedings such as mediation, conciliation, adjudication, and other similar alternative dispute resolution mechanisms have been on the rise. Nevertheless, arbitration remains, to date, the preferred option for resolving international commercial disputes within a formal procedural framework.

Although the advantages of arbitration may explain why it has flourished as the natural dispute settlement method in international commercial relations, this would not have been possible without substantial support of the international legal community. A cornerstone of the global development of arbitration is the New York Convention of 1958 on the Recognition and Enforcement of Foreign Arbitral Awards. With the removal of many national obstacles to the recognition and enforcement of arbitral awards, the New York Convention has provided the necessary guarantees enabling arbitration to gain the confidence of global economic players. Further major international support has been granted by the United Nations Commission on International Trade Law and, more specifically, the release in 1985 of the Model Law on International Commercial Arbitration. Finally, under the auspices of the World Bank, the creation in 1985 of the International Centre for Settlement of Investment Disputes through the Convention on the Settlement of Investment Disputes Between States and Nationals of Other States has demonstrated that arbitration is also a suitable forum for resolving cross-border disputes involving governmental organizations.

Beyond the formal international legal framework, the recourse to arbitration is, to a large extent, positively publicized by distinguished international organizations. For instance, the International Chamber of Commerce uses arbitration clauses in its various model forms. Another major reference is provided by the International Federation of Consulting Engineers, which includes arbitration clauses in its model Conditions of Contract used in international construction and infrastructure projects. Also worth noting is the work of the International Bar Association and its Arbitration Committee, which helps shape best practices and common standards in the field of transnational disputes.

Arbitration enjoys a global recognition through the crucial role played by international arbitration centers in organizing and facilitating access to arbitration. Aside from traditional arbitration institutions like the International Chamber of Commerce's International Court of Arbitration, the London Court of International Arbitration, the Stockholm Chamber of Commerce, the American Arbitration Association, the Swiss Arbitration Association, and the Vienna International Arbitration Center, the past decades have seen the assertion of major regional centers in developing economies; these centers include the Singapore International Arbitration Center, the Hong Kong International Arbitration Centre, and the China International Economic and Trade Arbitration Commission. The existence of reputable international arbitration centers is one of the reasons that the vast majority of arbitration proceedings are organized through these centers as opposed to ad hoc arbitration where the parties themselves arrange the arbitration rules and proceedings.

In view of the widespread use of arbitration to settle international disputes, arbitration contributes to the creation and evolution of transnational law. A salient example of this contribution is the fact that international arbitrators regularly refer to transnational legal principles, namely, the *lex mercatoria* (law of merchants), when rendering their awards. In so doing, arbitrators take part in the formulation and knowledge sharing of the *lex mercatoria*, which is itself a key component in the body of norms evolving in a globalizing economy.

In essence, arbitration is a product of globalization and, at the same time, arbitration is shaping the process of globalization.

Pierrick Le Goff

See also Conflict and Conflict Resolution; Global Economic Issues; Global Governance and World Order; Globalization, Phenomenon of; Law, International; Lex Mercatoria

Further Readings

Bortolotti, F. (2008). *Drafting and negotiating international commercial contracts—a practical guide.* Paris: ICC.

Friedland, P. (2007). *Arbitration clauses for international contracts* (2nd ed.). Huntington, NY: Juris.

Gaillard, E., & Savage. J. (Ed.). (1999). *Fouchard Gaillard Goldman on international commercial arbitration.* London: Kluwer Law International.

Poudret, J.-F., & Besson, S. (2002). *Droit comparé de l'arbitrage international* [Comparative law of international arbitration]. Brussels, Belgium: Bruylant.

Rowley W. J. (Ed.). (2006). *Arbitration world— jurisdictional comparisons* (2nd ed.). London: European Lawyer.

ARCHITECTURE

Generally, in architectural practice the word *global* is associated with the internationalization of finance capital that has resulted in a large number of Western architecture and urban design firms practicing across the world. But in academic circles, global architecture as a category of epistemic investigation has been gaining ground. In part, this stems from the recent curricular emphasis in including "non-Western" architecture as part of the core accreditation requirements of the professional architecture degree, but it is also a response to the increasingly globalized nature of architectural practice.

Types of Global Architecture Practice

Currently, two major types of architectural practices are usually described as being global. The better known of these are the high-profile practices of famous Western architects, particularly those located in Europe. These architects are often and increasingly invited to build iconic structures around the world, particularly in the rapidly emerging markets of East Asia, the Gulf, South Asia, and Southeast Asia. Often referred to as

Figure 1   The Walt Disney Concert Hall in Los Angeles, California. This iconic concert hall, designed by the famous global architect Frank Gehry, is known as one of the most acoustically superior concert halls in the world.

Source: Photo by Evan Janke.

"star-chitects," the practitioners include architects such as Rem Koolhaas (of OMA, the Netherlands), Jean Nouvel (France), Jacques Herzog and Pierre de Meuron (Switzerland), Renzo Piano (France and Italy), Norman Foster (United Kingdom), and Frank Gehry (United States). The iconicity of the architecture associated with star-chitects is a key element of their global demand. Civic agencies and public sector agencies are the usual patrons of star-chitecture.

Star-chitecture is also sometimes described as the Bilbao effect, a reference to the tremendous global attention focused on Bilbao, a small town in Spain, simply as a consequence of the Guggenheim Museum, which was built there by the U.S.-based architect Frank Gehry in 1997. This building, because of the iconicity of its architecture, made Bilbao a tourist and mercantile destination that transformed the economy of the town. This building's success opened the floodgates for iconic architecture worldwide as part of the accepted business practice of an urban economy trying to establish its place in globalization. As a consequence, the Guggenheim Bilbao was the building most frequently named in the 2010 World Architecture Survey of architecture experts as one of the most important buildings completed since 1980.

The second type of global architectural practice can be identified as that being done in the large, corporate architectural firms, an increasing portion of whose work is based outside the Western world. Firms such as Callison, NBBJ, SOM, KPF, Ellerbe Becket—all of which are primarily based outside the United States—maintain corporate offices in the major financial centers of the world, such as London, Shanghai, Hong Kong, Singapore, and Mumbai (besides their offices in the United States and Europe). Most of these firms specialize in several building types, such as hospitality, health, infrastructure, sports, and retail, and rely on efficiency and the signature branding of their work as their key marketing strategy. Their expertise is sought by clients who have projects that are financed by privatized capital infrastructures, including public-private partnerships, with specific investment expectations. Increasingly, architecture and design firms around the world are modeling themselves on major Western global corporate practices.

Most of the work done by both star-chitecture firms and large corporate offices relies on local professional partners for execution of projects. At a minimum, local partners function as the legal signatories in permitting processes, but more often than not, the local partners are also responsible for drafting the construction documents. Often, this is simply a function of financial efficiency: The Western global firm prepares the concept design at the international pay scales, while the local firm does the detailed construction documents utilizing local architects and draftspersons. However, it is also true that, in spite of the globalized nature of the design industry, the construction techniques utilized to make buildings in different parts of the world are significantly localized, usually designed to work with available construction techniques and management processes. Often, such localization involves significant innovation directed toward developing construction management techniques that can achieve the desired standard of the outcomes using significantly cheaper methods of construction that those prescribed by the architects originally.

Academia and Global Architecture

In the more academic register, the concept of "global" is usually connected to the broadening of the Western canon by including the non-West. The U.S. National Architectural Accrediting Board, the board responsible for accrediting professional architectural degrees, has recently introduced substantial changes to make architectural pedagogy more diverse and inclusive. These changes included the upgrading of the non-Western architecture requirement from "awareness" to "understanding," which requires that students develop competency in non-Western architectural history. The heading that the National Architectural Accrediting Board uses is "Historical Traditions and Global Culture," by which it means the study of "indigenous, vernacular, local, regional, national settings from the Eastern, Western, Northern, and Southern hemispheres in terms of their climatic, ecological, technological, socioeconomic, public health, and cultural factors" (NAAB 2009 Conditions for Accreditation, p. 22). In this sense, the study of the non-West in the academy derives largely from discussion of vernaculars.

The IASTE (International Association for the Study of Traditional Environments) conferences have been held every alternate year for more than 20 years. However, it is worth noting that, although devoted to "traditional" environments, IASTE conferences have routinely engaged topics on global themes designed to critically review the concept of the traditional as also that of the non-West in various registers. Recent conference titles have included "Interrogating Tradition," "Post Traditional Environments in a Post Global World," "(Un)Bounding Tradition," "The End of Tradition," and "Development Versus Tradition." The *Traditional Dwellings and Settlement Review*, a journal associated with the IASTE conferences, also publishes papers based on similar topics.

It is perhaps because of the lingering taste of 19th-century ethnography in some of the assumptions about global culture that the strongest critiques have come from cultural and postcolonial studies. From 1993 to 1999, a loose affiliation called "Other Connections" held a series of conferences explicitly devoted to developing "other," non-Eurocentric perspectives in architecture. The first of these was held in Singapore, the second in Chandigarh, the third in Melbourne, and the last in Beirut. Other Connections conferences were strongly influenced by studies in British cultural theory and postcolonial studies. Two books, *Postcolonial Space(s)* edited by Gülsüm Baydar Nalbantoğlu and Wong Chong Thai (Princeton Architectural Press, New York, 1997) and *Drifting: Architecture and Migrancy* edited by Steven Cairns (Routledge, 2004), were developed out of papers delivered at these conferences.

Although postcolonial studies have opened new venues for discussion, the emphasis has been largely on modernity and contemporary issues rather than on history. It has been only relatively recently that global has begun to be associated with the word *history* in the field of architectural history. Some of the first experiments were, however, hardly global but what one can call Euro+. *A History of Architecture: Settings and Rituals*, by Spiro Kostof, was recently reissued with a greater degree of non-Western content. But the first section of the book, titled "Part One: A Place on Earth," which has 10 chapters, has nine devoted to Western architectural history and only one to the rest, called "The World at Large: Roman Concurrences," within which Persian, Chinese, Indian, and American civilization is covered in broad strokes. The Euro+ model is even more explicit in the 2004 McGraw-Hill textbook, *Buildings Across Time: An Introduction to World Architecture*, by Marian Moffett, Michael Fazio, and Lawrence

Wodehouse. The difference between the older and newer editions of this book was the addition of chapters on India and China. Another example is the textbook *The Visual Arts: A History*, by Hugh Honour and John Fleming. In this book, too, "Buddhism, Hinduism and Far Eastern Art" is a chapter unto itself and precedes a chapter called "Early Christian and Byzantine Art."

In 2006, Wiley issued a textbook titled *A Global History of Architecture* by Francis D. K. Ching, Mark M. Jarzombek, and Vikramāditya Prakāsh. The book was designed to offer an architectural history that was truly global in scope. The book chapters are designated as time cuts. Thus, for instance, the chapter on 800 CE documents architecture around the world at this time. The time cuts are roughly about 200 years apart except in more modern times, where they are 100 years apart. Within each cut, the material is organized in short case studies, each one a mini-essay in itself. Each chapter begins at a different place, the argument being that because the earth is spinning, it does not really matter when the narrative begins because history is continually in flux. The chapters do not begin arbitrarily, however, but conform to certain arguments the authors make about the status of architecture at a particular time. Given the increased interest in global studies, other books are sure to come.

Since the beginning of the 21st century, one of the most important fronts in global studies has been driven by preservation with its own disciplinary approach to the topic of history. The United Nations Educational, Scientific and Cultural Organization (UNESCO) now has over 900 sites that range from buildings and landscapes to even "cultures." The research that goes into this is formidable and based on what UNESCO calls a site's "outstanding universal value." Because so many of the sites are tied in with the premises of global tourism, there will be increasingly strong debate about the merit of what is now called "the heritage industry." This industry drives art and architectural historical research away from global studies and toward histories with national perspectives. Just because preservation is now a global industry does not mean that it functions to open up new territories about global studies.

A genuine engagement with knowledge platforms that can truly be said to be non-Eurocentric or nonnationalist in nature, however, still is limited to the occasional conference paper. But it is also a reflection of the waning Eurocentrism in the discipline, at least in its historiographical parts, while the interests of design studios and architectural practices still tend to be largely Western centric in their aesthetic and intellectual interests.

Vikramāditya Prakāsh and Mark M. Jarzombek

See also Aesthetics; Cities; Eurocentrism; Globalization, Phenomenon of; Postmodernism; Tourism Sector; United Nations Educational, Scientific and Cultural Organization (UNESCO)

Further Readings

Cairns, S. (2004). *Drifting: Architecture and migrancy*. London: Routledge.

Ching, F. D. K., Jarzombek, M., & Prakāsh, V. (2007). *A global history of architecture*. Hoboken, NJ: Wiley.

Hewison, R. (1987). *The heritage industry: Britain in a climate of decline*. London: Methuen.

International Association for the Study of Traditional Environments. (2008). 2008 Working Paper Series. Available from http://iaste.berkeley.edu/2008wps.htm

Kostof, S., & Castillo, G. (1995). *A history of architecture: Settings and rituals*. Oxford, UK: Oxford University Press.

Moffett, M., Fazio, M. W., & Wodehouse, L. (2004). *Buildings across time: An introduction to world architecture*. Boston: McGraw-Hill.

Nalbantoğlu, G. B., & Wong, C. T. (1997). *Postcolonial space(s)*. New York: Princeton Architectural Press.

National Architectural Accrediting Board. (2009, July 10). *2009 Conditions for accreditation*. Retrieved August 31, 2011, from http://www.naab.org/documents/streamfile.aspx?name=2009+Conditions+FINAL+EDITION.pdf&path=Public+Documents%5cAccreditation%5c2009+Conditions+for+Accreditation%5c

Prakāsh, V. (Ed.). (1997). *Theatres of decolonization: Architecture, urbanism, and agency*. Seattle: University of Washington.

Sharpley, R. (1994). *Tourism, tourists and society*. Suffolk, UK: St. Edmundsbury Press.

Tignor, R., Adelman, J., Aron, S., Kotkin, S., Marchand, S., Prakash, G., et al. (2002). *Worlds together, worlds apart: A history of the modern world from the Mongol Empire to the present*. New York: Norton.

Urry, J. (1990). *The tourist gaze: Leisure and travel in contemporary societies*. London: Sage.

ART

Global art embraces any type of art, including paintings, sculptures, photography, cinema, video art, digital Internet art, as well as conceptual, installation, and performance arts, that participates in the international art world through cultural exchange or commerce. The exchange is not limited to one-directional transfers from dominant art cultures to indigenous sources. Rather, there exists a pluralism of active sources contributing to the reciprocal flow and mutually enhancing stream of art and its support systems, including art institutions, art publications, art criticism, and educational support. Contemporary art, as well as the traditional art forms of national and local cultures, have been influenced by globalism. The discussion here provides an examination of the changes brought about by global art as it relates to the art market and to cultural institutions such as museums and art *biennales*. Although the history of global art began with trade among the major civilizations in Asia, Europe, India, and the Ottoman Empire, this history is not repeated here.

Unlike the situation in the colonial era and during the period of 20th-century modern art, the global exchange of cultural influences today is no longer hegemonic. This means that the main currents of influence no longer flow from a dominant art-rich center such as Paris or New York to supplant or suppress the art in other regions. On the contrary, global art centers across the world, such as Beijing and New Delhi, compete successfully with European and American art centers as wellsprings of artistic innovation. However, instead of thinking and acting as cultural imperialists, the artists in the global era seem more content to share their art-producing strategies and their ideas with artists working in other cultures.

Cross-cultural exchange of art practices is not an entirely new development, as Western modern art has attracted the attention of Asian artists throughout the 20th century and before. For example, throughout the 20th century, artists, whose training might have begun with the study of Chinese traditional art forms, found in Western modern and contemporary art, such as Impressionism, Abstract Expressionism, and Pop Art, ways of developing their own art in new directions. At the same time, there exists a well-established tradition of Western artists, including avant-garde artists John Cage and Robert Rauschenberg and others in the United States, who look to Eastern art and philosophy for inspiration. The Guggenheim Museum's 2009 exhibition, The Third Mind: American Artists Contemplate Asia, 1860–1989, which showed the works of 110 artists, offers ample evidence of this development.

Globalization, Transnational, and World Art

Taken in the broadest sense, the term *global* means worldwide, universal, all-inclusive, complete, or exhaustive. Global art requires a narrower frame than this broad sense of global. Its network is worldwide, and it implies the possibility of some sense of universal art understanding, as it transcends particular national, regional, or local cultures. Still, global art is neither all-inclusive nor complete, because there are forms of art (e.g., amateur art, commercial art, local crafts, and art used solely in particular religious practices) that do not participate in transnational cultural networks.

Other terms might qualify as candidates for describing the processes that are referred to as global art, for example, *transnational art* instead of *global art*, as has been proposed by the philosopher Nöel Carroll. *Transnational* means going beyond national boundaries or solely national interests. Some scholars, however, prefer the term *global art* over *transnational art* for at least two important reasons: It is the language often used to discuss the dynamics of worldwide issues in other important cultural domains such as economics and politics. Furthermore, global is more suited to the nature of art practices taking place in contemporary geopolitical divisions where national boundaries are fluid and where pluralistic nation-states such as China, India, and the United States embrace diverse cultural and artistic practices. Given these considerations, *transnational* seems less useful than *global* for identifying the movement of art forces, which are currently taking place both within and across geopolitical boundaries. The term *world art*, previously used to characterize art museum and ethnographic museum collections of art gathered from around the world, also fails to capture the changes that art has undergone since the 1980s.

Agencies of Global Art

The contemporary agencies of global art include artists working in exile, art fairs, galleries, auction houses, and biennales, and also museums. The focus here is on artists intending to produce work aimed at making a contribution to culture through aesthetic or conceptual understanding and deemed to have artistic merit. It does not include the work of amateur artists made solely for personal expression or art produced solely for commercial purposes. In some cultures, there are many layers of artistic production: government-supported artists, artists who participate in regional and national art associations, members of art academies and university art departments, and free professional artists. It is the last group that figures most prominently in the contemporary global art world because the work of those artists is most likely to attract the interest of the museums and other cultural institutions and is also most attractive to the art market. These global individual artists often work in multiple geographic locations such as New York and Beijing.

International fine art fairs organized for the display and sale of art represent an important means of globalizing art. Art Basel, the Maastricht Art Fair in the Netherlands, Art Basel Miami Beach, Art Chicago, Art Dubai, London's Frieze Art Fair, Arco Madrid, Asia Pacific Contemporary Art Fair in Shanghai, and the Korea International Art Fair in Seoul are among the main vehicles for global art market transfers. Art dealers, collectors, and museum representatives frequent these gatherings to select artworks for their respective art enterprises and for the exchange of ideas.

Private art galleries and art auction houses located in virtually every metropolitan center across the world also contribute to the globalization of art. For example, one finds available in the Art Zone 798 section of Beijing artists from the United States, Europe, and other parts of the world, as well as offerings of Chinese artists. New York's Chelsea art district, as well as similar sites in Paris, Berlin, and London, regularly offers art from China, India, Japan, and elsewhere across the world.

Also important to the market distribution system for global art are the international auction houses such as Christie's and Sotheby's. With headquarters located in London and New York, these major action houses also have offices in cities throughout the world. For example, Christie's hosts offices in 30 countries and regularly holds art auctions in a wide range of places, including Beijing, Dubai, Moscow, Mumbai, New York, London, and other European and Asian cities. Sotheby's also offers auction services in the Americas, including major sites in Buenos Aires, Caracas, and Rio de Janeiro, as well as through its offices in Asia and Europe. Reportedly, worldwide auction sales grew more than eightfold between 2003 and 2007 (though there was a slight decline during the global economic downturn from 2008 to 2010).

A highly visible aspect of the contemporary global art world is the art biennale; by 2010, there were some 60 offered throughout the world. A biennale is a major international showing of works by up-and-coming contemporary artists held in an important city every 2 years. A biennale is normally international and noncommercial. The artists are invited by the organizing institution and are able to show, but not to sell, their works. A biennale typically has a theme and may spotlight artists of the host nation. The Venice Biennale, established in 1895 in Venice, Italy, is one of the oldest and most important. Other well-established biennales include the Whitney Biennale in New York and those in São Paulo, Brazil, and Sydney, Australia. (Documenta, held in Kassel, Germany, every 5 years, functions in ways similar to the biennales.)

The biennale circuit has contributed a nomad-like character to global art. Biennale artists tend to move from city to city presenting their works under the guidance of an international curator designated by the organizing city. Curators, who may have initially worked on museum collections and exhibitions or as art critics, also follow the path of nomadicity created by the constantly shifting geographic locations of the biennale circuit. Similarly, the transient character of the biennale circuit has impacted the shift from painting and sculpture as the preferred art media to photography, video art, and digital art. From a practical perspective, these media arts are more portable than paintings and sculptures and less susceptible to damage in transport.

Museums have also contributed to the development of global art, as they offer exhibitions drawing on artistic works from across the world. Lately, museums have offered exhibitions intended to reflect on the meaning of global art. Global

Conceptualism: Points of Origin (April 28, 1999, to November 6, 2000) opened at the Brooklyn Museum and traveled to the Walker Art Center in Minneapolis and the Miami Art Museum. This exhibition identified four key themes common to the global conceptual artists selected from Asia, Europe and the Soviet Union, Africa, Australia and New Zealand, North America, and Latin America. The themes were (a) the emergence of conceptual art from local circumstances instead of from a single international source, (b) prioritization of language over visuality, (c) critique of the institutions of art, and (d) dematerialization of art to focus on conceptual ideas. The curatorial staff of this global art project, under the leadership of its directors Louis Camnitzer, Jane Ferver, and Rachel Weiss, was equally global as it included, among others, Okwui Enwezor from Africa, Gao Minglu from China, and Carmen Ramírez from Latin America. In 2003 (February 9–May 4), the Walker Art Center in Minneapolis mounted an exhibition, How Latitudes Become Forms: Art in a Global Age, to explore how contemporary art is practiced in a global context. Among the questions considered were how global change impacts art, how there occurs a blurring of lines between disciplines, and how a global sensibility takes physical shape. The yearlong project at the Walker Art Center included programming in the visual arts, new media, film/video, and performing arts and was the culmination of 4 years of research and planning by a team of scholars and curators from across the world. Global Feminism, at the Brooklyn Museum (March 23–July 1, 2007), curated by Myra Reilly and Linda Nochlin, offered the works of 88 women artists from around the world. This exhibition included art in all media—painting, sculpture, photography, film, video, installation, and performance art. The exhibition presented feminism in a global perspective with a look at life cycle issues, identity, and emotions. The themes in these three exhibitions showed a progression from a focus on general characteristics of global art to its application to a particular theme showcasing women artists.

Impact of Global Art: Issues and Problems

The focus on globalization in art follows heightened attention to global economic and political discourse. This development raises issues important to the future understanding of art and its role in human experience. By focusing on the whole of artistic production worldwide, including the changes in local art, globalization draws attention to the diversity that exists in the arts as they function in different cultures and to the changes that are taking place. Recognition of diversity and change reinforces the need for an understanding of art that is broad and inclusive. This means that any definition or theory of art useful for a philosophical understanding of art must be in the form of an open concept instead of a closed definition. Any fruitful attempt to define art thus will look for correspondences among the various art practices without seeking conformity when examining the varieties of art that may come to be from time to time. Change and diversity offer important reasons for opting for an open concept of art. An open concept of art does not preclude the discovery of common or universal elements among the various practices because all art must serve some human need or interest.

Among the changes that have attracted attention today is the emergence of increasingly nomadic artists from across the world who participate in the seemingly endless stream of art biennales and art fairs showing new art. This development has prompted Carroll (2007) to propose that we are witnessing the emergence of a unified international art world, "something like a single, integrated, cosmopolitan institution of art, organized transnationally in such a way that the participants . . . share converging or overlapping traditions and practices at the same time that they exhibit and distribute their art in international coordinated venues" (pp. 136–141). Carroll finds in this development common themes such as "post-colonialism, feminism, gay liberation, globalization and global inequality, the suppression of free expression and other human rights, identity politics." Accompanying these common themes are sense-making strategies that are shared by artists, presenters, and their audiences. According to Carroll, these strategies might include "a battery of formal devices for advancing those themes, including radical juxtaposition, de-familiarization, and the de-contextualization of objects and images from their customary milieus" (p. 141).

This development represents one aspect of the overall globalization of art. But the themes and the strategies of the category of artists cited by Carroll offer a very narrow slice of art as it is being practiced in the current global world. The interests of these artists seem to be limited to a particular segment of the art world, and perhaps to an even narrower segment of art interests of the world population at large. Hence, the impact of global art cannot be gauged from this sampling alone.

A related set of issues is addressed in a series of conferences and publications on global art conducted by Hans Belting and others. Among the important questions raised by Belting's studies are these: To what extent is the new globalization of art prompting a critical reevaluation of the notion of mainstream art? How will the outcome of these developments affect the future role of the art museum as a barometer of cultural identity?

Of particular importance is the impact of globalization for the future of the art museum. Local and national museums across the world presently provide a measure of cultural identity for the local and national communities in which they are located, as well as a measure of cultural achievements and a banner of civic pride. Museums, in the Western tradition at least, are looked on as a main source of public access to art. In the West especially, but not exclusively, museums have had an important role in bringing art from across the world to their local constituencies.

Global art takes the discussion of contemporary art and art institutions one more step beyond postcolonial discourses on art. As Belting (2007) has noted, globalization of art brings forth a tension between the forces of "an aggressive localism that makes use of culture as a mark of otherness and as defense, and a transnational art, indifferent to claims of geography, history and identity."

With the latter claiming universality and the former holding on to local traditions, or seeking to embrace global art that is grounded in local or national traditions, the future of art worldwide remains in a state of transition. Thus, it is not possible to predict the future shape of global art at this time.

Accordingly, the push for global art raises complex cultural and psychological issues. Whether people who share the same visual environments and ownership of particular art practices will adapt to radical changes in art resulting in the abandonment of local cultures remains to be seen. There is some evidence from research in current neuroscience that sustained exposure to certain forms of visual conditioning may result in shifts in cognitive patterns, which supports the possibility of changes in local art practices with respect to both production and appreciation of art. Yet, other factors, including the pressures from economic and political interests, may also affect receptivity to changes in artistic practices. In any event, ongoing tensions from conflicting local and global interests in art will be important in shaping the future of global art.

Conclusion

The history of the globalization of art suggests that its results have not always been positive. There is the risk of local art being trampled or destroyed in the process of globalization. A second issue arises when art is considered a national treasure, which should be retained within its culture of origin. Auction houses, as well as museums, find themselves in the midst of international controversies over global transfers of works of art involving the disputed ownership of art believed to be looted or stolen, or otherwise improperly removed from its culture of origin. Such disputes often arise out of circumstances of long-standing duration. The transfer of the Elgin Marbles from Athens to the British Museum in the late 19th century is still disputed by the Greeks. A recent incident resulted in the Chinese government's condemning of Christie's auction house for the allegedly illegal sale of two bronze artifacts taken from a Chinese palace 150 years ago. The bronzes in question are of particular interest for a discussion of global art, because the artist of the two bronzes was a Jesuit who created the bronzes for the Qianlong Emperor of China in the mid-18th century. Interestingly, the bronzes were removed from the Chinese Palace by Anglo-French forces led by the Eighth Lord Elgin, whose father acquired the Elgin Marbles from the Parthenon.

Such examples abound. The Getty Museum, one of the most prestigious art institutions worldwide, has been in litigation with the Italian government over allegedly stolen items that found their way into the Getty collections. This long-standing dispute ended when in 2007 the

Getty Museum, under pressure from the Italian government, agreed to return some 40 disputed antiquities to Italy. A 6-year trial of ex-Getty curator Marion True, who had been charged with complicity in trafficking of stolen art, ended in October 2010 when the Italian judge determined that the statute of limitations for criminal prosecution had expired.

It is not yet clear what sorts of problems will ensue from the globalism of contemporary art. One area to watch will be the effects of the new developments on the museums and other cultural institutions charged with stewardship and preservation of culture for future generations. Another area of concern that is unresolved is the effects of the new globalization on the development of local art. Whether recent efforts toward the advancement of global art will help to resolve long-standing issues remains to be seen.

What is clear, however, is that contemporary global art has given new life to the international art market and has expanded the opportunities for innovative collaboration among the artists and cultural institutions of the world. On the positive side, global art increases the flow of ideas and art across cultural boundaries and advances the efforts toward mutual understanding among the peoples of different cultures. It endows individual artists with greater resources to create, using ideas, visual forms, and materials, irrespective of their particular cultural or geographic origins. This means that the artists have available an evolving universal vocabulary of artistic resources. Artists may then draw on the cumulative traditions of their own culture, as well as seize on innovations from other cultures in their creative undertakings. Similarly, audiences benefit increasingly from the rich variety of art that globalism continues to make available. The prospects for an increased interest in global art will continue to improve as the arts and culture take on a greater role in the global economy and are a greater concern for foreign policy.

Curtis L. Carter

See also Aesthetics; Artists; Cultural Hybridity; Culture, Notions of; Globalization, Phenomenon of; Heritage; United Nations Educational, Scientific and Cultural Organization (UNESCO)

Further Readings

Belting, H. (2007, January 25–27). Introduction to conference program. In *The interplay of art and globalization: Consequences for museums*. Vienna, Austria: Research Center for Cultural Studies. Retrieved September 13, 2011, from http://globalartmuseum.de/site/event/8

Belting, H., & Buddensieg, A. (Eds.). (2009). *The global art world: Audiences, markets, museums*. Ostfildern, Germany: Hatje-Canz.

Camnitzer, L., Farver, J., Weiss, R. (1999). *Global conceptualism: Points of origin, 1950s–1980s*. New York: Queens Museum of Art.

Carter, C. L. (Ed.). (2009). Art and social change. *International Yearbook of Aesthetics, 13*.

Carroll, N. (2007). Art and globalization: Then and now. In S. L. Feagin (Ed.), *Global theories of the arts and aesthetics* (pp. 131–143). Oxford, UK: Blackwell.

Eakin, H. (2009, May 14). The affair of the Chinese bronze heads. *The New York Review of Books, 56*(8).

Elkins, J. (2007). *Is art history global?* New York: Routledge.

Erjavec, A. (Ed.). (2004). Aesthetics of globalization. *International Yearbook of Aesthetics, 8*.

Munroe, A. (2009). *The third mind: American artists contemplate Asia, 1860–1989*. New York: Solomon R. Guggenheim Foundation.

Ratnam, N. (2004). Art and globalization. In G. Perry & P. Wood (Eds.), *Themes in contemporary art* (pp. 277–310). New Haven, CT: Yale University Press.

Reilly, M., & Nochlin, L. (Eds.). (2007). *Global feminism: New directions in contemporary art*. New York: Merrell.

ARTISTS

The globalization of artists and their work refers to the transfer of artistic practices and the works of art in various art media, such as the visual arts, performing arts, and media arts, from one culture to another. Through their migration, artists directly influence art beyond national or regional boundaries. Artists have an increasingly important role to play in the emerging field of global studies. Whether art is seen as a response on the part of artists to nature and the evolving manifestations of civilizations or is mainly a product of the artist's imagination, it holds an important place in the global world past and present. Together with language, works of art offer important symbolic means for human expression and communication of diversity and harmony both within and between cultures.

The movement of artistic practices from one culture to another often accompanies religious, commercial, or political interventions. Such efforts are not new to the 21st century. Western art first traveled to China by way of the Jesuit missionaries in the 16th century. In this instance, art was a part of the Jesuits' strategy for introducing Christianity to the Chinese. These efforts met with limited success, as Chinese viewers interpreted the symbols of Christian iconography, such as the Virgin Mary or Christ, as referring to Chinese Buddhist figures. On the other hand, Jesuit artist Giuseppe Castiglione, who came to China in 1715 and was appointed as court painter at the Imperial Palace in Peking under three successive emperors, successfully adapted his art to Chinese taste.

Western ventures into the Ottoman, Persian, and Arabic cultures involving the arts were more likely to follow the paths of commercial or diplomatic channels. For example, paintings of European artists depicting scenes with orientalist costumes and interiors were one manifestation of the globalizing connections between Europe and the Ottoman Empire during the Enlightenment in Europe. From the 1850s on, following the British occupation of India, art in India was officially guided by British-founded art schools in Calcutta, Madras, and Bombay. Hegemonic efforts of the British to dominate art in India by founding British-run schools and by presenting exhibitions of British art were offset in part by revival efforts of the Bengal renaissance in the early part of the 20th century reviving traditional Indian art. Today's Indian artists such as Surendran Nadir and Vivan Sundaram have established their places in the international art world.

Globalization was also evident in the movement of modernist art from Paris to New York at the beginning of the 20th century. The result was that Paris artists such as Marcel Duchamp, Pablo Picasso, and Henri Matisse dominated American art until the post–World War II era when American artists established Abstract Expressionism as the first original art movement in the United States. This movement featured American artists such as Jackson Pollock and Mark Rothko.

From the mid-20th century on, international contemporary art fairs, gallery representation of international artists in major cities across the world, and international museum exhibitions have advanced global art. Since the 1980s, a main path of global traffic has been between artists in the West and the East. For example, as Pop Art from the United States and England, based on Western commercialism and everyday life, became known in China, Chinese artists such as Wang Guangyi responded by developing their own Political Pop Art. At the same time, Chinese artists such as Xu Bing, Gu Wenda, and Wu Shanzhuan took their art to the urban centers of the United States and Europe and became active participants in the global art market as well as recognized museum artists of international stature.

One positive result of globalization is that it offers artists a greater choice of artistic means. Globalization opens the possibility for artists located virtually in any part of the world to draw on a broad stream of artistic knowledge as it has developed in the diverse artistic cultures. Global art thus enables individual artists to create, using the means available, without regard to national or regional limits. This means that artists have available an evolving universal vocabulary of artistic ideas and techniques contributed over time from the practices of artists working in many cultures across the world. Creating art today mandates that artists be free to incorporate into their work their own cultural histories as well as the culture histories of others. The outcome does not lie in creating a universal language for a new "International Style," reminiscent of the Euro-centered Western international style grounded in modernism, as a standard for future developments in art. Rather, the situation invites artists to continue to employ their creative imaginations in developing new ideas for art. For example, an artist working in China today has available the resources of traditional Eastern and Western art practices, as well as the pluralisms of modern and postmodern art.

There are also economic advantages working for the global artist, who may benefit from access to a wider audience. For example, a Chinese artist who works also in Berlin and New York has a much wider range of opportunities to participate in the art world of museums as well as the art market.

More important for the future of humanity, however, are the opportunities for global artists working today, in a fragile world of globally linked natural and social environments, to aid in expanding and deepening our understanding of the realities, both internal and external, natural and social, that will shape life into the future for human beings. What can artists working in a global context contribute toward alleviating the clashes of culture leading to war and other forms of social violence? Perhaps, with their special sensitivities and conceptual articulateness, artists are able to perceive and communicate aspects of these realities that might otherwise escape notice or be deemed unimportant until brought to attention in a striking visual image, a poem, a song, or a moment in the theater. Perhaps the evolution of art freed of national boundaries and informed by diverse cultures will better communicate values that all persons, irrespective of their particular cultures, can share.

Globalization opens the doors for border crossings where artists are no longer limited to national or local practices. Intercultural confrontations through art can be both informative and productive. At the same time, they require attention to the needs to respect and preserve important local and national art traditions while forging the path for the new.

Curtis L. Carter

See also Aesthetics; Art; Cultural Hybridity; Culture, Notions of; Globalization, Phenomenon of; Heritage; United Nations Educational, Scientific and Cultural Organization (UNESCO)

Further Readings

Belting, H., & Buddensieg, A. (Eds.). (2009). *The global art world: Audiences, markets, museums.* Ostfildern, Germany: Hatje-Cantz.

Craig, T. J., & King, R. (2002). *Global goes local: Popular culture in Asia.* Vancouver: University of British Columbia Press.

Erjavec, A. (Ed.). (2004). Aesthetics of globalization. *International Yearbook of Aesthetics, 8.*

Ratnam, N. (2004). Art and globalization. In G. Perry & P. Wood (Eds.), *Themes in contemporary art* (pp. 277–310). New Haven, CT: Yale University Press.

ASIAN TIGER PHENOMENON

The "Asian Tigers"—Hong Kong, Singapore, Taiwan, and South Korea—have had a considerable impact on the global economy. The influence of the region has had global dimensions since the Cold War, when Asian countries like Korea and Vietnam served as a battleground between two competing global forces. The region has since elevated to an economic power, affecting the rest of the world by setting business trends and leading capital movements. Throughout this period and beyond, observers have attributed the growth of this region to a number of factors, from application of traditional Eastern philosophy to economic policy to replication of manufacturing techniques. Regardless, the place of these countries in international relations has had no less of an impact, positive or negative, than established powers like the United States and the United Kingdom.

The 1950s and 1960s, when the Tigers' growth began, were a time when the state system and international relations were going through significant changes, including postwar shifts and decolonization. although there were similarities among the Tigers in their respective political economies, each had a different predicament. In economic terms, each Tiger started with very little capital and low savings rates, which, according to the Solow-Swan growth theory, are the key components for sustainable growth. While still a British colony, Hong Kong began exporting manufacturing goods such as textiles in earnest, while at the same time keeping labor costs low. In Singapore, growth accelerated in 1965 through foreign direct investment and a shift to an economy where the price of goods was based on the general economic principle of supply and demand (i.e., market-based economy). Also in the 1960s, postwar South Korea turned to a trade strategy similar to Hong Kong's in manufacturing labor-intensive goods at a low price. Finally, Taiwan shared similar growth origins with Singapore—it received significant foreign investment while using development aid (capital) from the United States to build its infrastructure.

The economic changes in each country were based on the changing political structures of each state. During the 20th century, decolonization and the Cold War affected the government, which affected the economy. In colonial Hong Kong, the government was made up of both British and Chinese officials in the 1970s, which, rather than having negative effects on coalition politics, turned out to be beneficial for the region. The Chinese had innate regional knowledge, which led to effective decisions in strategy, while the British allotted capital funding for the country. In postcolonial Singapore, the government led by Lee Kuan Yew and the People's Action Party, facing problems such as the brief union with Malaysia (in part due to issues over religion) and the threat of communism, adopted a policy of neutrality. The country sought foreign investment to increase capital stocks, which was seen as a basis for growth. To do this, the government had to create stability in the labor market (at the time, the country was known for labor strikes and disputes), which it did through legislation that limited the power of labor unions and worker disputes. For Taiwan, the Republic of China that governed the island sought closer economic ties with the world. Today, Taiwan's government is a head wearing "two hats": raising interest rates periodically, which has led to higher savings that are used to finance new businesses ("greenfield" investment). In addition, it encourages technological advancements in agriculture. This strategy followed the neoclassical economic theory of the production function stating that technology maximizes output through its effect on the factors of production (labor, capital). Like Taiwan, the government of South Korea broke from a Communist foe. Still, the government was shaped by military dictatorships up until the 1980s but sought technological progress and aided in the development of the export-oriented industries. Afterward, the government made strides to transform itself into a liberal democracy but has maintained its economic policies. In essence, the global political climate affected the domestic economies, and today the domestic economies of the Tigers affect the global political environment.

Each state has experienced growth in two arenas—exports and investment—which has helped establish a middle class and strong institutions. There are, of course, some drawbacks to domestic growth, for example, a widening wealth gap and traditional industries like agriculture being left behind. Still, the Tiger governments have attempted throughout the growth period to minimize elements of a "dual economy," which can cause wealth gaps. But the growth strategies have had a stronger impact internationally. In a positive way, they are still operating on the level of other "small open economies," which have little effect on the world market. Fluctuations such as an expansionary fiscal policy, which has the ability to raise the world interest rate (thus lowering investment), if carried out by the United States and the People's Republic of China, have little effect if carried out by the Tigers. In other words, they provide all the benefits of small open economies such as investment and trade but none of the drawbacks of larger countries. However, their closer integration with the world economy through interchanging capital outflows has made international capital markets more susceptible to issues in the region. The 1997 Asian financial crisis is a case in point. It began in Thailand but carried over to South Korea and Singapore. More interesting is the "double-edged sword" of the Asian Tigers, elements of their growth that have both positive and negative affects. This comes up in the trade patterns of the Tigers. The patterns are favorable as they focus on exporting goods based on their comparative advantage and importing scarce goods, thus abandoning import substitution industries. Still, the Tigers have been prone to bilateral trade agreements (e.g., Singapore is part of 12 bilateral trade agreements), which can cause trade diversion, a side effect of bilateral trade in which a third country that has the ability to produce goods and export at a better rate is unable to do so because it is left out of the initial trade agreement.

In the past 50 years, the Tigers have shown relentless growth, which has been attributed to economic growth strategies, the rise in capitalism, even luck. Beyond these valid arguments, sociologists also point to elements of traditional Asian culture as the fundamental roots of economic growth. Harmony in a person's life is held in the highest regard in the Confucian belief system that is prevalent in Asian culture. As globalization has led to ups and downs in the world economy, the Tigers have sought to preserve this harmony with its neighbors through trade in "like products" and organizations such as the Association of Southeast Asian Nations.

Emiliano Reyes

See also Economic Development; Global Economic
    Issues; Globalization, Phenomenon of;
    Industrialization

Further Readings

Amsden, A. H. (1989). *Asia's next giant: South Korea
    and late industrialization*. New York: Oxford
    University Press.

Dobson, W., & Chia, S. Y. (Eds.). (2002). *Multinationals
    and East Asian integration*. Ottawa, ON: International
    Development Research Centre; Singapore: Institute of
    Southeast Asian Studies.

Gill, I. S., Kharas, H. J., & Bhattasali, D. (2007). *An East
    Asian renaissance: Ideas for economic growth*.
    Washington, DC: World Bank Publications.

Heller, P. S. (1997). *Aging in the Asian "Tigers":
    Challenges for fiscal policy*. Washington, DC:
    International Monetary Fund.

Jorgenson, D.W., Kuroda, M., & Motohashi, K. (2007).
    *Productivity in Asia: Economic growth and
    competitiveness*. Cheltenham, UK: Edward Elgar.

Kim, E. M. (1998). *The four Asian tigers: Economic
    development and the global political economy*. San
    Diego, CA: Academic Press.

Masuyama, S., Vandenbrink, D., & Chia, S. Y. (2000).
    Restoring East Asia's dynamism. Singapore: Institute
    of Southeast Asian Studies.

Yam, T. K. (Ed.). (2002). *Asian economic recovery: Policy
    options for growth and stability*. Singapore: Singapore
    University Press.

ASSIMILATION

Assimilation is a much contested notion whereby on entering a new country immigrant groups are encouraged, through social and cultural practices and/or political machinations, to adopt the culture, values, and social behaviors of the host nation in order to benefit from full citizenship status. In this view of assimilation, over time, immigrant communities shed the culture that is embedded in the language, values, rituals, laws, and perhaps even religion of their homeland so that there is no discernible cultural difference between them and other members of the host society. This idea is in stark contrast to multiculturalism where ethnic and religious groups maintain strong links to their cultural heritage, and it is indeed understood that these differences contribute to the rich diversity of a successful society.

The most commonly understood form of assimilation is that of cultural assimilation. This involves ethnic groups taking on the cultural signifiers of the host nation. Here minority groups are expected to adapt to the everyday practices of the dominant culture through language and appearance as well as via more significant socioeconomic factors such as absorption into the local cultural and employment community. It is agreed that, in this regard, assimilation becomes easier for the children of immigrants who are invariably socialized and educated in the culture and history of the dominant society from a young age.

Although the assimilation of minority groups into dominant culture has taken place in many societies over the course of history, often over a long period of time, because of the history of immigration in the United States, much of the contemporary literature on assimilation has focused on U.S. community and race relations. In the U.S. model prevalent for the first part of the 20th century, new immigrants were encouraged to "Americanize" in order to achieve social stability and economic success and minimize so-called self-segregation between communities. In terms of social relations, it was thought that assimilation, or cultural homogeneity, would lead to less conflict between groups as they came together under one belief system. In economic terms, it was believed that the more diverse groups were able to integrate into dominant modes of production and consumption, the more chance there was for a stable economy. In this regard, assimilation has not always had negative connotations. It was seen as a way to enhance the social mobility and economic opportunities of new entrants into the country and contribute to the social and economic stability of the host nation.

The idea again gained political prominence in both the United States and the United Kingdom in the 1950s and 1960s when postwar immigration into these countries increased. For example, in the United Kingdom the integration/assimilation debate has raged since shortly after World War II, when Britain sought to increase its working population by encouraging migration from its former colonies. Politicians were keen to foster public support for this process by asserting the idea that migrant communities would simply fit into the dominant sociocultural norms of the United Kingdom. To lessen the effects of intergroup rivalry for jobs and other resources, some politicians believed that the assimilation of the new groups into the dominant culture could curb conflict. However, the idea became problematic for a new generation of scholars who considered that it created a hierarchy of citizenship, whereby those individuals or groups who were able to fully integrate could potentially achieve greater social status. These scholars argued that the more able a group was to *pass* in the dominant culture, the more successful would be their assimilation and the greater the benefits they would achieve. This had obvious consequences for those groups whose ethnicity made it more difficult to fit in. For example, studies have suggested that immigrant communities in the United Kingdom and United States will integrate with more ease if they originate from White European countries rather than from Afro-Caribbean or Indo-Chinese nations.

Despite these debates, how far migrant communities have ever assimilated into the host culture has been disputed by writers across many disciplines—including sociology, race and ethnicity studies, and postcolonial theory—from the 1960s onward. Instead, many writers accept that immigrant communities maintain a significant level of their cultural heritage, and indeed many first-generation immigrants reject the culture of their new country of residence and maintain their previous life in self-sufficient segregated migrant communities. Because of this, governments globally have once again sought to create policies that integrate immigrants into the host nation, for example, Community Cohesion in the United Kingdom. Perhaps this has never been more so than since the attacks on New York and Washington, D.C., in 2001 and the attacks on the London transport system in 2005, which generated new policies designed to limit the cultural freedoms of certain, mainly Islamic, groups. Indeed, the terrorist attacks have led to renewed interest in debates on citizenship across many Western nations, which have instigated legislation that requires incoming immigrants to complete citizenship tests. Referring to global events that have seen the rise in nationalism and fundamentalism in both Western and Islamic states, recent literature suggests that we

may see a new wave of policies that support assimilation on the global agenda.

Siobhan Holohan

See also Acculturation; Americanization; Citizenship; Cultural Hybridity; Diasporas; Identities in Global Society; Immigration; Immigration and Transnationalism; Multiculturalism

Further Readings

Alba, R., & Nee, V. (2003). *Remaking the American dream: Assimilation and contemporary immigration.* Cambridge, MA: Harvard University Press.

Joppke, C., & Morawska, E. (Eds.). (2003). *Toward assimilation and citizenship: Immigrants in liberal nation-states.* New York: Palgrave Macmillan.

Kivisto, P. (2005). *Incorporating diversity: Rethinking assimilation in a multicultural age.* Boulder, CO: Paradigm.

ASSOCIATION OF SOUTHEAST ASIAN NATIONS (ASEAN)

The Association of Southeast Asian Nations (ASEAN) is a regional organization that has emerged as a key component of global governance. ASEAN provides the mechanism through which its 10 member-states collectively respond to a range of regional and transnational problems that they are unable to address individually. Regional governance in Southeast Asia also involves member governments cooperating through ASEAN to position their respective states more advantageously in the global division of labor, in the process shaping the globalization phenomenon through their collective agency. As a result of these region-level governance activities, ASEAN has become an integral part of global governance. As a number of scholars have argued, global governance is not limited to what takes place through multilateral organizations or global regimes. Rather, global governance is also instantiated through "less-than-global" governing arrangements, including regional organizations such as ASEAN. However, the relationship between the regional and the global is rather more complex than the common reading of the former as either a building block or a stumbling block to global governance and globalization. These complexities in the regional-global relationship are clearly illustrated by the ASEAN experience.

History

Formed in 1967 by five countries—Indonesia, Malaysia, the Philippines, Singapore, and Thailand—ASEAN's membership has since increased to ten, with Brunei joining in 1984, Vietnam in 1995, Laos and Myanmar (Burma) in 1997, and Cambodia in 1999. The association was originally established to build trust and confidence among its members, who continue to engage in regular consultations with each other and with their external dialogue partners on a host of shared intraregional and external problems that impinge on regional peace, security, and economic prosperity. Regarded as one of the more enduring regional organizations in the developing world, ASEAN was instrumental in turning a once tense and violence-prone region into a zone of peaceful interstate relations. After 1990 and the end of the Cold War, ASEAN began to address new transnational problems that had begun to challenge states, particularly those grouped under the rubric of nontraditional security, such as maritime piracy, drug trafficking, terrorism, illegal migration, environmental destruction, and, more recently, food and energy security as well as human trafficking. ASEAN also began to pay closer attention to matters of economic cooperation, initiating the ASEAN Free Trade Area (AFTA) in 1992 and the ASEAN Economic Community (AEC) project in 2003. ASEAN has also negotiated bilateral preferential trading arrangements with countries outside the region. In addition to managing regional order in Southeast Asia through ASEAN, member-states have also actively managed the wider East Asian order by establishing broader frameworks for governance centered on ASEAN but extending beyond its membership. Through the ASEAN Regional Forum, the ASEAN Plus Three grouping, and the East Asian Summit, the ASEAN states work together with other states—including regional and global powers such as the United States, China, Japan, India, Russia, and the European Union—in ways that help secure ASEAN's external environment for its members. These sorts of regional governance activities ultimately impinge on global governance arrangements, although the regional-global relationship can take a number of forms.

Regional-Global Relationships

The literature on regionalism views the regional-global relationship in the following ways: (1) Regional governance arrangements are a mere subset of global governance arrangements, reinforcing the latter's norms and rules; and (2) regional arrangements constitute counter-governance arrangements through which states collectively resist the dominant norms and practices of global regimes and organizations. Moving beyond the building block–stumbling block dichotomy is a third view: (3) Regional cooperation arrangements combine elements of conformity and resistance as member-states use the regional level to mediate global developments and pressures in ways that secure the interests of local/national actors, whether firms, local communities, or governments, even if that means departing partially or for a limited period of time from global norms. Which type of global-regional relationship prevails in Southeast Asia depends on domestic sociopolitical and economic interests surrounding different issue areas as well as the prevailing ideational/normative framework, including the structure of regional norms. Although the specific dynamics of each issue area may differ, in general the ASEAN states negotiate between two very broad concerns when designing regional governance: how to avoid possible domination by global governance arrangements and the resultant loss of autonomy to govern domestically, and how to ensure that the ASEAN states are not excluded from that very same dominant (or hegemonic) global system that also offers attractive material gains to those who participate in its processes.

Of these three views of the regional-global relationship, the conventional perspective is that regional arrangements tend to reinforce global ones, with the former constituting building blocks to global order and governance. This has been true to some extent of ASEAN, which has been depicted as a security community, albeit a nascent one, by Amitav Acharya, who argues that the region has become pacified to such an extent that war between member-states to settle conflicts has become unthinkable. Consequently, ASEAN constitutes a zone of peace in the wider global system, effectively contributing to global order. Moreover, ASEAN's more recent efforts in addressing other transnational problems, such as drug trafficking, piracy, and terrorism, have the potential to contribute to global governance.

However, to see the global-regional relationship as simply one of conformity or of the regional as a surrogate of the global is too simplistic. Regional actors often choose to exercise their collective agency and structure regional governance in ways that reflect local political, economic, and sociocultural realities, as well as regional ways of doing things. In ASEAN, the principles of sovereignty and noninterference in the internal affairs of states remain central to the design of regional governance as do the "ASEAN Way" procedural norms that prescribe nonconfrontational bargaining styles, closed door consultations, and the practice of consensus. Although these norms have been relaxed to differing extents in some areas of cooperation, ASEAN member-states continue to uphold them as a set of foundational ASEAN norms against which departures are carefully considered and usually resisted. Member-states value these norms, which have helped them forge unity among a group of very diverse states, thereby enabling these states to exercise what Sarah Eaton and Richard Stubbs have termed *competence power*, or the capacity to shape their external environment to their benefit. By committing ASEAN members to respect the domestic autonomy of other members, these norms create shared expectations that none will be pressured to adopt positions and take actions that may be detrimental to domestic interests, including that of domestic regime security, still a core desideratum of all ASEAN members. Although these norms limit the effectiveness of ASEAN regional governance, they are nonetheless embraced by national governments that value these other political benefits. Thus, although ASEAN's cooperative efforts in various issue areas may rightly be regarded as building blocks of global governance—governance in parts—given broadly similar end goals, the means adopted to deal with the problem at hand can differ from practices in other regions as well as from the dominant rules and practices sanctioned by major powers and multilateral organizations.

Regional Liberalization

Regional liberalization and integration in ASEAN also reflect the links between the global and the national/regional. The decision in 1992 and 2003 to create a regional free trade area (AFTA) and an integrated regional economic community (AEC), respectively, were not attempts by these Southeast Asian states to step up intraregional economic interactions at the expense of interactions with the rest of the world or to close themselves off from the world economy. Instead, they were attempts to enhance the attractiveness of individual Southeast Asian economies to international investors, particularly in competition with China, through collectively presenting a large, regional space in Southeast Asia in which investors would establish regional production plants. *Open regionalism* as it was termed was, consequently, a form of economic regionalism aimed at strategically inserting the ASEAN states into advantageous positions within global production networks. Investment flows into the ASEAN region increased partly as a result of these liberalization and integration projects while Southeast Asian production networks took shape in a number of economic sectors. These outcomes suggest that even weak states are not necessarily without agency in the face of globalization forces, as commonly believed. The ASEAN experience instead shows that small or weak states may be able to manipulate these external forces through collective agency. ASEAN's pursuit of bilateral trading agreements with other states to secure market access and investment in the face of failure at the World Trade Organization to advance global trade liberalization reflects a similar self-help logic.

Despite recognizing the importance of regional economic integration to their economies, ASEAN member-states also subscribe to nationalist aspirations to develop local entrepreneurs and firms, which lead governments to be wary of liberalizing too fast lest fledgling domestic firms are wiped out by foreign firms. ASEAN governments have addressed these concerns in three ways: (1) Regional liberalization is usually designed to be flexible, thus allowing national governments substantial autonomy in deciding what sectors to liberalize and at what speed. (2) The ASEAN governments sometimes opt to accord market access and other privileges to ASEAN national firms (both state-owned and private-owned) before providing them to non-ASEAN firms, intending these temporary privileges to help fledgling ASEAN firms to develop into more competitive firms better able to meet competition from already established global corporations. (3) Bilateral trading arrangements allow negotiating partners to carve out sensitive sectors from liberalization agendas. ASEAN's flexible and developmental approach to regional liberalization, thus, combines elements of openness to the global economy and temporary or partial closure from it, thereby giving individual national governments the space to address domestic economic and sociopolitical priorities while still engaging with the outside world.

Regional Human Rights Governance

A regional governance project that clearly lies at the resistance end of the spectrum is that of regional human rights governance. In the 1990s, the ASEAN states rejected liberal, Western notions of universal human rights in favor of a set of rights considered to be more culturally specific to the Asian context. Although ASEAN states have since become more willing to acknowledge, to varying degrees, the liberal conception of human rights and established the ASEAN Intergovernmental Commission on Human Rights in October 2009, the commission is designed as a consultative body that conforms to the ASEAN norms of sovereignty and noninterference and adopts the organization's preferred nonconfrontational approach to addressing human rights violations. Given the questionable human rights record of many ASEAN states, especially Myanmar (Burma), civil society groups and rights activists have condemned the commission as a toothless tiger and criticized ASEAN for continuing to privilege the security and political interests of states and governing regimes while resisting calls to address issues of rights, political inclusion, and social justice. In recent years, ASEAN has seen conflicts within individual member-states exploding in pockets of unrest and violence, reflecting the failure of national and regional governance to address problems of exclusion and marginalization within member-states. Responding to these challenges will require ASEAN to rethink its state-centric governance agenda and its continued commitment to its sovereignty and noninterference principles.

Helen E. S. Nesadurai

See also Global Governance and World Order; Globalization, Phenomenon of; Regional Governance; Regional Identities; Regionalism; Sovereignty

Further Readings

Acharya, A. (2001). *Constructing a security community in Southeast Asia*. London: Routledge.

Ba, A. D. (2005). Contested spaces: The politics of regional and global governance. In A. D. Ba & M. J. Hoffmann (Eds.), *Contending perspectives on global governance: Coherence, contestation and world order* (pp. 190–212). London: Routledge.

Breslin, S., & Higgott, R. (2000). Studying regions: Learning from the old, constructing the new. *New Political Economy, 5*(3), 333–352.

Caballero-Anthony, M. (2005). *Regional security in Southeast Asia: Beyond the ASEAN Way*. Singapore: Institute of Southeast Asian Studies Press.

Eaton, S., & Stubbs, R. (2006). Is ASEAN powerful? New-realist versus constructivist approaches to power in Southeast Asia. *The Pacific Review, 19*(2), 135–155.

Khong, Y. F., & Nesadurai, H. E. S. (2007). Hanging together, institutional design, and cooperation in Southeast Asia: AFTA and the ARF. In A. Acharya & A. I. Johnstone (Eds.), *Crafting cooperation: Regional international institutions in comparative perspective* (pp. 32–82). New York: Cambridge University Press.

ASSOCIATIONS

Voluntary associations are an important backbone of global civil society and a key element of civil societies in democratic countries. Their role is crucial in democratic societies: The right of peaceful assembly and association is expressly guaranteed in Article 20 of the Universal Declaration of Human Rights. Although scholars still argue over whether it is possible to generalize about the social roles, functions, and effects of associations, given their plurality of forms and variety of purposes, it is clear that in most of the literature, associations are considered to enhance social integration, emphasize freedom, or strengthen democracy. Only recently have researchers started to explore specific conditions regarding some of the negative effects of associations and social networks, such as corruption or social exclusion.

A basic definition of associations is a collection of persons who have joined together for a specific purpose. The existing literature distinguishes between primary associations, such as families and friendships; secondary associations, such as civic groups, sports clubs, or religious associations; and tertiary associations, such as goal-oriented membership groups and professional organizations. Scholarly interest focuses on secondary and tertiary associations, because they involve the voluntary act of joining the association and are a step beyond the more intimate context of family and friends.

The literature on civil society focuses on the variety of democratic effects attributed to associations and on their role in facilitating social cohesion. Robert Putnam emphasizes the role of voluntary organizations as facilitators of face-to-face encounters that sow generalized trust and civic engagement. Recent empirical research also focuses on the socioeconomic payoffs of voluntary association involvement, such as easier access to new jobs, safer neighborhoods, or economic prosperity.

Democratic systems depend on the effects and functions of associations, in particular the representation and deliberation of opinions and interests, the counterbalancing of powers, the cultivation of political skills and the formation of public opinion. The recently emerging literature on multilevel governance claims that democratic systems in which politics has migrated beyond the level of the nation-state and toward an interplay among the local, regional, state, and international levels are more dependent on associations as an alternative form of governance.

The Democratic Effects of Associations

The claim that associations have democratic effects is supported mostly by normative and theoretical arguments. Many of those arguments are based on Alexis de Tocqueville's descriptions of the role of associations for democracy and social life in America. Effects mentioned in the literature include the formative and developmental effects on individuals (increasing their capacity to participate, to make decisions, and to judge autonomously), as well as effects on civic infrastructure and the public sphere (the embodiment of deliberation, provision of voice and public reasoning, and the contribution to political autonomy). Mark E. Warren also mentions the effects of associations on institutional conditions in providing political representation, enabling pressure and resistance, or organizing political processes. More specifically, the contributions of associations have distinct effects in building and sustaining social capital or in enhancing the democratic skills of its members, such as voting, developing democratic knowledge, and articulating political ideas.

Critics, however, question those democratic effects based on three main arguments. The first is that membership and member activities in associations are declining in many countries due to societal changes, the availability of more options in life in general, the economic pressures that result in more double-income families, or a general decrease in the values of collectivism and solidarity. Second, critics argue, associations have lost their pivotal role as schools of democracy, fostering the formation of democratic values and competencies in established democracies. In addition, some scholars argue that the organizational structure of an association does not meet the demands of individuals in today's societies. People want more flexibility and may favor a looser connection to organizations, with time-limited, project-oriented forms of participation (episodic volunteering). Associations and their often-bureaucratic structures do not typically provide sufficient options for active participation to satisfy those demands.

An Economic Theory Perspective on Associations

Voluntary organizations are centralized decision-making structures and differ from for-profit and governmental organizations in that their governance structures (goals, ownership, and decision-making procedures) are adapted to the requirements of collective action, allowing for the pooling of resources and provision of trust goods.

Economic theory defines voluntary associations as nonprofit organizations, based on the fact that they cannot distribute any profit among stakeholders. Other theories emphasize the lack of patrons' control over the association and the importance of multi-stakeholder interests on organizational behavior, or they underscore the importance of consumer control in situations where information asymmetries exist among the various classes of participants. Voluntary associations may also be understood as governance structures with specific coordination mechanisms that allow for alleviation of market failures or government failures. In this perspective, it can be argued that voluntary organizations use hierarchical mechanisms to coordinate their constituencies. In terms of transaction costs, this hierarchy may be more efficient than the market as a coordination mechanism.

Associations, Membership, and Social Capital

Associations are key social institutions for the production of common goods. Whereas public goods need to be universally desirable, for common goods it is sufficient that they be shared or held jointly by members of an association, according to Roger A. Lohmann. Social scientists argue that associations increase the social capital in democratic societies; they strengthen social cohesion and enhance the formation of mutual trust relationships among their members. This claim, among others by Putnam, argues from a socialization perspective that voluntary associations serve as educational institutions in which individuals learn social and democratic behavior ("schools of democracy").

One could also argue that Putnam somewhat overstates the amount of socialization taking place within associations. The primary contribution of voluntary associations might not lie in socializing individual members but in *institutionalizing* social capital. The strength and prevalence of the voluntary sector—the degree to which it permeates society and is perceived as a real infrastructure of collective action—is at least as important as the amount of time people spend meeting face to face. In this respect, passive membership in associations and multiple overlapping memberships, which result in cross-cutting ties between associations

and create networks, are membership-based indicators for the creation of a civic infrastructure. This infrastructure can be described by an institutional approach, which examines the structures, roles, and functions of social institutions and how they influence values and beliefs in society regarding solidarity, trust, reciprocity, or civic virtues.

The Dark Side of Associations

With the renewed public and academic interest in the social role of voluntary associations as producers of social capital, the awareness of potential negative effects of social networks has grown. Researchers studying the "dark side" of social networks and associations point to the fact that some associations promote extremist values and other networks enable further segregation of society by fortifying existing boundaries between socially marginalized groups and the wealthy middle class. Still others explore the relationship between strong social networks and the likelihood of corruption in a given society.

Associations expressing political opinions are in danger of being dominated by extreme voices, notes Morris P. Fiorina, such as religious extremist groups or groups that use violence to further their goals. Some strong social networks might also promote corruption—for example, by providing and enforcing social norms regarding bribery. Researchers, such as S. Seubert and Mary Daly and Hilary Silver, also examine the ways in which voluntary associations may reinforce social exclusion and constitute barriers for access to cultural, economic, and social resources. This may be particularly problematic for women living in poverty, as well as for marginalized youth and migrants, because existing networks rely on internal communication, are self-serving, and tend to fortify existing divides between "members" and "nonmembers" of the social network.

Global Perspectives on Associations

World politics has undergone a radical and often-overlooked transformation since the 1990s, resulting neither from the collapse of the Soviet Union nor from the rising tide of fundamentalism but from the unprecedented growth of nongovernmental organizations (NGOs) around the globe.

NGOs, or civil society organizations, have moved from back to center stage in world politics and are exerting their power and influence in every aspect of international relations and policymaking. NGOs have been a positive force in domestic and international affairs, working to alleviate poverty, protect human rights, preserve the environment, and provide relief worldwide. Few, therefore, have felt the need to take a critical look at the effectiveness and accountability of these organizations. Organizations such as Amnesty International, Greenpeace, and the International Campaign to Ban Landmines have helped bring international recognition to NGOs. Global perspectives on associations include international comparative data on associations, volunteering and membership, and international networks and platforms of national associations as well as those of internationally active associations (international nongovernmental organizations).

Comparative Data on Associations

The Johns Hopkins Comparative Nonprofit Sector Project (2004) has provided comparative data on volunteering and membership in voluntary associations and nonprofit organizations in 36 countries. The research team has found strong empirical evidence of the capacity of nonprofit organizations and voluntary associations to mobilize voluntary work. Helmut K. Anheier and Leister Salamon have proposed three core criteria for comparing the structures of the nonprofit and voluntary sectors: the number of employees in nonprofit organizations, the number of volunteers as a percentage of the workforce, and the percentage of the population holding memberships. The values for all three categories vary greatly across countries, depending on the social welfare system, as well as on traditions of membership and volunteering. On average, however, more than 40% of the nonprofit work is done by volunteers.

Global Networks of National Associations

As the total number of voluntary associations and NGOs is growing worldwide, their political influence on a global level is increasing: In 2009 more than 3,200 NGOs had official consultative status with the UN Economic and Social Council (ECOSOC). A number of international initiatives offer platforms for national volunteer associations, such as the Affinity Group of National Associations or the International Association for Volunteer Effort.

International Associations

International nongovernmental organizations (INGOs) are increasingly embedded in multilevel governance structures and processes. One entry point in international governance procedures and negotiations for NGOs is the Committee on Non-Governmental Organizations, a standing committee of ECOSOC established by the council in 1946, which reports directly to ECOSOC and considers application for consultative status submitted by NGOs.

In 2007–2008, research by Marin Albrow and colleagues indicated a total number of 21,443 INGOs. The UN web portal "Civil Society Network" has mapped 11,788 NGOs all over the globe, providing information about their fields of activity, organization type, and location.

The increase in numbers of NGOs and the growth in revenues for these organizations have enabled them to become a powerful force in global politics. But this proliferation goes along with a crisis of transparency and accountability: According to Albrow and colleagues, NGOs need new mechanisms to overcome the existing lack of transparency and accountability in terms of finances, agenda, and governance necessary to effectively perform their crucial role in a democratic global civil society.

Although INGOs operate around the globe, their headquarters and meeting venues mostly reside in the Northern Hemisphere, characterized by U.S. and western European prevalence. Some of those organizations have become real global players. Friends of the Earth International, for instance, is an international association of environmental organizations in 77 countries, representing 5,000 local activist groups with over 2 million members and supporters around the world (in 2009). Other associations, like the Coalition to Stop the Use of Child Soldiers, coordinate the efforts of their international member organizations, all major INGOs themselves (Amnesty International, Human Rights Watch,

Terre des Hommes International Federation, International Save the Children Alliance, and others). The combined forces addressing a particular topic strengthen the coalition's advocacy role in a global media environment. Other emerging forms are the so-called dot.causes, virtual global networks that use the Internet as the key medium for information exchange, event planning, and communication among their affiliated supporters. Those new emerging organizational forms, along with the rise in numbers, financial assets, and political weight are arguments for further efforts to resolve existing accountability and transparency issues to support international associations as they play their roles as conscience, advocate, watchdog, and service provider in the global civil society.

Andreas Schröer

See also Accountability; Civil Society, Global; Foundations; Social Capital; Social Movements; Transparency

Further Readings

Akuhata-Brown, M. (1999). *Civil society at the millennium.* West Hartford, CT: Kumarian Press.

Albrow, M., Anheier, H. K., Glasius, M., Price, M. E., & Kaldor, M. (Eds.). (2008). *Global civil society 2007/8: Communicative power and democracy.* London: Sage.

Anheier, H. K., & Salamon, L. (2006). The nonprofit sector in a comparative perspective. In W. W. Powell & R. Steinberg (Eds.), *The nonprofit sector: A research handbook* (2nd ed., pp. 89–116). New Haven, CT: Yale University Press.

Banting, K. G., & Brock, K. L. (Eds.). (2001). *The nonprofit sector and government in a new century.* Montreal, QC: McGill-Queen's University Press.

Daly, M., & Silver, H. (2008). Social exclusion and social capital: A comparison and critique. *Theory & Society, 37*(6), 537–566. doi:10.1007/s11186-008-9062-4

Fiorina, M. P. (1999). Extreme voices: A dark side of civic engagement. In T. Skocpol & M. P. Fiorina (Eds.), *Civic engagement in American democracy* (pp. 395–426). Washington, DC: Brookings Institution Press.

Florini, A. M. (2003). *The coming democracy: New rules for running a new world.* Washington, DC: Island Press.

Graeff, P. (2007, August). The dark side of social capital: Why and how do corruption norms facilitate illegal exchanges? Paper presented at the 2007 annual meeting of the American Sociological Association, New York.

Herman, R. D. (2005). *The Jossey-Bass handbook of nonprofit leadership and management* (2nd ed., pp. 4–26). San Francisco: Jossey-Bass.

Lewis, D. (2001). *Management of non-governmental development organizations: An introduction* (2nd ed.). Cornwall, UK: Routledge.

Lohmann, R. A. (1992). *The commons: New perspectives on nonprofit organizations and voluntary action.* San Francisco: Jossey-Bass.

McCarthy, K. D., Hodgkinson, V. A., & Sumariwalla, R. D. (1992). *The nonprofit sector in the global community: Voices from many nations.* San Francisco: Jossey-Bass.

Morgan, D. F., Green, R., Shinn, C. W., & Robinson, K. S. (2008). *Foundations of public service.* Armonk, NY: Sharpe.

Putnam, R. (2000). *Bowling alone: Collapse and revival of American community.* New York: Simon & Schuster.

Putnam, R., Leonardi, R., & Nanetti, R. (1993). *Making democracy work: Civic traditions in modern Italy.* Princeton, NJ: Princeton University Press.

Seubert, S. (2007). In schlechter Gesellschaft. Das Problem unzivilen Sozialkapitals [In bad company. The problem of uncivil social capital]. *Neue Soziale Bewegungen, 20*(4), 87–92.

Warren, M. E. (2001). *Democracy and association.* Princeton, NJ: Princeton University Press.

ASYLUM

The Universal Declaration of Human Rights, proclaimed by the General Assembly of the United Nations in 1948, states that everyone has the right to seek and enjoy asylum from persecution. This starting point leads to several important observations. The first is that the notion of asylum is linked to the development of international human rights, which followed World War II. It is also crucial that even in this original text, asylum is qualified. The right is limited to asylum "from persecution," a qualifier that politicizes the term. The Universal Declaration also states that asylum is not available to people fleeing legitimate prosecution or those who have acted against the principles and purposes of the United Nations. Finally, the right is to *seek* asylum and not to be *granted* asylum. From these starting points, international refugee law has developed.

The concepts of "refugee" and "asylum" are inextricably linked. Refugees are people to whom asylum is granted. Asylum is the protection granted to refugees. There have historically been some differences between countries regarding qualifications for this status, but these differences have now largely disappeared in favor of a widely respected international commitment.

Since 1951, there has been an international agreement regarding who qualifies as a refugee. A refugee is someone who is outside his or her country of origin and is at risk of being persecuted if he or she returns. The persecution risk must be at least partially for reasons of race, religion, nationality, political opinion, or group membership. The refugee definition, which sets out these key ideas, is the centerpiece of the agreement known as the Refugee Convention. Its formal name is the Convention Relating to the Status of Refugees. This is now one of the most widely ratified treaties in the world: by October 2008, 144 countries were party to this agreement.

When people leave their own country and ask another country to protect them as refugees, they are said to be seeking asylum. In some places, those seeking this kind of protection are called refugee claimants; in others, they are called asylum seekers. The terms are interchangeable in a legal sense, although they do tell us something about the national origins of those who use them. As the international definition of *refugee* is now widely accepted, there are no remaining differences between *refugee claimants* and *asylum seekers*. The vast majority of nations in the world use the refugee definition to determine who is entitled to asylum. There is, however, nothing preventing any nation from granting asylum on any other basis.

The main benefit of refugee status is protection against *non-refoulement*. This means that refugees cannot be returned to a place where they are at risk of being persecuted. In most cases, this is their home. This commitment means that refugees have a right to remain in the country that is protecting them, because is it virtually impossible to send them on to a place where they are neither citizens nor residents. In addition to this protection, the Refugee Convention establishes the human rights to which all refugees are entitled. These include, among others, freedom from discrimination, a right to work, access to education, and access to the courts. In general, refugees are not to be treated more harshly than citizens or than foreign nationals who have status under immigration laws. Refugees also must not be punished for entering any country illegally.

Asylum Claims

In 2007, just under 650,000 asylum claims were made around the world. This number is broadly similar to the annual total over the past decade. Most claims are made to governments; about 15% are made to the United Nations High Commissioner for Refugees (UNHCR), the UN Refugee Agency. Fewer than half of all asylum seekers are eventually recognized as refugees. In 2007, 209,000 people were found to be refugees after having made a claim for this status. Because refugee determination takes some time, these people are not the same as those who made claims in 2007, but the numbers can be compared in an approximate way.

It is extraordinarily difficult to estimate an acceptance rate for asylum claims. The UNHCR provides a compelling illustration of how rates vary (*2007 Global Trends*, p. 17). In comparing claims by Iraqis determined in 2007 in eight European countries, acceptance rates ranged from zero to 63%. Greece accepted none of approximately 4,000 claims; the United Kingdom accepted about 15% of 1,500 claims; Germany accepted 63% of almost 3,000 claims; and Sweden considered almost 10,000 claims and granted a status other than refugee status to 98%.

With more than 15 million refugees worldwide in 2007, the number of claims for asylum is low. The main reason for this is that, to make a claim for refugee status, a person must arrive in a country where such a claim will be heard. As travel is expensive and asylum claims are generally unwelcome, it is likely the case that many people who would like to make refugee claims in prosperous Western states are unable to do so because they cannot reach these states.

Over the past two decades, Western governments have introduced or strengthened a series of policies that make it harder to claim refugee status or asylum. These policies are to deter people from traveling in the first place, even those seeking refugee protection and those who, in the past, could have claimed asylum at the border and sought passage to a safe third country. They include visa requirements for travel by nationals of states that are producing high numbers of refugees and carrier sanctions imposed on corporations that transport individuals without proper travel documents. These policies began to develop in the mid-1980s after sharp increases worldwide in the number of people seeking asylum. In 2001, Australia implemented the most extreme policy of this nature, declaring parts of its sovereign territory to be "excised" from its territory for the purpose of refugee applications.

The Refugee Convention setting out the international rules regarding refugee status does not discuss any of these measures. What the Refugee Convention does require is that if a person reaches the state's sovereignty territory and makes a claim for refugee status, that claim must be heard and determined. This obligation means that acting to deter arrivals is a state's best way of controlling the number of claims it must determine. International lawyers now agree that someone who arrives at the border and asks to make a refugee claim must be admitted and allowed to remain until the claim is heard, even though the Refugee Convention does not contain an explicit right of entry.

Controversies

Asylum is a politically contentious issue in most Western states at this point in time. There are many reasons for this—some shared and some nationally idiosyncratic. At least two factors are common causes of contention in prosperous Western countries. The first of these is that because of the requirements of the Refugee Convention, asylum seekers can be deterred but not stopped altogether. The second is that asylum and migration flows are intertwined. This intertwining is increasingly important and deserves some further attention.

As recently as the outset of the 20th century, wanting to move in order to work hard and better one's life chances was acceptable. Over the past 100 years, however, migration has become a minutely regulated area of state control. Categories of acceptable migration are strictly limited. Most people who are destitute, or even simply moderately educated and poor, are not eligible. Unskilled workers are required worldwide as an economic ingredient, but fostering their migration is not generally politically palatable, at least not on a permanent basis.

The possibility of seeking asylum is the one exception to this tight global migration net. Whereas being poor and unskilled is not a requirement for refugee status, it is also not a bar to obtaining this status. The requirement that asylum claims must be taken seriously and adjudicated individually means that seeking asylum provides a legitimate means to enter another country and ensures at least some period of time that one can remain there. As other means for legitimate migration become harder and harder to access, states create incentives for people to seek asylum who otherwise would not. In current asylum flows, therefore, we would expect to find a certain number of people who think they are refugees and will be found to be refugees, a certain number of people who think they are refugees but will be found not to be, and a certain number of people who are pretty sure they are not refugees but who believe that life in a prosperous Western country will be good for them. The tighter the global migration net becomes, the more this latter category is likely to grow.

It is often difficult for people to know in advance if they are eligible for refugee status because refugee law is complicated. Given the number of asylum claims each year, the Refugee Convention is the most frequently interpreted international legal text in the world. A risk of persecution is the core concept in the refugee definition. Persecution is not defined in the law. It has been interpreted by judges over time to mean serious harm in breach of an individual's basic human rights. A harm is more likely to be seen as persecution if it is systemic or discriminatory. A decision maker has to look to the future and assess whether a person is likely to face persecution if he or she returns to his or her home. It is not necessary to prove that one has been persecuted in the past.

In addition, the refugee definition provides that the risked persecution must be for a particular reason. The acceptable reasons are persecution for one's race, religion, nationality, membership in a particular social group, or political opinion. The latter two categories have led to some important interpretation issues. For example, is a woman's decision to leave her husband in a traditional patriarchal society an expression of political opinion? Are transsexuals a particular social group? Over time, these questions have been answered in the affirmative. They provide examples of how one legal text that has not changed can address new situations.

Refugee protection is a surrogate protection provided by the international community when a country fails to protect adequately its citizens' basic human rights. For this reason, decision makers are also required to consider whether people seeking asylum can be adequately protected at home. People will be turned down for asylum if the decision maker finds that they can move to another region of their home country and live safely or that they can ensure their safety by seeking police protection.

In most countries, refugee determination decisions are made by bureaucrats. There is usually a way for the decision to be appealed, often to an administrative tribunal. As these decisions are made by the executive branch, they can be judicially reviewed in the courts. This review is very limited in comparison to an appeal. Canada is an exception to this pattern: In Canada, the initial decision is made by a tribunal, and there is no possibility for an appeal.

People who seek asylum but are found not to be refugees are usually asked to leave and return home. Some people do this voluntarily. Some do this with the government's assistance, for example, in paying for their airfare. Some refuse to return home and are deported. Some refuse to leave and are eventually granted some other status, or they remain indefinitely without permission.

Finding ways to ensure that failed asylum seekers will leave the country has become a major concern for most Western countries. Deportation is difficult and expensive. Liberal democracies have found it politically impossible to employ the draconian measures required to run an effective deportation system. The inability to ensure departures is a key feature of the contemporary angst about asylum and a key motivator behind the measures aiming to ensure that those seeking refugee status are unable to reach Western countries.

Catherine Dauvergne

See also Borders; Human Rights, International; Humanitarianism; Immigration; Immigration and Transnationalism; Inequality, Global; Refugees; Security; Undocumented Persons

Further Readings

United Nations High Commissioner for Refugees (UNHCR). (2007, December). *Statistical yearbook 2006: Trends in displacement, protection and solutions.* Retrieved August 6, 2011, from http://www.unhcr.org/cgi-bin/texis/vtx/home/opendocPDFViewer.html?docid=478ce2e62&query=statistical

United Nations High Commissioner for Refugees (UNHCR). (2008, June). *2007 Global trends: Refugees, asylum-seekers, returnees, internally displaced and stateless persons.* Retrieved August 6, 2011, from http://www.unhcr.org/cgi-bin/texis/vtx/home/opendocPDFViewer.html?docid=4852366f2&query=2007

United Nations High Commissioner for Refugees (UNHCR). (2008, October). *Asylum levels and trends in industrialized countries.* Retrieved September 22, 2011, from http://www.unhcr.org/49c796572.html

Website

United Nations High Commissioner for Refugees: www.unhcr.org

AUTHORITARIANISM

See Global Religions, Beliefs, and Ideologies

AWQAF

See Waqfs

B

BABY BOOMERS

Although technically a U.S. phenomenon, the Baby Boomer generation serves as a model of how societies around the world can handle large increases in the population across their life span—from employment to housing to health and leisure behavior. Baby Boomers, born between the years 1946 and 1964, and often subdivided into leading-edge (1946–1955) and trailing-edge (1956–1964) boomers, comprise more than one quarter of the U.S. population, according to the website GenerationBoomer. This age cohort is known for its strong generational identity, and marketing specialists often use Boomers as a barometer for tracking social, political, and economic trends, because Boomers account for 40% of all consumer spending, and the generation controls roughly 70% of the nation's assets.

Workforce and Employment Issues

Aging Boomers have changed the way that aging workers are treated and viewed in the workplace. Characterized as "reliable, compassionate, and honest" by the website Baby Boomer Care, Boomers have forced many companies to rethink policies on work scheduling, retention, and recruitment; these range from flexibility in hours to job sharing, postretirement reemployment, and consulting. According to Eve Tahmincioglu, an

estimated 69% of Boomers will spend their retirement years at work, delaying collecting Social Security or serving as mentors to new employees, who may have to take on roles they might previously have had an opportunity to grow into over a decade or more, potentially compromising productivity, quality, or safety.

Boomers are also seen as essential to successful transfer of leadership and authority to subsequent generations (commonly referred to as GenXers and Millennials) and, through interaction with newer employees, are learning new styles of communication, use of social media, how to work as a team, and how to use a wide range of technology. Casey Hawley found that Boomers provide benefits to many organizations and their coworkers because of their ability to take a long-term view, to overcome short-term downturns, to suppress negativity, to manage interoffice politics, and to negotiate better than their junior colleagues. Whereas newer generations of employees may demonstrate teamwork and social media savvy, Boomers model accountability and personal responsibility.

For those Boomers who wish to remain employed, career change is a viable option, as many spent more or part of their work life doing jobs that helped them survive as opposed to thrive. Among top employment opportunities are management analysts, postsecondary educators, logisticians, general and operations managers, and other medical, therapeutic, and health services professionals. Emerging employment areas include environmental technologies (green technologies) and energy industries as well as applications of environmental sustainability policies in many areas, such as housing.

Housing

One example of an area that is influenced by trends among Baby Boomers is housing. Dowell Myers and Sungho Ryu trace the impact of this generation on the housing market, where the economic recession during the early years of the new millennium demonstrated the impact that 78 million Boomers had on the price of homes (85% of the available inventory is existing homes) after dominating the real estate market for 30 years. Implications of downsizing, relocation, transportation, and myriad issues concern planners, real estate professionals, and providers of support services for aging Boomers.

Whereas many Boomers express a desire to "age in place," some opt for dual residences, spending a portion of the year in each. Kevin E. McHugh and Robert C. Mings (1996), for example, describe the term *snowbirds*, those who leave colder climates during winter months and relocate to warmer ones in the winter, as a cycle of separation, experience, and return that allows many older adults to claim multiple places as home, thereby making "the transition from vacationers, to tourists, to members of several communities" (p. 535). Both domestic and international locales are increasingly evident among this mobile group of older adults.

Additional factors that need to be considered in housing options for Boomers include reserving space for "boomerang" children (adult children who return to live with their parents), raising grandchildren, or caring for aging parents who may depend on living with Boomers; these factors may cause many Boomers to hold onto a larger home instead of downsizing. Proximity to health services, entertainment, parks and recreation facilities, education, and entertainment, along with affordable transportation options, presents important decision criteria for selecting housing as Boomers age.

Health and Leisure Behavior

According to Ethan Lyon (2010), "Boomers are seated at the very top of the world's largest, most powerful companies, and as established career professionals, they have tremendous buying power" (p. 1). Seventy-eight million Baby Boomers begin turning 65 in 2011, an average of 3 to 4 million each year, with an uncertain impact on financial institutions, investments, and social services, even though a recent study by Lisa A. Keister and Natalia Deeb-Sossa (2001) predicted that "baby boomers had, and will continue to have, considerably more wealth than their parents did at all stages of the life cycle" (p. 578). As Boomers draw on accrued savings and pension plans, they are spending money, and those industries benefiting include leisure, health care, and financial services. Mature adults increasingly seek to reinvest and wisely manage existing resources, often shifting from growth-oriented portfolios to investments that yield monthly incomes. Travel companies have benefited from Boomers' desire for affordable travel and new experiences. Hybrids that combine health and leisure outcomes are evidenced in emerging enterprises such as medical tourism, which offers individuals choices and options for higher quality and lower cost care in a variety of international destinations around the world. Suzanne Macguire, for example, describes the success of medical tourism in India and identifies significant benefits to the national economy. Many Baby Boomers also combine social justice, spiritual exploration, and international environmental/sustainability concerns with leisure travel—a complex practice that presents opportunities and challenges for the international community.

Global Implications

The manner in which Baby Boomers deal with aging holds global implications for social, economic, and political institutions, whether in the public or the private sector. Tracking the consumer behaviors of millions of Baby Boomers can identify useful trends throughout the international community, for example, the purchase of homes and health care outside the country of residence (Selingo, 2008). According to Michael J. Weiss, Boomers are less likely to leave inheritances to the next generation but are, instead, paying down debt and saving for possible medical emergencies. Patterns emerging from these analyses may be useful to developing nations as they attempt to predict and manage resources across the life span of large and increasingly healthy populations that will inevitably access international media and social networks, expect higher quality health care services, and insist on improved and sustainable standards of living.

Veda E. Ward

See also Aging Societies; Consumerism; Culture, Notions of; Family; Feminism; Peace Activism; Retirement Systems; Welfare State

Further Readings

Baby Boomer Care. (2007). *Baby boomers in the workforce.* Retrieved from http://babyboomercaretaker.com/baby-boomer/Baby-boomers-in-the-workforce.html

Graves, J. (2010). *Aging baby boomers.* Retrieved from http://www.wikinvest.com/concept/Aging_Baby_Boomers

Hawley, C. (2009). *Managing the older employee.* Avon, MA: Adams Business.

Keister, L. A., & Deeb-Sossa, N. (2001, May). Are baby boomers richer than their parents? Intergenerational patterns of wealth ownership in the United States. *Journal of Marriage and Family, 63,* 569–579.

Lyon, E. (2010, March 2). *Examining baby boomers: Stats, demographics, segments, predictions.* Retrieved from http://sparxoo.com/2010/03/02/examining-baby-boomers-stats-demographics-segments-pr

Macguire, S. (2008, October 18). *"Cure with care": The motto of Indian medical tourism.* Retrieved April 13, 2011, from http://ezinearticles.com/?Cure-With-Care-The-Motto-of-Indian-Medical-Tourism&id=331621

McHugh, K. E., & Mings, R. C. (1996). The circle of migration: Attachment to place in aging. *Annals of the Association of American Geographers, 86,* 530–550.

Myers, D., & Ryu, S. (2008). Aging baby boomers and the generational housing bubble. *Journal of the American Planning Association, 74,* 17–33.

Selingo, J. (2008, April 21). If only the dollar were stronger. *New York Times,* section SPG, p. 4.

Tahmincioglu, E. (2007). *Baby boomers will spend golden years at work.* Retrieved from http://www.msnbc.msn.com/id/20075038/ns/business-future_of_business

Weiss, M. J. (2003, May). Great expectations. *American Demographics,* pp. 26–35.

Website

GenerationBoomer: www.Generation4Boomers.com

BAHA'I

From its origins in the Middle East in the 1850s and 1860s, the Baha'i Faith has become transformed into a small-scale world religion with perhaps 5 million followers worldwide, drawn from almost every cultural and religious background and found in virtually every country. The Baha'i prophet-founder, Bahá'u'lláh (1817–1892), clearly saw his mission and message in global terms. Claiming to be the latest in the succession of divine messengers who had inspired the world's religions, he presented himself as the world redeemer for the present age who had come to bring God's message to the peoples of all the world and of all religions, providing them with the social and religious teachings for an approaching era of world peace and unity. Subsequent elaboration of these themes was provided by Bahá'u'lláh's eldest son and successor as leader, 'Abdu'l-Bahá (1844–1921).

For the Baha'i leaders, the modern world faced a dual crisis. Their own immediate world of the Middle East was mired in religious prejudice and ignorance and urgently needed enlightenment and modernization—'Abdu'l-Bahá, in particular, urged the leaders of his native Iran to embrace a more democratic form of government and promote education and justice. At the same time, the much-vaunted West was eroded by the poison of materialism and threatened by international hatreds that would surely lead to war and widespread destruction. What was needed, he said, was a dual reformation: first, a spiritual renewal at the individual and collective level which would reinvigorate moral life, bring people closer to God, and free them from superstition and the blind following of fanatical religious leaders, and, second, a far-reaching social transformation that would create the institutions and commitment to promote international harmony and cooperation; develop education and science; end the injustices of class and gender inequality; abolish racism; and create accountable and corruption-free political institutions. The problems that confronted humanity were so severe that, unless action was rapidly taken, the world's people were surely destined to experience severe and potentially catastrophic problems. Many of the Baha'i teachings relate to these global concerns and to the concept of a new age of justice and peace. Thus, Baha'i beliefs include the following: The whole of humanity is but a single family; unity should be promoted by the choosing and promotion of a single world auxiliary language; global regulation of those matters of human conduct that are of international concern (trade, environment, natural resources, conflict, crime, drugs and the like) is necessary; there must eventually be some form of world court and superstate coexisting with national governments; the extremes of wealth and poverty must be ended; and there must be fundamental gender equality. Other Baha'i teachings address the basic elements of moral and spiritual life: daily prayer and the bringing of oneself to account before God; fasting; concern for the poor; freedom from prejudice toward others; striving to live a better life, characterized by such virtues as truthfulness, trustworthiness, and chastity. Others again are theological: that God is beyond human understanding and, hence, that a lot of religious disputation results from the misguided belief that one's own limited view is the only right one; that the founders of the major religions are all "manifestations" of one God, directed to lead humanity forward toward a better world; and that it is essential for religion to be in harmony with science. There are also teachings concerning the organization of the Baha'i community itself, particularly the establishment of locally and nationally elected administrative councils ("spiritual assemblies"); the importance of resolving all issues through a process of open and honest consultation; and the role of loyalty to the central authority of the Baha'i Faith (since 1963, the Universal House of Justice) as a means of uniting a very diverse global Baha'i community.

Another fundamental concern is with "teaching the Faith"—the promotion of lay mission (the Baha'i Faith has no clergy). Indeed, a mission of global expansion was implicit in Baha'i teachings from the beginning. Exiled from Iran, Bahá'u'lláh first directed his message to the survivors of the earlier Babi movement of the 1840s, which had been suppressed by the Iranian authorities after a series of bloody confrontations. (Its founder, the Báb [1819–1850], had claimed to be the promised Mahdi, an implicit challenge to all existing religious and secular authority.) Writing from various places of exile within the Ottoman Empire (Iraq, Rumelia, and finally Akka in Ottoman Syria—close by the modern city of Haifa, which eventually became the Baha'is' chief headquarters), he also sent a series of proclamatory letters to contemporary world leaders and encouraged his followers to begin a cautious missionary outreach to the wider world. During his lifetime, however, the Baha'is remained confined to the Middle East and adjacent areas (notably British India and Russian Turkestan) where there were expatriate Iranians. Even so, the Baha'i community was already becoming more diverse, the original Babi core being joined by a growing number of Iranian Muslims, Jews, and Zoroastrians, as well as small numbers of Ottomans and Egyptians—Arabs, Turks, and Kurds, including Levantine Christians as well as Sunni Muslims.

A second stage of Baha'i expansion began in the 1890s with the initiation of a missionary project in North America. This was greatly encouraged by 'Abdu'l-Bahá—initially still an Ottoman prisoner, but later able to visit Europe and North America, inspiring the Western Baha'is and presciently warning of the approaching world war. The results of these efforts were very encouraging, with several thousand Americans and a few hundred Europeans becoming Baha'is or Baha'i sympathizers over the next few decades. Iranians continued to constitute the majority of the world's Baha'is, but the new Western Baha'is were intensely active and unhindered by the social constraints and repression imposed on their Iranian coreligionists. Able to travel the world, give public talks, and publish literature, the Westerners were able to spearhead the transformation of the Baha'i Faith into a genuinely global movement. This expanded distribution was particularly marked during the period of leadership of 'Abdu'l-Bahá's grandson, Shoghi Effendi (1897–1957) from 1922 on. Thus, by 1925, there was already a recorded Baha'i presence in 27 countries and colonial territories, but by 1930 this number had increased to 42, by 1939 to 64, and by 1949 to 90 (Smith, 2010). Shoghi Effendi also oversaw the extension of a system of local and national elected Baha'i councils by which the Baha'is continue to administer their affairs and the development of systematic expansion plans.

A third stage of expansion began in the late 1950s, with an increasing number of large-scale conversions in various parts of the world, mostly from among Third World villagers in countries as diverse as Bolivia, Uganda, and India. Growth in some of these areas was dramatic, representing a major shift in Baha'i demographics—from perhaps a little over 200,000 Baha'is worldwide in the early 1950s, most of them in Iran, to 4.5 million by 1988, most of them (87%) in South and Southeast Asia, Africa, and Latin America and the Caribbean (Smith & Momen, 1989). A series of global expansion plans has also ensured that there are now Baha'is in every country in the world (apart from the Vatican City and perhaps North Korea), so that the Baha'i Faith has become the second most widely spread religion in the world after Christianity. Overall numbers have further increased since the 1980s, but the predominance of the Third World Baha'is has continued, with the Middle Eastern Baha'is a significant minority and the Western Baha'is a small but intensely active element in the global Baha'i community. The severe repression of the Iranian Baha'is since the Islamic Revolutionary government took power in 1979 (with over 200 killings to date and widespread denial of civil rights) has forced the Baha'is there to dissolve their administrative institutions and suspend many communal activities.

Global expansion has encouraged and enabled the Baha'is to adopt a more active and visible international profile in the realization of their social objectives. Key events have included the establishment of a permanent office to represent the Baha'i International Community at the United Nations in New York in 1967; of a number of Baha'i radio stations in Latin America commencing in 1977; of an Office of Social and Economic Development at the Baha'i World Centre in Haifa in 1983; and of international Baha'i Offices of the Environment and for the Advancement of Women in 1989 and 1992, respectively. As a consequence of these and a large number of local and national Baha'i initiatives, Baha'i social teachings and practice have received increasing attention from academics, nongovernmental organizations, UN agencies, and some governments, and Baha'i work in such areas as education, community building, and the addressing of problems of social division and discrimination has become increasingly recognized.

Physical embodiments of Baha'i expansion are relatively few as the Baha'is have focused more on practical community needs than on specialized buildings. Nevertheless, in addition to the well-known Baha'i shrines and gardens in the Haifa-Akka area, there are now Baha'i temples ("Houses of Worship") at Wilmette, Illinois; Kampala, Uganda; Sydney, Australia; Frankfurt, Germany; Panama City, Panama; Apia, Samoa; New Delhi, India; and shortly to begin construction, Santiago, Chile. There are also a number of Baha'i schools in various countries that are open to children of any religious background. More intangibly, the Baha'is have sought to foster a genuinely global sense of community, evidenced in the polyglot and multiethnic gatherings at their international conventions and congresses.

Peter Smith

See also Communities, Transnational; Cultural Hybridity; Diasporas; Identities in Global Society; Immigration and Transnationalism; Multiculturalism; Religious Identities; Religious Movements, New and Syncretic; World Cultures; World Religions, Concept of

Further Readings

Momen, M. (2006). *Baha'u'llah: A short biography.* Oxford, UK: Oneworld.

Momen, W., & Momen, M. (2006). *Understanding the Baha'i Faith.* Edinburgh, UK: Dunedin Academic Press.

Smith, P. (2008). The global distribution of the Baha'is in the 1920s. *Baha'i Studies Review, 14,* 107–120.

Smith, P. (2008). *An introduction to the Baha'i Faith.* New York: Cambridge University Press.

Smith, P. (2009). The global distribution of the Baha'is in the 1930s. *Baha'i Studies Review, 15,* 115–132.

Smith, P. (2010). The global distribution of the Baha'is in the 1940s. *Baha'i Studies Review, 16,* 135–154.

Smith, P., & Momen, M. (1989). The Baha'i Faith 1957–1988: A survey of contemporary developments. *Religion, 19,* 63–91.

Warburg, M. (2006). *Citizens of the world: A history and sociology of the Baha'is from a globalization perspective.* Leiden, Netherlands: Brill.

Warburg, M., Hvithamer, A., & Warmind, M. (Eds.). (2005). *Baha'i and globalisation.* Aarhus, Denmark: Aarhus University Press.

Websites

The Bahá'í Faith: The International Website of the Bahá'ís of the World: www.bahai.org

Bahá'í World News Service: bahaiworldnews.org

One Country: The Online Newsletter of the Bahá'í International Community: onecountry.org

BANKING, OFFSHORE

Offshore banking centers are located in places that are outside the customer's home country. Offshore banking is relevant to the field of global studies because of the global distribution and international reach of these financial centers and because of its impact on the global economy.

In the film *Bourne Identity*, Jason Bourne, an amnesiac assassin, wonders what kind of person keeps money, six passports, and a gun in a safe deposit box in a bank in Zurich. *The Economist* magazine points out that in the popular imagination, as well as in Hollywood movies, the answer is obvious: customers of Swiss banks do. Although not literally "offshore," Swiss banks provide a safe haven free from the regulations of a depositor's home country.

All the requirements of the global financial system cannot be met by conventional banking services. The need for secrecy and the desire for shelter from taxation and regulation have led to the proliferation of offshore banking centers. These centers can also be attractive because of convenient time zone differences, sophisticated telecommunications networks, local skilled workers, and politically stable and supportive governments. Offshore banking provides discreet markets where currencies, bonds, loans, and other financial instruments can be transacted outside the attention of regulating authorities or competitors. Offshore banks offer low or no tax settings for savings, and some can be havens for both tax evasion of undeclared income and money laundering.

The term *offshore banking* initially applied to the Channel Islands because these islands were offshore from the United Kingdom. Although many offshore banking centers subsequently opened on islands (such as the Cayman Islands and Bermuda), not all did; some offshore banks are located in microstates (like Liechtenstein or Andorra), in small countries (such as Switzerland or Luxembourg), or even within a city like New York. As a major financial center, New York benefited in the early 1980s when the Federal Reserve authorized U.S. banks to establish international banking facilities in an effort to attract some of the Eurocurrency market to the United States. Eurocurrency is any currency that is deposited in a bank outside the country in which that currency is the unit of account.

Globally, it is possible to identify five main specialized offshore banking center nodes:

1. The Caribbean and surrounding area: including the Cayman Islands, the Bahamas, the British Virgin Islands, Antigua, and Aruba, with Bermuda to the north and Panama to the south

2. Europe: including the Channel Islands, the Isle of Man, Switzerland, Austria, Luxembourg, Monaco, Liechtenstein, Andorra, San Marino, and Cyprus

3. Southwest Asia (the Middle East): including Bahrain and Lebanon

4. East and Southeast Asia: including Hong Kong, Macau, Singapore, and Labuan

5. South Pacific: including Nauru, Vanuatu, and the Cook Islands

A variety of factors have facilitated the globalization of financial services in general and of offshore banking in particular. A crucial factor has been the advances in information and telecommunications technologies, allowing an incredible increase in the digital flow of global capital, that have significantly reduced the transaction and transmission costs associated with moving money internationally. Another has been the institutionalization of savings in richer countries (through pension funds and the like) that has established a large pool of capital managed by professional investors with few geographical allegiances. Another has been the trend toward "disintermediation" whereby borrowers (especially transnational corporations) raise capital and make investments without going through the traditional, intermediary channels of conventional financial institutions. Yet another, and probably more important, factor has been the deregulation of financial markets that occurred in many richer countries beginning in the 1980s (until the global financial crisis beginning in 2007).

As much as one half of the world's business transactions are estimated to flow through offshore banks. Lucy Komisar reports that 26% of the world's wealth, including 31% of the net profits of U.S. transnational corporations, is found in offshore banks despite the fact that only 1.2% of the world's population lives in these locations. The U.S. Internal Revenue Service (IRS) admits that it is difficult to quantify the amount of offshore assets but has estimated that some $5 trillion in assets worldwide may be held in offshore banks. With transfers from the United States representing a huge share of this wealth, estimates of the annual revenue loss to the IRS range from $700 to $100 billion.

Since the beginning of the recent global financial crisis and the budgetary crises of many governments worldwide, there have been increasing efforts internationally to crack down on offshore tax evasion. Even Switzerland has agreed to loosen its strict bank secrecy rules and to cooperate more in preventing tax evasion in a desperate effort to deflect the global crackdown on tax havens that is upsetting the offshore banking industry. The concern of offshore banks like those in Switzerland is that their reputation, which is crucial for gaining and keeping customers, may become tarnished, causing an outflow of customers and funds. *The Economist* article referred to at the beginning of this entry reported on the Swiss bank UBS and its run-ins with the IRS over demands to divulge the names of alleged tax dodgers and money launderers. *The Economist* article concluded wryly that, like other Swiss banks, UBS is not eager to have assassins as customers, but that amnesiacs are a different matter.

Linda McCarthy

See also Banks; Corporations, Transnational; Finance, Financial Systems; Globalization, Phenomenon of; Tax Havens

Further Readings

Bourne to survive: Offshore private banking. (2009, August 6). *The Economist.*

Corkill Cobb, S. (1998). Global finance and the growth of offshore financial centers: The Manx experience. *Geoforum, 29,* 7–21.

Knox, P. L., Agnew, J., & McCarthy, L. (2008). Services: Going global? In *The geography of the world economy* (5th ed., pp. 317–356). London: Hodder Arnold.

Komisar, L. (2003, Spring). Offshore banking: The secret threat to America. *Dissent Magazine,* 45–51.

Roussakis, E. N. (1999). Offshore banking at the close of the twentieth century. *Revista Latinoamericana de Administración, 22,* 99–112.

BANKS

Banks are a central component of local, national, and international financial industries, but the modern banking industry has changed due to the emergence of new technology, global economies, deregulation, and mergers. In addition to central banks, most nations also have full-service national, regional, and community commercial banks and specialized financial institutions such as savings and loans, trusts, mortgage bankers, and credit unions. Development banks and international banks such as the World Bank and International Monetary Fund have emerged as key sources of aid to developing countries. Banking regulation occurs mainly at the national level.

History

The early history of modern banking had its origins in international trading. The first Western banks appeared in Italy during the 14th century and mainly facilitated money exchanges and provided small loans to prevent the violation of Catholic Church prohibitions against usury, defined as lending money at interest. Other early financial centers were located in commercial trading centers in countries such as Switzerland, France, Belgium, and Holland. By the 18th century, banks had begun lending at interest as well as providing other new services, including savings accounts, the use of collateral to back loans, and the issuance of paper currencies. Banks appeared in the United States at the end of the 18th century and in Japan by the end of the 19th century.

Central banks have a history dating back to the late 17th century in Europe. Central banks are sponsored by national governments and can be either state or privately owned. Early functions of central banks included the financial support of national government spending, the standardization of national financial systems, the stabilization of currency value and exchange rates, and employment promotion. Central banks received government favor in return, and many were monopolies. One central debate surrounding central banks has been whether or not they should operate independently of national governments. Central banks later began to serve as depository institutions and lenders of last resort for other types of banks, which can help avoid national and global economic crises. They also help establish and oversee financial systems and monetary policies.

Central banks' role in the establishment of monetary policies had both domestic and international impacts. For example, these banks play a role in determining international currency exchange rate policies, help determine market investors' actions through their economic forecasts, and can aid in times of financial crisis through the raising or lowering of interest rates. Many developed countries that wish to aid developing countries see central banks as playing a key role in their economic development through their role in maintaining low inflation rates and stable currency values.

Changes in the Banking Industry

The late 20th and early 21st centuries saw a number of key changes in the banking industry, including globalization, consolidation, and deregulation. Deregulation in many countries had a global impact through its encouragement of banks' entries into foreign sectors of the market. Consolidation and mergers also led to the emergence of large national banks with an expanded global market presence. Mergers also took place between banks and insurance brokers because of deregulation, resulting in the offering of new services to bank customers. One popular new service was the banking industry's expansion into insurance and brokerage services, although some countries legally forbid banks from providing these services.

Deregulation and mergers were especially prominent in the United States and Japan, whereas the practice of combining other services such as insurance and securities with banking had already been common in the European banking industry. Deregulation and mergers also occurred at the international level, as banks from one country acquired banks from other countries and expanded to serve an international clientele. The 1994 General Agreement on Tariffs and Trade and subsequent meetings under the aegis of the World Trade Organization resulted in many member nations resolving to provide greater international access to their financial markets.

Commercial banks function at the individual, branch, and corporate levels. Individual banks that provide complete banking services with only one location have become increasingly rare in today's global society. The branch system is now the norm for much of the world as it allows for convenient multiple locations of a single bank to serve both individual and corporate clientele. Commercial banks serve as depositories of financial assets, facilitate cash transfers, provide trust services, and provide credit for individual and corporate clientele. A corporate headquarters oversees the branch operations. Corporate banks emerged in popularity in the early 21st century. A corporate bank is a single international company with no public dealings that facilitates corporate financial transactions and liabilities and can also serve as a corporate holding company.

The emergence of new global markets and international trade agreements such as the North American Free Trade Agreement (NAFTA) and the General Agreement on Tariffs and Trade and institutions such as the World Trade Organization have increased demand for international financial services. Technological innovations that have aided the global expansion of banking include the use of checks, credit cards, debit cards, electronic transfers, and automatic teller machines. Another key innovation has been the development of online banking services, which are especially beneficial to internationally based corporate customers.

Technological advances have allowed banks to provide all aspects of international financial services to their clientele within a single financial institution, facilitating the growth of international trade and the global economy. Commercial banks also facilitate international trade through the issuance of commercial letters (lines) of credit. The world's 10 largest banks based on Fitch Ratings of assets in 2010 were BNP (France), Royal Bank of Scotland Group (United Kingdom), HSBC Holdings (United Kingdom), Crédit Agricole (France), Barclays (United Kingdom), Bank of America (United States), Mitsubishi UFJ Financial Group (Japan), Deutsche Bank (Germany), JP Morgan Chase (United States), and Citigroup (United States). China was the only developing nation to make the top 50. The declining costs of technology have also allowed smaller banks to enter the international financial market.

The rise of international and online banking has also brought new problems to the banking industry. One is the lack of clear international regulations to parallel those that exist on the national level in many countries. The international outsourcing of financial and customer services hurt customers' opinions of banks. Customers and governments also became concerned over the security of online banking and the vulnerability of personal and corporate financial information as well as, potentially, the entire global economy to hackers and cyber-terrorism. National and global economies also faced increased risks of suffering the ill effects of personal and corporate bankruptcies and debt that could devastate the global banking industry. Banks began to search for alternative ways to manage national and global credit risks.

International banks and financial oversight institutions have emerged to oversee the global financial system. The World Bank offers loans, advice, and other financial resources to developing countries. The International Monetary Fund is an international governmental organization that oversees the global financial system and is a source of loans. Many developing countries suffer economically because of trade deficits and external debts to developed countries through international banks such as the World Bank or the International Monetary Fund.

Development Banks

Another key area of growth has come in the field of development banks. Development banks are financial institutions located in developing countries. These banks vary in size, funding, and services. Development banks can be either publicly or privately owned or a combination of both. Private ownership is minimal, however, when there are few domestic savings or little access to external financing. Most rely on corporate or institutional investors. Some development banks specialize in a single area, such as agriculture or industry, whereas others work in a multitude of areas.

Development banks have increased in number and popularity since the mid-20th century, often receiving international assistance through programs from developed countries as well as the International Bank for Reconstruction and Development and its affiliates, the International Finance Corporation, and the International Development Association. Development banks often play a crucial role in national development plans as they are used to spur economic growth and industrialization. A few development banks finance public and national development projects. Some critics argue that international economic aid such as that provided to development banks is a form of neocolonialism by which developed nations maintain control of their former colonial possessions.

Many development banks provide loans to entrepreneurs wishing to start their own businesses as a way to spur private sector economic development. Many of these are small loans to customers that would otherwise have no access to traditional commercial banks and are too small to qualify for many international assistance programs individually. Thus, their only alternative would be reliance on traditional moneylenders who charge excessively high interest rates. The expense of maintaining loans and subsequent reluctance to deal with small loan amounts, however, has given rise to the popularity of microfinance institutions in much of the developing world. Many development banks also provide customers with other forms of business assistance, such as technical, marketing, or accounting training.

Marcella Bush Trevino

See also Banking, Offshore; Bretton Woods Agreements/ System; Currencies; Economic Development; European Central Bank; Finance, Financial System; International Monetary Fund (IMF); World Bank

Further Readings

Barnet, R. J., & Cavanagh, J. (1994). *Global dreams: Imperial corporations and the new world order.* New York: Simon & Schuster.

Cassidy, J. (2009). *How markets fail: The logic of economic calamities.* New York: Farrar, Straus & Giroux.

Caufield, C. (1996). *Masters of illusion: The World Bank and the poverty of nations.* New York: Holt.

Chernow, R. (1990). *The house of Morgan: An American banking dynasty and the rise of modern finance.* New York: Atlantic Monthly Press.

Davidson, P. (2002). *Financial markets, money, and the real world.* Northampton, MA: Elgar.

Goodhart, C. (1988). *The evolution of central banks.* Cambridge: MIT Press.

Kojm, C. A. (1984). *The problem of international debt.* New York: H. W. Wilson.

Kurtzman, J. (1993). *The death of money: How the electronic economy has destabilized the world's markets and created financial chaos.* New York: Simon & Schuster.

Lavoie, M., & Seccareccia, M. (Eds.). (2004). *Central banking in the modern world: Alternative perspectives.* Northampton, MA: Elgar.

Mayer, M. (1997). *The bankers: The next generation.* New York: Truman Talley Books.

Mayer, M. (2001). *The Fed: The inside story of how the world's most powerful financial institution drives the markets.* New York: Free Press.

Moffitt, M. (1983). *The world's money: International banking, from Bretton Woods to the brink of insolvency.* New York: Simon & Schuster.

Moore, B. J. (1982). *Horizontalists and verticalists: The macroeconomics of credit money.* New York: Cambridge University Press.

Moyo, D. (2009). *Dead aid: Why aid is not working and how there is a better way for Africa.* New York: Farrar, Straus & Giroux.

Pierce, J. L. (1991). *The future of banking.* New Haven, CT: Yale University Press.

Posner, R. A. (2009). *A failure of capitalism: The crisis of '08 and the descent into depression.* Cambridge, MA: Harvard University Press.

Sampson, A. (1982). *The money lenders: Bankers and a world in turmoil.* New York: Viking Press.

Sowell, T. (2001). *Basic economics: A citizen's guide to the economy.* New York: Basic Books.

Teichova, A., Kurgan-van Hentenryk, G., & Ziegler, D. (1997). *Banking, trade, and industry: Europe, America, and Asia from the thirteenth to the twentieth centuries.* New York: Cambridge University Press.

BATTLE OF BADR

It could be said that the global expansion of Islam began with the Battle of Badr. The town of Badr, or Badr al-ḥunayn, lies southwest of Yathrib, later named Madīna, in the Arabian Peninsula (presently, the town, or its surviving environs, is situated in the province of al-Madīna al-Munawwara in Saudi Arabia). It was here that the Battle of Badr was fought on 17 (or 19 or 21) Ramadān in 2 AH/13 (or 15 or 17) March, 623 CE. This battle was the first great triumph of Muḥammad and his new followers against his hometown enemies in Mecca; that is, those members of the Quraysh tribe, Muḥammad's own super tribe, and the elite of Mecca, who rejected his claims to prophecy and revelation, culminating in his emigration (*hijra*) to Yathrib in 622.

While the medieval Muslim sources are rife with hagiographical accounts of the Battle of Badr and its heroes, the best attested traditional account is reported by the historian al-Tabarī (d. 923) in a purported letter from 'Urwa ibn al-Zubayr (d. 713) to the Umayyad caliph 'Abd-al-Malik ibn Marwān (r. 683–705). Having received reports of a loaded Meccan caravan returning from Syria, headed by Abū-Sufyān ibn Ḥarb, a progenitor of the later Umayyad Caliphate (r. 661–749), Muḥammad gathered a force of about 300 followers whom he marched to Badr to intercept and raid it; the raiding of caravans, while central to tribalism in Arabia, provided for the economic survival of Muḥammad's nascent polity (*umma*) in Madīna. Apparently aware of Muḥammad's machinations to attack his caravan, Abū-Sufyān messaged Mecca to provide him with reinforcements as the caravan was passing near Madīna. The Meccan reinforcements, led by Abū-Jahl (literally "Father of Paganism or Ignorance," so nicknamed by Muḥammad), the head of the Makhzūm clan, numbered some 1,000 men, nearly all of whom were from Muḥammad's super tribe, the Quraysh. Before reaching Badr, Abū-Jahl was informed that the caravan, by taking a route closer to the coast of Arabia, had safely eluded Muḥammad and his followers. Nevertheless, in a show of power, Abū-Jahl went forward to Badr, thinking that Muḥammad, given his small contingent, would not attack them or, better, that they would defeat him.

Muḥammad apparently did not know of Abū-Jahl's expedition until the night before the battle. The Meccans were camped behind a hill, not far from Muḥammad's followers. The notion that fleeing would be dishonorable appears to have persuaded Muḥammad's followers to remain and fight the Meccans on the next morning. After seizing all of the surrounding water wells and filling them, except for one, with sand, Muḥammad forced his Meccan rivals to fight for the only remaining water source. Details of the Battle of Badr are sparse. What is reported is that there were a number of duels followed by a mêlée. The Meccans, despite the superiority of their numbers, were defeated, with nearly 70 of them killed, including their leader Abū-Jahl, and another 70 taken as war prisoners later to be ransomed. As for the Muslims, who proved victorious, it is reported that only 15 were killed or martyred. Symbolically, this battle was a huge blow to the Meccans' prestige and honor. For Muḥammad and his followers, it was a vindication of God's providence for this emerging polity and of God's foretold punishment of the unbelievers, as evinced in the Qur'ān 8:42–44:

> When you were on the nearer bank, and they were on the farther bank, and the cavalcade was below you; and had you made tryst together, you would have surely failed the tryst; but that God might determine a matter that was done, that whosoever perished might perish by a clear sign, and by a clear sign he might live who lived; and surely God is All-hearing, All-knowing. When God showed thee them in thy dream as few; and had He shown them as many you would have lost heart, and quarreled about the matter; but God saved; He knows the thoughts in the breasts. When God showed you them in your eyes as few, when you encountered, and made you few in their eyes, that God might determine a matter that was done; and unto God all matters are returned. (Arberry, 1996, p. 202)

The Battle of Badr also introduced the idea of God's succor in the form of sending down angels to fight alongside the Muslims (Qur'ān 8:9,12):

> When you were calling upon your Lord for succor, and He answered you, "I shall reinforce you with a thousand angels riding behind you." . . . When thy Lord was revealing to the angels, "I am with you; so confirm the believers. I shall cast into the unbelievers' hearts terror; so smite above the necks, and smite every finger of them!" (Arberry, 1996, p. 198)

While the Battle of Badr confirmed Muḥammad's followers in the righteousness of their cause, it also led to an exaggerated sense of their military prowess, which played a role in the defeat of Muslims by the Meccans in the next battle at Uḥd in 625 CE. Nevertheless, the Battle of Badr appears to have allowed Muḥammad to consolidate his religio-political power in Madīna, leading, first, to the expulsion of two Jewish tribes and the annihilation of one from that town and, second, to the conquest of his native Mecca in 630 CE; and those who fought in the Battle of Badr were immortalized as the Badriyyūn, later receiving among the highest stipends of the new Muslim aristocracy.

For political Islamists, mainly those advocating militancy and violence, including Jihādī-Salafī groups like al Qaeda, who have drawn parallels between the Battle of Badr and the events of September 11, 2001, the global and modern significance of the Battle of Badr is most evident in their religio-political discourse about "the battle between Islam and the West." The Battle of Badr was a defining event of early Islamic history, which should be taken as a guide for (modern) Muslims as they engage in a religiously sanctioned war, or *jihād*, against a far more militarily (in terms of numbers and, more importantly, weapons), economically, and otherwise powerful enemy. These political Islamists, including the Egyptian Sayyid Qutāb (d. 1966), further argue that, if only Muslims truly believed in their religion (as the "Jews" have done in the case of Israel, a Jewish state), then victory and Islam's hegemony over the world would be ensured against all conceivable and inconceivable odds. The literature of modern Jihādī-Salafī hagiography has also attested to the appearance of God's angels on the battlefields in Iraq and Afghanistan. Additionally, the religio-political influence of the Battle of Badr may be seen in the appellations of Islamist organizations, including the Badr Organization or Brigade (*Munẓẓamat Badr*), so called after Badriyyūn (viz., those who participated in that historical battle), which is the paramilitary wing of the (recently renamed) Shī'ite Iraqi political group the Islamic Supreme Council of Iraq, which sought unsuccessfully to topple Saddam Hussein's regime before 2003.

Ahmed H. al-Rahim

See also Caliphate; Charismatic Leaders; Conquests; Identities, Traditional; Islam; Islam-Related Movements; Myths; Terrorism

Further Readings

Arberry, A. J. (1996). *The Koran interpreted*. New York: Touchstone. (Original work published 1955)

Bergesen, A. J. (2007). *The Sayyid Qutb reader: Selected writings on politics, religion, and society*. London: Routledge.

Guillaume, A. (1955). *The life of Muhammad: A translation of Ishāq's* Sīrat Rasūl Allāh. Oxford, UK: Oxford University Press.

Jabar, F. A. (2005). *The Shi'ite movement in Iraq*. London: Saqi Books.

Kepel, G., & Milelli, J.-P. (Eds.). (2008). *Al-Qaeda in its own words* (P. Ghazaleh, Trans.). Cambridge, MA: Belknap Press.

Muhammad Baqir ibn Muhammad Taqi Majlisi. (1850). *The life and religion of Muhammad, as contained in the Sheeah tradition of the* Hyat-ul-Kuloob (J. L. Merrick, Trans.). Ithaca, NY: Cornell University Library.

Watt, W. M. (1956). *Muhammad at Medina*. Oxford, UK: Oxford University Press.

BEIRUT

Beirut is one of the cities in the Arab Middle East that is heavily enmeshed with other places in the world; this is especially so due to its connection with networks of the Lebanese diaspora. By number, however, the population of approximately 1.5 million people in the metropolitan area is outnumbered by many other cities in the Middle East.

Beirut, the primary city and capital of Lebanon, is an old town. Excavations have uncovered ruins of the Phoenician, Hellenistic, Roman, Byzantine, Arab, Crusader, and Ottoman periods. However, in premodern times, Beirut was only a second-rate regional center. It was mainly with the rising influence of European colonial interests in the 19th century that Beirut grew in importance. Urged by European powers that saw themselves as protectors of the Christian communities in the region, in 1861, the Ottomans established a semiautonomous district, "Mount Lebanon." While still an Ottoman provincial capital, Beirut became a focal point of commercial and political ties from the Levantine coast with European powers—especially France. Also, Beirut became a center of evangelization activities. Many renowned educational institutions, such as the American University of Beirut, have their origins in that period. Beirut grew into a cosmopolitan center of the Levantine coast. The city attracted immigration from the surrounding rural areas. At the same time, Beirut became an important harbor for the outmigration from the Mount Lebanon areas and the Syrian hinterland to the New World. Today there is a huge diaspora of several million people with Lebanese origin (either holding Lebanese passports—often beside other ones—or at least with close ties to Lebanon) in North and South America, in Europe, in Africa, and, since the 1980s, also in a growing number or countries in the Arab Gulf as well as in Australia.

With the defeat of the Ottoman Empire in Word War I, France and Britain could expand their influence in the region and circumvented the establishment of a pan-Arab nation. Taking the Mount Lebanon region as a core, adding mostly Sunni-populated coastal towns, some mostly Shī'a-populated rural areas as well as the multiconfessional and cosmopolitan coastal town of Beirut as capital, the French created the Lebanese state in 1920. The Lebanese state was built on the basis of a balance of powers between the different sects. During World War II, Lebanon obtained full independence. Independent Lebanon kept the sectarian political system, which, in comparison to the authoritarian or monarchic neighboring states of the Arab Middle East, is a rather democratic political system and developed an open, liberal, service-based economy with hardly any state intervention. In the 1960s, Beirut became the major relay station for economic relations between North America/Europe and the Arab Middle East. Furthermore, Beirut turned into the first major tourist destination in the Arab Middle East, the cosmopolitan character and the summer resorts in the mountains attracted the economic upper classes of the Arab countries, and the image of a "Paris of the Middle East" fascinated European tourists. Last but not least, Beirut became the financial center of the Arab Middle East. Thus, the economy in Lebanon could indirectly profit enormously from the oil boom in the Arab Middle East.

Nevertheless, despite the favorable economic situation, Beirut saw growing social tensions in the 1950s and 1960s. With the first Arab-Israeli war, Lebanon became the host for thousands of Palestinian refugees. On the outskirts of Beirut, the United Nations established camps, most of which continue to exist in the 21st century. Continuing clashes between different militias and the Israeli army, as well as rural poverty, triggered waves of mostly poor, mostly Shī'a internal migrants who settled in the southern suburbs of Beirut. It was especially the precarious status of the Palestinian refugees which enhanced tensions between a pro-Western, conservative, mostly Christian, economic and political elite and a progressive, mostly pro-Palestinian and pan-Arab, mostly Muslim faction.

Internal tensions as well as external influences led to the outbreak of the Lebanese Civil War in 1975. Inner-city Beirut became a battleground, and the whole city rapidly became divided along the so-called green line between a mostly Muslim west and a mostly Christian east. During the civil war, other cities in the region took on many of the gateway functions of Beirut—in numerous ways, the civil war "disconnected" Beirut from the world.

After several rounds of fighting between shifting lines of conflict, fighting finally stopped in 1990. Rapidly, the inner city of Beirut became cleared and even buildings that had been damaged only lightly were demolished to make room for a new city center. In 1994, Solidere (Société libanaise pour le développement et la reconstruction de Beyrouth) was established, a private Lebanese stock company that became the owner of almost all of the inner-city properties (prior owners became mostly indemnified by shares). The Lebanese government gave Solidere the rights to plan and redevelop inner-city Beirut—all in all, the company became responsible for the development of 180 hectares (including a landfill of the sea). The key figure behind Solidere, the Lebanese-Saudi businessman Hariri, who has been prime minister several times, promoted this project with the geographical imagination of a Beirut as a hypermodern business and tourism center that may, to a large extent, retake its preeminent position in the Arab Middle East.

At the beginning of the 21st century, Beirut is again an important center for international Arab tourism and an important cultural center for the Arab world. The financial and the real estate sectors as well as the tourism industry profit enormously from the huge and often affluent Lebanese diaspora. However, for the moment, Beirut is far from regaining its regional position, and many social and political problems remain unresolved.

Georg Glasze

See also Arab League; Cosmopolitanism; Cultural Diversity, Convention on; Diasporas; Modern Identities; Nation-State; Sites, Global; Tourism Sector; War, Civil

Further Readings

Hourani, A., & Shehadi, N. (Eds.). (1992). *The Lebanese in the world. A century of emigration.* London: Tauris.

Schmid, H. (2002). The reconstruction of downtown Beirut in the context of political geography. *Arab World Geographer, 5*(4), 232–248.

Verdeil, E., & Faour, G., & Velut, S. (Eds.). (2007). *Atlas du Liban: Territoires et société* [Atlas of Lebanon: Territories and society]. Beirut, Lebanon: Institut français du Proche Orient.

BIOFUELS

Biofuels have been promoted as one alternative to the reliance on fossil fuels for the world's energy needs, but the use of biofuels is controversial. The term *biofuel* (or agro-fuel) refers to the conversion of agricultural crops into forms of liquid energy that can be blended with or substituted for gasoline and diesel fuel. There has been a phenomenal rise in industrial biofuel production in a short period of time, with intensely contested impacts. On one hand, advocates have promoted biofuels as a "green" process of harnessing solar energy in a way that simultaneously helps address global problems of declining oil reserves and climate change. On the other hand, mounting research has shown a host of negative environmental and social impacts rooted in dubious energy budgets, extensive land demands, and the market pressures associated with the rising competition for agricultural products. To the extent that the terminology of biofuels itself suggests a benign product, critics generally prefer agro-fuel, a discursive shift that seeks to center attention on the process of industrial agriculture.

Production

First-generation biofuels are ethanol produced from the fermentation of crop carbohydrates and biodiesel produced from a chemical reaction between edible oils and an alcohol. In temperate regions, the primary feedstock is grain for ethanol and oilseeds for biodiesel, and in tropical and subtropical regions, the primary feedstock is sugar for ethanol and palm oil for biodiesel. Low-ratio blends of 10% ethanol with gasoline (E10) and 20% biodiesel with diesel (B20) can power standard engines and are the typical commercial end use. High-ratio blends (E85 flex fuel and B100) require either modifications or special engines and are becoming more common.

Brazil was the first site of large-scale biofuel production, based on sugar-ethanol, which was established with strong state support in the face of the country's energy and foreign exchange crisis in the 1970s. As late as 2000, Brazil was the only major biofuel producer on a world scale. But in 2006, the United States overtook Brazil as the biggest producer, its biofuel boom spurred by extensive government subsidies and centered on corn-ethanol. By the end of the decade, roughly one quarter of the annual U.S. corn harvest went into ethanol, which was blended, mostly as E10, into one third of all gasoline pumped in the country. Led by the United States and Brazil, global biofuel production roughly quintupled between 2000 and 2009, with annual fuel ethanol production increasing from 17 to 73 billion liters and annual biodiesel production increasing from 1 to 15 billion liters.

Biofuel production is projected by the UN Food and Agriculture Organization to continue growing quickly. It is also expected to become more diversified as many countries have set ambitious targets for increasing the scale of biofuels in their energy supply. The extent of state subsidies in biofuels, particularly in the United States, has helped encourage investment and technological innovation by a range of transnational corporate interests, including those in grain and oilseed processing, agro-chemicals, automotive manufacturing, and oil and gas. But subsidies can only ever be part of the picture; there has to be more fundamental economic imperatives underlying them. In the case of biofuels, this hinges squarely on the looming scarcity of oil reserves, or peak oil.

Driving Forces and Justifications

Peak Oil

Peak oil refers to the fact that when all of the oil consumed by human economies since the late 19th century is added to current reserves, the world is either fast approaching or has already passed the halfway point of total oil consumption. It implies that the world's easiest-to-produce, lowest-cost oilfields have already been discovered and that extraction will become ever more difficult, costly, and energy intensive as they decline. At the same time, the second half of the oil supply will get consumed much faster than the first half because of the tremendous growth in economic activity.

The enormity of the challenges posed by peak oil is hard to overstate. Oil, natural gas, and coal are essentially ancient stores of photosynthesized solar energy that have been accumulated, buried, and compacted over a long geologic period, and together they account for four fifths of the world's total primary energy supply (i.e., all of the energy used in production, households, and transportation). Of these, oil is the most important, not only because it is the biggest source of energy by volume but also because it accounts for virtually all of the liquid energy fueling modern transportation systems and the compression of time and space so central to globalization. The basic hope with biofuels is to replace part of this pivotal and finite resource with renewable stores of photosynthesized solar energy that can be converted into liquid forms. Following from this, a common way that governments have justified their subsidization of biofuel production is with the claim that it will enhance domestic energy security.

Climate Change

Beyond the peak oil imperative, biofuels have been marketed as a response to climate change. This case for biofuels as "climate friendly" starts from the fact that the combustion of fossil fuels unlocks long-buried carbon and changes greenhouse gas concentrations in the atmosphere, the biggest cause of anthropogenic climate change. In contrast, advocates suggest that biofuel combustion mainly releases the carbon that was sequestered in plant growth, which amounts to a perpetual short-term carbon flux that does not affect the long-term volume in the atmosphere.

Criticisms

Behind this rosy imagery lies a much more problematic resource budget and atmospheric impact. To appreciate this, and the growing criticism of biofuels, it helps to start with the low or negative energy return on investment (EROI) in industrial agriculture. Industrial agriculture depends heavily on the consumption of fossil energy, from the running of farm machinery and irrigation systems to the production, transport, and application of industrial fertilizers and agro-chemicals. Producing, moving, and spreading nitrogen, phosphorous, and potassium fertilizers alone involves large amounts of oil and natural gas. The tremendous extent to which fossil energy is embedded in industrial grains and oilseeds has been well established, and the energy inputs into biofuels grow further with the post-harvest transport, processing, and fermenting and distilling process.

Though the EROI of biofuels varies from crop to crop, in general, scientific research is finding that often nearly as much—and in some cases more—fossil energy goes into the production of ethanol and biodiesel as the end product can replace. The EROI of corn-ethanol in the United States is especially damning, recalling how ethanol amounts to only a small share of national gasoline consumption (used mostly as E10 in one third of all gasoline) despite its voracious appetite for corn (one quarter of the annual harvest in 2009). Corn occupies far more land than any other crop in the United States and consumes the greatest volume of irrigation, fertilizers, and chemicals. In addition to its poor EROI, corn-ethanol also highlights the low output per land area that is characteristic of first-generation biofuels. At existing levels of biofuel output per land area, it is estimated that the United States and European Union would each have to devote roughly two fifths of their total cultivated land to biofuel feedstock in order to produce the energy equivalent of only 10% of their oil consumption.

This low output per land area, together with the fact that virtually all of the world's best arable land is in cultivation or pasture, means that the fast-rising use of agricultural crops for biofuels has become an important factor in international markets for basic food staples. The U.S. biofuel boom was widely identified as a factor in the volatility of international grain markets after 2006, as corn is the world's largest grain crop. The United States accounts for roughly 40% of all corn production and 70% of all corn exports, and the demand and subsidies for ethanol have impacted not only corn markets but also the cultivation of other grains.

Vulnerability to international grain price volatility is very uneven, as many low-income developing countries rely heavily on cheap grain imports (dependence that was fostered since the 1960s through food aid and subsidized trade). Thus, much of the criticism of biofuels, from a human perspective, has focused on their role in magnifying the profound inequalities of the global food economy and heightening the food security concerns of the world's poor. Many have condemned the use of grains and oilseeds to "feed" the cars of the wealthy while roughly 1 billion people are chronically malnourished, a global class dynamic the UN Special Rapporteur on Human Rights described as a "crime against humanity" in 2007. Biofuel growth has also been implicated in increasing efforts to expropriate or privatize public and common lands in many developing countries, which has been likened to a neo-imperial process of "land grabbing."

In addition to the social justice issues laden in the competition between food and fuel, the huge land area required, coupled with the poor EROI, also shatters the claim that biofuel growth is climate friendly. Critics have argued that if climate change mitigation were the real priority, the land currently given to biofuel feedstock would be ecologically restored to enhance its capacity to sequester carbon. Worse still is deforestation to expand the cultivation of biofuel feedstocks, as this releases carbon in the short term and reduces sequestration capacity in the long term—as well as having negative impacts for biodiversity. This is most disastrous where tropical rainforests are destroyed to make way for palm-oil plantations, as in Malaysia and Indonesia.

Researchers are working to improve the poor EROI and low biofuel output per land area with what have been termed second-generation biofuels. The key here is the development of enzymes that can derive ethanol from plant cellulose and not merely crop carbohydrates. The aim is to significantly expand the raw material feedstock to include such things as non-edible grasses, woody biomass, straw, and various waste by-products, which would, in turn, enable the use of permanent crops and reduce tillage, erosion, and energy while increasing the volume of biofuels that can be produced from a given amount of land. Although large uncertainties remain about their specific EROI, output per land area, and timeline to commercial viability, second-generation biofuels could constitute a considerable improvement for lands given to biofuel feedstock.

However, even if the EROI and output per land area of second-generation biofuels improve significantly, biofuels could only ever replace a small percentage of contemporary levels of oil consumption. One way to appreciate the limited potential for substitution is to recognize that the annual global combustion of fossil energy exceeds the net primary production of all plant biomass on Earth, a large share of which comes from ecosystems that are vastly more biologically productive than are agricultural landscapes. Thus, critics argue that the promotion of industrial biofuels is ultimately a false solution to peak oil and climate change, which serves to partially obscure the nature and magnitude of economic changes needed to really address them.

Still, the land area cultivated for biofuel feedstock is poised to continue growing with government subsidies fortifying lucrative new investment opportunities for large agricultural, chemical, automotive, and energy corporations. If this growth occurs on already cultivated land, it is bound to increase food prices in international markets. If this growth involves more land clearance, it will exacerbate climate change, which poses untold risks to agricultural production. Both of these prospects threaten to have terribly regressive human outcomes.

Tony Weis

See also Alternative Energy Sources; Climate Change; Energy Efficiency; Environmental Security; Global Environmental and Energy Issues; Oil; Petroleum Economy

Further Readings

Borras, S. M., McMichael, P., & Scoones, I. (Eds.). (2010). The politics of biofuels, land and agrarian change [Special issue]. *Journal of Peasant Studies, 37*(4).

Fargione, J., Hill, J., Tilman, D., Polasky, S., & Hawthorne, P. (2008). Land clearing and the biofuel carbon debt. *Science, 319*(5867), 1235–1238.

Giampietro, M., & Mayumi, K. (2009). *The biofuel delusion: The fallacy of large-scale agro-biofuels production*. London: Earthscan.

Pimentel, D., & Pimentel, M. H. (2008). *Food, energy, and society* (3rd ed.). Boca Raton, FL: CRC Press.

Rosillo-Calle, F., & Johnson, F. X. (Eds.). *Food versus fuel: An informed introduction to biofuels*. London: Zed.

Smith, J. (2010). *Biofuels and the globalisation of risk: The biggest change in North-South relationships since colonialism?* London: Zed.

BIOHAZARDS

Biohazards are biological agents—including pathogens such as bacteria, viruses, parasites, and fungi—that infect humans and are spread through a variety of transmission methods. These pathogens cause local and global outbreaks of a variety of diseases that impact billions of people annually, resulting in widespread death, illness, and economic losses. Biohazards may result from scientific and medical research, such as genetic engineering. Biohazards are also released intentionally in the form of biological weapons or bioterrorism. The global consequences of biohazards have spurred the national and international development of emergency response planning.

Natural Pathogens and Diseases

Pathogens such as microscopic bacteria, viruses, and parasites are biohazards that can result in infectious disease pandemics and foodborne and waterborne illnesses that claim millions of lives each year. These biohazards are spread through a variety of methods, including contact with domesticated and wild animals; insect bites; contaminated food, water, or blood; and through the air. Well-known historic pandemics included the Black Plague, caused by the *Yersinia pestis* bacterium in the 14th century; the transmission of smallpox and other European diseases that decimated the indigenous populations of the New World in the late 15th through the 18th centuries; and the influenza A H1N1, or Spanish flu, outbreak that spread globally in 1918 in part due to the return of soldiers after World War I.

Older diseases continued to spread in the modern era, including the avian influenza H5N1 (bird flu), the influenza A H1N1 (swine flu), tuberculosis, hepatitis, malaria, West Nile virus, and dengue fever. New diseases and strains have also emerged, including severe acute respiratory syndrome (SARS), Ebola, and Hantavirus. New drug-resistant strains, such as the methicillin-resistant *Staphylococcus aureus* bacterium, and drug-resistant tuberculosis have presented new challenges in medical treatment.

HIV/AIDS spread globally through unprotected sexual intercourse, illegal blood donations, inadequate blood donor screening, improper handling and disposal of medical waste, and the sharing or reusing of needles. HIV/AIDS claimed over 2 million lives globally in 2007, most in African countries, and left behind a growing population of AIDS orphans. Rates of sexually transmitted diseases have also remained high. According to 2004 World Health Organization statistics, there were 18.4 million global deaths due to communicable diseases.

Foodborne and waterborne illnesses annually sicken, malnourish, impair, or kill millions more worldwide. Bacteria such as *Salmonella, Campylobacter, Listeria*, and *Escherichia coli* (*E. coli*), as well as viruses such as the norovirus (Norwalk virus), cause periodic outbreaks of food poisoning. Contamination also results in recalls of associated products, causing large financial losses to agricultural producers, governments, corporations, grocery stores, and restaurants. A 1990s outbreak of bovine spongiform encephalopathy, commonly known as "mad cow disease," in Great Britain led to a search for its origin in infected feed, international bans on the importation of British beef, and fears of the spread of the disease's human variant, Creutzfeldt-Jakob disease.

Diseases spread through skin contact with, or ingestion or use of, contaminated water include cholera, caused by the *Vibrio cholerae* bacterium; typhoid fever, caused by the *Salmonella typhi* bacterium; and schistosomiasis, caused by the *Schistosoma* parasite. Water chlorination and improved sanitation have led to drastic reductions in waterborne illnesses in developed countries, but billions of people in developing countries still lack access to safe water and basic sanitary conditions. The dumping of raw sewage and medical wastes into waterways is another major source of contamination that results in waterborne illness.

Globalization has given rise to conditions that have facilitated the emergence and spread of diseases. Continued urbanization and population growth, especially in developing countries, have increased population density, allowing communicable diseases to spread more easily. International trade and travel have opened new global disease transmission routes while the importance of international tourism revenue has prevented countries from reporting epidemics, allowing them to spread further. Development and its concomitant destruction of native habitats have introduced diseases previously isolated in nature. Foodborne illness outbreaks have increased global implications as a result of the rise of transnational agribusinesses in the late 20th century. The increasing frequency of natural disasters related to climate change can lead to increased incidence of the disease outbreaks that often follow in their wake. Disease outbreaks and potential pandemics can also result in widespread public fear, panic, and ostracism of victims.

The possibility of global pandemics resulting in millions of deaths and severe negative impacts on the global economy has led to the rise of national and international emergency response planning and the use of new global technology to create early detection and warning systems. International problems include the tendency of some nations to cover up disease outbreaks, resulting in the prevention of research and implementation of measures designed to quickly halt its spread and the difficulty of quickly curtailing international travel in the advent of an outbreak. National governments face the difficulty of stockpiling needed antibiotics and other medications, coordinating local governmental and medical responses, and countering the possible overwhelming nature of a widespread pandemic.

Scientific and Military Biohazards

Groups such as the World Health Organization and the U.S. Centers for Disease Control and Prevention sponsor research into disease outbreaks, response, and prevention while drug and pharmaceutical companies spend billions to develop new drugs, vaccines, and antibiotics. Modern medicine has had one success in the global eradication of smallpox from the variola virus. Drawbacks to reliance on such medications include the high price that makes them unaffordable by much of the world's population and the rise of drug-resistant pathogens or new strains that require new drugs or vaccines. There has also been some controversy over whether some vaccines that are composed in part from the viruses they are meant to fight may actually cause illness in some people, and there are controversial links between vaccines and conditions such as autism.

Other forms of biological scientific research have raised concerns over laboratory safety and the creation of new possible biohazards. The application of human technology to biology, known as biotechnology, includes a variety of fields, such as genetic engineering and the genetic modification of plant and animal life. Pioneering genetic engineering research began in the mid-1970s when genetic engineers developed the ability to isolate genes and alter DNA molecules to correct errors or add new information. The now recombinant DNA (rDNA) could then be introduced back into the organism to correct diseases or genetic disorders, produce new chemicals, or fulfill other useful purposes. Scientists can also molecularly clone DNA to replicate genetic materials.

Genetic engineering also allowed for the commercial production of genetically modified plants and microorganisms for use in agriculture and food production. Scientists have developed biologically based pesticides and biofuels. The development of a process of irradiating foods resulted in public concerns over the safety of treated foods and international symbols to mark them for consumers. Public concerns also resulted in the global symbols for the labeling of genetically modified foods in the marketplace. As a result of growing public concern over the new technologies, many governments, organizations, and institutions developed research guidelines to protect public safety and the environment, ensure the safe handling and transport of biohazards used or created during scientific research, and govern the release of genetically modified organisms or food products.

Various nations and organizations have also conducted research into the military applications of biohazards through the development of biological weapons. The use of biological warfare has a long history, including dipping arrows or other weapons into contaminated fluids such as blood, introducing biological agents into wells or other water supplies, and contaminating blankets or other items with diseases such as smallpox. In the 20th century, countries such as the United States, Germany, Japan, Great Britain, the former Soviet Union, and Iraq have implemented military programs for the development and testing of biological weapons. Biological agents used for military purposes include anthrax, botulism, tularemia, cholera, typhoid, and the plague, as well as nerve toxins such as mustard gas, sarin, and ricin.

The dangers of biological weapons as well as their use on prisoners of war and civilian populations led to an international movement to ban their use. Many countries have signed and ratified the 1972 United Nations Convention on the Prohibition of the Development, Production, and Stockpiling of Bacteriological (Biological) and Toxin Weapons and on Their Destruction, otherwise known as the Biological and Toxin Weapons Convention. The treaty forbids research into the military purposes as well as the stockpiling of biological agents. Countries such as the United States have also passed stringent regulations for the shipment of biological agents that have potential uses as weapons. Remaining concerns include the safety and location of remaining stockpiles of biological agents, unsigned nations, and nations that have signed the treaty but violated its provisions or prevented UN inspectors from searching for evidence of programs or weapons.

The late 20th and early 21st centuries saw a rise in global terrorism and fears of potential terrorist use of biological agents and weapons. The best known instances of bioterrorism in the United States include the Rajneeshpuram cult's contamination of Oregon salad bars with *Salmonella typhimurium* in an attempt to influence local elections and the mailing of letters laced with anthrax around the time of the September 11, 2001, terrorist attacks, resulting in one death. Other well-known instances of terrorism include the Japanese cult Aum Shinrikyo's 1995 release of toxic sarin gas in Tokyo subway stations, which resulted in at least 20 deaths. International and national governments and nongovernmental organizations have developed emergency response plans for potential terrorist attacks involving biohazards.

Marcella Bush Trevino

See also Diseases; Global Environmental and Energy Issues; Global Health and Nutrition; HIV/AIDS; Viruses, Killer; Viruses and Diseases, Emerging; Waste Management

Further Readings

Boss, M. J., & Day, D. W. (2003). *Biological risk engineering handbook: Infection control and decontamination*. Boca Raton, FL: CRC Press.

Brickman, R., Jasanoff, S., & Ilgen, T. (1985). *Controlling chemicals: The politics of regulation in Europe and the United States*. Ithaca, NY: Cornell University Press.

Erickson, P. A. (2006). *Emergency response planning for corporate and municipal managers* (2nd ed.). Waltham, MA: Elsevier Butterworth-Heinemann.

Grady, S. M., & Tabak, J. (2006). *Biohazards: Humanity's battle with infectious disease*. New York: Facts on File.

Heinsohn, P. A., Jacobs, R. R., & Concoby, B. A. (Eds.). (1995). *Biosafety reference manual* (2nd ed.) Fairfax, VA: American Industrial Hygiene Association.

Jay, J. M., Loessner, M. J., & Golden, D. A. (2005). *Modern food microbiology*. New York: Springer.

Korenaga, T., Tsukube, H., Shinoda, S., & Nakamura, I. (Eds.). (1994). *Hazardous waste control in research and education*. Boca Raton, FL: CRC Press.

Krimsky, S. (1982). *Genetic alchemy: The social history of the recombinant DNA controversy*. Cambridge: MIT Press.

Krimsky, S. (1991). *Biotechnics and society: The rise of industrial genetics*. New York: Praeger.

Larson, R. A. (1989). *Biohazards of drinking water treatment*. Chelsea, MI: Lewis.

Layne, S. P., & Beugelsdijk, T. J. (2001). *Firepower in the lab: Automation in the fight against infectious diseases and bioterrorism*. Washington, DC: Joseph Henry Press.

Liberman, D. F. (1995). *Biohazards management handbook*. New York: Dekker.

Ryan, J. R., & Glarum, J. (2008). *Biosecurity and bioterrorism: Containing and preventing biological threats*. Waltham, MA: Elsevier Butterworth-Heinemann.

World Health Organization. (2003–2007). *Global health atlas*. Retrieved from http://apps.who.int/globalatlas

BIOLOGICAL DIVERSITY

What sets our planet apart from any other is not only the presence of life but life in an enormous variety. Our planet hosts a diversity of living forms that have resulted from about 4 billion years of evolution. Collectively over time, life has affected the chemistry and physics of the planet, including the composition of the atmosphere, the temperature of the planet, and the acidity of the oceans. The planet works as a biophysical system.

Understanding Biological Diversity

In recent decades, our understanding of biological diversity has advanced enormously so that the simple tree of life of schoolchild days (two big trunks: one for plants and the other for animals with microbes at their base) has been replaced with something that represents a low spreading bush with only a couple of twigs toward one end representing plants, animals, and fungi. All the rest is an astonishing array of microorganisms, many with strange metabolisms and appetites dating to the early history of life on Earth and with potentially great value as nontoxic elements in industrial processes.

The diversity—termed "endless forms, most beautiful" by Charles Darwin—is awesome. Science has described about 1.7 million species since

Linnaeus began the task in the 18th century, but there is no accurate sense of how many species remain to be discovered and described. In large degree, that is because exploring life on Earth has not risen to the level of recognized importance of discovering the subatomic particles, or space exploration, despite its direct relevance to human welfare and the fascination and excitement inherent in doing so. In addition, there is the complication that it is not easy to apply the definition of a species to microorganisms.

The total number of extant species remains an elusive number. Among widely accepted numbers are 3 to 5 million and 10 million, estimated in different ways by Baron Robert May of Oxford, of Oxford in the county of Oxfordshire. It could of course be higher, leading Edward O. Wilson to say we really do not know the number of species we share the planet with to an order of magnitude. Whatever it is, there is clearly a great frontier for exploring life on Earth.

Biological diversity is also a characteristic, in the sense that every ecosystem and biological community has both a characteristic species composition and species number. So, for example, a northeastern temperate forest in North America usually has somewhere between 20 and 30 species of trees, whereas a tropical rain forest in the Amazon has many hundred tree species.

This turns out to be very useful in environmental science and management. In the 1940s, freshwater ecologist Ruth Patrick determined that the number and kind of species in streams and rivers in the Middle Atlantic states reflected not only the natural physics and chemistry but also all the stresses from human activity on the watershed. In other words, biological diversity provides a direct measure of the sustainability of human activities within an ecosystem.

This "Patrick principle" applies to any kind of ecosystem and lies at the very heart of environmental science and management. In one sense, the reason is that by definition environmental problems affect living systems, and as a consequence biological diversity integrates all environmental problems. It makes it the perfect measure of course, but it also means that generically biological diversity is harder to conserve because it depends on addressing all environmental problems.

In its broadest sense, biological diversity encompasses diversity at all levels of biological organization from genetic diversity at the level of the organism, to diversity of ecosystems, to the big biological formations called *biomes* (e.g., desert is a biome). It is most easily understood in terms of diversity of species, so it is often used that way as shorthand, but it should always be understood to mean diversity at all levels.

Various kinds of organisms abound on the land, from the cornucopias of biological diversity that are the tropical forests of the world to the soils of the frozen dry valleys of Antarctica. The oceans are where life on Earth began to teem with life; all the major groups of living things (each one is called a *phylum* [plural, *phyla*]) occur in the oceans, and recently it has been discovered that seawater is so rich in microorganisms that their combined mass is equivalent to 280 billion African elephants. Freshwaters also are rich in biological diversity, from tiny algae and aquatic insects to organisms as large as manatees and crocodiles.

By the end of the 20th century, humanity had learned additional dimensions to life on Earth. Around thermal vents on the bottom of the ocean, there are entire communities that derive their energy from the primal energy of the planet—totally removed from sunlight, which powers most ecosystems through photosynthesis. Scientists have discovered that life can be found 2 miles below the surface of the Earth. There is every reason to believe there is a great deal more to discover.

Benefits of Biological Diversity

From the beginning of our history as a species, we have depended on other species in very direct ways, most obviously as food. Agriculture only transformed that dependence into a more complex one. Although agriculture, in turn, made human settlements possible, humans are still dependent on those particular species but also on their continued refinement. This often involves bringing in genetic material from wild relatives of the domestic species (e.g., genes from a wild perennial relative of corn, discovered in the 1970s, confer resistance to certain viral diseases of domestic corn), or it can involve pest management (e.g., an insect predator of the cassava mealy bug prevented famine in

Africa where cassava [manioc], a South American plant, had become a major crop).

Throughout human history, species have made important economic contributions, whether beaver pelts from North America (which provided the basis of the fortune of John Jacob Astor) or the value of whale oil, timber, rubber, spices, or medicinal plants. There is not a lot of awareness of the connection with wild species and ecosystems with our daily lives, even though every time someone goes to the pharmacy, the odds are the medicine derives in one way or another from nature.

We also benefit from ecosystem services, which derive from the diversity of species from which ecosystems are constructed. A series of elegant experiments by David Tilman and others at the University of Minnesota has demonstrated that an increasing number of species are directly related to an ecosystem's productivity, resilience to stress, and the amount of standing biological materials (biomass). This in turn means the benefits humans derive from ecosystems are directly derived from the biodiversity of the ecosystem.

Some ecosystem services are fairly obvious, like the provision of water reliable in both quality and quantity from a watershed; this led New York City to restore its Catskill Mountains watershed rather than build a water treatment facility at essentially 10 times the cost. Other services may be less obvious. For example, the American oyster population of the Chesapeake Bay, in addition to being a harvestable food resource, filters a volume of water equivalent to the entire bay about once a year. Before the decline in oyster populations for various reasons, the oysters did that once a week, making a huge difference in water quality.

On an even greater scale, the Amazon forest ecosystem contributes significantly to the productivity of the rivers, which drain the enormous basin (equivalent in size to the 48 contiguous U.S. states), and to the people who depend on those rivers for food. During high water months when the rivers rise 10 meters and more, many of the fish species swim into the flooded forest and feed on fruits and seeds and insects that fall into the water; for many of these species, this is the only food source for the entire year.

The forest itself makes roughly half its own rainfall. Traveling westward, moist air comes in off the Atlantic Ocean and drops as rain, which then is mostly evaporated off the complex surfaces of the forest and transpired by the leaves. It then turns into rain further to the west. Finally, when the moisture hits the high wall of the Andes, some becomes rain and feeds the river system, but the rest of the moisture is deflected north and south, the latter contributing to the agro-industry and hydropower in that part of Brazil and northern Argentina.

One of the least appreciated aspects of biodiversity is the way it functions as a living library. Each species represents a set of solutions selected by evolution to a set of biological problems and opportunities. That is what makes nature the biggest pharmaceutical factory on Earth. The origin of aspirin, the best-selling medicine of all time, is from willow bark, prescribed as an analgesic by Hippocrates. Its active ingredient is salicylic acid. Today it is produced synthetically, but the template came from nature. The concept of antibiotics, which is responsible for major improvements in medicine, came from observations of the inhibition of bacterial growth by mold accidentally contaminated in a culture dish. Vaccines came from observing the resistance of a cowpox-infected milkmaid to smallpox; indeed, the name comes from that of the cowpox virus, namely *Vaccinia*.

Impact of Humans on Biodiversity

No species can exist without affecting its environment through its needs for food or through production of its wastes. Humans have been doing it throughout our history. Indeed, one of the interesting revelations is the pervasive elimination of many bird species on islands by indigenous peoples. As our population has grown and our technology has magnified our impact per capita, we have developed to a global scale.

One way in which we affect biodiversity is by direct harvest. Brazil is named for a tree that produced a purple dye that today is very rare. Hunting eliminated the passenger pigeon, which existed in the billions in North America. It was also responsible for the extinction of the dodo on Mauritius; it represented an easy food source while it lasted, but it has been gone so long people think it is a fictional bird in *Alice in Wonderland*. Fishing pressure, both directly and through indirect catch, has drastically reduced more than 70% of all ocean fish stocks.

Another way humans affect biodiversity is by habitat destruction. Today huge amounts of tropical forest are cleared every year to produce timber and plywood, make way for agriculture and cattle, or simply get it out of the way. In previous centuries, it was the European and North American forests that fell to the axe; in the eastern United States, a lot of the forest recovered, especially in New England, when agricultural opportunity proved better in the Midwest. Most of the native grasslands of America are gone. With the elimination of habitat, biological diversity is lost. A general rule of thumb is that reducing a forest or other habitat by 90% will eliminate half of the species.

Introduced species often have unintended and massive impacts. The American chestnut was close to being eliminated from eastern North America, where it was a very important tree for wildlife by the arrival of the chestnut blight from Europe. Dutch elm disease has similarly eliminated most of the American elm, which was a favored street tree in 19th-century America. The only known specimens of the Stephen Island wren were collected by the lighthouse keeper's cat. A $250 million anchovy fishery in the Black Sea was reduced to economic extinction with the introduction via ballast water of a comb jellyfish from the Atlantic coast of the Americas. Today, magnified by modern transportation and travel, the opportunity for species to create havoc in novel locations is a runaway problem: Burmese pythons in the Everglades, zebra mussels clogging power plant pipes throughout much of the United States, the West Nile virus, and more.

Pollution also takes a major toll. Nitrogen from fertilizer use and other human activities moves through estuaries until eventually it ends up in coastal waters. One of the first places this was noted was in the Gulf of Mexico at the mouth of the Mississippi, where it created a "dead zone" with almost no oxygen and obviously eliminating fisheries. In recent years, the number of dead zones has doubled every 10 years around the world. Use of DDT and other chlorinated hydrocarbons affected birds such as peregrine falcons, bald eagles, and brown pelicans, because they became more concentrated at the end of long food chains. Acid rain from sulfuric acid from coal burning power plants created acid lakes and affected forest growth in New England. Veterinary use of pharmaceuticals on cattle in India and Pakistan has brought a number of Asian vulture species close to extinction.

On top of it all, there is now human-driven climate change, the imprint of which can be seen in nature all over the world. Previously, ecosystems had adapted to a 10,000-year period of unusual climatic stability. Now, with the planet 0.75°C warmer than preindustrial times, plant and animal species are changing their annual timing of things like flowering or egg laying. In addition, species are actually changing their geographical distributions.

There is already evidence of abrupt change in ecosystems—essentially ecosystem failure. A clear example is tropical coral reefs, where elevated temperature causes the fundamental partnership at the heart of the ecosystems—namely, between a coral animal and an alga—to break down. The coral rejects the alga, and the reef undergoes a bleaching event, causing a crash of the coral's productivity and diversity, which has serious consequences for the human communities that depend on them. Bleaching was first recorded in 1983 and is occurring with increasing frequency annually.

In North America, the coniferous forests in the West are experiencing massive mortality from native bark beetles because the summers are increasingly longer and more beetles survive the milder winters. From Alaska to Colorado, there are vast stretches of forest with up to 70% dead trees as a consequence.

Looking ahead, there are disturbing tipping points on the horizon. One of these involves the southern and eastern Amazon, which is subject to a drastic drop in rainfall. The Hadley Centre for Climate Prediction and Research originally projected that this drop in rainfall would occur at a 2.5°C increase in global temperature; revised modeling, however, has lowered that projection to 2.0°C. Further modeling involving deforestation and fire, as well as climate change (as the forest experiences them), suggests the tipping point could come at 20% deforestation (currently at 18%). The good news is the margin of safety could be built back by aggressive reforestation.

A Biologically Better Future

So what is to be done to stem this tide of biodiversity red ink and improve the prospects for a biologically better future for ourselves on this living planet? One of the key things is to greatly increase the area under strict protection—the relatively safe havens even though subject to pollution and climate change. There has been a strong upswing in creating new protected areas, but there are places where population is so dense, such as in Haiti or parts of South Asia, that it is hard to do. Similarly, there has at long last been the beginning of a major effort to create protected areas in the oceans, with the excellent ancillary effect of restoring fishery productivity in adjacent waters.

There needs to be a major effort to reduce the various stresses affecting biological systems, including preventing new invasive species, controlling the ones already present, and tackling pollution. A major way of tackling pollution is through the nitrogen cycle, because human activity has doubled the amount of biologically active nitrogen available on the planet. In addition, there is a veritable soup of man-made chemicals infused throughout the planet, the impact of which we understand very little. Although there is an international convention dealing with "persistent organic pollutants"—the Stockholm Convention on Persistent Organic Pollutants—it deals with only about half a dozen chemicals. The rise of green chemistry gives hope for a more rational approach in the future.

The specter of climate change is an enormous challenge but also suggests an entirely new approach to safeguarding the living planet. At the current rate, if the world manages to peak in emissions in 2016, a 2.0°C warmer—450 parts per million (ppm); we are currently at 390 ppm, and preindustrial was 280 ppm— world is inevitable. It is also clear that a 2.0°C *warmer* world will be brutal for ecosystems and thus for humanity. In addition, the last time the world was 2°C warmer, the seas were 4 to 6 meters higher.

So how might we avoid this? One way would be to pull carbon dioxide (CO_2) out of the atmosphere. There is one clear way to pull some of it out, namely, using biology, indeed natural biology as happened twice in the geological past (the first with the emergence of plants on land and the second the advent of modern flowering plants). In the past three centuries, modification of ecosystems has released 200 billion tons or more of carbon into the atmosphere. Indeed, we are continuing to do so, principally through tropical deforestation (perhaps 15% of current annual emissions).

An effort at a global scale to restore ecosystems has the potential to pull something like 40 ppm from the atmosphere into living systems over a 50-year period. That would be essentially half a billion tons a year each in reforestation, grassland/grazing land restoration, and modification of agriculture practices to restore soil carbon. This would have the additional advantage of making all ecosystems more resilient in the face of climate change and other stresses they will encounter and would mean that more biodiversity makes it through the constriction of human-driven impoverishment. It could also lead us more toward a model of existence in which human aspiration is embedded in the biology of the planet rather than the other way around. It would involve the long overdue recognition that the planet works not as a physical system but as a biophysical system and that the human future is best optimized by a biodiverse planet.

Thomas E. Lovejoy

See also Acid Rain; Alternative Energy Sources; Biosphere; Darwinism and Social Darwinism; Earth Summit; Environmental Change; Environmental Rights; Environmental Treaties, Conventions, and Protocols; Global Warming

Further Readings

Wilson, E. O. (1992). *The diversity of life*. Cambridge, MA: Harvard University Press.
Wilson, E. O. (2002). *The future of life*. New York: Knopf.

Websites

The Economics of Ecosystems and Biodiversity (TEEB): www.teebweb.org
Global Biodiversity Outlook 3 (GBO3): gbo3.cbd.int

BIOSPHERE

The biosphere is the planet's fragile ecosystem and environment where life exists. Its change during the Anthropocene era demonstrates globalization from an ecological perspective. The biosphere is relevant for global studies, as it is the crucial but increasingly damaged basis for all life on Earth with serious cross-disciplinary implications.

The biosphere is exposed to numerous natural and anthropogenic influences that affect its conditions and ecological functions and, thus, also life.

The maintenance of an equilibrium in favor of present conditions and life forms is challenging because of dynamics and multiple sources of harm and interests. Due to the biosphere's global dimension, complex transboundary interactions, vital impacts, and relevance for many disciplines and sectors, knowledge about the biosphere, its composition, its dynamics, and its fragility is a most important prerequisite for global studies.

Definition

The biosphere, or ecosphere, is the overall globally interacting ecosystem and environment of the Earth system, where life exists; that is, the outer litho-, pedo-, hydro-, atmo- and lower stratosphere. It provides and maintains most basic conditions of all life on Earth. Ecologically, it is the global biota and biocoenosis (as defined by de Chardin) or the sum of all organisms and their inhabited environment with which they interact and in which they form (and which may meanwhile be maintained by human intelligence—from geo- over bio- to noosphere, as per Vladimir Vernadski). Additionally, it may be a self-regulating "organism" itself, avoiding extremes for the benefit of life (the Gaia hypothesis of James Lovelock). Naturally, it is the global, dynamically stable, but nevertheless fragile ecosystem comprising all biodiversity with their biological functions (photosynthesis, respiration, decomposition, matter cycling) and vitally important local and global (sub-) ecosystem key processes, mechanisms, and services, such as (a) provision of water and food; (b) support of material cycling, pollination, and dispersal; (c) regulation of climate and disease; and (d) cultural services. The cover-like biosphere system around the Earth is not fully closed but basically determined by external cyclic solar energy and its transformation.

Conditions and Hazards

The fragile, temporarily balanced biosphere conditions are influenced by both natural processes and anthropogenic activities, which set the natural order increasingly at risk. Disturbances of the sensitive complex network interactions and the present energy, element, and information balance result in a spatiotemporal global biosphere change. All life forms have limited ecophysiological niches and depend on suitable conditions where their specific needs for survival are fulfilled. However, natural and anthropogenic hazards and changes in and of the biosphere affect many aspects of life. Despite the biosphere's enormous dimension, the buffer capacity and self-healing mechanisms against disastrous alterations are limited. Resource overexploitation, land-use change, deforestation and emissions of abundant fatal chemicals, genetically engineered organisms, or electromagnetic and radioactive radiation can cause ground, water, and air pollution; mutations, diseases, and death; biodiversity and ecosystem service loss; subsequent amplified feedback; and even global disasters. Some biosphere hazards and harms appear immediately, can decline, and are partly reversible or could be simply switched off. Others can cause delayed long-term reactions (e.g., xenobiotica, greenhouse and ozone-depleting gases) and/or multiply themselves and/or get permanently out of control (e.g., living engineered organisms, atomic technology, resistant toxic chemicals, diseases). Biosphere changes can affect, for example, health and life directly and promptly (toxic chemicals) or indirectly and delayed (climate change or cancer). Disturbances and/or effects can be local, regional, or global and specifically or generally effective, (non)reversible, accumulative, or synergetic. Like globalization, pollution and hazards do not stop at political frontiers, and regions of suffering are often different from those of origin. The serious risk and extent to which the natural biosphere and its organisms, food webs, and matter cycles have already suffered under human impact are reflected by the numerous international environmental agreements concerning, for example, oil pollution, radioactivity, long-range transboundary air pollution, greenhouse gases, or biosafety. For example, nearly 100 chemicals destroying the ozone layer are regulated alone by the Montreal Protocol. Many hazards depend on nonsustainable lifestyles and politics and underlie global and individual human responsibility—a fact that should be pointed out by researchers and educators of global studies across disciplines.

Challenges and Solutions

Sustainability means respecting the regenerative capacity of the biosphere. In the Anthropocene era, however, the exponential human population growth, consume- and growth-oriented economies, resource-demanding and biosphere-damaging lifestyles, and risky technologies and their globalization are serious nonsustainable challenges for the biosphere and biological, social, economic, and political life. Considering the biosphere's threats and limits, humankind requires faster and more sustainable instruments than current international environmental agreements and intrinsically confined growth-favoring development. So far, human intelligence and technology have failed to prevent pollution and hazards or to create self-sustainable artificial noospheres. Thus, nature conservation and prevention are still wise biosphere- and life-maintaining strategies. Furthermore, the overall life quality could be increased and many threats prevented if the "polluter pays" principle of the Organisation for Economic Co-operation and Development and the Agenda 21 principles could be enforced—that is, if the costs emerging from pollution, including control, accidents, and all consequential charges, would be paid by the polluter (e.g., long-term costs of risk technologies such as nuclear power) or at least addressed, as, for example, in the Kyoto Protocol. Additional wise solutions and instruments could be biosphere-sensitive politics, transboundary strategic environmental and social impact assessments, incentives, globally fair regulations and resource sharing, ecological footprint–reducing lifestyles, more efficient technologies, and strategies to reduce the fertile land and other resource demand.

Significance of the Biosphere for Global Studies and Vice Versa

The biosphere is the vital, first, and only home of all life prior to human geopolitical frontiers, cultures, or local homes. Global studies should thus address the ecological status and the responsibility of *Homo sapiens* for the entire biosphere, helping to stop the destructive impact of its activities on nature, natural systems, biodiversity, health, and life. They must scrutinize the interaction of globalization and offer sustainable alternatives. The functional understanding and protection of the biosphere are crucially relevant for the survival of present life forms, including humans. Global studies are predestined for a global ecological education addressing the multidisciplinary cross-sectoral responsibility for the globally interreacting and reacting biosphere. The study of the complex global biosphere ecology should become a cross-disciplinary standard in the global studies curriculum.

Thomas R. Engel and
Klaus Müller-Hohenstein

See also Biological Diversity; Climate Change; Deforestation; Earth Summit; Environmental Change; Environmental Rights; Environmental Security; Environmental Treaties, Conventions, and Protocols; Global Environmental and Energy Issues

Further Readings

Schulze, E.-D., Beck, E., & Müller-Hohenstein, K. (2005). *Plant ecology*. Berlin, Germany: Springer.

Smil, V. (2003). *The Earth's biosphere: Evolution, dynamics, and change*. Cambridge: MIT Press.

Stern, N. (2007). *The economics of climate change: The Stern Review*. Cambridge, UK: Cambridge University Press.

Vernadsky, V. I. (1998). *The biosphere*. New York: Copernicus. (Original work published 1926)

Wackernagel, N., Shulz, N. B., Deumling, D., Callejas Linares, A., Jenkins, M., Kapos, V., et al. (2002). Tracking the ecological overshoot of the human economy. *Proceedings of the National Academy of Sciences, 99*(14), 9266–9271.

World Wildlife Fund International. (2010). *Living planet report 2010: Biodiversity, biocapacity and development*. Gland, Switzerland: Author. Retrieved from http://assets.panda.org/downloads/lpr2010.pdf

Websites

Global Footprint Network: www.footprintnetwork.org

Intergovernmental Panel on Climate Change: http://www.ipcc.ch

International Geosphere-Biosphere Programme: http://www.igbp.net

Millennium Ecosystem Assessment: www.maweb.org/en/index.aspx

United Nations Environment Programme Ozone Secretariat: http://ozone.unep.org

United Nations Framework Convention on Climate Change: http://unfccc.int

World Rainforest Movement: http://www.wrm.org.uy

Birth Control

Birth control is at the center of global reproductive politics. The term *birth control* refers to a regimen of one or more sexual practices, medical devices, or medications that couples use to deliberately prevent unwanted pregnancy. Globally, millions of people have practiced birth control for centuries. Most modern scientific contraceptives were developed after Word War II. Recent studies of birth control come from various disciplines with different emphases, indicating the complexity of this subject, especially in the global context. Scholars from women's history and feminist studies to global history and foreign policy studies explore topics ranging from sexuality, women's health, and gender equality to social movements, contraceptive technologies, and geopolitics.

In recent decades, the term *birth control* has been used interchangeably with *contraception* or *family planning*, yet when American feminist Margaret Sanger (2006) invented this term, she highlighted women's agency in managing their reproductive powers: "The verb 'control' means to exercise a directing, guiding, or restraining influence. . . . It implies intelligence, forethought, and responsibility" (p. 4).

The ideas and practices of birth control that emerged in western Europe and the United States in the late 19th and early 20th centuries soon extended their global reach to the colonies and to other countries such as Japan and China. Various voluntary groups and individuals around the world promoted or opposed birth control for different reasons, ranging from women's liberation, maternal welfare, classism, racism, and eugenics to religious and moral concerns.

In the second half of the 20th century, the discourses, institutions, practices, and policies regarding birth control shifted from planned parenthood to family planning for population control, then to reproductive health care for women's empowerment. The global arena involved—including feminist activists, nongovernmental organizations, health professionals, private foundations, state governments, and intergovernmental organizations—increasingly recognizes that access to birth control is a basic human right and that couples, but especially women, should have the freedom to decide if, when, and how often to have safe sex and bear children.

Birth Control Movement, Neo-Malthusianism, and Eugenics

Early birth control advocates came from different groups with various rationales. Influenced by the English economist and Anglican clergyman Thomas Malthus (1766–1834), a group of early 19th-century elite White males, including Jeremy Bentham (1748–1832), Francis Place (1771–1854), and John Stuart Mill (1806–1873), saw a solution for poverty in the regulation of fertility. Whereas Malthus stressed moral restraint—delayed marriage and abstinence—on religious grounds, neo-Malthusians searched for more practical methods, such as coitus interruptus, vaginal douching, condoms, pessaries, and sponges. They mainly campaigned as single individuals in their freethinkers' circles until 1877, when Charles Drysdale (1829–2907) founded the Malthusian League in England and published a journal called *The Malthusian* to challenge Victorian sexual morality. Branches were established in Holland, France, and Germany in the 1880s and 1890s; the first International Neo-Malthusian Conference met in Paris in 1900.

Some feminists at the turn of the century shared with the neo-Malthusians the idea of legalizing contraception and making it more available, but to promote women's liberation and maternal welfare rather than on economic grounds. Leading figures include Aletta Jacobs (1854–1929) in Holland, Annie Besant (1874–1933) and Marie Stopes (1880–1958) in England, Helena Stoecker (1869–1943) in Germany, Emma Goldman (1869–1940) and Margaret Sanger (1879–1966) in the United States, and Ishimoto Shizue (1923–2001) in Japan. They wrote pamphlets and delivered public lectures to disseminate information about contraception. Significantly, they worked with female doctors to set up birth control clinics. The first centers in the Netherlands, the United States, Germany, and Japan were created in 1882, 1916, 1919, and 1922, respectively. These activists formed an informal transnational feminist network and influenced each other's work; they also sent information and supplies to dozens of countries. Like many pioneers, they faced harsh criticism. To some advocates of women's emancipation, the discourses and practices of the birth control movement seemed controversial and threatened to undermine their priority of women's suffrage; they refused to include the topic of birth control on their agendas. Medical professionals, predominantly male, also kept their distance from the movement. Eager to earn scientific endorsement for their work, the birth control campaigners turned to eugenicists and built an alliance with the eugenics movement.

Eugenicists took birth control seriously because of their concerns about differential fertility rates. Drawing on social Darwinism's counter-selection theories, they believed that selective breeding via birth control could achieve the goals of racial betterment and purity. Europe, North America, and Japan became involved in birth control in the early 20th century as a result of their intensifying national rivalries and fears of national decline. The birth control programs they established promoted some radical eugenic measures, including compulsory sterilization targeting "unfit" groups such as the poor, the feebleminded, or those with inheritable diseases. In colonies like Puerto Rico, South Africa, and India, the colonial authorities promoted birth control to curb the fertility of the poor, whether colored or White, while encouraging the White middle class to increase their birth rates.

In addition to promoting publications and personal networks, international conferences fostered the development of the birth control and eugenics movements. Scientists, doctors, and activists gathered to examine the latest theories and studies of population and contraceptive technologies. When the Sixth Neo-Malthusian and Birth Control Conference was held in New York in 1925, more than 1,000 people from 16 countries attended. The conference proceedings circulated ideas and information in and beyond the West. Today, transnationally oriented scholars investigate birth control movements active in at least 30 countries before World War II, the similarities and variances among different countries, how the movements were connected, and the circulation of ideas and devices between metropoles and colonies.

Birth Control and the Postwar Campaign to Limit Population Growth

By the end of World War II, eugenics had lost its public acceptability as a result of the Nazi and fascist regimes' notorious social engineering. Instead of focusing on the quality of the population at home, neo-Malthusians and former eugenics advocates then turned their attention to rapid population growth in the "Third World." Population experts received financial support, initially from private sources, such as the Rockefeller and Ford foundations, then from public funding to promote fertility control and family limitation overseas. In an effort to avoid "overpopulation," which would retard economic growth and exacerbate poverty, introducing birth control to the Third World became integral to postwar development projects sponsored by the developed nations. At the same time, feminist birth control advocates in the West also expanded their efforts. The International Planned Parenthood Federation (IPPF) was established in 1952, with Margaret Sanger as the first president. Although feminist views were imprinted in this organization, the IPPF also included former advocates of the eugenics movement and extreme population controllers like William Vogt (1902–1968) and Hugh Moore (1887–1972).

Scholars have observed that Western feminist birth control advocates and neo-Malthusians made strange bedfellows between the 1950s and 1970s. Although they shared the same goal—to bring contraception to the masses of the developing world—their motivations were completely different: Feminists believed that spacing and limiting childbirth could benefit individual women's well-being and status, whereas population specialists were convinced that reducing fertility rates could resolve geopolitical and societal crises. In the late 1950s, they disagreed about whether male or female contraceptive methods were more effective in mass application in the developing areas. Given the limited contraceptive technologies at hand, the population controllers joined feminists to sponsor research on the birth control pill, but they soon also invested in their ideal birth control methods that could be used on a national scale and be imposed on female users. Intrauterine devices and, later, injectable hormonal contraceptives were products of this population control framework, which could not be reversed by women themselves.

Beginning in the mid-1960s, the neo-Malthusian campaign to limit global population growth became a part of U.S. foreign aid programs. It garnered abundant resources as well as criticism and suspicion. The United Nations Fund for Population Activities (UNFPA) was established in 1969 to incorporate birth control into the packages of international development projects. The UNFPA maintained strong connections with the IPPF and several U.S. agencies and foundations, such as the United States Agency for International Development (USAID), the Population Council, and the Pathfinder Fund, which established regional offices in Asia, Africa, and Central and South America. Meanwhile, the Catholic Church condemned birth control as unnatural and immoral. Second-wave American feminists, more diverse and critical than their predecessors, criticized the White male domination, racism, and the eugenics implications in the population establishment. Whereas some developing countries undertook family planning programs sponsored by U.S. or other international organizations, others were reluctant to participate, viewing the motives of global population control as running counter to their cultural and national interests and/or as an imperialist strategy. The conflicting North-South standpoints on issues involving population and birth control were clearly evident at the International Conference on Population in Bucharest in 1974.

Eastern Europe and the Soviet Union, nevertheless, faced strikingly different demographic trends. The communist governments regarded declining fertility rates in these countries from the late 1950s on as threats to the labor force supply and planned economy and to socialist modernization. Pro-natalist policies were adopted, ranging from welfare and economic incentives to restrictions on access to contraceptives and abortion. In sharp contrast, in communist China, to reconcile China's anti-Malthusian stance with its rapid population growth, Mao Zedong and supporters invented the concept of "birth planning" in the mid-1950s to highlight the collective character of scientific fertility regulation in contrast to the individual nature of birth control in the West. The extreme version of Chinese birth planning is the draconian one-child policy, which has been varyingly in place since the late 1970s.

Birth Control, Reproductive Health, and Global Social Policy

The variety of newly invented contraceptives and the expanded access to birth control since the 1960s have undoubtedly liberated women's sexual lives and freed them from unwanted pregnancies. Yet, overemphasis on hormonal and other long-acting contraceptives had serious drawbacks: Users suffered from complications and health risks, including blood clots, circulation disorders, cancers, irregular bleeding, pelvic inflammatory diseases, uterine perforations, and septic spontaneous abortions. American feminists, health activists, and consumer advocates strongly denounced these medical scandals and called for government hearings and lawsuits, successfully pressuring regulatory agencies and drug companies to adopt more rigorous risk evaluations and to provide precautionary information. The women's health movements that emerged in the 1970s criticized the bias in contraceptive research: overwhelmingly targeted for female bodies; unwillingness to invent safer, more comfortable barrier methods; and greater concern for contraceptive efficacy than safety. These advocates not only cautioned against public family planning programs that imposed fertility control on American Indians and women of color but also drew attention to the contraceptive industries' lobbying, marketing, and close cooperation with the population establishment both at home and abroad.

Meanwhile, feminists, researchers, and activists from the global South started to organize and to make their voices heard in international forums. They challenged the conventional top-down paradigm of state-led family planning programs, co-shaped by their foreign donors, in which women's sexuality and fertility were closely linked with population control. By reflecting the diversity of regional experiences, Southern feminists (e.g., Development Alternatives With Women for a New Era) showed that women's reproductive roles and birth control practices were embedded in multilayered webs that implicate gender relations within households and communities, local social and political processes, and global inequalities. They argued that equal access to education, employment, and health care, as well as to birth control, should be part of alternative development models focusing on holistic, sustainable practices that empowered all people, but especially women.

The collaborative mobilization of the Southern and Northern feminists gained momentum at the International Conference on Population and Development held in Cairo in 1994. The concept of reproductive health—"a state of complete physical, mental, and social well-being and not merely the absence of disease or infirmity, in all matters relating to the reproductive system and to its functions and processes" (United Nations, 1994, p. 40)—became part of the dominant international discourse about population and birth control. According to this new paradigm, women and men have rights to have access to safe, effective, affordable, and acceptable birth control as well as to appropriate health care services. The Cairo Consensus—endorsed by leaders of 179 countries—meshes feminist and human rights rhetoric and has become a guideline for governments, international nongovernmental organizations, and donors (e.g., Population Council, USAID, governments of other developed countries), and multilateral agencies (e.g., UNFPA, World Health Organization, World Bank) that work on family planning and development programs.

In the first decade of the 21st century, birth control is a central feature of national and global social policies. Barrier methods are regaining public health experts' attention and becoming vital to preventing sexually transmitted diseases, especially in HIV/AIDS programs. Among the Millennium Development Goals, set in 2000 at the Global Summit Meeting for achievement by 2015, birth control is considered indispensable to combating HIV/AIDS, to reducing maternal mortality, and to providing women and girls universal access to sexual and reproductive health and rights. New global actors from diverse sectors, including the Advocates for Youth, the European Parliamentary Forum, Physicians for Human Rights, and the Bill & Melinda Gates Foundation, to name but a few, now join family planners, feminists, and human rights groups in negotiating the liberating power of birth control, which can truly promote gender equality and empower women.

Yu-ling Huang

See also Abortion; Activism, Transnational; Contraception; Feminism; Fertility; Global South; Health Care Access; HIV/AIDS; International Nongovernmental Organizations (INGOs); Malthusian Idea; Overpopulation; Population Control Policies; Population Growth and Population Explosion; Social Movements; Women's Movement; Women's Rights

Further Readings

Clarke, A. (2000). Maverick reproductive scientists and the production of contraceptives, 1915–2000+. In A. R. Saetnan, N. Oudshoorn, & M. Kirejczyk (Eds.), *Bodies of technology* (pp. 37–89). Columbus: Ohio State University Press.

Connelly, M. (2008). *Fatal misconception: The struggle to control world population*. Cambridge, MA: Belknap Press.

Corrêa, S. (1994). *Population and reproductive rights: Feminist perspectives from the South*. London: Zed Books.

Hartmann, B. (1995). *Reproductive rights and wrongs: The global politics of population control* (Rev. ed.). Boston: South End Press.

Hodgson, D., & Watkins, S. C. (1997). Feminists and neo-Malthusians: Past and present alliances. *Population and Development Review, 23*(3), 469–523.

Kammen, J., & Oudshoorn, N. (2002). Gender and risk assessment in contraceptive technologies. *Sociology of Health & Illness, 24*(4), 436–461.

Robinson, W. C., & Ross, J. A. (Eds.). (2007). *The global family planning revolution: Three decades of population policies and programs*. New York: World Bank Publications.

Sanger, M. (2006). *The pivot of civilization*. Middlesex, UK: Echo Library. (Original work published 1922)

Takeshita, C. (2011). *The biopolitics of contraceptive research: Population, women's bodies, and the IUD*. Cambridge: MIT Press.

Turshen, M. (2007). *Women's health movements: A global force for change*. New York: Palgrave Macmillan.

United Nations. (1994). *Report of the International Conference on Population and Development, Cairo, 5–13 September 1994*. New York: Author. http://www.unfpa.org/webdav/site/global/shared/documents/publications/2004/icpd_eng.pdf

Website

Women Deliver, Inc.: http://www.womendeliver.org

BLOGS

The collapse of the economic viability of print media across the world in the first decade of the 21st century signified a profound shift in global communications. A growing number of citizens, especially in the West, began to gain their news and information principally from online sources. During the previous century, newspapers, radio, and television provided a static relationship with the "truth," with little interaction with the consuming public.

The Internet interrupted this one-sided dynamic. "Online social media," argues Steve Anderson (2009), the national coordinator for the U.S.-based Campaign for Democratic Media, "represent something of a return to a pre-print oral culture—more of an ongoing dialogue than a form of production and consumption—in the form of commentary, anecdotes and shared stories" (para. 3). Blogs are one of the key tools of this revolution. There are literally hundreds of millions of bloggers around the world writing about personal issues, politics, sex, democracy, and freedom. There are no boundaries to what can be written or expressed. While bloggers in the United States may opine about the trials and tribulations of their own government, web users in Iran express support or criticism of the mullahs, often paying a high price for doing so. Readers are given the privileged opportunity to hear the whispers of once silenced voices.

In repressive states, blogs and websites have become essential sources of information on topics—from women's issues to sexual orientation, dating rituals to human rights—routinely shunned by channels for official propaganda. Western journalists are increasingly turning to these sources to gain insights into societies that are impossible to easily define or condemn. Blogs can entirely bypass the necessity of a foreign journalist representing the views of individuals, the mainstay of Western media conventions.

Cultural bias inevitably shades any understanding of our world. It is important for relatively privileged Westerners to see how the non-Western world views them, both as a comparison and counterpoint. We can learn directly where our tax dollars and weapons are going. Those on the receiving end of U.S.-backed dictatorships across the globe now have the means through which they can articulate their own perspectives to be read by both locals and the world. A private audience for online work has become virtually nonexistent. The very nature of these blog posts does not in itself make them fascinating or insightful, but bloggers in, say, Egypt or Saudi Arabia know that dissenting from the party line could bring prison or worse.

For example, China, the world's largest Internet market—over 400 million people and growing—has developed a diverse web community, although it remains highly regulated and censored, assisted by Western multinationals such as Google, Yahoo, Cisco, and Microsoft. How much is known about Yahoo's or Google's willingness to modify their behavior to please Chinese officials? Western executives of these companies have seemingly been comfortable with allowing their Chinese counterparts to self-censor thousands of sensitive keywords, far more than just *democracy* and *Falun Gong*. Moreover, they seem to be ignoring developments that some consider disturbing, such as Yahoo China's decision in 2008 to post images of wanted Tibetans on its home page after the Lhasa uprising before the Beijing Olympic Games.

Bloggers in China and in the Chinese diaspora regularly discuss these matters. Politics may often be the furthest thing from their minds, but connecting with friends has become an essential part of life. Many express general satisfaction with the regime's economic policies, so there does not appear to be a great desire for "democratization." The Internet does not automatically bring Western-style democracy or even the desire for it, but bloggers are able to initiate conversations that the mainstream media find either irrelevant or too time-consuming.

U.S. writer Clay Shirky (2008) explains in his book *Here Comes Everybody: The Power of Organising Without Organisations* that "communications tools (such as YouTube, Twitter, Facebook and blogging) don't get socially interesting until they get technologically boring" (p. 105). In other words, it is only now becoming possible to come across online the words of indigenous communities in Bolivia, dispossessed voters in Kenya, sex workers in India, or dispossessed Tamils in the diaspora.

The culture of blogging is unlike that of any previous social movement. Disjointed and disorganized, its aims are deliberately vague. While many want the right to be critical in the media, others simply crave the ability to date and listen to subversive music. That in itself is revolutionary for much of the world. However, many gaps remain in the blogosphere. The poor and illiterate, the vast bulk of the world, are not largely represented online.

The decline of well-financed establishment media is an opportunity, as well as a cause for concern. For millions around the world, the blogosphere has become a respite from the grandstanding of commentators and "insider" journalism. Women have been one of the key beneficiaries of the new technology, forcing into the open issues that patriarchal societies would rather keep hidden. The globalized world seems much smaller when these people are involved.

Blogs are not the answer to mainstream media woes, nor are they currently strong enough on their own to sustain necessary democratic transparency. They are merely one piece of the puzzle. In many ways, blogs have become a global phenomenon at the same time that the public's view of the corporate media has never been lower. They emerged almost by necessity. Many users ask why they should rely on an embedded mainstream reporter when an indigenous perspective is on the ground, more accurate and reliable?

Ultimately, bloggers in the non-Western world are challenging the West, not only for recognition but also for acknowledgment of their uniqueness. Bloggers in Latin America, Africa, Asia, and the Middle East are creating their own realities and visions for the future, ideas impossible to articulate in the state-run press.

Antony Loewenstein

See also Cyberconflict; Global Communications and Technology; Global Culture, Media; Internet; Knowledge Production Systems; Web 2.0

Further Readings

Anderson, S. (2009, May). Social media, social change. *Common Ground*. Retrieved October 18, 2011, from http://www.commonground.ca/iss/214/cg214_anderson.shtml

Jarvis, J. (2009). *What would Google do?* New York: HarperBusiness.

Morozov, E. (2010, September 16). The great Internet freedom fraud. *Slate*. Retrieved October 18, 2011, from http://www.slate.com/id/2267262

Shirky, C. (2008). *Here comes everybody: The power of organising without organisations*. London: Penguin.

Shirky, C. (2010, June 4). Does the Internet make you smarter? *Wall Street Journal*. Retrieved October 18, 2011, from http://online.wsj.com/article/SB100014240 52748704025304575284973472694334.html

Websites

Global Voices: http://globalvoicesonline.org
Jay Rosen's Press Think: http://pressthink.org
Mondoweiss: The War of Ideas in the Middle East: http://mondoweiss.net

Borders

Territorial borders are conventionally understood to mark the limits of nation-states' territory and legal jurisdiction, distinguish one state from another, and demarcate domestic from international realms. For this reason, territorial borders provided a key point of departure for 20th-century studies of global political life. Yet borders have rarely been as clearly demarcated as the lines drawn on maps imply. The history of the modern state system is a history of cross-border trade, sovereign disputes, and unclear territorial jurisdictions.

In the contemporary phase of globalization, borders have become increasingly fragmented—both more and less significant for different kinds of traffic. Global trade agreements facilitate freer cross-border movements of goods, finance, and business people. At the same time, however, borders represent the site of unprecedented policing against unwanted migrants and contraband goods. The changing role of borders—their dissolution, reconstitution, and disaggregation—is central to processes of globalization that are transforming contemporary states and societies. These dynamics are addressed by scholarship within the specialized field of border studies and are of crucial significance to global studies more generally.

The territorial border finds its origins in the history of the European state system that is generally dated to the Treaty of Westphalia in 1648. The treaty enshrined the principle of sovereignty within territorial limits, and borders were drawn to clearly distinguish the sovereign territory of one state from another. As Europeans colonized the Americas, Asia, Oceania, and Africa, new borders were drawn to divide new territories into the sovereign realms of various imperial powers. In the 20th century, anticolonial struggles established new borders again. Territorial borders generally rode roughshod over traditional systems for demarcating social, cultural, and political allegiances and only sometimes corresponded with existing geographic formations (or natural boundaries). Even today, territorial borders and centralized state authorities have only a partial grasp on the social, cultural, and political sensibilities of tribal, nomadic, and other traditional societies.

Histories of imperial conquest and modern state formation thus reveal that there is nothing essential or timeless about the borders of the past or those that we live with today. Some scholars refer to "bordering" as a process, to emphasize this point. From this perspective, borders cannot be taken for granted as self-evident dividing lines between one sovereign power and another. Rather, borders are made and remade through ongoing practices that serve, over time, to establish particular borders as matters of common sense and to frame the spatial environment through which we come to understand citizenship, governance, and other social phenomena. Approaches that emphasize this social construction of borders conceptualize borders in spatial *and* cultural terms. The border is interpreted as a "limit concept" in general, dictating the parameters of cultural identities as much as sovereign territories.

Understood in this way, the border is conceived as a site of political contestation. Different political actors may contest, on one hand, the position of the border in space. On the other, they may dispute the symbolic meanings invested in the border in terms of its relation to national, religious, or other social norms. Such disputes arose, for example, in the European context in the aftermath of World War I, when empires were carved into new sovereign states according to principles of national self-determination. Newly drawn borders were designed to mark the limits of distinct national homelands from which sovereign status was derived. Yet the populations within those states never corresponded to clear-cut distinctions in relation to nationality. The entire endeavor was consequently mired in disastrous tensions and violence between national majorities and minorities.

In the 1980s, the border between the United States and Mexico emerged as a focus for new theorizations of the spatial and cultural dimensions of borders. Pioneering scholars such as Gloria Anzaldúa challenged the notion of the border as a sharp line of difference in favor of the concept of "borderlands"—a zone of transgression where identities and territories are blurred. The concept was intended to capture a marginalized history of the border region—which included the annexation of traditionally Mexican territory and centuries of migration between Central and North America. Borderlands also referred to a hybrid sense of identity that could not be subsumed by prevailing cultural norms on either side of the border. In this way, what emerged as the field of border studies drew important links between the so-called hard borders of geopolitics and the soft borders of social group formation. The field critiqued the binary distinctions (us/them, inside/outside) through which borders derived their legitimacy by exposing a range of border-dwellers who could not be clearly categorized in terms of a binary schema.

In the 1990s, the question of borders again rose to prominence as part of a broader debate across the social sciences on the meaning and extent of globalization—a debate from which the field of global studies emerged. The question focused initially on a range of transnational forces and technological developments that appeared to undermine both the conceptual coherence and logistical capacities of territorial borders. Some scholars envisaged a world in which such borders were simply made redundant by the accelerated growth of a global marketplace. In this context, they contended that borders offered little protection against flows of global capital and a rapidly homogenizing global consumer culture. For some, this implied that borders and the sovereignty (and democracy) they guarded were increasingly under siege. For others, the shift toward a borderless world created much needed disincentives for interstate conflict by generating greater economic and cultural interdependence. Most scholars agreed that a range of challenges facing societies across the world (environmental destruction, nuclear technology, viruses and pandemics) could not be contained within borders and required coordinated global responses. From these perspectives, borders appeared to be rapidly fading as useful or meaningful demarcation points for global political life.

Other trends suggested that borders were reemerging in unexpected ways. Scholars began to identify reactionary responses to globalization, including the rise of a new identity politics. Right-wing forces across Europe, North America, and Australasia were reinvigorating traditional national tropes and calling, in some cases, for national economic protection. This national populism played out, in particular, around the issue of migration, with increasing calls for tighter sovereign defenses against a range of unwanted flows. In this context, strategies for border controls against irregular migrants shifted from the realm of domestic administration and into the realm of first-order global security issues. The geopolitical upheavals associated with the end of the Cold War and with global economic restructuring had produced new sources of mass displacement and population flows. Growing numbers of asylum seekers, refugees, and undocumented labor migrants attempting to find refuge and work now encountered increasingly elaborate and militarized means of securing borders against their spontaneous arrival. At the same time, however, state migration policies and corporate business models encouraged the hypermobility of highly skilled professionals, entrepreneurs, and students. Combined, these trends defied earlier predictions of a cosmopolitan, borderless world. Far from disappearing, borders had become disaggregated—increasingly restrictive for some types of people and increasingly irrelevant for others.

These trends had implications for scholarly debate. The terms of debate shifted from either/or scenarios between bordered and borderless worlds to more complex accounts of the transformation of borders. Borders, it seemed, were with us to stay, but their form and application were changing. This was evident, for many scholars, in the reshaped borders of the European Union. The practical function of internal borders had largely been removed through a series of intergovernmental negotiations. Yet the external borders of Europe were hardening into a new kind of boundary, dubbed "Fortress Europe," that was shifting the demarcation point for freedom of movement and cultural identification. Other scholars pointed to specific examples in which borders were being manipulated in ways that introduced uncertainty to their material and symbolic function. This trend was apparent, for instance, in the practice of offshoring. Offshoring occurs when states suspend the application of certain legal and regulatory codes from a portion of their territory. That territory operates, in effect, as if it were offshore. This strategy has been used, for example, to create a specific tax environment within the City of London (that does not apply elsewhere in the United Kingdom) in order to attract global financial business. It has also been used in Australia's island territories to evade legal obligations to provide refugee protection. These kinds of examples have been interpreted as indicative of the "bordering" processes that are reconstituting the relationship between states, borders, and territory and generating new spatial arrangements for citizenship, sovereignty, mobility, and governance.

Contemporary bordering processes such as offshoring are the focus of an emerging field of critical border studies, which investigates borders in relation to changing social and spatial imaginaries. Studies in this field have emphasized that borders not only are found at the edges of territory but surface in a range of administrative and policing practices well within and beyond the map-drawn border as such. Empirical foci include new technologies of surveillance and data control (such as biometrics) through which borders are erected against certain kinds of people in increasingly virtual or ephemeral ways that defy territorial logic. Critical border studies raises not only the prospect of deterritorialized borders but also the need for new methodologies and epistemologies that can capture the realities of existing and emerging borders. Building on the insights of earlier scholars such as Anzaldúa, scholars within this field explore conceptual tools that deviate from embedded territorial logics of inside/outside and us/them. They have begun to theorize borders in terms of new spatial frames and in terms of disaggregated *experiences* of control. The field thus lends itself to critical engagement with diverse expressions of power in geopolitical and biopolitical forms. Importantly, critical border studies also includes an emancipatory angle. Scholars ask how reconceptualizations of the border might generate new avenues of social change for those who currently find themselves on the wrong side of border lines.

At the broadest level, therefore, the study of borders is also the study of changing perceptions and experiences of space. These perceptions and experiences are crucial to the ontologies that shape who we are, the social formations we belong to, and the terms of reference through which societies are governed. If the field of global studies reflects a shifting consciousness from national to global socio-spatial relations, then the transformation of borders is central to its concerns.

Anne McNevin

See also Citizenship; Deterritorialization and Reterritorialization; Globalization, Phenomenon of; Immigration and Transnationalism; Migration; Security; Sovereignty

Further Readings

Albert, M., Jacobson, D., & Lapid, Y. (Eds.). (2001). *Identities, borders, orders: Rethinking international relations theory.* Minneapolis: University of Minnesota Press.

Anzaldúa, G. (1987). *Borderlands. La frontera: The new mestiza.* San Francisco: Aunt Lute Books.

Michaelsen, S., & David, E. J. (Eds.). (1997). *Border theory: The limits of cultural politics.* Minneapolis: University of Minnesota Press.

Newman, D. (2007). Boundaries. In J. Agnew, K. Mitchell, & G. Toal (Eds.), *A companion to political geography.* Chichester, UK: Wiley-Blackwell.

Ohmae, K. (1999). *The borderless world: Power and strategy in the interlinked economy.* New York: HarperPerennial.

Parker, N., & Vaughan-Williams, N. (2009). A line in the sand? Towards an agenda for critical border studies. *Geopolitics, 14,* 582–587.

Bretton Woods Agreements/System

The Bretton Woods system refers to the rules and norms governing international monetary and financial practice during the roughly quarter century following World War II. Although both the institutions and the practices of the Bretton Woods system focused on obligations between sovereign governments, they are generally credited with creating a congenial environment for the explosive growth of private international trade and investment that took place during subsequent decades; this growth in trade and investment became a central foundation of globalization.

The name refers to the town in New Hampshire where an international conference was convened in 1944 in order to formulate these rules and also to agree on the charters for two institutions intended to play central roles in postwar international economic governance: the International Monetary Fund (IMF) and the International Bank for Reconstruction and Development (World Bank). The promotion of international trade was a key normative objective of the Bretton Woods system. The system's commitment to stable exchange rates, with "fixed but adjustable" parities, was a second-order consideration, consistent with prevailing beliefs that floating exchange rates were inimical to liberal trade.

This belief about exchange rates was shared by the system's two primary architects, Harry Dexter White of the United States and John Maynard Keynes of the United Kingdom. These two men also agreed, at least for the most part, on the necessity of limiting cross-border capital movements in order to preserve a system of stable exchange rates and, hence, of relatively free trade. Their disagreements focused largely on how to promote economic adjustment among the participants in the resulting network of states, given at least a nominal commitment to exchange-rate fixity. Keynes, representing a country expected to run considerable deficits in its future balance of payments, pushed for international arrangements that would provide temporary financing of those deficits on lenient terms and that would permit changes in exchange-rate parities at the request of national governments. White, representing a country anticipating a continued surplus position, was not anxious to finance other nations' profligacy and, hence, resisted both of these initiatives. On these questions, the formal arrangements adopted at Bretton Woods tended to reflect the U.S. position, although there were key concessions to the British.

In subsequent years, actual exchange-rate practices varied rather substantially, despite the tendency to refer to the next several decades as "the Bretton Woods system." For example, in the period immediately after the war, the United States strongly discouraged exchange-rate movements and, consequently, deficit spending by IMF members. With the beginnings of the Cold War, the U.S. position softened considerably: The Marshall Plan provided substantial payments financing to European states, deficit spending was countenanced, and in 1949 the United States gave its assent to a major multilateral exchange-rate realignment. Beginning roughly 10 years later, when the U.S. balance of payments shifted from surplus to deficit, the U.S. government once again became intolerant of exchange-rate movements, fearing that these would undermine confidence in the dollar. These very different postures of the West's economic leader toward the question of exchange-rate flexibility, and the shifts in practice that accompanied these changes in posture, have led some observers to suggest that applying the moniker "Bretton Woods system" to the entire period is misleading.

One piece of evidence of the procrustean nature of the Bretton Woods system is the absence of scholarly agreement about when it came to an end. Some leading analysts claim that the system was terminated in March 1968, when national authorities of Western nations abandoned efforts to maintain the private price of gold at $35 an ounce (as had been agreed at Bretton Woods). Others insist that the system ended in August 1971, when the United States closed the "gold window" at the U.S. Treasury, meaning that foreign central banks could no longer redeem their dollar reserves for gold. Still others argue that the system ended in March 1973, when leading currencies around the world began to float against the dollar.

On the other hand, inasmuch as the underlying aim of the Bretton Woods agreement was to promote relatively liberal trading arrangements, and because international trade flourished even after the 1973 shift to greater exchange-rate flexibility, the essential commitments on which the Bretton Woods agreement was founded still obtain in the 21st century. One can thus distinguish between "the Bretton Woods system," meaning the particular commitment to fixed-but-adjustable exchange rates as agreed in 1944, and "the Bretton Woods order," meaning the larger set of understandings and objectives on which that agreement rested. Thus, whereas the Bretton Woods system is now over, the normative framework of the Bretton Woods order is still with us.

In addition, although the international financial institutions established at Bretton Woods—the IMF and the World Bank—still exist, their functions have changed. The original mandate of the IMF was to provide balance-of-payments financing to states experiencing temporary external deficits; ongoing external deficits were judged to be evidence of the necessity of structural adjustment, including but not limited to changes in the national exchange-rate parity. But this distinction made little sense in an era of widespread exchange-rate floating, and the IMF came to take on new functions, including multilateral surveillance of exchange-rate practices, emergency lending to countries experiencing balance-of-payments difficulties, and the sponsorship of structural adjustment programs. This last mission overlapped, at least potentially, with the traditional functions of the World Bank, whose mission was to promote long-term economic development. As a consequence, the end of the Bretton Woods system meant enhanced competition between the two Bretton Woods institutions for influence over policy making in developing countries.

David M. Andrews

See also Banks; Capitalism; Economic Crises; Global Economic Issues; Globalization, Phenomenon of; International Monetary Fund (IMF); World Bank

Further Readings

Andrews, D. M. (2008). *Orderly change: International monetary relations since Bretton Woods*. Ithaca, NY: Cornell University Press.

Gardner, R. (1969). *Sterling-dollar diplomacy*. New York: McGraw-Hill.

Helleiner, E. (1994). *States and the reemergence of global finance: From Bretton Woods to the 1990s*. Ithaca, NY: Cornell University Press.

British Broadcasting Corporation (BBC)

The British Broadcasting Corporation (BBC) is Britain's public broadcaster and one of the oldest and best-known global media corporations (GMCs). It possesses one of the world's largest news-gathering networks; reaches a wide global audience via radio, television, and its website; and is a key actor in the globalization of media. The international popularity of its programming is said to enhance Britain's cultural "soft power." The BBC has also played a key role in debates over British national identity.

The term *British Broadcasting Corporation* refers to a number of legally distinct but closely related organizations. The BBC began as a private commercial radio broadcaster, the British Broadcasting Company, in 1922. However, policymakers shared the view of the first director-general, John (later Lord) Reith, that radio's social and cultural impact was potentially so great that the medium should not be left to market forces. In 1927, the company was reformed by Royal Charter into a nonprofit public corporation. It is required to serve the public interest and is funded primarily by license fees levied on all U.K. owners of television sets. Parliament must periodically reapprove the Royal Charter, but it does not control the budget directly, a fact that is said to give the BBC a relatively high degree of editorial independence from political influence as well as from advertisers or corporate sponsors.

The BBC World Service is a separate legal entity launched in 1932 as the Empire Service to unite far-flung British expatriates and imperial subjects. In the postimperial era, the World Service targets a non-British audience, currently broadcasting in 33 different languages to an estimated 280 million households worldwide. It is often cited as a valuable source of relatively objective news for citizens in regimes practicing censorship. The World Service is funded directly by the U.K.'s Foreign and Commonwealth Office.

The BBC is particularly relevant to two major debates in the literature on media globalization. First, the cultural imperialism hypothesis suggests that as wealthy Western media organizations globalize, local media and cultural traditions in poorer countries will be undermined. This is predicted to have a homogenizing effect on media content and ultimately on the norms and values of non-Western audiences; the so-called McDonaldization of culture. Critics of this thesis note that the World Service did not succeed in its original task of holding the empire together. Further, the BBC has found it desirable to tailor specific programming to specific audiences, using local languages, relying on local staff, and, most recently, encouraging user-generated content for the online services, a process sometimes known as the "glocalization" of broadcasting.

Second, many scholars see media globalization as the result of neoliberal deregulation of national markets, leading to a concentration of power in a small handful of GMCs such as CNN (Cable News Network) and News Corporation. Commercial pressures are said to be causing GMCs to de-emphasize their democratic responsibilities to educate and inform in favor of more profitable entertainment. For example, U.S. television networks have cut back on international news reporting. Some see the BBC, with its public service ethos and relative freedom from commercial pressures, as uniquely placed to resist the trend toward dumbing down. Others argue either that the BBC's news content is no better than those of commercial GMCs or that it will ultimately be unable to afford extensive global operations.

The literature on soft power suggests that the BBC's high international reputation should confer diplomatic resources on the United Kingdom. However, there is little hard evidence for this, in part because of contradictions within the BBC's corporate identity. It is famous as a uniquely British cultural export, and the World Service claims to represent what it describes as British values, such as honesty and fair play; yet, the BBC also claims to be a global rather than national news organization, neutral rather than biased toward British interests. During the Falklands/Malvinas war between the United Kingdom and Argentina in 1982, journalists were required to refer to "British" rather than "our" troops, while the BBC was criticized for supposed bias toward European integration at the expense of national sovereignty during debates over involvement in the European Union. The BBC's desire for editorial independence from the state was illustrated in 2004, when a journalist made the on-air accusation that then prime minister Tony Blair's government had deliberately misled the public about Iraq's possession of weapons of mass destruction. Blair vehemently denied the charge. A subsequent inquiry supported the prime minister, finding the BBC guilty of editorial negligence. However, public opinion generally favored the BBC, and its international reputation for independence was enhanced.

The BBC has played a central role in shaping debates over Britain's national identity. From the imperial era until at least the 1960s, the BBC presented a highly traditional image of Britishness, reflecting and reinforcing dominant hierarchies of class, gender, religion, and ethnicity. White male announcers spoke and dressed formally. Christian religious services were broadcast, but Jewish and Muslim ones were not. Arts and drama programming catered overwhelming to middle- and upper-class interests. A special committee worked on linguistic homogenization, mandating the correct pronunciations of "BBC English" across the British Empire. The BBC also helped create many unifying national rituals, such as the monarch's Christmas Day message. Since the 1960s, however, the BBC has embraced multiculturalism with increasing enthusiasm, portraying a far greater degree of diversity in British society. The BBC's history thus demonstrates the degree to which national identities are not fixed but are subject to continuous interpretation and reinterpretation by dominant media in a global era.

Henry Laurence

See also Al Jazeera; Cable News Network (CNN); Global Culture, Media; Homogenization; Imperialism; Journalism; McDonaldization, McWorld; Media, Global; National Identities; News; Radio; Soft Power Diplomacy

Further Readings

Briggs, A. (1961). *The history of broadcasting in the United Kingdom* (5 vols.). Oxford, UK: Oxford University Press.

Herman, E., & McChesney, R. (1997). *The global media: The missionaries of global capitalism*. London: Cassell.

Kung-Shankleman, L. (2000). *Inside the BBC and CNN: Managing media organizations*. London: Routledge.

Websites

British Broadcasting Corporation: http://www.bbc.co.uk/news

BUDDHISM

Buddhism has been a global religion almost from its beginning, as its teachings and practices were soon transmitted to countries outside the Asian region where Buddhism originated and historically established itself. In the process of what Martin Baumann calls the "transplantation" of Buddhism, transactions have taken place in many parts of the world where people do not always share a common cultural heritage or religious background as that of its Buddhist transmitters.

At the advent of global migration that started in the early 20th century, Buddhist transmission took place when waves of Asians emigrated to the West Coast of the United States, Canada, and also to Brazil. These immigrants adhered to their traditional Buddhist faith as a means of preserving their ethnic and cultural identity, and social activities were focused on Buddhist temples as a way of keeping the groups together rather than disseminating to people of different faiths. In the last half-century, however, transplantation has been instigated by organizations or teachers from traditionally Buddhist countries in Asia to the West, and accelerated interactions have taken place with their host nations and communities. In such contexts, sectarian barriers among different Buddhist traditions of East Asia, Southeast Asia, and that of the Himalayas appear to be breaking down, creating an impetus for new interpretations of its teaching and wide adaptation of its practices. Consequently, a new breed of Buddhism has emerged in the West, invested with individualistic and rational features and an emphasis on neoliberal principles. As issues of environment, conservation of species, and human rights become more immediate, there is a growing sense of shared responsibility among Buddhists, making the notion of "socially engaged Buddhism" more relevant in the contemporary world. Meanwhile, Buddhism is also becoming increasingly "privatized," as many regard it as a faith of internal retrospection. This may be understood as a repercussion of increasing secularization that is forcing Buddhists in the postindustrial world to recede from the public domain of faith to the comfort of private worship or psychology. Such a trend is reflected in the rising popularity of Vipassanā meditation that has caught the attention of Western Buddhists. Similarly, there is an attempt to conflate Buddhist aspirations with moral purity and individual endeavor, encouraging vegetarianism and various types of abstinence as a means to distance practitioners from the world that is seen to be materialistic and corrupt.

Impact of Globalization

The activities of Buddhist communities today transcend national borders and regional communities, and the network of monastic recipients and donors (individuals, groups, and organizations) extends far beyond the boundaries of their original affiliation. Globalization has penetrated national borders even in countries such as Myanmar-Burma where the state authorities limit people from traveling or having access to the outside world. However, the growing influx of international tourists to historical Buddhist sites, spiritual seekers looking for teachers and going on retreats, the penetration of global technology, and consumerism are all having an impact on a traditional way of life in Buddhist societies. At another level, globalization that lays emphasis on market economy and mass consumption has turned Buddhism into a kind of commodity at the expense of local sensitivities and faith, commercializing sacred sites and ritual objects. Buddhist paraphernalia and objects of worship such as Tibetan *tanka*s, Buddha images, and even ancient scrolls are transformed into commodities, and ritual chants and recitations are sought after to relieve the stress of urban dwellers in developed countries.

Increased transactions and extending networks, nonetheless, have challenged Buddhists in Asian countries to come up with different responses. Traditionalists regard Buddhism as an important cultural heritage that should be passed down undisturbed and unchanged, whereas modernists regard its transformation and adaptations as necessary for its basic survival. The growing tension between traditionalists, who regard modernity as detrimental to their morality and communal stability, and modernists, who seek relevance of their beliefs and practices in the contemporary world, may be felt acutely today. Some Asian Buddhists hark toward the glorious past, when Buddhism was patronized by Buddhist kings, and express their concern for the degeneration and corruption of Buddhist morality as the result of rapid development and globalization.

The proliferation of Buddhism has also put certain pressures on its doctrine to become more philosophical and rational, lessening the importance of cultural practices and rituals that do not suit the spiritual aspirations of its new followers. Donald S. Lopez Jr. states that popular teachers such as the 14th Dalai Lama or Thich Nhat Hanh have become prominent proponents of Buddhist modernism by spreading universal messages of peace, compassion, and interdependence. As their moral gospel is disseminated in the global scene, Buddhism has become more modern and accessible, and, as a consequence, they have succeeded in reaching an international audience beyond the confinement of a single religious tradition. Meanwhile, the image of Buddhism being solitary and withdrawn has attracted a certain type of devotee in the West, who sees spiritual benefit in its more individualistic practices at the expense of congregational rituals, communal worship, and pantheon of deities. An increased standardization of doctrine has resulted in a homogenized version of "textbook Buddhism," placing much less emphasis on cultural diversity and the syncretic nature of traditional practices. Various patterns of worship and merit-making activities that have been essential for communal celebrations in traditional Buddhist countries have come to be downplayed in this form of modernist Buddhism popular in the West.

The global transmission of Buddhism is also taking place through a proliferation of Buddhist publications, sermon tapes, CDs, and DVDs, as well as through the Internet. Nonetheless, if people can access religious information through books and websites, it is up to every individual to "mix and match" whatever teaching is available and subsequently produce a blend of Buddhism that is eclectic, inconsistent, and without any specific context. The Internet, in particular, seems to have affected the relationship between the guru/master, who was the traditional repository of knowledge, and his disciples/audience. All of the practical skills and knowledge passed down for centuries from teacher to student—that is, traditional methods of memorizing passages, recitation with correct breathing and rhythm, and unique Buddhist homiletics—may eventually become extinct. As *dharma* knowledge becomes increasingly "virtual," the power of mantra and magical quality of chants may become less appreciated as an essential part of Buddhist ritual. Because there is no longer a central authority that controls the procedure to pass on the "secret doctrine," what used to be regulated by personal transmission in exclusive lineages is becoming free for all, as modernist Buddhists look to themselves for such authority. Language is another issue in the global transmission of Buddhism. Esoteric teachings, which used to be passed down in ancient Indian languages of Sanskrit or Pali, Tibetan, and Chinese, are now translated in many languages, and monks' sermons can be downloaded and listened to in English or in Asian vernacular over the Internet.

In the absence of an effective central authority, the media have come to play a prominent role. That is, the media not only communicate information about a religious teaching and ethics but at times act as a kind of moral judicator, criticizing corrupt monks and priests and suggesting future directions for Buddhist leadership. Media are also used by charismatic figures to spread their moral and political messages to the international audience. Tibetan Buddhists in exile, in particular, have been most active in using the virtual community in developing their Buddhist network, disseminating religious and political messages, and keeping in touch with their fellow Tibetans and sympathizers from all over the globe. Nonetheless, their activities are subjected to scrutiny by those threatened by their international network because their religious activities are seen to overlap with their political goals, and a virtual battle for control may take place in cyberspace.

In the context of transnational movements and transactions, there have been charismatic individuals whose vision and initiatives have had a wider impact on the development of Buddhism beyond the confines of regional community. An American theosophist, Henry Olcott, was an early example of such transaction; he helped instigate a Buddhist reformist movement in urban areas of Ceylon in the 19th century. D. T. Suzuki was instrumental in spreading interest in both Zen and Shin Buddhism in the West in the early 20th century. In the 21st century, Hyongak Sunim, an American Buddhist monk, started a revival movement in South Korea where Buddhism was in steady decline. Global transmission has also taken place as a result of monks and nuns studying in other Buddhist countries and taking the doctrinal tradition or lineage back to their own country, which has been the case of nun Dhammavati, who instigated the Theravāda revival movement in Nepal after having studied in Myanmar-Burma. In the case of Thai forest tradition, its ascetic practices were brought back to the West (the United States, England, and Australia) by Western monks and followers of charismatic Thai ascetics, but the transplantation of practices into an alien milieu appears to be much more challenging than doctrinal transmission, especially in the case of the strict forest tradition.

The flow of information and transnational interactions takes place not only in the West-East/East-West relationship, but East-East connections are developing increasingly, as wealthy Asian Buddhist nations take active interest in offering financial support and educational sponsorship to fellow Buddhists in developing countries. In a similar vein, missionizing activities have accelerated in the global scene, and Buddhist organizations from Japan, Taiwan, or Singapore have expanded their influence and established local branches in other parts of the world. In their expansionist scheme, however, worthy charitable causes, such as providing international relief work in the aftermath of natural disasters, become meritorious occasions to provide aid to victims and spread their particular Buddhist agenda. Competition with other religious groups, such as that with evangelical Christian organizations, has intensified as well as sectarian tension among these Buddhist groups, as local activities become transposed to the global scene.

Monasticism

The sangha (the monastic community of ordained monks) has been revered and worshipped as one of the three sacred symbols in Buddhism along with the Buddha and the Dhamma (his teachings). However, as secularization and global consumerism corrode the traditional monastic ideals and an ethical way of life, the very foundation of monasticism is threatened today. Moreover, the notion of *sangha* has come to be apprehended in the West as an exclusive, elitist, and male-centered institution. Buddhist organizations such as the Friends of the Western Buddhist Order have replaced the concept of *sangha* with that of *mitra* (friends) in order to make its community more accessible to the laity and female members. Many of these groups in the West regard the status distinction between the monastic and laity to be no longer relevant for their spiritual practices and monastic rules and regulations no longer applicable to their contemporary worship. Such liberal and modernist views, nonetheless, are not always shared by Buddhists in Southeast Asia or in regions of the Himalayas where Buddhists continue to uphold monasticism as the foundation of their faith, and interactions with monks and are nuns are seen to be an indispensable means for acquiring merit. The reverence the majority of Asian Buddhists have for their monastic members may be further downplayed by Western Buddhists who view it as anachronistic and conservative, creating a tension between the two. However, this does not mean that Asian Buddhists are not critical in their acceptance of the state of their monastic establishment.

As the process of laicization increases in degree, there have been several cases of traditional Buddhist authority being openly contested. Reformist groups, such as Santi Asoke in Thailand, have openly challenged the legitimacy of the sangha, exploring alternative ideals of Buddhist asceticism and moral practices outside the confinement of the monastic institution. The lay association of Japanese Soka Gakkai denounced the religious authority of Nichiren Shoshu priests in the early 1990s, reclaiming the sole authority to conduct ceremonies and initiate members in the organization. When the priesthood is made obsolete, however, the Buddhist organization is often left without ritual specialists of an "otherworldly" outlook, and there is always a danger of its ending up as a personality cult under a charismatic leader. While direct channels are sought by lay congregations to obtain enlightenment without the intervention of monastic intermediaries, the role of monks is undergoing review today as they come under increasing demands to assert a new kind of spiritual leadership that is applicable and relevant to the world today.

In the context of globalization, Buddhist women have been most effective in asserting their rights, working beyond borders, and opening new avenues for cross-fertilization. The international movement to revive higher ordination for Buddhist nuns started in earnest in the mid-1980s, originally instigated by Western Buddhist nuns and Asian Buddhist feminists, as a movement to uplift the position of nuns and close the gender disparity in the Theravāda and Tibetan sangha. The first higher ordination took place in 1996, conferred by Korean monks on Sri Lankan nuns. The second higher ordination took place in 1998, conferred by Fo Guang Shan, an active Taiwanese Buddhist organization promoting Humanistic Buddhism. Although the mixing of Mahāyāna and Theravāda ordination procedures was criticized by some, these occasions led to an international collaboration of Buddhist women who have succeeded in breaking down sectarian barriers, promoting education, and establishing an expanding network of Buddhist women. However, the issue of cross-fertilization between different traditions has raised the issue of Theravāda orthodoxy and split the monastic community into revivalists and anti-revivalists of the *bhikkhunī* lineage. It has also questioned the value of introducing liberal principles of gender equality and status parity into the religious domain of faith and piety, as many Asian nuns do not regard such measure of empowerment relevant to their spiritual life.

Conclusion

To make Buddhism into a world religion, Gavin Flood states the necessity to have it abstracted out of its historical and cultural context, treating it as a religious tradition that is characterized by certain universal characteristics common to all religions. In this process, nonetheless, Buddhism will become further decontexualized, and having eliminated its "idiosyncratic" features, such as propitiating the spirits and petitioning for protection in times of crisis, it undermines the power of deities and traditional role of oracles and mediums that have been an integral part of the tradition. Even the Buddha has become humanized; he is no longer a *bodhisattva* or a deity with magical powers, but only a historical teacher. Globalization seems to have accelerated the devaluation of cultural values and the separation of Buddhism from its historical and cultural tradition. The trend has also standardized Buddhism in its doctrine and practices, and the process has made it increasingly "soul-less." Interestingly, it has also provided an international context in which new idiosyncracies have emerged. For example, there is an increase of non-Tibetan *trulku*s (high reincarnate masters), both men and women, in the international scene. While people create a personally tailored form of idealized Buddhism, ironically there appears to be a strong longing for charismatic spiritual leaders and a new communal affiliation.

Globalization has had a different impact on the East-East relationship in contrast to the East-West relationship in the Buddhist world. For example, Buddhists from wealthy Asian countries, in awe of Tibetan lamas equipped with magical powers and healing skills, visit esoteric shamanic practitioners to regain what they consider to have been lost in their secular societies. The response of Asian Buddhists to traditional values preserved in the monastic community, such as the authority of guru, seniority, and hierarchy, may not appeal to their Western Buddhist counterparts who have replaced them with neoliberal ideals born out of their particular history of European Enlightenment. Meanwhile, we can anticipate that regional variations, cultural practices, and traditional concerns will become purposely subverted in favor of universal ones, and Buddhism could ultimately end up as a self-help therapy, a secular ideology, or a moral philosophy at the most. Globalization ultimately raises the issue of authority in regard to who decides about the future of Buddhism. It also makes us question the notion of "universalism" promoted by Western powers in the context of globalization, as "Buddhism," as we know it, can become ultimately devoid of its historical and cultural context in its universal application.

Hiroko Kawanami

See also Dharma; Ethics, Global; Humanity, Concepts of; Independence Movements; Migration; Peace Activism; Religious Identities; World Cultures; World Religions, Concept of

Further Readings

Baumann, M. (2001). Global Buddhism: Developmental periods, regional histories, and a new analytical perspective. *Journal of Global Buddhism, 2,* 1–43.

Bond, G. D. (2004). *Buddhism at work: Community development, social empowerment and the Sarvodaya movement.* West Hartford, CT: Kumarian Press.

Chandler, S. (2004). *Establishing a pure land on Earth: The Foguang Buddhist perspective on modernization and globalization.* Honolulu: University of Hawai'i Press.

Clarke, P. (2000). Success and failure: Japanese new religions abroad. In P. Clarke (Ed.), *Japanese new religions in global perspective* (pp. 272–311). London: Curzon.

Flood, G. (1999). *Beyond phenomenology: Rethinking the study of religion.* London: Cassell.

Goldstein, M. C., & Kapstein, M. T. (Eds.). (1998). *Buddhism in contemporary Tibet: Religious revival and cultural identity.* Berkeley: University of California Press.

Heine, S., & Prebish, C. S. (2003). *Buddhism in the modern world: Adaptations of an ancient tradition.* Oxford, UK: Oxford University Press.

Kawanami, H. (2007). The Bhikkhunī ordination debate: Global aspirations, local concerns, with special emphasis on the views of the monastic community in Burma. *Buddhist Studies Review, 24*(2), 94–112.

Learman, L. (Ed.). (2004). *Buddhist missionaries in the era of globalization.* Honolulu: University of Hawai'i Press.

Lopez, D. S., Jr. (1998). *Prisoners of Shangri-la: Tibetan Buddhism and the West.* Chicago: University of Chicago Press.

Machacek, D., & Wilson, B. (2000). *Global citizens: The Soka Gakkai Buddhist movement in the world.* Oxford, UK: Oxford University Press.

Prebish, C. S., & Baumann, M. (Eds.). (2002). *Westward dharma: Buddhism beyond Asia.* Berkeley: University of California Press.

Swearer, D. K. (1996). Sulak Sivaraksa's Buddhist vision for renewing society. In S. B. King & C. S. Queen (Eds.), *Engaged Buddhism: Buddhist liberation movements in Asia* (pp. 195–235). Albany: State University of New York Press.

Burial and Crematory Practices

Because burial and crematory practices in many traditions are related to particular places and cultures, the vast mobility and demographic shifts in the global era make many of these traditional customs problematic. However, there has always been a great deal of diversity in the way that the dead are treated and respected, and these practices are applicable in varying ways to the global age.

Corpse treatment and the ritual of passage to pay respects to the deceased are closely related, but it was exceptional in the past to pour great amounts of resources and labor into dealing with the corpse. The pyramids in Egypt and the tombs of ancient kings in East Asia are good examples of gigantic tombs. For the majority of people, however, individual graves have not been built. Leaving the corpses in nature, such as platform burials among Parsees and Tibetan people in which the corpse is defleshed by carnivorous birds and the exposure of corpses to the elements among nomadic people are the remains of simple funerals.

In India, cremation reflects the religious culture of the nation that encourages people to be a part of the cycle of life by returning the corpses to nature rather than keeping them within man-made spaces. In the past, burial in the ground, which is not the same as burial in a grave, was a means of consigning the corpse to the Earth rather than as a means of preserving the corpse. The places where the deceased were buried have often been revered as holy places, but they were not always associated with the preservation of individual corpses or building tombs.

As a class society formed and developed, the practice of preserving corpses and building tombs for persons with high social status and their families spread gradually. The tombs of saints were often thronged as the sites for pilgrimage (worship). Some kings and their liege lords left stately tombs and monuments. It became a matter of course for the rich, from feudal lords to influential people in a locality, to leave their names by building grand tombs. But these were the cases for few people. For the majority, even if they built their tombs expressing their individual characters, many were simple.

In the process of modernization, people became better off, and the ritualistic practice to carefully bury individual persons prevailed. Personal graves and family graves rapidly increased in number, and large-scale cemeteries were built. At the beginning, cemeteries were built in cities, and later, park-like cemeteries were built in suburban areas. In these cemeteries, lots are segmented as grave spaces for families and individuals, and the right to use the space is provided. In some cases, mausoleums were built to show off the wealth and the status of a family. Today, in developing countries, in part due to the global development process, the practice of using tombs for individuals and families is becoming more common. On the other hand, in developed countries, some people are no longer satisfied with individual and family tombs and are seeking new ways to carry out funerals.

The most common funerals in the world are earth burial and cremation. On the death of a person, the body is purified and is dressed in a special costume. Then the corpse is either put in a coffin and buried in the ground or cremated. Cremation has spread since the earlier days and has long been practiced among the Hindus in India. India has an extraordinary position in human history, as this practice has been carried on since olden times. Typically, the corpse is burned together with wood from the river on the riverbanks of the Ganges or other river, and the ashes are poured into the river. There is no tomb. It is believed that a return to the source of life, reincarnation, or emancipation from the earthly materiality can be achieved through this funeral. Belief in the cycle of life is in place here. The holy place on the riverbank, such as Varanasi (Benares), is well known as a place where people waiting for their death gather.

Earth burial is a way to express one's respect to the deceased through paying respect to the corpse and is a symbol of hope for the eternal life of the person after death. The psychology of fear of the corpse being destroyed is reflected in the burial. Christians and Muslims believe that corpses go to their god after the posthumous judgment, and it is the norm for them to leave corpses as they are. In Islamic regions, the body is laid with the head directed toward Mecca. In some Islamic areas, tree branches are placed on both sides of the body on the assumption that this will help the deceased to stand up on his or her feet after the judgment. In

Islamic countries, the style of burial varies from one place to another. In Egypt, stately tombs are built, whereas in Saudi Arabia, a marking stone is placed on the ground.

In China, Korea, and other Asian societies where earth burials prevail, the respect given to the corpses reflects the philosophy of Confucianism and ancestor worship. In Taiwan, Buddhist monks or Taoist priests are involved in funerals and in consoling the spirit of the deceased. In Korea, kin organizations take the lead in building a tomb and conducting respectful funeral services. Rituals for mourning and consoling the soul and visits to the tomb are conducted for many years. In Japan, where Buddhism has deeply permeated the people's life, the practice of cremation spread in the Middle Ages, and both cremation and burial have long been conducted in parallel. After the 17th century, the Confucian influence became stronger, and ancestor worship and consolation deepened and became stronger. Even in the case of cremation, fine graves were built, and the traditions of visits to the graves and holding memorial services have continued.

With the advancement of modernization are two notable trends in funeral rituals. On one hand, the tendency of expanding the scale of funerals or building expensive tombs to reflect the social status of individuals and families has spread. On the other hand, there is a movement to simplify funerals and tombs due to factors such as the rationalization of belief and the weakening of traditional beliefs as well as the mounting negative feeling toward the expansion of formalistic funerals and tombs. In the Western Christian cultural sphere of the West, the simplification of funerals and tombs is remarkable among the Protestant community, while the Catholic community tends to maintain solemnly ceremonial funerals and large tombs, and to visit their tombs earnestly.

The most notable change is the spread of the practice of cremation. Cremation does not require a large amount of space, as does burial in a coffin, and thus is sometimes viewed as a solution to the problem of space. Cremation is an answer to this problem, as it does not occupy a wide space. In Europe and North America, some people advocated cremation in the 19th century; however, it was in the 20th century that this practice rapidly increased. At the end of the 20th century, the ratio of cremation exceeded 50% of funerals in places such as Britain, Germany, and the Scandinavian countries. In the case of cremation, some put ashes in an urn and bury it in the ground, whereas others put ashes in an urn in a space called a *columbarium* in which box-like containers are overlaid in a wall-like structure. There also are cases in which the ashes of more than one person are laid together, or in which ashes are scattered in a specific space in a park-type cemetery. In these cases, tombs or tombstones identifying the dead do not remain.

A remarkable change along with the spread of cremation is the development of the funeral business. In the past, relatives and neighbors would conduct necessary proceedings for a funeral. As the process of industrialization progressed, a funeral services business grew and began to undertake the burial services immediately after death. In the United States, where this trend spread faster, instead of churches, halls owned by funeral agencies were increasingly used for funerals and receiving condolatory visitors. At the same time, a technique of embellishing the appearance of the corpses was developed. Even in places where this technique is not applied, holding funerals at halls owned by funeral business corporations in place of houses, religious facilities, or hospitals is on the rise across the world.

In eastern Europe, Russia, and China, funerals and tombs were simplified during the socialist period. After the collapse of the USSR, and along with the progress toward capitalism in China, there was a movement to revive traditional funerals and graves. In Taiwan and other Chinese communities and Korea, where cremation was infrequent in the past, cremation has been rapidly increasing since the end of the 20th century. In Japan, cremation became the preferred practice during the latter half of the 20th century, with the urns placed in the ground in a family grave space with a stone monument. Toward the end of the 20th century, a new trend of seeking different styles of funerals grew in Japan. These styles include ash scattering in the sea or in a forest together with planting a memorial tree (tree funeral), and laying ashes in a joint repository with those of nonfamily members. This trend may imply the transformation of a posthumous ritual strongly influenced by East Asian tradition whereby people continually conduct lavish religious services for deceased individuals in a family across generations, centered around a family grave.

Susumu Shimazono

See also Cultural Diversity, Convention on; Ethnic Identity; Family; Global Religions, Beliefs, and Ideologies; Heritage; Identities, Traditional; Memory Wars

Further Readings

Adams, R. L., & King, S. M. (2010). Residential burial in global perspective. *Archeological Papers of the American Anthropological Association, 20*(1), 1–16.

Gillespie, S. D. (2010). Inside and outside: Residential burial at formative period Chalcatzingo, Mexico. *Archeological Papers of the American Anthropological Association, 20*(1), 98–120.

Iqbal, Z. (2011). McDonaldization, Islamic teachings, and funerary practices in Kuwait. *Omega: Journal of Death and Dying, 63*(1), 95–112.

McAnany, P. A. (2010). Practices of place-making, ancestralizing, and re-animation within memory communities. *Archeological Papers of the American Anthropological Association, 20*(1), 136–142.

Nakamatsu, T. (2009). Conventional practice, courageous plan: Women and the gendered site of death rituals in Japan. *Journal of Gender Studies, 18*(1), 1–11.

Natali, C. (2008). Building cemeteries, constructing identities: Funerary practices and nationalist discourse among the Tamil Tigers of Sri Lanka. *Contemporary South Asia, 16*(3), 287–301.

C

CABLE NEWS NETWORK (CNN)

The Cable News Network (CNN) began modestly in 1980 in the United States as the first 24-hour, all-news television channel in the United States, transmitted on cable television systems. A few years later, it had changed not only the broadcasting landscape but also the daily TV information flow, which occurs without borders on a global scale.

Created in Atlanta, Georgia, by Ted Turner on June 1, 1980, CNN was based on a small, independent local cable channel. But a new era began with the all-news format distributed through a network of cable systems. In 1982, CNN created a second channel, Headline News, and in 1985, it added CNN International based in London, which initially aimed at European countries and later expanded globally. CNN provided an American alternative to the BBC as an English-language global news medium. The value of CNN as a 24-hour global news source became clear during the first Gulf War, when it began war coverage on January 17, 1991, during the terrorist attacks and subsequent events of September 11, 2001, and during the 2003 invasion and occupation of Iraq. In the meantime, however, CNN faced new competition as a global news medium from other cable and satellite news channels and from the Internet. The originality of CNN, with CNN Domestic also broadcasting in Canada and CNN International broadcast in more than 150 countries, lies in the construction of a network of permanent offices and journalists-correspondents throughout the world (including Moscow, Cuba, and Beijing), which provided TV information flow, including "breaking news" and investigative reporting. With the technologies of its time (cables in the vicinity and satellites covering the world), CNN created a network for its channels comparable with those constructed more than 100 years before by international press agencies like Havas (in 1832, becoming Agence France Presse [AFP] in 1944), Associated Press (AP, in 1848), Reuters (in 1851), or United Press Association (UP, in 1907). CNN's success can also be attributed to other aspects of the global media space, such as TV subscription managers, who included CNN in their subscription packages, and hotels, which until 1987 were the only private firms accessing CNN.

The global significance of CNN is that it created an opportunity for governments, elites, upper classes, international CEOs, English-speaking populations, travelers, and tourists to have access to 24-hour TV news regardless of the time in their local time zones. Many people around the world saw the space shuttle *Challenger* explode live on January 28, 1986, and most of the world's TV channels used CNN's footage of that event. Similarly, many viewed CNN broadcasts of the fall of the Berlin Wall and "the Romanian Revolution" in

1989, the Gulf War of 1991 (with live video feed from Baghdad, Riyadh, and Jerusalem), the O. J. Simpson trial in 1995, the congressional hearings during the Monica Lewinsky scandal in 1998, September 11, 2001, the Second Gulf War or Iraq war in 2003, the Tsunami in South Asia in 2004, the 2010 earthquake in Haiti, and the 2011 earthquake and tsunami in Japan.

Born in Atlanta, Georgia, in 1939, Ted Turner symbolizes a new example of a self-made man of the American Dream, especially in the world of the media. After his father's death in 1963, he inherited his billboard business, Turner Outdoor Advertising, which became Turner Communications, and he bought a radio station in Tennessee and two others in South Carolina and Florida. In 1970, he also bought a freelance cable TV network and two sports teams (basketball and baseball) in Atlanta. The broadcasting of the games of these teams enlarged the audience of the TV firm. In 1976, Turner integrated it into a satellite system, which brought a national audience to this local TV programming. In 1980, he created a new TV cable channel, specializing in nonstop information flow: CNN and later Headline News. The second developed the headlines of the daily news, especially these chosen and realized by the first one with its events in live television.

In 1986, Turner bought the cinema catalogue of Metro Goldwyn Mayer-United Artists. In 1988, he created Turner Network Television (TNT), his own TV cable network to better manage the satellite links with the viewers of all his channels. The breakthrough moment for CNN was the Persian Gulf War of 1991. CNNI, having negotiated with U.S. General Norman Schwarzkopf, commander of the Desert Storm Operation, the presence of its reporters on the war ground, covered the war "live from Baghdad," continuously for 17 days. Schwarzkopf made possible the "CNN effect," as the impact on the foreign policies and the world opinions of this 24-hour network TV was called, in live and permanent world broadcast, as well as preserving the exclusivity of CNN's reports and its footage. The "exclusive U.S. point of view" delivered by CNN was also an impetus for the creation of Al Jazeera, an Arabian information satellite TV channel, to create an alternative point of view with transnational viewership, in 1996 in Doha, the Qatari capital. Al Jazeera became a network

offering a 24-hour CNN-style news format in Arabic, with a focus on the Middle East. Although many key personnel in Al Jazeera had formerly worked with the BBC, the network was dubbed by many as "Arabian CNN." The U.S. government, during the administration of George W. Bush, responded to the challenge of Al Jazeera with another international channel, Al Hurra, or the free Arabic TV, also in Arabic and broadcasting live since February 2, 2004. It appeared just 1 year after the Saudian channel Al Arabiya was created by the Middle East Broadcasting Center (Dubai, February 19, 2003). Other international TV channels and networks include Fox News (the TV firm of News Corp. owned by Rupert Murdoch), BBC World, Euronews, and France 24. In 1996, Time Warner, the corporation formed from the 1990 merger of Warner Communication and Time Inc., bought TBS for US$7 billion. In 2000, Time Warner and AOL merged and became the first multimedia group in the world. This was also the period of increasing stock exchange speculation (1995–2000) in the new information and communication technologies (ICT and Internet) sector. After the Internet bubble burst, CNN went through several crises during the presidency of Steve Case, who was the founder of AOL. However, the new group became the second of the 50 leading audiovisual companies worldwide, after Walt Disney and before News Corp. and Sony. Since 2009, AOL and Time Warner are separate companies again.

In 1996, other future CNN competitors emerged. Businessman Rupert Murdoch (News Corp.) bought the 20th Century Fox corporation of Hollywood, after taking over the satellite operator British Sky Broadcasting (BSkyB) in 1990. The same year in the United States, Bill Gates's Microsoft Corporation acquired the TV channel NBC, a subsidiary of General Electric, and created the Microsoft National Broadcasting Corporation (MSNBC). In the same year, CNN also created special focus channels such as CNNfn (Financial) and CNNSI (Sports Illustrated), as well as multimedia services and participating activities for "citizen journalism" like CNN Interactive and CNN.com. However, Time Warner decided to stop CCN SI's activities in 2002 by creating a new joint venture with NBA TV and to replace CNNfn by websites in 2004 for profitability reasons.

At the beginning of the third millennium, CNN News Group was organized in six regional networks (North America, Latin America, Europe, Middle East, Asia, and South Asia), and it has nine main channels: CNN US, CNN en Español (USA), CNN Headline News or HNL (USA), CNN Airport Network, CNNI (world), CNN Chile, CNN Türk, CNN-IBN (India), and CNNj (Japan). Together, these channels reach more than 200,000 homes and 1 billion persons in the world. Nevertheless, CNN is no longer the leader in the European media space: Euronews, which has been broadcasting since January 1, 1993, became the leader, and its audience is considerably larger than that of CNNI. However, in 2011, it uses 11 languages, not exclusively English. The pace of global television development has moved beyond the initial global success of CNN and the "CNN effect" of the first Gulf War.

Michel Mathien

See also Al Jazeera; Global Communications and Technology; Information Age; Journalism; Knowledge Production Systems; Media, Global; News; Television

Further Readings

Flournoy, D., & Stewart, R. K. (1997). *CNN: Making news in the global market*. Luton, UK: University of Luton Press.

Mathien, M. (2005). Relations internationales et médias: CNN et les autres [International relations and media: CNN and the others]. *Questions Internationales, 16*, 105–112.

Semprini, A. (2000). *CNN et la mondialisation de l'imaginaire [CNN and the globalization of the imagination]*. Paris: CNRS Editions.

Volkmer, I. (1998). *News in the global sphere. A study of CNN and its impact on global comunication*. Lutton, UK: University of Luton Press.

CALIPHATE

The caliphate (Arabic: *khilafa*) refers to the historical institution of centralized religiopolitical authority in Islam, particularly in its Sunni branch. Traditionally and symbolically, the jurisdiction of the caliph—the title assumed by the office holder—was global in scope, and his authority applied to all Muslims worldwide. Although formally abolished as an institution 1924, the concept has received attention in the contemporary global era as a result of the rise of transnational Islamic social and political movements in the context of globalization—including several groups who posit the revival of the caliphate as an explicit political objective.

The first caliph, or "successor," was appointed in 632 at the time of the death of the prophet Muhammad. The question of who should lead the nascent Muslim state after Muhammad's passing prompted the initial manifestation of what would later become the main sectarian cleavage in Islam, between Sunni and Shī'a . Where the latter felt that leadership of the community should be vested in the Prophet's family, the former—who soon prevailed—argued for a model of political succession based on seniority and merit.

Reflecting the belief, central to Islamic political theory, that sovereignty ultimately belongs to God alone, the caliph was understood to function as a viceregent charged with the worldly enforcement of divine law (Shari'a). The first four caliphs, collectively known as the *rashidun* ("rightly guided"), carry special significance insofar as their rule (632–661) is regarded as a period of relatively enlightened governance. Even in the 21st century, the time of the rashidun caliphs is considered by Muslims to exemplify a pure form of religious society and, hence, a model worthy of emulation. The passing of these early caliphs marked the beginning of Islamic dynastic rule. As the Muslim world expanded geographically and culturally, it inevitably fragmented politically. Although the caliph remained a nominal constant throughout the medieval and early modern periods, his effective political monopoly over the *umma* (the world community of believers) ended by the 10th century as the Muslim world began to splinter into kingdoms and empires.

During this time, the minority branch of Islam, the Shī'a, recognized an entirely different line of leaders. The *imamate* was based on the aforementioned belief that the Prophet's family possessed superior religious authority. Beginning with 'Ali (also recognized by Sunnis as the fourth and final rashidun caliph), the Shī'a chart an alternative genealogy of religious authority that more closely approximates the Catholic apostolic tradition. Subdenominations of Shī'a Islam recognize imamate lineages of varying scale, but the majority branch acknowledges 12, the last of whom is understood to have left the world and entered a state of occultation in the 10th century. Shī'a in this tradition believe that the final imam will one day return in a messianic form known as the Mahdi to consolidate the rule of Islam around the world. Absent a living religiopolitical figurehead, authority in the contemporary Shī'a world is vested in the guardianship of a group of geographically and nationally diverse senior religious scholars, the *marja'iyya al-taqlid* ("sources of emulation").

Under the expansive and culturally diverse Ottoman Empire (1300–1922) the caliphate experienced a renewed period of cosmopolitanism. Ottoman Sultans carried the parallel title of caliph from the 16th century until the institution's abolition in 1924 at the hands of Mustafa Kemal with the founding of the modern Turkish republic. As a global civilization stretching from West Africa to the Malay archipelago, the geographic mandate of the caliphate took in much of what was soon to become the postcolonial world. Muslims of diverse backgrounds and political orientations, hence, took an interest in the fate of the caliphate in the years leading up to and immediately after World War I. In India, the Khilafat Movement, which would eventually play a far more significant role in the development of the nationalist movement in India, was founded initially to exert influence on the British to preserve the Ottoman formation of the caliphate after the war. Without invoking the institutional authority of the caliphate, Jamal ad-Din al-Afghani (1838–1897) established an anticolonial movement based on worldwide Muslim unity and "Pan-Islam."

The actual event of the caliphate's abolition in 1924 prompted something of a crisis among Muslim intellectuals. Some, such as Rashid Rida (1865–1935), argued that the caliphate was indeed a necessity but a form of governance inappropriate to the prevailing world order. His thinking was instrumental in laying the groundwork for what would soon become an effort to establish Islamic polities within the boundaries of modern nation-states, a political ideology known as Islamism. His intellectual opponent, 'Ali 'Abd al-Raziq (1888–1966), argued to the contrary that nowhere in Islamic sources was there to be found any institutional basis for the caliphate. He took the position that any form of government, including secular democracy, was acceptable as long as it was compatible with the basic principles of Islam.

Despite the political claims of various Muslim leaders in the wake of World War I and several semi-institutionalized efforts—such as the Muslim Congresses of the interwar period—the caliphate concept was quickly overtaken by the nation-state in the political imagination of Muslims worldwide. Even in the thinking of the major exponents of Islamism—the major ideological effort seeking to establish an Islamic political order in the nation-state era—the caliphate took on a different significance. Hassan al-Banna, the founder of the Muslim Brotherhood, for example, spoke little of the caliphate, figuring it as relevant only to a vague and distant future of Islamist activism. Abu'l Ala Maududi of Pakistan's Jama'at-i Islami popularized the caliphate, arguing that every Muslim carried the responsibilities of serving as God's viceregent on earth in the context of what he termed a "theo-democratic" model of government.

The caliphate has remained marginal to mainstream Muslim political thought into the 21st century. A minority position, such as the one contained in the salafi-jihadist worldview that lies behind the al Qaeda movement, has exploited the absence of a caliph to revise centuries of Islamic Just War tradition—which in its central facets closely resembles Just War Theory in the Christian West—to argue for an individual Muslim obligation to undertake jihad. Yet most Muslims view the caliphate as a historical and largely intangible ideal. A few isolated political movements, such as Hizb ut-Tahrir (the Party of Liberation), actively seek to reestablish the caliphate but have generally failed to gain a critical mass of support beyond their generalized critique of Western hegemony and geopolitics. Although a centralized world, Muslim political leadership seems unlikely to appear in this century; some have suggested that globalization and Muslim transnational networking may lend renewed relevance to the concept of a global Muslim community, or *ummah*.

Peter Mandaville

See also Global Religions, Beliefs, and Ideologies; Islam; Islam-Related Movements; Religious Politics; Shari'a (Islamic Law)

Further Readings

Enayat, H. (2004). *Modern Islamic political thought*. London: Tauris.

Mandaville, P. (2007). *Global political Islam*. London: Routledge.

CAPITALISM

The spread of "global capitalism" in the global era has been driven by multinational corporations and transnational corporations. It has also been nurtured by international financial institutions (IFIs) such as the International Monetary Fund (IMF), the World Bank, the Asian Development Bank, and free trade conventions such as the General Agreement on Trade and Tariffs (GATT) and its successor, the World Trade Organization (WTO), North American Free Trade Agreement (NAFTA), the European Union, and MERCOSUR (the Southern Common Market that includes Argentina, Paraguay, Uruguay, and Brazil)—just to name a few.

The term *capitalism* generally involves what may be called—depending on one's perspective—the "value-added use" or the "exploitation" of the factors of production, namely, land, labor, and money, in ways that are meant to generate surplus wealth known as profit. Capitalists invest their money in those enterprises that they believe will augment their wealth. Sometimes they win, and sometimes they lose. Capitalism therefore, assumes that there is an inherent risk when individuals (known as entrepreneurs) undertake actions that could possibly make them worse off.

In a capitalist system, producers aim to create consumers. Producers exploit natural and created resources (regarded as factors of production) to produce goods and services to satisfy the wants and needs of their customers. Advancements in the methods of production that accompanied the industrial revolution expanded the productive appetites of powerful industrialists and fueled their thirst for natural resources.

Laissez-Faire Capitalism

Market capitalism is associated with classical liberals such as Adam Smith and David Ricardo who promoted the doctrine known as laissez-faire or free market economics. Smith's exegesis, titled *The Wealth of Nations*, was released in the late 18th century during the heyday of a doctrine known as mercantilism. Under mercantilism, the state acted as both the principal entrepreneur and the principal agent that was in charge of regulating the economy. These dual roles were jointly undertaken by the government for the explicit purpose of maximizing state power. Holding to the view that the free market was the most efficient mechanism for allocating the world's wealth, Smith challenged the mercantilist assumption that free trade meant that one country's gains were realized at the direct expense of another's loss. Alternatively, Smith argued that the role of the state in the economy should be limited to preventing powerful firms from establishing oligopolies or monopolies that would pose a threat to free markets. Smith held that the purpose of the state, therefore, was to protect and defend market competition.

Sharing Smith's views on the free market, Ricardo articulated a theory known as comparative advantage that proposed that countries should specialize in certain areas of production where they enjoyed relatively superiority. Accordingly, since England enjoyed a relative abundance of machine-intensive industries when compared with India in the 17th and 18th centuries, England could produce manufactured goods such as finished textiles more efficiently. And since India, in contrast, enjoyed an abundant supply of labor and agricultural-producing land relative to England, India could produce raw cotton more efficiently. According to Ricardo's theory, India should specialize in growing and harvesting raw cotton and sell it to Britain. India could then turn around and use its newly realized profits to purchase finished cloth produced in Britain. Ricardo argued that the result of such an arrangement was a win-win outcome for both involved parties. Moreover, even if a given country could produce both raw cotton and finished cloth more efficiently than all others, Ricardo's theory suggested that countries focus their energies and resources in particular areas where they enjoyed a comparative advantage.

Although all share a similar kind of reverence for the notion of private property, one must bring out that there are in fact what political scientists Peter A. Hall and David Soskice refer to as "a variety of capitalisms." Unfortunately many explanations on the topic tend to gloss over the fact that there are substantial differences between capitalist systems in the United States as compared with France or those emerging in the 21st century in Asia. And the various forms of capitalism that have been developing in Latin America have involved strong doses of government-led industrial strategies that have caused them to resist the free trading ideals as originally espoused by Ricardo and Smith.

The Age of Managed Capitalism

The capitalist systems that developed and evolved in the United States and Britain after the Great Depression of the 1930s involved a great deal more government intervention than classical liberals could ever have envisioned. Leaders such as President Franklin D. Roosevelt in the United States sought to save capitalism from certain death by ushering in a new era of government regulation and assistance. Both governments oversaw unprecedented bailout packages of their respective country's floundering financial systems and the implementation of new regulatory systems in an effort to prevent future crises. This new form of managed capitalism was validated by the ideas advanced by economist John Maynard Keynes. Keynes proposed that governments could employ certain macroeconomic policy tools to prevent the subsequent occurrence of "boom and bust" economic scenarios. He argued that governments should increase public spending during economic downturns to spur growth and cut back spending when the economy might be growing too fast and in danger of overheating.

The widespread application of Keynesian ideas by various governments across the industrialized world, ranging from the United States to Europe all the way to Japan, caused many to refer to the period from 1945 to the 1960s as the golden age of managed capitalism. This period was characterized by the development of exchange rate regimes to promote stable international markets and the expansion of welfare states to protect labor and

the working poor. According to political scientist Peter J. Katzenstein, this form of capitalism enjoyed particular prominence among the small social democratic states such as Austria, Norway, and Denmark. Boasting strong levels of productivity growth and relatively low unemployment throughout most the golden era, these small democratic states seemed to demonstrate successfully that there need not be any contradiction between the dual pursuits of social justice and strong macroeconomic performance. The relatively small size of their economies compelled their industrial sectors to specialize in highly particular export-oriented products and services. This made their domestic industries heavily dependent on international trade for raw resources and market outlets for their finished goods. As a result, they were highly vulnerable to global economic shocks. They responded to these imperatives by adopting and implementing government-assisted industrial strategies aimed at promoting more flexible production profiles and agile labor markets. During periods of economic hardship or adjustment, labor union elites, peak business groups, and state officials worked together to bring about formal agreements whereby workers often accepted reduced wages from their private employers in exchange for receiving generous state-sponsored welfare packages for their domestic workers.

The onset of two massive oil shocks that occurred in early and latter parts of the 1970s, however, drove up the global price of crude, thereby increasing production costs and fueling inflation. During this period, traditional government-managed remedies of increasing government spending to propel demand seemed only to make matters worse as national deficits soared while productivity declined, leading to massive layoffs. Widespread disillusionment with golden-age demand management strategies inspired many to revert to more fundamentalist market capitalist ideas. Thus, the era of neoliberal capitalism was born.

Neoliberal Capitalism

Authors David Harvey and Naomi Klein indicated that neoliberal capitalism was associated with the rise of the so-called political New Right in the United States, Britain, and Chile in the late 1970s and early 1980s. Not unlike the broader notion of capitalism itself, the particular brand of neoliberal capitalism came in various forms and guises. Two of the most well-known strands of neoliberal capitalism included Laffer-Curve supply-side economics, which was embraced by U.S. president Ronald Reagan, and monetarism, which was championed by Chilean president Augusto Pinochet and British prime minister Margaret Thatcher.

Popularized in the 1960s and 1970s by Nobel Prize–winning economist Milton Friedman, monetarists took the view that the key to a sound economy rested fundamentally in stabilizing a country's money supply. For monetarists, then, the greatest threat to stable and sustainable growth was the looming and ever-present threat of inflation that they argued came part and parcel with the emergence of the previous so-called welfare state era associated with managed capitalism. Monetarists argued that the development and maintenance of large welfare states depended on increased taxes and large sums of government spending. Many of these politically popular and expensive social policies outpaced government revenues, forcing governments to borrow beyond their means, thereby fueling inflationary pressures. Fearing inflation above all else, Friedmanite monetarists were prepared to take draconian steps to gut many needed social welfare policies for the poor, including those pertaining to basic education and health care.

President Pinochet's dictatorial regime oversaw a series of monetarist-directed deregulation and privatization schemes that were part of a broader assault on Chile's social welfare state. Pinochet's regime subsequently abolished price controls in an effort to control the country's enduring hyperinflation problem as well as removed restrictions on imports to compel modernization of the domestic economy. In a calculated effort to minimize any political dissent that might impede the swift and decisive implementation of his monetarist reform agenda, Pinochet resorted to ruthless measures when dealing with members of the opposition.

Although much milder in her political approach, Thatcher's monetarist crusade involved concerted attempts to dismantle large chunks of her country's welfare state. Determined to fight inflation and slash deficit expenditure, her government initiated a series of a spending cuts aimed squarely at her country's welfare sector. In addition, Thatcher sold large portions of the country's public housing and public utilities sector into private hands, using the profits to pay down the country's public debts. Consistent with her monetarist leanings, Thatcher did all she could to promote unfettered market competition, which included undertaking a revolutionary effort to revamp Britain's waning financial sector. In an initiative known as Big Bang, the Thatcher government eviscerated long-standing trading restrictions and slashed sales commissions to attract new global business. Investors swarmed back to London's new globally competitive trading markets in search of higher returns. However, the euphoria generated by windfall profits that initially accompanied Big Bang inspired a massive stock bubble that ultimately burst on the now infamous Black Monday of 1987.

Neoliberal capitalism was briskly introduced into the U.S. White House by President Ronald Reagan in 1981. Named for the economist Arthur Laffer, Laffer-Curve supply-side economics (otherwise known as Reaganomics, trickle-down economics, or voodoo economics) asserted that governments needed to cut excessive taxes on private individual wealth to spur much needed private investment in the economy. Reducing taxes, they argued, would free up new capital that could then be redirected into private investment schemes. Although Reagan and other Laffer-Curve supply-siders were philosophically opposed to the growth of big government, they took a much more measured approach to welfare retrenchment than their monetarist counterparts. This in part stemmed from the fact that they were less worried about rising budget deficits and their potential for fueling inflation.

In the 1980s, the Reagan administration supported an initiative that deregulated the savings and loan (S&L) industry. Prior to the deregulation, S&Ls were in the business of lending out their customers' savings deposits to home loan borrowers. The deregulation strategy now allowed them to invest their customers' money in risky stocks and bonds so that they could seek greater profit returns. Investor-driven speculations fueled a 3-year-long bull market, which began in 1984. In the fall of 1987, however, the speculative bubble burst and the value of the New York Stock Exchange plummeted during an event now known as Black Monday, which echoed the experience of Thatcher's Big Bang.

Global Capitalism and the Washington Consensus

The second half of the 20th century saw the global economy shaped by an ideological battle or cold war between a so-called Marxist-inspired central planning model pushed by the Soviet Union and its Eastern bloc allies on one end of the spectrum and the market-oriented approach that was pressed by rich Western nations on the other end. With the collapse of the Soviet Union in the early 1990s, many developing countries belonging to the so-called global South began simultaneous moves toward more market-oriented systems. These movements encouraged many in the West to claim a victory for capitalism over all other systems prematurely. During this pivotal period, several powerful IFIs sought to enforce a particular set of capitalist objectives and concrete policy applications in the developing world. The Washington Consensus, as it became known, referred to the lowest common denominator of policy advice. Coined by economist John Williamson and championed by the IMF, the World Bank, the Paris Club, the London Club, and most neoclassical economists, the Washington Consensus suggested that economic relief be offered to assist countries whose economies were imperiled in exchange for faithfully adopting certain policy conditionalities. These conditionalities, in turn, required countries to adopt the following: prudent fiscal spending practices, tax reform that promoted entrepreneurial development, policies that liberalized government controls on the flow of capital moving in and out the country, realistic exchange rates, freer trade practices, enforceable laws that protected private property rights, and policies that promote basic education and health care to its poorest citizens.

By the mid-1990s, the Washington Consensus won over the sympathies of Russian president Boris Yeltsin. Indeed, Yeltsin's capitalist reform agenda directly reflected the policy recommendations outlined by the Consensus. The Russian president sought to put an end to communist-era price controls and implemented a massive privatization program that included the sale of nearly 250,000 state-owned companies. In addition, he took great strides to pry open the Russian market to foreign trade. Unfortunately, the case of Russia's Big Bang capitalist transformation seemed to depict a worst-case scenario of capitalism gone wrong. Poorly implemented privatization schemes allowed for the rise of ruthless oligarchs who became notorious for using their inordinate power and influence to undermine rather than support the development of healthy competitive markets.

Asian Developmental Capitalism

In 1993, the World Bank issued a report proclaiming the East Asian developmental capitalist model "a miracle." The report praised the governments of emerging economies of Thailand, Indonesia, Malaysia, South Korea, and the Philippines for promoting a cooperative rather than an adversarial relationship with the respective countries' business and labor sectors. The report highlighted the essential role that state elites played in helping countries develop and promote their export-oriented industrial sectors. Additionally, development economists such as Chalmers Johnson and Robert Wade have credited the success of the Japanese, Taiwanese, Singaporean, and South Korean economies, in particular, to "wise decisions" made by a group of enlightened national leaders and permanently appointed bureaucrats who possessed the sovereign authority to design and implement superior national industrial policies.

As articulated by Johnson, Wade, and others, the Asian developmental capitalist model involved selective government intervention in the private economy that helped bolster the global competitiveness of particularly favored high-growth industries. Indeed, government officials had the power to redirect their countries' capital financial resources toward particular export-oriented industries. In addition, these industrial policies often placed initial restrictions on free trade to protect their countries' budding domestic firms from cutthroat global competition. Once their domestic firms had grown strong enough, trade restrictions would be lifted.

By the middle-to-late 1990s, however, several governments within these East Asian economies began moving their developmental capitalist systems more into line with neoliberal directives. Japan took the lead in that effort. Under the leadership of Prime Minister Hashimoto, Japan pursued a vigorous deregulation drive that sought to revamp Tokyo's financial system in much the same way as Thatcher's Big Bang. The Hashimoto government overturned historic regulatory legislation that traditionally separated the business functions and practices performed by private banks, insurance companies, and securities firms. The deregulation reforms facilitated a whole new range of investment products and business opportunities that firms could now offer to their international customers. Initially, the Hashimoto's reforms seemed to be a great success as many international investors flocked to the Tokyo trading exchange to take advantage of these new business opportunities.

By the late 1990s, the governments of several Southeast Asian economies followed Japan's neoliberal tack by systematically liberalizing restrictions on international capital flows. In addition, they raised interest rates and pegged their currencies to the U.S. dollar in the hopes of courting additional international investment. Initially, their neoliberal efforts were received warmly by international investors who began pouring unprecedented amounts of wealth into their markets, thereby boosting stock and real estate values throughout the region. Speculative euphoria, however, quickly gave way to suspicions that stock and real estate prices had become overvalued. As speculative fears mounted, panicked investors began withdrawing their money at alarming rates, thereby igniting a full-blown regional financial crisis.

Third Way Capitalism

The election of Bill Clinton in the United States in 1992 and Tony Blair in Britain in 1997 ushered a "Third Way" form of capitalism onto the scene. First coined by London School of Economics and Political Science (LSE) Director Anthony Giddens, the Third Way approach to capitalism jointly emphasized an energized role for government in supporting private entrepreneurial-based growth on the one hand, while guaranteeing social provisions such as basic health care on the other hand. According to the Third Way, the policy agendas of progressive governments needed to be transformed from those that sought to give struggling families a handout via traditional long-term welfare payment

programs into ones offering them a temporary hand up via low-interest educational loans and grants. Third Way politicians often denounced short-term wage bargaining tactics characteristically used by traditional workers' unions to help their members cope with cost of living increases in favor of expanding tax credits to decrease income for individuals and families.

Capitalism and the Great Financial Crisis

Labeled the "greatest recession since the Great Depression," the so-called great financial crisis (GFC) of 2008–2009 fueled intense debates about global capitalism and its alternatives. Many individuals identified the infamous deregulation and liberalization of policies that were undertaken in the era of neoliberal capitalism as the main culprit for the crisis. In response, citizens around the world rallied for the return to the golden age of managed capitalism. Such voices demanded that governments institute new regulations governing financial markets and their trading practices. Remarkably, many neoliberal capitalists themselves ended up supporting public bailouts and takeovers of fledgling private banks, insurance companies, and manufacturing industries. If there are, indeed, a variety of capitalisms, then they may become incarnate in many other forms in the future.

Ravi K. Roy

See also Antiglobalization Movements and Critics; Economic Development; Global Economic Issues; Globalization, Phenomenon of; Ideologies, Global; Inequality, Global Economic; Investments; Liberalism, Neoliberalism; Marxism and Neo-Marxism; Mercantilism; World Economic Forum

Further Readings

Battersby, P., & Siracusa, J. M. (2008). *Globalization and human security*. Lanham, MD: Rowman & Littlefield.

Fulcher, J. (2004). *Capitalism: A very short introduction.* Oxford, UK: Oxford University Press.

Galbraith, J. K. (1952). *American capitalism: The concept of countervailing power.* Boston: Houghton Mifflin.

Giddens, A. (1998). *The Third Way: The renewal of social democracy.* Cambridge, UK: Polity Press.

Hall, P. A., & Soskice, D. W. (Eds.). (2001). *Varieties of capitalism: The institutional advantages of comparative advantage*. Oxford, UK: Oxford University Press.

Harvey, D. (1990). *The political-economic transformation of late twentieth century capitalism*. Malden, MA: Blackwell.

Harvey, D. (2005). *A brief history of neoliberalism*. Oxford, UK: Oxford University Press.

Hayek, F. A. (1975). *The pure theory of capital*. Chicago: University of Chicago Press.

Heilbroner, R. L. (1985). *The nature and logic of capitalism*. New York: Norton.

Johnson, C. (1982). *MITI and the Japanese miracle: The growth of industrial policy, 1925–1975*. Stanford, CA: Stanford University Press.

Katzenstein, P. J. (1985). *Small states in world markets: Industrial policy in Europe*. Ithaca, NY: Cornell University Press.

Klein, N. (2007). *The shock doctrine*. London: Penguin Books.

Marx, K., & Engels, F. (1967). *The communist manifesto*. London: Penguin Books.

Polanyi, K. (1944). *The great transformation*. Boston: Beacon Press.

Rostow, W. W. (1960). *The stages of economic growth: A non-Communist manifesto*. Cambridge, UK: Cambridge University Press.

Smith, A. (1776). *An inquiry into the nature and causes of the wealth of nations*. London: Strahan & Cadell.

Stiglitz, J. (2002). *Globalization and its discontents*. London, UK: Allen Lane.

Weber, M. (1930). *The Protestant ethic and the spirit of capitalism*. St Leonards, UK: Allen and Unwin.

Cartoons, Comix, Manga

Published under a variety of names, comics have long been an important form of local and global communication that has played a key role in internationalizing visual storytelling styles and genres. Various definitions of the comics form have been advanced by scholars, and no single conception seems to accommodate the vast breadth of the field. In general, comics are widely held to be narratives, constructed using the copresence of sequential images and, frequently, the text.

Each of the various terms commonly used to refer to the comics actually designates a different specific iteration of the form. *Cartoon* is frequently used to refer to nonsequential humor illustrations in newspapers and magazines. *Comic strip* designates works that appear in daily or weekly newspapers. *Comic book* refers to the American magazine format for comics popularized in the 1930s. *Comix* was widely used in the 1960s and 1970s to describe comics produced by and for the American counterculture. *Graphic novel* is a more recent marketing term referring alternately to collections of comic books produced for the book trade and to long-form comics intended for adult audiences. *Manga*, which is "whimsical pictures" in Japanese, is used to refer to all Japanese comics in translation. Although comics have been produced in all cultures, three national traditions—the United States, France-Belgium, and Japan—have most strongly shaped the evolution of the art form. The intersections of these various examples of the comics form highlights shifting conceptions of transnational culture at the current time.

Cartoons, Comic Strips, and Comic Books

The rise of the comics form is historically tied to the development of mass printing, and, in particular, to daily newspapers and illustrated magazines. Although nonreproductive narratives in images have a long history, including the Bayeux Tapestry, Trajan's Column, and Greek friezes, these proto-comics are often excluded from considerations of the form.

The Swiss writer-artist Rodolphe Töpffer is widely credited with the publication of the first books of comics. His *Histoire de M. Jabot* (Mr. Jabot's Story), first published in 1833, was the first of seven satires that he published during a period of 14 years. In 1865, Wilhelm Busch published *Max und Moritz—Eine Bubengeschichte in sieben Streichen* (Max and Moritz—A Story of Seven Boyish Pranks), which was a direct inspiration for Rudolph Dirks's early newspaper comic strip, *The Katzenjammer Kids* (1897). Across Europe in the latter half of the 19th century, there was an explosion of illustrated humor magazines incorporating comics and cartoons that contributed to the development of the comics form.

Richard Felton Outcault's creation of *Hogan's Alley* for Joseph Pulitzer's *New York World* in 1985 is widely regarded as the birth of the

American newspaper strip tradition. Comic strips became a major selling point of newspapers in the United States in the first decades of the 20th century. Popular characters, like Buster Brown, were widely marketed, later crossing over into radio, television, and film. American newspaper comics of the first half of the 20th century were divided between humorous gag strips and ongoing serialized narratives such as *Terry and the Pirates, Dick Tracy,* and *Little Orphan Annie.*

In the second half of the 20th century, the American newspaper strip began to focus increasingly on humor. The most successful strips were widely integrated into the mass media generally. Charles Schulz's *Peanuts,* which spawned an empire of marketing tie-ins, television specials, and films, was the model for a global entertainment brand for more than four decades. This example was followed by many others, including Jim Davis, whose *Garfield* appears daily in more than 2,000 newspapers around the world. Bill Watterson, whose *Calvin and Hobbes* was the most popular comic strip of the 1980s and 1990s, was one of the few cartoonists to have resisted the global commercialization of his characters.

The rise of the American comic book as a distinct form of magazine publishing can be traced to the mid-1930s. Initially, comic books were simply repackaged collections of newspaper comic strips. By the end of the 1930s, original material was much more common, and the unexpected success of *Superman* in 1938 contributed to the rapid expansion of comic book publishing. After World War II, comic books emerged as one of the biggest success stories of the American publishing industry, with comics appearing in a wide variety of genres, including crime, romance, humor, war, and the western. The consolidation of the comic book industry in the mid-1950s, largely because of the increasing importance of television, directed comics increasingly toward the superhero genre. By the 1980s, comic books had become virtually synonymous with superheroes in the United States.

Comix

The most important alternative to superhero comics in the mid-20th century was the underground comix movement of the mid- and late 1960s. Rooted largely in the San Francisco Bay area, comix were culturally integrated with the hippie youth culture scene. Underground comix were primarily concerned with topics, such as sex and drug use, that were taboo in a comics industry governed by a self-regulating code. The comix movement gave rise to several prominent artists, including Robert Crumb and Art Spiegelman, who would prove instrumental in globalizing comics as graphic novels.

Spiegelman's two-volume autobiographical comic book *Maus* was the work, more than any other, that transformed the popular image of what comics were and could be. In detailing his relationship to his father, who was a survivor of Auschwitz, in the comic book form, Spiegelman helped usher in an era of long-form comics for adults in the United States. The book was subsequently translated into dozens of languages and has sold millions of copies worldwide, making it one of few international comics successes targeted at an adult readership. After the success of *Maus* and other similar works, the graphic novel emerged as a distinct publishing category in the United States. The graphic novel has been used as a catchall marketing term for comic books collected in book format, as well for comics conceived as works with a novelistic density.

The rise of the graphic novel format in the United States owes a debt not only to the post-comix generation represented by Spiegelman but also to the impact of European comic books in English translation. Although the American graphic novel emerged from the parallel development of the comic strip and comic book traditions during the course of the 20th century, European comics developed much differently. Most European nations did not develop a newspaper comic strip industry of a size comparable with that of the United States. Rather, comics were most frequently published in magazines for children. In the 1920s, French artist Alain Saint-Ogan and Belgian Hergé (Georges Rémi) created popular comics series for children, while the 1930s saw the birth of several popular comics magazines, including *Journal de Mickey* (which published American newspaper strips in translation) and *Spirou.* Unlike American comic books, which were disposable magazines, popular French and Belgian comics were collected as hardcover books, termed "albums," which were kept in print as long as sales warranted, and generations of readers were exposed to the same stories. After World War II, the market for comics magazines expanded to include *Tintin*, *Vaillant*, and *Pilote*. After the general strike that brought France to a virtual standstill in May 1968, many comics artists sought to bring a new maturity to their work and created new publishing venues for adult comics. Unlike the American underground comix, which circulated through the counterculture, magazines like *L'Écho des savanes* and *Métal Hurlant* were mainstream successes. When the American magazine *Heavy Metal* began to translate this material in the 1970s, it helped to position European comics, and the album tradition in particular, as an important contributor to the new seriousness of an internationalized comics culture.

Manga

The third major national comics tradition is Japanese manga. Dating from the American occupation of Japan after World War II, manga originally evinced a high degree of American influence, notably the visual style of Disney animation. Manga artists in the 1950s, including Osamu Tezuka and Machiko Hasegawa, integrated comics (manga) production with animation (anime), developing cross-media entertainment platforms that flourished for decades. Manga for young people is roughly divisible into two types: shonen manga targeted at young boys featuring action-adventure stories, slapstick humor and sexuality; and shojo manga, aimed at young girls, which emphasizes romance and superheroines. Japanese comics are serialized in thick black-and-white weekly magazine anthologies, with the most popular series being collected into books called tankobon. Additionally, many popular manga series are adapted as television and film animation projects and also as licensed commercial properties.

Japanese comics were not widely available in the United States and Europe until the 1980s when a small number of works began to appear in translation. The popularity of Japanese animation in the 1990s paved the way for the global explosion of interest in manga, with works like *Akira*, *Dragon Ball*, *Pokemon*, and *Sailor Moon* finding large audiences around the world. By the 2000s, manga had become a dominant economic force in nearly all comics industries, and the international appetite for manga extended to works from other Asian countries, including Korean manhwa and Chinese manhua.

Globalized Outlook

In all three cultural contexts, comics have evolved from an art form primarily targeted toward children to one that seeks to attract all types of audiences. This transformation has occurred in different ways in each context and has, importantly, been reinforced cross-culturally by the circulation of "foreign" comics in new areas. In the United States, for example, the influence of the Franco-Belgian album tradition in the 1970s spurred an interest in comics dealing with more mature themes than were generally found in superhero comics. The rising influence of manga in the 2000s similarly pushed American cartoonists toward the exploration of new storytelling structures. To this end, a work like *Scott Pilgrim*, serialized in six volumes by Canadian cartoonist Bryan Lee O'Malley between 2004 and 2010 is instructive about the increasingly globalized outlook of the contemporary comics industry.

Scott Pilgrim tells the story of its titular hero, an unemployed 20-something living in Toronto who falls in love with a delivery woman named Ramona Flowers. Each volume in the series is modeled on the Japanese tankobon publishing format of black-and-white books of several hundred pages in length. The story itself shows the influence of the semiautobiographical slacker genre that arose in the 1990s in the wake of the success of *Maus*. At the same time, the book uses fantasy and science-fiction elements frequently found in Japanese shonen manga to develop its romantic plot, as well as a sophisticated humor reminiscent of recent work from the Franco-Belgian tradition. To this end, *Scott Pilgrim* can be read as an amalgam of intersecting comics traditions that are a result of an increasingly transnational media environment and as a harbinger of future globally hybrid comics productions.

Bart Beaty

See also Art; Cinema; Cultural Industries; Global Culture, Media; Radio; Television

Further Readings

Beaty, B. (2007). *Unpopular culture: Transforming the European comic book in the 1990s.* Toronto, ON: University of Toronto Press.

Gabilliet, J.-P. (2010). *Of comics and men: A cultural history of American comic books* (B. Beaty & N. Nguyen, Trans.). Jackson: University of Mississippi Press.

Gravett, P. (2004). *Manga: Sixty years of Japanese comics.* New York: Harper Design.

Lent, J. A. (2001). *Illustrating Asia: Comics, humor magazines, and picture books.* Honolulu: University of Hawaiʻi Press.

Lopes, P. (2009). *Demanding respect: The evolution of the American comic book.* Philadelphia: Temple University Press.

Schodt, F. L. (1986). *Manga! Manga! The world of Japanese comics.* Berkeley, CA: Stone Bridge Press.

Smolderen, T. (2009). *Naissances de la bande dessinée de William Hogarth à Winsor McCay* [Birth of the comics, from William Hogarth to Winsor McCay]. Paris: Les Impressions Nouvelles.

CHARISMATIC LEADERS

Charisma, the magnetic popular appeal exuded by some political leaders, is a term that comes from the Greek, meaning "gift of grace." In the classical tradition, the connection to the suprapersonal or "divine" is central to the hero's innate ability to lead signified by the Roman concept of *facilitas*. This refers to an oratorical eloquence inspired (in part) by a source external to the speaker. For Christians, charisma is the sense of the saint's intimate contact with God. However, that one person can gain charismatic power from claiming a highly personal connection to the divine presents a real threat to the established order, as was demonstrated in the events leading to the deaths of almost all followers of the Branch Davidian sect in Waco, Texas. R. A. Knox details the fraught history of such personal connections to the divine in his meticulous study of Enthusiasm. Charisma in political contexts is viewed as a capacity to embody an extraordinary suprapersonal power.

Whether the leader is viewed as having a connection to the divine (however that is culturally conceived), there is enduring emphasis on charisma defined by the personal qualities of the leader. Exceptional personal qualities and skills constitute "personalized charisma"—the least developed of sociologist Max Weber's two variants of charisma and the one most emphasized in this entry. The second variant, "routinized charisma," derives from institutional power accorded by social roles. It is not the central focus in this entry. In personalized charisma, there is the felt sense in the here and now of a leader's almost divine uniqueness in being extraordinarily empowered to draw others into participatory, selfless communion to bring about innovative social transformation. Within personalized charisma, there is a further subdivision: the leader embodies (Weber's "emulatory charismatic") and/or gives voice to (Weber's "prophetic or messianic charismatic") a vision of the future he or she convinces followers he or she can make real.

In his notion of personalized charisma, Weber outlines a charisma that "is opposed to all institutional routines, those of tradition and those subject to rational management" (1946, p. 52). According to Weber, "'Charisma' shall be defined to refer to an extraordinary quality of a person, regardless of whether this quality is actual, alleged or presumed. 'Charismatic Authority,' hence, shall refer to a rule over men, whether predominantly external or predominantly internal, to which the governed submit because of their belief in the extraordinary quality of a specific person" (1946, p. 295). Charisma defined by personal qualities is distinct from position, hierarchy, or social advantage, which underpin Weber's notion of routinized charisma. "Charisma is a gift that inheres in an object or person simply by virtue of natural endowment. Such 'primary charisma' cannot be acquired by any means" (Weber, 1922, p. 2).

The power accruing to the leader derives in part from the appeal of his or her exceptional personal qualities (which may be real or consensually ascribed). These attributes include personal magnetism, dominance, courage, and confidence in the moral righteousness of their convictions and a contagious emotional expressiveness.

Charisma's Relational Appeal

Charismatic appeal develops in a relationship, and while it may be prompted by the remarkable qualities of one person, sociologists emphasize the importance of context for the social validation of charisma. Charisma is relative to the perceiver. However, some attributes are more likely to have broad appeal in conjunction with a particular message or vision at a given cultural and historical moment. The charismatic leader is attractive thanks to might, message, and audience uptake. The intensity and breadth of appeal are in part a result of the timeliness, pertinence, and scope of the message to address and resolve shared threats and chagrins that are personally, historically, and culturally relevant at a given time.

The Charismatic Vision

The charismatic political vision is innovative, nontraditional, sometimes novel, outlining possibilities and implicating changes to the personal identity and social affiliation of followers, with ramifications for the system of meanings and institutional power within the host culture and wider political milieu. It can promote change within a system or change of a system. Ideology operates in charismatic relations through the leader: The vision is given a voice (Weber's notion of "prophetic charisma") or is embodied by the person and lifestyle of the leader (Weber's "emulatory charisma," also called "personalised leadership"). It is a charisma of the body. Presidents whose inaugural address contained words like *heart*, *dream*, and *hunger* were later judged to be visionary or charismatic. It is also inspired by the leader's nonverbal expressiveness, and is frequently intensified by the excitement and contagion of a group setting (which Hitler, for example, capitalized on). It makes a direct emotional appeal to the follower.

The Context of Charisma

Some suggest crisis is not required for charisma. However, historically charismatic relations are most likely to form and charismatic leaders to develop and be recognized as charismatic where there is some social crisis. Where there has been a threat to or disintegration in the structures of meaning that inform problem-solving attempts at personal, group, national, or global levels—charismatic power can develop. It can address threats by offering means to stabilize personal identity,

provide clarity of group belonging, and group status. Erich Fromm's analysis of Hitler's rise to power suggests that the weakening of Germany's pride as a result of postwar sanctions paved the way for the rise of Hitler as much as his personal attributes of malignant narcissism. Weber's (1922) analysis of charisma entails the occurrence of a social crisis involving a weakening of traditional values, an emergence of group conflicts, and a sharpening of class differences. The traditional order is then challenged by the emergence of a charismatic authority.

Three stages in personal change may develop prior to, or as a result of, contact with charismatic authority. Followers are rendered "charisma-prone" where (a) early or recent disruptive life circumstances induce some form of separation from identity-maintaining contacts and beliefs, thereby promoting potential followers' embarkation on (b) a phase of transition where social relationships, beliefs and ways of life are renegotiated. This is followed by (c) a reintegration of follower identity within a new group where problems are addressed from within a newly acquired or restructured ideology in the context of a social and cultural landscape frequently changed by the rise of the charismatic group around a leader. A follower's passage through these phases may be shaped by the charismatic appeal of a leader at any stage. With forcible or deceptive recruitment, the rupture of existing bonds may occur as a result of the intervention by the leader, his or her message, or representatives. Actual physical or psychological encapsulation may develop where normal contact with identity-sustaining social bonds is not permitted—for example how, in prisoner of war camps, the threat of informers in their midst prevented men from confiding in each other, resulting in a psychological group becoming a mere physical assemblage of men. Barring capture, the separation stage in personal change occurs in the course of contingent life circumstances.

Against a cultural and temporal backdrop of crisis, alienation, shallow bonds rather than real intimacy, loss of ideals, or weakening of values, charisma develops as a lock and key fit between leader and follower whereby a leader's qualities and message appeal to (and dynamically transform) the personal needs and ideological orientation of the follower.

The Charismatic Bond

The charismatic relationship is poised between love and leadership, elaborated empirically as "idealized influence" in contemporary transformational leadership research. Charisma is a cultural form of transference (whereby one attributes to a person in the present qualities and power that were in fact experienced in relation to a person in the past), where fears and longings mobilized in followers lead them to perceive and/or ascribe (sometimes idealized) exceptional capacities to a leader and to take unique, personalized significance from the leader's message, which forms an uncanny bond to both leader and the way of life he or she embodies. The boundaries between leader and follower are blurred or lost. The more conscious the leader is of the mechanisms of power, the less symmetric or mutual the loss of self. Although the follower may come to believe that he or she shares the attributes of the leader, the leader retains a clear awareness of personal boundaries and does not derive a grandiose sense of power from assimilating the follower.

Uncanny Mechanisms of Devotion

Little is known about how leaders have the remarkable and sometimes frightening effects they have on followers, such as inspiring them to die for a cause. Weston La Barre uncovers the mechanism by which selfless devotion develops. The message has to be sufficiently consonant with the (often unconscious) longings of the followers to produce the seemingly "magic" and "irrational" conviction of the leader's rightness and to produce a sense of there being a unique bond between leader and follower despite the group or mass following often in evidence. The leader's message taps unspoken and unacknowledged longings that are already there in the follower.

The Challenges of Charisma

A charismatic bond mobilizes attributes of followers motivating them to sometimes astonishing levels of commitment and sacrifice, sometimes of their lives, as they work to realize a vision of a future.

The impact of the charismatic bond can undermine the stability of the leader's personality, which plays a large role in determining the degree to which the transformative personal, cultural, and global outcomes are ennobling or destructive. The impact of the bond and the outcomes of gaining power also reveal the degree to which the charismatic's quest for power was narcissistically based. Many have been concerned by the destructive, dark side of charisma. Concern rose because of the murders carried out by the Manson Family in the late 1960s; the People's Temple mass suicides at Jonestown, Guyana, in 1978; and the rise of violent religious fanaticism as a mode of government. These occurrences suggest, notes Charles Lindholm, that "some human groups at least, are acting on principles that stand beyond ordinary understanding, and that explanations of these groups based on rational interest are wholly inadequate" (1988, p. 4).

Ensuring Positive Charisma

Whether charisma is destructive or positively transformative depends on several factors: the degree of narcissism of the leader's personality; the leader's capacity to delegate and retain dissenting voices within his or her inner circle optimizing corrective feedback concerning sources of discontent regarding the exercise of power rather than surrounding himself or herself with sycophantic advisors; the leader's humility, resisting a romanticization of leadership enabling the recognition of his or her role as catalyst rather than sole cause of social change, despite followers' wishes to view the leader as being in control. Charisma is more likely to be positive in outcomes where the vision of the future is socially inclusive, welcoming those currently recognized as out-groups; and ethically informed, transcending the self-interest of leaders and followers alike, and is dedicated to more than assuaging personal fears or those of the followers and the perpetuation of powerful influence itself. For transformational leaders to be truly charismatic, their messages must offer inspiration and innovation, with goals that transcend time, place, and the satisfaction of individual interests. Many attributes of the ethically aware, authentic transformational leader—such as concern for self and others, absence of manipulation and hypocrisy, and a vision that followers can accept or reject—demarcate a relative absence of narcissism.

Charismatic leaders unite groups, but they can also create out-groups and scapegoats if their vision is not inclusive. The division into "us" and "them" may develop from a leader's tendency toward "splitting," a tendency to view those who share one's vision as wholly good and those who do not as wholly bad. The mechanism of splitting is common in grandiosity of narcissistic origin. However, the ascription of all negative attributes to out-groups is more likely with the acquisition of unquestioned power where the leader comes to occupy a position of tyrant not subordinate to law or principles higher than himself or herself. Some suggest only ethically good leaders can truly be transformational. However, dark charisma can be equally transformative of the milieu of values within a nation, which in turn has global impact.

The outcome of charisma hinges on the leader's capacity for having insight into and conscious respect for the mechanisms of power. This conscious awareness is less possible the more narcissistic the leader or the more the situation lacks checks and balances for difficulties regarding the exercise of power to be voiced and redressed. The outcome of charisma also depends on how the extant social powers respond to the challenge it represents.

Doris McIlwain

See also Genocides; Leadership; Populism; Religious Conversion; Social Movements

Further Readings

Cherulnik, P. D., Donley, K. A., Wiewel, T. S. R., & Miller, S. R. (2001). Charisma is contagious: The effect of leaders' charisma on observers' affect. *Journal of Applied Social Psychology, 31*(10), 2149–2159.

Conger, J. A., & Kanungo, R. N. (1998). *Charismatic leadership in organizations.* Thousand Oaks, CA: Sage.

Erikson, E. H. (1958). *Young man Luther: A study in psychoanalysis and history.* New York: Norton.

Erikson, E. H. (1969). *Gandhi's truth: One the origins of militant nonviolence.* New York: Norton.

Friedland, W. H. (1964). For a sociological concept of charisma. *Social Forces, 43*(1), 18–26.

Friedrich, C. J. (1961). Political leadership and the problem of the charismatic power. *The Journal of Politics, 23*(1), 3–24.

Goldberg, S. (1983). Courage and fanaticism: The charismatic leader and modern religious cults. In D. A. Halperin (Ed.), *Psychodynamic perspectives of religion, sect, and cult* (pp. 163–186). Boston: John Wright, PSG Inc.

Greenfeld, L. (1985). Reflections on the two charismas. *British Journal of Sociology, 36,* 117–132

Hummel, R. (1975). The psychology of charismatic followers. *Psychological Reports, 37,* 759–770.

Katz, J. (1972). Deviance, charisma, and rule-defined behavior. *Social Problems, 20*(2), 186–202.

Knox, R. A. (1950). *Enthusiasm: A chapter in the history of religion with special reference to the XVII and XVIII centuries.* Oxford, UK: Clarendon Press.

La Barre, W. (1980). *Culture in context.* Durham, NC: Duke University Press.

Lindholm, C. (1988). Lovers and leaders: A comparison of social and psychological models of romance and charisma. *Social Science Information, 27,* 3–45.

Lindholm, C. (1990). *Charisma.* Cambridge, MA: Basil Blackwell.

McIlwain, D. (2009). *Impatient for paradise: Charisma, personality & charismatic new religions.* Saarbrücken, Germany: VDM–Verlag.

Popper, M. (2000). The development of charismatic leaders. *Political Psychology, 21*(4), 729–744.

Post, J. M. (1986). Narcissism and the charismatic leader-follower relationship. *Political Psychology, 7*(4), 675–688.

Shamir, B., & Howell, J. M. (1999). Organizational and contextual influences on the emergence and effectiveness of charismatic leadership. *Leadership Quarterly, 10*(2), 257–283.

Shils, E. (1965). Charisma, order, and status. *American Sociological Review, 30,* 199–213.

Smith, D. N. (1998). Faith, reason, and charisma: Rudolf Sohm, Max Weber, and the theology of grace. *Sociological Inquiry, 68*(1), 32–60.

Trice, H. M., & Beyer, J. M. (1986). Charisma and its routinization in two social movement organizations. *Research in Organizational Behavior, 8,* 113–164.

Weber, M. (1946). In H. Gerth & C. Wright Mills (Eds.), *Max Weber: Essays in sociology.* New York: Oxford University Press.

Weber, M. (1968). Charisma, its revolutionary character and its transformation. In G. Roth & C. Wittich (Eds.), *Economy and society.* Bedminster, NJ: Bedminster Press. (Original work published 1922)

CHARITIES, CHARITY

In a global context, there is no single concept of charity. Charity, as it is known to those nations belonging to the common law tradition, is defined by law rather than by religion. In that respect, it is different from its counterpart *zakat* and *sadaqa* in Islamic culture and from *tzedakah* in Judaism. It differs, also, from its equivalent in other Christian societies that are under civil law jurisdictions. (See the entry on Legal Systems in this encyclopedia.)

The word *charity* in a legal context differs from popular usage, which can range from its wider sense of "the good affections between persons" to its restricted sense of "relief of the poor"—often the deserving poor. It is also distinguished legally from "benevolent" and "philanthropic" purposes, which are regarded as having meanings that are narrower or broader than that permitted in law by "charitable purposes."

Background

Charity, as a social construct and legal concept, is confined to and defined by the common law. It dates from the Statute of Charitable Uses 1601 in England (43 Eliz. 1. Cap. 4), which laid the legislative foundations for the development of modern charity law. Others have traced the origin of the laws of charity back to Judeo-Christian traditions molded by the arrangements of the Catholic Church and its fraternities and reconfigured by Protestant theology as exemplified by a 14th-century poem *The Vision of Piers Plowman*, which closely resembles the Statute of Charitable Uses. There are intriguing similarities to the Hindu *math*, and returning crusaders sometimes established institutions, later regarded as charitable, which incorporated notions from the Islamic *waqf*.

The preamble to the Statute of Charitable Uses 1601 defined charity in terms of the following charitable purposes:

> Releife of aged impotent and poore people, some for Maintenance of sicke and maymed Souldiers and Marriners, Schooles of Learninge, Free Schooles and Schollers in Universities, some for Repaire of Bridges Portes Havens Causwaies Churches Seabankes and Highwaies, some for Educacion and preferment of Orphans, some for or towardes Reliefe Stocke or Maintenance of Howses of Correccion, some for Mariages of poore Maides, some for Supportacion Ayde and Helpe of younge tradesmen Handicraftesmen and persons decayed, and others for reliefe or redemption of Prisoners or Captives, and for aide or ease of any poore Inhabitantes concerninge payment of Fifteenes, setting out of Souldiers and other Taxes.

Thereafter, neither a government nor a court would regard a purpose as charitable unless it appeared on that list or could be defined as coming within "the spirit and intendment" of the preamble.

The concept was imposed by default in most of the British colonies, including Canada, Australia, New Zealand, Singapore, Malaysia, India, and Hong Kong. The law has developed through judicial precedent with most of the 60 or so common law jurisdictions having varying degrees of reference back to developing English precedents. The most notable of these was the case of *Commissioners for Special Purposes of Income Tax v Pemsel* [1891] AC 531 (*Pemsel's case*) in which the Preamble's disparate items were distilled into four "heads" of charity: relief of poverty, advancement of education, advancement of religion, and other purposes beneficial to the community. In addition, to be charitable, a purpose had to benefit the public. Only since the turn of this century has there been significant proposed and actual statutory intervention in the United Kingdom and some former colonies.

Since the quincentennial in 2001 of the modern English origins of the definition of charitable purposes there have been significant legal reform proposals to transfer the determination of core common law concepts largely from a judicial to a statutory basis by legislating for a new definition of what constitutes charitable purposes and public benefit in the United Kingdom and some of its former colonies.

The Charities Act 2006 (England and Wales) mostly took effect in early 2008. Under section 2 of that Act, the four common law heads of charitable purposes are increased to 13 statutory heads—the *Pemsel plus* set. Thus, a charitable purpose must fall within the following: (a) the prevention or relief of poverty; (b) the advancement of education; (c) the advancement of religion; (d) the advancement of health or the saving of lives; (e) the advancement of citizenship or community development; (f) the advancement of the arts, culture, heritage, or science; (g) the advancement of amateur sport; (h) the advancement of human rights, conflict resolution, or reconciliation or the promotion of religious or racial harmony or equality and diversity; (i) the advancement of environmental protection or improvement; (j) the relief of those in need by reason of youth, age, ill health, disability, financial hardship, or other disadvantage; (k) the advancement of animal welfare; (l) the promotion of the efficiency of the armed forces of the Crown, or of the efficiency of the police, fire and rescue services or ambulance services; and (m) other purposes that are currently recognized as charitable or are in the spirit of any purposes currently recognized as charitable.

The law had previously included a presumption that charities with the purposes of relief of poverty, advancement of education, or advancement of religion were for the public benefit. The Charities Act 2006 removed this presumption, so for the first time the law requires every charity to demonstrate explicitly that their purposes are for the public benefit.

Global Perspectives

Since 2001, the growing pressure for statutory intervention in all closely aligned English jurisdictions is working its way through each of the jurisdictions at different rates of progress. The final practical outcomes of the new legislative interventions will only be evident in the coming years. However, replacing common-law concepts with statutory definitions does inevitably signify a break with tradition. In the future, the legal definition of what constitutes charity will be much less amenable to judicial influence and more vulnerable to direct political control through the government use of a statutory amendment.

Scotland

Revenue law is applied uniformly across the United Kingdom, so for taxation purposes, Scotland has shared the legal definition of charity. However, in the general law of Scotland, the terms *charity* and *charitable* did not acquire a technical meaning and so in this respect diverged from the situation in England and Wales. Recent reforms have largely brought this divergence to an end.

The Charities and Trustee Investment (Scotland) Act 2005 (the CTI(S) Act) transfers responsibility for charitable status in Scotland from HM Revenue and Customs to the Office of the Scottish Charity Regulator (OSCR). OSCR has further regulatory responsibilities that include maintaining the Scottish Charity Register. Section 7(2) of the CTI(S) Act sets out 15 different charitable purposes, as well as a 16th category that encompasses any other purpose that may reasonably be regarded as analogous to any of those 15. The list almost duplicates the English *Pemsel plus* set. Perhaps noteworthy is that advancing any philosophical belief, whether or not involving belief in a god, is stated to be analogous to the advancement of religion.

Ireland

Charity law in Ireland is rooted in the common law and based on the Statute of Pious Uses 1634, which is not dissimilar to the English Statute of Charitable Uses 1601 noted. The English classification of charitable purposes was accepted in Ireland, and their judicial interpretation has developed along much the same lines. Although the Irish reform process was first mooted in 1996, it was not until 2007 that the Charities Bill was introduced in the Oireachtas (the Irish Parliament) to modernize the law and definition of charities. The bill was passed in 2009, becoming the Charities Act 2009. Under the new act, the Charities Regulatory Authority becomes the entity responsible for establishment and maintenance of a register of charities and overseeing the reporting regimes applicable to registered charities.

Section 3 of the new act retains but extends the common law definition of charitable purposes. In addition to enlarging the first head of charity to include prevention as well as relief of poverty, section 3 defines the fourth head, other purposes beneficial to the community, to include 12 specific subheads that are recognized as charitable purposes. These have similarities to those of the

English and Scottish acts, although it is perhaps noteworthy that there is no reference to amateur sport or to human rights in its definition of charitable purpose. Those that are recognized as charitable include the advancement of efficient and effective use of the property of charitable organizations, protection of the natural environment, and advancement of environmental sustainability. One purpose that is not expressly included in the English and Scottish acts is "integration of those who are disadvantaged, and promotion of their full participation, in society."

The new act requires proof of public benefit before a purpose can be declared charitable, although it retains the presumption that advancement of religion is for the public benefit—a presumption that is rebuttable.

Canada

Despite the English-speaking parts of Canada not adopting English statutory law at the time of colonization, much of the charity law in Canada reflects the English common law of charitable trusts. Various provinces, including Quebec, have their own definitions of what constitutes a charitable purpose. Under Canada's federated constitution, the responsibility for supervising charities rests with the provinces. However, the Canada Revenue Agency (CRA) has effectively become the gatekeeper to charitable status under the Income Tax Act 1985.

Charity law reform has been underway in Canada for more than a decade with the Ontario Law Reform Commission issuing a report in 1996. Since 2002, there has been a series of roundtables and joint government-sector working groups (e.g., the Joint Regulatory Table [JRT]). Some recommendations of JRT have been adopted by the government; however, little substantive reform has resulted.

Singapore

Charity law in Singapore is derived primarily from English law, but since attaining independence in 1965, Singapore has begun actively to develop its own body of law. Section 2(1) of the Charities Act 1994 defines charity as any institution, corporate or not, that is established for charitable purposes and is subject to control by the High Court in its jurisdiction over charities. "Charitable purposes" is defined as purposes that are exclusively charitable according to the law of Singapore. The courts interpret the meaning of these terms relying on the common law, as established largely through English precedents.

In October 2005, considerable media exposure of scandals involving the National Kidney Foundation and other organizations highlighted problems of governance in the sector. Following this, the Inter-Ministry Committee on the Regulation of Charities and Institutions of Public Character (IPCs) was established with a remit to examine the regulation of charitable organizations and IPCs. The result was a series of administrative and procedural reforms, but no alteration to the definition of charity.

Australia

Australia was stamped at its colonial birth with the imprimatur of English laws and followed the English common law of charities. By default, the primary regulatory authority in Australia is at federal level where the revenue agency, the Australian Taxation Office (ATO), regulates the fiscal environment, including charities, through the Income Tax Assessment Act 1997. The ATO follows established English precedents on definitional matters, deploying a generally conservative and defensive interpretation of *Pemsel's case* and the spirit and intendment rule. Unlike the English Charity Commission, the ATO has neither the remit nor the resources to undertake a strategic program for the development of charitable purposes.

The federal government launched the Inquiry into the Definition of Charities and Related Organisations in 2000. The Inquiry report in 2001 made 27 recommendations, some of which were remarkably similar to later charity reforms in England and Wales, including enacting a statutory definition of charity and establishing an independent charities administrative body. However, the reform process stalled, and only three relatively minor matters were addressed in the Tax Laws Amendment (2005 Measures No. 3) Act 2005: "The provision of child care services on a non-profit basis" is now a recognized charitable purpose; self-help groups can acquire charitable status provided they are "open and non-discriminatory"; and closed or contemplative religious orders are also deemed charitable.

New Zealand

New Zealand also took the hallmarks of English charity law until the introduction of the Charities Act 2005. Prior to that, under the Charitable Trusts Act 1957 charitable purpose meant "every purpose which in accordance with the law of New Zealand is charitable." Subject to some minor adjustments, the common law continues under the 2005 act.

There has been a longstanding and fundamental difficulty in fitting the charity law framework to Maori needs. This is because Maori communities are organized around blood relationships, and under common law, charitable purposes must benefit the public; any purpose that is limited in its reach by a requirement of blood connection or restricted membership does not meet the public benefit test. Under section 5(2)(a) of the Charities Act 2005, a purpose may still be charitable and satisfy the public benefit requirement, notwithstanding that the beneficiaries are related by blood.

The Inland Revenue Department has transferred to the newly established Charities Commission the power to grant an organization charitable status for income tax purposes only if that organization satisfies four requirements:

1. It must be carried on exclusively for charitable purposes.

2. It must not be carried on for the private pecuniary profit of any individual.

3. It must have a provision in its rules requiring the assets of the organization to be transferred to another entity with charitable purposes if the organization ceases to exist.

4. It must not have the power to amend its rules in such a way as to alter the exclusively charitable nature of the organization.

United States

The American Revolution led to repeal of English legislation including the Statute of Charitable Uses, thereby rendering all charities that had been established in the different states null and void. The U.S. Constitution leaves the definition and regulation of charity to the states, but the Internal Revenue Service (IRS) is the dominant influence in determining what is charitable.

Section 501 of the Internal Revenue Code 1986 lists two major sets of nonprofit organizations that are tax preferred. There are the section 501(c)(3) organizations, that is, what are commonly called charitable organizations, "organized and operated exclusively for religious, charitable, scientific, testing for public safety, literary, or educational purposes"; and a residuary group of noncharities such as social clubs, veterans' organizations, unions, chambers of commerce and other private member organizations. Although all section 501(c) organizations are exempt from income tax, donors to 501(c)(3) organizations may be eligible for income tax deductions for the value of the gift. Within section 501(c)(3), the law divides organizations into private foundations and public charities—the intent being to separate donor-controlled or closely held organizations from operating charities with broad-based donor or beneficiary constituencies, so that stricter controls can be placed on private foundations.

State courts tend to look at broader definitions of not-for-profit purposes to determine whether a corporation is an organization that deserves to be recognized as a charity or other beneficial nonbusiness organization. State courts also have jurisdiction to enforce provisions of charitable trusts.

Future Directions

The raft of reforms to the law and regulation of charity, led by England and Wales and spreading through former British colonies, is too recent to predict confidently how charity law will develop. The expansion of the heads of charitable purpose by legislation, coupled with revamped, quasi-judicial mechanisms for the interpretation of charitable purposes through tribunals or administrative fiat, will relieve some of the worst artificial confinement of the legal definition of charity.

The United States has largely left behind the *Pemsel* list and developed its own jurisprudential understanding of charitable purposes through its revenue laws. The European civil law traditions are different from the underlying jurisprudence of English charity law. However, those countries that are part of Europe will be under pressure to integrate into the European notions of nonprofit and foundation law in cross-border taxation exemptions, corporate forms, fundraising regulation, and accountability measures.

Myles McGregor-Lowndes

See also Civil Society, Global; Foundations; Humanitarianism; International Nongovernmental Organizations (INGOs); Legal Systems; Philanthropy; Poverty and Poverty Alleviation; Social Entrepreneurship

Further Readings

Anheier, H., & Ben-Ner, A. (Eds.). (2003). *The study of the nonprofit enterprise—theories and approaches.* New York: Kluwer Academic/Plenum.

Brody, E. (2002). The legal framework for nonprofit organizations. In W. W. Powell & R. Steinberg (Eds.), *The nonprofit sector: A research handbook* (pp. 243–266). New Haven, CT: Yale University Press.

Dal Pont, G. (2010). *Charity law in Australia and New Zealand* (2nd ed.). Melbourne, Australia: Oxford University Press.

Luxton, P. (2001). *The law of charities.* Oxford, UK: Oxford University Press.

Mitchell, C., & Moody, S. (Eds.). (2002). *Foundations of charity.* Portland, OR: Hart.

O'Halloran, K. (2007). *Charity law and social inclusion: An international study.* New York: Routledge.

O'Halloran, K., McGregor-Lowndes, M., & Simon, K. (2008). *Charity law & social policy: National and international perspectives on the functions of the law relating to charities.* New York: Springer.

Phillips, J., Chapman, B., & Stevens, D. (Eds.). (2001). *Between state and market: Essays on charity law and policy in Canada.* Montreal, QB: McGill-Queen's University Press.

Picarda, H. (1999). *The law and practice relating to charities* (3rd ed.). London: Butterworths.

Salamon, L. (1987). Of market failure, voluntary failure, and third-party government: Toward a theory of government-nonprofit relations in the modern welfare state. *Nonprofit and Voluntary Sector Quarterly, 16,* 29–49.

Warburton, J., Morris, D., & Riddle, N. F. (2003). *Tudor on charities.* London: Sweet & Maxwell.

CHILD TRAFFICKING

See Illegal Trade, Children

CHRISTIANITY

Christianity is increasingly a global religion, but it has had an explicitly global and translocal vision since its origins. In the New Testament Gospel of Matthew, Jesus charges the apostles with the "Great Commission," enjoining them to "go therefore and make disciples of all the nations, baptizing them in the name of the Father and the Son and the Holy Spirit" (Matthew 28:19, New American Standard Bible). The Great Commission began in earnest with Pentecost. Fifty days after Jesus's resurrection, the Holy Spirit descended in the form of a rushing wind and tongues of fire on the apostles, who had been hiding in fear of persecution, empowering them to preach to the various "nations" gathered at the market. This event marked the birth of a highly mobile charismatic religion, which spread quickly through Asia Minor, Greece, and North Africa. Wherever the apostles went in the Roman Empire, they performed wondrous works, allegedly healing the sick and expelling possessing evil spirits, as signs of the emergence of a new radically deterritorialized community, a "reign of God" that transcended traditional notions of belonging based on kinship and locality. As the Apostle Paul states, "There is neither Jew nor Greek, there is neither slave nor free man, there is neither male nor female; for you are all one in Christ Jesus" (Galatians 3:28). Christianity's theology combines what Max Weber describes as a universal religion of salvation: a strong emphasis on individual redemption through a personal encounter with the incarnate, historical figure of Jesus and on humanity's universal salvation.

Growth and Globalization of Christianity

The Christian religious tradition has proven highly flexible to social change and adaptable to globalization. It has certainly accompanied various periods of globalization not only through missionary activity but also through diverse translocal flows and processes, such as the circulation of relics and ritual artifacts, pilgrimages, wars, immigration, mercantilism, and colonialism. Although Christianity's attempt to take root in different localities has invariably involved the imposition of institutionally sanctioned orthodoxy, Christianity has often cross-fertilized with autochthonous religions, generating new, hybrid symbols, doctrines, practices, and forms of organization. This was certainly the case in the Americas, where an Iberian traditional popular Catholicism built around the cult of the saints and Marian devotions, with all its associated practices and beliefs, such as apparitions, everyday miracles, pilgrimages, and festivals, interacted with indigenous traditions and the religions brought by African slaves, which involved the veneration of ancestors, ritual sacrifice, and divination, to form new religions like Santería and Candomblé.

Christianity's capacity to become "glocalized," to preserve a universal eschatological message while incorporating the particular, explains Christianity's richness, which ranges from the apparition of the Virgin of Guadalupe to Juan Diego in Tepeyac, Mexico, just a few years after the Spanish conquest of the Aztecs, to the prophetic visions of Joseph Smith in Palmyra, New York, in the mid-1800s.

Despite the claims of the secularization paradigm, which predicted the widespread decline of religion in the public sphere and its increasing rationalization and privatization, Christianity is arguably now closer than ever to fulfilling the Great Commission. Relying on a powerful combination of the latest innovations in communication technology, including radio, television, DVDs, and the Internet, and old-fashioned door-to-door evangelization, Christianity has become one of the fastest growing world religions. Nowhere has the growth of Christianity been more explosive than in Africa, where the number of Christians has gone from 10 million in 1900—approximately 10% of the continent's population then—to 411 million in 2005 (46% of the population) (Jenkins, 2007). Christianity's rapid growth in Africa has brought it into tension with Islam, another religion with a strong global vision and a long historical presence in the region.

Christianity's growth extends beyond Africa into the global South. Approximately 60% of the estimated 2 billion Christians in the world live in Latin America (510 million), Africa (411 million), and Asia (300 million). Like in its early days, the Christianity that is spearheading this "southern" growth is "spirit filled." In particular, Pentecostalism in its various manifestations has been at the forefront of a vertiginous expansion in Latin America and Africa, notes Allan Anderson. For example, although Brazil continues to be the country with the largest number of Catholics in the world (128 million), Protestants have gone from 6.6% of the population in 1980 to 15.4% (26 million) in 2000. Approximately 70% of Brazilian Protestants identify themselves as Pentecostals. A similar picture emerges in Nigeria, where Christians are currently close to 48.0% of the population, up from 34.5% in 1963, the last census that collected information on religious affiliation. Interestingly, during the same period, the percentage of Muslims has gone up only by 3 points.

By the end of the 20th century, some of the most dynamic global Pentecostal churches have originated in the global South, particularly in Brazil, Nigeria, and Ghana. For example, Igreja Universal do Reino de Deus (the Universal Church of the Kingdom of God [UKCG]), founded by Edir Macedo, a retired lottery agent in Rio de Janeiro in 1977, claims to have temples in more than 170 countries in the world, ranging from the United Kingdom, the United States, and throughout Latin America to South Africa and Japan. Another example is the Nigerian-based Redeemed Christian Church of God (RCCG), started in 1952 by Josiah Akindayomi, a Yoruba-speaking pastor that emerged from the Aladura Movement. The RCCG may have as many as 3,000 parishes spread across more than 100 nations and bringing together more than four million members, reports Manuel A. Vásquez.

Shift in Christianity's Globalization

The UKCG and the RCCG represent the leading edge of what we may call a "reverse evangelization." The flows of Christianity from Europe and the United States to Latin America, Africa, and Asia characteristic of the period from the colonialism to the years immediately after the 1910

Edinburgh World Missionary Conference, which divided the world into mission fields and sought the "evangelization of the world in a generation," have now more than ever become polycentric and multidirectional, notes Lamin Sanneh. Through their missionary activities, dense transnational religious networks anchored in the global South are now revitalizing Christianity in the United States and Europe. Unlike classical Pentecostal churches that emerged in the 1910s in the United States, churches like the UKCG and the RCCG go beyond glossolalia (gift of tongues) as the first and definite evidence of baptism in the spirit. They both engage in open spiritual warfare with the Devil and its minions, viewing their exorcism as essential to the rearticulation of selves broken by the contradictions of late modernity. In that sense, both churches are part of a larger global neo-Pentecostal movement that operates through a nondualistic "pneumatic materialism," which links closely an immediate, intimate, and transformative encounter with the Holy Spirit and prosperity and physical well-being. This formula, often termed the "gospel of health and wealth" or the "prosperity gospel," is particularly attractive to vast sectors of the world's population who have been adversely affected by the current phase of economic globalization, which has been driven by neoliberal capitalism. These populations face increasingly precarious life conditions, and Pentecostalism's tight link between otherworldly salvation and this-worldly hope and success provides an invaluable resource to counter anomic forces like poverty, crime, drug addiction, domestic violence, and inadequate or nonexistent health care, according to Donald Miller and Tetsunao Yamamori. Some scholars, such as Nina Glick-Schiller, however, argue that prosperity gospels serve as ideologies that legitimate a "made in the United States" neo-imperialism, with pastors as global carriers of a new entrepreneurial and consumerist ethic.

The reverse missionary activity of churches like UKCG and RCCG dovetails with immigration patterns since the late 1960s, which have brought increasing numbers of Latin Americans, Africans, and Asians to Europe and North America. Latinos in the United States are a case in point. Constituting now approximately one third of the Catholic Church's membership, these immigrants and their children are not only forming their own ethnic

transnational congregations that keep them in contact with their countries of origin but also joining and transforming established native churches. According to a 2007 study by the Pew Forum on Religion and Public Life, Latinos are bringing a powerful spirit-filled and renewalist Catholicism, precisely at a time when the U.S. Catholic Church has been shaken by the series of sexual scandals. The impact of immigration on the rearticulation of Christianity is not restricted to the United States. Christian immigrants from Africa, Asia, and the West Indies are also changing the face of Christianity in places like the United Kingdom and France.

The change in Christianity's center of gravity has implications beyond Pentecostalism. Catholicism also shows a significant southward shift. From 2001 to 2006, the Catholic population in Africa grew more than 16%, while in Latin America it increased by 6%. In contrast, the Catholic population in Europe remained virtually unchanged. As of 2006, 67% of all Catholics (close to 750 million) reside in Latin America, Africa, and Asia. These data are more startling if one considers that 68% of the world's Catholics lived in Europe in 1900. This southward shift at the level of laity is still to be matched at the top echelons of the church hierarchy. Although in 2005, Latin America accounted for 43% of all Catholics, only 21 of the 117 cardinals eligible to elect the pope hailed from the region.

Partly in response to the dramatic advances of evangelical Protestantism in Latin America and Africa, Pope John Paul II called in the 1990s for a global "new evangelization." In practice, this new evangelization has meant a movement away from the focus on social concerns and internal reform that emerged out of the Second Vatican Council, a focus that was central to progressive Catholic movements in the Third World, including liberation theology, toward a stress on movements more narrowly concentrating on spiritual conversion and moral transformation such as the Catholic Charismatic Renewal Movement and Opus Dei. At the same time, John Paul II emphasized Marian devotions and the cult of the saints as a way to inculturate Catholicism. More than any other pope, John Paul II canonized many saints, valuing local traditions threatened by strongly Chisto-centric evangelical Protestantisms, while bringing these local beliefs and practices into the Church's institutional fold.

Tapping into his considerable personal charisma, John Paul II also traveled extensively and used mass media skillfully to advocate a "civilization of love," as an alternative to the individualism and consumerist materialism of Western capitalism and atheistic materialism of communism. Turning the tables on a modernity that has paved the way for radical postmodern relativism, John Paul II offered the Catholic Church as the legitimate holder of timeless universal values that transcend national divisions and ethnic strife that characterized the close of the 20th century. In that sense, John Paul II came to represent the figure of the pope "as the high priest of a new universal religion of humanity and as the first true citizen of a global civil society" (Casanova, 1997, p. 125).

John Paul II's call to spread the gospel through mass media has spurred global initiatives such as the Eternal World Television Network (EWTN), launched in 1981. Headquartered in Irondale, Alabama, the EWTN claims to be the largest religious media network in the world, reaching close to 150 million homes in 144 countries. Along with the Christian Broadcasting Network, which offers programming by cable and satellite to approximately 200 countries, the EWTN exemplifies the ways in which Christianity now circulates through global electronic media.

Pope Benedict XVI has also built on the legacy of his predecessor. However, he has gone beyond John Paul II by explicitly affirming that the Christian civilization of love must be anchored on a re-evangelized Europe. The re-evangelization of Europe has meant not only the need to struggle against secularization but also the effort to thwart the increasing influence of Islam in the continent, an influence that is dramatized by the presence of large Muslim communities and the potential inclusion of Turkey in the European Union. These efforts to re-evangelize Europe may be jeopardized by the furor over the sex abuse scandal, which has now affected churches throughout the world, from Ireland and the United States to Mexico and India.

Like Catholicism, the Anglican Communion has been deeply affected by the rapid rise of southern Christianities. The most visible case in point has been the rift between liberal Episcopalians in the United States and more socially conservative churches in Africa and Latin America over the election of gay bishop Eugene Robinson. This consecration has precipitated the split of several dioceses from the Episcopal Church, including those of Fort Worth, Texas; Pittsburgh, Pennsylvania; San Joaquin, California; and Quincy, Illinois, and their realignment with the Anglican Province of the Southern Cone. Other provinces in Kenya, Rwanda, and Nigeria have been supportive of this realignment, offering to accommodate dissenting dioceses in the United States, according to Miranda Hassett.

Philip Jenkins, a scholar of global Christianity, views the conflict and realignment of the Anglican Communion as the harbinger of a clash of Christianities that will challenge the hegemony of northern secularized Protestantism. According to Jenkins, southern Christianities generally profess "a much greater respect for the authority of scripture, especially in matters of morality; a willingness to accept the Bible as an inspired text and a tendency to literalism; a special interest in supernatural elements of scripture, such as miracles, visions, and healings; a belief in the continuing power of prophecy; a veneration of the Old Testament, which is often considered as authoritative as the New" (2006, p. 4). Here, Jenkins might be glossing over the diversity of Christianity in both the North and South, particularly when one takes into account Latin America, which exhibits liberal and conservative currents that sometimes even converge. In addition, he points to an overarching conservative shift in Christianity in reaction to its accommodation with an Enlightenment-based modernity that has failed to deliver on its promise of universal emancipation through human reason.

The final trend associated with the shift in Christianity's center of gravity has to do with the rapid growth of alternative Christianities in the South. The Church of Jesus Christ of Latter-day Saints, for example, claims to have 13 million members worldwide, of which only 5.7 million live in the United States. Although these figures are disputed by many scholars as being overinflated, they indicate the increasingly southern flavor of a Christianity that is quintessentially North American. It is projected that by 2020, only 1.3% of all Mormons will live in Europe (down from 5.6% in 1970). By sharp contrast, some independent scholars "estimate that by 2020, between half and two thirds of all Latter-day Saints on the church rolls will live in Latin America" (Phillips, 2006, p. 60). With 882,953 church members, Mexico now has the world's second largest Mormon population.

Similar trends are observed in among the Jehovah's Witnesses. Seven of the top ten countries with the highest numbers of baptisms in 2002 were in Latin America, Africa, or Asia, with Brazil leading the way. Russia and Ukraine were also on this list, pointing to an important geopolitical factor in the global spread of Christianity. Indeed, the fall of the Berlin Wall and the collapse of the Soviet Union opened a whole new evangelization frontier that Pentecostals, Catholics, and alternative Christians have aggressively pursued. This, in turn, has led to vocal denunciations by the Eastern Orthodox Church, which was severely persecuted in the Soviet Union but is experiencing considerable revitalization at the grassroots in post-Soviet Russia. Under the leadership of Patriarch Aleksy II, the Orthodox Church has reconstructed its relations vis-à-vis the postcommunist Russian state, positioning itself as the only authentic national faith.

Next Phase of Christianity's Globalization

A frontier that remains largely unexplored is China. Temples and house churches have proliferated, often aided by the remittances of a generally successful Chinese diaspora, particularly residing in the United States. The Center for the Study of Global Christianity estimates the number of Christians in China at 111 million, 90% of whom are Protestant (Allen, 2007). If these statistics are correct, China has the third largest Christian population in the world, just behind the United States and Brazil. It is hard to predict the future trajectory of Christianity in China. Estimating that there are 10,000 conversions to Christianity every day, the Center for the Study of Global Christianity projects that by 2050 there will be 218 million Chinese Christians. These numbers could be substantially inflated. However, given the size of population involved and the dramatic socioeconomic transformations China is undergoing, it is safe to assume that the country will play a key role in the next phase of the globalization of Christianity.

Manuel A. Vásquez

See also Christianity-Related Movements; Global Religions, Beliefs, and Ideologies; Mormonism; Religious Identities; Vatican; World Religions, Concept of

Further Readings

Allen, J. L. (2007, August 2). The uphill journey of Catholicism in China. *National Catholic Reporter.*

Anderson, A. (2004). *An introduction to Pentecostalism: Global charismatic Christianity.* Cambridge, UK: Cambridge University Press.

Casanova, J. (1997). Globalizing Catholicism and the return to "universal church." In S. H. Rudolph & J. Piscatori (Eds.), *Transnational religion and fading states.* Boulder, CO: Westview Press.

Garrard, J., & Garrard, C. (2008). *Russian Orthodoxy resurgent: Faith and power in the new Russia.* Princeton, NJ: Princeton University Press.

Glick-Schiller, N. (2005). Transnational social fields and imperialism: Bringing a theory of power to transnational studies. *Anthropological Theory, 5*(4), 439–461.

Hassett, M. (2007). *Anglican Communion in crisis: How Episcopal dissidents and their African allies are reshaping Anglicanism.* Princeton, NJ: Princeton University Press.

Jenkins, P. (2006). *New faces of Christianity: Believing the Bible in the global South* (Rev. ed.). Oxford, UK: Oxford University Press.

Jenkins, P. (2007). *The next Christendom: The coming of global Christianity.* Oxford, UK: Oxford University Press.

Miller, D., & Yamamori, T. (2007). *Global Pentecostalism: The new face of Christian social engagement.* Berkeley: University of California Press.

Pew Forum on Religion and Public Life. (2007). *Changing faiths: Latinos and the transformation of American religion.* Retrieved April 30, 2010, from http://pewforum.org/Changing-Faiths-Latinos-and-the-Transformation-of-American-Religion.aspx

Phillips, R. (2006). Rethinking the international expansion of Mormonism. *Nova Religio, 10*(1), 52–68.

Sanneh, L. (2007). *Disciples of all nations: Pillars of world Christianity.* Oxford, UK: Oxford University Press.

Vásquez, M. A. (2009). The global portability of pneumatic Christianity: Comparing African and Latin American Pentecostalism. *African Studies, 68*(2), 273–286.

CHRISTIANITY-RELATED MOVEMENTS

The global trajectory of Christianity has been propelled not only by the missionary outreach of the main branches of the tradition but also by the many smaller movements related to it. Although from the beginning, the small Jewish sect of Christians in Palestine reached outward to include uncircumcised gentiles in the Mediterranean world, to absorb Greek terminology, and to embrace Roman culture, the historical emphasis on the northward movement of Christianity to Europe has obscured the importance of global Christian movements in the Middle East, Africa, Asia, and the Americas. Recent historical research has allowed us to recognize global movements that have carried the vital center of Christianity beyond Europe.

The Christian-related movements that have emerged in response to the cultural conflicts of religious globalization have appeared in every part of the world, including Europe and the Americas. The millenarian peasant movements in Europe in the 19th century that historian Eric Hobsbawm described as "primitive rebels" comprised one recent example, the utopian Protestant communities in the United States another. Communes created by marginal Christian movements such as Christian Identity in 21st-century United States have been formed explicitly in protest against "the new world order" that they believe is being promoted by the globalization supported by mainstream Christianity.

Some of the most active movements, however, have been in non-Western parts of the world where responses to globalized Christianity have emerged both within and outside the communities of Christian converts. In South Pacific islands, cargo cults were formed, based on the notion that the fabulous cargo of European explorers' ships were the result of heavenly rewards that would return again to bestow wealth and blessings on faithful believers. In Africa and Asia, cultural contact created synthetic movements—new Afro-Christian movements that fused traditional African gods with Christian saints in forms of religiosity that came with enslaved Africans to the Western Hemisphere as Vodou, Santería, and Candomblé. In South Asia, expressions of Hindu Christianity merged traditional Indian religious practices with the religious culture brought by missionaries.

China also experienced the emergence of new movements for social reform, religious syncretism, and state protest as a result of Christian cultural contact. In the remainder of this entry, the focus will be on several of these Chinese examples to provide a specific sampling of the Christian-related movements that have responded around the world to religious globalization.

Chinese Rites Controversy

The globalization of Christianity is particularly striking in China, whose historical culture contrasts so starkly with Europe. China was the object of one of the most extensive cultivation efforts by Western missionaries from Europe and North America for four centuries (1550–1950). The establishment of Europe's global commercial links coincided with the burst of Counter-Reformation spirituality that inspired missionaries to go to all corners of the world. The Society of Jesus was founded in 1540 and produced highly educated Jesuits who attempted to carry out Jesus's command to "make disciples of all nations" (Matthew 28:19). Nearly a thousand Jesuits worked in China in the years 1579–1773. In confronting China's advanced society, economy, and culture, the Jesuits soon realized that it was necessary to adapt Christianity to China by blending the Christian message with essential elements of Chinese identity. Other less accommodating missionaries resisted this blending on the ground that it threatened the purity of the Gospel message.

One of the earliest confrontations involved how Christianity should treat Chinese ancestral rites. A great debate ensued over the meaning of ancestral rites and whether they were merely ritual acts of remembrance and expressions of filial piety or involved prayers to the spirits of the deceased ancestors for blessings. Although the common people tended to view the rites more as petitions, the literati tended to view them in a more rationalized way as memorials. Differences developed between the Jesuits who worked more with the literati and other missionaries who worked more with the common people. This Chinese Rites Controversy was referred to Rome, where European clerics ignored the arguments of Chinese literati, to rule in 1742 that ancestral rites were to be prohibited for Chinese Christians. This caused a great crisis in a country where family and ancestors were a crucial part of Chinese cultural identity. It was a victory of the Eurocentric wing of the Catholic Church, which did not take seriously the arguments of Chinese Christian literati. Indeed, the flawed character of the ruling was revealed when the ruling was reversed in 1939.

Antifemale Infanticide Movement

Another Christian-related global movement was generated by concern for the weak. This concern was quickly adopted by Chinese converts who supported the missionaries in opposing female infanticide. Many Buddhists had voiced strong protests against the practice of drowning or abandoning infant girls soon after their birth. However, the popular belief in Buddhist reincarnation provided an escape clause for many parents who viewed the act not in terms of ending a life but ending only one reincarnation in an existence involving innumerable reincarnations. In the rationalizations of many parents, the sin of drowning a girl was mitigated by the possibility of the girl's rebirth in a wealthy family in which she might have a better life or the possibility of her rebirth as a boy. The position of Confucianism in regard to female infanticide was even more conflicted than Buddhism. Several Confucian literati wrote essays opposed to the killing of girls, and Confucian scholar-officials made periodic attempts to enforce the laws against female infanticide. However, the favoritism of Confucian patrilineal ancestor reverence toward males worked to eliminate girls, and this was reinforced by a practical concern for reducing the expensive dowry that a bride's family was obliged to pay.

Roman Catholics were more active than Protestants in fighting female infanticide because of the Catholic emphasis on infant baptism. Unlike most Protestants, Catholics viewed the baptism of abandoned moribund infants as a priority because of their belief that infant baptism secured salvation. For related reasons, Catholics made far greater efforts than Protestants to establish orphanages. These Catholic orphanages, mostly established in the years 1850–1950, attempted to realize the Christian value of concern for the weak. However, they provoked a great deal of misunderstanding and resentment among the Chinese people, who viewed them as part of the imperialist intrusion of foreigners into China.

Another Christian-related movement in global history was generated by the Christian belief in racial and gender equality before God. St. Paul's injunction of Galatians 3:28 that before God humans are neither Jew nor Greek, slave nor free, or male nor female was implemented in the 19th century by both Christian abolitionists who opposed slavery and by women missionaries carrying the Christian message to other women throughout the world. The evangelizing of Chinese women by male missionaries was impeded by the seclusion of many Chinese women in their homes. The fact that female missionaries were more able to make contact with Chinese women created a ministry that attracted growing numbers of women from Europe and North America. By the 1870s in the United States and Europe, the feminist spirit was largely fused with worldwide Christian evangelization. Women were restless to break out of the narrow constraints imposed by farms and small town milieus in Europe and North America. In China, the numerical dominance among missionaries of males over females reversed itself in the last half of the 19th century. By 1890, women missionaries in China surpassed men in numbers, and by the early 20th century, women outnumbered men by more than 2 to 1. The establishment of schools was a crucial part of the Protestant missionary effort. Schools were viewed as a Christian ministry of caring for the poor, and Protestants were particularly active in establishing schools throughout the world. Schools for girls were a manifestation of an early form of feminism emanating from the United States.

Taiping Rebellion

One of the most powerful ideas that Christian missionaries carried around the globe was the Trinity. This is a teaching of the three in one by which the eternal deity contains the three different forms of Father, Son, and Holy Spirit (God, Jesus, and the Greek *Logos*). It is a mystical paradox that defies rational thinking, and yet it is also a transcendent vision with the power to cross cultural barriers. The power of the idea of the Trinity was revealed in its ability to stimulate a response in 19th-century China that absorbed and assimilated the idea by fusing it with fundamental Chinese ideas concerning family, politics, and the peasantry. However, this was a Chinese-led movement in which foreign missionaries played a limited role. This became the movement of the Heavenly Kingdom of Great Peace (*Taiping Tianguo*), which was a blending of the New Testament notion of a Heavenly Kingdom with the idealized goal of a world "Great Peace" that is mentioned in the Chinese classics. The Taipings absorbed the biblical notion of God as the creator of the world. But God was also a tribal deity to the Taipings, who viewed themselves, like the Old Testament Hebrews, as God's chosen people. As God's chosen people, the Taipings and not the Manchus (who had occupied the Chinese throne since their 1644 conquest) should rule China. God was believed to intervene in battles personally. However, God was also intolerant of idolatry. Taiping morality imposed a strict form of orthodoxy among the Taipings, including severe punishments for violating the separation of men and women.

The Taipings reinterpreted the Trinity by fusing the Old Testament notion of a Creator God with traditional Chinese ideas on fatherhood. However, Jesus was recast as the eldest son rather than as a divine figure. The Son was fully humanized by fusing Jesus with a Chinese sense of Confucian family order by making the Taiping founder, Hong Xiuchuan, the younger brother of Jesus. The Christian Holy Spirit was personalized by fusing the Taiping second-in-command Yang Xiuqing with the Holy Spirit. Christian concern for the weak was fused with Chinese attitudes toward social welfare expressed in the classic *Book of Rites*, in which the aged, orphans, widows, and disabled are all cared for in accordance with their need. The Taipings transformed Jesus' blessing of the poor and weak as well as the communal ownership of the New Testament church into the development of a sacred treasury system in which all property belonged to God. In the process, they blended the Christian idea with ancient Chinese tradition and the idea of communal granaries (*shecang*) discussed by the famous neo-Confucian philosopher Zhu Xi (1130–1200).

Underground Church Movement

Unlike most global cultures that European missionaries perceived as inferior to Europe, the comparable cultural and political status of China and Europe gave rise to a conflict between papal authority and the forces of Chinese nationalism. For more than four centuries, Chinese political leaders have resisted Rome's claim to ultimate authority in the Catholic Church in China, including particularly the appointment of bishops. This has caused the Catholic Church to be divided into an official church and an underground church, with Chinese authorities refusing to recognize bishops in the underground church appointed by Rome and Rome refusing to recognize bishops in the official church appointed by Beijing. On the Protestant side of Christianity, a large movement of unauthorized evangelical "house churches" has emerged throughout China since cultural regulations were relaxed in the 1990s. One possible resolution of both the Catholic and Protestant conflicts with the state that has been advocated by Chinese leaders is to treat the national church of China as a local church that is part of a Universal Church. In this perspective, the Vatican itself might be viewed as a local church that is part of the Universal Church. To what extent this represents a serious proposal versus a bargaining position remains to be seen, but clearly it reflects the reality of the globalization of Christianity and how it continues to evolve and create new movements in response.

D. E. Mungello

See also Christianity; Confucianism; Global Religions, Beliefs, and Ideologies; Religious Identities; Social Movements

Further Readings

Hobsbawm, E. (1965). *Primitive rebels*. New York: Norton.

Hyatt, I. T., Jr. (1976). *Our ordered lives confess: Three nineteenth-century American missionaries in East Shantung*. Cambridge, MA: Harvard University.

Liu, W. T., & Leung, B. (2002). Organizational revivalism: Explaining metamorphosis of China's Catholic church. *Journal for the Scientific Study of Religion, 41*, 121–138.

Mungello, D. E. (2008). *Drowning girls in China: Female infanticide since 1650*. Lanham, MD: Rowman & Littlefield.

Mungello, D. E. (2009). *The great encounter of China and the West, 1500–1800* (3rd ed.). Lanham, MD: Rowman & Littlefield.

Spence, J. (1996). *God's Chinese son: The Taiping heavenly kingdom of Hong Xiuquan*. New York: Norton.

Wang, P. C.-M. (Ed.). (2007). *Contextualization of Christianity in China: An evaluation in modern perspective*. Nettetal, Germany: Steyler Verlag.

CINEMA

With performances that can be simultaneously presented before millions around the world, cinema is a truly global entertainment medium. The ticketed screening of ten Lumière shorts at the Grand Café of Paris on December 28, 1895, is widely regarded as the birth of cinema, but the history of the medium is more complicated than this singular event implies. A series of discrete yet connected inventions led up to the moment: optical toys from the 17th-century magic lantern to 19th-century image-animating devices like the Thaumatrope and Zoetrope; development of still photography in the 1820s and 1830s by innovators like Nicéphore Niepce, William Henry Fox Talbot, and Louis Daguerre, and the subsequent experiments of Eadweard Muybridge and Étienne-Jules Marey aimed at capturing movement; George Eastman's evolving film stocks; Thomas Edison and William Kennedy Dickinson's search for motion picture cameras and projection systems (Kinetograph and Kinetoscope); and Auguste and Louis Lumière's combination of recording and projecting functions in the Cinématographe. This standard account presents cinema as a modern, Western technology of representation as well as its genesis as, in the main, a French-American event.

At first glance, this history seems accurate; yet two distinct complications, pertaining to the qualifiers "modern" and "Western," develop when we think of cinema in a global frame. Even if we acknowledge the centrality of capital to what we call the modern era, it is difficult to shore up the hypothesis of a unitary, universal modernity: Cultural differences will ensure divergent local experiences, generating a multiplicity of concurrent modernities. To argue otherwise will require we accept some version of a "stages" theory of modernization, according to which modernity emerges first in western Europe, then in the United States, and then gradually spreads to the rest of the world. In such a Eurocentric framework, the magic lantern or the Zoetrope can be absorbed easily into the history of cinema as a modern medium, but non-Western precinematic entertainment and narrative forms, such as Chinese shadow puppetry and Indian narrative scroll paintings, will produce cognitive hiccups and get jettisoned as premodern.

Limitations of the Hollywood and European Art Cinema Dichotomy

The bulk of scholarly and journalistic writings bolstered media histories and geographies in which Hollywood commercial cinema and, later, European art cinema get ensconced as the global benchmarks of two contrary modes. Overly distinguished by their imputed adherence to two polarized sets of conventions (commercial cinema's erasure of the means of production in the interest of taut, pleasurable, "slice of real life" narratives, in contrast to art cinema's reflexive, formally radical, discursively ambiguous and intellectually stimulating works), these two ideal types are then viewed as spawning their respective emulators. If Hollywood remains the undisputed model for various commercial film industries, their "derivative" status now obsessively reiterated by epithets like Bollywood and Nollywood, then more radical European formations such as Soviet Revolutionary Cinema or the French New Wave are celebrated as inspirations for Brazilian Cinema Novo or Taiwanese New Cinema.

The point is not to deny the global hegemony of Hollywood or the far-flung influences of Italian Neorealism and the French Nouvelle Vague. The point, rather, is to press for more global accounts of world cinema. If Hollywood principles of verisimilitude, continuity editing, and narrative economy are taken to be the universal standards, then Hong Kong martial arts and ghost genres or Indian melodramas with their epic digressions and musical numbers seem idiosyncratic, only partially evolved: These huge industries remain oddly marginal. What, then, is the place in global cinema of the Hindi film *Awara* (1951), now widely considered to be the most watched film in the world?

How do we appreciate the penetration of Hollywood action films by martial arts gestures—a development of which the *Matrix* trilogy (1999–2003) may only be the most legible signpost? Even today, as Hollywood is entering all kinds of transnational collaborations, the moniker "world cinema" routinely refers to a smorgasbord of non-Hollywood cinemas (thereby rivaling the absurdity of the category "world music"). Where and what is Hollywood, exactly? In what sense is *Moulin Rouge* (2001), a film about a group of fin de siècle Parisian bohemians producing a stage show set in India, co-produced by Twentieth Century Fox (United States), Angel Studios (Britain), and Bazmark Films (Australia-United States), with British, Australian, and Colombian-American lead actors, and directed by the Australian filmmaker Baz Luhrmann, a Hollywood film?

Multiple Models of Global Cinema

Reflections such as these index the insufficiency of established paradigms and underscore a need to acknowledge, document, and analyze the multiple folds along which cinema has developed as a global medium. Current research is moving in this direction, going beyond both West-centric myopia and the stale question of "influences," and postcolonial critiques of cultural imperialism and orientalist representation, to record the global efflorescence of cinematic genres and styles, circuits, and institutions. The signs of such a paradigmatic shift are increasingly more common. Thus, Sean Cubitt places the Marathi pioneer D. G. Phalke alongside the French Georges Méliès as progenitors of special effects; Toby Miller and colleagues investigate the global constitution of Hollywood; Corey Creekmur questions the undisputed preeminence of Hollywood and "provincializes" it via a rethinking of the musical genre in the light of Indian cinema. Peter Bloom and Priya Jaikumar record not only the colonialist agenda of French and British "empire cinemas" but also their tremendous productivity in forging modern globalities. Brian Larkin, Morris and colleagues, and Sudha Rajagopalan track the global reach of non-Hollywood cinemas (Hindi films in Nigeria and the Soviet Union, Hong Kong films in South India and Southeast Asia, and so on), while Hamid Naficy and Bhaskar Sarkar, among others,

map—in a variety of contexts and frameworks, from the hybrid, "accented" nature of diasporic and transnational independent films to the critique of modernist "foundational fictions" in terms of an epic melodramatic mode—the material relations and affective affinities among communities of a mutating global South.

Such approaches extend and deepen our understanding of the global in global cinema, while helping to globalize film scholarship. At the same time, they explore and often reproduce tensions between the global and the local, now with twists pertaining to the medium. Thus, for instance, what is known as Mexican cinema is a formation at once shaped by local concerns and translocal forces. In its professed golden age between the 1930s and the 1950s, typified in the works of Emilio Fernández and his cinematographer Gabriel Figueroa, this national cinema already combined the contradictions of Mexican society and local settings (haciendas, chapels, dancehalls, and brothels) with Hollywood-style plot structures and drew inspiration from Soviet filmmaker Sergei Eisenstein's use of Mexican folkloric idioms in *Que Viva Mexico* (1932). More recently, internationally recognized directors such as Alfonso Cuarón, Alejandro González Iñárritu and Guillermo del Toro stage the incongruities of being Mexican filmmakers in the era of global co-productions and expanding transborder audiences: films such as *Amores Perros* (2000) and *Y tu mama también* (2001) perform an "innate" Mexican-ness even as they tap into the vitality of emerging transnational markets, lifestyles, and sensibilities.

The Persistence of National Cinema

Here, we encounter one of the peculiarities of contemporary cinema: Even as the national is eclipsed by transnational collectivities, institutions, and channels, the rubric of "national cinema" persists. A qualifier derived from modernity's archetypal unit of political organization, the national came to denote cinema—like literature, art, and culture before it—as something of a collective patrimony. The invocation of the national, even when cinema existed in an uneasy relation to nationalist/statist ideologies, took on a performative role, seeking to institute a shared ethos and identity through reiteration. The linguistic basis of such presumed affiliations, reflected in familiar categories such as Italian Cinema or Spanish Cinema, is complicated by intranational linguistic differences (e.g., Italian auteur Pier Paolo Pasolini's use of Friulian) or competing nationalisms (e.g., Catalan and Basque cinemas in relation to Spanish cinema). And in a multilingual society such as India, "national cinema" amounts to an awkward bundling of multiple "regional" film industries corresponding to distinct languages: Bengali, Hindi, Kannada, Malayalam, Tamil, and Telegu, to name the most prominent. Despite all the contradictions at both subnational and supranational levels, this not-so-vestigial category continues to frame films in international circuits: Thus, Korean cinema enjoys a renaissance, a Thai filmmaker wins at Cannes, and so on.

Regional Cinema

In many ways, the lesson of cinema is the impossibility of sustaining any self-evident integrity of categories like the local and the global, or of related designations of the national, microregional (Bhojpuri, Catalan) or macroregional (East Asian, European) kind. Consider, for instance, cinema of the Middle East: How does it relate to cognate cinematic formations—Persian, Israeli, Arab, Maghrebi, Egyptian, or Beur? All the same, as long as these categories are not allowed to become immutable and sacrosanct, they remain useful heuristics encapsulating complex histories and geographies. They represent multiple acts of worldmaking that overlap, seep into, and jostle with each other, at once fracturing and thickening our understanding of world cinema.

Realism and Social Critique

That cinema conjures up entire worlds in fantastic genres (the historical epic and science fiction) is a commonplace. What remains less recognized is the role of more prosaic genres (family melodrama, romantic comedy) in shaping social institutions, modes of behavior and collective futures—indeed, the very idea of the human. Debates about cinematic realism often proceed from an assumption that the medium's role is to "reflect" reality, even as proponents of realist aesthetics routinely project what they would like reality to be. The history of world

cinema—of its various "movements," including the so-called radical modernisms—is full of struggles to shape reality. But this agonistic history does not imply a simple antagonism between cinema and capital: In fact, the medium has been a crucial component of the uneven experience of capitalist modernity. Not only has cinema recorded (i.e., reflected) the shock of the modern, but it has also reordered spatiotemporal relations and fabricated novel media ecologies. Miriam Hansen argued that locally grounded "vernacular modernisms" were as responsible as the various avant-garde movements in producing modern subjectivities, socialities, and worldviews, effectively working in tandem with the global processes of industrialization, urbanization, and migration. The medium has induced sensations of mobility and shaped aspirations; fostered connectivity around cinephilia and cosmopolitan ideals; generated spirited cultural interventions on behalf of social justice and equity; and served as the site for geopolitical realignments from imperial cinema to Third Cinema (a paradigm proposed in the 1960s as a politicized alternative to both neo-imperialist commercial cinemas and European "art cinema"). Although it is necessary to reveal, by means of careful materialist-ideological critique, mainstream cinema's role in the reproduction of the relations of global production, it is also important to acknowledge its considerable generative capacities.

Cinema as a Mirror of Globalities

Not the least of these capacities is the ability to project and materialize entire lifeworlds: in a profound sense, cinema is constitutive of modern globalities. Many social scientists still overlook this aspect, reducing films to epiphenomenal documents of a reality "out there." In actuality, cinema is directly imbricated in global mechanisms and patterns of transformation. Thus, cultural policies have undergone momentous shifts within a neoliberal ecumene. Both Luisela Alvaray and Cristina Venegas documented a new regionalism in Latin America in the wake of trade pacts and alliances such as North American Free Trade Agreement (NAFTA) and MERCOSUR: Regional collaborations such as Programa Ibermedia and RECAM mark the emergence of new media geographies. In a markedly different context, Mette Hjort analyzes how the cinema of Denmark, a "small nation," sought to overcome its limited market and cultural prestige with a two-prong strategy: posing the concept of "heritage" as something universal, imbued with broad humanist appeal (now taken up by the United Nations with respect to culture in general); and developing the aesthetically rigorous Dogme 95 film movement as a means of energizing world cinema.

The Impact of New Technologies

It is not as if cinema's material networks have become global only in this much-hyped era of globalization. The planetary circulation of Lumière, Edison, and Pathé film crews and shorts in the early years of cinema; international film festivals from the 1930s; "runaway productions" shot in foreign locales from the 1960s; connections fostered by film schools such as the one at the University of Southern California in Los Angeles and Cuba's famed ICAIC (the Cuban Institute of Cinematographic Arts and Industry): These are only a few significant moments in the medium's history that counter such presentism. Nonetheless, several contemporary developments expand and intensify cinema's global dimension. Central among these is the advent of digital media technologies, formats, and systems, revolutionizing all aspects of cinema and prompting hyperbole about "the death of cinema." The use of digital editing software, digital video and high-definition technologies, CGI (computer-generated imagery); outsourcing of postproduction work to multiple locations dispersed across the planet (creating translocal, "virtual" studios); increasing standardization of theatrical exhibition in terms of multiplexes with similar architectures, game arcades and concession stands, Dolby or THX sound systems, and digital projection; the proliferation of three-dimensional and IMAX screens to compete with popular immersive technologies like video games; the Internet purveying new platforms for experimental and short films and inducing the radical reorganization of commercial distribution in electronic formats directly to home and handheld devices; Web 2.0 intensifying the romance with interactivity and enabling user-generated media: these emerging media assemblages are surely marking the end of cinema as we know it.

At the same time, the new technologies and conduits have exacerbated illegal copying and distribution of media—piracy—underscoring the need for more stringent regimes of regulation. The World Trade Organization's global agreement on Trade Related Aspects of Intellectual Property Rights (TRIPs) seeks to achieve this, but global compliance runs into problems of competing interests and sovereignties at national and local levels. What is a problem for media industries is, on the other hand, a form of cultural activism for their critics, who decry the former's unmitigated greed for profits and extol the entrepreneurial pirates' role in expanding access to, and informally archiving, films. The shacks and carts of Beijing, Cairo, or Kuala Lumpur that offer a cornucopia of world cinema, sometimes even hard-to-find titles, mark the vibrant and irrepressible underbelly of globalization.

Preserving World Cinema and Global Social Responsibility

Two other sets of contemporary initiatives, both focusing on cinema and seeking to promote global understanding and civil society values, are worth mentioning. The first springs from the turn of the century interest in restoring, preserving, and archiving significant works of world cinema. The second involves transnational documentary movements, which seek to record, bear witness to, and mobilize publics against social suffering—often perpetrated by the state. Working with nongovernmental organizations and institutions such as the World Social Forum and taking advantage of the new modes of dissemination, these cine-initiatives promoting social justice and human rights constitute a significant part of globalization "from below." However, these emergent documentary archives also feed into a global frenzy for top-down humanitarian interventions: a tendency dramatically instantiated by the U.S. Holocaust Memorial Museum's recent Darfur Project. As the global community moves to adopt policies such as the United Nations doctrine of "Responsibility to Protect" (2005), cinema's role in furthering the cause of a global civil society—itself a deeply contested concept—remains ambiguous.

Bhaskar Sarkar

See also Academy Awards; Americanization; Artists; Civil Society, Global; Cultural Industries; Global Culture, Media; Globalization, Phenomenon of; McDonaldization, McWorld; Mumbai

Further Readings

Alvaray, L. (2008, Spring). National, regional, and global: New waves of Latin American cinema. *Cinema Journal, 47*(3), 48–65.

Bloom, P. (2008). *French colonial documentary: Mythologies of humanitarianism.* Minneapolis: University of Minnesota Press.

Creekmur, C. (2002). Picturizing American cinema: Hindi film songs and the last days of genre. In P. R. Wojcik & A. Knight (Eds.), *Soundtrack available* (pp. 375–406). Durham, NC: Duke University Press.

Ďurovičová, N., & Newman, K. (Eds.). (2009). *World cinemas, transnational perspectives.* London: Routledge.

Hansen, M. (2009). Vernacular modernism: Tracking cinema on a global scale. In N. Durovicová & K. Newman (Eds.), *World cinemas, transnational perspectives* (pp. 287–313). London: Routledge.

Hjort, M. (2005). *Small nation, global cinema: The new Danish cinema.* Minneapolis: University of Minnesota Press.

Jaikumar, P. (2006). *Cinema at the end of empire: A politics of transition in Britain and India.* Durham, NC: Duke University Press.

Larkin, B. (2008). *Signal and noise: Media, infrastructure, and urban culture in Nigeria.* Durham, NC: Duke University Press.

Miller, T., Govil, N., Wang, M. R., & Wang, T. (2008). *Global Hollywood 2.* London: British Film Institute.

Morris, M., Leung Li, S., Chan Ching-Kiu, S., & Sai-shing, Y. (Eds.). (2006). *Hong Kong connections: Transnational imaginations in action cinema.* Durham, NC: Duke University Press.

Naficy, H. (2001). *An accented cinema: Exilic and diasporic filmmaking.* Princeton, NJ: Princeton University Press.

Pang, L. (2007). *Cultural control and globalization in Asia: Copyright, piracy, and cinema.* London: Routledge.

Rajagopalan, S. (2009). *Indian films in Soviet cinemas: The culture of movie-going after Stalin.* Bloomington: Indiana University Press.

Sarkar, B. (2010). Epic melodrama, or cine-maps of the global south. In R. Burgoyne (Ed.), *The epic film in world culture* (pp. 263–295). London: Routledge.

Sarkar, B., & Walker, J. (Eds.). (2009). *Documentary testimonies: Global archives of suffering.* London: Routledge.

Venegas, C. (2009). Thinking regionally: Singular in diversity and diverse in unity. In J. Holt & A. Perren (Eds.), *Media industries: History, theory, and method* (pp. 120–130). West Sussex, UK: Wiley-Blackwell.

CITIES

In the global era, the city has emerged as a strategic site for understanding some of the major new trends reconfiguring the social order. The city and the metropolitan region have become locations where major macrosocial trends materialize and hence can be constituted as an object of global studies. Each of those major trends has its own specific contents and consequences. The urban moment is but one moment in their often complex multisited trajectories.

The city has long been a strategic site for the exploration of many of the issues confronting society. But it has not always been a heuristic space—a space capable of producing knowledge about some of the major transformations of an epoch. In the first half of the 20th century, the study of cities was at the heart of sociology. This is evident in the work of Georg Simmel, Max Weber, Walter Benjamin, Henri Lefebvre, and most prominently the Chicago School, especially Robert Park and Louis Wirth, both deeply influenced by German sociology. These sociologists confronted massive processes—industrialization, urbanization, alienation, and a new cultural formation they called "urbanity." Studying the city was not simply studying the urban. It was about studying the major social processes of an era. Since then, the study of the city, and with it urban sociology, gradually lost this privileged role as a lens for the discipline and as a producer of key analytic categories. There are many reasons for this, most important among which are questions of the particular developments of method and data in sociology generally. Critical was the fact that the city ceased being the fulcrum of epochal transformations and hence a strategic site for research about nonurban processes. Urban sociology became increasingly concerned with what came to be called "social problems."

The worldwide resurgence in the 1990s of the city as a site for research on these major contemporary dynamics is evident in multiple disciplines—sociology, anthropology, economic geography, cultural studies, and literary criticism. In the global era, economists have begun to address the urban and regional economy in their analyses in ways that go beyond older forms of urban economics. Globalization has given rise to new information technologies, the intensifying of transnational and translocal dynamics, and the strengthening presence and voice of sociocultural diversity. All of these are at a cutting edge of change. These trends do not encompass the majority of social conditions; on the contrary, most social reality probably corresponds to older continuing and familiar trends. Yet, although these trends involve only parts of the urban condition and cannot be confined to the urban, they are strategic in that they mark the urban condition in novel ways and make it, in turn, a key research site for major urban and nonurban trends.

The City as Exemplar of the Global Information Economy

The concept of the city is complex, imprecise, and charged with specific historical meanings. A more abstract notion might be centrality, present in all cities, and, in turn, something that cities have historically given to societies. For most of known history, centrality has largely been embedded in the major city of a region or a country. One of the changes brought about by the new communication technologies of the 21st century is the reconfiguring of centrality: The central city is today but one form of centrality. Important emerging spaces for the constitution of centrality range from the new transnational networks of cities to electronic space. What are the conditions for the continuity of centrality in advanced societies in the face of major new technologies that maximize the possibility for geographic dispersal at the regional, national, and indeed global scale, and simultaneous system integration?

A second major challenge for thinking about the city as a site for researching major (including nonurban) contemporary dynamics concerns the narratives we have constructed about the city and how those narratives relate to the global economy and to the new technologies. The understandings and the categories that dominate mainstream discussions about the future of advanced economies imply that the city has become obsolete for leading economic sectors given electronic networks. We need to subject these notions to critical examination. At least two sets of issues need to be teased out if we are to understand the role, if any, of cities in a global information economy and, hence, the capacity of urban research to produce knowledge about that larger economy. One concerns the extent to which these new types of electronic formations, such as electronic financial markets, are indeed disembedded from social contexts. The second set of issues concerns possible instances of the global economy and of the new technologies that have not been recognized as such or are contested representations.

Finally, and on a somewhat more theoretical level, certain properties of power make cities strategic. Power needs to be historicized to overcome the abstractions of the concept. Power is not simply an attribute or a sort of factor endowment. It is actively produced and reproduced. Many studies on the local dimensions of power have made important contributions to this subject. One of the aspects today in the production of power structures has to do with new forms of economic power and the relocation of certain forms of power from the state to the market, partly as a result of deregulation and privatization. In the case of cities, this also brings with it questions about the built environment and the architectures of centrality that represent different kinds of power—the civic power of the grand bourgeoisies of the late 19th century and the aggressive power of the new rich of the 1990s. Cities have long been places for the spatialization of power. More generally, we might ask whether power has spatial correlates, or a spatial moment. In terms of the economy, this question could be operationalized more concretely: Can the current economic system, with its strong tendencies toward concentration in ownership and control, have a space economy that lacks points of physical concentration? It is hard to think about a discourse on the future of cities that would not include this dimension of power.

To some extent, it is the major cities in the highly developed world that most clearly display the processes discussed in this entry. However, these processes are present in cities in developing countries as well: But they are less visible because they are submerged under the megacity syndrome—sheer population size and urban sprawl create their own realities. Size and sprawl do not prevent the new power equation described; however, the spatial correlates (e.g., gentrification and the building of a new glamour zone) are less visible in a city of 20 million inhabitants. The geography of globalization contains both a dynamic of dispersal of people and activities and a dynamic of centralization. Most of the attention has gone to dispersal patterns. But the massive spatial dispersal of people and economic activities has itself contributed to a demand for new forms of territorial centralization of top-level management and control operations. The fact, for instance, that firms worldwide now have approximately 1 million affiliates outside their home countries signals that the sheer number of dispersed factories and service outlets that are part of a firm's integrated operation creates massive new needs for central coordination and servicing. This is one of the major trends leading to the emergence of global cities. In brief, the spatial dispersal of economic activity made possible by globalization and telecommunications contributes to an expansion of central functions *if* this dispersal is to take place under the continuing concentration in control, ownership, and profit appropriation that characterizes the current economic system.

The city enters the discourse at this point. Cities regain strategic importance because they are favored sites for the production of these central functions. National and global markets as well as globally integrated organizations require central places where the work of globalization gets done. Finance and advanced corporate services are industries producing the organizational commodities necessary for the implementation and management of global economic systems. Cities are preferred sites for the production of these services, particularly the most innovative, speculative, internationalized service sectors, but more provincial cities play this role as well, although for less complex versions of these services.

Furthermore, leading firms in information industries require a vast *physical* infrastructure containing strategic nodes with hyperconcentration of facilities. We need to distinguish between the capacity for global transmission/communication and the material conditions that make this possible. Finally, even the most advanced information industries have a production process that is at least partly place bound because of the combination of resources it requires even when the outputs are hypermobile; the tendency in the specialized literature has been to study these advanced information industries in terms of their hypermobile outputs rather than the actual work processes, which include top-level professionals as well as clerical and manual service workers.

When we start by examining broader dynamics in order to detect their localization patterns, we can begin to observe and conceptualize the formation, at least incipient, of transnational urban systems. The growth of global markets for finance and specialized services, the need for transnational servicing networks as a result of sharp increases in international investment, the reduced role of the government in the regulation of international economic activity, and the corresponding ascendance of other institutional arenas with a strong urban connection—all these point to the existence of a series of transnational networks of cities. These are of many different kinds and types. Business networks are probably the most developed given the growth of a global economy. But we also see a proliferation of social, cultural, professional, activist, and political networks connecting particular sets of cities.

To a large extent, the major business centers in the world today draw their importance from these transnational networks. There is no such entity as a single global city—and, in this sense, there is a sharp contrast with the erstwhile capitals of empires. A global firm, an international museum, or a global civil society organization need not be one perfect global city but many. The networks of major international business centers constitute new geographies of centrality. The most powerful of these new geographies of centrality at the global level binds the major international financial and business centers. In the 1980s, these networks were centered on New York, London, Tokyo, Paris, Frankfurt, Zurich, Amsterdam, Los Angeles, Sydney, and Hong Kong, among others. By the late 1990s, they had added Mumbai, Bangkok, Seoul, Taipei, Shanghai, São Paulo, Mexico City, and Buenos Aires. By 2011, they included more than 100 major and minor global cities.

The intensity of transactions among these cities, particularly through the financial markets, trade in services, and investment, has increased sharply, and so have the orders of magnitude involved. There has been a sharpening inequality in the concentration of strategic resources and activities between each of these cities and others in the same country. This has consequences for the role of urban systems in national territorial integration. Although the latter has never been what its model tells us, the last decade has observed a subsequent acceleration in the fragmentation of national territory. National urban systems are being partly unbundled as their major cities become part of a new or strengthened transnational urban system.

But we can no longer think of centers for international business and finance simply in terms of the corporate towers and corporate culture at their center. The international character of major cities lies not only in their telecommunication infrastructure and foreign firms: It lies also in the many different cultural environments in which these workers and others exist. This is one arena where we have observed the growth of an enormously rich scholarship.

Cities and Political Subjectivity

It is helpful to consider Max Weber's *The City* to examine the production of political subjectivity signaled by the preceding section. In his effort to specify the ideal typical features of what constitutes the city, Weber sought out a certain type of city—most prominently the cities of the late Middle Ages rather than the modern industrial cities of his time. Weber sought a kind of city that combined conditions and dynamics that forced its residents and leaders into creative and innovative responses/adaptations. Furthermore, he posited that these changes produced in the context of the city generated transformations that went beyond the city and could institute often larger fundamental transformations. In that regard, the city offered the possibility of understanding far-reaching changes that could—under certain conditions—eventually encompass society at large.

There are two aspects of Weber's *The City* of particular importance in this entry. Weber helps us understand under what conditions cities can be positive and creative influences on peoples' lives. For Weber cities are a set of social structures that encourage individuality and innovation and, hence, are an instrument of historical change. There is, in this intellectual project, a deep sense of the historicity of these conditions. Modern urban life did not correspond to this positive and creative power of cities; Weber viewed modern cities as dominated by large factories and office bureaucracies. The Fordist city that was to come much later and culminate in the 1950s and 1960s can be viewed as illustrating Weber's view in the sense that the strategic scale under Fordism is the national scale and that cities lose significance. Unlike medieval times, it is not the city, but the large Fordist factory and the mines that emerge as key sites for the political work of the disadvantaged and those without or with only limited power.

Struggles around political, economic, legal, and cultural issues centered in the realities of cities can become the catalysts for new transurban developments in all these institutional domains—markets, participatory governance, rights for members of the urban community regardless of lineage, judicial recourse, cultures of engagement, and deliberation. For Weber, it is particularly the cities of the late Middle Ages that combine the conditions that pushed urban residents, merchants, artisans, and leaders to address them and deal with them. These transformations could make for epochal change beyond the city itself: Weber shows us how in many of these cities these struggles led to the creation of the elements of what we could call governance systems and citizenship.

Today a certain type of city—the global city—has emerged as a strategic site for innovations and transformations in multiple institutional domains. Several key components of economic globalization and digitization concentrate in global cities and produce dislocations and destabilizations of existing institutional orders and legal/regulatory/normative frames for handling urban conditions. The high level of concentration of these new dynamics in these cities forces creative responses and innovations. There is, most probably, a threshold effect at work here.

In contrast, from the 1930s until the 1970s, when mass manufacturing dominated, cities lost strategic functions and were not the site for creative institutional innovations. The strategic sites were the large factory at the heart of the larger process of mass manufacturing and mass consumption, and the government as site for making a new social contract (e.g., legal protections for workers and the welfare state). The factory and the government were the strategic sites where the crucial dynamics producing the major institutional innovations of the epoch were located. With globalization and digitization—and all the specific elements they entail—global cities emerge as such strategic sites but with a project of concentrating power and wealth and an opposing actor consisting of a mix of immigrants, minoritized citizens, and other disadvantaged. Although the strategic transformations are sharply concentrated in global cities, many are also enacted (besides being diffused) in cities at lower orders of national urban hierarchies.

Current conditions in global cities are creating not only new structurations of power but also operational and rhetorical openings for new types of political actors that may have been submerged, invisible, or without voice. A key element of the argument here is that the localization of strategic components of globalization in these cities means that the disadvantaged can engage the new forms of globalized corporate power, and second, that the growing numbers and diversity of the disadvantaged in these cities take on a distinctive "presence."

This entails a distinction between powerlessness and invisibility/impotence. The disadvantaged in global cities can gain "presence" in their engagement with power but also vis-à-vis each other. This is different from the period between the 1950s and the 1970s in the United States, for instance, when White flight and the significant departure of major corporate headquarters left cities hollowed out and the disadvantaged in a condition of abandonment. Today, the localization of the global creates a set of objective conditions of engagement, for example, the struggles against gentrification, which encroaches on minority and disadvantaged neighborhoods and which led to growing numbers of homeless beginning in the 1980s and the struggles for the rights of the homeless, or demonstrations against police brutalizing minority people. These struggles are different from the ghetto uprisings of the 1960s, which were short, intense eruptions confined to the ghettos and causing most of the damage in the neighborhoods of the disadvantaged themselves. In these ghetto uprisings there was no engagement with power but more protest against power.

Conclusion

The conditions that today make some cities strategic sites are basically two, and both capture major transformations that are destabilizing older systems organizing territory and politics. One of these is the rescaling of the strategic territories that articulate the new politicoeconomic system. The other is the partial unbundling or at least weakening of the national as container of social process resulting from the variety of dynamics encompassed by globalization and digitization, but also by the fact of growing inequalities—the making of global elites and the impoverishment of the modest middle sectors. The consequences for cities of these two conditions are many: What matters here is that cities emerge as strategic sites for major economic processes and for new types of political actors.

What is being engendered today in terms of political practices in the global city is different from what it might have been in the medieval city of Weber. In the medieval city, we observe a set of practices that allowed the burghers to set up systems for owning and protecting property and to implement various immunities against despots of all sorts. Today's political practices may have to do with the production of "presence" by those without power and with a politics that claims rights to the city rather than protection of property. What the two situations share is the notion that, through these practices, new forms of political subjectivity (i.e., new notions of citizenship/membership) are being constituted and that the city is a key site for this type of political work. The city is, in turn, partly constituted through these dynamics. Far more than a peaceful and harmonious suburb, the contested city is where the civic is getting made. After the long historical phase that saw the ascendance of the national state and the scaling of key economic dynamics at the national level, the city is once again a scale for strategic economic and political dynamics.

Saskia Sassen

See also Antiglobalization Movements and Critics;
Capitalism; Citizenship; Connectedness, Global;
Empires, Modern; Immigration; Inequality, Global;
Power, Global Contexts of; Social Networking;
Urbanization; War, Urban

Further Readings

Abu-Lughod, J. L. (1999). *New York, Los Angeles,
Chicago: America's global cities.* Minneapolis:
University of Minnesota Press.

Amen, M. M., Archer, K., & Bosman, M. M.
(Eds.). (2006). *Relocating global cities: From the
center to the margins.* Boulder, CO: Rowman &
Littlefield.

Castells, M. (1972). *La question urbaine* [The urban
question]. Paris: Maspero.

Cordero-Guzmán, H. R., Smith, R. C., & Grosfoguel, R.
(Eds.). (2001). *Migration, transnationalization, and
race in a changing New York.* Philadelphia: Temple
University Press.

Friedmann, J., & Wolff, G. (1982). World city formation:
An agenda for research and action. *International
Journal of Urban and Regional Research, 15*(1),
269–283.

GaWC. (1998). *Globalization and World Cities Study
Group and Network.* Retrieved October 17, 2011,
from http://www.lboro.ac.uk/gawc

Gugler, J. (2004). *World cities beyond the West.*
Cambridge, UK: Cambridge University Press.

Hagedorn, J. (Ed.) (2007). *Gangs in the global city:
Exploring alternatives to traditional criminology.*
Chicago: University of Illinois Press.

Hall, P. (1966). *The world cities.* New York:
McGraw-Hill.

Harvey, D. (1985). *The urbanization of capital.* Oxford,
UK: Blackwell.

King, A. D. (Ed.). (1996). *Representing the city. Ethnicity,
capital and culture in the 21st century.* London:
Macmillan.

Krause, L., & Petro, P. (Eds.). (2003). *Global cities:
Cinema, architecture, and urbanism in a digital age.*
New Brunswick, NJ: Rutgers University Press.

Sandercock, L. (2003). *Cosmopolis II: Mongrel cities in
the 21st century.* New York: Continuum.

Sassen, S. (2001). *The global city: New York, London,
Tokyo.* Princeton, NJ: Princeton University. (Original
work published 1991)

Sassen, S. (2011). *Cities in world economy* (4th ed.).
Thousand Oaks, CA: Sage/Pine Forge.

Sennett, R. (2003). *Respect in an age of inequality.*
New York: Norton.

Soja, E. W. (2000). *Postmetropolis: Critical studies of
cities and regions.* Oxford, UK: Blackwell.

Stren, R. (1996). The studies of cities: Popular
perceptions, academic disciplines, and emerging
agendas. In M. Cohen, B. Ruble, J. Tulchin, & A.
Garland (Eds.), *Preparing for the urban future: Global
pressures and local forces.* Washington, DC: Woodrow
Wilson Center Press (distributed by Johns Hopkins
University Press).

Taylor, P. J. (2004). *World city network: A global urban
analysis.* London: Routledge.

Valle, V. M., & Torres, R. D. (2000). *Latino metropolis.*
Minneapolis: University of Minnesota Press.

CITIZENSHIP

Emerging global contexts have affected the concept of citizenship. They have shifted, altered, and created new forms of individual political membership and activity that call into question the traditional link among citizenship, national polity, and individual freedom in democratic theory.

Whereas in the late 1970s scholarly interest in the concept of citizenship had all but died, by the 1990s, it had come back in fashion among political thinkers, and in the first decade of the new millennium, interest in citizenship has grown across the spectrum of disciplines as scholars of democracy, international relations, new institutions, public law and policy, constitutionalism, justice, identity, race, and ethnicity seek to understand empirical shifts, provide normative analysis, and offer new theories of the transformation of citizenship.

Several empirical observations today throw traditional understandings of citizenship into question. One set of observations concerns the large-scale transnational flows of migrants. International migration patterns have the foundational conception of citizenship as a single loyalty of political and social membership in that migrants maintain cross-border ties that link sending and receiving countries through remittances, social networks, and increasingly, political decision making. These social, economic, and political memberships that transcend state boundaries give rise to multiple legal statuses that diffuse and expand the notion of citizenship as a bundle of rights and duties. What have come to be known as "diasporic" or "nomadic" citizenships unhinge the connection between community and space.

A second set of observations concerns the shifting nature of sovereign authority. The regulation of transnational flows of goods and capital have spawned a dense web of legal rights and judicial administration through the proliferation of quasi-national or transnational courts that have given individuals access to assert rights within, beyond, and through national states. The rise of supranational bodies such as the European Union, the secession or devolution of federated states into smaller ethnic communal localities, and the connections between regions or global cities as economic and political centers call into question the secular national state as a sovereign authority. In addition, networks of global political, economic, and social actors now form a global civil society that exerts authority over the national state, calling into question the connection between citizenship and republican governance as popular sovereignty.

A third set of observations concerns the division between global entrepreneurs who operate through privately owned security, education and social services, and legal networks that bypass the state bureaucratic institutions and, at the other extreme, global workers who are increasingly denied such public services and are, thereby, excluded from the state and public sphere. These dialectical global forces have dislocated traditional understandings of citizenship concerning place and belonging, equality, and right. Disenfranchised and socially excluded immigrant communities experience a disconnect between the grant of citizenship, as a formal status, and the full status of membership that comes through substantive equality and community belonging. All these various observations regarding the globalized world necessitate an examination of the historical progression of citizenship and the normative discussions regarding its transformation.

The core claim is that globalization dislocated the traditional understandings of exclusive or quasi-exclusive political membership and that there has been an expansion of institutions and legal structures to facilitate and legitimize new forms and multiple memberships such that national citizenship may be obsolete. Yet, at the same time, national citizenship seems to have gained currency

as a valuable political and social commodity in the globalized world of limited resources and heightened security, which have increased the costs of nonmembership. Behind both these claims is the normative understanding of citizenship in democratic theory as a transformation of the individual into a political actor possessing the power to make communal decisions and, thereby, actualize individual freedom. The question, then, is how the observations mentioned concerning the globalized world have either altered this understanding or shifted its attainment to new centers and modes of political belonging. In other words, how do we understand the transformation of citizenship that has taken place, and what does this say about the nature of political relations and democratic institutions that have traditionally been understood in terms of freedom actualized through unitary membership and rights in a polity? After a discussion of the transformation of citizenship within the historical context of the evolution of the modern national state, this entry examines the scholarly debates regarding ways in which new global trends and events have altered the traditional normative understandings of citizenship as either a "good" or as a "right." A concluding section discusses new theories of global citizenship.

Historical Evolution of the Modern National State

In the historical evolution of the modern national state, citizenship developed as a response to papal, dynastic, and monarchal authority and is, therefore, closely connected, in the early theorizing on citizenship in Thomas Hobbes, John Locke, Jean-Jacques Rousseau, Immanuel Kant, and Georg Wilhelm Friedrich Hegel, to specific historical power struggles and political contexts and stages of national development. In the progression of political theory on citizenship from the 17th-century birth of the Westphalian European state system to today, we view citizenship as a challenge to religious authority, a revolution against estatism, an assertion of individual rights, a call for equality, an expression of universal moral imperative, and more recently, reformulation of the meaning of communication and diversity.

With the settlement of Westphalia in 1648, which ended the Thirty Years' War, emerged the

European State system as a patchwork of sovereign national authority. However, citizenship, as a theory of democracy, came a bit later and flourished in the 18th century through the philosophy of the Enlightenment, which claimed reason as the basis for authority. The principles of the Enlightenment, such as individual right, liberty, and equality, gave rise to public law as separate from papal and monarchical authority and gave birth to the constitutional state premised on secular rule of law and popular sovereignty. Through revolutions and proclamations of independence, such as the French Declaration of the Rights of Man and Citizen and the U.S. Declaration of Independence, the concept of citizenship located the individual as a free and morally responsible political actor. Although still a limited status reserved mainly for male property owners, this stage significantly altered the power of papal, dynastic, and monarchal authority and situated sovereign authority in the status and rights of the individual and rule of law.

In its second stage, corresponding to the late 19th-century and early 20th-century industrial revolution and the expansion of rights beyond propertied White males, citizenship located the individual as a rights-bearing member of a national territory. In this stage, a connection was made among state, territory, and rights. During this stage, the emerging industrial democracies embarked on a period of imperial colonization. Citizenship was enacted into public law in order to better define and secure national borders and deal with new colonial territories and increased migration. Citizenship policies were based on either a birthright or territorial (*jus soli*) principle or a descent-based (*jus sanguinis*) principle, or a combination of the two. Both approaches to citizenship were responses to the global migration system produced through colonial expansion and industrialization. For example, birthright citizenship provided for the absorption of migrants into countries such as the United States, where industrialization and vast empty lands required the entry of migrant labor, and in the United Kingdom, where colonial subjects were needed on the mainland. Descent-based policies in labor-exporting countries such as Germany permanently extended membership to descendants when they emigrated to other countries. During this stage, Western liberal national states such as the United Kingdom

and France developed the status of "nationality" as distinct from citizenship, which they extended to colonial subjects. Whereas, in the United States, nationality and citizenship were synonymous, in France citizenship, as rights and duties of membership, remains distinct from nationality, as membership in a national state.

After World War II, a new stage began to unfold as colonization gave way to a right to self-determination inscribed in 1948 in the Universal Declaration of Human Rights and citizenship became understood as the right to membership in one's sovereign nation. In this way, citizenship became closely associated with a territory, a national people, and guarantee of rights. The state system became encompassed within an international human rights order that, through international treaties and institutional structures such as the International Court of Justice and the European Court of Human Rights, sought to guarantee individuals human rights and protection against statelessness. In other words, it sought to guarantee state citizenship for everyone. During the 1980s, national and supranational courts in Europe and the United States extended liberal civil and social rights to those present in a territory and linked extended residence to entitlements that approximated residency to formal citizenship status. The post–World War II economic expansion and increase in the flow of labor migration through guest-worker policies resulted in a growing number of noncitizens as long-term or permanent residents in advanced Western liberal democracies. In some situations, naturalization was not available because of restrictive citizenship policies (e.g., Germany and Austria), while in others, it was available, but first-generation immigrants increasingly chose not to naturalize (e.g., United Kingdom and United States). In both cases, noncitizens possessed full access to liberal civil and social rights. Scholars connected the growing percentage of "foreign" populations in Western liberal democracies with a "devaluation" of citizenship, while others focused on developing a concept of multicultural citizenship for liberal democracy.

In the late 20th century came the collapse of European communism and the fragmentation of national borders into smaller ethnic units. At the same time, the international system of human rights had developed to provide a legal structure for the acquisition of rights beyond national borders. Thus, scholars proclaimed the end of the Westphalian system of national states and the birth of postnational citizenship. Others, who still viewed the national state as the primary political form of membership and sovereign authority, recognized citizenship as bifurcated or multiple. During this period, empirical research showed the convergence of Western liberal citizenship policies. States that held onto a descent-based definition of membership, such as Germany, Austria, Greece, and Switzerland, and that acquired sizable populations of guest workers during the 1960s and 1970s, revised national laws to grant citizenship based on territorial birth; those that had easy access to citizenship through birth on the territory and that had acquired sizable populations of former colonial subjects revised policies to restrict the grant of citizenship.

Scholarly Debate

Having a sense of the historical progression of citizenship provides the basis on which to understand the transformation of the two core normative models that have animated discussion in the Western tradition. The first is a Greek participatory model that views citizenship as a good or value. In fifth and fourth century BCE Athens, citizenship was a concept used to divide private and public life. The citizen was free of the household or private sphere, free of the world of things. The assumption was that humans are political by nature. Citizenship was a vocation or a practice. Being fully human and free meant ruling yourself. Democratic citizenship, in this understanding, required requisite civic virtues needed to participate in the polity. In contrast, the Roman model from the third century BCE and first century CE views being human as relating to the world of things (the *res*) as the medium in which humans live and relate to each other. In this understanding, citizenship is the freedom to act by law and the freedom to ask and expect the law's protection. The relation among things raises the need for law. Thus, in the Roman juridical model, citizenship is a legal status or bundle of rights, and the Roman citizen was a rights-bearing individual. This concept suited life in the Roman Empire, where the need was to obligate citizens across vast territories. The Greek model suited the Greek city-state, where territory was small.

Both models place the individual at the center of political life, where, either as a rights holder or through the status and practice of membership, the individual forms into a community of citizens and society embodies a common right (Cicero) or achieves the common good (Aristotle). The difference is that in the Greek model, the "good life" and freedom stem from participation, and therefore, citizenship is viewed as an activity, whereas in the Roman model, the emphasis is on the individual's ability to choose the "good life" for himself absent interference or domination (Pettit). In the 18th century, the modern concept of citizenship was born as a concept central to democratic theory and freedom of the individual through a constitutional government based on a social contract and popular sovereignty that would guarantee noninterference.

The modern concept of citizenship has been understood in several ways that find their foundations in either the Greek or Roman tradition. For example, some view citizenship as membership in a social community where membership is limited to those who possess ascriptive, exclusive, or organic bonds. In this view, citizenship is not tied to territory but to a common ethnicity, religion, race, culture, or shared language. Others view citizenship as membership in a civic national community bound together as "a people" that is inclusive but where inclusion is formed through tradition and assimilation. National holidays, patriotic songs, shared history of a founding moment, a common language, and the belief in the common good and political institutions all comprise the essence of this secular understanding of *peoplehood*. Those who view citizenship as membership in a civic polity emphasize rule of law, social contract, and popular sovereignty as the essence of citizenship. Individual liberty, reflection, and choice are central and guaranteed through a concept of citizenship premised on participation in public decision, democratic deliberation, individual rights, and responsibilities. Yet, for others, modern citizenship is premised simply on a connection to a territory and is acquired at birth or through long-term residence within the territory of a state regardless of personal attributes. And, finally, some view citizenship as the condition of universal human rights and personhood that transcends state boundaries and is grounded in humanity and a common civilization. Whereas the first three view citizenship as a "status," the second two associate citizenship with a "bundle of rights." Within each of these broader categories, a discussion has developed regarding the effect of globalization on citizenship.

Among those who ascribe to the Greek tradition of citizenship as a status, civic nationalists focus on the transformation of the civic connection to the nation under conditions of globalization; there are communitarians, civic republicans, and civic multiculturalists. What these theorists have in common is the discussion of citizenship as the need for a common identity and social cohesion, as well as the way in which international migration, increased diversity, and globalization have rendered the common basis for membership and agreement regarding the "common good" difficult in the traditional national state construct that links a national people with a territory. This view argues that there are transnational rights and structures for membership but that the membership of individuals, even in this transnational structure, is mediated through the organization of the state. They respond to the global world by highlighting the threat that devalued citizenship has for individual freedom that comes from national membership. For those who view citizenship as a legal status, there cannot be a global citizenship since the status derives from the state. Moreover, those who hold this view see the world as a place of scarce resources and membership in a political community as the best way in which to find security. Only under global libertarianism or global socialism would the distribution of membership not develop.

On the other side of this debate are scholars who argue that the current system of state sovereignty exists alongside an increasingly transnational institutional system through which individuals possess multiple memberships. Multiple memberships fuel a "deterritorialized" citizenship transcending geographically defined political and legal entities. This position looks at the sending and receiving contexts—emigrant and immigrant status of international movement of people. There is also a discussion of dual citizenship.

Other scholars view citizenship within the Roman tradition as a bundle of rights and argue that the expansion of universal liberal rights has produced a transnational citizen anchored in the global world through the growing international court system. The bundle of rights position often begins from the premise of T. H. Marshall's seminal work on England during the rise of the welfare state. For Marshall, citizenship is "a status bestowed on those who are full members of a community. All who possess the status are equal with respect to the rights and duties with which the status is endowed" (1998, p. 102). Marshall viewed the transformation of citizenship and development of universal citizenship as a result of the growth of capitalism as a system of inequality and state responses to that inequality. He questioned the relationship of citizenship to inequality and social class and noted an expansion of citizenship through a progression of rights from civil to political to social. According to Marshall, in the feudal society of the 16th and 17th centuries, the state did not exist or administer life. Instead, feudal lords took care of those who lived on their land. The Magna Carta signed in the 13th century granted basic civil rights, and once the feudal order broke down, rights developed in stages: The 18th century was characterized by the extension of civil rights, the 19th century by political rights, and the 20th century by the extension of social rights and the overall expansion of citizenship beyond class, race, and gender. Marshall viewed the emerging global capital world as a place where the status of the rights-bearing individual was an aid to capital development because civil rights confer the legal capacity to strive for things one would like to possess but do not guarantee the possession of any of them. He accurately noted that legal status did not guarantee freedom in practice absent social welfare and that the 20th century's contribution to citizenship was the incorporation of social rights in the status of citizenship, the extension of the area of common culture, and common experience and enrichment of the universal status of citizenship. At the same time, as long as citizenship remained a concept of the national state, Marshall predicted that inequalities would persist since status differences receive "the stamp of legitimacy in terms of democratic citizenship provided they do not cut too deep, but occur within a population united in a single civilization" (Marshall, 1998, p. 110).

Postnationalists drawing on Marshall's progression of rights predicted the end of the national state as the global capital economy in conjunction with human rights and that global courts would sever the rights-bearing individual from his or her ties to the national state. This postnational school posits that state sovereignty has been rendered obsolete by supranational institutions and global human rights norms. In a slightly different version, cosmopolitans argue that rights should transcend national boundaries. Also drawing from Marshall but arriving at a different conclusion, liberal nationalism argues that although liberal rights have a universalizing tendency, these are not so easily severed from the national state administrative apparatus and that individual rights are best guaranteed within the context of the national state. Instead, liberal nationalism posits that the status of citizenship will wither away as a meaningful distinction between citizens and residents. Others argue that liberalism guarantees freedom of movement among states either as a property right or, stemming from John Rawls, through a global view of the original position.

New Theories

New theories attempt to ground citizenship in a global constitutionalism (cosmopolitan hospitality that recognizes porous national borders) or a republican understanding of world citizenship as nondomination.

Galya Benarieh Ruffer

See also Civil Rights; Humanity, Concepts of; Identities in Global Societies; Immigration; Immigration and Transnationalism; National Identities; Nation-State; Sovereignty; Undocumented Persons; Westphalia, Treaty of, and the Post-Westphalian World

Further Readings

Aleinikoff, T. A., & Klusmeyer, D. (Ed.). (2001). *Citizenship today: Global perspectives and practies.* Washington, DC: Carnegie Endowment for International Peace.

Balibar, E. (2008). Historical dilemmas of democracy and their contemporary relevance for citizenship. *Rethinking Marxism, 20*(4), 522–538.

Beiner, R. (Ed.). (1995). *Theorizing citizenship.* Albany: State University of New York Press.

Benhabib, S. (2004). *The rights of others: Aliens, residents and citizens.* Cambridge, UK: Cambridge University Press.

Bohmann, J. (2007). *Democracy across borders.* Cambridge, UK: Cambridge University Press.

Bosniak, L. (2006). *The citizen and the alien.* Princeton, NJ: Princeton University Press.

Dagger, R. (1997). *Civic virtues: Rights, citizenship, and republican liberalism.* Oxford, UK: Oxford University Press.

Hanson, R., & Weil, P. (2002). *Dual nationality, social rights and federal citizenship in the U.S. and Europe: The reinvention of citizenship.* New York: Berghahn Books.

Jacobson, D. (1996). *Rights across borders: Immigration and the decline of citizenship.* Baltimore: Johns Hopkins University Press.

Kostakopoulou, D. (2008). *The future governance of citizenship.* Cambridge, UK: Cambridge University Press.

Kymlicka, W. (1995). *Multicultural citizenship: A liberal theory of minority rights.* Oxford, UK: Oxford University Press.

Kymlicka, W., & Norman, W. (Ed.). (2000). *Citizenship in diverse societies.* Oxford, UK: Oxford University Press.

Sassen, S. (2006). *Territory authority rights.* Princeton, NJ: Princeton University Press.

Shafir, G. (Ed.). (1998). *The citizenship debates.* Minneapolis: University of Minnesota Press.

CIVIL AVIATION

Civil aviation has unique characteristics compared with other industries: It is not only wide-ranging but also an instrumental force of globalization. The term *civil aviation* refers to the operation of any civil aircraft and related activities for the purpose of transportation by air. In other words, civil aviation covers all aviation activities except military operations. Although generally the design, development, and production of a civil aircraft is considered separately as in the aerospace industry, in a broader sense, civil aviation and the operation of a civil aircraft refers to the design, development, production, and use of aircraft and all related activities and facilities for serving some kind of transportation activities by air.

Unlike many other fields that grow domestically first and then expand to other countries, the civil aviation industry has had an international character from its beginning. This verity is partly a result of the uniqueness of air transportation. Travel through air has naturally a beyond-border character and needs some legal requirements between countries. In addition, safe and secure air navigation and air transportation between countries require standardized special equipment, facilities, and operational procedures. Another reason for the international characteristic of civil aviation is the industry's massive need for financial investment. Generally, the domestic markets of individual countries are not strong enough to finance the needed investments.

History

Civil aviation and globalization move in tandem. That means civil aviation has always fostered globalization, while also being affected by globalization. To understand this interaction, one needs to look back in aviation history. The dawn of the modern aviation industry started on December 17, 1903, with the first successful powered, controlled heavier-than-air machine flight. With that 12-second flight of the Wright Brothers, aviation was born and began to develop. World War I and World War II were the accelerating phases of civil aviation. After these wars ended, many countries began looking to use these military aircrafts for commercial purpose, such as transporting mail, cargo, and passengers. The first small airlines began carrying mail, cargo, and passengers in the early years after World War I. After World War II, many countries had a large number of new airplanes and airfields equipped with the latest technology. Using these assets as a starting point, international airlines emerged and international air transport grew rapidly. Technical innovations like the introduction of turbo-propeller aircraft in the early 1950s, the introduction of jets in the late 1950s, and high bypass and faster engines in 1970, greater size and range and more efficient unit costs contributed to the growth of the industry. All these developments made possible long-range, regular, and cheaper public transportation. Combined with increased real incomes and more leisure time, the effect was an explosion in demand for air travel. Hence, air transportation became the dominant transportation mode of long-haul passenger travel, especially in developed countries. Nevertheless,

international regulations were required to keep the pace of growth strong and healthy.

Regulating Civil Aviation

World War I revealed the negative aspect of aviation. The reality of aviation being a potential threat to national security brought the issue of regulating civil aviation to the international agenda. The legal framework for international civil aviation rights was initiated at the 1919 Convention for the Regulation of Aerial Navigation (Paris Convention), which was a part of the Paris Peace Conference. As an outcome of the conference, an International Commission on Aerial Navigation was established with the object of drawing up a convention on international civil aviation and to establish uniform rules and standards for inter alia aircraft registration, airworthiness, personnel licensing, maps and charts, rules of the air, and procedures for flying. Although there were some attempts to regulate aviation previously, by the Paris Convention, the basic principle that every nation has absolute and exclusive sovereignty over the airspace above its defined territory was recognized.

This principle was confirmed in 1928 at Havana and in 1944 at the Chicago International Civil Aviation Conference, which produced the Chicago Convention. The convention, signed on December 7, 1944, by 52 signatory states, resulted in an international framework based largely on national interests, favoring bilateral air transport agreements over multilateral accords with respect to issues such as routes, frequency, and capacity. The convention's achievements included an agreement by the signatories to grant each other two of the so-called five freedoms of air transport. These freedoms give states the right to fly across other states without landing and the right to land for nontraffic and traffic purposes. Later, these agreements expended to eight freedoms, but only the first five freedoms are internationally accepted, and the last three have not yet been fully implemented. In the European Union, the eighth freedom, known as cabotage, was adopted when the single market in air transport came into force on July 1, 1997.

The Chicago Convention established the International Civil Aviation Organization (ICAO) to regulate the safety, communications, and technological aspects of international civil aviation.

ICAO is a specialized agency of the United Nations, which is headquartered in Montreal, Canada, and is responsible for worldwide regulation of aviation. The agency is charged with responsibilities regarding both air navigation, which relates principally to the technical and operational aspects of aircraft movement, and air transport, which relates to the transportation of passengers, baggage, cargo, and mail by air. The organization serves as a global forum for member-states to work together toward the safe, secure, and sustainable development of civil aviation. The prime objective of ICAO is promoting aviation safety (technical and operational safety of flight) and at the same time improving security (safeguarding civil aviation against acts of unlawful interference). The convention is supported by 18 annexes containing Standards and Recommended Practices (SARPs) to regulate civil aviation effectively. The annexes are the basic rules of civil aviation and are amended regularly by ICAO.

There are some other regional or international organizations that regulate civil aviation. For example, the European Aviation Safety Agency (EASA) is responsible for promoting the common standards of safety and environmental protection in civil aviation in the area. The Federal Aviation Administration (FAA) is an agency of the U.S. Department of Transportation with authority to regulate all aspects of civil aviation. Every other country has its own civil aviation authority that regulates civil aviation in the country. For internationally accepted aviation systems, all these regulations must be in harmonization with international air rules standards.

Civil Aviation Activities

Civil aviation activities, as proposed by the ICAO, include commercial air transport, general aviation, airport services, air navigation services, civil aviation manufacturing, aviation training, maintenance and overhaul, regulatory functions, and other activities. Air transportation in a broad sense means travel by air, but in a narrow sense it represents commercial air transportation, especially airlines. ICAO defines commercial air transport as "an aircraft operation involving the transport of passengers, cargo or mail for remuneration or hire." The International Air Transport Association (IATA) is an organization that represents and serves the world airlines and establishes commercial standards of the global aviation system. One duty of IATA is to ensure that people and goods can move around the global airline network as easily as if they were on a single airline in a single country. Today, as a result of code-sharing agreements, a passenger can travel around the globe with different airlines but with the same flight number on one's ticket and without seeing one's baggage.

The other large interest area of civil aviation is general aviation. ICAO defines general aviation as "an aircraft operation other than a commercial air transport operation or an aerial work operation." Aerial work is "an aircraft operation in which an aircraft is used for specialized services such as agriculture, construction, photography, surveying, observation and patrol, search and rescue, aerial advertisement, etc."

Airport services are another segment of civil aviation activities. Almost all aircrafts need a designed surface (land, water, ice, etc.) for takeoff and landing, so landing strips are essential parts of any transportation system. Today's airports are more than just a place for takeoff and landing; they have various services such as banks, bookstores, gift shops, restaurants, social and cultural services, and many more. Today's metropolitan areas need global-scaled airports to meet the needs of liberalization and globalization. Some hub airports, which connect global cities like London, Paris, and Hong Kong, can serve 50–60 million international passengers in a year; in many cases, these airports are in a competition to capture international connection traffic.

Impacts of Globalization

Civil aviation is one of the main contributors to today's global system. Technological developments that reduce air transportation costs have resulted in relatively inexpensive, rapid, and safe transportation of goods and people over prolonged distances. This has led to increased trade flows between continents and countries as well as an integrated world economy. Today, commercial aircrafts can make nonstop long-haul flights. Such long-range air transportation services that link the world's global cities has been "shrinking the world" and integrating the world economy. Civil aviation is one of the indispensible elements of today's global economic system. Through linking prolonged distances it has also played a role in the operation and expansion of transnational corporations. Air transportation has enabled the global flow of many new and perishable commodities and has fostered international and global commerce. Manufacturers, especially those producing perishables, time-sensitive materials like newspapers, high-value goods like microelectronics, gems, and live animals like race horses, rely heavily on air transport to tie together spatially disaggregated operations. Today, many manufacturers have global-scale production, supply chains, and sales networks that highly depend on air transportation. By enabling easy transportation, civil aviation has linked different nations and cultures and has fostered social and cultural globalization. The extended linkages between people and places that are facilitated by jet transportation and relatively inexpensive air transport have also fostered the growth of tourism.

Civil aviation is a global industry but also has characteristics distinct from other multinational industries. Since World War II, international air services between countries have operated under the terms of bilateral air service agreements (ASAs) negotiated between two countries. Typically, these ASAs specified which airlines could operate between the two countries, the routes carriers could operate (e.g., which airports they could fly to), whether carriers could offer beyond services (fifth freedom rights), and limits on the frequency and capacity (seats) that the carriers could operate, and they often placed controls over airline pricing. In addition to the bilateral agreements, many countries have placed foreign ownership and control restrictions on the airlines. For these reasons, civil aviation is unique in that it remains regulated at the international level largely by bilateral agreements between governments. But especially since the late 20th century, liberalization, transnationalization, and globalization have affected international air transportation services. Air transport services have become more liberal and more commercialized, as well as borderless. Several regional and transnational ASAs that create geographically localized blocs

sharing common aviation rules, such as the European Union, have emerged. Bilateral ASAs have transformed into multilateral ASAs. In Asia and Africa, initiatives regarding common aviation blocs have been proposed.

With the advent of these changes in the structure of the civil aviation industry, airlines, airports, and other aviation businesses have also become more borderless. Internationalization and globalization are illustrated in the civil aviation industry with the location of operations beyond national borders and the emergence of global alliances. Today, most airlines are in airline partnership groups, called alliances, such as Star, Oneworld, and Skyteam. These alliances enable airlines to expand their networks globally, creating a seamless network and more frequent flights for passengers. Civil aviation services like airport operations and management have also become more commercialized and borderless. Airports have become autonomous entities or even private companies. Although the management and ownership structure of airports have changed, foreign ownership and management options have also emerged. Today, some large airport companies operate airports around the globe while sharing their expertise with newly privatized or commercialized airports. Likewise, airport management companies have partnerships and alliances with other countries. Commercial aircraft manufacturing is one example of beyond-border or global supply chains. The high technology, expertise, and finance needs of the aerospace and aircraft manufacturing industry have led to cross-cultural teaming for design, development, manufacturing, and marketing.

A factor that is having an increasing impact on civil aviation is growing environmental consciousness. Besides its positive contribution to the global system, civil aviation is a part of global environmental concerns, as there is a general perception that the aviation sector may be contributing largely to environmental problems. However, today civil aviation remains a large and growing industry that is at the forefront of globalization by facilitating economic growth, world trade, international investment, and tourism, and therefore, it is a broad field of global studies.

Ferhan Kuyucak and Bijan Vasigh

See also Air Travel; Airlines; Globalization, Phenomenon of; International Air Transportation Association; Shrinking World Concepts; Transportation Systems

Further Readings

Button, K., & Taylor, S. (2000). International air transportation and economic development. *Journal of Air Transport Management, 6,* 209–222.

Forsyth, P. J. (2005). International aviation: Globalisation and global industry. In P. Gangopadhyay & M. Chatterji (Eds.), *Economics of globalisation* (pp. 181–190). Aldershot, UK: Ashgate.

Hanlon, P. (2007). *Global airlines: Competition in a transnational industry* (3rd ed.). Amsterdam, Netherlands: Elsevier Butterworth Heinemann.

Kassim, H. (1997). Air transport and globalization: A sceptical view. In A. Scott (Ed.), *The limits of globalization: Cases and arguments* (pp. 202–222). London: Routledge.

Yergin, D., Vietor, R. H. K., & Evans, P. C. (2000). *Fettered flight: Globalization and the airline industry.* Cambridge, MA: Cambridge Energy Research Associates.

Websites

International Air Transport Association (IATA): http://www.iata.org

International Civil Aviation Organization (ICAO): http://www.icao.int

CIVIL RIGHTS

Civil rights are a subject of concern both nationally and globally, and they are the most basic legal guarantees a state must bestow for its citizens to possess the status of free and equal citizens. Historically, the ascent of the concept is associated with the institutionalization of political power in form of the modern nation-state, which began in the late 18th century. Today, however, the term *civil rights* is used in a variety of interrelated yet slightly distinct ways.

For students of global studies, three main uses of the term should be of interest. First, as a category of legal and/or moral entitlements, civil rights have been a common object of study by scholars of Western political thought. Second, civil rights have commonly been identified as the demands put forward by marginalized societal groups engaged in a political struggle for equal citizenship that go beyond formal equality (such as the civil rights movement in the United States). Third, as far as positive (international) law is concerned, the understanding of civil rights has been permanently shaped by the adoption of the International Covenant on Civil and Political Rights (ICCPR) in 1966.

Civil Rights as Privileges

Etymologically, the word *civil* derives from the Latin *civilis* (relating to public law or life), which in turn derives from *civis* (citizen). In ancient Rome, full citizenship was granted only to privileged classes according to a complex system of rules that relied on the dichotomy between citizen and foreigner (with differential citizenship given to *latini* and *peregrini* and next to no rights granted to *barbari*). Civil rights were the rights that Roman citizens enjoyed by virtue of being a member of Roman society. This concept of citizenship and civil rights was fundamentally challenged by ideas of the European Enlightenment. Soon, civil rights were still held to be reserved for a privileged class but became universal in aspiration. They were attributed not because of membership of one specific state but because of membership in society more generally.

Civil Rights as Universal but Not Natural

The British writer Thomas Paine published his influential *Rights of Man* in 1791, partially defending some of the claims to universal rights that were made during the French Revolution against its critics, most notably the conservative Edmund Burke. While doing this, Paine contrasted natural rights with the civil rights of man. In his account, the natural rights of man (following a natural law tradition and in the spirit of Enlightenment ideas) are those rights that appertain to man by virtue of being human: rights of mind and all those rights that enable men to act as individuals without infringing the liberty of others. Civil rights, by contrast, are those rights that are bestowed on man as a consequence of his being a member of society. Therefore, civil rights build on a foundation of inalienable natural rights—but are in need of societal institutions to be properly implemented. In this regard, the French Revolution therefore represented a struggle for civil rights. Nevertheless, Paine considered both classes of rights to be universal (for males, at least), which is why his account caused political uproar and led to his persecution in England.

The premise that all men are created equal underlies most Western constitutions to this day. It might be helpful to view these core constitutional rights predominantly as negative rights—rights whose realization relies on the state merely abstaining *from* something, so that, following Thomas Hobbes, freedom is enabled through the "silence of the law." Positive rights, by contrast, could be associated with political, social, and cultural rights and tend to be rights *to* something (formally, this is somewhat similar to the distinction of positive and negative liberty by Isaiah Berlin).

The simple distinction between positive and negative rights is only a rough distinction that has been disputed by many political thinkers. Although some claim that civil and political rights are relatively easy to institute, others dispute this by arguing that their implementation and enforcement requires as much the right *to* something as positive rights. Nonetheless, in much of political theory (particularly liberal theory), civil rights are most often associated with the basic liberties each member of society needs to enjoy for an institutional setup of a society to be considered just. Rights relating to the securing of (material) welfare are commonly held to be of a secondary order only, as for example in John Rawls's lexicographical ordering of equal basic liberties (in the first principle of justice) *before* the distribution of social and economic inequalities (in the second principle of justice).

T. H. Marshall and the Development of Citizenship

There is wide disagreement on what the scope of civil rights is and should be and how these rights should be implemented. To find answers to these challenges, it does not suffice to survey positive law today, but the approach also needs to be sociological and historical. In his famous 1950 essay *Citizenship and Social Class*, T. H. Marshall put

forward an argument about the continuous progress of the "developing institution of citizenship" and its impact on social inequality. Principally with large advanced industrial societies in mind—particularly England—Marshall argued that there had been a shift in the understanding of what it means to be a citizen and what constitutes basic equal membership in society. These three different layers of citizenship were civil rights, political rights, and social rights. Marshall assigned their core formative period to the 18th, 19th, and 20th centuries, respectively. The label of civil rights was used to describe the rights necessary to guarantee individual freedom, ranging from liberty of the person to freedom of speech, freedom of thought, freedom of faith, the right to property, and the right to due process of law. The most comprehensive struggle for these universal civil rights was rooted in the aftermath of western European Enlightenment, and particularly in the struggle for political emancipation in the period before, leading up to and after the French Revolution. Marshall singles out the role that courts played in this first universal struggle for civil rights. He argued that only subsequently, these civil rights were augmented to include political rights—that is, the right to participate meaningfully in the political process (e.g., through active and passive voting rights). And indeed, today many legal cultures treat voting rights as civil, not as political, rights—something unimaginable in the formative period of civil rights. Under social rights, Marshall understood those rights that enabled citizens to attain an adequate standard of living, including for instance the right to education and social services (economic and welfare rights).

The different layers of citizenship play fundamentally different roles. The core purpose of civil rights is to contain violence and, hence, to make the establishment of social order possible. Political rights, in turn, serve the function of limiting the power and influence of elites. Last, social rights are geared toward counterbalancing the socioeconomic inequalities arising from a market economy. What is common to all layers, however, is their aspiration to be universal: Citizenship brings with it rights to *all* members of the citizen-body. This view differs from the notion of citizenship in the Greek polis, in Roman law, or in medieval and early modern times. Civil rights are not conceptualized as a privilege and are becoming ever more inclusive—not only with respect to the content of the rights subsumed but also with respect to who counts as a citizen in the first place.

Of course it is easy to challenge this simple account: The categories of rights are neither jointly exhaustive nor mutually exclusive—and it might be naïve to think of citizenship as having undergone a simple linear development and to disregard major countercurrents during the centuries. Similarly, the alleged universality of civil rights in their formative period can be disputed—women, for instance, were left out of civil rights for a long time, not being permitted to hold public office or to vote.

Civil Rights: Struggle and Social Norms

Today, civil rights are most often associated with the civil rights movement in the United States in the 1960s and the political struggle of African Americans for effective equality before the law (partially inspired by parallel decolonization movements in other parts of the world).

In 1865, the Civil War ended, and with the Civil Rights Act of 1866, all persons born in the United States were automatically regarded as citizens, regardless of their race. This was constitutionally enshrined, and the Thirteenth, Fourteenth, and Fifteenth amendments to the Constitution were added to guarantee the civil rights of all Americans. Nevertheless, particularly in the South, racism was endemic, and racial segregation (Jim Crow laws) existed de jure on the local and state levels, degrading African Americans to second-class citizens. The doctrine of "separate but equal" justified the segregation of the African American population so that effectively, African Americans were formally free but not substantively equal before the law. Starting in the 1950s, a broad political movement formed, spearheaded among others by Martin Luther King Jr. and Rosa Parks, who fought for the end of segregation by means of protest marches, acts of civil disobedience, boycotts, sit-ins, and other nonviolent means. Several court cases (e.g., *Brown v. Board of Education*, 1954) challenged elements of segregation such as the separate but equal doctrine. The legal transformation culminated in the landmark Civil Rights Act of 1964, which outlawed racial segregation and prohibited all forms of discrimination on the basis of race, religion, or sex.

The civil rights movement in the 1960s was first and foremost a struggle for formal equality before the law. But it was also much more. Will Kymlicka called it a movement of "civil rights liberalism": It was a challenge of widespread social norms, touching on issues of fundamental human dignity, socioeconomic equality, cultural diversity, and fairness that went beyond a narrow reading of what civil rights are. The civil rights movements aimed at more than the mere rectification of inequality before the law—but focused on the social norms that were reproducing this unjust fragmentation of citizenship.

Civil Rights in International Law

The understanding of civil rights has been increasingly shaped by the development of the International Bill of Human Rights within international law since the end of World War II, which comprises the Universal Declaration of Human Rights (1948), the ICCPR (adopted 1966), and the International Covenant on Economic, Social and Cultural Rights (ICESCR, adopted 1966).

With the creation of the United Nations in 1945, a declaration was initially planned that would comprise all rights "essential to man." It became quickly evident, however, that nations had different opinions on what these essential rights were. This disagreement resulted in two distinct covenants, one dealing with more negative civil and political rights and another with more positive economic, social, and cultural rights. By 2010, the ICCPR had been signed and ratified by 166 members of the United Nations, committing the parties to respect civil and political rights of individuals, such as the right to physical integrity, right to a fair trial, and several individual liberties (freedom of expression, thought, religion, movement assembly, and association).

Following the slogan of the French Revolution *Liberté, Égalité, Fraternité*, Karel Vašák categorized the development of human rights into three different generations: The first generation (Liberté) refers to civil and political rights, and the second generation (Égalité), to economic and social rights. In contrast to Marshall's interpretation, Vašák goes further to include so-called third-generation human rights (Fraternité) in his narrative. These rights include, among other things, rights to cultural membership and heritage. The ICCPR is indeed a good reflection of Vašák's model of the development of civil rights, as it contains, in Article 27, precisely those third-generation civil rights of cultural membership (including, for instance, rights to preservation of institutions, linguistic practices, and the rights to exercise some degree of political autonomy).

These developments in positive law shaped the way in which the term *civil rights* is being understood and used. In the ICCPR, just as in most UN documents, the term *civil rights* is nearly exclusively used in conjunction with political rights, and a definition, which would single out civil rights by themselves, is never provided. This shows how the concept of civil rights has been transformed into an ever more inclusive concept. Kymlicka pointed out that since the work on the ICCPR, we have indeed been living in a world in which human equality is unquestioned. Political movements have progressively contested the remnants of older, obsolete beliefs about ethnic or racial hierarchies in society. And beyond this, the belief in human equality has led to contestations of other hierarchies based on gender, disability, age, or sexual orientation.

The cosmopolitan belief in this human, moral equality transcends borders. Civil rights—somewhat paradoxically, given the history of the concept—are now granted to noncitizens as well. Civil rights are increasingly understood not as rights that citizens of one state hold in contradistinction to those that foreigners are lacking (as in ancient Roman law) but as rights that a state bestows on persons generally, regardless of whether they are citizens. Civil rights are being understood as human rights—rights that accrue to persons as a function of their humanity, rather than as a consequence of having a certain passport.

Robert Lepenies

See also Anti-Apartheid Movement; Antislavery Movements; Citizenship; Cosmopolitanism; Democracy; Enlightenment, The; Free Speech; French Revolution; Gay Rights; Human Rights, International; Justice Movements, Transnational; Nation-State; Women's Rights

Further Readings

Kymlicka, W. (2007). *Multicultural odysseys: Navigating the new international politics of diversity.* Oxford, UK: Oxford University Press.

Marshall, T. H. (1950). Citizenship and social class. In *Class, citizenship and social development.* Westport, CT: Greenwood Press.

Paine, T. (1791). *Rights of man: Being an answer to Mr. Burke's attack on the French Revolution.* London: Jordan.

Vašák, K. (1977). *Human rights: A thirty-year struggle: The sustained efforts to give force of law to the Universal Declaration of Human Rights.* UNESCO Courier 30. Paris: UNESCO.

Waldron, J. (1993). *Liberal rights.* Cambridge, UK: Cambridge University Press.

CIVIL SOCIETY, GLOBAL

Civil society has assumed new relevance in the context of globalization, as not only economies but also societies are becoming more intertwined. Few concepts in the social sciences can look back to an intellectual history longer than that of civil society—and few have experienced more prolonged periods of neglect, even obscurity, and fewer still have achieved a more spectacular revival. Indeed, a term little known among social scientists and policymakers until the 1980s, civil society has become a central policy issue around the world and a major theme in academia.

At one level, civil society has an intuitive meaning and connotes aspects of public civility, compassion, and voluntary participation of citizens in the infrastructure of communal and professional networks, associations, and organizations. At another level, civil society is also an abstract term that, in the words of Jürgen Habermas, constitutes a public sphere outside the state (as the seat of power) and the market (as the manifestation of self-interest).

The terms also have both an intuitive appeal and an abstract meaning in a globalizing world, where local communities are often under threat, where the role of government is undergoing a major reappraisal, where public administrations are shifting some of their tasks to voluntary associations, and where market forces, combined with technological developments, are shaping people's lives, often beyond their control. Today, and perhaps more so than in the past, the concept of civil society is employed for a variety of purposes, many of them normative, spanning the political spectrum. For example, politically conservative positions view civil society as the bulwark against the dominant state, emphasizing the capacity of society for self-organization, whereas the political left regards civil society as the locus of social participation, solidarity, and community building in the context of anonymous market forces.

In a globalizing context, the term *civil society* is used across national and cultural borders and historical periods, often as convenient shorthand to refer to whatever is part of neither government/state administration nor market firms/corporate capitalism at a particular place or time. Yet the diffuseness and flexibility of the term is as much its enemy as the normative use to which it is frequently put, and for many observers the concept seems to obscure as much as it reveals.

What Is Civil Society?

Many different definitions of civil society have been suggested, particularly in recent years, although much overlap exists among core conceptual components. Although civil society is a somewhat contested concept, definitions typically vary in the emphasis they put on some characteristics of civil society over others; some definitions primarily focus on aspects of state power, politics, and individual freedom, and others focus more on economic functions and notions of social capital and cohesion. Nonetheless, most analysts would probably agree with the statement that civil society is the sum of institutions, organizations, and individuals located between the family, the state, and the market, in which people associate voluntarily to advance common interests.

Civil society is primarily about the role of both the state, that is, the seat of political power, and the market, that is, the sphere of economic power, relative to that of citizens and the society they constitute. The intellectual history of the term is closely intertwined with the notion of citizenship, the limits of state power, and the foundation, as well as the regulation of market economies. The prevailing modern view sees civil society as a

sphere located between state and market—a buffer zone strong enough to keep both state and market in check, thereby preventing each from becoming too powerful and dominating. In the words of Ernest Gellner, civil society is the set of institutions that is strong enough to counterbalance the state, and, while not preventing the state from fulfilling its role of keeper of peace and arbitrator between major interests, it can, nevertheless, prevent the state from dominating and atomizing the rest of society. Civil society is not a singular, monolithic, separate entity but a sphere constituted in relation to both state and market, and indeed permeating both.

Civil society is self-organization of society outside the stricter realms of state power and market interests. For Habermas, civil society is made up of more or less spontaneously created associations, organizations, and movements, which find, take up, condense, and amplify the resonance of social problems in private life and pass it on to the political realm or public sphere. Lord Ralf Dahrendorf views the concept of civil society as part of a classic liberal tradition and as characterized by the existence of autonomous organizations that are neither state-run nor otherwise directed from the center political power.

As a concept, civil society is essentially an intellectual product of 18th-century Europe, in which citizens sought to define their place in society independent of the aristocratic state at a time when the certainty of status-based social order began to suffer irreversible decline. The early theorists of civil society welcomed these changes. For Adam Smith, trade and commerce among private citizens created not only wealth but also invisible connections among people, the bonds of trust of social capital in today's terminology. Others like John Locke and Alexis de Tocqueville viewed civil society less in relation to the market and more in political terms and emphasized the importance of democratic association in everyday life as base of a functioning polity. Friedrich Hegel sounded a more cautionary note about the self-organizing and self-regulatory capacity of civil society and emphasized the need of the state to regulate society. For Hegel, state and civil society depend on each other, yet their relation is full of tensions and requires a complicated balancing act. The role of the state relative to civil society was also emphasized in the writings of

Charles de Montesquieu, Lorenz von Stein, and other thinkers, who viewed the rule of law as the essence of state-society and society-market relations.

In the 20th century, civil society became associated with notions of civility (Norbert Elias), popular participation and civic mindedness (Sidney Verba), the public sphere (Jürgen Habermas), social capital (Robert David Putnam and James Samuel Coleman), culture (Antonio Gramsci), and community (Amitai Etzioni). The various concepts and approaches emphasize different aspects or elements of civil society: values and norms like tolerance in the case of civility, the role of the media and the intellectual, the connections among people and the trust they have in each other, the moral dimensions communities create and need, and the extent to which people constitute a common public space through participation and civic engagement.

The complexity of civil society and the many relations and intersections it has with the economy, the state, and institutions like the family, the media, or culture, make it possible and almost necessary to examine the concepts from different perspectives and orientations. Some analysts adopt an abstract, systemic view and view civil society as a macrosociological attribute of societies, particularly in the way state and society relate to each other. Others take on a more individualistic orientation and emphasize the notions of individual agency, citizenship, values, and participation, using econometric and social network approaches in analyzing civil society. There is also an institutional approach to studying civil society by looking at the size, scope, and structure of organizations and associations, as well as the functions they perform. The different perspectives of civil society are not necessarily contradictory, and the various approaches to understanding it are not necessarily rival; to the contrary, they often differ in emphasis, explanatory focus, and policy implication rather than in principle.

Defining society as "the sphere of institutions, organizations, and individuals located between the family, the state and the market, in which people associate voluntarily to advance common interests" has important consequences for measurement for two reasons. First, the "sphere" of civil society is an analytic category, and as such, it typically does not exist as a separate, identifiable element in reality like some physical infrastructure or geographic feature. Although there might be "pure" expressions of civil activism and engagement, civil society, like the market or the state, is usually intermingled with other aspects of human and organizational behavior.

Global Civil Society

The growth and expansion of global civil society as a phenomenon seems closely associated with a major shift in cultural and social values that took hold in most developed market economies in the 1970s. This shift saw a change in emphasis from material security to concerns about democracy, participation, and meaning, and it involved, among others, a formation toward cosmopolitan values such as tolerance and respect for human rights.

These values facilitated the cross-national spread of social movement around common issues that escaped conventional party politics, particularly in Europe and Latin America, and it led to a broad-based mobilization in social movements, with the women's, peace, democracy, and environmental movements as the best examples of an increasingly international "movement industry."

The 1990s brought a political opening and a broad-based mobilization of unknown proportion and scale, which coincided with the reappraisal of the role of the state in most developed countries and growing disillusionment with state-led multilateralism in the Third World among counterelites. In addition to this broadened political space, favorable economic conditions, the vastly reduced costs of communication, and greater ease of organizing facilitated the institutional expansion of global civil society in organizational terms.

By the 2000s, the changed geopolitical environment and the economic downturn challenged both the (by then) relatively large infrastructure of global civil society organizations, and the broad value base of cosmopolitanism in many countries across the world, in particular among the middle classes and elites. As a result, new organizational forms and ways of organizing and communicating have gained in importance, with social forums, Internet-based mobilization, and transnational networks as prominent examples. These developments, like the expansion of global civil society generally, are accompanied by a resurgence of religion in some parts of the world and a change in state-religion relationships, creating a more conflict-prone and highly diversified complex sphere of ideas, values, institutions, organizations, networks, and individuals.

Manifestations of Global Civil Society

One of the main characteristics of global civil society, celebrated by some yet deplored by others, is its multifaceted nature. The different manifestations play different roles in the triad of market, governance, and civil society. The political tools and organizational means of global civil society have changed.

The first is the new public management manifestation, which is part of the so-called modernization of welfare states. At the international level, new public management is replacing conventional development assistance policies and seeks to capitalize on what is viewed as the comparative efficiency advantages of nonprofit organizations through public-private partnerships, competitive bidding, and contracting under the general heading of privatization. The main actors, according to this approach, are the professionalized organizational component of global civil society, in other words, the nongovernmental organization (NGO) or international nongovernmental organization (INGO). Prompted in part by growing doubts about the capacity of the state to cope with its own welfare, developmental, and environmental problems, political analysts across the political spectrum have come to view NGOs as strategic components of a middle way between policies that put primacy on "the market" and those that advocate greater reliance on the state. Institutions like the World Bank, the United Nations, or the European Union, along with bilateral donors and many developing countries, are searching for a balance between state-led and market-led approaches to development and are allocating more responsibility to NGOs. In fact, service provision has been the fastest growing area of INGO activities since the 1990s.

A second manifestation is an increasingly corporate manifestation of global civil society. This has to do with the "corporatization" of NGOs as well as the expansion of business into local and global civil society. Corporations use extended social responsibility programs to provide, jointly with nonprofits, services previously in the realm of government (e.g., health care, child care, and pensions, but also community services more widely), and the international community. In contrast, NGOs "professionalize"; under pressure from management gurus, they increasingly adopt corporate strategies, as well as being increasingly open to partnerships with business.

Given that more than one third of the world's 100 largest "economies" are transnational corporations (TNCs), there are growing "points of contact" between global businesses and global civil society organizations, in particular INGOs like GreenPeace, the World Wildlife Fund, Oxfam, and World Vision—the global brand names of civil society. TNCs and INGOs work together in addressing global problems (e.g., environmental degradation, malnutrition, low skills, and education levels) but also many local issues in failed states and areas of civic strife and conflict.

Yet, it is not only in the developing world that global business and INGOs are developing partnerships. In some ways as a backlash to, in other ways as an implication of, neoliberal policies and "lean states," public opinion in developed market economies is expecting greater corporate responsibility and "caring" about the societies in which they operate. Increasingly, this goes beyond adherence to principles of corporate governance and some core of conduct; it implies greater emphasis on service delivery to employees and their communities (e.g., educational programs and child care), addressing negative externalities or "bads" of business operations (e.g., pollution and resource depletion), and public goods (e.g., health and sustainability). Willingly or reluctantly, companies and NGOs team up to divide responsibilities that the state is failing to meet.

A third manifestation is social capital or activist manifestation. Here, the emphasis is not so much on management as on building relations of trust and cohesion. The idea is that norms of reciprocity are embodied in transnational networks of civic associations. What is important, according to this approach, is that self-organization across borders creates social cohesion within transnational communities. Here, the main actors are social movements, transnational civic networks, and social forums. They are a source of dissent, challenge, and innovation, a counterveiling force to government and the corporate sector. They serve as a social, cultural, and political watchdog keeping both market and state in check, and they contribute to and reflect the diversity, pluralism, and dynamism of the modern world.

The Infrastructure of Global Civil Society

The infrastructure of global civil society includes a vast array of NGOs, voluntary associations, nonprofit groups, charities, and interest associations, in addition to more informal or less permanent ways of organizing such as Diaspora networks, dot.causes, or social forums. The growth of INGOs since the 1990s and their greater organizational presence is, of course, not equally spread across the world. Europe and North America show the greatest number of INGOs and higher membership densities than other regions of the world. And even though cities in Europe and the United States still serve as the NGO capital of the world, a long-term diffusion process has decreased the concentration of NGOs to the effect that they are now more evenly distributed around the world than ever before.

To illustrate this process, it is useful to review some basic patterns of NGO locations over time and to go back briefly to the beginnings of modern NGO development. According to statistics compiled by the Union of International Organizations, in 1906, only two of the 169 INGOs had their headquarters outside Europe; by 1938, 36 of the total of 705 INGOs existing at that time were located outside Europe. By 1950, with a significant increase of U.S.-based INGOs, and with the establishment of the United Nations, 124 of the 804 existing INGOs were not based in Europe. With the independence movement and the generally favorable economic climate of the 1950s and early 1960s, the number of INGOs increased to 1,768, of which 83% were located in Europe, 10% in the United States, and between 1% and 2% in Asia, South America, Central America, Africa, the Middle East, and Australia.

By the 2000s, much of this concentration has given way to a more decentralized pattern around an emerging bipolar structure of INGOs, with two centers: western Europe and North America.

Europe still accounts for the majority of INGO headquarters, followed by the United States, but other regions like Asia and Africa have gained ground. Nonetheless, among the ten countries hosting the greatest number of intercontinental organization headquarters in 2001, there are eight European countries (United Kingdom, France, Switzerland, Belgium, Netherlands, Germany, Italy, and Austria), next to the United States and Canada.

In terms of cities, the traditional role of Paris (729 INGOs), London (807), Brussels (1,392), Geneva (272), and New York (390) has not been diminished in absolute terms. They are, however, less dominant in relative terms: more than ten other cities in four continents have more than 100 INGO headquarters, and another 35 on five continents have more than 50.

There are thousands of scholarly associations and learned societies that span the entire range of academic disciplines and field of human learning. Likewise, there is a rich tradition of business and professional organizations reaching across national borders, forming international chambers of commerce, consumer associations, and professional groups in the field of law, accounting, trade, engineering, transport, civil service, or health care.

Today, value-based NGOs in the areas of law, policy and advocacy, politics, and religion make up the second largest activity component, with a total of 23% all NGOs. This is followed by a service-provisions cluster, in which social services, health, and education together account for 21% of INGO purposes. Smaller fields like culture and the arts (6.6%), the environment (2.9%), and defense and security make up the balance.

Yet next to a greater emphasis on values, the changes in the composition of purposes that took place in the 1990s brought a long-standing yet often overlooked function of INGOs to the forefront: Service delivery has become a visible and important part of INGOs. Indeed, the social services as a purpose grew by 79% between 1990 and 2000, health services by 50%, and education by 24%. This function of INGOs is primarily connected to the public management manifestation of global civil society, outlined previously.

Although INGOs provide only a partial picture of global civil society, looking at INGO data shows that the infrastructure of global civil society has expanded significantly since 1990, in terms of both scale and connectedness (Anheier, 2005, chap. 15). The relative focus on these organizations, taken together, shifted more toward value-based activities and service provision. Overall, the expansion of INGOs and the value-activity shift imply both quantitative and qualitative changes in the contour and role of global civil society organizations. Throwing some light on these changes will be the task in the next sections, where value changes in Western societies from the 1970s onward, transnationalism, and the rise of civil society in the 1990s are examined.

The Value Map of Global Civil Society

Social, cultural, and political values show significant variation within and across countries and cultures, but at the same time, the resulting value patterns are relatively stable over time and typically change more between than within generations. Shifts in basic value patterns are relatively rare, and if they happen, they are full of consequences and carry many implications—for social and economic behavior, politics, and the institutions of society at large. However, one such value shift took place in many Organization for Economic Cooperation and Development (OECD) countries between 1970 and the late 1980s, as social scientists have shown.

Researchers have used several different labels to describe this value shift, and the precise extent and sustainability of the changes involved continue to be debated among experts in the field. Although there are many sociological correlates to this value shift and its causation, it is associated with the rise of cosmopolitan values, a preference for democratic forms of governance, and an appreciation of cultural diversity. In other words, cosmopolitan values, such as tolerance, respect for others, and emphasis on human rights, have become increasingly important.

This shift in values goes beyond the traditional left-right cleavage in politics. Instead, beginning in the 1960s and more forcefully and widespread in the 1970s, many people began to engage in new forms of political activity and to participate in social movement, in particular the women's, environmental, and peace movements. The new social movements provide the institutional connection between the shift in values and the growth of global civil society. These new movements emerged in developed countries from the 1960s onward: The civil rights and anti-Vietnam movements of the 1960s, the environmental movement, the women's movement of the 1970s, the peace movement and human rights movement of the 1980, and the antiglobalization movements of the 1990s—are all related to value shifts.

Importantly, the value set connected with the new social movements had from the beginning a transnational element, particularly in Europe (environment, peace, and women), Latin America (human rights), and Australia (indigenous rights) but less in the United States, where the value shift and the changes in social structure could more easily be linked to a renewal of some form of domestic democracy or revival movements. In Europe, by contrast, the value shift coincided with the development of the European Project (from the Common Market to the European Community to the European Union) as the next step in a modernization process that points to a more peaceful and prosperous future and that necessitates the evolution of nation-states and national societies into a framework of European cooperation and integration.

Participation in Global Civil Society

Across the Western world, the value changes of the latter half of the 20th century consequently implied a greater mobilization of society around issues advocated by the new social movements: civil rights, gender equality, environmental protection, Third World development, peace and democratization—issues typically outside the realm of established party politics. By the very nature of the issues involved, these movements implied greater internationalism and linked value changes in the West to developments in Latin America or Africa, and vice versa. The new movement of international solidarity was less linked to the workers movement and the traditional political left. It was far more about human rights and democracy, more about equity than equality, and more about self-determination of the individual and society than about power politics and the state. Activists for democratization in Brazil, Chile, and Argentina, or those fighting apartheid and neocolonialism in Africa, were frequently either part of, or linked to, the emerging and highly educated postmaterial middle class of the Western world.

The mobilization effect around the events of 1989 and the fall of state socialism is perhaps the clearest expression of this "marriage" of changes in value patterns, social movements, and transnationalism. Others are the redemocratization of many countries in Latin America, the South African resistance to apartheid, the women's and environmental movements, or the human rights movement generally.

Unfortunately, little systematic comparative data exist for membership and participation in the types of associations and groups linked to social movements and transnationalism that would allow one to explore changes for the 1970–2000 period, although useful case studies exist that show how movements began to cross borders more frequently and more widely than in the past. However, with the help of the 1990 and 2000 European and World Value Surveys, it is possible to examine changes during the previous decade. Indeed, from the 1990s onward, people were more likely to join voluntary associations in the fields of Third World development, environmental protection, community organizing, peace, and human rights than in the past, as both members and volunteers.

The greater participation in NGOs coincided with favorable political opportunity structures throughout the 1990s and 2010s, with the political opening in central and eastern Europe and the redemocratization of Latin America perhaps the best examples. At the same time, many other parts of the world become more open and accessible for transnational organizations, such as Japan, South Korea, or South Africa. Of course, there were exceptions in the Balkans and in central Asia, but generally it seemed that the world was on a course for greater political openness that welcomed citizen participation and involvement to an extent unknown in the past.

Issues

Although much has been achieved in improving our understanding of global civil society, more remains to be done. Shortcomings that require proper attention and correction include the following: the failure to take into account other non-Western civil society traditions; the failure to address the relationship among global civil society, conflict, and violence; and, closely related, the neglect of the notion of civility.

Recent work has begun to address the first shortcoming. Heba Raouf Ezzat and Mary Kaldor examine differences and commonalities in the concept and constitution of civil society in Europe and the Arab world; Marlies Glasius and colleagues offer an overview of civil society in a broad cross section of countries. Although one wishes for the existence of a more systematic, comparative analysis of differences and similarities in concepts, patterns, and trends, the prospects for this to happen are good, in particular as civil society research has taken root in many non-Western countries.

The second shortcoming, too, can be addressed, chiefly through a greater recognition of the sociology of conflict. Studies of conflict have shown that violent conflicts have pronounced institutional path dependencies and desensitizing effects at the individual level. Conflict behavior is learned behavior, as are nonviolence and civility. Although wars might be fought in the name of free society, when won, such has been their intrusion into rights and behavioral patterns that there is an aftermath from which democracy and civility have to struggle to emerge again.

Sociologists like Dahrendorf remind us that conflicts are manifest tensions that develop from perceived disagreements, as opposed to latent conflicts where parties may be largely unaware of the level of threat and power capabilities. Once conflicts are manifest, the conditions for communicating, mobilizing, and organizing are critical for the process and outcome of conflicts. It is precisely the wider availability of information technology such as the Internet, combined with a steep decline in communication costs, that facilitates the transformation of latent into manifest conflicts. Political entrepreneurs, activists, and ideologues of many kinds find more and easier access to mobilization than in the past. What is more, with the end of the Cold War and a weakened system of international governance, many conflicts became reenergized and new ones engendered, whereas the capacity to keep movements in check and violence free has not kept pace.

Modern societies are conflict prone. They are also adept at seeking ways and means of managing, that is, institutionalizing, conflicts (through panels, hearings, political parties, social movements, the judiciary, etc.) rather than seeking settlement though power domination alone (Dahrendorf, 1994), including violence. Such institutionalized conflicts are viewed as creative conflicts that reduce the amount of tensions that could otherwise build up because of major societal cleavages. Such tensions could threaten the social fabric of societies, while managed conflicts contribute to social stability and "tamed" social change.

Could we think of global civil society as a means of institutionalizing conflicts and preventing them from becoming violent? Overinstitutionalization of conflicts can create inertia and stifle social change and innovation, whereas under-institutionalization can lead to a spreading of the conflict into other fields and the generation of unintended consequences. Moreover, deep-seated core conflicts (e.g., labor-capital, value conflicts, and ethnic conflicts) have a tendency to amass complicating factors around them that in the end can make some conflicts intractable. Such basic insights into the sociology of conflict are useful as they allow us to probe deeper into the alternating relationship between violence and civil society.

Institutions that mitigate violence within states are strengthened by the state's successful assertion of a monopoly of the means of legitimate violence. But the international system of sovereign states has also developed mechanisms to reduce the likelihood of war. Alliances, security pacts, and a framework of law for the settlement of disputes in addition to an American hegemony in conventional armed forces have reduced the incidence and likelihood of international disputes culminating in war.

At the same time, a new challenge has developed and threatens state institutions and hence civil society. In part, it develops from, and is assisted by, the same set of globalizing forces that favor the rise of civil society, and this affinity is sufficient for many to discredit the "civilizing power" of civil society altogether. Terror groups operate across borders employing all the newest means of communication, transportation, media, and messaging, including smart weapons. They appeal to values that are beyond the nation-state and at the same time exploit the freedoms of movement, association, and speech that the democratic state serves to protect. They attack nonmilitary targets and the civilian population. They are indeed an even greater challenge to civil society than they are to the state.

Helmut K. Anheier

See also Accountability; Democracy; Global Governance and World Order; Human Rights, International; Social Capital; Social Movements; State–Civil Society Relations; Values

Further Readings

Anheier, H. (2005). *Nonprofit organizations: Approaches, management, policy* (Chap. 15). London: Routledge.

Anheier, H., & Themudo, N. (2002). Organizational forms of civil society: Implications of going global. In M. Glasius, M. Kaldor, & H. Anheier (Eds.), *Global civil society: 2002.* New York: Oxford University Press.

Chandhoke, N. (2002). The limits of global civil society. In M. Glasius, M. Kaldor, & H. Anheier (Eds.), *Global civil society: 2002.* New York: Oxford University Press.

Clark, J., & Themudo, N. (2006). Linking the web and the street: Internet-based "dotcauses" and the "anti-globalization" movement. *World Development, 34*(1), 50–74.

Dahrendorf, R. (1990). *The modern social conflict: An essay on the politics of liberty.* Berkeley: University of California Press.

Ezzat, R. H., & Kaldor, M. (2005). "Not even a tree": Delegitimising violence and the prospects for pre-emptive civility. In M. K. Marlies & H. Anheier (Eds.), *Global civil society: 2006/7.* London: Sage.

Glasius, M., Lewis, D., & Seckinelgin, H. (Eds.). (2004). *Exploring civil society: Political and cultural contexts.* London: Routledge.

Kaldor, M. (2003). *Global civil society: An answer to war.* Cambridge, UK: Polity Press.

Keane, J. (2003). *Global civil society.* Cambridge, UK: Cambridge University Press.

Union of International Associations (UIA). (1905–2005). *Yearbook of international organizations.* Munich, Germany: K. G. Saur.

CIVILITY

One effect of globalization is an increase in the frequency of interaction among diverse individuals, organizations, societies, and cultures and, with it, greater potential for friction, tension, and even conflict. To counteract or, better yet, stave off the potential for differences to escalate into violent conflict or disengagement, a set of norms and behaviors well beyond simple acts of courtesy (i.e., civility) should govern these interactions. Identifying these norms and behaviors and understanding the meaning and functions of civility are thus key tasks for global studies.

The term *civility* has a long and impressive history in the social sciences and the humanities that reflects different uses and changes in meaning over time. Like many complex concepts, civility can easily become normatively charged and used for different ideological purposes. Differences in perspectives on what some view as a much needed normative foundation and others interpret as a moral bias are at the core of the emerging debate about the meaning, role, or function of civility in societies facing globalization processes.

Definition

Nicole Billante and Peter Saunders identified three elements that together constitute civility. The first is respect for others, or as Edward Shils elaborated, respect for the dignity of and the desire for dignity of others. This diverges with the conceptualization of respect as obedience, given that one can be disobedient while remaining respectful. A second element is civility as public behavior toward strangers. Neither love nor hate is needed in order to be civil toward others in everyday life. Here, the notion of privacy and personhood are reflected in the treatment of the other as a fellow human regardless of status. Finally, the third element refers to self-regulation in the sense that civility requires putting one's own immediate self-interest in the context of the larger common good and acting accordingly. Civility is an attitude that expresses readiness to moderate particular, individual, or parochial interests and a mode of action that attempts to strike a balance between conflicting interests and conflicting demands. As Paul Dekker points out, it is required when agreement cannot be reached and people must continue to coexist despite their conflicting interests and views of the common good.

Along similar lines, Adam McClellan emphasized three criteria that must be met in a relationship for there to exist a mood of civility: The individual actors acknowledge their own and the others' humanity, recognize their mutual interdependence, and are capable of finding—if needed or wanted—common cause. Following this line of thought, civility, as Christopher Bryant formulates it, does not require us to like those whom we deal with civilly, and as such it contrasts strongly with the warmth of communal, religious, or national enthusiasms.

Civility is learned behavior, embedded in the social and cultural codes of society, and it requires positive reinforcement. Like social capital, in particular interpersonal and institutional trust, civility requires acknowledgment and maintenance in actual social life. It can be learned as well as unlearned, and it can increase and decrease over time. There is a valid risk of forgetting that learned behavior and socialization processes will be challenged in the event of a drastically changed environment, where personal security is threatened. A drastically changed societal structure would be followed by changed human attitudes and behavior.

What, then, is the role or function of civility? As Norbert Elias suggested, the modern Western notion of civility developed beginning in the Middle Ages as economic ties across localities and regions spread and the demand for greater stability and predictability in social and political relations increased. The result was the creation and protection of nonviolent, institutional spaces and behaviors that facilitated interaction among the various individuals and societies that were increasingly coming into contact with one another. One could argue that similar processes took place in other parts of the world, for example, China, Japan, Persia, and Turkey, where political and economic development demanded violence-free zones and greater routinization and institutionalization of behavior, including conflict management.

Civility, therefore, can be said to facilitate social interaction and cooperation more generally, and it is vital for the development of bridging social capital in modern societies. As Shils suggested, civility serves to locate different human beings as equal members of the same inclusive public, whereas incivility is a device of exclusion. Others such as Melanie White, however, take a more critical view and point out that civility reinforces distinctions at the same time as it seeks to ameliorate them. It gives priority to particular forms of conduct and specific spaces for political action at the expense of others, at the same time as it works to constrain people in an effort to balance power relations in political engagement.

Scholars such as John Rawls and F. A. Hayek suggest that civility serves a deeper purpose in modern pluralist societies, which refers to the relationship between means and ends or methods and objectives in diverse societies, especially if people primarily follow their self-interest. Hayek, for example, argues that when individuals can disagree on ends, but agree on means that can serve a great variety of purposes, including their own interests, even very diverse societies can achieve a reasonable level of peace and nonviolence. Civility is one set of such means. Similarly, Rawls conceived of a "modus vivendi," related to civility, for reducing the collision of "unrestricted liberties" in modern, diverse society. One could make similar references to Jürgen Habermas's notion of the public sphere as a violence-free and equal space of communication.

Historical Background

The term *civility* derives from the Latin *civilitas* and *civilis*, meaning "relating to citizens." In this early usage, the term referred not only to the status of being a citizen of Rome but also to the behavior that is expected of a "good citizen." By the 16th century, as Elias noted, the notion of civility moved away from its focus on citizen status and began to emphasize formal politeness and courtesy in behavior and speech. As this change took place in the court societies of Europe's interconnected aristocracy, the meaning of civility in English, French (*civilité*), or German (*Zivilität*) remained fairly close, and the term soon acquired elitist connotations. Civility became a quality associated with elite status and separated elites from all others, becoming a symbol of exclusion.

What is more, during modern colonialism, especially during the 15th century to early 17th century, civility as a form of individual behavior became closely tied to the broader concept of civilization, and the notion that the West has a civilizing mission toward the world. The people and societies of Africa, Asia, the Americas, and Oceania were to be civilized and turned from "savages" into "civilized human beings." This process involved diverse institutions and organizations, and it existed in a variety of imperial frameworks but was typically rooted in some sense of superiority.

Thus, by the middle of the 20th century after colonialism, world wars, and genocides, the term *civility* had lost its allure and meaning, had become elitist and corrupt, and was viewed as antiquated and reactionary. Some postcolonial authors such as Patrick Chabal and Jean-Pascal Daloz attributed a racist connotation to the term, particularly when applied in non-Western contexts. In recent years, however, issues surrounding the changing social fabric of modern societies, the alleged decline of social capital, and perhaps most important for global studies, modes of interaction among and coexistence of diverse and pluralist societies resurrected the term in the social sciences and essentially detached it from connotations with Western civilization and elitism.

Research on Civility

Although much of today's popular literature focuses on civility as the opposite of rudeness, scholars tend to link it more closely to notions of community, sociability, responsibility, and mutual dependence and attempt to either measure its scale or understand its origins and functions. Taking as a given that civility has its roots and is embedded in a particular country, most of this literature focuses on individual behavior within specific—mainly national—boundaries.

Attempts to measure civility tend to use population surveys and operationalize the concept either in terms of self-discipline, restraint, and the sacrifice of ego-enhancing behavior or in terms of trust and tolerance. For example, using the U.S. General Social Survey and focusing on the restraint aspects, Abbott Ferriss found that in the United States, civility was highly associated with education, occupation, and health but not gender, race, or locality. In their proposal to develop a Global Civil Society Index, Helmut K. Anheier and Sally Stares suggested calculating a civility indicator using questions in the World Values Survey or the European Values Survey relating rather to tolerance, namely, the proportion of people who would not object to having immigrants or foreign workers as neighbors and the proportion of people who say that tolerance is an important quality to encourage in children.

More recent historical and cultural analyses have sought to build on Elias's seminal study of the codes of conduct taught in western Europe between 800 and 1900 CE or have examined civility in non-Western cultures. Benet Davetian's study bridges the historical development of civility in England, France, and the United States since the Middle Ages with its contemporary expressions, concluding that the ways in which trust, distrust, and pride are managed are the ultimate measures of a culture's civility. In her examination of Japanese aesthetic networks from the 1600s to the mid-1800s, Eiko Ikegami found that civility helped shape a zone of social relationships between the intimate and the hostile and that, through civil practices within this zone, network leaders acquired social and cultural capital that enabled them to have a broader impact.

Key Issues

Despite these and other efforts to measure and understand the origins and role of civility, it is still primarily viewed (and researched) in the context of national societies, especially in its capacity to help "manage" diverse communities. However, in the context of globalization, civility could play a similar role in the many emerging transnational arenas of economy and society, including culture and politics. Civility, as often tacit, culturally embedded "agreements to disagree agreeably," allows for the routinization of collaborative behaviors that may involve actors that are different in a variety of respects. Civility creates predictability and builds social capital through successful encounters across national, cultural, political, economic, and linguistic borders. It promises to create the nonviolent, stable, and predictable zones needed for institutions, organizations, and individuals to operate and flourish in transnational contexts.

What is missing, however, is a research agenda that focuses on civility beyond national borders. To what extent and under what conditions can such zones of nonviolence and predictability be created, maintained or expanded not only at the local or national level but also at the international and transnational levels? Which actors can or should play a role? In a globalizing world, knowledge about the diverse notions of civility, how they are practiced, and how they are brought to bear on the increasing interaction among individuals and societies is critical to dealing with the tensions and frictions that accompany it.

Helmut K. Anheier and Anael Labigne

See also Civil Society, Global; Conflict and Conflict Resolution; Cosmopolitanism; Human Rights, International; Social Capital; Values

Further Readings

Anheier, H., & Stares, S. (2002). Introducing the global civil society index. In M. Glasius, M. Kaldor, & H. Anheier (Eds.), *Global civil society 2002* (pp. 241–254). New York: Oxford University Press.

Billante, N., & Saunders, P. (2002). Why civility matters. *Policy, 18*(3), 32–36.

Chabal, P., & Daloz, J.-P. (1999). *Africa works: Disorder as political instrument*. Oxford, UK: Oxford University Press.

Davetian, B. (2009). *Civility. A cultural history*. Toronto, ON: University of Toronto Press.

Dekker, P. (2010). Civicness: From civil society to social services? In T. Brandson et al. (Eds.), *Civicness in the governance and delivery of social services* (pp. 19–40). Baden-Baden, Germany: Nomos.

Elias, N. (1939). *Über den prozess der zivilisation. Soziogenetische und psychogenetische untersuchungen* [On the process of civilization: Socio-genetic and psycho-genetic examinations]. 2 Bde., 17 Edition. Haus zum Falken, Germany: Basel.

Ezzat, H. R., & Kaldor, M. (2007). Not even a tree: Delegitimising violence and the prospects for preemptive civility. In M. Glasius, M. Kaldor, & H. Anheier (Eds.), *Global civil society: 2006/7* (pp. 18–41). London: Sage.

Ferriss, A. (2002). Studying and measuring civility: A framework, trends, and scale. *Sociological Inquiry, 72*(3), 376–392.

Habermas, J. (1991). *The structural transformation of the public sphere*. Cambridge: MIT Press.

Hayek, F. A. (1976). *Law, legislation and liberty: Vol. 2, The mirage of social justice*. Chicago: University of Chicago Press.

Ikegami, E. (2005). *Bonds of civility: Aesthetic networks and the political origins of Japanese culture*. New York: Cambridge University Press.

McClellan, A. (2000). Beyond courtesy: Redefining civility. In L. Rouner (Ed.), *Civility*. Boston University Studies in Philosophy and Religion. South Bend, IN: University of Notre Dame Press.

Rawls, J. (1993). *Political liberalism*. New York: Columbia University Press.

Shils, E. (1997). *The virtue of civility : Selected essays on liberalism, tradition, and civil society*. Indianapolis, IN: Liberty Fund.

White, M. (2006). An ambivalent civility. *Canadian Journal of Sociology, 31*(4), 445.

CIVILIZATION

The concept of "civilization" presages the ascent of global modernity while also challenging its apparent universality because it is bounded by both history (temporality) and place (culture). Civilization indeed once stood for world-historical progress and domination. Encounters and conflicts between civilizations acted as spurs toward processes of internationalization that prefigured the present vogue for spatial categories—the notion of the *globe*.

The term *civilization* stems from *civilize*, that is, to make civil that which implicitly is unruly or barbaric, hence, also implying an existing nature of some kind. A common term used broadly, *civilization* often elides proper definition and understanding, representing variously projected images of who we are and what we have become in different epochs. Its etymology gives some clue to its historical force and relevance, particularly as its genealogy is inextricably bound up with Europe and its imperial colonial expansions. To civilize a person or people, a phenomenon related to the earlier *civilité* (and civil), meant to institute a form of life that is closely associated with the political structure of the city or a settled complex society that the Latin *civitatum* once represented.

This entry discusses several important features that characterize this type of existence that has been variously discussed by historians, anthropologists, social scientists, and thinkers.

One predominant characteristic of its trajectory is its inexorable unintentional encompassment of oppositions or contradictions, for example, civilized and "savage," refined and vulgar, domesticated and wild, fraternal unity and estranged otherness, and advanced and primitive. Hence, under its canopy of complexity, there lie internal tensions and boundary delineations that forever attest to the essential contestability of the concept. Its inevitable contestability has once more prompted forms of resistance and self-assertion in the combat against perceived cultural grievances perpetrated largely by dominant Western (secular) philosophies and institutions.

Before 1750, civilization was associated with the practice of cultivating—derived from organic tilling and husbandry—carrying all the connotations of the Latin *Cultura*. (*Kultura* in German later becomes distinct from *Zivilization* as exemplified by the works of Immanuel Kant.) To cultivate is a deed involving nature, and this would later be extended, importantly, to the nature of civil life itself where human sociability (*sociabilité*) was enhanced by means of the rule of law, science, and the arts. Yet religion was pivotal to its conception from the beginning because sociability had to be preserved from the "false civilization" or evil that would inevitably develop. It is no coincidence that along with the Marquis de Mirabeau, Issac Newton, Benedict de Spinoza, and Immanuel Kant conceived their task of explaining the world in either philosophical or scientific ways as activity grounded in the religious worldview. After circa 1750, the bifurcation of civilization misleadingly led to the proposition that *Cultura* was something higher and superior to the base, materialist crudity of civilization. Letters, language, poetics, drama, theology, music, and mathematics were elevated in status to that which sustains and elevates the "spirit" of humankind—elements that were also previously encompassed by the older connation of civilization. Each of these elements was considered fitting for the task of refining or polishing what nature had endowed humans with. The dominion over other creatures, like the lower instincts and passions of humans, was integral to the formation of a civilized (or humanized) human animal; and the mark of such an achievement was the degree to which one seemed polished and refined (thus also educated) in the company of others.

By the close of the 18th century, the courtier had surpassed both the knight and the hero in evaluative symbolic norms. Emerging from the grand courts of dynastic Europe—especially France—courtly behavior and standards of high culture eventually spread to the middle classes, which by means of revolution themselves incorporated such standards with modifications of their own. Hence, the much celebrated industrial revolution of western Europe was surmounted by the importance of other forces of self-transformation of a less materialist kind. The symbolic moral milieu was a realm of importance beyond merely the discursive exercises of moral philosophers, for it helped transform the understanding of individuals' modes of conduct and their estimations of others (i.e., within and between classes, tribes, and societies). Manners, codes of presentation, and representation in complex networks of social intercourse—including the attendant disciplining of one's instincts and passions—were also integral to modern notions of improvement and advancement and, therefore, civilization.

Civilized-Barbarian Dyad

Those dissimilar to one's own kind, particularly when considered unpolished in their ways, were deemed uncouth and often barbaric foreigners. This refers to the second element of the concept: how symbolic frameworks and configurations of power form principles of division and distinction: the *civilized-barbarian* dyad. This dyad of two antagonistic groups represents a universal axis of sorts because it is found among almost every settled, complex political society on earth, and it was bequeathed to us from ancient tribes and cities that either vanished or became absorbed into dominant civilizations. We know from the hieroglyphic era that the alien was an important figure for the formation of distinctive civilizations (identities) as those who lie outside (the boundary of membership) were ipso facto untethered to the cosmic metaphysical vision of one's kind. Norms of social and moral conduct were not applicable

to the "barbarian" and as a consequence vicious violence was a common weapon against those who threatened the community.

Barbarism lies within the heart of civilization even while "superior men" lay claim to divine providence, destiny, or learned wisdom to justify their claim to a higher existence. Violence and religiosity are therefore not necessarily antithetical to each other; yet religious worldviews also contest the exclusionary practices of states and war machines because their transcendental principles mostly embody an ethic of hospitality. The heathen or pagan unbeliever is also one's "brother" (or sister); thus it becomes evident how both axes of the particular universal instance work to produce tensions within civilizational complexes. Instead of simply cultures or societies, one can more rightly speak of having complex constellations of underlying and formal logics of identification that produce particular tensions. Such tensions can best be conceived within the conceptual terms of *processes* rather than discrete entities or units in space.

Temple-Sacral Space

A third element of civilizations refers to a more primordial, premodern phenomenon that predates even the emergence of states: the temple-sacral space divined by religious guardians (priests) who mediate between the earthly and cosmic orders. In this sense, civilizations are not necessarily city or state centered, nor do they presuppose a post-tribal form of existence. When ancient astrologers, shamans, and mystics read the sky and its extramundane orders of reality, they were propelling the forces of human civilization. Nature and the divine order were incorporated into their radical revelations of the true origins of time, life, creation, and being; and their respective scriptural techniques and spiritual practices and rituals incorporated many former animistic, folklore, and sage beliefs of ancient peoples. Primitiveness is an outdated 18th-century concept—intimately connected with imperial power and Judaeo-Christian prejudices—that falsely denigrates the cosmologies and symbolic technologies of manifold communal-tribal societies.

The primitive-modern dichotomy that plagued anthropology, development studies, foreign policy, and art began to collapse only with the arrival of the magisterial work of Levi Strauss, the famous French structural anthropologist. It revealed simultaneously two points: The "savage" is needed for the aggrandizement of the "civilized" colonizer, who evinces a severe lack of knowledge, and every native society has a complex array of symbolic and material techniques (knowledge) that conjoin with complex cosmologies that are richly interwoven with intricate webs of social interaction and filial bonds. More contemporary understandings of civilizations emphasize the plurality of forms of civilization, dispensing with problematical traditional Eurocentric views of tribal (native) societies. Through numerous encounters, conflicts, and exchanges, the global perspective of civilizational difference has given rise to a renewed appreciable interest in world religions and nontheist belief systems. The groundbreaking work of the French sociologist Émile Durkheim in the early part of the 20th century showed how aboriginal peoples possess distinctive frames of meaning and cosmological orientations. Hence, before the Greeks, Persians, and Chinese, aboriginal peoples were developing formative ideas of how nature and the divine order intersect, sustain life, and imbue human life with purpose.

The denaturalization of the cosmos via the sacred and its concomitant symbolization of organic life led to adventures and breakthroughs that would reverberate for millennia. To that extent, civilization is irreducible to empire, state tyranny, domestication, and polished standards; it represents humankind under the canopy of extrahuman elements (i.e., earth, sky, gods, fate, and spirit-souls) that mingle with the sublime unconscious of a group or individual. Destiny, future, and present are inextricably linked to the past, historical time, and ancestral being, hence giving the species *Homo sapiens* a radically different (yet also similar) trajectory to other natural beings. The animality of humans was a relatively late modern discovery that was made possible only after nihilism ("death of God") cleared the way for natural science. Yet one kind of sciencing is not necessarily a timeless, abstract, universal activity of investigation.

Positivist science does suppose this, yet a civilizational studies approach would find sciencing to occur in different ways and methods at different times for variable purposes and ends (e.g., values). In this regard, the history and philosophy of science are akin to the history and philosophy of religions; an analogue exists between the two because world orientations are neither homogenous nor divisible into separate compartments of cosmological axioms. Religion and science, like nature and society, are wedded; it follows that the global predominance of one kind of science or (a)theism is not necessarily going to remain permanent; impermanence as the becoming of something new or different or merely temporal is the mark of civilizational analysis. By contrast, globalism presents itself as a permanent, irreversible phenomenon founded largely on a spatial rather than a temporal category. The "modern" is thus bound up with territoriality and its transcendence.

Constellation of Processes

It is therefore of interest that civilizational analysis—while capable of explaining globalizing forces—is not locked into reductive schemas, including those centered on spatial units or substances. A fourth fundamental element exists here: The unity of any civilizational identity is only temporally formed in and through several formative processes that manifest a coalescence into a *complex*. Instead of a whole organism or political unity, one can think of a civilization as a constellation of processes forming a temporally contingent complex. That is to say, civilizations are not substances extended in space such as cells within an organism: They vanish and appear and yet have a presence within historical time. Their formation results from a complex network of interlocking processes—material, moral, political, ecological, and metaphysical (spiritual). No singular landscape, language, or religion defines the unstable formative processes that give rise to civilizational complexes such as ancient Hellas and Rome, Ming China, and the Inca, among others. It is correct to say that heterogeneity marks the internal as well as the external constellation of relations of such complex societies. That being so, sociocultural complexes of this kind are in fact wholly porous things with extremely elastic margins of inclusivity and therefore moral exclusion. Yesterday's barbarian may rapidly become tomorrow's fellow citizen or neighbor—"it is only a matter of time," as the cliché has it.

Processes of national independence may, for instance, intensify and widen as a result of forces or changes specific largely to that civilizational constellation in time (e.g., Europe in the 1990s). Nation building and postcolonial independence are therefore not anathema to the project of civilization but integral to its modern operations. As processes, they can be understood as much more than mere "political" phenomena since the emergence of the Westphalian state-system resulted from the broader unity of an absolutist-Christendom-aristocracy constellation of *Europa*. This example of civilizational processes also exemplifies the fact that they cannot be bounded by a single constellation for too long; they thrust themselves beyond symbolic frontiers that often serve to define the insider-outsider boundary when ideology, belief, or political interest necessitates it. In this light, one can observe that the circumnavigation of the globe acted as an impetus to globalization but only from the proper vantage point of the *agent*— the phenomenon being the result of actions and ideas of concrete subjects who were acculturated by particular symbolic designs and logics. Processes—whether global or not—always require substantiation and agency, hence the critique of abstract globalism as espoused by lay and technical observers. Without agents of culture—valuation, sociability, or self-interpretation—there could not have been phenomena such as internationalization or globalization.

Cyclic Worldviews

Finally, the idea of civilization antedates the modern era; consequently, modern precepts such as "progress" should not be read back into them. Notable in this regard is the tension between the prejudice for progressive advancement—a legacy of 19th-century natural science—and the orientation of other ages and peoples that largely conformed to the movements of the cosmos and nature. The former inclination—traditionally Western and European—tends to confer an instrumental attitude toward nature onto other (or previous) civilizations. Power and appropriation have certainly been common to most complex societies, yet different cosmologies or belief systems incorporated

and elevated the importance of *cyclical* seasons and forces within nature herself. Time was also cyclical, and the ravages of nature—as catastrophic science would later acknowledge—confirmed the decidedly fragile fabric of social life. Birth, growth, decomposition, death, and rebirth were all vital facets of the civilizational processes of expansion and contraction (akin to the patterns of the global economy today). The regeneration of the universe was commonly conceived to be intertwined with the life cycle of one's particular community—an insight regained today through ecological science.

Human development, not to mention technological innovations, occurred mostly within the symbolic parameters of such cyclic worldviews. Indeed, preceding the modern instrumentalist view of nature—a domination of nature through predictive powers decreed as impartial knowledge—one finds two essential elements of overcoming the dangers of wild animal life emerged: specialization and vertical differentiation or social hierarchy. A heightened division of labor (including the creation of surplus and relative organic stability through agriculture) and with it a greater differentiation between social types/functionaries was propelled by worldviews other than the linear conception of time that progress was thought to represent. Kings and palatial officials took care of civil matters on the basis of divine authority, which itself explained earthly natural events in the terms of its own cosmology.

Higher specialization and divisions within society gradually altered religious world understandings even while these understandings were originally foundational for the forming of complex civilized societies. Each mutually influenced and (largely) reinforced the other—a point often forgotten in broad references to so-called global phenomena. Complexity and differentiation in all kinds of spheres of life is a hallmark of human civilization(s), as are also domination and the desire for increased power and security over time. However, it is important to conceive of these phenomena as emerging from and manifesting themselves out of so many discernible as well as indiscernible processes. Technological change, for instance, may hold sway over our lives today, and yet not all of its (underlying) processes are clearly known to us. Hence, the unconscious still plays its sui generis role in tamed, domesticated life, where existence is no longer simply a given.

John Mandalios

See also Colonialism; Culture, Notions of; Empires; Enlightenment, The; Global Religions, Beliefs, and Ideologies; Global Village; Humanity, Concepts of; Modernization; Myths; Otherness; Pariahs, Global

Further Readings

Arnason, J. (2003). *Civilizations in dispute: Historical questions and theoretical traditions*. Leiden, Netherlands: Brill.

Daedalus. (1975). Wisdom, revelation, and doubt: Perspectives on the first millennium B.C. *Daedalus, 104* (2).

Eisenstadt, S. (2003). *Comparative civilizations and multiple modernities*. Leiden, Netherlands: Brill.

Elias, N. (2000). *The civilizing process* (Rev. ed.). Oxford, UK: Blackwell.

Nelson, B. (with T. E. Huff, Ed.). (1981). *On the roads to modernity: Conscience, science, and civilizations*. Totowa, NJ: Rowman & Littlefield.

CLASS

Class theories are important in analyses of the contemporary globalizing world, both in the Marxist structural version and in Weberian studies of class as socioeconomic status or stratification. Yet there is no single generally agreed-on definition of class. Moreover, class skeptics argue that class is of declining relevance since, for example, class identity is no longer as helpful a predictor of certain behaviors, like voting, as it once was. Even so, both globalization and the worldwide economic crisis that began in 2008 have stimulated several class analyses as the inner workings of world capitalism and its contradictions become more evident.

Marxist Definitions of Class in a Globalizing World

Marxists emphasize that the current "globalizing" world is capitalist and understand class relationships within that context. They maintain that capitalism has undergone different historical phases with varieties of capitalism within each phase. If capitalism has long been a world system, it has now entered a new global phase. Yet, even in a globalized world, nation-states continue to matter as sites of political compromise in the ongoing struggle between antagonistic classes.

Marxists argue there is an international or global capitalist class, one that owns the means of production, that is, the finances and equipment used to produce goods and services for sale on the market. Despite inevitable tensions within capitalist factions and capital's short- and long-term interests, the capitalist class has a degree of political unity worldwide. For within capitalism, the capitalist class has a structural interest in maximally exploiting workers since lowered wages and increased productivity are necessary to sustain the profits on which the survival of capitalist enterprises depends. Hence, class is an inherently unequal, antagonistic social relationship. In the current phase of global capitalism, capital mobility worldwide has enhanced capital's relative power over labor and the state.

The class composition of today's working classes, made up of those who sell their labor power for a wage or salary to make a living, is complex and ambiguous. Workers labor in more or less autonomous employment situations, with more or less access as consumers to "middle-class" lifestyles. They are employed in the private or public sectors, in unionized or nonunionized workplaces, in service or manufacturing employment, and in the formal or informal sectors. Moreover, class is analytically but not empirically and descriptively distinct from the social facts of gender and race. These differences affect worldwide class formation and struggle.

For Marxists, class struggle is the major engine of social change, contributing to the emergence of different phases and varieties of capitalism. Class struggle will determine the shape of the world political economy beyond the current global phase and ultimately that of a noncapitalist future.

Weberian Definitions of Class in a Globalizing World

Anglo-American versions of class inspired by Max Weber emphasize stratification within the contemporary world polity. Such accounts analyze rankings among individuals occupying higher and lower categories across different measures, like occupation, education, and income. Individuals in these categories or classes are not viewed as antagonistic, apart from seeking to remain in higher rather than lower nominal categories. This conceptualization reflects the classical Weberian notion of class as a set of people with similar power to mobilize resources that will enhance their "life chances," that is, their access to food, shelter, health, education, and so on. For example, lawyers harness specific, certified technical skills, selling them on the market to gain advantages, including enhanced income, compared with nonskilled workers.

For Weber, class is simply one basis for social organization. Important noneconomic bases for inequality include status distinctions based on social esteem or honor. Thus, Weberian accounts of the contemporary world political economy describe class-based inequalities alongside others, based on race, ethnicity, gender, and religion, arguing that inequalities are growing along many dimensions worldwide. Some neo-Weberian accounts emphasize the existence of a transnational elite, based on shared status achieved through similar cosmopolitan consumption habits.

Weberian notions of class are often viewed as conflicting with Marxist accounts, but they may be complementary. For example, Pierre Bourdieu observes that inequalities are socially reproduced, in part, through distinctive class cultures that maintain social distance. This collapses the class-status distinction since the correct display of status markers typically depends on class origin. At the same time, the relative power of antagonistic classes, in the Marxist sense, can be viewed as the determinants of the global socioeconomic differences and inequalities described in Weberian approaches.

The International History of Class Relationships

Class-based accounts of today's world political economy emphasize that their current international character has a long history. In particular, world systems theorists maintain that the capitalist political economy has been a world political economy since Columbus "discovered" the Americas,

beginning a centuries-long process of incorporating distant populations into class relationships with the imperial center. Early on, for example, indigenous peoples of North America sold furs used to make felts for hats in London, linking them as independent commodity producers with mercantile capitalists in the distant heart of the British Empire. Similarly, transnational capitalists have existed for centuries. The early transnational enterprises, like the British, Dutch, Danish, and French East India companies, were established in the 1600s for long-distance trade in spices, tea, coffee, and textiles. At the same time, working-class labor has long moved across borders. More than 100 years ago, working-class people immigrated from Europe, China, and Japan to places like Canada, Brazil, and South Africa, where they built the railways and roads and operated laundries, restaurants, and other services. Racialized and gendered working-class relationships have stretched across the world capitalist system since its inception. Furthermore, as Karl Marx's famous injunction "workers of the world, unite!" reminds us, world consciousness has been part of organized working-class movements for well over a century. Unions like the American-based Industrial Workers of the World, established in 1905, are additional evidence of the international aspirations of working-class factions since at least the early 20th century.

Capital's Growing Relative Power Worldwide

Many factors contributed to the increased relative power of capital over the working class and the state, historically the privileged site for the political negotiation of class compromises since the economic crisis of the 1970s. New transportation and communication technologies, themselves spurred by the search for increasing productivity and profits, have enabled capital mobility. Whether realized in practice, the *credible threat* of capital flight directly and indirectly disciplines working-class movements. Labor is more reluctant to make demands in direct negotiations with the employer, when the employer may move jobs to another part of the world, with a cheaper or more cooperative workforce. States are less willing to accommodate working-class demands if capital suggests these are discouraging for investment. For example, strengthened protections for workers from layoffs may be cited by capital as a reason for relocating to another local or national jurisdiction with more flexible labor regulations. Many enterprises are now transnational, operating across national jurisdictions to minimize labor, environmental, and other costs, and to maximize profits. Finance capital is especially mobile and volatile, able to make second-by-second investments and disinvestments, in the amounts of trillions of dollars per day.

Mobile capital's structural advantage over labor is enhanced by self-conscious political organizing by capital factions. Capital is not simply a class "in itself" with shared structural interests but to some degree a class "for itself" organized politically to pursue shared interests. Worldwide capital is represented in international associations like the World Economic Forum (WEF), founded in 1971. The WEF members are global enterprises with billions in annual turnover. The WEF's annual meeting in Davos, Switzerland, routinely brings together members with heads of states, international policymakers, and academics in a self-conscious effort to shape the world political economy.

Both outside and through such organizations, capital has developed class policies. Since the 1970s, these have emerged as a familiar package of initiatives that aim to expand markets, which are often referred to as "neoliberalism." Neoliberal advocates call for the privatization and commodification of formerly public goods and services and for the implementation of rules facilitating the movement of industrial and finance capital. Typical policy directions include, for example, the privatization of (aspects of) formerly public health and education services or even the military, as with the use of private security firms by the United States in its occupation of Iraq. Other standard policies include trade liberalization or free trade and the elimination of national barriers to foreign investors to facilitate international flows of goods and capital. Such policies are unevenly pursued in practice, but capital has been largely successful in organizing a near worldwide consensus around neoliberal ideas. Not only Western states but also the former Soviet states and developing world have adopted neoliberal programmes to varying degrees, often as a condition for receiving loans through the World Bank and International Monetary Fund (IMF).

In pursuing neoliberal policies, capital is supported by organic intellectuals, including mainstream economists who hold important policy positions in nation-states and at the World Bank, the IMF, and so on, as technical experts, finance ministers, and trade ministers. These organic intellectuals argue that neoliberal policies are in the general interest, not just capital's interests. For example, they argue that the expansion of private education and health care is not only to open new markets (and generate more profits) for capital but also to create choice for citizens as consumers. Neoliberal policies fostering capitalist markets are said to enhance democracy, bringing about and deepening liberal democratic political forms.

Most WEF members and practicing economists are White men. Moreover, most major capitalist transnational enterprises worldwide have headquarters in the developed world. Yet, the capitalist class holds fundamentally, structurally similar interests, no matter its color or gender composition. No capitalist can indefinitely ignore the profit imperative; otherwise, he will be out of business. Nonetheless, the current degree of gender and racial cohesion in the capitalist class and a shared international cosmopolitan lifestyle facilitates political cohesion and capital's ability to act as a class for itself.

Yet, capitalist class ideology, specifically neoliberalism, is not necessarily consistent with the interests and actions of all capitalist fractions. For example, American capital advocates free trade but then pressures its government to adopt protectionist measures in textiles and agriculture since it cannot compete on an open market with enterprises producing these products in the developing world. Nor are neoliberal policies necessarily compatible with capital's longer term interests. In the economic crisis beginning in 2008 and after the 1994 Mexican and 1997 Asian crises, elements of capital argued for financial capital controls, suggesting that the "deregulated" economic environment precipitates financial panics, destabilizing whole regions and even the world economy with sudden, massive disinvestment.

The Declining Relative Power of the Working Class

Class theorists argue that neoliberalism is not in the general interest but instead hurts the world majority's life chances. Yet, the world working class is not homogenous. Declining relative working-class power since the 1970s has different effects on working-class men and women across the world. For example, the privatization of public health and education services in developed countries has meant the loss of well-paying, secure employment for women workers, who are overrepresented in public-sector employment. Since women workers entered the workforce later than men, union-negotiated agreements stipulating "first hired, last fired" mean that women in unionized private employment are more likely to be laid off if a company closes or relocates. Temporary work, especially for women, has grown in North America and Europe, partly as a result of capital's successful efforts to make labor regulations more flexible. Often, women's temporary work is viewed as a supplement to a male breadwinner's, justifying lowered wages. Temporary workers are particularly vulnerable to industrial accidents.

Most nations now have special export processing zones (EPZs) with favorable tax, environmental, and labor rules for capital to attract foreign investment. Such EPZs frequently employ racialized women workers, given assumptions about their efficiency and docility. Thus, the *maquiladora* zones along the U.S.-Mexico border disproportionately employ female Mexican workers in precarious working conditions at low wages. Nations with nondiscrimination policies for foreign capital and goods typically maintain sharp distinctions between citizen and noncitizen workers and their rights. Chinese workers employed by subcontractors for large foreign firms, like the Walmart chain, have few possibilities to negotiate meaningfully with their foreign employer since they are not American citizens and have no political rights in the country where their employer is based. In the United Arab Emirates, foreign workers make up as much as 80% of the workforce. Their negotiating position is weakened since they lack the formal political rights of citizen workers. Undocumented workers worldwide do not have documented workers' minimal rights, which include the rights to organize a union, receive a minimum wage, and limit the hours in the working day. There are some exceptions. Documented European citizens have some formally guaranteed rights as workers across contracting nations in the European Union.

For the working class, the consequences of their declining power are both visible and hidden class injuries. Visible injuries include negative life chances in various domains. In developed and developing countries, more neoliberal welfare states, with relatively less successfully organized working-class populations, show higher rates of inequality than more social democratic states with stronger working-class representation. They have higher rates of infant mortality and infant death, decreased longevity, higher rates of injury and death in the workplace, and worse educational outcomes, including literacy rates, compared with more social democratic welfare states. In contrast, the more social democratic Indian state of Kerala is significantly more equal, with better health and basic education outcomes than many richer, more neoliberal regions. At the world level, inequality is increasing partly because the wealthiest are capturing an increasingly large percentage of world income and wealth. The consequence is diverging life chances depending on class origin.

Hidden injuries of class include the psychic difficulties of routinely undertaking boring, dangerous, low-paying jobs with little autonomy, while having the responsibility for "making something of yourself." Insofar as work remains an important area for defining selfhood, low-status work in particular is difficult to reconcile with a positive idea of self. Many workers stress that work is only a small part of their identity—as parents, neighbors, children, and so on, they survive, make decisions, and participate, to the extent their wages allow, in a consumer culture that enables them to recapture a sense of middle-class respectability absent in the work place. Working-class people must define themselves against the social experience of work if they are to develop a positive self identity. Moreover, in working-class families, parents encourage their children to aspire to a life different from what they can provide, so that current circumstances seem shameful and undignified in contrast with the hoped-for future. Better paid workers with more autonomy and status may suffer from the pressures of self-exploitation because failure (like success) is an individual and not collective achievement.

Working-class people across the globe resist these injuries in ways that range from ambiguous, local acts drawing on a weak class identity to more self-conscious political movements. Workers manipulate information about their family status, nationality, and legality to secure jobs. They draw on stereotypes to reject dangerous, demeaning work, for example, by calling on notions of feminine helplessness. Sometimes, workers organize collectively to protect jobs but make distinctions between national and foreign workers, viewing the latter as competitive threats. More clear-cut examples of class solidarity include calls for one day or rotating general strikes against neoliberal policies affecting a range of workers and working-class rights, with instances during the last few decades in places like Canada, Korea, South Africa, and France. In the World Social Forum, held to coincide with and challenge the World Economic Forum organized by capital, working-class people offer an international challenge to the neoliberal vision of globalization advocated by capital. Yet, they do not do so as a politically unified, self-conscious working class. Working-class politics, in the contemporary global world, is not synonymous with a White, male unionized manufacturing class located in the developed nations. Rather, it reflects the diverse, actually existing situations of working-class people worldwide, as well as the multiple aspirations of human beings whose potentially unalienated expression translates into political demands that go beyond their status as workers.

Class theory provides unique insights into the global political economy. Yet, globalization also poses a challenge to class theory, a challenge to become even more cosmopolitan, with rich analyses of transforming class relationships in declining and emerging states and in the ever-changing world system itself. Class theory must itself become more globalized.

Elaine Coburn

See also Capitalism; Labor; Liberalism, Neoliberalism; Marxism and Neo-Marxism; World Economic Forum; World-Systems Perspective

Further Readings

Bonacich, E., Alimahomed, S., & Wilson, J. (2008). The racialization of global labor. *American Behavioral Scientist, 52*(3), 342–355.

Bourdieu, P. (2007). *Distinction: A social critique of the judgement of taste.* Cambridge, MA: Harvard University Press.

Friedman, J. (2000). Globalization, class and culture in global systems. *Journal of World Systems Research, 6*(3), 636–656.

Marx, K., & Engels, F. (1985). *The Communist manifesto.* London: Penguin Books.

Navarro, V. (2007). Neoliberalism as a class ideology; or, the political causes of the growth of inequality. *International Journal of Health Sciences, 37*(1), 47–62.

Ross, R., & Trachte, K. C. (1990). *Global capitalism: The new leviathan.* Albany: State University of New York Press.

Sandbrook, R., Edelman, M., Heller, P., & Teichman, J. (2007). *Social democracy in the global periphery: Origins, challenges, prospects.* Cambridge, UK: Cambridge University Press.

Sennett, R., & Cobb, J. (1972). *The hidden injuries of class.* New York: Vintage Books.

Wallerstein, I. (2000). Globalization or the age of transition? A long-term view of the trajectory of the world system. *International Sociology, 15*(2), 251–267.

Weber, M. (1978). Status groups and classes. In G. Roth & C. Wittich (Eds.), *Economy and society* (pp. 302–307). New York: Oxford University Press.

CLIMATE CHANGE

The global environmental crisis of climate change has resulted from a process called the greenhouse effect. This is a disturbance of the energy balance of the Earth that results in a rise in surface temperature when there is an atmospheric increase in the concentration of greenhouse gases such as carbon dioxide (CO_2).

As humans burn fossil fuels and deforest the land, CO_2 is released, altering the chemistry of the atmosphere for a long time. This change in atmospheric composition has led to a discernible human influence on our planet's climate, to what is referred to as global climate change. It represents changes over time in the averages and variability of surface temperature, precipitation, and wind, as well as associated changes in the Earth's atmosphere, oceans, and natural water supplies, snow and ice, land surface, ecosystems, and living organisms. The climate is a complex system evolving under natural and anthropogenic forces; its change produces a variety of impacts felt all over the world. This entry discusses the changes and impacts, as well as other concerns, associated with climate change on the Earth.

Global Nature of Climate Change and the Greenhouse Effect

The presence of greenhouse gases (particularly water vapor but also carbon dioxide, ozone, and methane) in the atmosphere leads to an Earth temperature significantly warmer than it would otherwise have been without their greenhouse effect. As human activities add more or new greenhouse gases (chlorofluorocarbons, for instance), the Earth's average temperature increases.

The Earth is naturally warmed by solar (shortwave, SW) radiation absorption and cooled by emission of infrared (longwave, LW) radiation. It is the balance between the warming from SW absorption and the cooling from LW emission that governs the Earth's temperature. When this balance is altered, the Earth's temperature adjusts to the new equilibrium. Such perturbation of the Earth's energy balance is called a radiative forcing, and the greenhouse effect is the main perturbation whereby the presence of greenhouse gases in the atmosphere blocks the emission of LW radiation to space, therefore reducing the cooling this escaping radiation normally causes. This process leads to a warming of the Earth.

Of the CO_2 emitted by human activities, nearly half is quickly taken up by land and ocean, and the remainder is transported by atmospheric motion around the globe. This CO_2 remains in the atmosphere for hundreds of years before being taken up by chemical weathering on land and sediments deposition in the ocean over geological time scales. CO_2 can therefore be considered as having a long lifetime, and the location where it is added to the atmosphere has essentially no influence over where the greenhouse effect will occur. The greenhouse effect occurs globally.

Regionalization of the Warming

Surface observations averaged over the entire globe show a general temperature increase (~0.8°C) during the last century as is expected from the greenhouse effect. A map of surface temperature changes during the last several decades, however, displays some spatial variations in the warming (Figure 1). In particular, the high latitudes of the Northern Hemisphere display a warming two to three times larger than the globally averaged one. These spatial variations do not result from local greenhouse or other radiative forcing but are the consequence of a regional feedback (a self-reinforcing reaction to a forcing that either enhances or reduces the original forcing) process that tends to regionalize the warming. The so-called snow/ice albedo feedback effect is responsible for the large temperature increase in Northern Hemisphere high latitudes. In regions covered by snow or ice, a large part of the radiation from the sun is reflected (the surface is said to have a high albedo), and little radiation penetrates into the surface. As the surface temperature increases from the greenhouse effect, some snow or ice melts, exposing the surface (whether land or ocean) and allowing solar radiation to penetrate the upper layer where the radiation can be absorbed and warm it. This induces an additional melting of the adjacent snow/ice covered areas, giving rise to more solar radiation absorption. This self-enhancing process is called a positive feedback: Under an initial fluctuation (the warming from increased CO_2 in this case), a domino effect gets established that expands the original melting. The result is a larger temperature increase in these regions than in surrounding regions not covered by snow or ice.

Another source of regionalizing of the temperature change originates from other radiative forcings. One major example is the addition of aerosols (particles suspended in the air) resulting from industrial activities and the burning of wood, or from natural processes such as volcanic eruptions or sandstorms. Their impact on climate differs from that of greenhouse gases in two major ways. First, the aerosol lifetime is short (on the order of weeks to months, except for volcanic aerosols that can last a few years in the stratosphere); thus, they do not have time to extend globally, and therefore, their impact remains more regional. A consequence of this short lifetime is that their impact can decrease or even disappear as soon as the source of emission is reduced or eliminated. This is not the case for CO_2 that, once in the atmosphere,

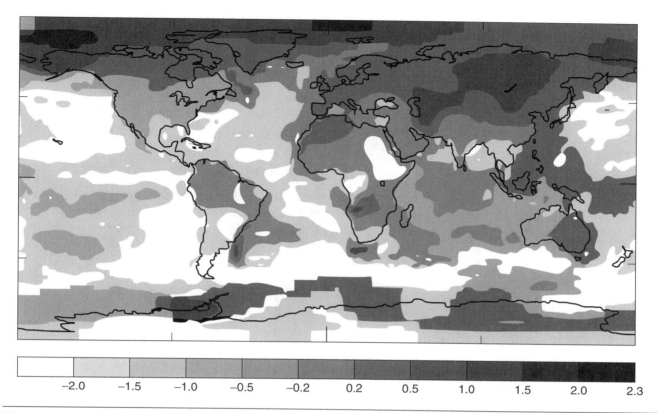

−2.0	−1.5	−1.0	−0.5	−0.2	0.2	0.5	1.0	1.5	2.0	2.3

Figure I   Annual mean temperature anomaly (°C) for the period 2001–2007 from the reference period 1951–1980.

Source: National Aeronautics and Space Administration Goddard Institute for Space Studies (NASA GISS), data.giss.nasa.gov/gistemp/references.html.

Note: Global mean = 0.54.

can remain there long after the source of emission has disappeared. Second, most aerosols have a cooling effect on the surface. This is particularly true with the prevailing aerosols, including the sulfate aerosols (SO_4) produced through the burning of sulfur-containing coal. The cooling effect of aerosol can in part compensate for the greenhouse warming and therefore mask its real strength. So, as we "clean" our atmosphere from aerosols, for health or other reasons, we might experience a larger warming from the greenhouse effect.

Global Climate Changes

Sea Ice Melting, Glaciers Retreating, and Sea Level Increase

A major aspect of climate change is the melting of sea ice and the retreat of glaciers as a result of the enhanced warming in high latitudes resulting from the snow/ice albedo feedback. These effects have already been observed in most parts of the globe, with varying intensity and timing. Maybe the most compelling example is the rapid melting of Arctic ice. The extent of Arctic ice, at its minimum in September, has generally been decreasing, one year after the next with, however, some recovery over short periods of time (e.g., in 2008). Ice, however, has been thinning everywhere. The consequences are multiple on humans and natural systems. The animals accustomed to living on sea ice must adjust to smaller ice areas in the summer. For instance, polar bears have to modify their habits as the large ice platforms from which they hunt are reduced to almost nothing and they now have to swim over longer distances to reach their prey. Fishing conditions and catches are also modified, and people have to adapt to those, while they can enjoy longer crop-growing seasons.

Melting glaciers is different in its nature, and it can add large amounts of fresh water to the ocean, increasing the sea level, which is not the case for sea ice. Only a negligible sea level increase occurs when ice already in the water melts. Glacier melt and its associated retreat occurs in both the Arctic and Antarctic. Shorter glaciers flow faster, which results in glaciers breaking up and large icebergs detaching from the ice sheet. Other processes such as melt water percolation through pores and fractures can accelerate the glacier flow through lubrication of its base.

Because the Antarctic is a continent covered with a thick layer of ice (in fact the thickest one in the world), only glacier retreat occurs. Already, nearly 90% of glaciers have retreated. But the retreat of these glaciers cannot be entirely attributed to global warming, and the slowing down of the retreat in the late 1980s and early 1990s is still unexplained.

Ocean Heat Accumulation, Expansion, and Sea Level Change

The ocean plays a major role in climate, storing heat in the tropical regions, redistributing it toward the poles and exchanging it with the atmosphere. It also plays a role in the carbon cycle as it absorbs a significant part of the CO_2 emitted by human activities, as mentioned. As the greenhouse effect adds heat to the Earth system, it is in the ocean that the heat is accumulated and the ocean warms. This has two major effects. First, a warmer ocean evaporates more, therefore putting additional water vapor in the atmosphere. Because water vapor is a greenhouse effect, this leads to an additional warming and therefore this is a positive feedback, possibly the most important one. The second effect of the ocean warming is ocean expansion. This expansion is the second component that induces sea level rise: Ice melting and ocean expansion have contributions nearly similar to this rise.

Temperature Extremes and Extreme Events

Atmospheric temperatures are expected to change in most places in the world, with extremes (both low and high) becoming more common and periods of heat waves occurring more frequently and over longer periods during the summer in many locations. The Northern Hemisphere is more likely to experience these heat waves and, because of the higher population density, their impacts will be more severe.

Warmer ocean surface temperatures are expected to lead to increased hurricane intensity and duration, possibly leading to enhanced devastation, particularly in highly populated and more developed coastal regions.

Hydrological Cycle

Despite these major changes in temperature, it is probably the changes in the hydrological cycle that will be affecting human and natural systems the most. Precipitation distribution and intensity have already been modified, and the prediction is for direr changes with, in particular, reduced precipitation in already rain-deficient regions such as the sub-Saharan regions, the Mediterranean surroundings, and the southwestern United States, associated with enhanced likelihood of wild fires. Higher precipitation in northern midlatitudes and in the tropics associated with flooding and landslides are also forecasted. In general, when precipitation falls, it will be more abundant and separated by longer periods of reduced or no rain.

Another major aspect of the hydrological cycle change relates to the nature of precipitation. In a warmer atmosphere, precipitation will fall more often as rain instead of snow. This will lead to a reduction of the snow pack and its ability to store water over long periods of time before it is released when it is the most needed in spring and summer. When combined with glaciers melting discussed previously, regions that rely on alpine water sources, such as the countries at the foot of Himalayas, could experience floods followed by water shortages.

Other climatological changes related to shorter scale variability of the atmosphere are expected to occur but are more difficult to predict because of the chaotic nature of atmospheric dynamics. Among them, intense mesoscale wind events are expected to occur more frequently but have limited predictability.

Human-Induced Changes?

One question often asked is as follows: How do we know that climate change has an anthropogenic origin because climate has always changed?

The first thing to note is that the observed temperature change is much faster than any ever observed in the past. Second, the observed increase in carbon dioxide (CO_2) concentration from 280 to nearly 385 parts per million (ppm) has been clearly documented since the beginning of the 20th century as intense industrial activities by emitters of CO_2 was ramping up. Moreover, an analysis of carbon isotopes in CO_2 allows us to verify its origin as that produced from burning fossil fuels or burning forests. But because correlation is not causation, the third element of this argumentation is that a theory—the greenhouse effect—links CO_2 (and greenhouse gases) increase with temperature increase. Finally, it has been suggested that the sun could be responsible for a large part of the observed warming. This can be assessed by jointly examining the temperature changes at the surface and in the stratosphere. In the case of a greenhouse-induced change, the stratospheric temperature decreases with increasing CO_2, while for a sun-induced effect, it increases, like at the surface. Observations can therefore help us differentiate an observed warming as a result of the greenhouse effect from one originating mostly from solar variability; the temperature change observed during the last few decades in the stratosphere clearly indicates a decrease.

Some Significant Impacts Resulting From Global Changes

Ocean Acidification

Approximately one third of the CO_2 emitted by human activity has already been taken up by the ocean and thus moderated the atmospheric CO_2 concentration increase and consequently global warming. In addition, as CO_2 dissolves in sea water, carbonic acid is formed. This has the effect of acidifying, or lowering, the pH of the ocean. Although not directly caused by warming, acidification is related to it because, like the greenhouse effect, it is the result of the increase of CO_2 in the atmosphere. Ocean acidification has many impacts on marine ecosystems, most of them highly detrimental to a substantial number of species ranging from corals to lobsters and from sea urchins to mollusks and will eventually affect the entire marine food chain.

Ecosystem Modification and Adaptation and Biodiversity Reduction

The list of impacts of climate change on ecosystems, plants, and animals is long. Combined changes in temperature and precipitation, as well as changes in extremes, can have an impact on the survival of species and lead to a rapid reduction of biodiversity. Ecological niches can disappear or the survival of some species can be at risk because of the appearance of new pests that can survive milder winter, for instance. But not all changes: A lengthening growing season in higher latitude, as discussed before, could be beneficial for some crops; increased CO_2 concentration can, up to a certain point, have a fertilizing action. Overall, however, the modification of ecosystems will affect the services they provide such as the provision of food, clean water production, waste decomposition, regulation of diseases, nutrient cycles, and crop pollination support, or even spiritual and recreational benefits. Those services rely on complex interactions among many species, each species having its unique function and DNA that has evolved to help it respond to natural challenges. Once a species goes extinct, however, it does not come back. And some losses of biodiversity then become irreversible.

Ecosystems can adjust over time to their climatic environment. Individual species making an ecosystem can adapt by moving away from detrimental conditions. To avoid increasing temperatures, they can grow further north in the Northern Hemisphere and/or at higher altitude. Species that cannot adjust fast enough or have nowhere to go (e.g., alpine ecosystems) will become stressed and at high risk of extinction. Such range shift has happened in the past but during long periods of time. The growing rate of both CO_2 concentration and temperature is now occurring at a faster pace than ever before, and this might be too fast for some species; entire ecosystems might disappear as a result.

Climate Change Predictions

One question of significance for society is, How much CO_2 in the atmosphere is too much considering that CO_2 concentration is already well outside the envelope of the concentration that has occurred during the past 1 million years?

An associated question is, How large a temperature increase is too large? Although no definitive answer can be offered to those questions because of the complexity of the climate system, they can be addressed from a probabilistic perspective using data from paleo-climatological records for guidance based on what has happened in the past and climate models for predictions.

Climate models suggest that if we continue to use fossil fuel energy to fuel our economic growth at the current rate, the global temperature change by the end of the century would be between 2°C and 6°C with a most likely value around 4°C. Most scientists agree that if the temperature increases beyond 2°C, the climate might change in dramatic yet unknown ways. This is why this 2°C figure has been selected as part of recent international discussions. CO_2 emissions that would correspond to a 2°C increase would correspond to releasing approximately twice as much CO_2 as we have done thus far, a far cry from the five times that are predicted if we continue on our current energy usage trajectory. Almost all computations converge to a needed cut of 80% to 85% in CO_2 emissions in highly emitting countries and 50% globally if we want to avoid dangerous climate change.

Additional Concerns: Known Unknowns

Several unknowns in the climate system can potentially trigger rapid and possibly irreversible global changes. One important one is the possibility of methane release as a result of permafrost—the soil that remains frozen year round in high latitudes—melting. The top layer melts in the summer. This melting has been observed to be expanding with time from rapidly increasing surface temperature. Large amounts of methane are stored under the permafrost, and as it melts, this very powerful greenhouse gas escapes into the atmosphere, significantly adding to the greenhouse effect because it is approximately 25 times more potent than CO_2.

The exact amount of permafrost hydrate methane is not known so this process is among the known unknowns about which our knowledge might improve over time. However, this is a powerful feedback process that cannot be stopped once it is initiated by a general warming such as that produced by increasing CO_2 concentration.

And, naturally, there are unknown unknowns as well, about which not much can be said except that we know they will develop at some point.

Conclusion

Global climate change connects people across space by its global nature and time from the long CO_2 lifetime. If unabated, it will be felt by future generations well over the next century. Although climate change is one of the foremost issues of our time that needs immediate attention, it is also the manifestation of another significant concern, that of the overuse of the Earth's resources and their near-term exhaustion that may usher us into unknown territory.

Catherine Gautier

See also Alternative Energy Sources; Biosphere; Environmental Carrying Capacity; Environmental Change; Environmental Security; Environmental Treaties, Conventions, and Protocols; Global Environmental and Energy Issues; Global Warming; Greenhouse Gases; Petroleum Economy

Further Readings

ACIA. (2005). *Arctic climate impacts assessment scientific report*. Cambridge, UK: Cambridge University Press.

Gautier, C., & Fellous, J.-L. (Eds.). (2008). *Facing climate change together*. Cambridge, UK: Cambridge University Press.

Solomon S., Qin, D., & Manning, M. (Eds.). (2007). *IPCC fourth assessment report: The physical science basis*. Cambridge, UK: Cambridge University Press.

COAL

See Extractive Industries Sector

COLD WAR

The Cold War, which largely defined global politics in the latter half of the 20th century, was waged on many fronts. The first front, broadly referred to as the East-West confrontation, had two related but not completely identical components. The first and the most important component was the superpower conflict. The United States and the Soviet Union confronted each other globally as leaders of the competing camps, engaged in the nuclear arms race, and competed ideologically as models of modernity for developing nations. The second component of the East-West confrontation was the conflict between the West European alliance, headed by the United States, and the Soviet Union and its East European satellites. Although the East and the West confronted each other militarily in the contest of the two competing military alliances, each camp had to manage its alliance within itself. This two-layered East-West confrontation constituted the central core of the Cold War.

The second front of the Cold War was waged in Asia. China played a unique role, injecting an important element in the structure of the Cold War not only in Asia but also globally. The victory of the communists in China in 1949 expanded the area of the East-West conflict beyond Europe. But the Sino-Soviet conflict that had initially begun as a ideological contest developed into a state-to-state conflict and contributed to the "strategic triangle" in the 1970s with China serving as a pivot between the two superpowers. Furthermore, unlike the East-West conflict in Europe, two hot wars—the Korean War and the Vietnam War—were waged in Asia.

The Third World conflict was the third front of the Cold War. Decolonization of former colonies was placed in the Cold War context in the Third World. The United States and the Soviet Union competed with each other in expanding their influence in the Third World. The Cold War exacerbated the regional conflicts, while it imposed limitations on conflicts so as not to have these conflicts go beyond regions.

Last, the fourth front of the Cold War was fought on the domestic home fronts of each side. The Cold War was not merely confined in international relations, but it spilled over into domestic policies, culture, and popular consciousness.

Stages of the Cold War

The First Stage: 1945–1953

In the first stage, the Grand Alliance during World War II was transformed into the Cold War. Signs of impending East-West conflict emerged immediately after World War II ended. With Joseph Stalin's Bolshoi Theater speech (February 1946), Winston Churchill's "Iron Curtain" Speech (March 1946), and the Truman Doctrine (March 1947), conflict became intense, and differences widened. At the core of this conflict were divergent ideologies and misperceptions that each held about the motivations of the other side. In his Long Telegram (March 1946) and "Mr. X" article in *Foreign Affairs* (July 1947), George Kennan formulated a strategy of containment that became the foundation of U.S. policy toward the Soviet Union throughout the Cold War. But the Cold War did not begin until the Marshall Plan in 1947. Viewing the Marshall Plan as the West's challenge to the Soviet Union, Moscow responded by creating the Cominform in 1947, and Andrei Zhdanov proclaimed that the world was now divided into two hostile camps, socialist and imperialist. From then on, the break was complete, and neither side expected to gain from negotiations. Germany became a focal point of the East-West conflict. Stalin's gamble of the Berlin blockade, countered by the Western airlift in 1948, eventually led to the division of Germany into the Federal Republic Germany (West German) and the German Democratic Republic (East Germany) in 1949. After 1947, Stalin began transforming the East European states into communist satellites, precluding the possibility of "Finlandization" of Eastern Europe. To prevent Soviet expansion into Western Europe, the West formed the North Atlantic Treaty Organization (NATO). The Soviet Union responded by forming the Warsaw Treaty Organization (Warsaw Pact) in 1955, as a reaction not to the formation of the NATO but to the rearmament of West Germany. The East-West conflict thus came to bear military confrontation with nuclear weapons pointed at the other side.

Soviet failure in Germany was soon offset by two major events in 1949. First, the Soviet Union succeeded in detonating the atomic bomb, breaking the U.S. monopoly on nuclear weapons. Second, the Chinese communists succeeded in completing the revolution, establishing the People's Republic of China (PRC). In 1950 Stalin and Mao Zedong concluded a treaty forging an alliance. Although East and West confronted each other in Europe, the focus of the Cold War shifted to Asia. With the tacit approval of Stalin and Mao, Kim Il Sung of North Korea invaded the South, provoking U.S. intervention. The Korean War ended in stalemate, dividing the Korean peninsula into North Korea (Democratic People's Republic of Korea) and South Korea (Republic of Korea) throughout the Cold War and beyond. With the outbreak of the Korean War, the United States committed itself to defending Taiwan, thus preventing the completion of China's unification. Taiwan became a thorny issue between China and the United States.

The Second Stage: 1953–1964

After Stalin's death in 1953, new Kremlin leaders initiated a new foreign policy to ease East-West tension. They ended the Korean War, concluded the Austrian Neutrality Treaty, and normalized relations with West Germany and Japan. Nikita Khrushchev's policy of peaceful coexistence was partly based on the revision of the Stalinist doctrine on the inevitability of war. After having ousted his rival, Georgii Malenkov, Khrushchev appropriated his opponent's thesis that with the advent of the nuclear weapon, it became possible to attain peaceful coexistence with the imperialist camp, although Khrushchev never abandoned the conviction that the socialist system would eventually prevail over the capitalist system.

Khrushchev's de-Stalinization, however, created serious problems within the socialist camp. His secret speech denouncing Stalin's "cult of personality" at the 20th Party Congress in 1956 caused unrest in Poland and Hungary. Although Khrushchev managed to avoid a crisis in Poland by installing national communists in power, he had to send tanks into Hungary to suppress the revolution. From this moment on, East European satellites presented a difficult challenge for the Kremlin in search of methods to maintain its outer empire by propping up a regime that lacked legitimacy. Moscow had to allow the ruling communists to liberalize their domestic policies, but ultimately the maintenance of the outer empire depended on the threat of military intervention.

Khrushchev's secret speech also contributed to the Sino-Soviet split. Mao Zedong made sure that the criticism of the cult of personality would not be extended to the Chinese communists, and he voiced opposition to Khrushchev's peaceful coexistence. Mao created two Taiwan Strait crises by bombarding the offshore islands in 1954–1955 and 1958. Furthermore, against the advice of the Soviet leaders, Mao launched the "Great Leap Forward," an ambitious and irrational economic policy that threw the Chinese economy into utter chaos. The Soviet Union reneged on its commitment to provide China with a sample and the technology of the nuclear weapon and eventually withdrew all its advisers from China. From 1960 on, the Soviet Union and China began to attack each other, using the surrogates of Yugoslavia and Albania, but soon their criticisms became directed at each other.

Although pursuing a policy of peaceful coexistence, however, Khrushchev initiated a series of adventurous policies on his own, challenging the United States and its Western alliance. To prevent East German citizens from escaping into West Germany, Khrushchev issued an ultimatum to the West to conclude a peace treaty with East Germany and hand over the control of Berlin to the East German government. The Berlin crisis eventually led to the construction of the Berlin Wall in 1962, which served as a symbol of the East-West division over Germany and over Berlin.

Khrushchev's contradictory policy was partly based on his confidence and insecurity about Soviet nuclear capabilities. During the 1950s Khrushchev was instrumental in carrying out the "nuclear revolution" in the Soviet military doctrine. Rejecting Stalin's military doctrine that downgraded the importance of nuclear weapons, Khrushchev placed nuclear weapons at the center of the new Soviet military doctrine. But he was fully aware that the Soviet nuclear arsenal was far inferior in quality and quantity to that of the United States. To conceal this inferiority, Khrushchev engaged in disinformation, calculated to magnify the Soviet nuclear capability far more than its reality. For this purpose, Khrushchev exploited the success of the satellite *Sputnik* in 1957 to intimidate the United States.

The problem was it worked too well. This disinformation provoked a sense of crisis in the United States, first, as the fear of the bomber gap, and then of the missile gap, that the United States was lagging behind the Soviet strategic military buildup. Although it was clear to U.S. presidents Dwight D. Eisenhower and, then, John F. Kennedy that the United States was still far ahead, Kennedy used the issue of the missile gap for domestic political purposes and launched a large-scale modernization of U.S. strategic forces.

Kennedy's robust modernization of U.S. strategic forces pushed Khrushchev into a corner. To redress the strategic inferiority, Khrushchev decided to install medium- and intermediate-range nuclear missiles in Cuba in 1962. Kennedy's reaction was swift. He used the naval blockade, euphemistically calling it "quarantine," and demanded the total withdrawal of Soviet missiles from Cuba. It was the closest encounter during the Cold War with a nuclear holocaust. But the crisis was averted by Khrushchev's withdrawal of missiles.

The Cuban Missile Crisis was a major turning point in the Cold War. Both Kennedy and Khrushchev realized the danger of nuclear confrontation. This triggered a series of crisis management measures, including the installation of the "hot line" connecting the White House with the Kremlin. It also contributed to the conclusion of the Partial Test Ban Treaty, the first major arms control agreement between the United States and the Soviet Union. More importantly, both sides tacitly agreed to recognize each other's sphere of influence. From then on the Cold War was fought outside the European core of the conflict.

Khrushchev also turned Soviet attention to the Third World, assisting the national liberation movements, even if they were not led by communists. The Soviet Union insinuated itself into the Middle East conflict, supporting Egypt, Syria, and Iraq. The United States countered by invoking the "Eisenhower doctrine," and militarily intervened in Lebanon. In Africa, the Soviet Union and the United States supported competing political factions in the Congo. At this stage, however, Soviet assistance to national liberation movements, on the whole, proved ineffective.

The Third Stage: 1964–1972

Khrushchev's failure in the Cuban Missile Crisis cost his job, leading to the formation of the Brezhnev-Kosygin collective leadership. Generally, Leonid Brezhnev represented a hard-line policy, allied with the military and hard-liners within the Politburo, while Aleksey Kosygin represented a softer line, supported by the economic elite and the scientific community. Kosygin's attempt at economic reform was offset by Brezhnev's relentless arms buildup.

The most important event that took place during this stage of the Cold War was the Vietnam War. At the Geneva Conference in 1954, the Eisenhower administration under its secretary of state, John Foster Dulles, rejected the general election in Vietnam. Subscribing to the domino theory, which speculated that the fall of Vietnam under communism would lead to the communist takeover in Southeast Asia, and beyond, the United States backed Ngo Dinh Diem in the South. John F. Kennedy escalated the Vietnam conflict by sending the "U.S. military advisers" to South Vietnam to suppress the National Liberation Front (NLF), which was directed by North Vietnam. The assassination of Ngo Dinh Diem in 1962, which was engineered by the military junta and tacitly approved by the United States, destabilized South Vietnam. Lyndon Johnson, who became president after the assassination of Kennedy, decided to escalate the war after the Gulf of Tonkin Incident in 1964. Johnson authorized the bombing of the North and dispatched 47,000 ground troops in May 1965. The "Americanization" of the Vietnam War began, and the United States became stuck deeper in the quagmire of the war.

The Vietnam War delayed a decisive break in Sino-Soviet relations, as both China and the Soviet Union were compelled to help North Vietnam. It also delayed détente between the United States and the Soviet Union. It gave Mao Zedong the luxury of launching the Cultural Revolution. It contributed to the erosion of U.S. prestige and facilitated multipolarization of international relations.

Despite the erosion of U.S. prestige, however, the Soviet Union could not decisively capitalize on the U.S. failure to its advantage. Partly, it was because the Soviet Union itself faced a crisis in its outer empire. In 1968, Czechoslovakia under Alexander Dubcek initiated internal reform under the slogan "socialism with a human face." Invoking the "Brezhnev Doctrine," which justified Soviet military intervention when the Kremlin viewed a security threat in the satellite countries, the Soviets brutally suppressed the Prague spring with military intervention. Soviet military intervention in Czechoslovakia made it impossible for East European countries to engage in gradual reforms within the socialist system.

Another important reason the Soviet Union could not turn the U.S. failure in Vietnam to its benefit was the worsening of Sino-Soviet relations. After the Soviet intervention in Czechoslovakia, Mao considered the Soviet Union not only an ideological but also a security threat. In 1969, the Chinese attacked the Soviet border troops in Zhenbao Island. The border clashes in that year meant that the Sino-Soviet conflict was elevated to a state-to-state conflict.

The Fourth Stage: 1972–1979

During this period of détente, East-West relations made clear progress. West German Chancellor Willy Brandt's Ostpolitik achieved a major reconciliation with the Soviet Union and Eastern Europe, and the relaxation of tension was further facilitated by the Helsinki Accords in 1975. Another important achievement was the arms control negotiations between the Soviet Union and the United States. In 1972, they signed the SALT I. To the Soviet leaders, it was a crowning moment because the Soviet Union was recognized by the United States as a superpower.

The Sino-Soviet border clashes in 1969 provided an opportunity for the United States to explore the possibility of reaching rapprochement with China. On the Chinese side as well, the time was ripe to end the self-imposed isolation of the Cultural Revolution. A meeting between Henry Kissinger and Zhou Enlai prepared the way for U.S. president Richard Nixon to visit China in 1972 and achieve historic rapprochement. It seemed that the United States skillfully maneuvered the strategic triangle to use the China card to extract concessions from the Soviet Union in pressuring North Vietnam to end the war and in concluding SALT I. In the end, however, it was China that benefited from this diplomatic revolution. The PRC was admitted to the United Nations with a permanent seat on the Security Council. Despite its weak economic and military status, China leapt onto the world arena as one of the great powers.

Détente, however, suffered setbacks in the second half of the 1970s. Henry Kissinger treated détente as an extension of containment, while the Soviet leaders celebrated it as the sign of the Soviet Union gaining advantage in correlation of forces. Moscow pursued relentless arms buildup within the constraints imposed by SALT I. In particular, the SS-18s, powerful MIRVed weapons, seem to place the U.S. land-based missiles at risk. The conservative Committee on Present Danger publicized "the window of vulnerability" and campaigned against SALT II, which Brezhnev and U.S. president Jimmy Carter signed in 1978.

Another crisis took place in the Third World. Using the Cuban brigade, the Soviets were expanding their influence in Angola, Ethiopia, and South Yemen. Combined with its extended influence in India and Vietnam, the Americans became alarmed by what Zbigniew Brzezinski, Carter's National Security adviser, called "the arc of crisis." The United States, on the other, faced the Iranian hostage crisis, further diminishing its prestige.

The Soviet invasion of Afghanistan took place in this context. To Carter, it was the last straw. Abandoning détente, Carter invoked the Carter doctrine, justifying U.S. involvement in the Persian Gulf, scuttling SALT II, and boycotting the Moscow Olympics. Détente was over.

The Fifth Stage: 1979–1985

A new Cold War, replacing détente, began under Carter. All the elements of the military buildup—development of MX missiles, Trident SSBNs, B1 bombers, and deployment of Euromissiles to counter the SS-20s—had been initiated under Carter. But the new Cold War was stepped up by successor Ronald Reagan. Under the bellicose rhetoric against the Soviet Union as "the evil empire," he called for "a crusade against communism." He abandoned SALT negotiations altogether, pursued arms buildup, deployed Euromissiles, and proposed the Strategic Defense Initiative (SDI). Having encountered antinuclear movements in the United States and Western Europe, he proposed the Strategic Arms Reduction Talks (START) and demanded the total dismantlement of SS-20s in order to cancel the deployment of Euromissiles. Defense Secretary Caspar Weinberger adopted a strategy to "prevail in nuclear war," and Admiral James Watkins "maritime strategy," by which the United States was to launch preemptive attacks on the vulnerable strategic weapons in the Far East at a time of crisis. The Soviet leadership was alarmed by the new strategic policy adopted by Reagan and concluded that the

United States was preparing to launch a surprise attack on the Soviet Union.

Reagan's military policy was also accompanied by his Third World policy. The United States stepped up its military aid to the mujahedeen in Afghanistan, providing sophisticated Stinger surface-to-air missiles to Afghan rebels.

The Soviet Union was clearly on the defensive. It faced a crisis in Poland, where General Wojciech Jaruzelski had to impose martial law to suppress the widely popular Solidarity movement. In protest, Reagan proposed economic sanction against the Soviet Union. The Soviet Union was further weakened by a transition in leadership. Brezhnev died in 1982, succeeded by ailing Yuri Andropov, who died in 1984, and was succeeded by another ailing leader, Konstantin Chernenko.

The Sixth Stage: 1985–1991

In March 1985, Mikhail Gorbachev succeeded Chernenko as general secretary of the Communist Party and initiated perestroika and glasnost, which, ironically, ended up destroying the Soviet Union. But his contributions to ending the Cold War should not be underestimated. He pursued a bold foreign policy under the new political thinking, which consisted of two key concepts: mutual security and interdependence. He proposed that common human values shared by both socialists and capitalists should take precedence over class struggle. This concept finally broke the fundamental contradiction that lay at the foundation of deterrence and paved the way for the historic START agreement as well as the intermediate-range nuclear forces (INF) agreement.

Nevertheless, his policy often ignored power politics and inherent Soviet strategic interests. His premature withdrawal of troops from Eastern Europe in 1988 deprived the Soviet Union of important leverage to make a smooth transition of East European regimes into noncommunist regimes in the East European revolutions in 1989 that would not threaten the security of the Soviet Union. He allowed the reunification of Germany by West Germany absorbing East Germany and maintaining its membership in the NATO without much protest.

Another important achievement of Gorbachev was rapprochement with China. Gorbachev's visit to Beijing, however, took place when Chinese students demanded democracy in China. When the world media focused on Gorbachev's forthcoming visit to Beijing, the Chinese students exploited this occasion by demanding democratization of the rigid communist rule, staging demonstrations on Tiananmen Square. Deng Xiaoping decided to suppress the democratic movement by the use of force. Zhao Ziyang's moderate course was an alternative that Deng and the Chinese leadership deliberately rejected. The Tiananmen Incident set the clock back in China's democracy, casting a dark shadow on its modernization effort. Gorbachev's achieving rapprochement with Japan was crucial in securing its financial and economic assistance to aid his economic reform, but he failed to make necessary concessions on the territorial question to satisfy overly intransigent Japanese. To compensate his failure in Japan, he rushed to achieve rapprochement with South Korea in return for its promise of economic assistance, thus sacrificing the Soviet leverage with North Korea. North Korea's decision to acquire nuclear weapons originated from its diplomatic isolation.

Gorbachev's foreign policy was at the epicenter of the fundamental restructuring of international relations and the most important factor in ending the Cold War, but it was also accompanied by his inability to turn his diplomatic success into successful reform at home. His perestroika ended up with the collapse of the Soviet Union.

Legacies of the Cold War

The big loser in the Cold War was clearly the Soviet Union, but it does not mean that the United States and its Western alliance won the Cold War. The Cold War militarized the economy, science, and technology in the Western world. Many lives were lost in the Korean War, the Vietnam War, and other conflicts. The United States intervened in Third World conflicts, often supporting brutal dictators in order to combat the spread of communism.

Given the ideological differences between the United States and the Soviet Union, East-West conflict would have been inevitable after the end of World War II. Nonetheless, this does not mean what happened had to happen. Misperceptions of the other side's motivations closed off the better choices that might have been made.

Contemporary conflicts that emerged in the post–Cold War period had their origins in the Cold War period.

Cold War Studies

Since the early 1990s, study of the Cold War has made great strides. First and foremost, with the opening of the archives in the former Soviet Union, Eastern Europe, and China, historians have reexamined and reinterpreted Cold War history on the basis of solid archival evidence that has not been available before. Second, in contrast to the previous Cold War studies that were predominantly U.S. centric, focusing on U.S.-Soviet rivalry mainly based on U.S. archives, historians have expanded their inquiry into the roles played by third parties. Third, historians have expanded the scope of inquiry from narrow diplomatic history into wider areas, including culture and gender issues. The study of the Cold War has increasingly become a study of global social and political developments in the 20th and 21st centuries.

Tsuyoshi Hasegawa

See also Communism, as International Movement; Global Conflict and Security; Global Historical Antecedents; Globalization, Approaches to; Hegemonic Power; Ideologies, Global; Marshall Plan; War

Further Readings

Chen, J. (2001). *Mao's China and the Cold War*. Chapel Hill: University of North Carolina Press.

Cold War International History Project Bulletin. Retrieved October 17, 2011, from http://www .wilsoncenter.org/publication-series/cwihp-bulletin

Craig, C., & Logevall, F. (2009). *America's Cold War: The politics of insecurity*. Cambridge, MA: Belknap Press.

Gaddis, J. L. (2006). *The Cold War: A new history*. New York: Penguin Books.

Garthoff, R. (1994). *Détente and confrontation: American-Soviet relations from Nixon to Reagan* (Rev. ed.). Washington, DC: Brookings Institution.

Hasegawa, T. (Ed.). (2011). *The Cold War in East Asia, 1945–1991*. Washington, DC/Stanford, CA: Wilson Center Press/Stanford University Press.

Leffler, M. (2007). *For the soul of mankind: The United States, the Soviet Union, and the Cold War*. New York: Hill & Wang.

Lüthi, L. M. (2008). *The Sino-Soviet split: Cold War in the communist world*. Princeton, NJ: Princeton University Press.

McMahon, R. J. (1999). *The limits of empire: The United States and Southeast Asia since World War II*. New York: Columbia University Press.

McMahon, R. J. (2003). *The Cold War: A very short introduction*. Oxford, UK: Oxford University Press.

Painter, D. S. (1999). *The Cold War: An international history*. London: Routledge.

Westad, O. A. (2006). *The global Cold War: Third World interventions and the making of our times*. Cambridge, UK: Cambridge University Press.

Westad, O. A., & Leffler, M. (Eds.). (2010). *Cambridge history of the Cold War* (3 vols.). Cambridge, UK: Cambridge University Press.

Zubok, V. (2008). *A failed empire: The Soviet Union in the Cold War from Stalin to Gorbachev*. Chapel Hill: University of North Carolina Press.

COLONIALISM

Colonialism is both a practice and a worldview. As a practice, it involves the domination of a society by settlers from a different society. As a worldview, colonialism is a truly global geopolitical, economic, and cultural doctrine that is rooted in the worldwide expansion of West European capitalism that survived until well after the collapse of most colonial empires.

Historically, colonies in the strict sense of "settlements" had existed long before the advent of global capitalism; the English word *colony* is derived from the ancient Latin term *colonia*, denoting an outpost or settlement. However, colonialism as a principle of imperial statecraft and an effective strategy of capitalist expansion that involved sustained appropriation of the resources of other societies, indeed regions, of the world for the benefit of the colonizing society, backed by an elaborate ideological justificatory apparatus, is a modern, West European invention *par excellence*, emerging from the 15th century onward.

Colonialism involved a combination of several processes, recurring with remarkable consistency across various instances. Some of these were as follows:

- Encounter and repeated/sustained contact between the Western "discoverers" and the rest of the world, typically involving invasion, conquest, strategic genocide, the relegation of local rulers to subservient roles, and, eventually, some form of settlement by West Europeans.
- The surveying and scientific analysis of the geography, resources, peoples, and customs of the colonies, with the explicit intent of facilitating resource extraction and/or unequal exchange through forced trading.
- The imposition of extractive enterprises, such as plantations, mining, and other forms of raw-material-yielding activities, and the deployment of nonfree "native" labor in such enterprises.
- The systematic destruction of indigenous industries to transform the colonies into captive markets for European goods.
- Triangular trade (the hawking of European commodities to Africa, enslaved people to the Americas/the Caribbean, and plantation products to Europe).
- The establishment of modernizationist projects, such as the construction of elaborate transportation and information infrastructures, the introduction of private property in land, specific forms of taxation, and colonial law with the purpose of enabling the extractive and disciplinary apparatus of the colonial administration.
- The forced transfer and circulation of enslaved or indentured labor between colonies, or between regions within the same colony, disrupting culturally articulated modes of interaction between nature and people, and creating buffer populations between the colonizers and the locals.
- Creation of collaborationist/comprador colonial elites, mass educational systems, and public cultures that systematically facilitated the explicit alignment of ideas such as knowledge and progress with Western civilization, thereby producing the illusion of European superiority and the normalization of colonial relations.
- Continuous and systematic framing of colonized populations as the backward, inferior, dehumanized "other" of the enlightened European/White "self," and the use of the discourse of scientific racism to this end.
- In later phases of colonialism, warfare using colonial populations from one colony in armed incursions against other (potential) colonies.
- Prevention of the access of colonial subject populations to Europe.

Because it involved the superimposition of the rule of an alien social order on another, violence inhered in all aspects of colonialism. As Aimé Césaire has pointed out, colonialism allowed the routine practice of all elements of what later came to be decried as Nazi violence within Europe, on non-European populations overseas.

Although colonialism was certainly a total system, for analytical purposes, it may be useful to approach it as a compound effect of three interconnected fields of domination: political-economic, social-institutional, and representational-symbolic. Each of these three fields is considered briefly in the following sections.

Political Economy

Given the tendency within much Western scholarship to view the rise of capitalism as a phenomenon largely rooted in the dynamics of feudalism in Europe, it is difficult to grasp the significance of colonialism in both the emergence of global capitalism and the making of what western Europe is today. Immediately before the colonial period, western Europe was a relatively small, spatially marginal, and economically, not particularly noteworthy appendage on the vast interlocking Afro-Eurasian system of trade. According to the estimates made by economic historian Angus Maddison, between the years 1000 and 1500 (i.e., before the full onset of colonialism), Africa and Asia jointly accounted for 75% to 80% of the total economic output of humankind; by contrast, western Europe's share hovered between 9% and 18%. With the construction of overseas colonial empires centered in western Europe, by 1820, Africa's and Asia's joint economic weight in the world decreased to 64%, while western Europe's grew to approximately 23%.

The 19th century saw two major transformations in the structure of colonial domination of the rest of the world by western Europe that brought further changes in the relative fortunes of these areas. On the one hand, a groundswell of successful independence movements in the first half of the century led, in most cases, by creole elites, in Latin America drastically diminished the colonial holdings of Spain and Portugal. On the other hand, the colonial penetration of South and Southeast Asia mainly under the British, the French, and the Dutch, and Africa by several West European colonizing powers intensified considerably, bringing new areas under direct colonial rule and leading to a scramble among the imperialists to carve out vast areas of these two resource-rich continents. As a result, by 1913, Africa's and Asia's joint share of the world's income diminished to a near-catastrophic level (less than 28%), while western Europe, reaching the zenith of its colonial rule, commanded an unprecedented one third of the total value produced in the world.

How did this happen? Plainly put, colonialism launched two relatively separate processes of global structural transformation. One could be called colonial value transfer, and the other could be called the devastation effect. The first involved the unleashing of economic, legal, and logistical mechanisms that would ensure transfer of natural resources from the colony to the metropole (e.g., deposits of minerals, most prominently silver and gold, plus, along with industrialization in western Europe and North America, other metals such as iron ore). West Europeans also initiated the production of crucial commodities such as cotton, spices, tea, and coffee and exploited slave, hence, by comparison with Europe, strikingly low-cost labor in the colonies. Extremely tilted systems of taxation and manipulation of currency rates further devalued colonial labor vis-à-vis West European capital, and they ensured the uninterrupted flow of value from the colonies to the metropole. The significance of such colonial activities cannot be overstated: For instance, it is estimated that the slave-labor-based plantation product output of the relatively small island of Saint-Domingue (later known as Haiti) alone accounted for two fifths of the entire foreign "trade" revenue of France before the Haitian revolution of 1791.

The second process instituted by colonialism resulting in the relative improvement of the global economic position of western Europe involved the destruction of the social, legal, political, proto-industrial, agrarian, and other technological structures of the colonized society. Imperial warfare; the displacement or murder of significant portions of populations; the destruction of the technologies, circuits of trade, and economic institutions of the indigenous societies; the forced importation of West European products; and the imposition of legal schemes alien to the existing legal practices of the colonized society, such as the enforcement of private property in land where communal access to land was the norm (introduced, to a large measure, in order to be able to impose colonial taxation on rural agricultural production) were disparate elements of colonial policy that worked together to weaken the economic, political, and social capacities of the colony. In a particularly heinous example of intentional destruction, the British East India Company, possessing a monopoly on trading opium grown in India, systematically saturated China—a powerful non-European empire that had successfully resisted colonization—with the highly addictive substance in defiance of the repeated, explicit bans on the importation and sale of opium. The amount of opium smuggled into China by the British increased almost 100 times between the 1730s and the 1830s, resulting in an addiction epidemic of colossal magnitude, effectively undermining the Chinese state's capacity to act. The Chinese reaction was used as an excuse to wage two wars on China by the British Empire in the 19th century, contributing to the effective destruction of the Chinese Empire despite the inability of the Western powers to gain territorial control beyond a few islands and port cities.

In sum, the colonial value transfer and the incapacitation effects jointly enabled western Europe to expand its geopolitical and economic sway during the colonial period and to reap the benefits of dependencies produced during that period well after the end of formal colonial dominance. This process has been widely documented in the scholarly literature on economic, political, technological, financial, and aid dependency. The striking contemporary poverty of some of the erstwhile colonial societies is deeply rooted in these twin political economic processes of colonial value transfer and devastation as practiced throughout the centuries of colonial rule.

Social Institutions

Colonialism also produced social forms in the colonies that were distinct from those in place in Europe, even though in both contexts the driving force was the rise and expansion of capitalism. Within western Europe, the establishment of the rule of private property and the commodification of all social realms involved the production of what Antonio Gramsci called hegemony—a combination of compromise, persuasion, and the judicious use of strategic violence—through the gradual transformations of the educational, legal, religious, political, and cultural institutions as well as the structures of the public and private spheres. Colonial administrations, by contrast, bypassed most of these intervening mechanisms, routinely resorting instead to the use of force and imposing what Ranajit Guha has aptly called dominance without hegemony.

One aspect of colonial dominance without hegemony can be observed in the massive dislocation of human beings—achieved through physical, juridical, legal, or economic force—in the service of the capitalist production process. Colonialism generated three main institutionalized forms of human displacements: first, a large outward movement of soldiers, merchants, requisitioning agents, convicts, prospectors, administrators, farmers, missionaries, teachers, and increasingly from the early 19th century, social scientists from Europe. A second displacement involved the capture and sale of human beings as chattel slaves mainly from Africa to the Americas, the Caribbean, and to a lesser extent from South Asia to colonies in Southeast Asia, until the abolition of slavery in the mid-19th century. Third, colonial empires practiced the forced displacement of bonded and convict labor among various, often geographically distant, regions. Bonded labor was destined to work in plantations, in mines, in the building of infrastructure (such as the use of Chinese coolie labor to build the railways in North America), and in other forms of construction (such as the use of convict labor from South Asia in the early construction of the city of Singapore) throughout the 19th century.

Colonies were also treated by the colonizers as experimental spaces. Many West European ideas regarding policing (including such innovations as fingerprinting and the passport), the law, education, medical science, and technology (including psychiatric experiments) were first carried out on the "disposable" populations of the colonies. Such experimentation was made possible by the introduction of sharp, putatively ontological contrasts between metropole and the colony, the colonizer and the colonized—a worldview that turned on a very specific, hierarchical understanding of the comparative worth of populations, with European White groups at the top and all others below.

"Race" thus takes colonial difference to the level of biopolitics. It grafts moral qualities onto observed phenotypic variation and posits difference as natural and, hence, immutable. Although the 19th-century understanding of the innate, biological nature of racial difference has been proved to be baseless, these ideas have acquired a dynamic of their own and continue to shape social relations in the postcolonial world.

Social relations under colonialism were also deeply gendered and involved explicit sexual exploitation. Most early Europeans arriving in the colonies were men, with specific fantasies about "native" women. Although the sexual and caretaking labor of women of colonized populations—who shared a variety of relationships with European men ranging from slavery to common law marriages—was central to the very reproduction of colonial workforces in an alien world, discussions about native women as represented in colonial records, memoirs, and travelogues are typically trivialized by placing them within a larger discourse of the eroticism, sexual abandon, and general lack of morals in the colonies. Similarly, the construction of native men as effeminate or lesser men sanctioned multiple forms of subjugation—including sexual exploitation—to be imposed on them. Perhaps the most egregious examples of such exploitation involved the forced mating of enslaved men and women with the sole purpose of reproducing the labor force in a context in which marriage and family formation among the enslaved was forbidden. Sexual exploitation of the enslaved by owners was also a widespread practice.

These kinds of dehumanizing diminution of the non-European other eventually produced a range of reactions in colonized societies and a variety of strategies and experiences of anticolonialist struggles. Some, such as the Algerian resistance against the French, have embraced violent insurgency as a necessary and even salutary element of anticolonial liberation. As Frantz Fanon argued, anticolonial violence can provide a catharsis for the colonized in contexts where respect, dignity, and even humanity have been systematically denied to them. Others, such as Mohandas K. Gandhi in his struggle against British rule in India, insisted on the importance of nonviolence as a symbol of the moral superiority of the non-West over the violence of the West. Although these two movements reflect different moments in the history of anticolonial struggles, it is worth noting that both of these instances involved a process of first imagining an "inside," the idea of a nation beyond the reach of the colonizers, and a sense of "we-ness," based on which the political struggle against colonial rule—no matter what form it took—could be launched.

Representations

As Gayatri Spivak argues, representation has two interlocking aspects: *vertreten* (approximately meaning "step in someone's place, represent politically in the formal sense") and *darstellen* (roughly "re-present, place there, portray"). The tortuous history of colonial representations unfolded in a field of power marked by these two dimensions: The former severely limited the contexts in which the colonized subject could represent herself, and the latter ensured that representations were neither natural nor innocent, as they were always implicated by colonial social relations.

As the first voyages of discovery, ostensibly for God, gold, glory, and spices, were being imagined, the question of the potential conversion of natives was very much among the key preoccupations of the early colonizers. However, the practice of colonial expansion, involving such immoral acts as the robbing, slaying, and enslavement of native populations, were clearly at odds with a view of the colonial other as not only human but potentially Christian. As a result, European representations of the colonized soon acquired new configurations that locked the other increasingly into eternal savagery. By the 19th century, it was but a small step to move from this image of the irredeemably savage/heathen to a portrayal of the colonized other as naturally and immutably inadequate—a racially inferior human being.

Over time, as West European colonial rule both deepened and stabilized in various parts of the world, explicit discourses about native customs, drawing on observations and interpretations made by colonial administrators, medical doctors, educators, missionaries, and anthropologists, emerged to form veritable systems of knowledge about other societies. Indeed, European social sciences developed separate branches for studying specific colonized societies within a larger discursive framework—Orientalism, in Edward Said's formulation, portrayed colonized cultures as eternal (hence, fixed in time and unfit for change), feminine, sensual-erotic, weak, inefficient, and essentially inferior. Colonial exhibitions, newspaper accounts, travel narratives, popular novels, guidebooks and vade mecums, operettas, popular songs, photographs, postcards, and personal accounts by former colonial personnel returning from the colonies worked together to stabilize such images of the colonies, justifying their continued subjection for the metropolitan publics.

Since the contemporary world is a direct heir to the colonial-imperial order, especially to the logic of the overseas empires centered in western Europe, the legacy of colonialism in all its dimensions—political-economic, social, and symbolic—has become a integral part of the common history of humankind, explained partly by the powerful presence of colonial patterns of representation in modern West European public cultures. These factors gave colonial ideas a life of their own so that even those areas of the world that had no direct experience of being either the colonized or the colonizer have not escaped the moral, intellectual, and aesthetic impact of colonialism.

József Böröcz and Mahua Sarkar

See also Empires; Enlightenment, The; Global Historical Antecedents; Global Religions, Beliefs, and Ideologies; Hegemonic Power; Humanity, Concepts of; Imperialism; Knowledge Production Systems; Liberalism, Neoliberalism; Myths; Neocolonialism; Otherness

Further Readings

Césaire, A. (1972). *Discourse on colonialism*. New York: Monthly Review Press. (Original work published 1955)

Fanon, F. (2006). *The wretched of the Earth*. New York: Grove Press. (Original work published 1961)

Guha, R. (1997). *Dominance without hegemony. History and power in colonial India*. Cambridge, MA: Harvard University Press.

Loomba, A. (1998). *Colonialism/postcolonialism*. London: Routledge.

Maddison, A. (2010). *Statistics on world population, GDP and per capita GDP: 1–2008 AD*. Retrieved September 22, 2010, from http://www.ggdc.net/MADDISON/Historical_Statistics/horizontal-file_02–2010.xls

Said, E. (1978). *Orientalism*. New York: Vintage.

Spivak, G. C. (1988). "Can the subaltern speak?" In C. Nelson & L. Grossberg (Eds.), *Marxism and the interpretation of culture* (pp. 271–313). London: Macmillan.

COMMUNICATIONS AND TECHNOLOGY, GLOBAL

See Global Communications and Technology

COMMUNICATIVE POWER

Communicative forms and power are inextricably linked, and within global studies, analyses of communication provide a window into how power is created and maintained. Power is both exercised by the use of communicative forms and shaped by the norms of those communicative forms. Ideologies of gender, for example, infuse communicative forms from basic folktales to political documents that create and maintain institutions, communities, and nation-states.

Linguistics is the study of various aspects of language, including the lexicon, grammar, and semantics. The ethnography of communication involves the study of factors such as participants, setting, intentions, norms, and genres of particular speech events. A skilled political agent can use any and all of these factors to support his or her agenda. A United Nations speech will be directed to multiple audiences and will be heard in multiple languages. Samoan leaders at a traditional *fono* will use a specific variety of Samoan that is phonologically different from that used in churches, one that has different norms and expectations. Both English and Bangla speakers can employ specific grammatical forms that de-emphasize responsibility, for example, Ronald Reagan's phrase, "Mistakes were made."

One example of the interplay between the use of specific forms and larger cultural systems is how communicative power is gendered. In the United States, many western European countries, and often elsewhere, the tradition has been that men speak in attention-grabbing monologues in public and women speak in participatory dialogues in private. When women do speak in public, studies have shown that they may be perceived as talking more even when they speak less than their male counterparts. Even when speaking styles are different, if males are in power, female speech is devalued. In the New Guinea village of Gapun, men pride themselves on their calm, deliberative speaking style while the *kros* is a low-status bilingual and obscenity-filled rant used by women. These rants are not without power, however, as the ranter may achieve what she wants by ranting.

Communication forms also have indirect power, socializing individuals into the general ideologies of a society, which of course have implications about who has access to power and resources. The most basic examples of this are stories such as the Anansi the Spider stories of Ghana and the Caribbean; Apache, Salish, and other Native American Coyote tales; and Western fairy tales. These stories are told and retold, taught to children, and where there is literacy, written down on paper and in other formats. Tales such as *Cinderella* are clearly recognizable as being gendered. The heroine sits by the fire, cleans up after her stepfamily, and endures her lot patiently. For this, she is rewarded with a visit from a fairy godmother, given a pretty dress and shoes, and given a handsome but characterless Prince Charming. Different versions have different twists—in American versions, Cinderella's stepfamily gets forgotten; in the French 17th-century Charles Perrault version, Cinderella finds husbands for her stepsisters; and in the haunting German version collected by Jacob Grimm, the stepsisters get their eyes pecked out by pigeons—but all contain similar messages about the role of women in society. Female power here is constructed as being an indirect power related to the authority and wealth of the men in their lives.

The Italian and now widely known children's story *Pinocchio* reflects the construction of male power, particularly the differences between the settled leaders of a community and the outcasts and criminals. Pinocchio, the wooden puppet come to life, does not live up to the expectations of his carpenter father, runs off to hang out with various unsavory folks, turns into a donkey, and finally is saved by the (good) Blue Fairy. This focus on the division between men has echoes today in the discussion of street gangs and the mythic but stigmatized world of young men living apart from society's rule. Young men in the world of Pinocchio and elsewhere are supposed to attach themselves to wise older men, be the soldiers in their battles, and by doing so gain the rights and privileges of older men. These fairy tales discount the power of the men (and with increasing frequency, women) who establish their own groups and set up their own governments such as Garibaldi's Red Shirts or the African National Congress. Revolutionary documents such as the American Declaration of Independence are often designed to create solidarity where little may have existed before as between elite and less privileged White men but do so in part by creating divisions, in this case by ignoring White women, the enslaved, and Native Americans.

All communicative power is linked with other cultural resources, including food, land, market goods, and monetary and social capital. But these resources in turn are always connected to texts that justify and explain, that create commonalities and heighten divisions. All texts are partial, highlighting some aspects of the world while ignoring others. Communicative power is the use of these texts by political actors to entreat, cajole, argue, or force others to accept their points of view, political positions, and rights to resources.

Leila Monaghan

See also Civility; Elites; Feminism; Inequality, Global; Leadership; Linguistic Identities; Power, Global Contexts of; Social Capital

Further Readings

Anansi Masters. (2009). *Anansi masters*. Retrieved August 12, 2010, from http://www.anansimasters .net/e_home.html

Colodi, C. (2005). *The adventures of Pinocchio* (C. D. Chiesa, Trans.). (Original work published 1883). Retrieved August 12, 2010, from http://publicliterature .org/books/adventures_of_pinocchio/xaa.php

Dundes, A. (1982). *Cinderella: A folklore casebook*. New York: Garland.

Duranti, A., & Goodwin, C. (Eds.). (1992). *Rethinking context: Language as an interactive phenomenon*. Cambridge, UK: Cambridge University Press.

Kulick, D. (1993). Speaking as a woman: Structure and gender in domestic arguments in a New Guinea village. *Cultural Anthropology, 8*(4), 510–541.

Reagan, R. (1986). *State of the union address*. Retrieved August 12, 2010, from http://www.american -presidents.com/ronald-reagan/1986-state-of-the -union-address

Tannen, D. (2001). *You just don't understand: Women and men in conversation*. New York: HarperCollins. (Original work published 1990)

Walker, G. (2008). *Coyote stories/poems*. Retrieved August 12, 2010, from http://www.indigenouspeople .net/coyote.htm

Wilce, J. (2006). The grammar of politics and the politics of grammar: From Bangladesh to the United States. In L. Monaghan & J. Goodman (Eds.), *A cultural approach to interpersonal communication* (pp. 134–144). Malden, MA: Blackwell.

COMMUNISM, AS INTERNATIONAL MOVEMENT

Communism is a global social, political, economic, and cultural movement that dominated the 20th century, embracing transnational and international organizations and institutions as cognitive scripts and communist and socialist parties as essential national organizational features and as a part of the international workers' movement. Communism, named first in Etienne Cabet's utopian dream *Travels in Icaria* (1840), has existed as an international movement since the mid-19th century. Whereas political organizations (parties, internationals, and federations) had priority, the communist movement created its proper Lebenswelt with multifold associations for social purposes and/or particular strata of the worker's movement (including youth and women), mass organizations or peripheral special sympathizing, and transnational or regional/continental bodies (e.g., labor unions) on a global scale.

This entry treats communism as an internationally organized movement. Communism as a transnational social movement should be taken into account in parallel, while communism as state or government system is described only marginally. With Marxism (-Leninism) as a main form of thinking and also as a dogmatic ideological corpus, the continually changing history of international communism from 1848 to 1989/1991 can be broken down into eight periods.

1847–1889

The League of Communists (1847–1952) acted as the first internationalist and transnational workers' organization, in accordance with Karl Marx's maxim in the *Communist Manifesto* (1848), "Workers of the world, unite!" yet of a clandestine nature. In 1864 the International Workingmen's Association (IWA), called the First International, was founded (based in London, later New York). Its foundational articulation was the *Inaugural Address of the IWA*, drafted by Marx and adopted by the General Council as its highest body. Strongly influenced by British union leaders, the left pluralistic IWA had also been firmly established in central and southern Europe. Apart from communist, it also amalgamated socialist, mutualistic, anarchist, and unionist intellectual currents (Pierre-Joseph Proudhon, Louis Auguste Blanqui, Mikhail Bakunin, Paul Lafargue, Friedrich Engels, and Friedrich Adolf Sorge). After conducting seven congresses, the IWA was dissolved by the Philadelphia Congress in 1876, mainly as a consequence of the split between Marxists and Anarchists, called "Bakunists," at the Hague Congress of 1872.

The IWA's strategic thrust toward a unification of the European and American workers, on the one hand, and then again the prevention of the use of foreign workers as blacklegs, on the other hand, can be regarded as globally significant and pathbreaking. The long-term objective was the abolishment of classes by eliminating wage through a combined social and political revolution. The Paris Commune (1871) empirically provided the global prototypes of "dictatorship of the proletariat" as a new form of government, comprising direct democracy and a working class organized as political force.

The IWA acted as a school for the practice of global solidarity and equity, as well as a way of life and a normative identity code in times of the global growth of workingmen. Although the possibilities of realizing all of the IWA's goals were something of an illusion, the movement was charged with enthusiasm and an incentive for creativity in bringing these ambitious goals to fruition.

Historically, the IWA corresponded in time to the epoch of the second empire of Napoleon III, ending through the unification of Italy and Germany and the Paris Commune. After that, communism as an international movement acted as a global political and class-based movement, combating anarchist, mutualist, or syndicalist currents. The construction of solid political party organizations on a national scale became the next task to move beyond an International that served in many respects as a discussion club, with National Federations as anticipations of the ideal society, and to assemble a new and strengthened instrument for global change during the next stage of the communist movement.

1889–1914

The IWA's successor during the dramatic acceleration of industrialization and the emergence of classic imperialism and colonialism as new global trends after the 1880s was the Workers' International, also the Second or Socialist International, founded in 1889. Its largely autonomous socialist, or, respectively, social democratic, parties as member sections were initially linked institutionally only by international congresses (nine until 1914). Not until 1900 did an International Socialist Bureau start operating (in Brussels) as a permanent, information-providing body. As a result of the growth of mass parties aiming at the unification of nations in a federal world socialist republic, and due to the personal charisma of political leaders like Jean Jaurès, Wilhelm and Karl Liebknecht, Clara Zetkin, Jules Guesde, Lenin, Trotsky, Julius Martov, Victor and Friedrich Adler, James Keir Hardie, Camille Huysmans, and Karl Kautsky, the Workers' International achieved global status. By 1914, it included 3.5 million members in 29 countries of Europe, South and North America, Asia (Japan), and Australia, among them the Russian Mensheviks and Bolsheviks and the German Social

Democratic Party (SPD, which became the largest party of the Reich), the Jewish Bund, and the British Labour Party, totaling 9 million votes.

Besides a transnational practice of solidarity acts and campaigns—including May Day as a first global mass campaign and movement in both hemispheres—the movement turned to parliamentary elections, and many of their social, political, and economic goals were achieved by parties and labor unions at the ballot box. From 1900 onward, coordinated activities against war, militarism, and colonialism increased. But the expulsion of the Anarchists (1896), who opposed parliamentary and legal means to struggle against capitalism, made visible early fault lines. Besides the original internationalist mainstream, a "centristic," reformist, and nationalist wing was formed (the Bernstein revisionists). One consequence of this was that the rejection of colonialism met reservations on the part of those positive about a socialist colonialism. At the outbreak of World War I, the program adopted at the International Socialist Congress of Stuttgart (1907) to avoid the war at all costs was abandoned, rousing the European nations to global actions to end the war once it had started, and thereby accelerating the decline of capitalist class rule. Instead, most socialist parties in 1914 (with the exception of Russia and Serbia) became war parties themselves, for example, by approving the war credits of their respective national governments (as the German SPD, the Austrian SDAP, or Social Democratic Workers Party, and the Labour Party did).

This downfall, known as *Burgfrieden*, pushed socialist global practice ad absurdum in favor of particularization and nationalism. It disintegrated the Workers' International, marking a break with the humanistic tradition of international brotherhood and world peace as the basic principles of progressive thinking inherited from the 18th-century Enlightenment. After 1914, the globally oriented Marxist and "defeatist" minority movement (Rosa Luxemburg and Lenin, among others) took over the fight against the sterilization of the workers' movement.

1914–1919

The struggle against World War I as Europe's slaughterhouse was of crucial importance for the rise of a new global communist movement. Initially, in consequence of the breakup of the Workers' International and the failure of an antiwar opposition in the belligerent and neutral nations (Bern Conference 1915), the internationalist movement was reduced and isolated. Nevertheless, as a consequence of transnational manifestations of protest (including youth and women), the Swiss conferences of Zimmerwald (1915) and Kiental (1916) were convened, establishing an International Socialist Commission and demanding the reconstruction of a new Workers' International. Still, more than 20 socialist and syndicalist parties and groups took part (especially from eastern Europe and Russia); statements of support were sent by the Socialist Labor Party of America and the International Socialist League of South Africa. Vital actors of these international minority movements were Robert Grimm, Clara Zetkin, Karl Radek, Trotsky, Fritz Platten, Angelica Balabanoff, and Christian Rakovsky.

After several initiatives for international peace conferences failed, the Zimmerwald Movement, weakened by state repression, confined itself to information and mutual support, rather than massive antiwar campaigns. Two transnational undercurrents against "capitalist war" were represented in the Zimmerwald Left: the pacifist Centrists (Giuseppe Modigliani, Alphonse Merrheim, and Georg Ledebour) and the Zimmerwald Left influenced by Lenin and the Bolsheviks.

However, declarations like the Kiental manifesto *To the People Driven to Ruin and Death*, in which joint international mass strikes and the formation of a new Workers' International were called for, had some effect. The successful October Revolution provided a further boost. Journalistic commitment to Soviet Russia increased and preparatory steps were taken, especially by the Russian and eastern European members, to create a new Workers' International.

1919–1943

The Third Communist International, also known as the Comintern (1919–1943), was many things: a contemporary expression of labor internationalism, a concrete option and tool of the Bolsheviks to globalize the October Revolution, a global politico-cultural community, and a vision of Russia as a new Icaria (utopia) leading to European and world revolution. Initially, it directly opposed the League of Nations, the Versailles System, and the creation of new national states. It was also a bureaucratic Babylon undermined by Stalinism as one of the Soviet channels to influence governmental state structures.

The Comintern's transnational institution building comprised 60–80 legal and illegal national communist parties with up to 1.2 million members (not counting the Russian party), each of them maintaining its own multifunctional (political, unionist, cultural, and sociopolitical) network. As a transnational vertical and horizontal network, the multicultural Comintern was not a state organization, although it was never beyond the purview of Russian influence. Its leading figures, like Lenin, Trotsky, Grigory Zinoviev, Nikolai Bukharin, Viacheslav Molotov, Dmitri Manuilsky, and Georgi Dimitrov, were mostly Russians; the Comintern's Executive Committee (ECCI) was directly linked with the Politburo of the Russian Communist Party (CPSU). With Stalinism, Soviet patterns of government like personal networks and patronage prevailed.

Until the mid-1920s, multifold strategic alignments for reaching a world federation of Socialist Soviet Republics beyond European revolutions were the anticolonial national liberation struggle proclaimed by the Baku Congress (1920) and the Bolshevik "affirmative empire" strategy advancing the interests of national minorities in the new national republics and the eastern and southern border states of the Soviet Union. The defeat suffered in Europe (the German revolution in particular) during the postwar crisis of 1918–1923 labeled Russification a structural device of international communism. The Russian Revolution creating a multinational state delayed further disintegration of the tsarist empire but was confined to the periphery, especially to the "East." The administrative bureaucratic caucus of the CPSU shed centralism and bureaucratic rule for the Comintern; the new Stalin and Bukharin paradigm of "Socialism in one country" implied the validity of the national and territorial principle. The VII World Congress (1935) recognized formally—under the banner of *popular fronts*—a withdrawal from the original revolutionary Bolshevik project in the capitalist centers and also of the "Baku objectives." Emancipation of national minorities finally transformed into the punishment of peoples.

Privileged importance was attached to the Moscow-Berlin connections more than to the Moscow-Paris line. German and French communist parties meanwhile developed proper communist milieus based on their traditions and regional leadership cults (Ernst Thälmann, Maurice Thorez, also Harry Pollitt in the UK) in line with the global Stalin cult. The Comintern, giving up its role as a global player (including the endorsement of the modernization of the Soviet Union), was progressively converted into a self-legitimizing sounding board of a new great-Russian statehood to exert pressure and confusion on national governments. In the 1930s, the Comintern was on the verge of being destroyed as a result of the "great purges." Antifascist openings (France, Spain, and Chile) were counteracted by incremental control and repression of radical social movements, individual terror, caudillismo, offhand uprisings (e.g., in Brazil in 1935), or espionage for the Soviet Union in all areas. The repressive transformation gave birth to several intermediate oppositionist communist formations (the left, the "Ultraleft," and the "Right opposition"). Each of them sought a transnational or even international center, like the formation of a Fourth International prepared by the Trotskyist current against revolutionary degeneration and corruption of international communism.

The Stalin-Hitler Pact of August 1939, as a strategic pact for a new world order, signified the end of left solidarity and antifascism. In 1941, this was again overturned by the German attack against the Soviet Union and the communists' engagement in the European resistance, and was supplanted by the Soviet Union's victory in World War II. The Comintern's dissolution in 1943 was meant to assure the western Allies and to offer greater flexibility for the communist parties in a new postwar order.

Although national coalitions with "bourgeois" partners were the main objective in the metropolis, major contradictions were created by the hegemonic pretension of Soviet politics marking global relations with the peripheries and the colonial world. Revolutionary playgrounds and/or alliances with nationalist movements and progressive caudillos (in Latin America) were allowed or tolerated, as anti-imperialist claims dominated until the mid-1930s (e.g., the South African Communist Party and the National Congress). However, Popular Front politics after 1935 marked the acceptance of colonial mandates of the great powers (e.g., the cases of Syria and Lebanon) and the curbing of anticolonial movements. In 1939, anti-imperialism was once again intensified as a result of the Stalin-Hitler Pact against France and Great Britain. In contrast, after the German attack against the Soviet Union in 1941, anticolonial movements were slowed down and subordinated to the interests of the anti-Hitler coalition, and the movements disciplined, sometimes opposing the communist parties to the national liberation movements (e.g., in India and the Arab countries). After 1945, however, extensive support was given to these movements, sometimes to the detriment of the domestic communist parties.

The ideological, organizational, and political alignment to the CPSU and "Marxism-Leninism" ("Bolshevization" and "Stalinization") occurring during Russia's transition to terror and nationalism under Stalin led to a degradation of the original transnational networks, implementing a secret and sealed off bureaucratic structure. The disintegration of social morphology by dissolving the horizontally oriented Comintern networks as "soft skills" (sociopolitical, cultural, and intellectual associations from within, especially the so-called Münzenberg Trust) were sealed off against transnational influences involving secret cadre control and secret services.

The Comintern's institutional charisma, its initially avant-garde practice, was the subject of a global ideological and cultural transfer under Stalinism that mythologized and ritualized language, emblematic symbols, and slogans like *international solidarity, antifascism, danger of war, anti-imperialism*, and *fight for peace* as assets for personal cults of the communist leaders. The rank and file developed an identitarian language with corresponding slogans, symbols, and matrixes for everyday life (folklore and songs), organizing an interchange of delegations and contacts. Despite Stalinism, the attraction of the Soviet Union and the general conviction not only among the communist left to defend her through an antifascist reflex secured a remaining influence of sterilized global party communism and public perception worldwide.

1943–1947

From 1941 on, the communist movement propagated renewed and full engagement in the anti-Hitler resistance of the European nations. Simultaneously, Stalin intended to appease the Allies, who postponed their decision to open up a second front in the West, therewith also protesting Stalin's brutal proceedings in Poland and elsewhere.

Even after the Comintern's formal dissolution, communism as an international movement was not disbanded. During World War II and in the immediate postwar period, it experienced multiple transformations. The dissolution, intended to create better conditions for the communist parties in national coalitions of the European anti-Hitler resistance and to counter the argument that they were "Moscow's agents," was illusory in that Comintern structures for international broadcasting, training courses for resistance, diversion, sabotage, partisan activities, and prisoner of war agitation (*Antifa*, or antifascist, schools) were kept alive, disguised as "research institutes," some of which continued after the global turning point of 1945. In personal continuity with the Comintern, control was taken over by the Department of International Relations of CPSU's Central Committee (first led by Dimitrov and later by Mikhail Suslov), including the allocation of financial resources to the communist parties. Its status was higher than the Foreign Ministry, and it acted as a controlling body for the *Sovinformburo*, the Press Agency TASS, the foreign broadcasting department, the Society for Cultural Relations with Foreign Countries (VOKS), the workers' unions, and the All-Slavic and Antifacist committees.

After the war, partisans and militias were ordered to lay down their arms, and the communist parties participated in rebuilding their respective nations. Initially, the communist movement propagated a Western-style "new democracy," aiming to construct National Fronts including bourgeois parties (France, Belgium), in favor of national unity (Italy) and rejecting revolutionary changes. In Eastern Europe, the transition from military power to civilian governments of people's democracies (Albania, Bulgaria, Hungary, the German Democratic Republic, Romania, Poland, Czechoslovakia, and Yugoslavia) occurred mostly under Soviet occupation. Communicated in soft tones to the world, it was enforced by repressive measures. In 1946, Stalin still refused Yugoslav party leader Tito's offer to create a new international organization. Instead, international communist world or mass organizations for special purposes were considerably enlarged in 1945–1946, among them, besides the International Federation of Trade Unions, ten worldwide youth and women's organizations, solidarity or professional associations for resistance fighters, journalists, students, scientists, lawyers, and media professionals.

With the Marshall Plan and the U.S. declaration of intentions to stay in Europe, Stalin's expectation of a strategic pan-European control under the slogan of democratic antifascist unity in the West failed. With the new bipolar world order a formally democratic intermediate period of the international communist movement was closed.

1947–1956

In September 1947, the Information Bureau of the Communist and Workers' Parties (Cominform or Informbureau) came into existence in total secrecy. Founded in Sklarska-Poreba, Poland, and seated in Belgrade, Yugoslavia (later in Bucharest, Romania), it served as a new coordination body for the international communist movement with ten member parties (the Soviet Union, Czechoslovakia, Poland, Hungary, Romania, Bulgaria, Albania, and until 1948, Yugoslavia). Observer status was granted to communist parties of France, Italy, and the German Democratic Republic. Gradually, a governing apparatus was established according to the statutes, including a secretariat and a chancellery. Besides the CPSU representatives Suslov and Andrei Zhdanov, party leaders like Mátyás Rákosi (Hungary), Władysław Gomulka (Poland), and Klement Gottwald (Czechoslovakia) emerged.

Conceived as an answer to the Marshall Plan and the Truman Doctrine, Cominform marked a caesura in the international communist movement closing the takeover period (e.g., in Czechoslovakia), installing *realsocialism* in east-central, eastern, and southeastern Europe and Asia. Cominform reflected bipolarity and ideological cold war, officially legitimated by the Zhdanov-Doctrine replacing internationalist concepts by the theory of the two world camps in conflict: one anti-imperialist and democratic and the other imperialist and antidemocratic.

Serving as an instrument of Sovietization, the new control and information agency organized conferences and published an international press organ in more than twelve languages (*For Permanent Peace and People's Democracy!*). Beyond the member parties, Cominform practically and ideologically fed the global movement of the Partisans of Peace.

According to Stalin's geopolitical concept, new revolutionary aims were not to be pursued. Instead, the USSR's sphere of influence fixed in Yalta had to be secured, solidifying hegemony over Eastern Europe. Cominform was not only a tool against national particularisms in the East but also should have helped to build a post against the United States and Great Britain in Western Europe formed by the communist parties of France and Italy. This was the reason for Stalin's harsh criticism of Communist Party of France leader Thorez's withdrawal from the government in 1947, and the Russian imposition of a new radical offensive tactics, including the fight against social democracy. Although this influenced radical French workers, it led to the isolation of the Western communist parties.

New dependency mechanisms for the people's democracies were installed against potential centrifugal tendencies, as Czechoslovakia, for example, wanted to attend the Marshall Plan negotiations and Yugoslavia after 1947 not only demanded an equal treatment of the parties but also favored regional Danube and Balkan Federation plans and supported Greek revolutionary partisans, unlike the Soviet Union. The effective Soviet-Yugoslav schism occurred in 1948; the League of Communists of Yugoslavia was expelled from Cominform, and Moscow used this to openly proclaim the liquidation of Titoist and Trotskyist heretics, organizing purges in the Eastern bloc (including trials against László Rajk, Rudolf Slánský, and others).

The period of limited independence and flexibility of the parties was definitely ended by this bloody continuity from Comintern to Cominform; the once proclaimed "national path to socialism" became a distant dream while the international communist movement had become a fiction. During the Cominform period, the ideology of Pan-Slavism superseded internationalism, and the relations between center and periphery became stricter than during the Comintern period.

Meanwhile, the victory of Mao Zedong in the civil war against the nationalist camp with support of the Soviet Union (the Chinese revolution), and the proclamation of the People's Republic of China (1949)—and also (North) Korea in 1948 and Vietnam in 1954—brought a significant expansion and produced a second epoch of international communism, which seemed to confirm the achievement of a communist world domination (also reaching the decolonizing peripheries). But this did not meet the objectives of the internally morbid world communist movement. As part of the logic of economic catch-up development and the goal of reciprocity ("peaceful coexistence"), the formally invoked "world socialist camp" was approaching its final triple disintegration in Soviet Party Marxism, Maoism, and Eurocommunism.

Stalin's regional policy of rallying Europe against the Marshall Plan failed. Moscow's more stringent approach hindered Italian communist party leader Palmiro Togliatti from becoming secretary of the Cominform, which was dissolved after Stalin's death in 1953, shortly after the CPSU's 20th Party Congress in April 1956.

1949–1956

Significantly, despite the dissolution of the Cominform, the international communist world organizations remained active. From 1949 onward, the World Peace Council, inspired by Suslov and founded in 1949, functioned as a central link. It asserted itself in 1950 with the Stockholm Appeal, calling for a proscription of nuclear weapons.

Excluding the World Peace Council (not based on individual memberships), the world organizations counted approximately 15 million members globally. Their strategic orientation emphasized nationalism or neutralism rather than internationalism. The affinity with Soviet politics was disguised by the fact that the Soviet Union did not provide any leading staff members, showing more presence in the working staffs.

The Soviet predominance, resulting in withdrawals and refoundations of noncommunist representation as members of the world organizations, led to global ideological hardening and confrontation. After the 20th CPSU Party Congress in 1956 and the uprising of the East Berlin workers in 1953, during Nikita Khrushchev's attempts at de-Stalinization bearing massive implications for the communist parties, a new field of international communist politics was opened as the Soviet Union switched to again supporting noncommunist nationalist parties and liberation movements, especially in the Third World. In contrast, controversies within the peace movement about the armed suppression of the Hungarian anti-Stalinist Revolution of 1956 had negative consequences. And still more flexible international peripheral peace organizations were created, for families, journalists, and other groups, following a "Matryoshka doll" principle of nesting entities within similar organizational bodies.

The new focus on the peripheries corresponded, in the 1960s, to continental attempts (e.g., in Latin America and Africa), with the Cuban Revolution (1959) as a new stimulus, at creating federations of trade unions or educating Africans and Asians within the Soviet bloc.

Nevertheless, international communism further eroded, from the top downward. Although these were to mirror the vanguard of the movement, dissent and splits had already surfaced at the international conference of the communist parties in 1957, attended by 67 parties, of which 12 ran governments. Mao, for example, opposed the strategy against nuclear war (which, he thought, would lead to global socialism). Even when the process of erosion was blurred by an official confession for unity, in view of Yugoslavia, Albania, and China, Soviet revisionism became the major enemy. In 1960, the 12 parties of the Soviet bloc met—first separately in Budapest, and only later in Moscow where 81 parties conferred. The Chinese delegation openly spoke against the revisionist decisions and anti-Marxist positions of the 20th Party congress and the "Khrushchev Clique." The schism in world communism, signifying the final disbandment of communism as global movement (even in its bureaucratic form), was introduced in 1961 with Albania but remained unmentioned in the Budapest appeal "to the peoples of the world."

1964–1989/1991

Although the Soviet Union geopolitically strived for détente (through the SALT treaties and Helsinki Accords in 1975), the disintegration of communism as an international movement accelerated during the Brezhnev era (1964–1982), stimulated by the official doctrine of limited sovereignty of the people's republics. Initially, this was to be countered through the convocation of international party congresses (Moscow 1965 and 1969 with only 75 attending), but the brutal repression of the Prague Spring, aiming at a "socialism with a human face" by Warsaw Pact forces (1968) followed by "normalization," nurtured multiple scissions and antagonisms of communist parties and régimes, affecting both periphery and core. A larger explosion likely did not take place in 1968 because the Western and Eastern zones of influence were still mutually respected.

In addition to the split of international communism carried out by China, Albania, North Korea, and North Vietnam, opposition and dissent emerged from Yugoslavia and Romania. The emergence of the Euro-communist parties in the West included the high-ranking Italian Communist Party, which abandoned the Soviet model. Eurocommunist and Chinese attempts to boost their influence by creating their own international networks and consortiums were only partly successful (e.g., continental outfits in the Afro-Asiatic regions). In fact, at the Moscow conference in 1969, half of the communist parties became "renegade," as a definitely final document was issued in the name of the international communist movement using rhetorical internationalism. Thereafter, only regional conferences dealing with partial problems were held: Karlovy Vary 1967 and Berlin 1976 on questions of peace and international security.

The World Peace Congress, renamed the World Congress of Peace Forces, remained the hub of international activities supporting socialist and national movements in Asia, Africa, and Latin America. It was central, however, to backing Soviet foreign policy, especially in Africa, when in the 1960s and 1970s technical advisers and soldiers were sent to support liberation movements (but also established dictatorships) especially in the Horn of Africa and Angola. Worldwide anticolonial solidarity movements were organized or supported by the communist parties, such as the Portuguese Communist Party. Locally, however, proxy wars were fought with only short-term goals directed against the influence of China and the United States. In Latin America, also in the 1960s,

Guevarism emerged as an alternative guerrilla tactic outside Soviet influence followed by other intellectual currents and serving as a symbol of identification for the New Left in Europe and the United States. Simultaneously, it was used for global self-legitimation of anti-communist rightwing dictatorships.

Accelerated by the practice of the Polish oppositional and Solidarity movements in the 1970s and 1980s, a decisive blow occurred against the communist power apparatus and the remaining international structures. The Gorbachev years led to the renunciation of the Brezhnev doctrine, in praxis closing the history of the Soviet Union and the erosion process of communism as an international movement. During the celebrations of the 70th anniversary in honor of the October Revolution (Moscow 1987), the Communist Party representatives were pure show. Gorbachev's particular interest was hitherto focused on progressive world opinion, which could support his plans for perestroika, contributing to the implosion of the Soviet Union.

Bernhard H. Bayerlein

See also Capitalism; Cold War; Communist International; Industrialization; Labor; Social Movements; Socialism; Solidarity Movements

Further Readings

Adibekov, G. M., Bayerlein, B. H., & Mothes, J. (Eds.). (2002). *Das Kominform und Stalins neuordnung Europas* [The Cominform and Stalin's reorganization of Europe]. New York: Lang.

Bayerlein, B. H. (2004). Das neue Babylon. Strukturen und Netzwerke der Kommunistischen Internationale und ihre Klassifizierung [The new Babylon: Structures and networks of the Communist International, and their classification]. *Jahrbuch für Historische Kommunismusforschung*, 181–270.

Braunthal, J. (1967). *History of the international* (2 vols.). New York: Praeger.

Broué, P. (1997). *Histoire de l'unternationale Communiste* [History of the Communist International]. Paris: Flammarion.

Brown, A. (2009). *The rise and fall of communism.* London: Bodly Head.

Kernig, D., et al. (Ed.). (1966–1972). *Sowjetsystem und demokratische Gesellschaft. Eine vergleichende*

Enzyklopädie [The Soviet system and democratic society. A comparative encyclopedia]. Freiburg im Breisgau, Germany: Herder.

Kriegel, A. (1964). *Les internationales ouvrières (1864–1943)* [The Workers' Internationals]. Paris: PUF.

Mandel, E. (1993). *The place of Marxism in history.* Atlantic Highlands, NJ: Humanities Press.

Ponomarev, B., et al. (1980–1987). *The international working-class movement. Problems of history and theory* (7 vols.). Moscow: Progress.

Priestland, D. (2009). *The red flag. Communism and the making of the modern world.* London: Lane.

Ulam, A. B. (1992). *The communists: The story of power and lost illusions, 1948–1991.* New York: Scribner.

Van Holthoon, F., & Van der Linden, M. (Eds.). (1988). *Internationalism in the labour movement 1830–1940* (2 vols.). Leiden, Netherlands: Brill.

COMMUNIST INTERNATIONAL

The Communist International was threefold: an organizational part of the workers' movement, a global-politico-cultural intermediate community, and a tool of the Bolsheviks and international communists for globalizing the Russian Revolution as part of what they thought would be the imminent European and world revolution. Reflecting an ambiguous picture of both universal brotherhood and bureaucratic Babylon, the Communist International (known as the Comintern) directly opposed the League of Nations, the Versailles System, and the new world order arrangements in consequence of World War I. It lasted from 1919 to 1943.

As a high number of documents of the Comintern archives have been released, the historical contextualization of the Comintern is now possible, helping to elucidate the following issues: center-periphery relations or (relative) independence of the communist parties, ties with Soviet foreign policy, the stress of Stalinism and terror, and the (dis-)continuity from the Leninist to Stalinist epochs. As a transnational vertical and horizontal institutional network, the Comintern was not a state organization and not completely beyond the purview of states. Not only through its leading figures Grigori Zinoviev and Nikolai Bukharin—both fired by Joseph Stalin—as well as Viacheslav Molotov, Dimitri Manuilsky, and Georgi Dimitrov but also through its Russian delegation, it was linked with the Soviet Politburo.

The Comintern's institution building evolved to a transnational grid, composed by seven world congresses (1919, 1920, 1921, 1922, 1924, 1928, and 1935) and 13 plenary sessions, the governing and auxiliary bodies of its executive committee in Moscow (ECCI), and its apparatus with functional departments, country secretariats, bodies for budget, support, archives, cadre control, regional bodies, foreign bureaus, international mass and sympathizing organizations, and editorial and knowledge bodies (International Lenin School for cadres, the communist universities). Its progressive media empire for mass propaganda comprised publishing houses, journals, press agencies, and broadcasting stations. The Department of International Relations, the Comintern's nerve center, maintained another global network of bureaus.

Despite ideological defeats and increasing bureaucratic rulings, think tanks and specialized bodies for world continents, prior to Stalinization, acted as laboratories for global change and analysis of capitalism integrating ethnic differences. Comintern sections included 60–80 (legal and illegal) communist parties in all core and many (semi) peripheral or (semi)colonial countries, formally obeying Democratic Centralism and maintaining themselves as another multifunctional political, cultural, and sociopolitical network. Total membership (without Russia) decreased dramatically from 900,000 in 1921 to 328,000 in 1934 (excepting Germany), increasing again to an estimated 1,200,000 in 1939. With Germany as epicenter (until 1933) and extending to Asia (China and India) and Latin America, communist movements were also active social movements in Czechoslovakia and Norway, and politically relevant in France and Greece. Nevertheless, these parties still represented a minority in relation to Social Democrats and sometimes Syndicalists. In the 1930s, relative growth was achieved in France, Spain, Chile, and (semi)colonial countries in Asia, Latin America, and Africa, supported by peripheral bodies such as the League Against Imperialism or the Red International of Labour Unions. Beyond these mobilizations, a notable tradition of Marxism as cultural code existed in countries like the United Kingdom, Austria, Poland, and the Netherlands.

Roughly three periods of the Comintern's history are distinguishable. Until the mid 1920s, the World Federation of Socialist Soviet Republics was to be implemented by (a) the stimulation of European revolutions like the German Revolution, the Hungarian, Bavarian Republics of Councils with the Russian-German nexus as central axis; (b) the adoption of an "affirmative empire" strategy for the new territories and border states of the Soviet Union in the East and the South; and (c) the anticolonial national liberation of the (semi)colonial countries proclaimed by the Baku Congress of the Peoples of the East (1920). Whereas partial successes were achieved by the affirmative empire strategy, as a result of the defeats of European revolutions and most of these geostrategic realignments, the Russian Revolution was confined to the periphery. For this, in Europe, Vladimir Lenin and Leon Trotsky pushed against the leftist mainstream of the Comintern (Karl Radek, Bela Kun, Arkadi Maslow, Ruth Fischer, etc.), implementing the more defensive United Front tactics and worker's governments.

In the second period (1925–1934), the new paradigm of "Socialism in one country" provoked strong inner-party battles among transnational strategies. The Comintern lost revolutionary momentum because of the defeat of left oppositionists headed by Trotsky and Zinoviev. Organizational Bolshevization and political Russification adjusted the Comintern to Stalin's power; the defense of the Socialist Fatherland threatened by war became a leitmotif. Combined revolutionary activities were replaced by eclectic or opportunistic practices (the Anglo-Russian Committee 1926), control of social and anticolonial movements, or insurrectional attempts (China 1927). After proclamation of a Third Period (beginning in 1928), Social Democrats were denounced as social fascists while the National Socialists became only a secondary enemy, and defensive programs for national and social liberation alternated with revolutionary plans. In the anticolonial and national struggle, the Comintern supported anti-communist nationalists like the Chinese Kuomintang. Contemporaneously Soviet civilizing missions, exceptionalism, and multicultural coexistence were overshadowed by new Great-Russian strategies implying technical and cultural colonialism.

Beginning in 1934, during the third period, the Comintern partly overcame divisionism but abandoned its part as global player in favor of the integration of the communist parties into nation-states, developing antifascist popular or national fronts (whereas the Soviet Union maintained relations with the Mussolini and Hitler regimes). Left and right oppositionists split definitely, with Trotsky aiming at a Fourth International. The Comintern and Soviet Union intervened in the Spanish Civil War, organizing international brigades. Early victories were counterbalanced by struggles against real and imaginary Trotskyists, a process that accelerated the final defeat of the Republicans. The Soviet Great Terror (1936–1939) put at risk the Comintern's existence as an organization with independent, self-determined foreign relations. Meanwhile, Stalinism led to the liquidation of the transnational, more horizontal cultural networks (the Muenzenberg Empire) and deportations of entire peoples and national minorities. After the Stalin-Hitler Pact was concluded in 1939, the Comintern gave up antifascism; Stalin planned the Comintern's dissolution as a last gift to mollify Hitler, only to reactivate it after the German assault. The cessation of the Comintern's activity in raising combatants for the European Résistance and serving Stalin's policy during World War II (including espionage and individual assassinations) was a concession to the Allies but also a prevention of centrifugal movements by the communist parties after World War II.

In particular for global studies, beyond the study of transnational institutions and cultural transfer, the Comintern's path as a final example of a revolutionary institution acting through global networks to domination by Russian nationalism and Stalinism is an unprecedented basic historical pattern of the 20th century, focusing on the rise and the long erosion of communism.

Bernhard H. Bayerlein

See also Communism, as International Movement; Ideologies, Global; Labor; Revolutions; Socialism; Socialist International; Solidarity Movements

Further Readings

Adler, A. (1980). *Theses, resolutions and manifestos of the first four congresses of the Third International.* London: Atlantic Highlands.

Bayerlein, B. H. (2004). Das neue Babylon. Strukturen und netzwerke der Kommunistischen Internationale und ihre klassifizierung [The new Babylon: Structures and networks of the Communist International, and their classification]. *Jahrbuch für Historische Kommunismusforschung*, 181–270.

Bayerlein, B. H. (2006). *"Der Verräter, Stalin, bist Du!" Vom Ende der linken solidarität: Komintern und kommunistische parteien im Zweiten Weltkrieg 1939–1941* ["The traitor, Stalin, is you!" On the end of left solidarity: Comintern and communist parties in the Second World War, 1939–1941]. Berlin: Aufbau-Verlag.

Broué, P. (1997). *Histoire de l'internationale Communiste* [History of the Communist International]. Paris: Flammarion.

Chase, W. J. (2001). *Enemies within the gates? The Comintern and the Stalinist repression, 1934–1939.* New Haven, CT: Yale University Press.

James, C. L. R. (1993). *World revolution 1917–1936: The rise and fall of the Communist International.* Atlantic Highlands, NJ: Humanities Press.

McDermott, K., & Agnew, J. (1996). *The Comintern. A history of the Comintern from Lenin to Stalin 1919–1943.* Basingstoke, UK: Palgrave Macmillan.

Rees, T., & Thorpe, A. (1998). *International communism and the Communist International 1919–1943.* Manchester, UK: Manchester University Press.

Weber, H. (1966). *Die Kommunistische Internationale Eine Dokumentation* [The Communist International]. Hannover, Germany: Dietz.

COMMUNITARIANISM

The number and importance of transnational problems have increased since World War II compared with the decades that preceded it, especially compared with earlier ages. These include terrorism, environmental degradation, illegal immigration, contagion of financial crises, and transnational mafias. As a social philosophy with a global reach, communitarianism offers an approach to such problems. It builds on the assumption that the definition of the good should be social. It is often contrasted with liberalism, which assumes that each person should individually determine what is right or wrong. Communitarianism stresses that people have responsibilities to the common good (e.g., to the environment) while liberalism stresses that individuals are endowed with rights.

Although communitarianism is a small philosophical school, it has a measure of influence on public dialogues and politics, especially as an antidote to the kind of laissez-faire conservatism championed by Margaret Thatcher in Britain and Ronald Reagan in the United States. Barack Obama gave voice repeatedly to communitarian ideas and ideals in his book *The Audacity of Hope* and during the 2008 presidential election campaign. Obama called his fellow citizens to "ground our politics in the notion of a common good" (2006, p. 9) and suggested that "if we aren't willing to pay a price for our values, if we aren't willing to make some sacrifices in order to realize them, then we should ask ourselves whether we truly believe in them at all" (2006, p. 68). Obama, like other public leaders who have embraced similar themes, especially Tony Blair in the United Kingdom and Bill Clinton in the United States, never used the term *communitarian* itself; many consider it awkward and evoking misleading associations. Although communitarianism has mainly dealt with communities and national societies, more recently, it has also been applied on the international and global levels.

Academic Communitarianism

In the 1980s, communitarian thinking was largely associated with the works of political philosophers such as Charles Taylor, Michael Sandel, and Michael Walzer. (Others sometimes associated with this group include Alasdair MacIntyre, Seyla Benhabib, and Shlomo Avineri.) These scholars called attention to the mistaken assumptions about the nature of the self that liberal philosophy rested on. Liberalism views the human self as divorced from all its moral commitments and communal attachments as a disembodied, atomized self. Communitarians challenged this view, instead depicting the self as "encumbered," "situated," or "contextualized." Although these terms seem to imply that the self is constrained by social order, actually, communitarians—especially sociologists such as Émile Durkheim and Ferdinand Tönnies, who preceded the academic communitarians—stressed that individuals within communities not only flourish as human beings but also are more reasonable and productive than isolated individuals. Only if social pressures to conform rise to excessively high levels do they undermine the development and expression of the self.

Academic communitarians argued that the nature of the political community was misunderstood by liberalism. Whereas liberalism spoke of a neutral framework of rules within which a diversity of commitments to moral values can coexist, communitarians showed that such a "thin" conception of political community was both empirically misleading and normatively dangerous. Good societies, these authors showed, rested on much more than such neutral rules and laws. They relied on shared moral culture, historical identities, and other communal values.

Some academic communitarians argued even more strongly on behalf of particularistic values, suggesting that, indeed, these were the only kind of values that mattered and that it was a philosophical error to posit any universal moral values. Walzer, for instance, initially argued that concrete universal values were philosophically illusory and that societies could be measured only according to their own particularistic moral standards. As the debate over abstract universal values gave way to a discussion about cross-cultural justifications of human rights, the problems of such a relativistic position came to be widely (though not universally) acknowledged. In the 1990s, responsive communitarians developed a position that accommodated both particularistic *and* universal values (see the subsequent discussion).

Oddly, Taylor, Sandel, and Walzer systematically avoided the term *communitarian*. Arguably, this was the case because the term used to be, and to some extent still is, associated with authoritarian communitarianism.

Authoritarian Communitarianism

Authoritarian communitarians, often referred to as "East Asian" communitarians, argue that to maintain social order and harmony, individual rights and political liberties must be curtailed. Some believe in the strong arm of the state (e.g., former Singaporean Prime Minister Lee Kuan Yew and Malaysian head of state Mahathir bin Mohamad), and some in strong social bonds and the voice of the family and community (especially the kind of society Japan had, at least until 1990). Among the arguments made by authoritarian

communitarians is that what the West calls "liberty" actually amounts to social, political, and moral anarchy; that social order is an important value to individuals and to society; that curbing legal and political rights is essential for rapid economic development; and that legal and political rights are a distinctively Western idea that the West uses to impose its own vision on other cultures, which have their own preferred values. Over time, East Asian communitarians moderated many of these claims, made more room for individual rights, and were increasingly eclipsed, at least in the West, by the responsive communitarians.

Responsive Communitarianism

Early in the 1990s, a new group was founded by Amitai Etzioni, working with William A. Galston, which took the communitarian philosophy from a small and somewhat esoteric academic debate and introduced it into public life, and recast its academic content. The group, variously referred to as "responsive" or "political" communitarians, stressed the importance of society and its institutions above and beyond that of the state and the market, the focus of other public philosophies. It emphasized the key role played by socialization, moral culture, and informal social controls rather than state coercion or market pressures. Responsive communitarianism stressed that strong rights presume strong responsibilities, and one should not be neglected in the name of the other. It therefore served as a major correction to authoritarian communitarianism.

The group started by forming a platform, whose drafters included Mary Ann Glendon (law); Thomas Spragens Jr., James Fishkin, and Benjamin Barber (political science); Hans Joas, Phillip Selznick, and Robert Bellah (sociology); and Alan Ehrenhalt (writer). The platform was initially endorsed by more than 150 public leaders from across the political spectrum. The voice the group raised was soon found in numerous op-eds, public lectures, and on TV and radio programs in a considerable number of countries. The group also issued several position papers on subjects such as organ donation, character education, and HIV testing. In the 1990s, several members of this group worked with the New Democrats and advocates of the Third Way in Europe.

The ideas of the group were further developed, both on the public side and on the academic side, in books (especially *The New Golden Rule*) and an intellectual quarterly, *The Responsive Community*. These works stressed that social institutions and public policies should reflect shared values and the common good in addition to aggregation of individual preferences, which themselves are culturally penetrated. Beyond universal principles, communitarianism emphasizes particularism, the special moral obligations people have to their families, kin, communities, and societies.

Responsive communitarians showed that society is best understood not as composed of millions of individuals but as pluralism within unity. That is, subcultures and loyalties to various ethnic and regional communities do not undermine the integrity of society as long as a core of shared values and institutions—such as the Constitution and its Bill of Rights, the democratic way of life, and mutual tolerance—are respected. These observations are of special import today for societies that are in the process of coming to terms with mass immigration (e.g., many European societies and Japan), and in which minorities are questioning their place in the national whole (e.g., Québecois, Scots, Basques, and Iraqi Sunnis).

Communitarians of all brands draw on the core assumption that societies have multiple and incompatible needs. Societies cannot be designed, and public policies should not seek, to maximize one value to the neglect of all others. Responsive communitarianism holds that a good society is based on a carefully crafted balance between liberty and social order, between particularistic (ethnic, racial, and communal) and society-wide values and bonds. In that sense, far from representing a Western model, the communitarian good society combines "Asian" values (also reflecting tenets of Islam and Judaism that stress social responsibilities) with a Western concern for political liberty and individual rights.

Although this model of the good society is applicable to all of them, different societies at different moments in history may be failing in different ways. Hence, they may need to move in *different* directions to approximate the *same* balance. Thus, contemporary East Asian societies require moving toward much greater tolerance for individualism and pluralism, while in the American society, as Robert Bellah and his colleagues along with many others have shown, excessive individualism ought to be reined in.

Communitarianism and International Theory

As noted, transnational problems continue to grow with increasing globalization. Yet, there has been no significant change in the institutions that form policies to deal with these problems. Most transnational problems are still tackled by the Old System—by national governments and the international organizations managed by their representatives and funded by their allotments. But, in most cases, this Old System is has proven inadequate to face these problems. Recent attempts to apply communitarianism to the international level suggest how global institutions may be constructed.

Development occurs on several levels. The formation of transnationally shared norms and values is taking place as a result of transnational moral dialogues. These norms include sharp international condemnation of nations that invade the territory of other nations, which are advised to expect such intervention when genocides are taking place; an increased shared concern for the environment, climate change, and the protection of endangered species; and opposition to landmines, whale hunting, "White slavery," trade in antiquities, and traffic in nuclear arms and the materials from which they can be made. These evolving shared normative understandings provide one important foundation for the formation of new transnational institutions such as the International Criminal Court, the Internet Corporation for Assigned Names and Numbers (ICANN), the Proliferation Security Initiative, and some parts of the World Trade Organization. They also add to as the legitimation of older institutions (especially the United Nations) and actions such as the intervention to stop ethnic cleansing in Kosovo.

These values reflect a synthesis of Western ideas about human rights and liberty and "Eastern" ideas about spiritually, authority, and the common good.

The inchoate global community is also reflected in the rise of many thousands of transitional voluntary associations, social movements (e.g., in support of women rights), and associations of professionals and civil servants serving the same public needs.

Communitarianism points to a growing need for supranational institutions. The term *supranationality* refers to a political body that has acquired some of the attributes usually associated with political communities or nations, such as political loyalty and decision-making power—based not on an aggregate of national decisions or those made by representatives of the member-states but on those made by the supranational bodies themselves.

Amitai Etzioni

See also Civil Society, Global; Civility; Community; Global Village; Identities in Global Societies; Individualism; Publics and Polis, Global; Social Movements; Values

Further Readings

Avineri, S., & de-Shalit, A. (Eds.). (1992). *Communitarianism and individualism.* Oxford, UK: Oxford University Press.

Bell, D. (1993). *Communitarianism and its critics.* Oxford, UK: Clarendon Press.

Bell, D. (2000). *East meets West: Human rights and democracy in East Asia.* Princeton, NJ: Princeton University Press.

Bellah, R., Madsen, R., Sullivan, W. M., Swidler, A., & Tipton, S. (1985). *Habits of the heart.* Berkeley: University of California Press.

Benhabib, S. (1992). *Situating the self: Gender, community, and postmodernism in contemporary ethics.* New York: Routledge.

Communitarian Network. (1991). *The responsive communitarian platform.* Retrieved from http://www .gwu.edu/~ccps/rcplatform.html

Ehrenhalt, A. (1995). *The lost city: Discovering the forgotten virtues of community in the Chicago of the 1950s.* New York: Basic Books.

Etzioni, A. (1996). *The new golden rule.* New York: Basic Books.

Etzioni, A. (2004). *From empire to community.* New York: Palgrave MacMillan.

Frazer, E. (1999). *The problems of communitarian politics.* Oxford, UK: Oxford University Press.

Glendon, M.-A. (1991). *Rights talk: The impoverishment of political discourse.* New York: Free Press.

MacIntyre, A. (1984). *After virtue.* South Bend, IN: University of Notre Dame Press.

Mulhall, S., & Swift, A. (1992). *Liberals and communitarians.* Oxford, UK: Blackwell.

Obama, B. (2006). *The audacity of hope.* New York: Crown/Three Rivers Press.

Sandel, M. (1981). *Liberalism and the limits of justice.* Cambridge, UK: Cambridge University Press.

Selznick, P. (1992). *The moral commonwealth.* Berkeley: University of California Press.

Slaughter, A.-M. (2004). *A new world order.* Princeton, NJ: Princeton University Press.

Taylor, C. (1989). *Sources of the self: The making of the modern identity.* Cambridge, UK: Cambridge University Press.

Walzer, M. (1983). *Spheres of justice.* Oxford, UK: Blackwell.

COMMUNITIES, TRANSNATIONAL

The idea of a transnational community is based on a cross-border network of nonstate actors (or a "beyond border" network, as the prefix *trans* implies). These communities developed within a context of capitalist globalization, itself facilitated by the development of both information technology and relatively affordable and efficient means of international travel. The idea developed out of scholarship in two main areas, the first being transnational labor migration (and associated family reunion migrations) and the second, and more recent, being Internet-facilitated transnational civil society networks, often activist networks, grouped around global(ized) identity politics (including professional identities) or shared political projects.

The defining characteristics of transnational communities—and whether, and how, they differ from past migrant communities or other forms of transnational interaction—have been much debated. From these debates emerges a series of five definitional parameters, conditions of transnational interaction that are necessary for a transnational community to be said to exist: First, its actors must already be constituted as large groups that are identifiable as specific communities having a sociopolitical identity within national contexts—postmigratory minorities or other identity or interest groups. Second, the transnational interactions of these groups are both voluntary and reciprocal. Third, the interactions are associated with a bidirectional (or multidirectional) mobility of persons, resources, and ideas—virtual and/or physical—that is perceived as characteristic or representative of the communities in question. Fourth, the transnational interactions in question add dimensions to the nationally based communities that they otherwise would not have had, whether in cultural, socioeconomic, or political terms. Finally, to be constitutive of transnational communities, the interactions must form patterns that are sustained over time rather than being individualized, idiosyncratic, or temporary phenomena.

Labor Migration

The first understanding of a transnational community—that associated with the effects of labor migration—is clearly tied closely to both ethnic belonging and binational identifications with the idea of "home" as being connected simultaneously with the country of origin and the present and/or past country or countries of residence. It could be argued that such transnationalism existed well before the application of the term *transnational community* to these groups, and indeed it goes back to the beginnings of transnational labor migration, whether within colonial, postcolonial, or noncolonial contexts. A closer look, however, reveals that prior to the 1990s, when the concept of transnational communities started to gain currency in academic circles, transnational migrant communities did not entirely fit the five criteria outlined. Some were perceived as only temporary by both country of origin and host country and, indeed, by the migrants themselves. This is the case, for example, of many so-called postcolonial migrants of the first generation: Algerian workers in France, Turkish workers in Germany, Mexican workers in the United States, or Filipino workers in North America, the Middle East and East and Southeast Asia. Or, if permanently resettled, migrants were not particularly mobile, either physically or culturally, as in the case of interwar British migrants who traveled to Australia on assisted passages, or postwar Greek or Italian migrants. It was generally assumed that postmigratory communities would assimilate into the host society and culture (even if they also inevitably became agents of hybridization or transculturation within the host country). Or the transnational interaction has

not been sustained within a perceivable network of reciprocal transactions adding new dimensions to the communities in question that would not have otherwise occurred within national borders. Or the migration was largely forced, as in the case of refugee migration and slave migration (whether we are speaking of colonial slavery or more modern forms such as trafficking in women for prostitution or domestic service): In this case, the term *diasporic communities*, or simply *diasporas*, is usually more appropriate.

The term *diaspora*, as distinct from the idea of transnational community, comes from a Greek term meaning "scattering of seeds"; it has come to us from the Ancient Greek translation of the Hebrew Bible. Within that context, it referred to the forced exile of Jewish populations across the Middle East, North Africa, and Europe after the Babylonian captivity, from the 6th century BCE. Disaporas are thus displaced populations. The term is commonly used today by populations, notably postcolonial populations, that are not technically refugees but that associate their transnational locations with some idea of involuntary exile as a result of economic hardship or political instability in the home country. Jewish transnationals and overseas Filipino workers, for example, have typically identified as diasporic, resulting from a collective memory of centuries of expulsions, pogroms, and genocides in the first case and of promotion, by a dictatorial state, of worker emigration as a source of revenue in the second. Such collective and historically informed understandings hold even if in more recent decades the migrations and postmigratory communities formed are demonstrably closer to the idea of transnational communities than diasporas per se. More recently, the term *skilled diasporas* has gained currency in academe to refer to an increasingly cosmopolitan population of highly skilled professionals who live outside the country in which they grew up, often changing countries according to job prospects, and who identify with transnational communities at both ethnic and professional levels. Information technology workers from Hong Kong, nurses from the Philippines, or teachers of English as a foreign language from Australia, the United States and the United Kingdom would all be identified as skilled diasporas within such a definition. The use of the term *diaspora* in this way has, however, been criticized as both conceptually and politically inappropriate because it obliterates the original understanding of the term as associated with an experience of exile, even statelessness, that has been far from fully chosen.

The sorts of transnational networks in which transnational postmigratory communities are engaged are multidimensional. They may be financial, less via the traditional migrant-worker remittances (even if such interactions continue) than via trade and business networks as well as international solidarity networks of the sort that were deployed during the 2010 and 2011 earthquakes in Haiti and Chile. They may be cultural, such as transnational cultural or literary festivals, organizations, or networks that may exist at local, national, or regional levels. They may be political, such as the campaign conducted by transnational Filipino communities around the 2010 Philippine presidential and legislative elections. They may also involve increased physical mobility, not only of the postmigratory community in "visits home" and reciprocal visits to the new "home" by members of the family and community left behind, but also of mobile professionals, traders, community activists, or students who form networks during temporary education-, activism-, or business-linked visits or relocations in both directions. All these interactions, however, reside on a shared understanding of ethno-national origins and shared language as a basis for transnational community and, as such, as the key framing mechanism for continued transnational activity.

Shared Identities

The second understanding of transnational communities, as founded in shared identities and/or projects that are not ethno-national or ethno-linguistic in character, begs the question of what the limits are to community. Are all sustained, relatively large-scale, voluntary, and reciprocal transnational interactions around shared interests by individuals and groups who demonstrably have an identity characteristic or political allegiance in common, constitutive of transnational communities? Are all environmentalists, for example, or all human rights activists members of transnational communities? Are all workers in transnational corporations members of transnational communities?

Is self-perception of membership of a community essential?

It can be argued that at the core of this second understanding of transnational community is the idea of not simply an identity but a common project and/or common desire for belonging around which all those who identify with the transnational community converge and that defines the parameters of who is and is not a member of that community. It can also be argued that the more numerous and interlinked the connections (personal, professional, economic, cultural, philosophical, and political), the stronger the common identity or political purpose, and the more widely distributed and sustained over time the core philosophies and activities generated by the community, the more clearly identifiable it is as a transnational community. So that, for example, the Islamic notion of *umma*, or community of believers, constitutes a transnational community of Muslims, or lesbian, gay, bisexual, and transgender (LGBT) constitutes a transnational community of people who recognize themselves as not fitting within heteronormative ideas of gender and sexuality. Or, to take a less identity-focused example, a transnational feminist community of peace activism exists that has grown out of movements such as the Greenham common women's peace camp of the 1980s and Women in Black, which is now a transnational women's peace movement founded in Jerusalem in 1989.

Self-identification with the community as a determinant of its existence seems to be less important, or to become less so over time, in identity-based transnational communities than in purely politically based or professionally based ones. This is because transnational identities contain a presumed intrinsic, inalienable commonality based on shared cultural traits, which has been articulated over time by key political actors on the global stage, usually to some political purpose associated with a need for cohesion. Such identities thus accumulate a symbolic capital that is a stronger determinant of community than personal desire for belonging and that is reminiscent in some ways of the creation of "imagined communities" that has underpinned the construction of modern nations. Thus, the umma can happily exist conceptually as a transnational community even if significant numbers of Muslims in the world do not personally identify with it, or indeed, even follow the Muslim faith (i.e., they identify ethnically or culturally rather than religiously as Muslims). Similarly, the transnational LGBT community is characterized as much by political division and questioning—for a variety of reasons—of the LGBT identity tag by many deemed to be that community's members, as it is by commonality of identity, experience, or goals.

The idea of a community that does not meet with the same level of desire for belonging from all its members may seem paradoxical. All communities, however, from the physicality of the local borough, village, or street to the imagined communities of the nation, have always had their dissenters, marginals, eccentrics, black sheep, and outcasts: Such nonconformist individuals or subgroups are part of what enables the community to define itself and demarcate itself from other communities. There is no reason why such phenomena should not also exist transnationally. The dilemma, in definitional terms, of transnational communities is that the more the community is virtualized rather than existing in the same time-space, the bigger the scale at which the community operates, and the more diverse and numerous its networks, the greater the possibilities of divergence and, thus, the greater the difficulties of border patrol. But then, the idea of the transnational is itself going beyond borders. Hence the paradox: Community implies a stability of the always-knowable and delimitable, whereas the transnational implies a destabilizing of borders and of presumed homogeneity.

Bronwyn Winter

See also Civil Society, Global; Community; Cosmopolitan Identity; Diasporas; Identities in Global Societies; Immigration and Transnationalism; Migration

Further Readings

Al-Ali, N., & Koser, K. (Eds.). (2002). *New approaches to migration? Transnational communities and the transformation of home.* London: Routledge.

Anderson, B. (1983). *Imagined communities: Reflections on the origin and spread of nationalism.* London: Verso.

Castles, S. (2000). *Ethnicity and globalization: From migrant worker to transnational citizen.* London: Sage.

Kaldor, M. (2003). *Global civil society: An answer to war.* Cambridge, UK: Polity Press.

Moghadam, V. M. (2005). *Globalizing women: Transnational feminist networks.* Baltimore: Johns Hopkins University Press.

Portes, A., Guarnizo, L. E., & Landolt, P. (Eds.). (1999). Special issue on transnational communities. *Ethnic and Racial Studies, 22*(2).

Vertovec, S., & Cohen, R. (Eds.). (1999). *Migration, diasporas, and transnationalism.* Cheltenham, UK: Elgar.

COMMUNITY

Community is a fundamental concept of social coherence and political identity around the world. It is also the basis of social division. Most nation-states are characterized by multicultural conflicts among and between communities. In the first decade of the 21st century, approximately 56 armed conflicts between ethnic communities were counted annually in 44 locations around the globe. If the concept of conflict is enlarged to include a variety of severe intercommunal and intracommunal multicultural conflicts, these incidents are found all over the globe, including Australia, Belgium, Britain, Canada, France, India, Israel, Pakistan, and many other countries.

What Is a Community?

Community is a collective of human beings that is more unified around networks of solidarity than a usual social association—to use the classic distinction between community (*Gemeinschaft*) and organization *(Gesellschaft)* made by Ferdinand Tönnies in 1887. Community is characterized by specific culture, identities, practices, organizations, definition of a prime collective good, and boundaries between it and the nation-state as well as various other institutions. Various subcategories of communities are based on their main characteristic: national communities, religious communities, ethnic communities, and so forth. Communities may be nonruling (namely minorities) or ruling communities (often majorities).

After the demolition of some totalistic secular ideologies toward the outset of the 21st century and the inability of any concrete culture to be endorsed in all localities as a global transnational culture, the importance of communities as pillars in globalization is crucial. Communities have been crucial as sources of support, empowerment, and struggles for equality. Accordingly, communities are not merely symptoms of multiculturalism; rather, they generate and empower multiplicity of identities and their practices. A community is a bounded space of power, culture, and practices that may be real, imagined, mythological, or practical.

Importance

Why are communities so important in our life and to democracies? First, they are sources of identity construction, individual empowerment, and identity articulation. Our identities are significantly shaped by communities, which is especially important if communities aspire to maintain cultures and identities that are not endorsed or represented by the nation-state. Second, communities are necessary for generating social struggles for either reallocation of public goods or changing the structure of political power to gain more sociopolitical equality and to resolve issues of discrimination and deprivation. In other words, communities are important for the development and generation of civic societies and civic engagement.

Third, communities are crucial for democratic trust. Communities are the foci of social capital, and once governments crush the autonomy of nonruling communities, more violence may take place. Fourth, communities regard law and justice as flexible and relative terms, and therefore, they enable legal pluralism. In actuality, communities may provide more pluralization to definitions of rights and other collective goods that need to be promoted. Fifth, communities are narrative tellers and are bounded spaces of legal knowledge, legal consciousness, and legal culture. Hence, they might be major structures and agents of particularistic contexts in the conflict over what we think law is and what we think that we know. Communities provide us with prisms for relativity of law and culture, and hence, they are important constitutive sources of multiculturalism.

There is a discrepancy between the sociopolitical significance of communities and the way in which contemporary liberalism and liberal jurisprudence may perceive communities because liberalism often considers itself as a paradigm for promoting individual good as necessarily the prime collective good that is preferable over all other social goods. It might be a justified preference but debatable in democracies when conflicts between democracies and minorities are at stake in the age of globalization.

State and Communal Political Legal Strategies

Communal legal culture as a political culture is neither a complete autonomous entity nor merely the product of state ideology and state power. Legal culture is an interactive set of practices shaped by state hegemony, sometimes against it, and contingent on legal consciousness, social class, and identities, such as ethnicity, nationality, religiosity, gender, and sexual preferences. Therefore, state and communal strategies are interactive and often with fascinating results, for example, states that create or generate communalism to better control or to marginalize some identities that might challenge the state.

On the one extreme, communities may be a source of violence. Violence is not necessarily physical; rather, it is a systematic attempt to eliminate the other's hermeneutics and practices, according to Robert Cover. Communities need not be violent more than any other collectivity. Many communities are heterogeneous and in actuality fight against violence as pacifist communities and feminist communities. Yet, communities can present a few facets of violence as part of their legal culture. One facet of violence may be a means to produce intracommunal hegemony in nonhegemonic communities to enforce communal law, practices, and communal discipline on community members without a national sovereignty. Examples include communal police forces among ultra-Orthodox Jews, tight family control among the Amish, and military undergrounds as among the Catholics in Northern Ireland and the Palestinians in the West Bank and Gaza.

Another facet may be violence targeted against outsiders as a means of exclusion, for example, gated communities and/or closed communities that restrict access by outsiders. An additional facet of violence is a counterhegemonic force to state violence, as part of a larger effort of the community to mobilize resources up to altering the regime power structures through sociopolitical resistance.

Most often, a community will not be violent but a source of legal mobilization; that is, communities may use social activism to affect state law and/or communal law to attain more equality and/or access to public resources. Communities themselves are aware of the issues of boundaries between them and the nation-state and between them and other communities, and therefore, one may sense ambivalence in communities regarding the issue of how to approach state liberal legal ideology. On the one hand, liberal legal ideology may generate more individual rights, even limited group rights, but on the other hand, it also may atomize communities and fragment them into different and contradictory interests of individuals. This contributes to legal mobilization and litigation being prominent types of political participation of communities. The ambivalence of communities toward state law may generate a sociopolitical calculus that uses law as a form of political participation.

Communities often calculate from a sociopolitical point of view how and whether to litigate without acknowledging state legitimacy. It is primarily a dilemma of national minorities, but also it is a dilemma of religious fundamentalists and critical feminists. The dilemma is how to gain justice through the state's legal ideology without granting legitimacy to the state that frames that ideology. Theoretically, it is an oxymoron, which makes the logical conclusion simple: either litigate or delegitimize the state. Practically, minorities are especially ambivalent about that since they are weak and subjugated. The result is a great deal of unexpected political coalitions amid globalization, for example, Taliban women in Afghanistan who seek the assistance of the liberal international community, Palestinian women who seek the help of Zionist feminists, or African American feminists who justify the intervention of the White male-justice police to subdue domestic violence. What seems to observers as analytically mutually exclusive categories is in practice a set of ambivalent communal sociopolitical practice.

Another community consideration involves legality. Community members may consider whether litigation may not construct communal grievances as unlawful and, hence, legalize the communal predicament. This consideration is different from other types of legal strategies since the consideration is whether a community may not stigmatize itself through litigation.

Hence, communities may choose to change or ignore state law instead of pursuing litigation. Such "demobilization" often emerges from lack of trust in state law and may lead to bypassing state law through creation of alternative systems of communal laws like those proposed by religious communities, both directly and through Internet sites and chat rooms. It may lead also to grassroots activities that are remote from state law, or significantly within its shadows, for example, feminists helping battered women, assisting prostitutes, and raising consciousness groups. Many of these activities are performed without mobilizing state law and even protesting against and resisting it.

However, with the development of various discourses about labor rights and human rights in general, along with the responses to neoliberal economic globalization, communities may also deal with legal mobilization that may be directed either at changing the structure of the political power or aiming to alter allocation of public goods and gain more sociopolitical equality. From a communal perspective, mobilization is perceived as an incremental sociopolitical process. On the one hand, there is a communal pressure on the law to attain legal remedies that offer social relief for community members, and on the other hand, there is a perception that accumulation of individual rights will construct a level of actual groups' rights that can challenge the structure of the nation-state and generate more equality for community members.

Mobilization by communities is not isolated but connected with litigation in national and international courts. Often, communities may use globalization in litigation through localization of international law and what may seem to be international norms in domestic courts. On the other hand, through litigation in international venues that is becoming more common after the outset of the 21st century, as in the International Court of Justice (ICJ), the International Criminal Court (ICC), and the European Court of Human Rights (ECHR), communities may externalize internal conflicts, grievances, and issues regarding the abuse of human rights and cases of discrimination to internationalize communal interests and grievances. Hence, constructive rights litigation is a means of globalizing the localities and of localizing the globalities.

Communities may challenge not only state law but also each other through using different legal hermeneutics against each other. In terms of Robert Cover's legal sociology, the conflicts over nomos—in this case, normative world visions of the good society—are not only between state and communities but also between various communities in any given state. Hence, communities are the main carriers of multicultural conflicts in modern multicultural settings, notes Will Kymlicka.

Boundaries Between Communities and States

Violence and the legal mobilization of communities amid globalization bring to the fore the question of boundaries between communities and the nation-state. More specifically, the dilemma is whether liberal values should be preferred and even imposed by the nation-state on nonliberal communities.

What if the community—be it any kind of collectivity (e.g., Christian, Jewish, or Muslim)—is nonliberal and its particularistic obligations that it is imposing on its members may oppose and even contradict liberal obligations of the nation-state amid globalization? Communities should not be excessive in a way that makes them regimes of dictatorship. But, surely not all nonliberal communities are in that undesirable category. Freedom of choice in liberal philosophical and political context is only one type of individual freedom since individuals in nonliberal communities, who are embedded in a different culture, have significant intracommunal personal autonomy and enjoy social support from other community members and from community organizations.

Often, in nonliberal communities the intracommunal freedoms exist, but the choices are different from those in liberal settings as a result of the different culture. Freedom of choice is by itself a matter of choice, because of cultural relativism. Therefore it is problematic and undemocratic to exclude particularistic obligations in nonliberal communities solely based on a relative criterion like freedom of choice.

Nonliberal particularistic obligations have created democratic conflicts between communal cultures and liberal values. For example, religious minorities that have unified clothing as an integral part of their cultures have been challenged by court rulings and legislation in countries like France, where wearing a Muslim headscarf is prohibited. That legalistic prohibition has generated a communal protest against what may be viewed as a state intervention in communal ways of life. What liberals may perceive as an interruption to freedom of choice, community members may conceive as a choice to be viewed differently. Although the state may have an interest in regulating the public sphere, communities may assert that multiculturalism means maintaining diversity of particularistic obligations amid globalization of values and practices that are not necessarily Western. Those who propound this position try to protect the community from losing the diversity of cultural expressions that many of its members wish to preserve in a democratic context. The headscarf controversy in France creates one example of the local resistance to state attempts to enforce a particular cultural express. For some communities around the globe unified clothing is a crucial part of their collective identity, embedded in intergenerational cultures and traditions and marking the self-perceived necessary boundaries between the communities and their surroundings. Because an important part of globalization is dependent on liberal values, the conflicts between liberal values and nonliberal communities have become more prominent since the 1990s.

The possible collisions between nonliberal communities and globalization of liberal values may be around issues of intracommunal ethnic discrimination, subjugation of women, disobedience to state rules, violence, private education, private judging, and systems of punishment. The state is justified in intervening in communal affairs to prevent the abuse of community members if no other choice exists. The legitimate existence of nonliberal communities in Europe, the Middle East, Africa, Asia, Latin America, North America, Australia, and New Zealand, with their own nonliberal cultures, is a challenge to modern public policy and democratic theory.

In particular after the attacks of September 11, 2001, and on the verge of yet additional unfortunate violence, in the midst of a Zeitgeist of terrorism and counterterrorism, the practices of communities and their particularistic obligations may have a lot of significance. Indeed, communities are both, contingently and contextually, a source of suppression and a source of redemption. But we have to recall that community is a premodern and modern concept that may last well after nation-states.

Gad Barzilai

See also Global Justice and Legal Issues; Legal Systems; Multiculturalism; Nation-State; Racial Identity; Religious Identities; Xenophobia

Further Readings

Barzilai, G. (2003, 2005). *Communities and law: Politics and cultures of legal identities.* Ann Arbor: University of Michigan Press.

Bhikhu, P. (n.d.). *A commitment to cultural pluralism.* Retrieved from http://kvc.minbuza.nl/uk/archive/commentary/parekh.html

Bhikhu, P. (n.d.). *What is multiculturalism.* Retrieved from http://www.india-seminar.com/1999/484/484%20parekh.htm

Carnes, J. H. (2000). *Culture, citizenship, and community.* Oxford, UK: Oxford University Press.

Coleman, D. L. (1996). Individualizing justice through multiculturalism: The liberals' dilemma. *Columbia Law Review, 96,* 1093.

Cover, R. (1992). Nomos and narrative. In M. Minow, M. Ryan, & A. Sarat (Eds.), *Narrative, violence, and the law: The essays of Robert Cover.* Ann Arbor: University of Michigan Press.

Crenshaw, K. (1995). Mapping the margins: Intersectionality, identity politics, and violence against women of color. In K. Crenshaw, N. Gotanda, G. Peller, & K. Thomas (Eds.), *Critical race theory* (pp. 357–383). New York: New Press.

Etzioni, A. (1995). *Rights and the common good: The communitarian perspective.* New York: St. Martin's Press.

Gutmann, A. (2003). *Identity in democracy.* Princeton, NJ: Princeton University Press.

Hirschl, R. (2004). Constitutional courts vs. religious fundamentalism: Three Middle Eastern tales. *Texas Law Review, 82,* 1819–1860.

Kymlicka, W. (1995). *Multicultural citizenship: A liberal theory of minority rights.* Oxford, UK: Oxford University Press.

McCann, M. W. (1994). *Rights at work: Pay equity reform and the politics of legal mobilization.* Chicago: University of Chicago Press.

Renteln, A. D. (2004). *The cultural defense.* Oxford, UK: Oxford University Press.

Scheingold, S. (2004). *The politics of rights: Lawyers, public policy, and political change.* Ann Arbor: University of Michigan Press.

Selznick, P. (1992). *The moral commonwealth: Social theory and the promise of community.* Berkeley: University of California Press.

Shachar, A. (2001). *Multicultural jurisdictions: Cultural differences and human rights.* Cambridge, UK: Cambridge University Press.

Tönnies, F. (1887/1957). *Community & society (Gemeinschaft und gesellschaft).* East Lansing: Michigan State University Press.

COMPUTING

Although basic computation devices have a long history, the global impact of computing became widespread in the late 20th century after the development of personal computers, networking, and the Internet. An estimated 1.7 billion people or 26% of the global population had Internet access by 2009 according to the UN agency International Telecommunication Union (ITU). Although Internet access is less prevalent in developing countries, its availability is spreading. Computing and the Internet have revolutionized a variety of areas, including business and the economy, education, and social interactions but have also given rise to new ethical and security concerns.

Development

Basic computation devices have been present throughout much of recorded history, beginning with the abacus. Computing relies on either analog or digital technology to retrieve and communicate data. Analog computing uses a steady stream of data, which is modulated to transmit information, such as the telephone's conversion of audio signals into electronic transmissions and back again. Modern digital computers use a binary numeric system of ones and zeros to manipulate discontinuous groups of data or events. In digital computers, these discontinuous groups are known as bits, which can be on or off and combined in numerous ways to approximate analog events. Digital computers also use Boolean arithmetic and logic.

Although analog computing is still used and generally less expensive, most modern computers rely on digital technology. Analog computing provides greater accuracy, as digital computations are approximations of analog information, but digital systems can store and manipulate information much more easily. Some computing functions, such as the use of the Internet, require a conversion of information from digital to analog and back. The first modern computers were so large they took up entire rooms. The development of microchips and microprocessors increased the speed of computers and allowed for the development of small desktop or personal computers (PCs) and portable laptop computers that made widespread use more practical and affordable.

The development of the Internet was one of the most revolutionary technological advances in computing. Computers linked to the Internet transmit discrete batches of information through the Transmission Control Protocol (TCP) or the Internet Protocol (IP). Each Internet website has a unique address, known as a Uniform Resource Locator (URL). The U.S. Department of the Defense's Advanced Research Projects Agency Network (ARPANET) of the 1960s, which also included links to university research computers, was a key early experiment in networking. Academic, corporate, and commercial use soon followed.

Significant advancements that broadened the Internet's commercial and popular use include the use of peer-to-peer rather than hierarchical networks, the ability to be used with a variety of unspecified applications, the ability of each networked organization to maintain control of its own operations, and the development of local area networks (LANs), hypertext links, and electronic mail (email). Search engines and network browsers such as Google, Bing, Netscape Navigator, Microsoft Internet Explorer, AltaVista, and Lycos facilitate the search for information. Most people access the Internet via subscription Internet Service Providers (ISPs), such as America Online, Netscape, Yahoo! and Microsoft. Many people also subscribe to Internet-based social networking sites such as MySpace, Sonico Facebook, and Hi5.

ISPs provide subscribers with Internet access and an email address through formats such as a dialup modem using telephone wires, a high-speed cable modem, or a wireless broadband router. Wireless technology has made free or fee-based WiFi Internet service available within public places such as libraries or coffee shops, making access more portable and convenient. High-speed mobile broadband access surpassed fixed broadband access in 2008, with an estimated 640 million mobile and 490 million broadband subscribers by 2009. Drawbacks include a lack of guaranteed availability in all locations, expense, and periodic disruptions or periods of slow speed.

Twenty-first-century developments in computing include mobile computing, which gives users the ability to perform computing functions such as word processing, updating a calendar, obtaining directions, checking email, or surfing the Internet on handheld devices. Ubiquitous or smart computing, which is also known as embedded technology, has begun to allow the placement of computers into a person's environment, such as a house, office building, appliance, or automobile. For example, so-called smart buildings or houses using an operating system run by a personal computer can control air temperature or switch lights on or off without the user's immediate interaction. These technologies are in limited use but will most likely spread as costs lower and needed infrastructures are built.

Global Impact

According to statistics gathered by the ITU, Internet access rates have experienced steady annual growth in the 21st century. This growth has produced significant changes in all aspects of global society. Most businesses have reorganized or significantly changed the way they operate, from manufacturing through sales and marketing, based on the use of computing and the Internet.

Corporate use benefits include increased productivity, availability and flexibility through email, access to office files from home or on the go, and Internet-based meetings. Commercial uses include websites that allow businesses to promote themselves; provide directions, store locators, and product catalogs; send coupons; and conduct sales over the Internet. New Internet-only business models emerged, even affecting global financial markets as investors created the so-called dot-com technology stock market bubble in the 1990s. Drawbacks include service and manufacturing interruptions and security breaches of sensitive information. Businesses such as the music and entertainment industries have faced copyright protection battles as a result of the ease of sharing song, television, graphics, images, and other files over the Internet.

The spread of personal computing and the Internet has also opened up new educational and social uses. Educational uses include research on a variety of scholarly or informational topics, the availability of e-books and virtual reference, and online courses. Social uses include social networking, chat rooms, message boards, and online matchmaking sites that allow people to communicate with distant friends and family or people who share a common interest.

The openness of social networking, however, also makes potentially damaging personal or health information open to employers or others. Potential problems include the anonymity of the Internet, making it possible for people to hide their true identities and making some more likely to engage in behavior they otherwise may not have. The Internet has opened new avenues to criminal behavior, such as cyber-stalking, cyber-bullying, and its use by child molesters to contact potential victims.

The global reach and importance of computing and the Internet have raised a series of ethical questions and concerns for those working within computing and related fields. Professional organizations in the field, such as the Association for Computing Machinery (ACM), the Institute of Electrical and Electronics Engineers Computer Society (IEEE-CS), and the Association for Information Technology Professionals (AITP), have all developed codes of ethics for their members. Ethical considerations include quality control of software and other computing requirements where safety is a critical concern, the responsibility to inform the public of technological advances and their use, the responsible social use of such advances, and the responsibility to report observed illegal or unethical behavior by companies or individuals.

Global security concerns include safeguards for personal information and the threats of hacking, cyber-terrorism, and other criminal uses of computing and the Internet. As global wireless communications have increased, the security of personal information, banking records, passwords, health information, credit card numbers, and other sensitive information submitted online has emerged as a major concern. Although technological advances have allowed for the encryption of such information and the use of secured websites, security breaches still occur. Computer systems are vulnerable to hackers and cyber-terrorists who breach security systems or launch viruses through email attachments or other means that disrupt operating systems. The expansion of networking means that a single virus infecting a single computer can quickly spread to become a global threat, shutting down businesses or disrupting critical online systems.

The globalization of Internet use has raised the issues of freedom of speech. There are also arguments over how varying and sometimes contradictory national laws governing freedom of speech should apply in the international reaches of cyberspace and how to enforce such laws if so desired. Global controversies have developed over the decisions of some nations, such as China, to censor Internet content originating in other countries. Computer software filters allow institutions such as schools and libraries to limit access to certain websites such as those containing pornography, leading to public controversies over what should be censored and who should make that determination.

Increased reliance on computers and the Internet throughout much of the developed world has led to concerns over the lack of telecommunications infrastructure and Internet access in many developing countries, known as the digital divide. This is especially noticeable in rural areas. The cost of Internet service is often higher in countries with a lesser infrastructure, such as many African nations. These same nations rank among the lowest in per capita income levels, further limiting access to those few wealthy enough to afford it.

ITU statistics show that although the developing world is experiencing the highest annual rates of Internet access growth, 64% of the population in developed countries has Internet access as compared to only 18% of the population in developing countries as of 2009. The ITU provides an international public-private partnership focusing on developing networks and services and achieving consensus on information and communication technology issues. The ITU uses Internet penetration as a key measure of a nation or region's economic development and global integration.

Marcella Bush Trevino

See also Computing, Personal; Connectedness, Global; Email; Global Communications and Technology; Internet; Knowledge Management Systems; Microsoft; Web 2.0

Further Readings

Aspray, W. (Ed.). (1990). *Computing before computers.* Ames: Iowa State University Press.

Bowyer, K. W. (2001). *Ethics and computing: Living responsibly in a computerized world.* New York: IEEE Press.

Ceruzzi, Paul E. (2003). *A history of modern computing.* Cambridge: MIT Press.

Forester, T., & Morrison, P. (1990). *Computer ethics: Cautionary tales and ethical dilemmas in computing.* Cambridge: MIT Press.

Hunter, R. (2002). *World without secrets: Business, crime, and privacy in the age of ubiquitous computing.* New York: Wiley.

Ifrah, G. (2001). *The universal history of computing: From the abacus to the quantum computer.* New York: Wiley.

Sarkar, T. (2006). *History of wireless.* Hoboken, NJ: Wiley-Interscience.

Sutherland, K. (2000). *Understanding the Internet: A clear guide to Internet technologies.* Boston: Butterworth-Heinemann.

Young, M. L. (1999). *Internet: The complete reference.* Berkeley, CA: Osborne/McGraw-Hill.

Zysman, J., & Newman, A. (2006). *How revolutionary was the digital revolution? National responses, market transitions, and global technology.* Stanford, CA: Stanford Business Books.

COMPUTING, PERSONAL

The personal computing (PC) industry is highly global in its structure and competition. Most of the core innovation occurs at the component and software level in global industries led by major suppliers in the United States, Japan, Korea, Taiwan, Europe, and elsewhere. A global network supports system-level innovation by leading U.S. and Asian PC vendors that focus on incorporating component innovations into new products. At the firm level, high-level architectural design and product management are kept inside by PC makers, while physical development and manufacturing are generally outsourced mostly to Asia. At the national level, higher value analytical, design, and management activities are usually done in the home country of leading firms, whereas the development and manufacturing of the physical product, along with the more routine product and process engineering, are done in Taiwan and China. Finally, the competitive environment is global as well, with non-U.S. vendors dominating many national markets and in some cases competing in international markets as well.

Personal computing devices include desktops, portables (laptop, notebook, and netbook), servers, and various handheld devices such as personal digital assistants (PDAs), smart phones, and portable music players. Worldwide revenues for such products totaled US$282 billion in 2008, including US$107 billion for desktops, US$144 billion for portables, and US$31 billion for PC servers (IDC, 2008).

Unit sales reached 302 million in 2008, including 148 million desktops, 146 million portables and 8 million servers. The United States is the largest single country market with 69 million units shipped, followed by the Asia-Pacific region (excluding Japan) at 77 million units, western Europe at 70 million, Japan at 15 million, and the rest of the world at 71 million (IDC, 2008). The United States is home to the top two PC vendors, HP and Dell, and to Microsoft and Intel, which continue to set the key technology standards for the global industry. It is also home to Apple, which is widely regarded as the most innovative PC company.

Competition in the industry is increasingly global, with non-U.S. firms holding seven of the top ten spots (Table 1) since IBM's PC division was acquired by China's Lenovo in 2004. However, the leaders are all U.S., Japanese, or Asian firms. The only significant European competitor is Fujitsu Siemens, which is partly owned by Japan's Fujitsu and which does not compete outside of Europe. In other regions such as Latin America, South Asia,

Table 1   Worldwide PC Market Share

Company	Market Share (%)	
	Q3 2008	2005
HP	18.9	15.7
Dell	16.4	18.2
Acer	9.7	4.7
Lenovo	8.0	6.3
Toshiba	4.5	3.5
Apple	3.6	2.3
Asustek	2.9	NA
Fujitsu/Fujitsu Siemens	2.4	4.1
Sony	1.8	1.6
Samsung	1.1	NA

Sources: For 2008, adapted from IDC (2008). For 2005, adapted from IDC (2006).

and Africa, there are smaller domestic brands and many nonbranded "white box" makers who compete in single countries or localities.

There are no data on employment in the PC industry, but U.S. employment in the broader computer and peripherals industry totaled 181,700 in January 2009 (Bureau of Labor Statistics, 2009). This compares with 242,000 in 2002 (Bureau of Labor Statistics, 2002), reflecting a decline in U.S. employment in the computer industry that has gone on since the end of the dot-com boom in 2000. Given that PC hardware and peripherals account for at least two thirds of all computer sales, it is reasonable to estimate that a similar share of these employees are in the PC sector. Worldwide, employment in the industry is much larger, as most PC manufacturing is done outside the United States. In China, Taiwanese contract manufacturers employ hundreds of thousands of workers turning out PCs, iPods, peripherals, and other personal computing products.

The PC industry value chain is explained first in this entry. Next, the globalization of the production and product development are discussed. Finally, trends in the industry are considered.

PC Industry Value Chain

The PC industry is a complex network of companies involved in different industry segments, from microprocessors and other components to complete systems to operating systems and applications. These firm activities can be classified using a taxonomy that draws on Treacy and Wiersema (1993). This model groups a company's activities into three areas:

- *Product innovation* includes research and development (R&D), design, market research, and new product introduction.
- *Production/operations* include process engineering, manufacturing, logistics, information technology (IT), finance, and human resources.
- *Customer relations* include marketing, sales, advertising, distribution, customer service, and technical support.

Figure 1 groups the activities in the PC industry value chain under these three categories. As the figure illustrates, PC companies are only a small part of the overall value system. However, they are the focal point of the value system, coordinating the activities of other players in the network.

Globalization of Production

The personal computing industry is highly globalized, with final assembly in dozens of countries, but manufacturing is increasingly concentrated in the Asia-Pacific region (Figure 2). The globalization of the industry was present almost from its inception, as early PC makers sourced several components from Asian suppliers. Later in the 1980s, leading PC makers such as IBM, Compaq, Apple, and Dell set up assembly operations for desktops and notebooks offshore, with production in each major world region.

Subassemblies such as motherboards were sourced from Asian suppliers or U.S. contract manufacturers that located production near the major vendors. Final assembly also has been outsourced or offshored by most PC makers with time-critical production located in regional markets and less time-sensitive build-to-forecast production, mostly in China.

Although desktop production was already offshore, U.S. PC makers only began moving notebook production offshore in the early 1990s. Taiwan developed a homegrown industry focused on notebook PC production, led by a set of original

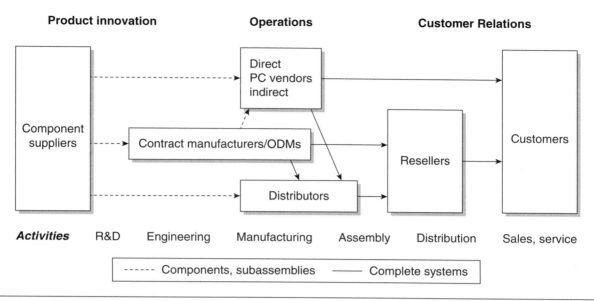

Figure 1   PC industry value chain.

Source: Adapted from Figure 3 of Curry & Kenney (1999).

design manufacturers (ODMs) such as Quanta and Compal, who offer design as well as manufacturing services. These firms developed specialized technical knowledge in issues critical to notebook performance such as battery life, heat dispersion, rugged mechanicals, and electromagnetic interference. Production was in Taiwan or Southeast Asia, but as pricing pressure increased on the ODMs, the Taiwan government removed restrictions on manufacturing notebooks in China, and the Taiwanese notebook industry moved to the Shanghai/Suzhou area of eastern China. By 2009, nearly 93% of the world's notebook computers were produced by Taiwanese firms, almost entirely in China.

Globalization of Product Development

The branded U.S. PC makers did product development in-house and onshore in the 1980s, but in the notebook market they fell behind Japanese competitors, which had superior skills in miniaturizing components and developing small, light, thin products. IBM reacted to Japanese competition by moving notebook development to its IBM Japan subsidiary, which came up with the very successful Thinkpad design. Compaq worked with Japan's Citizen Watch Company to engineer its notebooks and produce key subassemblies. Apple contracted with Sony for one of the original Powerbook models.

In time, however, most PC makers turned to Taiwanese suppliers for manufacturing, partly because of the lower costs as well as to avoid dependence on Japanese partners who could become competitors. The Taiwanese manufacturers gradually developed specialized engineering skills and began to take over product development as well. Companies such as Dell and Gateway entered the notebook market by working with the ODMs on design and development, taking advantage of capabilities nurtured by their competitors.

As for the ODMs, they have been moving engineering work to China along with manufacturing. Their design teams in Taiwan are still responsible for the development of advanced technologies and new products that provide competitive advantage. As these products mature, development of product variations, incremental improvement, and life cycle support has moved to China to be close to manufacturing and to take advantage of lower costs.

Notebook PC makers and ODMs have shifted more new product development activities from Taiwan to China, a trend that is driven both by the cost of engineers in China and the value of proximity to manufacturing. The shift of development to Taiwan and China depends not only on the stage of the activity but also on the maturity of the product. The Taiwan design centers of U.S. PC makers are mostly involved in developing new

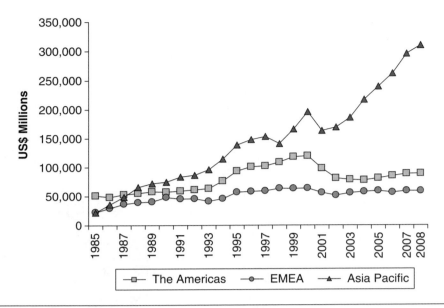

Figure 2   Computer hardware production by region, 1985–2008.

Source: Adapted from Reed Electronics Research (2007).

models based on existing product platforms, while development of new form factors or incorporation of new technologies is still led by teams in the United States. Taiwanese ODMs tend to keep development of new product generations in Taiwan, where they have close working relationships with key component suppliers such as Intel.

The activities that are not being moved from the United States and do not seem likely to move in the near future are R&D, concept design, and product planning. R&D tends to be concentrated in the home country for any company, whether American, Japanese, Korean, or other. Product design benefits from proximity to leading markets where new innovations are first adopted. As long as the United States remains the leading market for innovations in the PC industry and its companies remain leaders in the industry, it is likely that these functions will remain mostly in the United States, at least for U.S. companies.

Trends in the Industry

The PC industry is highly global, with U.S. companies dominating in microprocessors and software, and there is strong competition among U.S. and Asia-Pacific firms in systems and most components. A high concentration of production (final assembly, components manufacturing) is in the Asia-Pacific region. More recently, product development and even design have been migrating to Taiwan, China, and elsewhere in the region.

Although the relationship between U.S. firms and the Asian supply chain has been complementary, the region is also a source of new competition. Lenovo's purchase of the IBM PC business and the growing market share of Acer and Asustek illustrate the growing challenge to U.S. companies from that region. Acer's recent purchase of Gateway and Packard Bell has launched it into third place globally and gives it scale that may add to Asia's continuing challenge to the U.S. computer industry.

Another trend shaping the industry is the increasing convergence of computing with communications and entertainment as all of those technologies become digital. Although convergence in the home moves slowly, divergence in computing devices is proliferating, with new specialized devices being developed such as music and video players, PDAs, Internet access devices, voice recognition, satellite radio, GPS, language translation, and electronic books. The most successful specialized device has been Apple's iPod, which sold much more than 100 million units and spawned other devices aimed at taking music and video off of the computer.

In contrast, a trend toward greater convergence can be viewed in the smart phone market.

Originally aimed at the business market with products such as RIM's BlackBerry and Palm's Treo, the smart phone has entered the consumer market with Apple's introduction of the iPhone. Opening up the iPhone to independent application developers has turned it into a specialized computing device as well as a phone. Other smart phone platforms, such as Windows Mobile, BlackBerry, and Google's Android, are also encouraging application development, changing the landscape in the personal computing industry.

Another innovation is in the low-end netbook category, with small devices capable of simple PC tasks selling for US$200 to US$400. Sales of netbooks took off in 2008 when 10 million units were sold. Aimed originally at the developing country education market, these devices are now sold to consumers in all countries and seem to be cutting into sales of full-fledged laptops. Netbooks also promise to open up new markets of lower income consumers around the world.

With all this innovation around new devices, is it possible that the Wintel-based PC will become obsolete? Google is not only trying to organize all of the information in the world, it is also suggesting that users only need a simple terminal, netbook, or smartphone to access the Internet. In their vision, user applications and user data will reside online, as well as all the information encompassed by the World Wide Web. Even traditional computer companies such as IBM are touting similar concepts such as cloud computing, software-as-a-service, and virtualization (in which the individual PC is no longer a physical device). Will Google and others succeed in this grand vision, or will users and device makers stick stubbornly to their more intelligent stand-alone devices? As of 2009, there does not seem to be a simple answer.

Nearly 300 million PCs were sold in 2008—more than ever before in history—so it looks as if all of the new devices are supplements rather than substitutes for the PC. Instead of converging on one type of device or approach to computing, the market is expanding with a wider array of options than the traditional categories of desktop and laptop. Personal computing is now mobile and increasingly ubiquitous, and those options will likely keep expanding in the future.

Jason Dedrick and Kenneth L. Kraemer

See also Computing; Connectedness, Global; Global Communications and Technology; Information Age; Internet; Knowledge Management Systems; Media, Global; Social Networking; Technology Sector; Web 2.0

Further Readings

Bureau of Labor Statistics. (2002). Retrieved from ftp:// ftp.bls.gov/pub/news.release/History/empsit.01102003 .news

Bureau of Labor Statistics. (2009). Retrieved from ftp:// ftp.bls.gov/pub/suppl/empsit.ceseeb3.txt

Curry, J., & Kenney, M. (1999). Beating the clock: Corporate responses to rapid change in the PC Industry. *California Management Review, 42*(1), 8–36.

Dedrick, J., & Kraemer, K. L. (1998). *Asia's computer challenge: Threat or opportunity for the United States and the world?* New York: Oxford University Press.

Dedrick, J., & Kraemer, K. L. (2005). The impacts of IT on firm and industry structure: The personal computer industry. *California Management Review, 47*(3), 122–142.

Dedrick, J., & Kraemer, K. L. (2006). Is production pulling knowledge work to China? A study of the notebook computer industry. *Computer, 39*(7), 36–42.

International Data Corporation (IDC). (2006). *Worldwide PC market: 4Q05 and 2005 review.* Framingham, MA: International Data Corporation.

International Data Corporation (IDC). (2008, December). *Economic crisis response: Worldwide PC 2008–2012 forecast update.* Framingham, MA: International Data Corporation.

Juliussen, E. (2006). *Worldwide PC market: May, 2006 version.* Arlington Heights, IL: eTForecasts.

Reed Electronics Research. (2007). *Yearbook of world electronics data, 2007.* Surrey, UK: Author.

Treacy, M., & Wiersema, F. (1993, January–February). Customer intimacy and other value disciplines. *Harvard Business Review,* pp. 84–93.

CONFLICT AND CONFLICT RESOLUTION

The term *conflict*, as it relates to global studies, refers to the actual or perceived incompatibility of values, identity, resources, and/or access to power between two or more parties that leads to disagreement. The study of conflict, in general, has been divided into different types, namely, intrapersonal, interpersonal, intragroup, intergroup, and international. International conflict is the type of conflict normally associated with global studies because its effects often have immediate global significance. As the nature of conflict has changed and become more readily globalized, the category "international conflict" has increasingly encompassed interpersonal and intergroup conflicts.

International *conflict resolution* is the academic discipline that examines international conflicts. International conflict resolution is rooted in the larger field of study and practice called conflict resolution. As both a field of study and a practice, conflict resolution is interdisciplinary in nature. It draws from diverse disciplines, such as psychology, sociology, political science, and economics. Despite its name, conflict resolution recognizes that not all conflict needs to be resolved. Instead, it combines theory, research, and practice in an attempt to manage, transform, and/or resolve conflict.

International conflict resolution examines (a) the nature of conflict that has global significance; (b) the various methods available to address international conflict, for example, negotiation, conciliation, mediation, diplomacy, arbitration, adjudication, and reconciliation; and (c) the effects the conflict has (or may have) on parities directly and indirectly involved, including the social, cultural, political, economic, environmental, psychological, and medical effects.

Development of International Conflict Resolution

Resolving conflict and maintaining peace have been employed as long as there has been international conflict. However, international conflict resolution as an academic field of study and practice began to emerge only after World War I (1914–1918). The development of international conflict resolution has four phases. Phase one (1918–1945) is shaped by the experiences of World War I and World War II, traditional wars that were between nation-states or groups of nation-states. Much of this early work on international conflict resolution was done in the field of international relations, which was an emerging subject field in political science. After World War I, the focus was on ways to prevent another world war through security, disarmament,

and international dispute resolution. It was during this period the first international body devoted to international peace was developed, the League of Nations, which was the precursor to the United Nations. With the emergence of World War II (1939–1945), and the subsequent collapse of the League of Nations (1946), it became apparent that there were problems with the early efforts of conflict resolution, and much of the work on conflict resolution came to a standstill.

Phase two (1945–1965) is marked by institutional growth of conflict resolution. Following World War II, the central concern of international conflict resolution was on how to ensure international peace and the protection of human rights within sovereign nation-states. As a result, 50 country representatives came together in 1945 to draw up the Charter of the United Nations, which laid the framework for the United Nations, an international organization with the explicit mandate to work for international peace.

During this phase, the Cold War developed as a rivalry between groups of nations practicing two different ideologies. On the one side, the United States and its allies constituted the Western bloc, which promoted the ideologies of capitalism and democracy. On the other side, the Soviet Union constituted the Eastern bloc, which promoted the ideologies of socialism and communism. In the 1950s and 1960s, at the height of the Cold War, scholars and practitioners in Europe and North America were trying to understand and manage conflict in light of the experience of the end of World War II and the emergence of the Cold War. Academic journals and centers devoted to the study of conflict resolution were established. For example, in the United States, Kenneth Boulding, an economist at the University of Michigan, helped establish *The Journal of Conflict Resolution* and the Centre for Research on Conflict Resolution at the University of Michigan. In Europe, Johan Galtung, a sociologist, founded the *Journal of Peace Research* and the International Peace Research Institute, associated with the University of Oslo, in Norway.

Phase three (1965–1989) is a period of expansion of international conflict resolution. It was a period deeply shaped by the intensification of the Cold War and the threat of a nuclear war. The focus was predominantly on nation-state resolution. In the 1970s and 1980s, there was an increase in undergraduate and graduate programs at universities throughout Europe and North America, the development of departments and institutes of conflict resolution at universities, and the creation of independent organizations dedicated to conflict resolution. It was during this period that various theories and methods associated with international conflict resolution were developed.

The theories and methods of international conflict resolution are based on the fact that conflict is a dynamic process, and as a result, there is not just one theory for examining the nature of conflict on the global scene, nor is there just one method for resolving international conflict. It is more accurate to say that there are numerous theories and methods of international conflict resolution. For example, there is not just one single school of thought or a single theory of international conflict resolution. It would be more accurate to suggest that as a result of the experience of the Cold War, conventional international conflict resolution was an approach to international conflict. It was influenced by three often-converging trends in the Western tradition, namely materialism, political realism, and secularist political philosophy.

Philosophically, materialism refers to preoccupation with the material world, as opposed to intellectual or spiritual concepts, or to the theory that physical matter is all there is. In conflict resolution theory, this meant that if the sociopolitical and socioeconomic causes of the violence could be identified and redeveloped, then subsequent violence might possibly be avoided.

Secularism is an ideology that holds that religious issues should not be the basis of politics, or in the extreme, that religion has no place in public life. Although modern secularists disagree on many matters, they did share the common belief that, with the rise of secular institutions and scientific reasoning, religion would become increasingly irrelevant in people's lives. As a result, international conflict resolution tended to focus on secular matters, with little consideration of religion, and religion has been left out of international conflict resolution theories and processes.

Realist political thought, or *realpolitik*, emphasizes that politics is based on practical concerns rather than theory or ethics. Realism assumes that conflict and power struggles are intrinsic to human nature. It emphasizes the role of the nation-state and assumes that nation-states are motivated by national interests. For states to maintain their power, they must preserve their political autonomy and their territorial integrity, and they must do this through a balance of power. As a result, international conflict resolution theories emphasize the state as the key actor and international diplomacy as the conventional game plan for maintaining stable relations.

International conflict resolution has an intellectual history that not only mirrors the dominant Cold War schools of thought by focusing on statist means of resolving conflict but also reflects the liberal, Western intellectual tradition that emphasizes socioeconomic concerns (materialism), and secularism as means of resolving conflict. As a result, international conflict resolution theory has conventionally focused on economic, social, and political transformation.

Numerous methods can be used for resolving international conflict. Most methodological approaches to conflict resolution recognize that because of the dynamic nature of conflict, conflict progresses through various stages. For example, the stages of conflict tend to include conflict emergence, conflict escalation, stalemate, deescalation, dispute settlement, and postconflict peacebuilding. These stages are nonlinear; the stages can be repeated, or sometimes the conflict primarily moves between two or three stages. Each stage has corresponding strategies to help minimize violence and to help resolve and transform the conflict. For example, conflict emergence occurs when competing interests, needs, or values manifest. To prevent the conflict from escalating, methods such as conciliation, negotiation, mediation, or arbitration would be explored. Conflict emergence may be dealt with through a settlement or resolution, such as a peace accord, or it may be followed by subsequent escalation. The stalemate stage is when neither party in the conflict can win and neither side wants to back down or accept loss. In international conflict, the stalemate stage is often the high point of war, and methods such as peacekeeping or humanitarian intervention are considered. The deescalation stage can be temporary, or it can be part of a broader trend toward settlement or resolution. Here, the intention is to decrease violence and generate agreements among different parties through methods such as negotiation, conciliation, or mediation. The dispute settlement stage is when the underlying causes of the conflict are dealt with. At this stage, peace accords may be negotiated, new constitutions may be developed, and democratic elections are often held. Once a settlement or resolution is agreed to, the conflict moves to a postconflict stage where the focus is on repairing the damage that was done with a long-term goal to work for sustainable peace. A variety of strategies are used at this stage, such as criminal prosecutions, lustrations, truth commissions, amnesty, and reconciliation processes.

The fourth phase (1989–present) of the development of international conflict resolution is rooted in the major shifts in the nature of international conflict post–Cold War. It is at a stage of reconstruction, where responses to the changing nature of international conflict are still being worked out. This phase has been shaped primarily by two interconnected transformations that have occurred after the Cold War and have substantially changed the nature of international conflict. The first transformation is the shift from a bipolar world to a unipolar world. During the Cold War, the conflict between the two major superpowers shaped the global world and essentially created a bipolar world. The focus of international relations was on a balance of power between the two superpowers, which meant that intergroup conflicts were essentially kept in check. However, with the end of the Cold War, the United States emerged as the lone superpower. As a result, a power vacuum was created around much of the world, and there was no superpower to control domestic and global affairs. Under the Cold War, ethnic and religious identities had been held down around the world under the communal mentality of communism. However, with no superpower to keep things in check, regional intergroup conflicts, with ethnic and religious dimensions, began to flourish. Conflicts in the Balkans, Bosnia, and Rwanda are examples of the fallout from the transformation of a bipolar to a unipolar world.

The second transformation that took place after the Cold War is associated with the movement toward economic, political, cultural, and technological global integration associated with globalization. After the Cold War, borders opened, and a ripe arena for global integration of markets, nation-states, cultures, and technologies developed. Little research has been conducted on the relationship between conflict and globalization. What research has been done has focused on the debate regarding the impact of globalization on the world. On one side of the debate, there are advocates of globalization who praise it for its free market capitalist economic system and the technological advancements that have globally integrated the world. On the other side of the debate, there are critics who suggest that globalization is detrimental because the Western homogenization it purports damages culture, and it perpetuates poverty by increasing the gap between the rich and the poor, particularly in the poorer nations of the world.

Current Research

The many changes in the global system after the Cold War have transformed how individuals, societies, and states interact with each other. In terms of international conflict, the number of international conflicts has decreased dramatically, whereas the number of internal, intergroup conflicts has increased. These conflicts tend to be identified as ethnically based conflicts in which the key actors are nonstate actors, and the key issues are based on identity, culture, and/or religious nationalism. Yet the conceptual theories employed by conflict resolution theorists are still rooted in materialist, realist, and secularist assumptions, and they have, for the most part, been unable to address the complexities of contemporary conflict that include ethnic cleansing, civil war, religiously inspired violence, and a global War on Terror. As a result of the changing nature of international conflict, the field of international conflict resolution has slowly responded, and the current work being done tends to focus on four areas.

The first area focuses on strengthening the role of the state. Although this may seem to be rooted in political realism, it does not solely focus on the traditional realist method of conflict resolution of balancing power between states. Instead, it responds to the fact that the newly integrated global order has presented many challenges to the concepts of national sovereignty and state autonomy, and by extension international order. In the post–Cold War era, the number of failed states has risen, and as a result, the field of international conflict resolution has focused on two interrelated areas. The first area looks at how to prevent failed states, and the second area focuses on issues associated with humanitarian intervention. Both areas focus on failed states and the issues of human security; the role of the state in conflict resolution; and the role of international organizations, like the United Nations, and nonstate actors within failed states.

The second area of work being done by contemporary conflict resolution scholars to respond to the changing nature of international conflict focuses on the role of nonstate actors. This area of work directly challenges political realist assumptions in that it is based on the assumption that states are not the only key actors in politics and by extension, in international conflict. It focuses on two areas related to nonstate actors. The first area examines the role of nonstate actors in violence and perpetuating international conflict. It examines terrorist organizations, such as al Qaeda; organized crime networks, such as drug cartels; and rebel groups, such as armed militias and warlords. The second area of work examines the role nonstate actors play in international conflict resolution processes. It focuses on regional, national, and transnational nongovernmental organizations (NGOs), multinational corporations (MNCs), civil society, faith-based actors and organizations, business communities, and media conglomerates.

The third area of work examines the role religion can play in international conflict resolution. This field of study developed out of the resurgence of religious nationalism on the international scene and the rise in religious terrorism. This area of international conflict resolution is referred to as religious conflict resolution. It directly challenges realist-secular assumptions that claim that the role religion would play in the world and in people's lives would decline and that only state actors should be involved in politics and conflict resolution. The basic thesis of religious conflict resolution states that if religion plays a role in people's lives and if it played a role in perpetuating the conflict, then it should at least be accounted for in the resolution. Without accounting for religion, the conflict resolution mechanisms and theories fail to deal with the elements of the conflict and miss the potential peacebuilding sources found in the religions themselves.

The fourth and final area on which international conflict resolution research focuses is technology. The technical revolution has created both challenges and opportunities for international conflict resolution, particularly in terms of globalized information and communication technology in the form of the Internet. Although this area is relatively new in international conflict resolution, scholars and practitioners are primarily focusing on two areas. The first area examines the effects that the advancements in technology have on violence and conflict on a global scale. This research examines the role of the Internet in international affairs, as a medium both for proliferating political propaganda and rhetoric and for establishing transnational networks that support political violence. The second area focuses on how information technology can be used as a peacebuilding tool. This area examines how the technological revolution has changed socialization and communication patterns and the impact this can have in conflict zones. It focuses on how global access to information technology can build transnational peace networks; assist in diplomacy and dialogue; help bridge the growing gap between developed countries and developing countries; and aid government, private-sector organizations, and nonstate actors in conducting their work.

Megan Shore

See also Cold War; Ethnic Identity; Globalization, Phenomenon of; International Relations; Religious Identities; Security; Terrorism; United Nations; War

Further Readings

Boulding, K. E. (1957). Organization and conflict. *Journal of Conflict Resolution, 1*, 122–134.

Cheldelin, S., Druckman, D., & Fast, L. (Eds.). (2008). *Conflict: From analysis to intervention* (2nd ed.). New York: Continuum.

Deutsch, M., Coleman, P. T., & Marcus, E. (Eds.). (2006). *The handbook of conflict resolution: Theory and practice* (2nd ed.). San Francisco: Jossey-Bass.

Galtung, J. (1965). Institutionalized conflict resolution: A theoretical paradigm. *Journal of Peace Research, 2*, 348–397.

Jeong, H.-W. (2000). *Peace and conflict studies*. Aldershot, UK: Ashgate.

Juergensmeyer, M. (2008). *Global rebellion: Religious challenges to the secular state, from Christian militias to al Qaeda*. Berkeley: University of California Press.

Kriesberg, L. (2007). The conflict resolution field: Origins, growth, and differentiation. In I. W. Zartman (Ed.), *Peacemaking in international conflict: Methods and techniques* (pp. 25–51). Washington, DC: United States Institute for Peace.

Kriesberg, L. (2007). *Constructive conflicts: From escalation to resolution* (3rd ed.). Lanham, MD: Rowman & Littlefield.

Paczynska, A. (2008). Globalization. In S. Cheldelin, D. Druckman, & L. Fast (Eds.), *Conflict: From analysis to intervention* (2nd ed., pp. 217–220). New York: Continuum.

Ramsbotham, O., Woodhouse, T., & Miall, H. (2005). *Contemporary conflict resolution: The prevention, management and transformation of deadly conflicts* (2nd ed.). Cambridge, UK: Polity Press.

Shore, M. (2009). *Religion and conflict resolution: Christianity and South Africa's truth and reconciliation commission*. Aldershot, UK: Ashgate.

Stern, P. C., & Druckman, D. (2000). *International conflict resolution after the Cold War*. Washington, DC: National Academy Press.

Conflict and Security, Global

See Global Conflict and Security

Confucianism

Confucianism is a philosophical system of beliefs, sometimes referred to as a religion, instituted in varying degrees during the past 2,500 years throughout several East Asian nations—including China, Japan, South Korea, Taiwan, Hong Kong, Singapore, and Vietnam—and globally through Asian diaspora communities. The English word *Confucianism* can be traced back to 16th-century Jesuit missionaries in China who used the term to describe a tradition that had Chinese philosopher Kung-Fuzi (551–478 BCE) as its figurehead.

Because Confucianism evolved within several different cultures concurrently, there are cultural differences in doctrinal emphases, expressions, and manifestations. However, the positing of humans within correct social and moral structures to achieve harmony remained foundational within the Confucian worldview. Sources often refer to early or classical Confucianism, Neo-Confucianism, and modern New Confucianism, which points to various Confucian practices and philosophies spanning different time periods. Confucianism has had to coexist, although not always without tension, with several other philosophies/religions/belief systems, and it has been integrated into sociopolitical and economic structures of the East Asian countries mentioned. Academics are investigating the prevalence and relevance of Confucianism today as it encounters modernity for the East Asian nations mentioned, their diasporic communities, and the global community.

Early Confucianism

Kung-Fuzi (Confucius) was born in eastern China to an aristocratic family during the Zhou Dynasty. Supposedly founding his own school when he was 22 years old and teaching up to 3,000 students, Confucius is most commonly associated with the *Analects of Confucius (Lunyu)*, a collection of his sayings composed by his followers between 500 and 300 BCE. Confucius believed he was rediscovering and promoting a philosophy that extended back to ancient times. This philosophy tried to explain the roots and develop theories of human relationships to promote collective and individual stability, prosperity, and harmony. Confucius did not make theological assertions about deities, gods/god, or the afterlife, although Confucianists did discuss heaven's relation to humanity. Confucius's work, along with that of his followers Meng-zi (Mencius) (372–289 BCE), author of the *Four Books* (*Si Shu*), and Xun-zi (310?–211? BCE), formed the backbone of classical Confucian thought. Confucius has been referred to as "the sage of all times."

Generally, collective well-being was prioritized over fulfilling individual desires and aspirations. Humans were essentially social creatures who could attain fulfillment by perfecting their individual and social moral natures, which was a self-realizing process. Confucian scholars debated the essence of human nature, whether it was inherently good and moral (Mencius) or not (Xunzi), and whether all individuals had the potential to reach sagehood. They stressed several values believed to be unchanging in natural laws and essential in forming social bonds: humaneness/humanity/compassion (*ren*), ritual/propriety/etiquette (*li*), righteousness/moral sense (*yi*), wisdom (*zhi*), and faithfulness/honesty/heart (*xin*). In addition, the Way (*dao*), virtue (*de*), filial piety/love for the family (*hsiao*), loyalty (*chung*), reciprocity, empathy (*shu*), and courage (*yung*) were central. Each of these concepts tended to be broadly interpreted, encompassing numerous aspects and forms.

Within the Confucian worldview, a ranked pattern of society was visible—of rulers over subjects, parents over children, and husbands over wives. Observing these clearly defined hierarchical relationships, which could include the deceased, and one's duties maintained social, and therefore divine, harmony. In general, subordinates were expected to respect their superiors, and Mencius asserted that those of "higher order" were to protect those below, displaying "benevolent hegemony"/humane government (*ren sheng*) along with socially and morally exemplary behavior. Confucianists believed that this true moral virtue of the rulers could effectively govern and maintain order. Emperors were said to be "Sons of Heaven" (*tien tzu*) and were expected to uphold the "Mandate of Heaven." Proper conduct, morality, virtue, and ethics, along with each individual's fear of "loss of face" or shame, would necessarily ensure obedience to authorities. That said, mass uprisings against particular governments have occurred in Vietnam and China on the basis that rulers were not acting benevolently or virtuously.

Confucianism has experienced waves of popularity, imperial support, and institutionalization throughout its history. Where China's Qin Dynasty (221–206 BCE) saw the persecution of Confucian scholars, Confucianism served as the state and educational systems' intellectual basis during the subsequent Han Dynasty (206 BCE–220 CE). Several Confucian schools emerged, classic texts were annotated, and the Grand Academy established; Confucianist thought disseminated through all levels of Chinese society. Confucianism was then transported to other East Asian nations during China's Wei-Jin dynasties (220–420). Entering Korea from China in the 4th century (when Buddhism was also introduced to Korea), Confucianism

provided tools for government administration and academic and artistic development. Korea's National Academy was established in 372 CE, and Confucian studies were established during the Silla Kingdom (365–965). As in China, Korean officials emphasized social structures, obligations, and harmony. The *Analects* were brought to Japan possibly around 400 CE by a Korean scholar, and 200 years later, the nation witnessed the incorporation of Confucian ideas into its constitution. China had meanwhile introduced a formal civil service examination system, which tested candidates on their writing skills and on their knowledge of Confucian classics and philosophy.

Confucian Renaissance

Confucianism was revived during China's Song Dynasty (960–1279) and is referred to as a renaissance of Neo-Confucianism. The "cultivation of the gentleman" (*junzi*) became an important theme, and Confucius and Mencius were, as the prime fulfillers of the potentiality of human nature, iconic sage-gentlemen. Chinese aristocratic education, heavily imbued with Confucianist doctrine, was thought to cultivate appropriate behavior, leadership skills, and morality. Sagehood was therefore realized through both study and a conscious process of self-cultivation. Moreover, the pursuit of "gentleman-ness" was to be aligned to principles of heaven eventually culminating in the unity of heaven and humanity. Aristocratic education, with the ultimate goal of *ren*, involved learning in six arts: rites, music, archery, charioteering, writing, and arithmetic. Important rites of passage included those of adulthood, marriage, mourning, and burial, and ancestral veneration became widely practiced as a family ritual at all social levels. The elite literati class that emerged from state educational practices was powerful politically and socially, but social class was not hereditary, nor was social stratification ultimately fixed in Chinese society.

Up until the end of China's Qing Dynasty (1644–1911), the Confucian "canon" was expanded on; civil servants were increasingly recruited through the examination system; and several new movements, schools, shrines, and trends of Neo-Confucian thought were instituted. This occurred alongside (although often in contention with)

Buddhism, Daoism, geomancy, Mohism, and other local religious practices and philosophies, with elements of different belief systems sometimes being practiced together or being criticized. Jesuit missionary Matteo Ricci (1552–1610) is particularly noted for introducing Neo-Confucianism to Europe through his correspondence and for integrating some Confucian ideas with Christianity. It was he who after learning that Confucian scholars were the society's aristocrats, dressed himself as a Confucian sage and educated himself about Confucianism while working on his mission. He tolerated several Neo-Confucian practices and rituals, including ancestor veneration. Academics have stated that Neo-Confucianism remained the dominant school of philosophical thought within Chinese culture until the 20th century.

Neo-Confucianism became influential in Korea, Vietnam, and Japan, with highly regarded scholars and forms of state institutionalization emerging out of each culture. Korea's National Confucian Shrine (Munmyo), established in 1392 in Seoul toward the end of the Koryo Dynasty (918–1392), acted as a ritual site for paying homage to Confucius and other Confucian sages, but friction between Confucianism and Buddhism grew. It was also in this period that Korea introduced its version of the civil service examination and built a national university that helped to inculcate Confucian values. Similarly, Vietnam instituted public civil service examinations modeled on the Chinese examination system, which continued into the 19th century. As in China, Vietnam's ruling elite was recruited from the examination system, which necessarily required knowledge of Confucian ethics and political theory. In Tokugawa Japan (1603–1867), a Neo-Confucian worldview was propagated, affecting both the elite and the popular levels of society. Tokugawa Yoshinao (1601–1650) had a Confucian temple built on the site of a shogunal palace, and Confucian intellectuals such as Fujiwara Seika (1561–1619) and Hayashi Razan (1583–1657) helped to establish several Neo-Confucian schools within Japan, separate from Shinto and Buddhist authorities.

Confucianism in the 20th and 21st Centuries

Imperial, state, and popular support for Confucianism/Neo-Confucianism has not always remained consistent, and the last 150 years offer several examples of anti-Confucian movements. In China, it encountered resistance during the May Fourth Movement, and its relationship with Marxism was particularly contentious as people became increasingly suspicious of imperial ideologies and feudalism. Furthermore, Confucianism was condemned as having caused the country's prerevolution "economic backwardness." More recently, anti-Confucianism was linked with the anti-Lin Biao movement (1973) when certain political leaders were accused of following Confucian policies. Alternatively in Japan, both pro- and anti-Confucian arguments were used to support Meiji nationalism, the first using Confucian principles in support of state and the latter condemning Confuciansim as a foreign import.

Some critics have claimed that Confucianism is outmoded, patriarchal, incompatible with a scientific worldview, and a barrier to democracy, liberalism, and modernization. Tu Wei-Ming, who is often associated with 20th- and 21st-century Confucian humanism, states Confucianism can bring authentic meaning to the world and that it has global appeal, not just within East Asia. He argues it is relevant and adaptable to modernity because it provides an ethical framework in which to act. Similarly, Japanese thinker Takehiko Okada states that Confucianism could help integrate human values into modern society as scientific and technological developments should consider the ethical nature of humanity and show sensitivity to human life.

Academics analyze Confucianism's interaction and negotiation with modern issues. For example, some have used Taiwan as a case study to examine how democratic liberalism and capitalism develop within a Confucianist society. It and the other "Big Four"/"Asian Tigers" (referring to the economic strengths of Taiwan, Hong Kong, Singapore, and South Korea, although some economists have suggested adding other Asian nations to the list) have likewise been used as examples to suggest that there is nothing inherent in Confucianism that impedes modernization or capitalism. Some studies show that Confucianism has influenced and continues to influence several East Asian cultures. Confucius's birthday, September 28, is celebrated annually as a national holiday, Teacher's Day, in Taiwan; in South Korea, vocabulary terms such as "filial piety" and "losing face" are still used; Singapore had plans to introduce Confucian moral education in its school system; and Taiwanese and Singaporean politicians continue to draw on Confucian ideas to gain popular support. How Confucianism interacts with current salient issues, such as globalization, cosmopolitanism, democracy, communism, liberalism, nationalism, capitalism, authoritarianism, anti-authoritarianism, education, gender stratification, modernization, transnational identities, and technological development, continues to be investigated by Confucian and non-Confucian scholars alike.

Jackie Larm

See also Diasporas; Global Religions, Beliefs, and Ideologies; Identities, Traditional; Religious Identities; Religious Politics; Values

Further Readings

Adler, J. (2002). *Chinese religions*. London: Routledge.

Dirlik, A. (1995). Confucius in the borderlands: Global capitalism and the reinvention of Confucianism. *Boundary, 2,* 229–273.

Katz, P. R. (2003). Religion and the state in post-war Taiwan. In D. L. Overmyer (Ed.), *Religion in China Today* (pp. 89–106). Cambridge, UK: Cambridge University Press.

Ling, L. H. M., & Shih, C.-Y. (1998). Confucianism with a liberal face: The meaning of democratic politics in postcolonial Taiwan. *The Review of Politics, 60,* 55–82.

Louie, A. (2000). Re-territorializing transnationalism: Chinese Americans and the Chinese motherland. *American Ethnologist, 27,* 645–669.

Rozman, G. (Ed.). (1991). *The East Asian region: Confucian heritage and its modern adaptation.* Princeton, NJ: Princeton University Press.

Taylor, R. (1990). *The religious dimensions of Confucianism.* Albany: State University of New York Press.

Tu, W.-M. (1978). *Humanity and self-cultivation: Essays in Confucian thought.* Boston: Asian Humanities Press.

Tu, W.-M., Hejtmaner, M., & Wachman, A. (Eds.). (1992). *The Confucian world observed: A contemporary discussion of Confucian humanism in East Asia.* Honolulu, HI: Program for Cultural Studies, The East-West Center.

Yao, X. (2000). *An introduction to Confucianism.* Cambridge, UK: University of Cambridge Press.

Zhonglian, S. (1997). The dual economic function of Confucianism. In Y. Xuanmeng, L. Xiaohe, L. Fangtong, Z. Rulun, & G. Enderle (Eds.), *Economic ethics and Chinese culture, Chinese philosophical studies XIV* (pp. 15–23). Washington, DC: The Council for Research in Values and Philosophy.

CONNECTEDNESS, GLOBAL

Connectedness and globalization are closely linked, in the sense that a growth in international and transactional activities leads to greater connectedness across borders. This network phenomenon exists at the personal, organizational, and nation-state levels, and it implies ties to other people, groups, firms, and agencies abroad. Connectedness, greatly facilitated by the Internet, social networking sites, and mobile devices, involves not only the number of connections but also their reach and volume in terms of a multiplex transnational network. David Held differentiates among the following:

- *Extensity* as a measure of the geographical stretching of activities, indicated by the number of "nodes" (organizations, networks, and people) that constitute the overall spread of connections. Extensity refers to the range of globalized social structures generated by such ties across the different continents, countries, and regions of the world.
- *Intensity* or the overall density of the network among entities in terms of the number and types of connections involved among the various nodes they constitute. Intensity indicates how densely elements are connected among each other.
- *Velocity* of the overall network as a measure of the frequency with which connections are made or used among network nodes. Velocity refers to the volume of interactions among actors and organizations. It is a flow measure.

Examples include trade networks, supply chains and distribution channels, epidemics, commercial flights, academic conference circuits, migration patterns, communication flows, and friendship and acquaintance networks. Transnational corporations, states, nongovernmental organizations, activist networks, and individuals—all participate and communicate in a plethora of international exchanges, conventions, meetings, organizations, coalitions, and above all networks of all kinds, serving as the infrastructure of global regimes and allowing for the travel of flows of a variety of types (e.g., money, goods and services, knowledge and information, people, and drugs).

Background

Connectedness is a central theme in the study of globalization. Daniel Yergin and Joseph Stanislav use the metaphor of the "woven world" to express how transnational actors connect formerly disparate entities and issues, so that everything becomes relevant everywhere. James Roseneau describes global governance as a framework of horizontal relations between states and between nonstate actors. Held's notion of global governance denotes a complicated web of interrelated global issue networks. Ulrich Beck proposes to examine the scale, density, and stability of regional-global networks, the social spaces they create, and the cultural images they carry. In his view, the continued expansion and contraction along local-global axes creates patterns of varying density and centrality in these global networks. Most notably, Manuel Castells argues that networks increasingly form meta-networks at the transnational level and create a system of decentralized concentration, where a multiplicity of interconnected tasks takes place in different sites. Since the 1970s, Castells points out, enabling technologies such as telecommunication and the Internet brought about the ascendance of a network society, whose processes occur in a new type of space, which he labels the "space of flows." This space, comprising a myriad of exchanges, came to dominate the "space of places" of territorially defined units of states, regions, and neighborhoods as a result of its greater flexibility and compatibility with the new logic of network society. Nodes and hubs in this space of flows construct the social organization of this network society. For Castells, this new space is at the core of the globalization process—and for understanding global civil society within the larger process of a shift from "place" to "flows," networks are the central concept.

Connectedness and Structural Patterns

Global connectedness forms structures and patterns, based on different types of actors—individuals such as citizens, activists and scientists, organizations, governments, corporations, as well as others. Structures bound the possibilities of action; they prevent some actions from occurring but encourage and facilitate other actions. In contrast, action defines and modifies structure—actors can create new links, altering through their actions the structure, and as a result also the repertoire of actions available to them. Researchers have tried to identify characteristic patterns and explored their implications in terms of power, influence, and competitive advantages.

The power of network patterns resulting from connectedness can be illustrated by way of an example: Consider that an average person has 36 contacts abroad, and if each of these 36 had, let's say, the same number of contacts, the resulting network would link 1,296 people. If each of these had 36 in turn, their total count would reach 46,656, and if we continued this thought experiment further, we would by step 4 reach the population of Great Britain, and by step 5 almost one third of the world's population today.

Of course, we assumed so far that no overlapping ties exist among these connections. The structural image of the group is that of a radial network with 36 nodes in the center, and many more arranged along multiple lines of connectivity that branch out by the thousands and then millions without ever crossing. Yet our everyday experience (as well numerous sociological studies) shows that lines do cross and that there are overlapping connections among our friends, acquaintances, and colleagues past and present.

Assume that at each step, 18 of the initial 36 contacts had ties not with only one of the proceeding ones, but also among any of the other contacts already in the network. So in effect, at each step, we would add 18 new ones and allow for 18 existing contacts to connect with others at random. The resulting network would have a smaller scale or reach (68 million contacts at step 5), but it would have *structure*: Some parts of the network would be denser, others less so; some would be relatively isolated, and others well linked. Overall, the network would resemble a clustered set of "islands of connectivity," denser in the core, and sparser toward the periphery.

It is these island-like structures that span countries, organizations, communities, groups, and families that allow the power of transnational networks to unfold. These networks may have begun small and in one location or country, but they then spread out across borders, linking different groups, professions, and other advocacy networks, encountering opposing groups, or making allies. The result is a complex web of affiliations that integrates network members in manifold ways into other groups, and thereby it creates opportunities for action locally as well as globally.

Sociologists call the "small world phenomenon" the likelihood that our own personal contact network (often unexpectedly to us) overlaps with that of someone else's we encounter seemingly at random, and we discover common friends and acquaintances (the intersection of two networks). They also point to the tendency of networks toward homophily (i.e., to become self-referential in terms of social class, professional, religious, or ethnic background), as we tend to associate with people who are more like rather than unlike ourselves (McPhearson et al., 2001).

In the past, homophileous networks remained largely contained in national class structures and were strongly patterned by religious, ethnic, or other divisions. In a globalizing world, however, these lines cross in ways that are not only exceedingly complex but also that achieve their own patterns or island-like structures. Social movement activists make use of such structures in furthering their cause in transnational advocacy coalitions, as do marketing experts in developing transnational advertising campaigns, or social network sites in appealing to large numbers of subscribers that come from very different locations and nations.

The connectedness of today's world is not a passive or inert phenomenon. To the contrary, it is created, in part, and used by political, social, and economic entrepreneurs. Some network configurations facilitate entrepreneurship more than others, thereby making successful coalition-building and advocacy more likely. One is called the weak-tie phenomenon (Granovetter, 2005). Assuming that two networks present strong friendship ties, a plotted line between them represents a weak tie such as mere acquaintance, rather than some form of friendship between persons A and B. Along such weak ties, information can jump from one "island" to another, facilitating innovations and diffusion processes. Weak ties allow entrepreneurs to take advantage of the mobilization potential of two networks without integrating them. For example, a particular artistic style in one country's music culture can be connected to that in another country via a weak tie link, often via migrant groups.

The structural hole is another configuration (Burt, 2005). Here, the entrepreneur spots a missing link between two clusters and connects them. The entrepreneurial act of person X is one of closure and brokerage between two groups that would otherwise be unrelated. The structural hole is filled, and the separate networks are now connected. For example, a music student discovers synergies between styles among two unconnected music scenes and connects them accordingly.

A third configuration is the structural fold (Verdes & Stark, 2010). In this case, entrepreneurs are located in two or more groups at the same time. Formally, the entrepreneur is located in the intersection of groups rather than being the interlocutor above. This allows for internal as well as external influence, and the act is one of intercohesion within and across groups. An example here would be a musician participating in two otherwise unconnected music scenes.

Of course, connecting weak ties, closing structural holes, and creating folds for intergroup cohesion are not exclusive options. Successful "connection entrepreneurs" take advantage of all three—and in varying combinations over time, as do marketers, advertising agents, and communications specialists. Indeed connectedness is more than a social phenomenon linked to globalization; it is ultimately an economic as well as a political resource.

Helmut K. Anheier

See also Civil Society, Global; Class; Communities, Transnational; Entrepreneurship; Global Communications and Technology; Globalization, Phenomenon of; Identities in Global Societies; Markets; Social Movements; Social Networking

Further Readings

Beck, U. (1999). *What is globalization?* Cambridge, UK: Polity Press.

Burt, R. (2005). *Brokerage and closure.* Oxford, UK: Oxford University Press.

Castells, M. (2000). *The rise of the network society, the information age: Economy, society and culture*

(Vol. 1, 2nd ed.). Cambridge, MA: Blackwell. (Original work published 1996)

Granovetter, M. (2005). Business groups and social organization. In N. Smelser & R. Swedberg (Eds.), *Handbook of economic sociology* (2nd ed., pp. 429–450). Princeton, NJ: Princeton University Press.

Held, D., McGrew, A., Goldblatt, D., & Peratton, J. (1999). *Global transformations: Politics, economics, and culture*. Stanford, CA: Stanford University Press.

McPhearson, M., Smith-Lovin, L., & Cook, J. M. (2001). Birds of a feather: Homophily in social networks. *Annual Review of Sociology, 27*, 415–444.

Rosenau, J. N. (1995). Governance in the 21st century. *Global Governance: A Review of Multilateralism and International Organizations, 1*, 13–43.

Verdes, B., & Stark, D. (2010). Structural folds: Generative disruption in overlapping groups. *American Journal of Sociology, 115*(4), 1150–1190.

Yergin, D., & Stanislav, J. (1998). *The commanding heights*. New York: Free Press.

CONQUESTS

Conquests have played a significant role in empire building and imperial strategy from ancient times to the global era, as peoples and countries with superior resources, military might, or advantageous geographical locations have looked to expand their influence. Other reasons have included the belief in cultural superiority and desire to spread civilization. The impacts of imperial conquest have included the diffusion of diseases, foods, religion, culture, and knowledge; the development of regional and global economic and commercial networks; and the political, economic, and cultural oppression of conquered peoples and subsequent rise of colonial independence movements. Modern neocolonialism is the belief that military conquest has been supplanted through economic dominance.

Conquests in Early History

There were a variety of commercial, political, legal, cultural, and religious motivations for conquest in the ancient and medieval worlds. The development of a lucrative trade with Asia for silks, spices, and other valuable goods and a slave trading network with Africa provided commercial incentives for early exploration and conquest. Expanding an empire's boundaries through conquest also increased its tax rolls, plunder, and possible military conscriptions. The growing dominance of Christianity beginning in the Roman Empire and continuing into the medieval period gave rise to political and religious attempts to spread the Christian faith through both missionary work and conquest. The rise of Islam fostered similar attempts to spread the Muslim faith and culture.

Conquests were a key component in the building of early empires such as the Roman and Persian empires and Imperial China. Early religious-based conquests included those of the Muslims in the Near East, those of the Ottoman and Mughal empires, and the Christian Crusades in the Holy Land during the 12th and 13th centuries. Muslims (Moors) later advanced into Spain and Portugal, where they were eventually expelled. Genghis Khan of the Mongols (Tatars) and his elite military force created one of the world's largest empires in the 13th century, covering parts of present-day China, Korea, Russia, and eastern Europe. Subsequent Mongol rulers extended the Mongol Empire's conquests even further before internal dissension eventually broke up the empire by the late 14th century.

The Viking chieftain Rollo was granted territory in present-day France, and he and his descendants adopted French culture and became known as the Dukes of Normandy. The Normans then engaged in a series of conquests, such as an invasion of Sicily and southern Italy in search of wealth. The most famous of the Norman conquests was that of William the Conqueror, who conquered England in 1066 in an attempt to secure the crown he believed belonged to him. Scandinavian Vikings also led exploration and raiding parties into Europe, Greenland, and North America.

Conquests often resulted in cultural diffusion through the imposition or adoption of the conquering power's cultural practices. Knowledge was similarly spread. The lucrative Asian trade opened up commercial ties and extensive trade routes that linked numerous peoples. The maintenance of large empires proved difficult because of the need for a large government bureaucracy and military force to control diverse geographical locations and populations. The Roman Empire offered citizenship and its benefits to conquered peoples to gain their loyalty. These needs drained treasuries and sparked periodic wars and rebellions among conquered peoples.

European Conquest and Colonization in the Early Modern Era

European conquest and colonization during the early modern era of the 15th through 18th centuries made the leading European nations dominant political, economic, and cultural global powers. Improvements in shipbuilding and navigation facilitated the possibility of overseas exploration. Technological advances in land and naval weaponry, notably the use of gunpowder, fueled international European rivalries and provided the means for conquering large new territories and populations. Genoese mariner Christopher Columbus, funded by King Ferdinand and Queen Isabella of Spain, launched the new era in 1492 with his first expedition in search of a shorter trade route to the Indies (Asia). Economic, religious, and political motives impelled his and subsequent voyages in the Age of Exploration and Discovery, usually summed up in the phrase "gold, God, and glory."

Economic motives included the search for precious metals or other forms of material wealth, access to Asian trade routes, entry into the African slave trade, and the belief in mercantilism. Under the economic system of mercantilism, colonies would provide a nation with mineral wealth and natural resources as well as ready markets for manufactured products. Religious motives included the missionary desire to spread Christian religions to the indigenous peoples of the New World, commonly viewed as heathen savages. Political and social motives included the expansion of national empires and wealth, rivalries with other European nation-states, and the establishment of personal landholdings, wealth, or recognition. Developing anthropological beliefs in humankind's progression from primitive to civilized societies provided an important justification for conquest and colonization of what were viewed as more primitive cultures.

European competition for colonial possessions spread to the New World following Columbus' voyages. Spanish conquistadors explored and colonized Mexico, Central and South America, and parts of the Caribbean and North America, conquering the Aztec and Inca empires in Mexico and Peru, respectively, among other indigenous populations. Portugal colonized Brazil while the Netherlands established the colony of New Amsterdam in the area that later became New York. Britain and France competed for supremacy in North America and the Caribbean. Meanwhile, these same European nations were active elsewhere, including Africa, Indonesia, the Philippines, and Asia.

European conquests in the early modern era had numerous lasting global consequences. European nations emerged as dominant world powers in a time when the peoples and nations of the world were becoming increasingly interconnected. Global awareness and expansion led to the development of early international laws to govern international relations. These laws were to be established by the European Christian nations that represented the height of civilization.

The economic wealth, especially silver, obtained from the New World and shipped in treasure fleets enriched European nations and facilitated international economic relations. New World products such as tobacco, coffee, sugar, rice, and indigo proved highly profitable. New European wealth facilitated entry into the established Asian trade in spices and other valuable goods, draining European treasuries of their silver. The slave trade connecting Europe, Africa, and the New World proved highly profitable as a result of colonial demand for plantation laborers to grow cash crops in the New World. Newfound wealth financed the numerous international wars between European powers and their colonies that broke out during this period, which also burdened national treasures.

European conquests also facilitated a bidirectional cultural exchange of diseases, flora, and fauna generally known as the Columbian exchange, a term coined by historian Alfred Crosby. Military conquests, alliances, and involvement in European colonial wars, enslavement, the spread of diseases such as smallpox, religious conversions, and European cultural beliefs in the superiority of civilization and the White race led to the widespread destruction of indigenous peoples and cultures in Africa and the Americas. The voluntary and forced intermixture of peoples resulted in new populations through intermarriage, such as mestizos and

Creoles, as well as the blending of European, indigenous, and African religious beliefs and cultural practices.

Conquests and the Colonial Legacy in the Modern Era

Military conquest continued to join trade and diplomacy as key means of empire building and imperialism. Modern empires and nations that have used conquests have included the British Empire, the United States, Nazi Germany, Imperial Japan, and the Soviet Union. The early modern British Empire greatly expanded in the 18th and 19th centuries to the point that the phrase "the sun never sets on the British Empire" became a standard description. Military conflicts arising out of imperial conquests became global phenomena, best evidenced by World War I and World War II. Military occupations have included the post–World War II occupation of Germany and Japan and the early 21st-century occupation of Iraq and Afghanistan.

The rise of modern professional standing armies and navies, weapons using the technologies of industrialization, and the large military bureaucracies and logistics were key components in the rise of modern imperial powers. Also key were developments in transportation and communications, from railroads, steamships, canals, and telegraphy to automobiles, airplanes, and telephony. Increased reliance on fossil fuels such as coal and oil caused nations less well endowed with natural resources, such as Germany and Japan, to obtain them in part through colonial conquests and possessions. Cultural motivations for conquest included the belief in cultural, political, and religious supremacy, such as British belief in the White Man's Burden to spread democracy and civilization or Nazi Germany's attempts to create a pure Aryan race.

The study of conquests and their justifications, such as racial or cultural superiority, has given rise to scholarly debates over the definition of culture and equality among world cultures as well as the importance of other factors, such as geographical position and natural resources, in the rise of empires. Conquest in part built the empires whose military, naval, commercial, and financial power helped globalize the economy. Scholars have also debated the reasons for the fall of empires built in part through conquest, weighing the importance of such factors as the attempt to build too large an empire, environmental damage, the difficulty of maintaining the loyalty of disparate groups of people, and the increasingly destructive nature of warfare and the rise of nuclear weapons.

The legacy of colonial conquest and oppression among colonized peoples has also been widely debated. Conquests have fueled the voluntary and involuntary migrations of peoples throughout the world, aiding cultural diffusion and hybridization and giving rise to multicultural societies. Many scholars feel that colonial oppression gave rise to despotism, colonial rebellions and the rise of colonial independence movements, and a legacy of distrust and anger, as well as environmental degradation, poverty, and lower standards of living in much of the developing world. Others note that colonial powers brought political and economic stability that eroded into ethnic violence and battles for political control after independence, as evidenced in many African nations, such as Nigeria and Rwanda.

Scholars of modern conquest have also looked at the rise of neocolonialism in the wake of decolonization. Neocolonialism is used critically as the control of former colonial possessions through economic reliance, pointing to developing countries reliance on international aid from developed countries or global organizations such as the World Bank, International Monetary Fund, and World Trade Organization. These impacts have helped give rise to modern global peace and human rights movements as well as various international nongovernmental organizations dedicated to economic self-sufficiency, education, and other development programs in developing countries.

Marcella Bush Trevino

See also Colonialism; Empires; Empires, Modern; Global Historical Antecedents; Hegemonic Power; Humanity, Concepts of; Imperialism; Liberalism, Neoliberalism; Neocolonialism; War

Further Readings

Abernethy, D. B. (2002). *The dynamics of global dominance: European overseas empires, 1415–1980.* New Haven, CT: Yale University Press.
Bernstein, P. L. (2000). *The power of gold: The history of an obsession.* New York: Wiley.

Boatwright, M. T., Gargola, D. J., & Talbert, R. J. A. (2004). *The Romans, from village to empire*. New York: Oxford University Press.

Chasteen, J. C. (2001). *Born in blood and fire: A concise history of Latin America*. New York: Norton.

Chua, A. (2007). *Day of empire: How hyperpowers rise to global dominance—and why they fail*. New York: Doubleday.

Crosby, A. (1972). *The Columbian exchange: Biological and cultural consequences of 1492*. Westport, CT: Greenwood Press.

Diamond, J. M. (2005). *Collapse: How societies choose to fail or succeed*. New York: Viking.

Diamond, J. M. (2005). *Guns, germs, and steel: The fates of human societies*. New York: Norton.

Fuentes, C. (1992). *The buried mirror: Reflections on Spain and the New World*. Boston: Houghton Mifflin.

Kiernan, B. (2007). *Blood and soil: A world history of genocide and extermination from Sparta to Darfur*. New Haven, CT: Yale University Press.

Marks, R. B. (2007). *The origins of the modern world* (2nd ed.). Lanham, MD: Rowman & Littlefield.

Meinig, D. W. (2004). *The shaping of America: A geographical perspective on 500 years of history*. New Haven, CT: Yale University Press.

Pakenham, T. (1991). *The scramble for Africa, 1876–1912*. New York: Random House.

Sowell, T. (1999). *Conquests and cultures: An international history*. New York: Basic Books.

Spence, J. D. (1990). *The search for modern China*. New York: Norton.

Stannard, D. E. (1992). *American holocaust: Columbus and the conquest of the New World*. New York: Oxford University Press.

Topik, S., Marichal, C., & Frank, Z. (Eds.). (2006). *From silver to cocaine: Latin American commodity chains and the building of the world economy, 1500–2000*. Durham, NC: Duke University Press.

Tyerman, C. (2006). *God's war: A new history of the Crusades*. Cambridge, MA: Belknap Press.

Weatherford, J. M. (2004). *Genghis Khan and the making of the modern world*. New York: Crown.

CONSTITUTIONALISM

Constitutionalism has a variety of meanings in the global era, and neither is limited to specific historical connotations nor qualifies as an exclusively normative structure or institutional arrangement. Whereas the term *constitution* in a broad sense has been used to describe the "status" of a political community, determined by geopolitical, cultural, social, political, economic, or legal factors, *constitutionalism* is a more demanding and recent innovation in the history of political thought.

The concept has descriptive and prescriptive, formal and substantial, as well as procedural and institutional dimensions. Used in a descriptive way, it describes the historical struggle for a limited government as well as fundamental rights and freedoms including political participation of the people. This historical struggle is most significantly reflected by the American and the French revolutions, which, being successful, caused constitutional movements all over Europe. The first half of the 19th century thus can be described as an "age of constitutionalism." The U.S. federal Constitution is often viewed as a model for constitutionalization processes: The constituent power of the relevant people was brought to bear in constitutional conventions leading to the adoption of the relevant constitution. The subsequent exercise of constituent power could then be effectuated by either enacting constitutional amendments or, on an informal day-to-day basis, through manifold forms of political participation. The latter finds expression in a famous quote by French philosopher Ernest Renan: a *plébiscite de tous les jours* [a daily plebiscite] (in *Qu'est-ce qu'une nation?* [*What is a nation?*], 1882). Regardless of all the detours and setbacks faced by the idea of constitutionalism when confronted with fascist or communist totalitarianism, it had a new momentum after the breakdown of the Iron Curtain in 1989–1990 and finally gained universal recognition by the end of the 20th century.

Prescriptive Features

The modern-day universality of constitutionalism is first and foremost based on its prescriptive nucleus: the notion that any form of government (or governance) has to be legitimized as well as limited in its powers. In such a Lockean sense, constitutionalism serves to define what empowers and limits the legitimate exercise of governmental authority. Among the essential legitimizing features, the sovereignty of the people and as the obvious result thereof, the people's constituent power, rank first. Abbé Sieyès, on the eve of the French Revolution, acclaimed the emancipatory potential of this constituent power in his pamphlet *What Is the Third Estate?* (1789) and furthermore made the classic division between the constituent and constituted power of the people. However, because plurinational, multi-ethnic, and multireligious societies comprise heterogeneous citizenship endowed with constituent power, rather than homogeneous people, the sovereignty of the people has to be reframed as the "sovereignty of the citizens," and constitution building becomes an ongoing, open process of political integration by the citizens. The substantive guarantees of such "procedural constitutionalism" are often based on the notion of human dignity, which encompasses basic human rights ensuring freedom and equality (before the law). The orientation toward the common good has substantive as well as procedural elements. The same is true for another core principle of constitutionalism: the rule of law. Among other elements, it embraces the ideals of material justice, impartiality and fairness, legal certainty and proportionality, and in particular due process guarantees. Constitutionalism finally requires a formal mechanism for the enacting of laws (legality) and institutional safeguards for the three separate branches of government: legislative, executive, and judicial. Regarding the last named, constitutional justice and the idea of judicial review are nowadays universal features of constitutionalism. In general, all the aforementioned criteria work as a blueprint of constitution-building processes in emerging democracies and as structural prerequisites of a secular, reason-based polity.

National Level

Given the traditional state-centered framework of public authority, the modern state is the undisputed domicile of constitutionalism and still the most important guarantor of its relevance. However, the linkage between statehood and constitutionalism is an obvious one only at first glance. In the 21st-century architecture of worldwide economical and sociopolitical interdependencies as well as of globally intertwined policy structures, the constituent power of the people (the citizens) is embedded in the larger suprastate complexes of constituent forms, forums, and powers. Thus,

collective decision making by the citizens is not limited to the boundaries of the nation-state; common interest is more and more linked to the common interests of all humankind. Consequently, constitutional functions are fulfilled not only by domestic but also by regional (supranational) and international law. This is not meant to abolish the state in a postnational period but to strengthen cooperatively the guarantee functions of statehood in a world beyond the state.

Regional Level

On the regional level, the supranational European Union is the most advanced example of a nonstate constitutional community in the making. It is the supranational nature of the union—that is to say, the power to create law that is not only binding on the member-states but also without any subsequent act of transformation within the member-states—that raises manifold structural questions as to the European Union's far-reaching authority and competencies vis-à-vis member-states. These questions led to an intensive debate on constitutionalism, democratic legitimacy, sovereignty, and reversibility of the union's powers. The member-states, viewing themselves still as the "masters of the treaties," articulated constitutional constraints of their own. The most adequate scheme to comprise the intertwined polities on the national and the European level—not to be viewed in a hierarchical way though—is *multilevel constitutionalism* reflecting multilevel governance. Multilevel constitutionalism describes and tries to illustrate an ongoing process of establishing new structures of government. These are at the same time complementary to and building on changing existing forms of self-organization of the people or society. There is a parallel between the national and the European constitution(s): The citizen is the ultimate source of legitimacy for public authority. The European constitution is being composed by the national constitutions and the European treaties. It reflects the aforementioned core elements of prescriptive constitutionalism—first and foremost, its human rights basis. The European Constitution, being a constitutional architecture beyond the state, qualifies as a dynamic process driven by the citizens. These citizens, of course, might have multiple identities (as locals, nationals, or Europeans) and rely on multiple forms of belongingness, but they share common constitutional values: human rights, the rule of law, and democracy. European constitutionalism thus aims for a political system that ought to be responsive to the needs, desires, interests, and values of its constituents—to their notion of the *bonum commune*, or common good.

Global Level

Given all the real-world phenomena of globalization and consequently the ever-decreasing autarkic regulatory capacity of nation-states, both causing new multilayered structures of governance, dramatic extensions from the constitutional tradition can be observed, and the notion of *transnational constitutionalism* comes into play. The idea of legitimizing as well as limiting public powers (or what might be tantamount to their quality even though exercised by private actors) is being rethought in light of political globality. Influential substate groups, international organizations, transnational corporations, or nongovernmental organizations transcend and thus transform the national constitutional arena. The formerly clear distinction between "inside" and "outside" the domestic sphere has been blurred. New legal structures such as global constitutional law and global administrative law are discussed. Various notions of a global "civic" or "societal" constitution, driven by powerful—but nonstate—global players in the fields of economy or communication technology find resonance in a worldwide lex mercatoria (see the entry on Lex Mercatoria in this encyclopedia) or "lex digitalis" of the Internet (Internet Corporation for Assigned Names and Numbers [ICANN]; see the entry on Internet Corporation for Assigned Names and Numbers in this encyclopedia). Some advocate World Trade Organization constitutionalism; others attribute some constitutional quality to the United Nations charter. Notwithstanding some conceptual inconsistencies and inherent tensions—especially when it comes to the notion of a holistic constituent power missing on the global plane—the matrix of constitutionalism is, at least to a minimum extent, a useful tool for shaping the world beyond the state. It strives for a global legal community and public order that is based on a universal rule of law, framed by common values and directed toward a common good of humanity. Since the state is no longer the sole and unchallenged guarantor of its citizens' common interests, (institutional) compensation has to be provided for at regional and universal levels.

Conclusion

What human rights–based modern-day constitutionalism—reflected on the national, the regional, and the international levels—most precisely makes clear is the instrumental character of all political and legal structures. The aim is to serve the individual citizen. The human being is the ultimate addressee of law. Law has to function in the interest of the human being, and constitutionalism is composed by and composed of the following functions: to safeguard external as well as internal peace and security, to serve justice in relations between individuals and collectives, to guarantee and protect human rights, to establish a rule of law, and to promote public purposes. Of equal importance, however, is the control function. Constitutional structures control social reality in general and public powers in particular. Therefore constitutionalism has, following the classical ideas of Montesquieu, established functional safeguards that make a system of checks and balances possible. Not an abundant use of constitutional language, only a precise reference to these functions, can live up to the great expectations of constitutionalism since the 18th century's great revolutions.

Markus Kotzur

See also Civil Society, Global; European Union; Global Governance and World Order; Law, International; Legal Systems; Legitimacy; Lex Mercatoria; Nation-State; Regional Governance; State–Civil Society Relations; Universalism

Further Readings

Bogdandy, A. V. (2006). Constitutionalism in international law: Comment on a proposal from Germany. *Harvard International Law Journal, 47,* 223–247.

Dobner, P., & Loughlin, M. (Eds.). (2010). *The twilight of constitutionalism?* Oxford, UK: Oxford University Press.

Habermas, J. (2001). *The postnational constellation: Political essays* (M. Pensky, Ed. & Trans.). Boston: MIT Press.

Klabbers, J. (2004). Constitutionalism lite. *International Organizations Law Review, 1,* 31–58.

Loughlin, M., & Walker, N. (Eds.). (2007). *The paradox of constitutionalism: Constituent power and constitutional form.* Oxford, UK: Oxford University Press.

Peters, A. (2006). Compensatory constitutionalism: The function and potential of fundamental international norms and structures. *Leiden Journal of International Law, 19,* 579–610.

Teubner, G. (2004). Societal constitutionalism: Alternatives to state-centered constitutional theory. In C. Joergens, I.-J. Sand, & G. Teubner (Eds.), *Transnational governance and constitutionalism.* Oxford, UK: Hart.

Tomuschat, C. (1999). International law: Ensuring the survival of mankind on the eve of a new century. General discourse on public international law. In *Recueil des Cours 281* (pp. 10, 25). Leiden, Netherlands: Brill.

Walker, N. (2002). The idea of constitutional pluralism. *Modern Law Review, 65,* 317–359.

Walter, C. (2001). Constitutionalising (inter)national governance: Possibilities for and limits of the development of an international constitutional law. *German Yearbook of International Law, 44,* 170–201.

Consumer Protest

In a global economy, consumer protest is also global. Even before the global economic era, moreover, international orgnizations were formed to foster consumer rights and give an international voice to their concerns.

Consumer protest refers to the campaigns, tactics, and organizations of consumers that are designed to promote the interests of either the consumers themselves or any other group in society for which the consumers feel an affinity or allegiance. Since we have an infinite number of relationships with goods and services, and since almost any political point can be made through consumption, the range of consumer protests is seemingly endless. Although many might be familiar with consumer protests such as the boycott of South African products during the era of apartheid, the concept must include too those far less progressive causes of consumers that have been motivated by feelings of nationalism and racial prejudice.

For all this diversity, however, consumer protest can be divided into three broad types. The first is that associated with the 19th century and includes those moral and political campaigns to protect the interests of groups other than those doing the actual consuming. The classic example here is that of the antislavery movement. Women in Britain and America purchased brooches, badges, ribbons, pins, buttons, and jewelry bearing the legend, "Am I not a man and a brother," to protest against the slave trade around the turn of the 19th century. Later, they boycotted slave-grown sugar, inspiring many other forms of consumer protest: from the bazaars held by supporters of the Anti-Corn Law League to the exclusive dealing campaigns of the Chartists who put pressure on shopkeepers to vote for radical candidates.

In Britain, in 1887, Clementina Black of the British Women's Trade Union Association set up a Consumers' League. This was an antisweating campaign modeled on the efforts of the Knights of Labour in the United States, and although it proved short-lived, it was taken up again across the Atlantic where a Consumers' League was formed by the Women's Trade Union League in New York in 1890. Other chapters soon appeared across the United States until a National Consumers' League was formed in 1898. This then inspired the *Ligue Social d'Acheteurs* in France, the *Käuferbund Deutschland* in Germany, and similar organizations in Switzerland, Italy, Belgium, and the Netherlands. As organizations of mainly middle-class women, the consumers' leagues proved popular with philanthropically minded sympathizers of labor. They would be followed by a whole variety of consumer protest groups, including the League of Women Shoppers (1935) in the United States, but also by an expanding number of women's organizations around Europe concerned with domestic issues.

The second type of consumer protest is one that seeks to defend the interests of consumers themselves and that evolves into a general consumer movement. Two examples stand out: the cooperative movement and the comparative testing movement. Beginning in the north of England in the

1840s, the dividend-on-purchase, consumer cooperative ethos of the "Rochdale Pioneers" spread throughout Europe as an alternative to the capitalist marketplace. By the outbreak of World War I, there were literally thousands of local societies across all of Europe. Cooperation was subsequently weakened through its own institutional and parochial failings, the interference of totalitarian regimes, and the competition of more dynamic capitalist firms, but it was still a vociferous presence in Europe and Japan after World War II. Even today, some estimates claim that, worldwide, cooperation still attracts around 900 million members.

By the mid-20th century, a new form of consumer protest emerged. The comparative testing movement began in the United States in the late 1920s and spread to Europe after World War II. It was most commonly known for its best buys found in *Consumer Reports*, *Which?* and *Que Choisir*, although it would gain greater prominence through such figures as Ralph Nader. In 1960, the leaders of the main European and U.S. groups came together to found the International Organisation of Consumers Unions (IOCU). Its growth is a testament to the spread of organized consumerism across the developing world. By 1970, IOCU's membership consisted of consumer groups across Asia, Africa, and Latin America. Today, Consumers International, as IOCU is now called, is represented in more than 100 countries. Much of its expansion had been overseen by Anwar Fazal, a product of the Malaysian consumer movement and president of IOCU from 1978 to 1984, although other developing world activists have subsequently directed the global consumer movement from Indonesia, Brazil, and Kenya. In the 1980s, IOCU was a prominent player in global civil society, not least in the consumer campaigns it coordinated through the International Baby Food Action Network (1979), Health Action International (1981), and Pesticide Action Network (1982).

In recent decades, the comparative testing consumer movement has been overshadowed by a third type of consumer protest: that associated with green, ethical, and fair trade consumerism. In many ways, these protests represent a return to the campaigns of the 19th century since the consumer acts on behalf of others, but because they have become so prevalent and are predicated on a consumer consciousness that is focused on not one issue but on a whole range of issues (often associated with the umbrella term *globalization*), it requires separate identification. The modern era of consumer protest began in the 1960s with the rise of green consumerism. It was bolstered by the renewed interest in the boycott, particularly that associated with South Africa, and gained momentum with the interest in fair trade, often promoted by nongovernmental organizations such as Oxfam and Christian Aid. By the beginning of the 1990s, the ethically minded shopper could draw on a range of publications to assist his or her decision making, could purchase a range of certified goods through, for example, the Fairtrade Foundation (UK) and Max Havelaar (Netherlands), and could make such purchases from a range of retail outlets.

In the global era, fair trade has entered the mainstream, such that "protest" is as routine an act as is the weekly shopping trip. Moreover, the modern consumer is expected to be engaged with the politics of consumption through so many other options: the slow food movement, culture jamming, downsizing, recycling, farmers' markets, and so on. Indeed, the pace of commodity capitalism has been seemingly matched by the pace of innovation in ever new forms of consumer protest. "Carrot mobbing," whereby mobs of consumers show their preference for the more ethical business, is but one of several recent tactics invented by citizens ever more aware of their own role as consumers and the range of political protests that can be made through consumption.

Consumer protest is not going to go away. It may not be able to achieve all of its objectives; it may encompass protestors from opposite ends of the political spectrum; and it often lacks the coherence we usually associate with social movements. Indeed, it is best understood as a tactic, except in those instances of cooperation and comparative testing when it has taken on the role of a movement as well. Yet what is clear is that consumer protest is not something that is brought to the marketplace from external sources. It is as much a fact and a part of consumer society as shopping is itself.

Matthew Hilton

See also Capitalism; Civil Society, Global; Consumerism; Economic Ethics; Environmental Movement; Ethics, Global; Global Economic Issues; Global Health and Nutrition; Labor; Social Movements; Value/Commodity Chains, Global

Further Readings

Glickman, L. B. (2009). *Buying power: A history of consumer activism in America.* Chicago: University of Chicago Press.

Hilton, M. (2009). *Prosperity for all: Consumer activism in an era of globalization.* Ithaca, NY: Cornell University Press.

Micheletti, M. (2003). *Political virtue and shopping: Individuals, consumerism and collective action.* London: Palgrave.

CONSUMERISM

The global spread of consumerism is a pervasive feature of culture in the global era, but it also has extensive historical roots. Consumerism can be roughly defined as a deep interest in acquiring material items not necessary to even reasonably ample subsistence and judging one's own well-being (and sometimes that of the society around one) partly on the basis of acquisitions. Enjoyment and personal investment in the process of selecting the items—shopping, in short—can be an important corollary of this basic commitment.

Premodern Consumerism

Signs of consumerism crop up very early in the human experience. Some hunting and gathering societies clearly used material objects to help denote status, as in placing ornaments alongside the buried bodies of presumably elite tribesmen, even children. As aristocracies formed in early civilizations, again diverse material adornments—in housing, furnishing, clothing, and jewelry—resulted from their prosperity but also served to mark their privilege both to other members of the class and to society at large. Many early efforts at interregional trade resulted from the same acquisitive interests, on the part of the wealthy. Thus

various Middle Eastern and Mediterranean societies sent merchants to what is now Afghanistan, the only source of lapis lazuli. Gold and various precious stones served as major trading items. By the time of the classical period, what historians have labeled the Silk Roads, running from western China to India, Persia and the rest of the Middle East, and the Mediterranean, served elite consumer trade first and foremost. By the time of the Roman Empire, use of Chinese silks to embellish clothing for the wealthy, including the prestigious though by now politically impotent Roman senators, was well established for men and women alike. Soon, Chinese silks, as objects of consumer-oriented trans-regional trade, were joined by Chinese porcelains and vividly colored printed cotton cloth from India. By the postclassical period (600–1450), elite consumerism as a foundation of rising trade and production was well established. Mongol leaders used rare bird feathers from East Africa as fashion symbols, while wealthy women in western Europe adopted conical hat styles that had first emerged in China. European travelers to China, like Marco Polo in the 14th century, were astounded and deeply attracted by the consumer living standards in major cities, and the same thing applied to Western crusaders when they encountered the urban opulence of the Middle East. Consumerism, in other words, goes well back in human history, and it served as a major economic motivation well before modern times.

There were also, however, several limitations on premodern consumerism that distinguish the early stages of the phenomenon from what has developed, globally, in more recent times. In the first place, is it important to recognize that the boundary line between essentials and consumer items is not always easy to establish. Romans and others developed a deep interest in pepper from India, but this largely reflected the dubious preservation of many foodstuffs, whose early deterioration could be masked by spices. Interest in wine—and the Mediterranean was trading wine widely not just within the region but to the Indian Ocean by the later classical period—could obviously surpass any kind of necessity, but drinking weak wine also helped provide an alternative to polluted drinking water.

Early consumerism clearly affected only a small minority of any agricultural society, for most people simply did not have the means to buy beyond subsistence requirements. Lines could be fuzzy here as well, particularly as successful merchant classes developed, for example in the cities Marco Polo visited. Although aristocrats (after their early warrior phase) were the most obvious consumerist class, other prosperous urban groups could join in. Still, premodern consumerism was clearly a highly selective interest, leaving the vast majority of the population out. Additionally, the consumer riches of the upper class rarely seem to have sparked popular protest, at least in any direct way. People protested, occasionally, about food scarcities or about aristocratic control of desirable land, and once in a while—as in western Europe in the 14th century—they might more generally voice concerns about inequality. But consumerism was not on any specific protest list, which suggests that not only did the majority not participate in consumerist behavior, but consumerist motives had yet to spread widely as well.

Furthermore, many societies, both officially and often in fact, were far more interested in devoting extra resources to spiritual or political purposes than in any kind of personal consumerism. If anything, the spread of major religions during the postclassical period increased the focus on using funds to build mosques, churches, or temples. The ostensible purpose here was otherworldly, the praise of God or the celebration of the divine essence. It is possible to argue that the opportunity to see beautiful tile work or stained glass windows could have satisfied a consumer taste as well, for people who could not afford much if anything on their own, but the overall phenomenon, of public or religious spending, was different from consumerism in any literal sense.

Extra resources also might be used for group identity and bonding rather than individual satisfaction. Many artisans, in Japan, the Middle East, and western Europe, thus bought costumes to wear in public parades or guild meetings, and also afforded travel opportunities for workmen in training. The goal, however, was uniformity and group presentation, not consumerism in the more modern sense. Many of the same characteristics surrounded village festivals; popular cooking, for example, emphasized group meals at planting or harvest time rather than individualized or family enjoyment. A fair amount of

investment might go into these group efforts, which were thus really alternatives to consumerism per se although possibly satisfying some similar basic human needs.

Finally—and in many ways this sums up the spiritual and group alternatives to consumerism, as well as the confinement of most consumerism to specific social classes—premodern societies often turned against signs of consumerism in their own ranks. The Italian Renaissance, which produced new signs of urban consumerism in clothing and other items, also generated fierce attacks, mainly religiously inspired, in which luxuries were tossed onto public bonfires. The Chinese state periodically turned against individuals (both men and women, mainly from wealthy business ranks) who demonstrated too much commitment to showy furnishing and clothing, putting some to death. Many societies passed sumptuary laws that kept luxury spending down and enforced rigid consumer lines among defined social classes—for example, prohibiting efforts to imitate aristocratic styles. Active hostility to consumerism was part of the traditional legacy of many agricultural societies.

Modern Consumerism

Many of these hesitations about consumerism have persisted into modern times. Consumerism is still not equally available across wealth lines (or regional lines, for that matter); it is important not to overdo ubiquity of access. Objections to consumerism on grounds of the primacy of spiritual concerns persist, although many religious groups—even evangelical Protestants in the United States—have made a kind of peace with consumerism and have come to view it as one of the signs of divine favor. Group identities continue to war with individual whim in consumer tastes, although formally uniformed groups, aside from the military and some schoolchildren, are largely a thing of the past. And there are some societies that turn against consumerism on grounds of greater public needs, enforcement of class lines, or a traditionalist sense of decorum, although usually without putting consumerist icons to death.

In the main, however, modern societies have developed a different stance and potential toward consumerism than was true during the bulk of the hunting and gathering and agricultural periods of human history. The turning point toward more modern forms of consumerism began to emerge, first in western Europe, in the 17th and 18th centuries. This consumerism was distinguished from past patterns in several ways. It began to attract a mass (though not immediately universal) social following, and it was buttressed by a whole variety of novel commercial practices. It also acquired a more individualistic flavor, with people seeking to distinguish themselves from others by specific taste choices (even if, in past, they often parroted wider commercial models). A new level of faddism also entered in, with both consumers and their suppliers eager to discard past models (even from just a few years back) in favor of something at least superficially different. And the level of importance of consumerism in personal ratings of life almost certainly ratcheted up.

Attention initially focused on new food items, home furnishings, and clothing—not surprisingly, areas close to subsistence concerns. A huge fad for tulips emerged in 17th-century Holland, with people striving for new varieties, driving prices up, and buying pictures and decorations of tulips when the real thing was out of season. Interest in brightly colored clothing soared. By the 18th century, in places like Britain, a lively secondhand market and a notable increase in thefts of clothing indicated that, in true modern consumer fashion, passions sometimes outstripped financial means. Food consumerism involved growing interest in imports like sugar, tea, and coffee, as well as associated serving items. Imports of porcelain increased so much that in the 17th century the word *china* entered the vocabulary of materialism. Pots and cups became essential, and while urban families set the tone here, the interest spread gradually but inexorably to rural households as well. During the 18th century, a new European commitment to comfort arose, marked by interests like better home heating and umbrellas. And while a few critics railed that umbrellas undermined British virtue—a real man would simply get wet—the interests of comfort easily prevailed. Perhaps most important of all is the evidence that consumer items could take on real personal meaning. Wills, particularly from women, increasingly designated particular items—a serving utensil, a cabinet—for a favored niece or granddaughter, with the assumption that the material good carried an emotional value that would be obvious to the recipient.

Not surprisingly, in an increasingly commercial age, the consumer apparatus changed rapidly as well. It is not always easy to determine which came first—new sales pitches or new consumer interest—a conundrum that is still associated with interpreting consumerism. Shops began to proliferate, replacing the occasional itinerant salesperson, and they began to develop more eye-catching signs and window displays. Storekeepers offered loss leaders—an item sold under cost in order to lure customers to the store where they would buy other things—and began to extend easier credit. Advertisements appeared in the new outlet of weekly newspapers, often featuring endorsements from the rich and powerful—even for items as humble as a razor strop. Manufacturers, like the porcelain maker Josiah Wedgwood, began to test markets to see what models would sell in one place in order to determine larger production and sales strategies. Truly, at least rudimentary forms of virtually all contemporary consumer gimmicks were in operation in western Europe by the end of the 18th century.

It is important to note that the discovery of modern consumerism's point of origin is a recent and fundamental historical finding, as against older impressions that consumerism followed from the industrial revolution and came into play only in the later 19th century. Historians have spent a fair amount of time trying figure out the causes for the arrival of modern consumerism. Because of growing manufacturing and both regional and foreign trade, more Europeans had some margin of earnings above subsistence. The attraction of new imports—like coffee—helped spur novel tastes. Some scholars have pointed to the rise of a more sentimental or romantic culture, affecting practices like courtship, that simultaneously encouraged growing interest in items relating to appearance or home. The sheer pace of social change—with the massive population growth of the 18th century, for example—shook up established relationships. More young people could not gain familiar access to land inheritance or to craft mastership, but they could earn money wages: Consumerism provided substitute status and satisfaction. Women, increasingly pressed out of certain kinds of urban jobs, could view consumerism as a way to gain new voice in the household. Consumerism, in other words, was not merely a frivolous response to new earnings or new shopkeeper wiles: It had real meaning for many participants, providing opportunities for expression and even freedom outside traditional hierarchies.

Opposition inevitably surfaced. Moralists complained about misplaced priorities. Many conservatives lamented (and exaggerated) the extent that lower classes could now dress like their betters, wasting money in the process. Women came in for a lot of criticism, even though men were avid consumers too. Aristocrats and intellectuals often criticized what they saw as debased mass taste.

By the 19th century, however, consumerism was so well established in western Europe that it continued to accelerate despite hesitations. Two developments were crucial, from the basis already set: First, within the West itself, consumerism reached definable new levels. Second, modern consumerism began to spread to additional regions.

The first department store emerged, in Paris, during the 1830s as both cause and symbol of consumerism's movement to additional heights. Department stores, initially just groupings of clothing shops, provided new opportunities to display masses of goods to dazzle and lure consumers. Not surprisingly, department stores, along with more intense consumer passions, began to generate a brand new disease *kleptomania* (diagnosed soon after 1850), in which people—particularly middle-class women—would steal items that they did not objectively need and that they often could have afforded to buy outright. Along with department stores, thanks to improvements in printing, came increasingly glossy advertisements, with more visual and emotional inducements to buy: The first formal advertising agencies were established in the 1870s in the United States.

Consumerism's advance was signaled by a growing range of products, including more imported furniture (from the Middle East, for example, with a new passion for Persian rugs) and the addition of some high-investment items, like pianos (a must for any middle-class home), bicycles, and by the end of the century automobiles. It was also signaled by the rise of a more consumerist leisure pattern, with growing numbers of people buying entertainment as a main means of dealing with hours outside of work and sleep. Professional

sports, music hall, and ultimately movies were fruits of this important shift.

The new stage of consumerism was not simply the fruit of rising wages and falling hours of work, or the new talents of commercial manipulators to get people to buy unnecessary objects. It resulted as well from a new need to view in consumerism a reward for increasingly unrewarding work. In the working classes, many people began to realize that industrial jobs were less intrinsically interesting than their traditional counterparts, and sometimes, in the factories, downright nasty: But protests about work rarely succeeded, whereas demands for higher pay had a decent chance of winning. So many workers became what are called *instrumentalists*, accepting boring work as an instrument for a better consumer life off the job. Middle-class people, increasingly crammed into management hierarchies or white-collar slots, losing any shot at independent entrepreneurship, also turned to more abundant and explicit consumerism. Rising consumerism, in other words, was increasingly compensatory—which provided a new set of meanings.

Global Consumerism

The global spread of consumerism was a vital development in its own right. It depended on Western example and on the range of products available in world trade including the new outpourings from industrial factories; but it could also win independent appeal, to groups like young people for whom it gave welcome opportunities for expression. American interest in consumerism began to follow western European examples as early as the 18th century, and by the middle of the 19th century, the nation was becoming a consumer leader. A vast market and the lack of strong, preconsumer traditions helped propel the nation, and by 1900, American products and style were beginning to gain a strong foothold in various consumer markets around the world. Complaints about excessive Americanization emerged in consequence. American chain stores, like the dime store, and American movies (Hollywood was the clear global popular movie capital as early as 1919) were examples of pervasive American influence.

Department stores began to spread to Russia by the 1850s, catering admittedly to a small upper-class audience for whom foreign styles and shopping patterns had particular appeal. The stores reached Japan and Western-controlled Chinese cities like Shanghai by the 1890s. Again, they did not quickly appeal to everyone, even among those with some margin above subsistence. Many Chinese shoppers preferred traditional shops and items, finding little in the new stores that was not both foreign and useless. In contrast, enthusiasm for Western-style clothing made inroads in many urban settings. Commercial sports activities spread as well, with soccer associations forming in many regions, including Latin America, from the middle of the 19th century onward, and international federations developed soon after 1900. African cities, by the 1920s, generated something of a middle class, associated with business or with colonial administration and often partly Western-educated, who similarly internalized new consumer habits and often preferred them to extended family obligations that increasingly seemed expensive and distracting. Consumerism was going global.

Other forms of resistance responded as well. During the early part of the 20th century, the Japanese government took deliberate steps to discourage undue personal consumerism, attacking what it termed "luxury and indulgence" and urging a frugality that would build savings that could serve the state and society as a whole. Indian nationalists developed boycotts against consumption of Western goods as part of their independence struggle. The Soviet Union, after the Russian revolution, offered a somewhat ambivalent stand on consumerism. The nation developed new, state-run department stores, and some rhetoric implied that a communist society would extend consumer benefits more widely than capitalism managed. In fact, shortages and a desire to please department store workers, more than customers, led to limited consumer opportunities and often gruff service, in contrast to patterns outside the communist orbit. A bit later, many Islamic fundamentalists opposed key forms of consumerism: Leaders of the Iranian revolution of 1979 blasted consumerism as "corruption," particularly when it linked with sexual license, arguing the need for a religious alternative to a "hideous and most dangerous evil."

Particularly after World War II, however, global consumerism continued its advance in most regions of the world. Regional patterns varied, and not just because of different economic levels. Japanese and Chinese consumers continued to place more emphasis on savings than did their Western counterparts. Europeans put more stock in increasing leisure time, particularly vacations, whereas Americans relied more directly on acquisition of goods. No single model applied.

At the same time, however, consumerism became an important feature of globalization more generally. International conglomerates like McDonald's or Disney generated consumer experiences across a host of regional and cultural boundaries. Shopping malls, first introduced in the United States, gained access to newer consumer havens like Dubai. Christmas symbols, around Santa Claus and gift-giving, easily transcended religious affiliations. Japan became a major leader in generating international consumer styles in games and animation. Many regions, to be sure, combined local elements with international themes—as in the movie productions of Bollywood, in India, or modifications of fast-food menus to include traditional components. Huge variations in living standards greatly differentiated access to consumerism still. New concerns, particularly in the environmental area, generated new reasons to attack the phenomenon. But there was no question that consumer behaviors and aspirations constituted an important and often growing component of the contemporary experience on a worldwide basis.

Peter N. Stearns

See also Capitalism; Economic Ethics; Ethics, Global; Global Economic Issues; Global Health and Nutrition; Globalization, Phenomenon of; Inequality, Global; Peasant Economies; Social Movements; Trade; Value/Commodity Chains, Global

Further Readings

Breen, T. H. (2004). *The marketplace of revolution: How consumer politics shaped American independence.* New York: Oxford University Press.

Brewer, J., & Porters, R. (Eds.). (1993). *Consumption and the world of goods.* New York: Routledge.

Daunton, M., & Hilton, M. (2001). *The politics of consumption: Material culture and citizenship in Europe and America.* New York: Berg Press.

Rocci, F. (2003). *La Americanización del consumo: Las batallas por el mercado Argentino, 1920—1945*

[The Americanization of consumption: The battle for the Argentine market, 1920–1945]. Buenos Aires, Argentina: Universidad Tocuto Di Tella.

Stearns, P. N. (2006). *Consumerism in world history* (2nd ed.). New York: Routledge.

Tobin, J. (1992). *Re-made in Japan: Everyday life and consumer taste in a changing society*. New Haven, CT: Yale University Press.

Watson, J. (Ed.). (1998). *Golden arches East: McDonald's in East Asia*. Stanford, CA: Stanford University Press.

CONTAINERIZATION

Containerization—freight transport within a standard-sized box enabling intermodal transfer between marine and land modes efficiently and in large volumes—has revolutionized worldwide cargo shipping during the past 50 years. The modern manufacturing system and the contemporary global division of labor would not have occurred without containerization and its attendant impacts.

Modern-day containerization began on April 26, 1956, when a converted tanker, *Ideal X*, carried fifty-eight 35-foot metal truck trailer boxes from Newark, New Jersey, to Houston, Texas. The man behind the experiment was Malcolm Maclean, an American trucker, frustrated by slow and inefficient operations at dockside. In short order, he acquired other converted ships to carry his boxes. In 1960, he created Sea-Land Services, which became the world's largest container shipping company, and in 1999, it was absorbed by today's largest container line, APM-Maersk. In 1966, Sea-Land inaugurated a transatlantic service bringing the new technology to what was then the world's busiest shipping lane.

Between 1968 and 1970, the International Standards Organization adopted resolutions to standardize the design, size, and strength of containers enabling ships, ports, and land modes to handle the box uniformly. The standard size adopted was 8 feet wide and 8 feet high, with lengths of 10, 20, 30 or 40 feet. In time the 20-foot and 40-foot units came to dominate. Today, the standard unit of container ship capacity and port throughput is the 20-foot unit (TEU).

Containerization brought many changes. Time savings in ports were enormous. Where previously a ship would spend days in port to unload and load general cargo, now the time was reduced to hours. Security was enhanced also. Ports were reconfigured to handle the box. Large open terminals with long linear quays replaced covered sheds and finger piers. Special shore cranes were built to lift up to 40-ton capacity boxes; intermodal transfer stations were strategically placed to speed the transfer of containers. Port labor saw the elimination of thousands of longshoreman jobs. Ships were special built with cargo slots to accommodate the boxes. Ships grew in capacity from handling less than 1,000 TEUs to ships today handling more than 10,000 TEUs. These largest ships, called postpanamax, are larger than the constricting size of the Panama Canal, a disadvantage the Panama Canal Authority is addressing with the addition of larger locks set to open in 2014/2015. Changes also took place in rail transport. A real breakthrough in handling efficiency took place in 1984 with the introduction of double-stack train service—two containers on one railway flatcar—between Los Angeles and Chicago. Such service is now common throughout North America.

With time savings and economies of scale transport costs per ton of cargo declined relative to cargo values. In essence, the negative effect of distance on transporting goods decreased. Goods not previously traded were now able to enter trade. Those already in trade reached markets faster and more cheaply. As a result, consumer demand increased. This, combined with the wholesale shift of manufacturing to cheap labor areas in Asia, stimulated world trade and contributed to the globalization phenomenon.

Not only were the changes infrastructural, but they were also organizational. Rather than freight movement being viewed in distinct and separate parts, containerization became part of supply chain management in which physical distribution, materials management, marketing, and strategic planning were integrated into a cohesive whole. Consequently, merchandise in containers today moves through an integrated management system involving intermodal coordination.

The United Nations Conference on Trade and Development (UNCTAD) estimates that 143 million TEUs of containerized ocean freight were carried in 2007, a fivefold increase from 1990. The tonnage carried in 2007 was more than 1.2 billion.

The busiest containerized sea lanes are Asia–Europe, Asia–North America and Europe–North America. Combined, these routes see approximately 40% of the world's containerized freight. However, the trade on the lanes is not balanced with exports from Asia dominating. The Asia–Europe trade is overwhelmingly via the Suez Canal; the Asia–North America trade crosses the Pacific to/from West Coast ports or it passes through the Panama Canal to/from East Coast ports. A small proportion travels via Suez and the Atlantic Ocean. The world's container shipping fleet has a capacity of almost 15 million TEUs on approximately 9,500 ships. The major container shipping lines represent the global nature of containerization. Four of the top 10 companies are European: APM-Maersk (Denmark), MSC (Switzerland), CMA CGM (France), and Hapag-Lloyd (Germany). The remaining six are East Asian: Evergreen (Taiwan), COSCON (China), APL (Singapore), CSCL (China), NYK (Japan), and MOL (Japan). Interestingly, none of the major companies is U.S. based, largely because of domestic taxation and operating regulations. East Asia also dominates the port tables in container handling. Singapore, Shanghai, Hong Kong, and Shenzhen all handled more than 20 million TEUs in 2007. The busiest European port was Rotterdam (11 million TEUs); the busiest American port was the combined operations of Los Angeles–Long Beach (15 million TEUs).

The world recession in the first decade of the 21st century had negative effects on containerization. Approximately 10% of the container fleet was laid up; orders for new building were cancelled, and there were consolidations and mergers of major shipping lines. Increasing oil prices were also of concern. Although the long-term future of containerization may be uncertain, it is certain that what Malcolm Maclean envisioned and he and others brought about since 1956 has revolutionized how general cargo has moved around the world.

Robert J. McCalla

See also Global Economic Issues; Globalization, Phenomenon of; Industrialization; International Maritime Organization; Railroads; Standards and Standard Setting, Global; Trade; Transportation Systems

Further Readings

Levinson, M. (2006). *The box: How the shipping container made the world smaller and the world economy bigger.* Princeton, NJ: Princeton University Press.

Notteboom, T. (2004). Container shipping and ports: An overview. *Review of Network Economics, 3*(2), 86–106.

Slack, B. (1998). Intermodal transportation. In B. Hoyle & R. Knowles (Eds.), *Modern transport geography* (2nd ed., pp. 263–288). Chichester, UK: Wiley.

United Nations Conference on Trade and Development. (2008). *Review of maritime transport 2008.* New York: United Nations.

CONTRACEPTION

Although contraceptive use involves an individual's decision to have safe sex and control fertility, trends at both global and local levels are greatly affected by culture, religion, gender relations, medicine, and state policy. Contraception, the deliberate use of various methods to prevent pregnancy as a consequence of sexual intercourse, has been practiced since ancient times. Yet it was not until the second half of the 20th century that contraception became an issue of global importance out of a concern for both overpopulation and reproductive health and rights. Easy access to safe, effective, and affordable contraceptive methods is a crucial part of reducing unintended pregnancies and unsafe abortions; it also has brought about the so-called sexual revolution.

Contraceptive methods range from natural ones like rhythm, withdrawal, vaginal douching, and prolonged lactation to artificial ones such as sterilization, the birth control pill, injectable/implant, intrauterine devices (IUDs), vaginal barrier methods, and condoms. In the 19th century, coitus interruptus was the most widely used, followed by vaginal douching. The condom, because of its original association with prostitutes, its rough material, and its costs, was not attractive to many couples at the time. Birth control movements led by feminists in the early 20th century advocated female methods to separate sex and pregnancy, ensuring women full control of their bodies. These early advocates circulated contraceptive information and set up clinics to provide their clients with diaphragms, spermicidal cream, and jelly, which were banned in some countries under obscenity laws or pronatalist policies, such as the United States and Japan, respectively. The well-known fruit of the movements—the pill (a female hormonal contraceptive)—was invented in 1960 by reproductive scientists based in the United States who received financial support from the famous birth control activists Margaret Sanger and Katharine McCormick as well as pharmaceutical companies like Syntex and Searle.

In the 1960s and 1970s, anxiety about unchecked world population growth was pervasive worldwide. Developed countries, the United States in particular, were concerned that "overpopulation" in poor countries could cause social turbulence and lead to dwindling natural resources, undermining geopolitical security and the environment. Developing countries worried that rapid population growth might hinder their economic development. Some governments, private foundations, and international organizations argued that reducing the fertility rate was necessary for sustainable development, yet some developing nations asserted that the real problem was underdevelopment rather than population growth. In 1974, at the World Population Conference in Bucharest, Romania, the delegates from Third World nations championed the idea that, with adequate international aid, development itself was the best contraceptive for poor countries. Despite these controversies, international funding poured in, supporting research in long-acting and permanent contraceptive methods—especially IUDs and female sterilization—and spreading them in the developing regions. The large-scale promotion of contraception through national family-planning projects emphasized efficacy, convenience, and cost-effectiveness. However, a lack of adequate medical counseling was not uncommon, and this often resulted in less attention to safety issues, thus compromising women's well-being.

It was not until the 1970s that the rise of the women's health movement brought women's reproductive health and choice into public discussions about population control and access to contraception. Women's health activists not only worked for stricter risk evaluation for female contraceptive methods, but they also pressured the World Health Organization (WHO) to invest research monies in male methods, such as "the male pill," which is still under development. Through their advocacy in the International Population Conferences in 1984 in Mexico City, Mexico, and in 1994 in Cairo, Egypt, women's empowerment and reproductive health and rights gradually came to form the ground rules for both governments and nongovernmental organizations that were providing and assessing family-planning services. In addition to the women's health movement, the HIV/AIDS prevention and treatment programs around the world play a critical role in disseminating information about contraception and providing cheap or free contraceptives (usually condoms). Contraception has become an essential part of global public health policies.

According to UN data for the first decade of the 21st century, the contraceptive prevalence (the percentage of married women 15–49 years of age currently using contraception) is around 70% in the more developed regions and greater than 60% in the less developed regions. Although the average contraceptive rate in developing countries has risen substantially from approximately 10% in the 1960s, the proportion of women with unmet need is still large in sub-Saharan Africa, western Asia, and Oceania. Only 28% of African women are using contraceptives. Worldwide, most couples rely on modern methods, although their choice differs significantly between more and less developed areas. For example, the most common methods globally are female sterilization and IUDs, but the two methods are used more often in less developed countries (22.3% and 15.1%, respectively) than in more developed areas (8.1% and 9.1%, respectively). By contrast, the use of the pill and condoms are more common (18.1% and 16.1%, respectively) in more developed countries than in less developed ones (7.2% and 4.4%, respectively). The difference in the prevalence of female and male methods is also noteworthy. Less than 7% of contraceptive couples in the less developed regions use condoms and withdrawal, compared with 30% in the more developed regions. This means that globally, only around one tenth of contraceptive couples use male methods, leaving women to shoulder most of the burden of fertility control.

Since the 1960s, many nongovernmental organizations have worked with the WHO and the United Nations to provide contraceptives around the world. The International Planned Parenthood Federation based in London was formed in 1952 at the Third International Conference on Planned Parenthood. The Population Council, the Guttmacher Institute, and Pathfinder International are based in the United States yet operate globally. The U.S. Agency for International Development has been the largest donor to their projects, which bears witness to the shift from population control to reproductive health and rights among institutional advocates of contraception. It is estimated that more than 26 billion new couples will need contraceptives in the first half of the 21st century. The global medical and health communities are still working on training family-planning professionals as well as developing new methods, such as male hormonal contraceptives and antifertility vaccines, to offer safer, more convenient, and more accessible contraception.

Yu-ling Huang

See also Abortion; Birth Control; Fertility; Population and Demographic Change; Population Control Policies; Population Growth and Population Explosions; Women's Movement; Women's Rights; World Health Organization

Further Readings

Collier, A. (2007). *The humble little condom: A history.* Amherst, NY: Prometheus Books.

Jütte, R. (2008). *Contraception: A history.* Cambridge, UK: Polity Press.

Oudshoorn, N. (2003). *The male pill: A biography of a technology in the making.* Durham, NC: Duke University Press.

United Nations, Department of Economic and Social Affairs, Population Division. (2009). *World contraceptive use 2009* (POP/DB/CP/Rev2009).

Watkins, E. S. (1998). *On the pill: A social history of oral contraceptives, 1950–1970.* Baltimore: Johns Hopkins University Press.

COOPERATION

Cooperation is essential for survival on all levels, from interpersonal to global. Cooperation refers to interactions between two or more creatures, individuals, or systems that happen in purposeful intention and often provide a benefit for the actors involved. At the same time, it is a basis for achievement and progress as it often also involves communication, coordination, and collaboration. Although the ideal case is mutual cooperation, some situations are also characterized by forced cooperation or deception. The crucial importance of cooperation often comes into focus when solutions fail because of unsuccessful cooperation.

On the global level, an oft-cited example of when cooperation is essential for survival is the ongoing negotiations on climate change. This example, among many others, highlights the importance and imperative of understanding cooperation on all levels of society. For scholars and students of global studies, the processes and various outcomes of cooperation are just as interesting as the associated cultural backgrounds, values, and interests of the cooperation partners.

Theoretical Models

Several scientific disciplines carry out research on cooperation and have established models for understanding it. Whereas biology focuses on symbiotic cellular processes or colony-forming insects, cultural and social studies deal with phenomena of interactions among individuals, among organizations and institutions, and among nations, on both a regional and a global level.

One of the most prominent approaches to human cooperation is outlined in Robert Axelrod's study on the evolution of cooperation. For his experiment, he invited internationally renowned scholars to propose solutions to an iterated interaction on the basis of the well-known prisoner's dilemma. The "tit for tat" strategy, where members of the group cooperate only with others who also cooperate and exclude those who do not, was the most successful.

Axelrod identified three necessary conditions for cooperation. First, the likelihood of meeting sometime in the future instills a basic level of accountability for actions taken: If there is no chance of future interaction, there are no repercussions for not cooperating. Second, the ability to identify one another also contributes to ensuring future accountability. Third and finally, a record of past behavior allows the individual actors to judge future behavior and determine whether cooperation will be beneficial. Axelrod thus concluded that cooperation portrays not only a successful method of goal-achievement without the need for prior agreements but also a very rational one.

In his study on the logic of collective action, Mancur Olson added another twist to these insights. Olson challenged the accepted wisdom that people will naturally act collectively to pursue common interests by identifying the "free rider" problem, under which individuals in a group will not cooperate when the group is seeking to provide public goods. A rational individual will join and contribute to a group only when the individual can gain a separate, private benefit reserved strictly for group members. In sum, without selective incentives for participation, cooperation is unlikely to take place even when the actors share common interests.

Another theoretical approach based on the analytical meso level that considers institutions and organizations is that of a commons. This ancient form of cooperation has experienced a renaissance in contemporary discourse. Propelled by the work of Nobel Laureate in economics Elinor Ostrom, the commons refers to resources that are collectively owned and are shared, used and managed cooperatively. These resources traditionally referred mainly to natural resources (e.g., land, forests, and rivers) but now extend to culture, public goods, such as education, and even knowledge and software (e.g., Creative Commons). This theoretical framework places issues such as global public goods and the global commons at center stage.

Cooperation in Societal Spheres and Internationally

Modern societies are heavily dependent on cooperation, as reflected in every societal sphere. All types of economic activities are based on cooperation, among a company's personnel, between companies forming joint ventures, and, in its perhaps strongest form of expression, in cooperatives or cooperative societies, which are associations of freely affiliated individuals who pursue common economic interests with direct democratic rules and arrangements. Similarly, within organized civil society, associations depend on the participation and cooperation of their members, and other nonprofit organizations rely on the involvement of their funders and other stakeholders to meet their collective aims. Finally, in the political sphere in democratic societies, cooperation is required even among competing political parties and interest groups to pass legislation and implement policy.

It is at the international level, however, where cooperation becomes of particular interest to scholars and students of global studies. The highest instance of international cooperation among nation-states takes place at the United Nations, along with its family of affiliated institutions dealing with specific issues and interests. Other intergovernmental instances include the International Organization for Standardization, the Organization for Economic Cooperation and Development, the range of "Group of . . ." entities, and the various regional assemblies, among them the European Union, the Organization for African Unity, and the Organization of American States. Furthermore, numerous nongovernmental international associations and unions have emerged to facilitate cooperation in business, the professions, science and social science research, environmental protection, and various other global issues.

Current and Future Issues

Amid expanding globalization processes and ever increasing access to information, the necessary conditions for cooperation outlined by Axelrod—likelihood of future encounters, actor identification, and record of past behavior—certainly exist at the global level. Furthermore, numerous institutional instances that should facilitate cooperation have emerged during the past decades. Given the persistence of certain global problems such as climate change, inequality, and conflict, these conditions are not necessarily sufficient in the absence of incentives and will.

Nevertheless, with cooperation at the global or international level, much progress and many successes have been achieved. For example, the worldwide effort to promote the prevention and treatment of HIV/AIDS has contributed to a significant reduction in new infections, and similar initiatives for other diseases have had positive results.

Among the many open questions are, if the necessary conditions for cooperation exist, what conditions or elements prevent it from happening?

What are the incentives and disincentives to international cooperation? What factors bring to the cooperation table issues that have been lingering for years? When does cooperation fail? As mentioned at the outset, the effort to find cooperative responses to the climate change phenomenon—as well as the many other pressing global issues—may serve as an object for analyzing many of these questions.

Martin Hölz

See also Associations; Darwinism and Social Darwinism; Global Commons; Individualism; International Nongovernmental Organizations (INGOs); Interpol; Labor; North Atlantic Treaty Organization (NATO); Organisation for Economic Co-operation and Development (OECD); Public Goods, Global; Solidarity Movements; Trade; Trade Agreements; United Nations; Wikipedia

Further Readings

Argyle, M. (1991). *Cooperation: The basis of sociability.* London: Routledge.

Axelrod, R. (1984). *The evolution of cooperation.* New York: Basic Books.

Olson, M. (1965). *The logic of collective actions. Public goods and the theory of groups.* Cambridge, MA: Harvard University Press.

Ostrom, E. (1990). *Governing the commons. The evolution of institutions for collective action.* Cambridge, MA: Cambridge University Press.

CORPORATE IDENTITY

Corporate identity is an important global and institutional phenomenon. Within the corporate marketing domain, it is viewed as a central and necessary concept. In international contexts, corporate identities are significant, prominent, and omnipresent, and they are central to our comprehension of the global landscape.

The discovery and explication of identities are central to academic research, and from time immemorial—and from all parts of the globe—many of the great themes of intellectual inquiry have identities as their foci. Marketing and management scholars are no different in this regard, and in recent years, many marketing and management scholars have begun to scrutinize institutional identities.

Corporate identity is a central—if, sometimes, underappreciated—global and institutional concern. Importantly, corporate identities have a key role in defining the self vis-à-vis the creation of an individual's identity as a customer, employee, and company shareholder.

Two Schools of Thought

In scrutinizing the area or corporate identity, it is important to realise that corporate identity is a multifaceted construct. As such, corporate identity can be associated with the following two schools of thought:

An *organization's outward identification* refers to the multiple ways an organization communicates its essence—real, envisioned, or desired—with its key stakeholders. This includes a plethora of planned and unplanned forms of communication. Historically, emphasis has been accorded to symbolic communication, especially corporate visual identification (company logos) along with sensory identification. This entry focuses on visual corporate communications. The field of integrated corporate communications grew out of those earlier developments.

An *organization's essence* encompasses those identity attributes that imbue an entity with distinctiveness via a set of inimitable characteristics. In their totality, these identity anchors offer penetrating insights into, among others, an organization's purposes, activities, markets and geographic presence, constituencies, philosophies, corporate style, and organizational form. This identity perspective is viewed as a central tenet of corporate marketing since corporate brands, communications, reputations, and a stakeholder association with an entity need to take account of an organization's defining attributes.

Outward Identification

Institutions have long been concerned with communicating identity and ideology via integrated visual and symbolic communication. From the earliest times, brand marks were used to indicate ownership and provenance. One important means through which we comprehend the world is via symbolism and logos. In addition, we should not lose sight of the importance of verbal identification: Company names are, invariably, the most powerful forms of outward identification from organizations.

Sensory Identification

Of course, we receive information via all five of our senses: sight (vision), hearing (audition), taste (gestation), smell (olfaction), and touch (tactition); institutions marshal all, or many, of these to communicate, inculcate, and reinforce corporate tenets, beliefs, and ideologies. Corporations, along with monarchies, religions, universities, and other corporate bodies, often prescribe the forms of sensory identification to be used, and often, these can form an important part of their symbolic vernacular.

Corporate Visual Identification

This being said, most attention in this area is rightly given to corporate visual identification. The desirability, indeed strategic necessity, of having a distinctive corporate visual style/visual communication has characterized institutional life since the earliest times. The importance of the territory is not a new phenomenon, and juridical insights shed light on the economic value and strategic importance of corporate visual identification.

Heraldic and Trademark Law

The ancient laws of heraldry are testimony to the importance of visual symbolism (specifically coats of arms, heraldic crests, badges, and mottoes) as identifiers for corporations: The Court of the Lord Lyon in Scotland is still active. Increasingly, from the 19th century onward, organizations relied on trademarks as means of reaching out to customers and others, and legal protection was soon sought for these identifying marks. The United Kingdom led the way in passing trademark legislation (the Trade Mark Registration Act of 1875).

The Value of Visual Identification

Drawing on heraldic law, the value of an organization's identifying visual symbol (a coat of arms or its modern equivalent such as a logo) can be seen in that it is viewed as inheritable property and

moreover is invested with commercial, economic, and emotional value. Among scholars there is a consensus that visual identification has value and can be used to articulate corporate strategy, corporate culture, corporate communications, and a more fashionable visual identity. Moreover, logos and company names can be signs of assurance and indicators of quality (corporate brand identity). They have considerable reach: A single company van in 1 year may bring a company's visual identity to millions of people.

Visual Identification Past and Present

The advent of the industrial revolution in Britain, followed by other countries, meant that a largely agrarian society shifted to one that quickly became industrialized. This presented difficulties for manufacturers: The distance between manufacturers and users became progressively more distant and led to corporate anonymity and obscurity. Visual communication, along with advertising and corporate brand-building, helped to bridge this gap and communicate both corporate and corporate brand identity to customers. The same phenomenon characterizes newly industrialized nations of today. Today, many Western companies outsource the manufacture of products or the provision of support services. As a consequence, visual identification has a new role: as an identifier for the corporate brand.

Visual Identification and Graphic Design

Today, visual identification is viewed as an important branch of the design profession, and its roots, arguably, can be traced back to the establishment by the British government in 1837 of a design training system: the South Kensington System, in which technical proficiency, aesthetic sensitivity, and design discrimination were emphasized.

Design Schools and Philosophies

The late 19th and early to mid-20th centuries observed the emergence of several influential design schools and philosophies: These schools resulted in some benchmark corporate visual identities, some of which still endure. England's Arts and Crafts Movement (1890–1914) emphasized simplicity and drew on traditional craftsmanship and medievalism. Germany's Jugendstil Movement (early 20th century) was inspired by its English forerunner and advanced the cause of total graphic design coordination *Gesamtkunstwerk*. In Italy, the Movimento Comunita (pre-1945) not only embraced design integration but also emphasized the importance of company culture and the wider societal roles of corporations.

Leading figures of this movement include Edward Johnston, whose celebrated typeface for the London Underground still endures (Arts and Crafts); Peter Behrens's pioneering integrative visual communications strategies for AEG, at the time the world's largest electrical company (Jugenstil); and Adriano Olivetti's much broader identity work for his family's firm of typewriter/computer fame (Movimento Communita).

Since 1945, the prominence and importance of corporate visual identification and the graphic design profession have burgeoned in global contexts. Increasingly, the analytical and strategic aspects of graphic design—and the need for coordinated design—were emphasized by leading graphic design and identity consultants. One point of note: Until the 1970s, the label "House Style" was commonly used to describe an organization's coordinated visual design scheme. However, as a result of U.S. influence, the corporate identity concept began to hold sway.

The importance of integrated graphic design can be viewed as a precursor of the field of integrated corporate communication and integrated identity coordination. However, the value of corporate logos is in what they represent rather than in their intrinsic design quality, and outward identification is, clearly, a manifestation of a deeper notion of identity. This brings us to a deeper and more substantive notion of identity: that which relates to an organization's essence.

Essence

Informed, principally, by a functionalist perspective, this school of thought views corporate identity in terms of an organization's defining identity traits. An organization's attributes are viewed to be substantive, and their effects are deemed, in part, to be observable. This identity viewpoint increasingly informs the work of marketing/corporate marketing scholars, especially those in the Euro-American world.

This perspective is also informed by juridical notions of identity, and one of its roots resides in an arcane, although extant, branch of law: canon law. Canon law (the law of the church) has, since time immemorial, regarded the Catholic Church's corporate identity to exist in perpetuity and views it as a unique identity type. This legal notion was influential in other branches of global jurisprudence in terms of the identity of nations (constitutional law) and importantly, in the context of this entry, vis-à-vis the identity of organizations (commercial law).

Today, drawing on the precepts of canon law, both corporate marketing scholars and jurists are mindful that corporations have a separate, and potentially perpetual, legal identity. Importantly, it is an identity type that is different from that of its owners and, moreover, from the collective identity of its organizational members. For this reason, organizations have the status of a legal person and can sue and can be sued. In juridical terms, corporations are regarded as *legal persons* with rights and responsibilities that are distinct from organizational members.

Although legal documents of incorporation articulate many key corporate identity attributes, they are, necessarily, limited. As such, complementary approaches in articulating core corporate identity attributes have been the focus of identity scholars. French scholars Jean-Paul Larcon and Roland Reitter have argued, for instance, that an institution's identity traits bestow a corporation with *specificity, stability, and coherence*. In a similar vein, albeit later, U.S. scholars Stuart Albert and David A. Whetten have postulated that an organization's real or perceived corporate identity attributes articulate an institution's *central, distinctive*, and *enduring* characteristics. However, there are likely to be difficulties in defining what an organization "is." Thus, it may be efficacious to refer to comparative identities: in other words, to articulate an institution's essence not so much by what it is but by what it is not.

Corporate Identity Management and Corporate Personality

Significantly, this school of thought takes account of the view that senior managers do effect material change to an institution's identity attributes through changes in ownership and legal status, core purposes and activities, working practices, and so on, even including the sale of its corporate brand. A core tenet of this school is that of corporate identity management: the strategic necessity of ongoing identity management. For instance, in the formative years of a corporation's existence, company purpose, rationale, and character are typically, clearly articulated by the organization's founders, and this comprises the corporate personality. As a consequence, there is normally little ambiguity in this regard. However, when the organization's founders leave and the organization enters a technocratic stage of development, there is a need to find a surrogate for the founder's personality with a managed corporate personality. The responsibility for this is very much a senior management concern, notes Olins.

Corporate Identity: A Necessary Concept

Only when an organization is established—where a corporate identity has a separate legal existence—can a corporate brand develop (corporate brands are a related but distinct category of identity) and customer, employee, and other types of identification with the organization develop. It also provides a foundation for corporate-wide action and coordination (unity of management and purpose).

Moreover, because an institution's corporate identity—a firm's defining attributes—provides a platform on which corporate communications policies are developed, corporate reputations are built, and corporate images and associations are formed. Identity is a central organizational construct: Other concepts are contingent on identity. This is why corporate identity is viewed as a central tenet of corporate marketing and of our comprehension of contemporary organizations in global contexts.

John M. T. Balmer

See also Aesthetics; Communicative Power; Consumerism; Corporations, Transnational; Global Communications and Technology; Global Economic Issues; Homogenization; Identities in Global Societies; Marketing

Further Readings

Albert, S., & Whetten, D. (1985). Organizational identity. In L. L.Cummings & B. Straw (Eds.), *Research in organizational behavior* (pp. 263–269). Greenwich, CT: JAI Press.

Balmer, J. M. T. (2008). Identity based views of the corporation: Insights from corporate identity, organisational identity, social identity, visual identity and corporate image. *European Journal of Marketing, 42,* 879–906.

Balmer, J. M. T. (2009). Corporate marketing: Apocalypse, advent and epiphany. *Management Decision, 47,* 544–572.

Balmer, J. M. T., Stuart, H., & Greyser, S. A. (2009). Aligning identity and strategy: Corporate branding at British Airways in the late 20th century. *California Management Review, 51,* 6–23.

Larcon, J. P., & Reitter, R. (1979). *Structures de pouvoir et identité de l'entreprise* [Structures of power and corporate identity]. Paris: Nathan.

Olins, W. (1978). *The corporate personality: An inquiry into the nature of corporate identity.* London: Design Council.

CORPORATIONS, TRANSNATIONAL

The term *transnational corporation,* also known as *multinational corporation,* refers to an enterprise composed of wholly owned or partially owned entities that operate in more than one country. A transnational corporation (TNC) originates in a particular national economy and then expands abroad over time. TNCs are central actors in the globalization of the production of goods and services. Until approximately 50 years go, TNCs tended to be involved with richer countries in producing industrial products and with less developed countries in agriculture and extractive industries. In contrast, in recent decades, TNCs have become important to the emergence of developing economies as major participants in the production of industrial goods and services for global markets.

In 2008, the world's top 100 nonfinancial TNCs, ranked by foreign assets, had 57% of their assets and 58% of their employees outside their home countries (United Nations Conference on Trade and Development [UNCTAD], 2008). These companies therefore had a strong global presence while

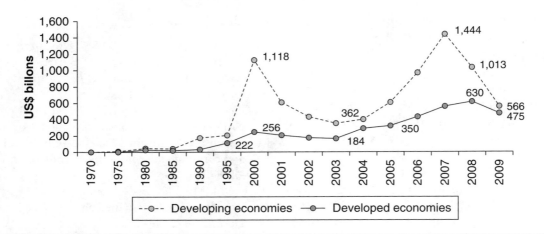

Figure I   Foreign direct investment to developed and developing countries, 1970–2009.

Source: UNCTAD. Foreign Direct Investment database, http://unctadstat.unctad.org (2011).

maintaining significant roots in their home bases. Among these top 100 TNCs, 18 were based in the United States, 15 each in the United Kingdom and France, 13 in Germany, and 9 in Japan. The other 30 companies among the top 100 were in 18 different countries, including 5 in Switzerland, 4 in Spain, and 3 in Sweden. In terms of industrial classifications, 11 of these corporations were in automobiles, 10 each in petroleum and utilities (electricity/gas/water), 9 each in pharmaceuticals and electrical/electronic equipment, and 7 each in telecommunications and food/beverages/tobacco.

A prime measure of the role of TNCs in countries other than their own is foreign direct investment (FDI). Figure 1 shows the amounts of FDI in nominal U.S. dollars to developed and developing economies from 1970 to 2009. Although the data in the graph are not adjusted for inflation, they nevertheless show the enormous growth in FDI to both developed and developing economies that has occurred in the last two decades.

The United States is by far the world's leading country in outward FDI with 17.4% of the world total in 2007, 17.1% in 2008, and 22.5% in 2009. The United States is also the leading country for inward FDI with 12.7% of the world total in 2007, 18.3% in 2008, and 11.7% in 2009. China is the largest recipient of FDI among developing economies, and in many years second to the United States among all economies. Not including Hong Kong, China received 4.0% of world FDI in 2007, 6.1% in 2008, and 8.5% in 2009. In addition, Hong Kong's share was 2.6% in 2007, 3.4% in

2008, and 4.4% in 2009. By comparison, India's share was 1.2% in 2007, 2.3% in 2008, and 3.1% in 2009.

The data displayed in Figure 1 also show that FDI to developed countries has been extremely unstable since the late 1990s. The sharp increase in FDI to the developed economies in the late 1990s was the result of telecommunications deregulation and the Internet boom, including the rollout of global optical fiber networks. When the Internet boom turned to bust in 2001, FDI plummeted as TNCs cut capital expenditures and several major service providers went bankrupt. Then from 2003 to 2007, there was another boom in FDI to developed economies, driven by both financialization and globalization. The prime form of FDI in this boom was cross-border mergers and acquisitions (M&A), with a heavy involvement of private equity firms and hedge funds. With an increase in global financial activity related to derivative trading, there was an unprecedented amount of FDI related to financial services. Although approximately 90% of the FDI to developed countries came from other developed countries, several TNCs from developing economies invested in greenfield sites in the developed countries.

A considerable proportion of the FDI that was undertaken in the 2003–2007 boom was driven by speculation, as evidenced by the dramatic decline in FDI to developed countries in 2008 and 2009. FDI to developed countries declined by 29% in 2008 and then by 44% in 2009, while FDI to developing countries continued to increase in 2008 before declining by 24% in 2009. The emergence of the BRIC (Brazil, Russia, India, and China) countries as major developing economies was both cause and effect of the boom of FDI to developing countries.

The growth in FDI during the past two decades reflects a dramatic change in the ways in which the large established industrial corporation extends its operations from its home country to foreign countries. Historically, in the era of protectionism that prevailed in the first half of the 20th century before being dismantled in the post–World War II decades, TNCs set up or acquired facilities abroad to jump trade barriers. TNC investments in manufacturing facilities tended to be in fully integrated plants located in the developed countries of the world where there were large markets for an industrial corporation's final products. TNC investments in less developed countries tended to be in mines and plantations for the extraction of natural products. TNCs were not viewed as dynamic forces for development in the poorer countries of the world and indeed were often viewed as rapacious exploiters of the natural resources of Third World countries.

This TNC "business model" for less developed countries began to change in the 1960s with the microelectronics revolution. Semiconductor companies invested in assembly and testing facilities abroad in low-wage areas of the world, especially in many Asian countries where they found a literate female labor force to do hand assembly and other shop-floor work as well as indigenous university-educated personnel to serve as managers and engineers. Since semiconductor devices were high in value relative to their weight, transportation costs of the goods-in-process to and from the host nations was not an important consideration in the location of plants. Important location criteria for TNCs were, however, the availability of an educated labor force and the political stability of the host country.

By the early 1970s, every major U.S. semiconductor manufacturer had set up assembly plants in Asia, which replaced Mexico as the main offshore location. The most favored Asian nations were Taiwan, South Korea, Singapore, and Hong Kong, as well as fast-rising Malaysia after it set up its free enterprise zone in Penang in 1972. At this time, wage rates were lower in these Asian countries than in Mexico and other Latin American countries, while in Asia the TNCs had access to a better educated labor force.

Over time in a favored host country such as Malaysia, TNCs in the electronics industry such as Intel and Hewlett-Packard upgraded their operations to engage in higher value-added activities, with the result that they not only demanded workers with greater skills but also invested in the acquisition of those skills. These companies expanded the number of indigenous people they employed and paid them higher wages, thus contributing to increases in standards of living of the economy as a whole. In Malaysia, as a prime example, FDI in the electronics industry was a major force in raising GDP per capita (in 1990 U.S. dollars) from US$2,289 in 1972 to US$5,132 in 1990 and US$9,584 in 2006 (Maddison, 2010).

In South Korea and Taiwan, FDI in the electronics industry from the late 1960s helped lay the foundation for the emergence in the 1980s and 1990s of indigenous companies—for example, Korea's Samsung and Taiwan Semiconductor Manufacturing Company—that themselves became major global TNCs and, through their high-end investment strategies, helped drive per-capita incomes in their home nations even higher. Many of the managers and engineers who became prominent in these home-grown companies began their careers working for Western, and especially U.S.-based, TNCs that had set up offshore operations in their countries. Complementing the capabilities of these TNC-trained personnel were those countrymen who returned from working abroad with higher education degrees and work experience with foreign companies. These accumulated capabilities enabled the returnees to contribute to indigenous innovation as employees at national research institutes and indigenous companies. At some point, the most successful indigenous companies themselves became TNCs.

Meanwhile, in the 1980s and 1990s, the Uruguay Round of the General Agreement on Tariffs and Trade (GATT) and then the World Trade Organization (WTO) were breaking down trade barriers. As we have observed, under the old TNC business model trade barriers had actually encouraged FDI as companies located abroad to jump over the barriers. Characterizing the new TNC business model that developed out of microelectronics industry were what became known as "global value chains" in which TNCs would off-shore the manufacture, assembly, and testing of a product's components to various parts of the world and then act as systems integrators in delivering the final assembled and tested product to buyers. Developments that have lowered the costs and increased the speed and reliability of global transportation and communications systems have further encouraged the creation of global value chains. TNCs that organized global value chains wanted to observe goods and services flow easily and inexpensively around the world, without trade impediments. A global economy based on the principles of free trade is, therefore, consistent with the new TNC business model.

Even with TNC capital flowing to employ people around the world, activities that involve complex learning processes and strategic decision making tend to remain located in home country of the TNC. Nevertheless, during the past two decades TNCs have been offshoring a great deal of activity that is classified as research and development (R&D). The amount of R&D expenditures is geographically distributed even though developed countries have had relatively higher shares. According to UNCTAD's 2005 World Investment Report, throughout the period 1994–2002, the role of developing countries as a whole increased from 7.6% to 13.5%. The top gainers of R&D shares during this period were as follows: China, Singapore, Hong Kong (China), Malaysia, and the Republic of Korea. The number of FDI projects in R&D provided by UNCTAD for the period of 2002–2004 also demonstrates the increasing importance of developing economies, as almost 48% of 1,773 projects were undertaken in developing Asia and Oceania. In terms of employment opportunities, India and China were the top two countries in which new jobs through those R&D-focused investments were created.

Industries differ in terms of markets, technology, and competition, and as a result, different industries hold out different possibilities for economic development through the involvement of TNCs. A key industry for both developed and developing economies is the automobile industry. UNCTAD's 2008 list of the 100 largest nonfinancial TNCs by assets includes 11 automobile producers: Toyota (ranked number 5), Volkswagen (11), Ford (16), Honda (20), Daimler (21), BMW (28), Nissan (34), Fiat (52), General Motors (53), Volvo (57), and Hyundai (79). Volvo AB was the leader in the proportion of its assets (79%) and employment (72%) abroad. At the other end of the scale for these 11 companies, Hyundai had only 34% of its assets abroad and BMW 26% of its employment abroad.

The globalization patterns for the leading companies differ markedly. In 2009, Toyota had 49% of its vehicle production in Japan, 12% in the United States, 8% in China, and 6% in Thailand. The global production figures for Volkswagen were 35% in Germany, 21% in China, 13% in Brazil, 9% each in Spain and the Czech Republic, and 5% in Mexico. As a U.S.-based company, Ford had 30% of its vehicle production in the United States, 16% in Germany, 10% in China, 8% in Belgium, 7% in Brazil, 6% in Spain, and 5% each in Canada and Mexico (OICA, 2010).

China looms large in the global strategies of these three automotive TNCs as well as several others. The Chinese government has encouraged TNCs to have joint ventures, including international technical centers, with indigenous companies in China. In 2009, China was by far the world's largest motor vehicle producer with more than 22% of the world total, followed by the Japan with 13%, the United States with 9%, and Germany with 8%. But virtually all the 13.7 million motor vehicles that China produced in 2009 were for its home market; China is a major host to automotive TNCs but has yet to develop its own indigenous companies that can invest around the world.

Of the other emerging giant, in 2009 India had only 4% of world motor vehicle production, and remained of relatively minor importance to the global investment strategies of automotive TNCs. Nevertheless there exists a proliferation of government initiatives and international joint ventures to develop the Indian automotive industry. Among developing countries, Brazil, with more than 5% of global production, was of greater importance than India in the motor vehicle industry.

Through FDI and the construction of global value chains, TNCs have become a major force for the transformation of once poor countries into emerging rich countries. As stated previously, the key conditions for developing countries in gaining the advantages of TNCs are investment in an educated labor force and the maintenance of political stability. When, as in the case of China, TNCs covet access to not only low-cost productive labor but also an expanding home market, there is an opportunity for the host country to "trade markets for technology," which in turn can foster indigenous innovation and global expansion. A prime example in China is the communications equipment company, Huawei Technologies, founded in 1988, which employed 95,000 people at the end of 2009, with only 35% of these employees from its home country (Huawei Technologies, 2010).

As for the developed countries, it is not clear that they remain the main beneficiaries of TNCs. In the 2000s, U.S.-based TNCs, including many in high-tech industries, showed a marked tendency to expand their presence in developing countries through FDI while using their profits to repurchase billions of dollars of stock to boost their stock prices in the United States (Lazonick, 2009; Milberg, 2008). Much of the potential gains from globalization are thereby lost to the U.S. labor force. The result has been growing employment opportunity in developing countries and declining employment opportunity in the United States. A combination of global value chains and financialized corporate behavior seems to be changing the role of TNCs in the rapidly changing balance of power between the developed and developing world.

William Lazonick and Ebru Bekaslan

See also Antiglobalization Movements and Critics; Capitalism; Economic Crises; Economic Development; Global Economic Issues; Globalization, Phenomenon of; Inequality, Global Economic; Investments; Law, Transnational; Liberalism, Neoliberalism; Value/Commodity Chains, Global; World Economic Forum; World Social Forum

Further Readings

Buckley, P., & Ghauri, P. (2004). Globalisation, economic geography and the strategy of multinational enterprises. *Journal of International Business Studies, 35*(2), 81–98.

Cantwell, J., & Mudambi, R. (2005). MNC competence-creating subsidiary mandates. *Strategic Management Journal, 26*(12), 1109–1128.

Huawei Technologies. (2010). *Corporate citizenship.* Retrieved from http://www.huawei.com/corporate_citizenship/corporate_responsibility_report_2009/people.do

Kapler, J. (2007). The theory of the firm, the theory of competition and the transnational corporation. *Competition & Change, 11*(4), 287–306.

Lazonick, W. (2009). *Sustainable prosperity in the new economy? Business organization and high-tech employment in the United States.* Kalamazoo, MI: Upjohn Institute for Employment Research.

Milberg, W. (2008). Shifting sources and uses of profits: Sustaining U.S. financialization with global value chains. *Economy and Society, 37*(3), 420–451.

Miozzo, M. (2000). Transnational corporations, industrial policy and the "war of incentives": The case of the Argentine automobile industry. *Development and Change, 31*(3), 651–680.

Okada, A. (2004). Skills development and interfirm learning linkages under globalization: Lessons from the Indian automobile industry. *World Development, 32*(7), 1265–1288.

UNCTAD. (2005). *UNCTAD/Erasmus University database. Transnational corporations and the internationalization of R&D. World investment report.* Geneva, Switzerland: Author.

UNCTAD. (2008). *The world's top 100 non-financial TNCs, ranked by foreign assets, 2008 a, 22/07/10 (WIR/2010/TNCs).* Geneva, Switzerland: Author.

Yeung, H. (2009). Transnational corporations, global production networks, and urban and regional development: A geographer's perspective on multinational enterprises and the global economy growth and change. *Perspective Review, 40*(2), 197–226.

Cosmopolitan Identity

One of the most trenchant by-products of globalization is the revival of cosmopolitanism in popular imagination and scholarly analysis. The term, originally derived from the Greek denoting the fusion of cosmos (world) and polis (city), has a venerable history. In its principal philosophical articulations, cosmopolitan identity represents a global outlook that extends a kind of world citizenship that transcends narrower communal identifications. In its contemporary versions, this expansive cosmopolitan social contract revolves around a set of universal values such as shared environmental concerns and human rights norms. Cosmopolitan identity here stands at the intersection of the global and the local, encompassing inclusive views of the other, openness toward different cultures, and concern regarding the global commons. Some philosophers have posited somewhat utopian assumptions about cosmopolitanism, especially when the world community is perceived as the primary circle of identification (Nussbaum, 1994).

Social scientists have been more circumspect about the possibility of such global citizenship and have conceptualized cosmopolitan identities as a set of cultural dispositions and practices that are tied at the interstices of global familiarity and corresponding local experiences. Cosmopolitan dispositions are based on boundary, transcending feelings and affiliations, involving cultural competencies and aesthetic preferences that are reinforced through ongoing exposures to global flows of information and imagery. Command over different cultural vocabularies is sustained by mobility, transnational experiences, and consumption patterns. Whatever differences might exist considering the exact nature of these cosmopolitan dispositions, there is a widespread agreement among scholars of cosmopolitanism that identities are no longer confined to the national or local but that they can be extended globally.

However, some scholars have raised doubts about the global reach of communal attachments, suggesting that cosmopolitan identifications are not possible because identity cannot be extended beyond the national. Globalization is perceived as dissolving collective identities and as setting up inauthentic and rootless substitutes in its stead. Anthony Smith puts it as follows:

> A timeless global culture answers to no living needs and conjures no memories. If memory is central to identity, we can discern no global identity in the making. . . . This artificial and standardized universal culture has no historical background, no developmental rhythm, no sense of time and sequence. . . . Alien to all ideas of "roots," the genuine global culture is fluid, ubiquitous, formless and historically shallow. (Smith, 1995, pp. 22–24)

Smith's statement is emblematic of two recurring assertions: (1) It restricts identity to the symbolic boundaries of the nation, and (2) it situates identity in a normative dichotomy of real life experiences and inauthentic mediated representations.

These contentions seem problematic, considering that national identity itself was the historical outcome of continuous enlargements from smaller circles of affiliation. The same arguments thrust against the expansion of identity beyond the nation were used in reaction to the idea of nationhood in the transition from *Gemeinschaft* to *Gesellschaft*, or from organic local communities to the new artificial nationwide political and economic structures of modern society. Then (as now), objections to these broader circles of affiliation were predicated on the notion that they were soulless as they were driven by impersonal means of communication, like newspapers. But the sociologist Ferdinand Tönnies's dichotomy of community and society (like the misleading juxtaposition of the national and the global) turned out to be a romantic and nostalgic one. Mechanical representations (newspapers then, the Internet now) did not stand in the way of strong identifications but actually promoted them.

In his seminal book *Imagined Communities*, Benedict Anderson describes how the nation was made into a "horizontal society" through the representation of symbols. It was precisely the now-lambasted impersonal media that produced the requisite solidarity through a constant repetition of images and words. Technological changes in the means of communication are thus of central importance for the structuration of identities. Both national and cosmopolitan identities seem implausible unless we perceive identity as a product of multidimensional and relational processes resulting in the re-imagination of new communities. And both are dependent on mediated representations. If the mass circulation of the print press was a key representational mode for the formation of national identity, there is no reason to dismiss the potential global representations carry for the emergence of cosmopolitan identities.

The nation-state, at the turn of the 20th century, depended for its coming into existence on a process by which existing societies used representations to turn themselves into new wholes that would act on people's feelings and on which they could base their identities—in short, to make them into groups that individuals could identify with. The ability of representations to give a sense to life is not ontologically but sociologically determined. So if the nation is the basis for authentic feelings and collective identities—as the critics of global culture seem almost unanimous in maintaining—then it cannot be upheld that representations are a superficial substitute for authentic experiences. The nation was literally inconceivable without an imagined community. On the contrary, representations are the basis of that authenticity. And there is nothing inconceivable, theoretically or empirically, about their providing such a basis for a globally available cosmopolitan identity, especially when the nation-state is no longer the uncontested and privileged site for the articulation of collective identifications.

Cosmopolitan and National Identities

The proliferation of global studies has contributed to a more refined approach, moving away from the dichotomy in which the global is perceived as the negation of the national. Instead, global flows of images and people are addressed in terms of their transformative potential for transnational and multicultural forms of identification. In this epistemological environment, a social-scientific literature exploring various facets of cosmopolitanism has flourished, mostly in the United Kingdom. Rather than being mired in the aforementioned normative conundrums of philosophical approaches to cosmopolitanism, this emerging field focuses on the analytic purchase of a cosmopolitan perspective. A starting point for this research orientation, which is primarily associated with the work of Ulrich Beck, is a critique of methodological nationalism. This nation-centric focus, which has dominated the social sciences, reveals conceptual limitations for the explanation of the multidimensional changes associated with globalization and the potential for broader forms of collective identification. A critique of methodological nationalism concerns the argument that a national ontology can no longer serve as a self-evident point of departure. By reexamining, reconceptualizing, and empirically establishing the transformations spurred by global processes, critical cosmopolitanism represents an emerging research trajectory in global studies.

To be sure, the emergence of cosmopolitan identity should not be mistaken for an end of national identity. Rather it suggests a reflexive interrogation of the validity of a historically specific and thus malleable conceptualization of the national and relational quality of identity. Critical cosmopolitanism contests the prevailing national-territorial notions in the social sciences by focusing on processes of de-territorialization and attendant mechanisms of de-nationalization. According to this view, globalization should not be reduced to external relations between increasingly interconnected national societies; instead, it carries transformative effects on the inner grammar of cultural and political identities. To specify the distinctiveness of such processes of "globalization from within," Beck introduces the concept of cosmopolitanization, which implies an interactive relationship between the global and the local.

Cosmopolitan identity comes into sight at the interstices of global orientations and particular attachments designating the emergence of new, denationalized social spaces and imaginaries. As indicated earlier in this entry, cosmopolitan identity does not entail a denial of the persistent reality of the nation for social actors. Instead, it suggests that forms of neo-national closure are a reflex to the reality of cosmopolitan identifications and can be understood only if the social scientist adopts a cosmopolitan perspective. This methodological gestalt shift derives its analytical force from elucidating the relationship between actual cosmopolitan identifications and the persistence or resurgence of political self-descriptions that are tied to a nationalist normativism.

Cosmopolitan identity remains an essentially contested concept torn between the binary assumptions of particularism (the national) and universalism (the global). Accordingly, nationalists have frequently used the term *cosmopolitanism* pejoratively, deploying it to label opponents as enemies to the national community. Paradoxically, some defenders of cosmopolitanism have inadvertently contributed to such a dichotomous perception by celebrating the cosmopolitan as a necessary antidote to nationalism. Consequently, the normative statements about the virtues and limitations of cosmopolitanism by philosophers and political theorists have, for the most part, juxtaposed an idealized open global cosmopolitanism with a closed national chauvinism. Certain cosmopolitan approaches have further reproduced this dualism by way of projecting cosmopolitanism as a universalism juxtaposed to the particularistic qualities of national or other communal attachments. The Enlightenment imperative, functioning as a cultural deep-structure of this universalistic universe, so to speak, has a long tradition of rejecting particular attachments as anachronistic. In its contemporary variant, the particular is frequently perceived as an impediment if not an outright contaminant to the cosmopolitan project. In particular, the more normative accounts tend to fall back on a Kantian conception of cosmopolitanism that is rooted in a universalism that has no conceptual and actual space for the persistence of particular attachments.

However, a dichotomy of national and cosmopolitan identities must be avoided. Contrary to the universal Enlightenment view, the analytic approach to cosmopolitanization refers to a process in which universalism and particularism are no longer exclusive "either-or" categories but instead a coexisting pair. This is premised on the notion that meaningful identities are predicated on particular attachments, as one's identity is always embedded in the story of the communities from which identities are constructed. On this view, particularism becomes a prerequisite for a cosmopolitan identity. Rather than treating cosmopolitanism as negating nationalism, social scientists can see particular national attachments as potential mediators between the individual and the global horizons against which identifications unfold. Particular identities are thus not an obstruction to cosmopolitan identities but in many ways are mutually constitutive, according to Gerard Delanty.

Real Existing Cosmopolitanism

For the most part, this "cosmopolitan turn" revolves around the emergence of a global discourse shaping global and local institutions, organizational forms, and political and moral principles. There is, by now, a substantive mass of research that explores these developments focusing on the institutionalization of human rights as a world cultural norm and the attendant maturation of international law. This human rights regime is evidenced in the inscription of cosmopolitan principles into numerous global institutions and networks of action. What is less

explored, though, is whether and how this cosmopolitanization of global institutional networks affects existing forms of collective identification. According to Kate Nash,

> Sociologists of cosmopolitanism can not be satisfied, however, with assuming that the cosmopolitanization of institutions in broadly multicultural or even post-national societies is matched in a general way by the cosmopolitanization of identities, especially in relation to law and politics. What is needed are concrete, empirical studies of how iterations of cultural norms in relation to institutional changes lead to disidentifications and the formation of new identities, or to the modification or the reactive consolidation of established identities, and what relation they bear to a cosmopolitan ideal of justice. (Nash, 2007, p. 432)

This disjuncture has been widely noted, and the empirical challenge remains how to operationalize the distinctive features of cosmopolitan identities and the specific meanings cosmopolitanism holds for those who subscribe to it.

Cosmopolitan orientations have been attributed to a wide range of actors. Historically, certain collectivities, especially in the context of their minority existence under imperial rule during the late 19th and early 20th centuries, have frequently been identified as carriers of cosmopolitan outlooks. Among them were Jews, Armenians, and other ethnic groups with mobility and involvement in mercantile networks. Members of the European nobility and various intellectuals have expressed their cosmopolitan leanings. More recently, in the context of the post–Cold War global age and the ideological currents of neoliberalism, certain politicians and business professionals, commonly referred to as members of the "airport culture," have been designated as citizens of the world. Here cultural competence over global repertoires and cosmopolitan dispositions are assets largely confined to elites. Recent research efforts have attributed cosmopolitan dispositions to nonelites, such as transnational migrants. However, straddling between two countries, a central feature of transnational experiences, might not necessarily yield to the kind of cultural openness that is the defining trait of cosmopolitan identity.

Although systematic explorations of the origins, conditions for, and diffusion of cosmopolitan identification are still in their infancy, a nascent body of research has started analyzing the constitutive features of cosmopolitan identities, its carriers, and their global interconnectedness. Ian Woodward, Zlatko Skrbis, and Clive Bean note,

> One of the widely accepted consequences of globalization is the development of individual outlooks, behaviours and feelings that transcend local and national boundaries. This has encouraged a re-assessment of important assumptions about the nature of community, personal attachment and belonging in the face of unprecedented opportunities for culture, identities and politics to shape, and be shaped by, global events and processes. (Woodward, Skrbis, & Bean, 2008, p. 207)

In a recent study based on social survey data (from Australia) investigating how globalization affects negotiations over belonging, Woodward, Skrbis, and Bean (2008) develop a set of cosmopolitan scales that can be identified in daily practices and referred to as "banal cosmopolitanism." They show how cosmopolitan practices, defined as outlooks that value cultural difference, "are shaped by social structural factors, and how forms of identification with humanity and the globe are fractured by boundaries of self and others, threats and opportunities, and the value of things global and local" (p. 207). More specifically, they suggest that

> there are multiple cosmopolitanisms, each defined by a particular mode of cultural engagement, and that each mode is favoured differentially. Cosmopolitan outlooks develop from the expression of universal sentiments to which most in the globalizing world have access, but they are also ruptured and skewed by the peculiarities of discourses within the nation and by social-cultural location, both of which necessarily mediate the production and reception of cosmopolitan sentiments in particular locales. (p. 223)

Arguably, the intensity and extensity of cosmopolitan identifications will vary a great deal not only within the nation but across states, depending largely on country-specific path-dependencies and on the type of prevailing majority-minority relations and related conceptions of otherness.

Globalization and Solidarity

Much of the debate on cosmopolitan identities (and the analytic means to identify the cosmopolitan) revolves around implicit or contested understandings of belonging. This is, according to Rogers Brubaker and Frederick Cooper (2000), compounded by the fact that the very notion of identity is a vague concept. Caught up in a national container, the sociological enterprise focuses on mechanisms of exclusion and inclusion, which is about social groups and solidarity. Strong forms of belonging are predicated on a naturalized image of the nation, with manifestations such as communitarianism and ethno-nationalism, to name but two possible modes. In contrast, cosmopolitanism is characterized (both in its normative version and by its nationalist opposition) as the breakdown of boundaries, referring to humans rather than to embedded people. Underlying this dualistic perception is the assumption that belonging operates primarily (or sometimes even exclusively) in the context of communal allegiance expressive of thick solidarities.

Conversely, we need not succumb to the opposite fallacy that presents cosmopolitan identity "as freedom from social belonging rather than a special sort of belonging, a view from nowhere or everywhere, rather than from particular social spaces" (Calhoun, 2003, p. 532). A second potential dimension of this fallacy is a liberal bias that privileges individual choice, normatively and analytically. Calhoun argues that "an approach that starts with individuals and treats culture as contingent cannot do justice to the legitimate claims made on behalf of 'communities,' and the reasons why 'thick attachments' to particular solidarities still matter" (p. 532). In both national and cosmopolitan cases, the success of identification with distant others is ultimately predicated on a balanced notion from thick attachments with concrete others (e.g., kin or local) to thinner versions of solidarity (e.g., the nation or the global). As indicated earlier in the discussion about the propensity of cosmopolitanism to propagate a universalism that comes at the expense of particularism, the point is not that we can or should dispense of thick forms of belonging but that we should explore identities as the coexistence of thick attachments and thin orientations.

The concept of "rooted cosmopolitanism" can be expressive of such a disposition as it entails no contradiction between particular loyalties and general openness. One way of capturing this dynamic and of avoiding the pervasive dualism of the national and the cosmopolitan is to replace the assumption of post-nationality (which is often invoked in conjunction with the cosmopolitan) with a process-oriented notion of de-nationalization. Saskia Sassen suggests that we go beyond binary schemes of the global-national or local and focus on interactive dynamics that may induce foundational transformations with regard to the national. She depicts those as an "incipient denationalization." Conceived along this interactive dimension, the recent cosmopolitan turn has made significant contributions to our understanding of the potentialities globalization affords to both the rejection and the construction of new and expansive forms of identification.

Daniel Levy

See also Communities, Transnational; Community; Cosmopolitanism; Ethnic Identity; Globalization, Phenomenon of; Identities in Global Societies; Immigration and Transnationalism; National Identities; Solidarity Movements

Further Readings

Beck, U. (2001). The cosmopolitan perspective: Sociology of the second age of modernity. *The British Journal of Sociology, 51*(1), 79–105.

Beck, U., & Sznaider, N. (2006). Unpacking cosmopolitanism for the social sciences: A research agenda. *British Journal of Sociology, 57*(1), 1–23.

Brubaker, R., & Cooper, F. (2000). Beyond "identity." *Theory and Society, 29*(1), 1–47.

Calhoun, C. (2003). "Belonging" in the cosmopolitan imaginary. *Ethnicities, 3*(4), 531–568.

Delanty, G. (2006). Nationalism and cosmopolitanism: The paradox of modernity. In G. Delanty & K. Kumar (Eds.), *Handbook of nations and nationalism* (pp. 357–368). London: Sage.

Nash, K. (2007). The Pinochet case: Cosmopolitanism and intermestic human rights. *British Journal of Sociology, 58*(3), 417–435.

Nussbaum, M. (1994). *The therapy of desire: Theory and practice in Hellenistic ethics.* Princeton, NJ: Princeton University Press.

Sassen, S. (2006). *Territory, authority, rights: From medieval to global assemblages.* Princeton, NJ: Princeton University Press.

Smith, A. (1995). *Nations and nationalism in a global era.* Cambridge, UK: Polity Press.

Woodward, I., Skrbis, Z., & Bean, C. (2008). Attitudes toward globalization and cosmopolitanism: Cultural diversity, personal consumption and the national economy. *British Journal of Sociology, 59*(2), 207–226.

COSMOPOLITANISM

Cosmopolitanism is, on the one hand, a collective term used to denote various forms of global thought developed in the history of philosophy since Greek antiquity and, on the other hand, a concept that has emerged in recent debates on moral responses to (economic) globalization. Both notions are nondoctrinal, as there is no specific school or center of cosmopolitanism. The term sometimes represents notions of a sophisticated globalized privileged consumerist lifestyle. In a more pejorative sense, cosmopolitanism also refers to selfish moral indifference, a lack of affection for a specific place or culture, and a compassionless attitude of belonging nowhere. Hence, cosmopolitanism can both refer to ideas of extreme individualism and to collective and global consciousness.

The peak of the discourse on cosmopolitanism as a philosophical concept, a moral value, and a societal value was the late 18th century. Largely fallen into oblivion and stigmatized during subsequent centuries, it resurfaced after the Cold War, when the dissolution of the bipolar power structure and the process of globalization called for intellectual and political responses. Since then, the term has been intensively debated in global studies and political philosophy and new research into its origin, and different representations has been carried out.

Classical Origins of the Concept

The theory of cosmopolitanism was developed during the pre-Hellenistic period (before 323 BCE). Materialist philosopher Demokritos (ca. 460 BCE to ca. 370 BCE) expressed the idea that the globe lies open to the sage and that the universe is the haven of good souls. Most significantly, the historical roots of cosmopolitanism lie in a much-quoted reply by Greek Cynic philosopher Diogenes of Sinope (ca. 412 BCE), who allegedly answered the question of where he came from with *kosmopolitês*, a city embracing the world or as it has been interpreted, a citizen of the world. True citizenship was realized in cosmos, totality. There is an inbuilt tension in this reply insofar as the term combines the universality and harmony of natural order as represented by the *kósmos* with the particular and contested man-made order of society, the Greek city-state *pólis*. It remains uncertain whether the term in its original context referred to the cosmos of Greek civilization only or if it denoted an idea of universal humanity, also integrating the so-called barbarian, non-Greek cultures. The question relating to the potential universal applicability of norms and concepts developed within Europe remains heavily debated in the contemporary discourse (mainly in postcolonialism and critique of modernity).

Cosmopolitanism seems, however, to imply to cross narrowly defined territorial borders and to embrace universal space positively, uniting the individual rational being with a citizenship in the whole, a global consciousness. With the expansion of Hellenistic rule under Alexander (peaking in the period 323—146 BCE), followed later by the Roman Empire (27 BCE–476 CE), an all-embracing perception of humanity across space gained new significance. Roman emperor and Stoic Marcus Aurelius (120–181 CE) viewed logos and reason as universally perceivable categories of thought and deduced that there existed a shared human morality. In his eyes, this morality was the basis for a common law and hence all human beings were to be regarded as citizens in a common state, the world as a whole constituted one entity. For Marcus, the basis of philosophical reasoning was Stoicism, a philosophy embracing all humankind regardless of origin and societal rank, with strong features of recognition of a divine order and destiny, the control of passions with the ultimate goal of a balanced and virtuous lifestyle. Within stoic cosmopolitanism, the idea emerged that a human being has a dual identity, a personal and at the same time a universal, relating him to humankind with an ethical ideal of universal benefit to humanity. The proximity between Stoicism and Christianity in the Roman Empire might help explain why Christianity perceived itself as an all-embracing and universal religion, the original meaning of the word *catholic*. Christianity in its ideological essence refuses particularity; all humans are equal in Christ. Internal differentiation between nations was an invention of the organization of medieval church hierarchy. It fueled perceptions of territorial particularity that were taken into the ideological struggles of reformation. The Westphalian (post-1648) state order manifested these ideas of particularity, strengthened by discourses on natural law in which the autonomous position of the individual and its liberty and in extension the autonomy of the individual state are constitutive. Theories of climate were drawn on to explain differentiations between nations and political systems, which was developed into an entire doctrine by Montesquieu in his *The Spirit of the Laws* (1748). Climate theories in combination with humoral pathology cemented collective stereotyping, which remains a powerful figure of thought in contemporary discourse. As a consequence of the strengthening of individual states, 17th-century jurists like Hugo Grotius and Samuel Pufendorf identified the need for international law, regulating mutual relations between single states. But this tiny common bond between states was based only on the similarity of autonomy and its reciprocal recognition, not on a shared joint system of values.

The Enlightenment and Cosmopolitanism

The political discourse of the 17th century was dominated by an aggressive dichotomy between the two branches of western European Christian belief, Catholicism and Protestantism. During the negotiations that led to the Peace of Westphalia in 1648, however, theories of natural law had an important impact on the concepts of European space that were predominant at least until the Vienna Congress in 1815. One basic element of political theory was the European territorial state, with its right of self-determination and independence. Along with that line of ideas, it had to be explained intellectually how and why European states could differ from each other. Self-determination becomes explanatory only when it is based on *difference*, and difference (to make any distinction between the qualities of the One and the significant Other) is a key element of identity and identification.

Unlike such concepts and ideas, counterconcepts evolved during the age of Enlightenment, all containing the basic ingredient *similarity*, or *egalité*. In particular, Freemasonry, which spread from 1717 to Europe and the world, embraced ideas of similarity and global community without initially referring to the term *cosmopolitanism*. In 1736, Fellow of the Royal Society André Michel de Ramsay (1686–1743) outlined these ideas in a famous lodge oration in Paris where he claimed that the entire world was a great republic, every nation a family, and each individual a child, a definition very close to the one offered in the later French *Encyclopédie* (1751–1772). Adding to ideas of mutual affinity and harmony, Ramsay outlined an encyclopedic vision where knowledge was shared universally. Invoking the idea that Freemasons were dispersed across the surface of the globe, cultural practices emerged within the craft that allowed members of Masonic lodges to live out cosmopolitan ideas. Although Freemasonry in essence was not an international organization, passports for the purpose of travel were issued, and printed directories of lodges worldwide facilitated global contacts with local nodes. The idea of global brotherhood was constantly hailed in Masonic poems, songs, and orations throughout the century and later reiterated in romantic concepts of fraternal cosmopolitanism. In 1785, an article appeared in a Masonic journal in Vienna, arguing for the adoption of cosmopolitanism as a moral duty for every Freemason. Apart from universal love and benevolence, the article called for eclecticism in the quest for truth and attacked sectionalism and sectarianism alike. Three years later, German author Christoph Martin Wieland (1733–1813) published a lengthy article in which he claimed that cosmopolitanism was a universal and inherent value, potentially to be discovered within every human being. All humans, all rational beings, were members of the same family. Everybody had a part in the rights of natural law. Based on individual precondition, everybody was obliged to work on the perfection of the whole, which implied the obligation to diminish evil and to augment good. For Wieland, no secret doctrine was attached to the concept; on the contrary, cosmopolitanism was accessible to all and constrained only by ignorance. Patriotism and cosmopolitanism were opposed to each other and irreconcilable. Although Wieland calls for political neutrality and acceptance of the respective form of government, implicitly he at the same time argues that cosmopolitanism has to be integrated within good governance.

Only a year after Wieland's article, the French Revolution erupted and profoundly changed the political landscape of Europe. Even moderate Enlightenment writers like Wieland would ardently oppose the use of violence during the revolution, but the change of cosmopolitanism from an apolitical to a political position was reflected in different ways during the period. Not only was the French Declaration of the Rights of Man extended to all men, but the French concept of *citoyen* was potentially universal in its scope.

Fougeret de Monbron (1706–1760) described himself in an autobiographical travelogue, *The Cosmopolitan* (1750), as a self-centered stranger traveling in the world, detached from every particular culture, observing it from his very own perspective. Although he has an appetite to cross the borders of his native land, a lively interest in the world, his judgments are based on personal prejudice rather than on all-embracing and eclectic tolerance. Against such a view, for Immanuel Kant (1724–1804), cosmopolitanism implied a universal hospitality that surrounds humankind, sharing the surface of the world. In his quest to define the parameters of a perpetual peace as the foundation of a world republic, the idea of cosmopolitanism is connected with universal political and international rights, especially related to the right of visitors and the right of the host. Every individual is entitled to rights and to live in a community ruled by law. Kant introduced the category of world citizen (*Weltbürger*) in his philosophy, relating back to the Stoic concept of a dual identity, particular and universal. In personal reason, the world citizen is placed above the world, whereas in the perspective of external reason, individuals are situated within the world as fellow citizens, where legal norms are mutually agreed. Kant's ideas on cosmopolitanism have three elements. The difference of the foreign Other has to be recognized without any conditions. The freedom of the individual has to be guaranteed by cosmopolitan law that regulates the relationship between individuals and states on a global scale. This legal order has to be protected by institutions such as a league of nations. Finally, cosmopolitanism will encourage a positive aesthetic experience of difference.

The Contemporary Discourse

Since the end of the Cold War, the term *cosmopolitanism* has developed from its historical basis to embrace ideas relating to concerns about contemporary global political order, neo-imperialist agendas, or ethical positions in a globalized society, dominated by the needs of omnipresent markets. Cosmopolitanism in this sense is pointing to the future of humankind. The end of the polarized world of the Cold War era called for a renegotiation of past concepts. German sociologist Ulrich Beck (b. 1944) argues that cosmopolitanism can be considered a reply to economic globalization, the attempt to balance liberal market forces with a globally shared ethos. Beck's ideas are built on Kant's call for tolerance of otherness. Another dimension of the term is the discussion of natural and universal human rights; cosmopolitanism can function as the normative basis of an international system of law and order. In a globalized world order, the nation-state and its previously well-defined geospatial entity are exposed to considerable tension, challenged by both neo-imperialist agendas and international networks. Searching for a transgression of the formerly constitutive position of states and relations between them, cosmopolitanism replaces a traditional international approach. Migration, forced and voluntary, has grown on an unprecedented scale. Both the question of global responses to national or local warfare and conflicts and the handling of displaced persons and environmental challenges have called for the adaptation of universal standards of conflict/disaster prevention and solution. In an increasingly entangled world culture, the relationship between the universal and the particular is gaining new relevance. Cosmopolitanism, in the terminology of Manuel Castells, might imply a homogenizing centripetal force of globalization (e.g., in calls for standardization). At the same time, it can be understood as facilitating diversity, bringing postmodern eclecticism and

tolerance to a new global and centrifugal level balancing any potentially homogenizing world order. The discussion of multiculturalism or a pluralistic society is related to the cosmopolitan ideal of mutual respect for cultural differences, intercultural coexistence. When observing early 20th-century immigrant communities in Chicago, Jane Addams branded a moral attitude based on the acceptance of difference in unity as cosmic patriotism. This impression has been intensified by ongoing developments of information and communication technology (ICT), reinforcing the idea of instant and global dissemination of culture. World citizenship can thus be understood from a communications perspective, with participation in the global information society as its foundation. ICT also facilitates global cyber-activism of nongovernmental organizations and other transnational advocacy networks, bundling activities ahead of and during events such as G-8 meetings or UN summits. This activism derives its sense of legitimacy from ideas resembling cosmopolitanism, a well-developed global consciousness demanding responsibility and sustainability for the planet (its climate and environment) and for humanity as a united and interrelated whole. From such a sense of membership in a global civil society and moral universalism generally follows support of global or transnational institutions in a cosmopolitan democracy. In contrast, transnational terror is organized similarly, representing violent global activism directed against democracy and the open society (in its Western fashion), based on shared values and particular belief systems. Furthermore, the vision of cyber-activism in a global cosmopolitan democracy has been impaired by state regulation and censorship of ICT as well as by a digital divide between online and offline communities based on access to resources. In the discussion of cosmopolitanism as a viable philosophy to balance economic globalization, it has also been queried whether ethical universalism is possible at all. David Östlund has recently argued that Eurocentric positions became entangled with colonialist and imperialist agendas. Hence, following the critique of modernity, it is possible to question the viability of a concept of cosmopolitanism that is rooted so heavily in European values and perceptions of humankind.

Within postmodern philosophy, the discussion of cosmopolitanism has been revitalized by Emmanuel Levinas (1906–1995) and Jacques Derrida (1930–2004), especially in encountering and interacting with the foreign Other. Like Kant, Levinas identifies cosmopolitanism as a position that enables full recognition of and infinite responsibility for the Other. The formation of identity, language, and culture is related to these encounters and is the basis for the acceptance of otherness. Derrida also draws on Kant's concept of hospitality and discusses how the foreign Other, especially the refugee, has an unconditional right to share resources and how, at the same time, the right of residence has to be limited.

Taxonomy of Cosmopolitanism

Pauline Kleingeld has introduced a conclusive categorization of different forms of cosmopolitanism. Originally researching varieties of late German Enlightenment discourse, she distinguishes among six forms of cosmopolitanism that also are recurring in the contemporary debate:

1. *Moral cosmopolitanism* represents the view that all human beings form a single moral community and that there exist moral obligations to all other human beings regardless of differentiations between them.

2. *International confederative cosmopolitanism* adds to this idea a political theory advocating forms of world governance, for instance as represented by a strong federation of states with coercive powers.

3. *Cosmopolitan law* represents the ideas formulated by Kant on the necessity of a legal framework regulating the relationship between states and individuals of foreign states, such as migration or business across borders in the spirit of general hospitality.

4. *Cultural cosmopolitanism* embraces the (anthropological) idea of mutual recognition of cultural differences, rejecting relativism as much as essentialism.

5. *Market cosmopolitanism* is built on the belief that free trade, unrestrained economic relations between people, will make state intervention and oppressive governance obsolete, contributing to a peaceful world order.

6. *Romantic cosmopolitanism* is in a sense a further emotional development of moral cosmopolitanism, stressing the global interconnectedness of people, shared fate, and values.

Andreas Önnerfors

See also Activism, Transnational; Cosmopolitan Identity; Enlightenment, The; Ethics, Global; Freemasons; Globalization, Phenomenon of; Identities in Global Societies; Otherness; Universalism

Further Readings

Appiah, K. A. (2006). *Cosmopolitanism: Ethics in a world of strangers.* New York: Norton.

Beck, U. (1997). *Was ist globalisierung?* [What is globalization?]. Frankfurt am Main, Germany: Suhrkamp.

Beck, U. (2006). *The cosmopolitan vision.* Cambridge, UK: Polity Press.

Derrida, J. (2001). *On cosmopolitanism and forgiveness.* London: Routledge.

Jacob, M. C. (2005). *Strangers nowhere in the world: The rise of cosmopolitanism in early modern Europe.* Philadelphia: University of Pennsylvania Press.

Kemp, P. (2010). *Citizen of the world: Cosmopolitan ideals for the 21st century.* New York: Humanity Books.

Kleingeld, P. (1999). Six varieties of cosmopolitanism in late eighteenth-century Germany. *Journal of the History of Ideas, 60,* 505–524.

Lettevall, R., & Linder Klockar, M. (Eds.). (2008). *The idea of kosmopolis. History, philosophy and politics of world citizenship.* Stockholm: Södertörn Academic Studies.

CREATIVITY AND INNOVATION

In recent discussions of global economic competitiveness, creativity and innovation have become central issues. In particular, notions such as the global knowledge society or the knowledge economy have given rise to deeper engagement with the topic. Besides this economic perspective, a second approach is that in a global era creativity is (once again) seen as important for mental well-being and that creativity helps the individual adjust to societal changes. In this way also, globalization is an important factor: Growing cultural diversity obliges people to deliberately choose their life-styles, albeit within certain limits. Characteristics related to creativity, like open-mindedness, help capitalize on this diversity and combine its ingredients in new ways.

Definitions of creativity are manifold, but most comprise at least two aspects: Work, ideas, products, and the like, are labeled creative if they are, first, novel or original, and second, appropriate or useful to the solution of some type of problem. To become an innovation, creative ideas have to be implemented in praxis. Creativity and innovation can be expressed in such different fields as the arts, new ideas for social action, expansion of knowledge in the sciences, and product and process innovations in business. Although creativity as such is conceived as universal, some authors claim that creativity in the East tends to be more "objective" and product-oriented, focusing on the innovation aspect, while in the West it is more "subjective" and process-oriented.

Key Concepts in Creativity Research

As is the case with many other topics in the broader field of global studies, creativity research is interdisciplinary and multifaceted. It is therefore important to trace these different facets and perspectives before dealing with the global dimension of creativity.

Two perspectives on creativity are often distinguished: "small-c" versus "big-C" creativity, or personal versus cultural creativity. Although the former concerns something that is new only to the creator such as children's play, the latter denotes something new for humankind. This distinction is important because it defines that creativity is not only an attribute of a few select geniuses or the basis for brand-new innovations in science and technology. Instead, it can be part of our everyday life, allowing us to adapt to rapid cultural evolutionary changes. At first sight, it seems easy to draw a line between the two perspectives. In many instances, however, this distinction is not all that clear. For example, companies often introduce new

processes that really are adaptations from other companies (Ronald S. Burt showed the importance of networks across so-called structural holes for such information brokerage). The new process is certainly an innovation for the company, but how much change is needed to speak of a real innovation (big-C) instead of a mere transfer of an idea? A similar question develops with regard to the patenting of indigenous knowledge.

Mel Rhodes proposed in 1961 a later popular way to structure the different approaches to creativity with his four Ps: person, process, press (environment), and product. Person includes research, mainly from psychology, on personal characteristics or personalities of creative people. Process deals with behavior and the generation of new ideas. The still influential stage model of Graham Wallas from 1926 plays an important part in this. He distinguishes among the four/five stages of preparation, incubation, intimation (a substage), illumination, and verification. Press, comprising mostly the research from sociology and economics, looks at the interaction of people and their environment. Teresa M. Amabile, for example, analyzed promoters and inhibitors of creativity in different organizational settings. The category product, finally, summarizes research about the output of creativity such as patents.

Although the approach of person focuses on specific traits of individuals, often attributing creativity to certain people only (dispositional perspective), the approach of press emphasizes the context (situational perspective), sometimes even arguing that creativity is the sole result of the social system or the context. Looking at products as an indicator of creativity might be regarded as objective and relatively easy to measure, but it misses some important forms of creativity, including small-c creativity, or process innovations, in companies. Additionally, to refer to Max Weber's famous distinction, one might be able to "explain" creativity by connecting it to certain characteristics of the creative person and its context, as is done, for example, by historiometry. Still, creativity cannot be "understood" without considering the processes leading to a product as well. Generally, each one of the four approaches is useful for certain studies. However, the complexity of the concepts creativity and innovation can be captured only by combining all approaches.

The Importance of Creativity and Innovation Today

Some claim that creativity has never been as important as it is today. On the individual level, people describe themselves as being creative—in job interviews, for instance. On the organizational level there are rankings of the most creative and innovative companies or sectors. Cities want to be creative hot spots, following Richard Florida's analysis of the "creative class." The innovative capacity of countries is assessed in comparison to that of others. In 1996, the World Commission on Culture and Development produced a report titled *Our Creative Diversity*, and the Commission of the European Communities declared 2009 to be its "Year of Creativity and Innovation."

Although most of these initiatives have a clear economic motive, the idea of individual and social well-being is often implied as well. First, with regard to the economy, it is argued that creativity and innovation are prerequisites for economic growth for at least two reasons. One is globalization: In particular for economies in industrially developed countries, ideas are becoming ever more important, as labor and other factors of production are much cheaper in other regions. The other reason is the increasing importance of the knowledge economy, in which success can no longer be based on selling more of the same, but on permanent improvements in products and production processes alike. The credo is that one has to change constantly to survive in the marketplace, and innovation is necessary for successful change.

Second, creativity is viewed as important for mental well-being. In traditional societies, creativity had its important but limited space, and too much innovation was often recognized as disruptive. In modern times, however, creativity helps individuals, communities, and societies alike tackle the new challenges that constantly confront them. Globalization, in combination with other factors like growing media consumption, leads increased cultural heterogeneity and change. Creativity, with its emphasis on open-mindedness and flexibility, may help deal with this diversity and even benefit from it by supporting the development of new and hybrid cultural forms. Creativity, therefore, can be viewed as a specific form of human capital.

Creativity and Innovation in Global Perspective

The global dimensions of creativity and innovation have at least three different aspects: creativity as a global phenomenon, international comparative studies of creativity and innovation, and the impact of globalization on creativity.

First of all, creativity is a truly global phenomenon. Curiosity, as a human trait, is the basis for creativity, and accordingly, creative individuals can be found all over the world and during all times of human history. One example of this is the existence of eminent geniuses worldwide as shown by historiometrics. Second, it is, however, equally the case that creativity is understood differently in various cultures and that creativity, and especially the transformation of new ideas into innovations, is heavily influenced by these contexts. When analyzing creativity and innovation, historical and cultural contexts have to be taken into account accordingly. Third, processes of globalization may have important impacts on creativity all over the world. To explore these three global aspects of creativity, it makes sense to distinguish different levels of analysis: individuals (micro level), organizations and cities/regions (meso level), and countries (macro level).

Most research on creativity comes from psychology and focuses on the individual level as the basis for all creative processes. Joy P. Guilford's 1950 presidential address to the American Psychological Association is often recognized as the starting point for this scientific study of creativity. International comparisons show that research in many countries today is still heavily influenced by the classic work of Joy P. Guilford, E. Paul Torrance, and other U.S. researchers. James C. Kaufman and Robert J. Sternberg therefore comment that, although "different cultures have different perspectives on what it means to be creative, it is nearly always the American or Western perspective that is represented in the psychological literature" (Kaufman & Sternberg, 2006, cover). It is therefore an open empirical question how valid lists of individual characteristics that foster creativity in the Western sense (e.g., flexibility, sensitiveness, autonomy, and ego strength) are when compared across cultures. Nonetheless, one can observe a global competition for creative people, in certain contexts labeled "brain drain/gain."

A wide array of educational initiatives is trying to implement such creativity, fostering personal characteristics in children and adults. Education is probably the most important field of applied creativity research. However, there are certain national differences in the means and aims of this stimulation, based on different notions of creativity as well as the emphasis put on either creativity or innovation, as research suggests that both need slightly different sets of attitudes.

There is a third relationship between the individual and creativity. An emphasis on individualism, at least in the developed countries of the Western Hemisphere, imposes the demand on everybody to be unique. In this sense, creating our own identity in a self-reflexive creative manner is an imperative of today's world. Individual creativity thus becomes an ideology. Although some authors hail the advent of the creative class, one should not neglect the downside of the pressure to be someone new every other day for many people—stress or a feeling of being uprooted, for instance.

Research from economics and sociology is much more directed toward the meso and macro levels of creativity and is often mainly concerned with the application of new ideas in the form of innovation. One important field of the former is creativity in organizations, and specifically in companies. Another aspect is the interest in what is called the "creative city." Comparing different contexts with regard to their influence on creativity incorporates the press perspective much more strongly than the previously described psychological research. Looking at organizations, regional clusters, and cities has the additional advantage of being able to circumvent the "methodological nationalism" of much sociological comparative work.

Studies about the influence of different organizational cultures on creativity are one way to take contexts into account. Research suggests that creative companies share certain characteristics that can foster creativity, including a mistake-friendly climate, a certain amount of pressure, and relative autonomy for employees. With regard to the background of employees, Ricarda B. Bouncken claims from her case studies that cultural diversity can be, but seldom is, used as a strategic resource. The term *innoversity* tries to grasp this relationship between innovativeness and diversity.

Another important area of research looks at regional creative capabilities, especially in the context of creative cities, but also with regard to regional cultural traits. Most of this work focuses on the economic impact of creativity and innovation, often in the context of the creative industries. Although some authors claim the "death of geography" because of increased availability of global information and communication technologies, others emphasize the role of clustering in certain places like Silicon Valley and the importance of supportive institutions for creativity and innovation. Some interesting initiatives, however, also look at the social consequences of creativity on cohesion and identity in a broader sense, including the arts and everyday creativity.

Equally, global economic competition has generated a vast amount of research about the creative capacities of nations on the macro level. Different global empirical indices exist. One example is the Global Innovation Scoreboard of the European Union or the Index calculated by the National Innovative Capacity Project. Important indicators used are the number of patents, research and development (R&D) expenditures, or the distribution of educational levels within populations. The data suggest that there is a handful of leading countries at the creative edge: the United States, certain European countries (Germany, United Kingdom, and some Scandinavian countries), Japan, and, when dynamic patterns are taken into account, other Asian countries as well (Singapore, e.g., is often labeled the new "creative hub" of Asia). Different theoretical approaches to National Innovation Systems have been developed as well. The main idea behind these approaches is that apart from investment in R&D or education, a certain combination of institutions plays a crucial role in shaping creativity and its transformation in innovation. However, as the models often become complex, empirical testing is difficult.

Conclusions

Generally, the relationship between creativity and globalization is reciprocal. Creativity is increasing globalization, by facilitating the development of new information and communication technologies for instance. Globalization contributes to creativity and innovation by increasing exchange and stimuli. However, some authors object that there might be limits to the adaptability of people and organizations to constant change.

The current interest in creativity and innovation, fueled mainly by economic motives, has resulted in intensified research on the topic and produced many insights, some of which were summarized in this entry. However, one should be cautious interpreting rankings of creative cities or nations, as cultures differ in their interpretation and their expression of creativity. An additional problem for empirical analysis is the fact that creativity also changes these cultures. Even so, more comparisons over regions and over time are needed to gain insights into the role that different contexts, such as structures, institutions, and culture, mean for creativity. Although the global dimensions of creativity and innovation make them a natural field of inquiry for global studies, the discipline also has the cultural and historical sensitivity as well as theoretical and methodological tools to contribute important findings to this research.

Michael Hoelscher

See also Aesthetics; Art; Artists; Cities; Creolization; Culture, Notions of; Genius, Notion of; Intellectual Property Rights; Knowledge Production Systems; Modernization; Nobel Prize; Think Tanks; Universities and Higher Learning; Utopia, Dystopia

Further Readings

Anheier, H. K., & Isar, R. (Eds.). (2009). *Cultural expression, creativity and innovation: Vol. 3, Cultures and globalization series*. London: Sage.

Bouncken, R. B. (2004). Cultural diversity in entrepreneurial teams: Findings of new ventures in Germany. *Creativity and Innovation Management, 13*(4), 240–253.

Florida, R. (2005). *The flight of the creative class. The new global competition for talent*. New York: HarperCollins.

Hoelscher, M. (2009). Measuring creativity and innovation. In H. K. Anheier & R. Isar (Eds.), *Cultural expression, creativity and innovation*. London: Sage.

Kaufman, J. C., & Sternberg, R. J. (Eds.). (2006). *The international handbook of creativity*. Cambridge, UK: Cambridge University Press.

Runco, M. A. (2007). *Creativity. Theories and themes: Research, development, and practice*. Boston: Elsevier Academic Press.

CREDIT CARDS

See Finance, Financial Systems

CREOLIZATION

Creolization refers to processes of cultural syncretism or transformation, especially of people, language, and social customs around the world. The term derives from the Portuguese word *crioulo* and gained common usage in Spanish plantation societies in the Americas during the 16th century. It is often used to refer to "mixing," but it originally referred to children of Spanish parents born in the New World. Later, it developed a range of specific local and historical meanings in the Americas. Creolization is used to refer to the global processes of hybridization and interculturation. However, this broader usage has been criticized for divorcing the term from its sociohistorical context, rendering it too general to be analytically useful.

In the late 16th century, the word *Creole* referred to a Spaniard born in the New World rather than in Europe. At that time, it was widely believed that the natural environment of the New World caused babies born there to be inferior to those born in Europe. Thus, a child born in Europe was viewed to be superior to his or her full sibling born in the New World. Creole children were excluded from the upper rank of colonial societies.

By the early 17th century, *Creole* had been extended to refer to any plant, animal, or person born in the New World but of Old World parents. It was used to distinguish slaves born in the Americas from slaves born in Africa. The growth of independence movements in the 18th century and the abolition of the slave trade in the early 19th century heralded a transformation in the meaning of the term. *Creole* came to refer to any person who was both locally born and locally loyal. This provided colonial societies with an oppositional identity with which to differentiate themselves from Europe, creating a local culture and society.

Creolization thus came to mean the process by which elements from the Old World were combined in the New World to create a cultural synthesis that incorporated elements of the past, yet with a distinctly local character. Exactly who or what is defined as Creole varies throughout the region. In Haiti, generally only people of primarily African descent are described as Creole; yet the language Haitian Kreyol is a mixture of both French and West African languages. In Martinique, Creole refers to any person who cannot claim to be of purely European heritage.

In Trinidad, there is a tension between mixing within people and mixing within the nation. Historically, the term has referred to the descendents of Africans and Europeans but has excluded Indians. Since Trinidad gained independence in 1962, it has attempted to define the nation, rather than the people, as Creole. This definition does not require intermarriage to take place. Instead, creolization refers to the creation of a national culture out of distinct elements.

Clearly, significant variations are observed in the meaning of creolization across time and space. Nevertheless, it has it become a key analytical concept across the region and indeed the globe for three main reasons.

First, the term is useful in the Americas because it points to shared historical circumstances as well as diversity. It provides a tool with which to think about how new societies and cultures were created out of the forced displacement of Africans and their replacement in a world dominated by European socioeconomic and administrative structures. Because creolization refers to a process, it allows us to think about these social changes as an ongoing process rather than as an historic event.

Second, creolization has political and conceptual application across the region. Since Simón Bolívar fought for the creation of Gran Colombia in the early 19th century, creolization has been central to efforts to develop a pan-American identity. Although this unification has had limited success, creolization is one of the few tools with which to conceptualize such an identity. This has become possible because creolization is now used primarily to refer to positive processes of cultural creativity rather than to inferiority. Furthermore, creolization refers as much to the stabilities that develop over time as to changes and adaptations.

Third, the concept of creolization has provided a model for theories of cultural contact and transformation under globalization. The long history of scholarly discussion of creolization in the Americas has provided ways of thinking about how transnational and local factors and the power differentials that accompany them affect processes of cultural transformation. When discussing global cultural transformation, *creolization* is often used interchangeably with words like *hybridity*, *syncretism*, and *mixture*.

It is widely recognized among social scientists that these issues are not confined to ex-slave societies but refer to cultural transformation globally. All societies in all times undergo cultural transformation, not just populations that have experienced radical social disembedding and reterritorialization. However, critics argue that applying the term *creolization* to this broader context deprives it of the sociohistorical context that makes it an analytically meaningful term. Creolization is most meaningful when it is used by people to describe themselves as well as by scholars to describe broader historical and geographical processes.

Erin B. Taylor

See also Connectedness, Global; Cosmopolitanism; Cultural Hybridity; Deterritorialization and Reterritorialization; Diasporas; Multiculturalism; National Identities; Racial Identity

Further Readings

Enwezor, O., Basualdo, C., Meta Bauer, U., Ghez, S., Maharaj, S., Nash, M., & Zaya, O. (2003). *Créolité and creolization: Documenta 11_Platform 3.* Ostfildern-Ruit, Germany: Hatje Cantz.

Hannerz, U. (1987). The world in creolization. *Africa: Journal of the International African Institute, 57*(4), 546–559.

Khan, A. (2007). Good to think? Creolization, optimism, and agency. *Current Anthropology, 48*(5), 653–673.

Stewart, C. (Ed.). (2007). *Creolization: History, ethnography, theory*. Walnut Creek, CA: Left Coast Press.

Trouillot, M.-R. (2002). Culture on the edges: Caribbean creolization in historical context. In B. K. Axel (Ed.), *From the margins: Historical anthropology and its futures* (pp. 189–210). Durham, NC: Duke University Press.

CRIME, TRANSNATIONAL

Borders are a key element in the consideration of transnational crime. A border is a port of entry, an exit route, and a governed barrier. A border crossing offers opportunities for trade, cross-cultural benefits, migration, and crime. As demand for precious resources—drugs, diamonds, and oil, among other things—increases, individuals and organized criminals cross borders, often moving from depressed nations into more affluent countries that offer attractive opportunities for illegal acts. Borders have often been sites of conflict and unease, especially when they separate groups with deep, long-standing hostility, an enmity often based on ethnocentrism, religious differences, or searing memories of age-old conflicts.

Borders separating countries throughout history were established as barriers that could help protect nationals from exploitation by criminal groups from outside and from individuals seeking to elude restrictions and regulations of their own countries. The borders cannot be perfectly guarded so that those sufficiently intent on crossing them can slip through at porous points or through the creation of clandestine routes. Smugglers traditionally have been able to discover routes to get their wares across national boundaries and into black market outlets.

It is arguable whether countries are protected from transnational crime by an absence of boundaries shared with contiguous nations. New Zealand, for instance, has a very low crime rate; its nearest neighbor, Australia, is 1,200 miles away. But, in contrast, Switzerland, sharing borders with France, Germany, Austria, Lichtenstein, and Italy, also registers a very low crime rate. Its crime rate may be attributable to a liberal culture that maintains limited amounts of prohibition and regulations. Like all manner of crime, an increase in regulation and law accompanied by enhanced police activity facilitates an increase in crime. As crime rates reflect law enforcement actions, increases in transnational crime have been enhanced by increased focus on international criminal activities. A stimulated global economy that results from the deregulation of importation requirements creates increased trade. The amplified rate of global commerce is followed by an equally robust increase in the illicit global economy.

Technology and Transnational Crime

Technological advances have contributed dramatically to the form and likely the extent of transnational crime. Two developments in particular have played a prominent role in the reconfiguration of a considerable portion of such crime: electronic technology and international shipping. The arrival of advanced electronic communications, such as the Internet, produced a major surge in transnational white-collar crimes. Computers provide access and a curtain of anonymity behind which a person can commit a variety of larcenous and fraudulent acts. Internet opportunities effectively evade barriers such as fixed borders. For example, Wall Street investment banks took advantage of the flow of currency worldwide through electronic mediums to unload toxic derivatives based on a subprime real estate market that was riddled with fraud. The movement of money has become so complicated, given innovative markets and open access, that laws governing international financial transactions have proven ineffectual. The economic meltdown that began in the United States in late 2008 reverberated worldwide and often was characterized by activities that were or should have been treated as criminal offenses.

As a further example, the Internet has allowed the development of a flourishing number of gambling enterprises that are headquartered in Caribbean countries such as Antigua and accept wagers from persons in other jurisdictions, most notably in the United States. In a David versus Goliath dispute, Antigua won a decision in 2004 by the World Trade Organization that efforts by the United States to criminalize such activity represented a violation of the General Agreement on Trade and Services (GATS), which was based on a treaty adopted in Uruguay in 1984 and to which the United States is a signatory. The case illustrates that when crime goes global nations may come into conflict on the basis of variant definitions of what their laws designate as crimes.

The massive increase in global shipping has led to increased fraud by importers and customs brokers looking to evade regulations on tariffs and trade. Increased manufacturing of durable goods overseas means that heavily trafficked global trade routes can be exploited by smugglers. Within the tens of thousands of oceanic containers, people, drugs, weapons, and items on embargoed lists can be hidden and brought into seaport transfer points.

Globalization has aroused public awareness and concern regarding harmful behavior that crosses national boundaries. Six criminal activities epitomize the transnational aspects of crime today: drug trafficking, trade in human organs, human smuggling, maritime piracy, extraordinary rendition, and white-collar or economic scams. The remainder of this entry focuses on the transnational elements in each of these illegal enterprises.

Drug Trafficking

The prohibition of certain classified narcotics in the United States has created a demand for substances that are manufactured elsewhere. Cocaine, sourced predominantly in the South American countries of Colombia, Peru, and Bolivia, and heroin, grown and manufactured primarily in the Asian countries of Afghanistan, Iran, and Thailand, are transferred through multiple borders to reach the North American market. The transfer of illegal narcotics has become the enforcement focus of a vast amount of federal resources in the United States.

International and U.S. laws have addressed successfully the drug smuggling that took place via Caribbean countries and Florida. Until the 1990s, most of the drugs coming into the United States were routed from Colombia to island nations in the southwest Atlantic, such as the Dominican Republic, Panama, Jamaica, and the Bahamas. Additionally, the U.S. territories of Puerto Rico and the Virgin Islands have been used as transit points where drug cargoes are transferred from the Cali drug cartel in Bogotá, Colombia, to the North American market.

An intense focus of U.S. federal resources on containing the flow of illicit drugs into the ports of entry in the southeastern portion of the United States has led to the rerouting of those substances across the deserts of the southwest United States. There have been explosive accounts of border violence near El Paso, Texas, Nogales, Arizona, and Otay Mesa, California. But unlike the Colombian-centered cocaine-fueled gang wars of the 1980s that permeated Florida, the flow of methamphetamine, heroin, and marijuana cargoes moved by members of Mexican drug cartels across the southwest border towns induced anti-immigration sentiment. The southwest border is being targeted for blockade measures by anti-immigration forces. Transnational crimes, as these developments indicate, can often be employed for political and ideological ends.

Arizona S.B. 1070, a highly controversial measure signed into law in Arizona in 2010, was significantly impelled by a belief that unchecked border crossings from Mexico into Arizona was aiding and abetting traffic in narcotics and increasing the level of regional violence. The Arizona legislature elected to add criminal penalties to an administrative violation with a policy that allowed law enforcement personnel to stop civilians and demand papers demonstrating their citizenship status. Mexico's president, Felipe Calderón, called the Arizona law "racial profiling" and said that drug trafficking from his country to the United States would not occur if the United States took more effective steps to curb rampant recourse to the consumption and distribution of illegal narcotics. Calderón maintained that the origin of the violence begins with the fact that Mexico is located next to the country that has the highest level of drug consumption in the world.

The Mexico and Colombian drug cartels supply approximately 90% of the illegal cocaine that reaches the United States. Members of these cartels employ sophisticated mechanisms for evading barriers implemented by border patrols. One example is the development of self-propelled semisubmersible (SPSS) vessels that can transport 7 to 10 tons of drugs at one time. The drugs are moved from Colombia to Mexico, then loaded onto fishing boats before being placed on the SPSS. Additionally, Mexican drug traffickers have constructed more than 1,000 tunnels along the more than

2,000 miles of land border between their country and the United States.

The transnational nature of drug trafficking was exemplified by the invasion of Panama by U.S. armed forces in late 1989. Manuel Noriega ran a military dictatorship in the country from the late 1950s to 1989. Noriega had been a spy for the Central Intelligence Agency (CIA) that at the time turned a blind eye to his drug trafficking until it decided that he was also feeding information to Cuba, working as a double agent. Later personnel from the CIA and the U.S. Army stipulated at Noriega's trial, where he was charged with eight counts of drug trafficking among other crimes, that they had paid him US$320,000; Noriega said that the figure was nearer US$10 million. In early 2010, after his release from prison in the United States, Noreiga was extradited to France, where he faced charges of laundering drug money through the purchase of Paris apartments valued at US$3 million.

The flow of drugs across borders is not limited to scheduled narcotics. There has been a significant increase in the illegal importation of pharmaceutical products that are sold on the black market or through web-based commerce sites. The trafficking of pharmaceutical drugs often violates customs laws regarding the importation of chemicals and substances by way of fraudulent documentation and mislabeling of substances in violation of health regulations. The distribution of counterfeit pharmaceuticals is largely accomplished via Internet-based, offshore front companies. The level of criminal activity is clearly enhanced by the presence of technology, which provides not only a venue for marketing products but also a method for concealing jurisdiction and identity.

Maritime Piracy

There have been many recent reports of maritime piracy that picture it as a return of an ancient scourge. Much of the media focus has been on the piracy that occurs off the coast of Somalia in Africa. Despite extensive coverage of individual piracy cases, there has been little focus on the crucial elements of what causes, stimulates, and sustains piracy. Somali piracy today is a reaction to the inability of Third World nations to prevent fishing fleets from First World countries, such as South Korea, Japan, Norway, and Denmark, from invading their waters and poaching on fishing in their ancestral sea domains. Pirates in Somalia, with tacit support from a weak government unable to mount other defensive measures, respond to the threats to their livelihood by harassing merchant vessels that transit their waters after passing through the Suez Canal. Enterprising groups within Somalia quickly learned they could capture and temporarily hold those vessels in exchange for sizable ransom payments. Owners of merchant ships realized that the likelihood of their individual vessel's becoming victim to piracy was remote.

As a contrast, pirates in the Pacific Ocean, at work off the coasts of Asian nations, steal cargoes for transfer on the black market. In this way, they are acting as pirates have done in centuries past. There has not been much political and media focus on piracy in Asian waters as merchant vessels do not want states to interfere with practices that have prevailed in the world's oceans for centuries. These practices include ignoring embargoes and passing through prohibited waters. Increased scrutiny of pirates might also lead to an increase in regulation of all maritime vessels.

Despite the fact that there has been so much attention paid to maritime piracy, very few ships worldwide are ever under threat of being seized by pirates. Less than 1% of the ships traveling anywhere in the world are successfully pirated. This fact, accompanied by the legal, political, and economic pressures to promote trade, often surpasses any need to employ force to obtain the release of a solitary vessel that may be captured when a ransom payment can be viewed as little more than a routine cost of doing business.

Smuggling Human Beings

In 2004, the U.S. federal government created a Human Trafficking and Smuggling Center as part of the Intelligence Reform and Terrorism Prevention Act of 2004. According to the Department of State statistics, approximately 600,000 to 800,000 persons were trafficked worldwide during any recent year, while between 14,500 and 17,500 persons were smuggled into the United States. Most individuals who are transported by organized crime groups will be employed, usually against their will, in the sex trade. They are in effect working as slaves. Typically, if such an individual has a passport, it will be confiscated by the criminal gang so that he or she cannot leave the country and will be possibly literally chained to a destructive form of employment.

The smugglers use altered documentation, and they corrupt border officials. This crime continues to increase despite strengthened border patrols and stricter laws. In part, this is attributed to the expansion of an illicit global economy that demands the illegal transfer of legitimate goods as well as the illegal transfer of illegitimate goods such as human beings.

Trafficking in Human Body Parts

Transnational crimes that involve the harvesting and the sale of human body parts typically take the form of an interchange among Third World countries, whose residents supply body parts such as the cornea, kidney, liver, or other organ, and a First World country whose residents purchase and have them implanted in their own body. The medical operation may be carried out in a third country where there are first-class medical facilities and where the procedure is legally permissible or, more likely, oversight is weak.

One such incident involved half a dozen medical personnel in South Africa who performed more than one hundred kidney transplants in the early 2000s at St. Augustine's Hospital in Durban. The donors tended to be Brazilians who were flown to South Africa. The recipients were most likely to be from countries where there are low numbers of organ donors, sometimes because of cultural and religious beliefs. The transactions violated South Africa's Human Tissues Act of 1983, which required the certification of a social relationship between the donor and the recipient before the body part transplantation could be performed. Participants in the South African scheme had to attest fraudulently to such a relationship.

Most published reports of murder to harvest and transport body parts tend toward sensationalism. But there have been compelling, if not strongly supported, indications of such trafficking from the African nation of Mozambique. The accusations escalated when a female missionary was brutally strangled to death in 2004 after she had sought government intervention in what she claimed were 125 murders of children committed to obtain their body parts. The corpse of a 12-year-old had been recovered with her tongue, eyes, heart, liver, and kidneys missing. Speculation was that the body parts were being flown to Zimbabwe or South Africa and sold to needy recipients from these and other countries. No known prosecution of such events has taken place, as evidence of these crimes seems anecdotal or circumstantial.

White-Collar Crime

The global interlocking of the economic health of the nations of the world was clearly demonstrated by reverberations from the disastrous default on subprime mortgages in the United States in late 2008. Like stacked dominoes, European and Asian markets tumbled in response to the U.S. meltdown. It became clear that banks overseas had been intimately intertwined with the U.S. investment giants and with many complicit in the misjudgments, greed, recklessness, and criminal negligence that brought about the collapse. The globalization of the marketplace is demonstrated by the fact that the ten largest law firms in the world locate more than half of their attorneys at sites other than their home country.

The risks that this may create were indicated in the 1995 collapse of the Barings Bank of England, when Nick Leeson, manager of its Singapore branch, speculated on Japanese bonds and ultimately ran up a loss of US$1.3 billion. The fact that the offender was far from his homeland and remote from direct supervision and accountability demonstrates the blueprint for disaster that can be associated with the globalization of commerce.

A major ingredient of international white-collar and corporate crime was recently pinpointed by a Japanese judge when he awarded US$170 million in damages against the board of directors of the Daiwa Bank, with headquarters in Tokyo and Osaka. The judge stressed that the failure of the bank executives to abandon traditional Japanese customs when operating in a venue with different legal requirements was unacceptable and costly.

Extraordinary Rendition

The tentacles of transnational crime were on display in a series of extraordinary renditions, acts by which one country, typically the United States, kidnaps a person in a friendly country who is suspected of ties with terrorists in foreign countries. The person is then transported to a third county, where he is tortured.

A landmark case took place in 2003 in Milan, Italy, involving Abu Omar, a Muslim imam who was kidnapped, then flown from the U.S. air base in northern Italy to Ramstein in Germany and then on to Egypt. Omar was picked up off the streets by a team of U.S. CIA agents and Italian police as he was making his way to a mosque for noon prayers. In Egypt, he suffered an interrogation regimen that included electric shocks to his genitals, being hung upside down, being bombarded with loud noises, and being moved from a hot sauna into a refrigerated cell.

In another case, Khaled El-Masri, a German-born Lebanon citizen, was on vacation when he was removed from a bus at a border crossing into Macedonia in 2003. He had been mistaken for an al Qaeda operative with a similar name. El-Masri was held for 5 months in solitary confinement in Afghanistan. A Council of Europe report later concluded that allegations that he was beaten, drugged, and sodomized were essentially correct. When finally released, he was left in a desolate area in Albania.

A third man, a resident in Canada for 17 years but Syrian-born, was intercepted by U.S. officials at John F. Kennedy airport in New York City en route home to Montreal from Tunis. He was transported to Syria, where he was placed in a small, damp cell. To gain relief from torture, he confessed to training with a terrorist group in Afghanistan, although he had never been in the country. Ultimately he was released, never having been charged with any crime.

Karen K. Clark and Gilbert Geis

See also Borders; Economic Crises; Global Economic Issues; Illegal Trade, Arms; Law, International; Legal Systems; Policing Systems; Power, Global Contexts of; Security; Sovereignty; Terrorism; Trade

Further Readings

Albanese, J. (Ed.). (2000). *Transnational crime*. Whitby, ON: de Sitter.

Andreas, P. (2009). *Border games: Policing the U.S.-Mexico divide*. Ithaca, NY: Cornell University Press.

Bussmann, K. D. (Ed.). (2007). Crossing the borders: Economic crime from an international perspective. *Monatsschrift für Kriminologie und Strafrechtsreform, 90*, 77–285.

Cherry, M. J. (2005). *Kidney for sale by owner: Human organs, transplantation, and the market*. Washington, DC: Georgetown University Press.

Ellingwood, K. (2004). *Hard line: Life and death on the U.S.-Mexico border*. New York: Pantheon Books.

Mayer, J. (2008). *Dark side: The inside story of how the war on terrorism turned to a war on American ideals*. New York: Doubleday.

National Drug Intelligence Center. (2008). *California border alliance group drug market analysis: 2008*. Washington, DC: U.S. Department of Justice.

CRUSADES

The Crusades constituted a global event for their times and provided a term that continues to be applied to strident, zealous effort. The Crusades were a set of religiously motivated military campaigns that occurred primarily from the 11th to the 13th centuries and that had the principal goal of recovering the Holy Land from non-Christians, especially the Muslims. The Crusades, with all their ideological, economic, and social characterizations, exerted formative influence on European history and on the relationship between East and West, between Islam and Christendom, having a lasting effect until the present day. In modern times, the term *crusade* has been revived for use both as a call for a concerted effort toward a particular goal (e.g., Campus Crusade for Christ) and as a metaphor for efforts and ambitions that try to establish the supremacy of one's own worldview.

The historic Crusades are of interest for scholars and students of global studies in many respects. For one, the Crusades represent an impressive example of the use of a special kind of rhetoric for legitimating and enforcing particular claims, which may shed light on the rhetoric employed in many of today's global initiatives. In addition, the period saw not only intense conflict and tension, especially between the Islamic and Christian faiths and cultures, but also the reopening of exchange between East and West and the expansion of commerce and geographic exploration.

Historical Overview and Context

The initial spark and public appeal for the Crusades was given by Pope Urban II at the Church Council of Clermont in 1095, mobilizing the faithful to liberate Jerusalem and the Holy Land more broadly. The situation in medieval Europe at the time was ripe for such an initiative. Among other factors, historians note the presence of armed warriors as a result of the Christianization of the Vikings and Slavs and the breakdown of the Carolingian Empire at the end of the 9th century. Given the relative stability of borders at the time, these warriors turned their energies to terrorizing each other and the local populations. In addition, although Western Christians had been making pilgrimages to Jerusalem, in particular the Holy Sepulchre, for centuries, the Muslim rulers of the time made it increasingly difficult for pilgrims. To complete the picture, although the Byzantine Christians and Roman Catholics continued to be at odds, the Byzantine emperor Alexios I called on the Catholic pope to send mercenaries to help defend the remains of the Byzantine Empire from a new wave of attacks from the (Muslim) Seljuk Turks.

Thus, the Crusades were conceived of and instigated as liberation movements and an expression of the Christian faith, along with (re)installation of its power; in the Christian rhetoric, participation was promoted as a (penitential) pilgrimage. The first crusaders set off from France and Italy in 1096, arrived at Jerusalem in 1099, conquered the city, massacred the majority of the inhabitants, and subsequently established four crusader states. The retaking of Edessa, one of the four crusader states, by Muslims in 1144 led to a call for the Second Crusade, which began in 1147. From here, historians debate the number of subsequent Crusades, ranging from a total of seven to nine, with several other military campaigns with religious goals taking place in between. Traditionally, the fall of Acre in 1291 marks the end of the Crusades, but some historians extend them to 1798, when Napoleon expelled the Knights Hospitaller from Malta.

Aftermath and Legacy

Whether the Crusades were the most important events of the Middle Ages, as some historians would contend, there is no dispute that they contributed greatly to changes in Europe and indeed the world.

Although the Crusades did not succeed in winning back the Holy Land, they did strengthen pontifical authority and fostered a view of Christendom as a united entity. In addition, papal intervention had the effect of channeling the violent energies of warring knights toward a common enemy and succeeded in reducing war within Europe.

The Crusades also had a positive impact on economies and trade, particularly in western Europe. The massive preparations for foreign war stimulated production. Trade in new types of goods opened up, especially once the Crusader states in the East were established.

Many historians also point to the impact of the Crusades on culture. Crusaders coming from the farthest reaches of Europe came into contact with new cultures and brought back with them novel ideas. These cultural transfers are manifested in western Europe through literature, for example Dante's *Commedia*, art, and architecture, such as the crusader castles. Some even attribute the origins of geographic explorations such as those of Marco Polo to the crusaders returning to Europe with knowledge of Asia.

Modern Views

In modern usage, a crusade refers to an effort or a campaign with a specific goal. In its positive connotation, crusades are launched against diseases or poverty. But today, crusades have also been linked to expansionary and colonizing activities, among them the Second Gulf War or the World Trade Organization's initiatives.

Furthermore, the Crusades won renewed interest following the September 11, 2001, terrorist attacks in the United States. Many of the commonly held beliefs about the causes and impacts of the Crusades were revisited, especially in light of Osama bin Laden's purported criticism of the U.S. "War on Terror" as a new crusade. Clearly, the Crusades have had and will continue to have an influence on East-West and Muslim-Christian relations.

Martin Hölz

See also Christianity-Related Movements; Conquests; Diasporas; Empires; Global Religions, Beliefs, and Ideologies; Islam; Islam-Related Movements; Religious Politics; September 11, 2001 (9/11); Vatican; War

Further Readings

Asbridge, T. (2010). *The Crusades. The war for the Holy Land*. London: Simon & Schuster.

Heston, A. (2003). Crusades and jihads: A long-run economic perspective. *The Annals of the American Academy of Political and Social Science, 588*(1), 112–135.

Lawrence, T. E. (1988). *Crusader castles*. Oxford, UK: Oxford University Press.

Lock, P. (2006). *The Routledge companion to the Crusades*. New York: Routledge.

Mastnak, T. (2002). *Crusading peace: Christendom, the Muslim world, and Western political order*. Berkeley: University of California Press.

Nicholson, H. (2004). *The Crusades*. Westport, CT: Greenwood Press.

Qureshi, E., & Sells, M. A. (Eds.). (2003). *The new crusades: Constructing the Muslim enemy*. New York: Columbia University Press.

Setton, K. M. (Ed.). (1969–1989). *A history of the Crusades*. Madison: University of Wisconsin Press.

CUISINE

Cuisine is an important manifestation of the impact of globalization on cultural practices. Defined as a style of cooking, cuisine is a boundary-marking mechanism for different societies, demarcating "us" from "them." Margaret Mead asserted that "food habits are seen as the culturally standardized set of behaviors in regard to food manifested who have been reared within a given cultural tradition" (Mead, 1943, p. 21). Foodways in general are a highly revealing lens through which to examine the diversity of human social formations and cultural practices.

Everybody must eat, so the production, consumption, and exchange of food are the most basic economic activities for families throughout the world and shared social activities in all cultures. As Claude Levi-Strauss has asserted, cuisine as a subset of foodways is perhaps the most basic of cultural activities, where nature is transformed (from raw food item) into a cultural artifact (cooked or prepared food).

Moreover, food production, exchange, and consumption are crucial to contemporary global political and economic issues. Solving food insecurity is listed as the first of the United Nations Millennium Development Goals, a situation that is paradoxical given the world's production capabilities; indeed, 1998 Nobel Prize–winner Amartya Sen's conclusion of the primary source of famine as human, and not as natural, underscores that while humans have had the technological ability to feed the world, they have not had the social and political will to solve global hunger. Food production and consumption have also become central in many different topics of environmental debate—from issues of access to clean food and water and the use of agricultural inputs to the introduction of genetically modified organisms and its possible ecological impact.

The influence of cuisine illustrates the central paradox of globalization. Although globalization seems to homogenize cultural practices, as societies seem to be converging toward what Benjamin Barber (1995, p. 9) refers to as the "numbing and neutering uniformities of industrial modernization and the colonizing culture of McWorld," it is also resulting in the resurgence and power of local cultures and traditions. From a cursory examination of the spread of different particular national and regional cuisines (and the accompanying cookbooks and cooking shows), it is clear that the local also transforms the global. Cuisine gives us a platform from which to observe how people in different areas of the world, in contrasting social contexts and historical experiences, are cooking up different solutions to the challenges presented by globalization.

Food Versus Cuisine as a Marker of Identity

In various world and indigenous religious traditions, food can be recognized as drawing a sharp border between different social groups, as shown in the kosher restrictions of the Jewish tradition, halal rules in Islamic tradition, food purity rules in the Hindu tradition, or food totemic practices in various indigenous religious traditions. For Christianity, the symbolic use of a shared meal of the body of Christ as the focal point for ritual underscores the importance of food as a marker of identity. In nonreligious contexts, a differentiated pattern of food consumption was also used historically to distinguish aristocracy from commoners, or higher from lower social classes, a difference that in history was sometimes codified through sumptuary laws and in contemporary times is understood through informal, culturally specific understandings.

The use of food as a marker of identity is slightly different from that of cuisine because of the process by which cuisine develops and spreads, and its association with identities that political scientist Benedict Anderson refers to as "imagined communities" (nation-states). Cuisine as a marker of identity involves processes of objectification and standardization through media such as cookbooks: "The existence of cookbooks presupposes not only some degree of literacy, but often an effort on the part of some variety of specialist to standardize the regime of the kitchen, to transmit culinary lore, and to publicize particular traditions guiding the journey of food from marketplace to kitchen to table" (Appadurai, 1988, p. 3). As Arjun Appadurai demonstrates in the case of India, a national cuisine emerges from heterogeneous regional cuisines as an urban middle class becomes both disconnected from the traditional kinship patterns that passed on culinary knowledge and connected to wider networks of multiethnic urban professionals who consume a similar globalized popular culture. Although the development of a national cuisine Appadurai describes for India is closely linked to the historical specificity of a postindustrial, postcolonial context, the development of national cuisines has accelerated with globalization. National cuisines continue to be further objectified and standardized as they spread beyond borders to satisfy the palates of global cosmopolitans.

Cuisine and Food Production

Although anthropological studies of the 19th and early 20th centuries primarily examined so-called primitive foodways through topics in religion (such as totemism or sacrifice), studies from the 20th century looked at food from a functionalist perspective that connected foodways to particular social structures. One such pioneer, Audrey Richards, boldly asserted that "nutrition as a biological process is more fundamental than sex" (1932, p. 1); a lesser-known statement by Richards is perhaps more crucial to understanding how cuisine shapes culture: "Of all the biological impulses nutrition is

that which is most dependent on the formation of a *habit complex* in the individual's lifetime" (1932, p. 3, emphasis added). Although this approach was later expanded on by Pierre Bourdieu through an examination of consumption, food production also strongly shapes culture. Anthropological studies of the latter half of the 20th century focused on the role of food from a materialist perspective of production (including authors such as Sidney Mintz or Marvin Harris), whether through agricultural work, studies of hunting and gathering societies, or through food preparation. Jack Goody, author of a canonical text in the anthropological study of food, concluded that since food "is linked to the mode of production of material goods, the analysis of cooking has to be related to the distribution of power and authority in the economic sphere" (1982, p. 37).

Although there has been a macroeconomic shift away from the predominance of agriculture in the global economy (first toward the industrial sector, then toward the service sector), food production continues to be an important source of livelihood for many people (especially in the developing world). Like many other economic sectors in this age of globalization, agricultural production has increasingly become consolidated into a smaller number of worldwide firms. This consolidation has been made economically feasible because of the expansion and reliability of global agricultural commodity chains—the integrated system of food production that connects a farm in one locale to the consumer in another. The economic implications of global food commodity chains (consolidation of agricultural production, tight vertical integration, and the squeezing out of small-scale farmers) have been thoroughly explored and debated, but these global networks of food have also made global cuisines—or more perhaps more precisely, the spread of local cuisines in global locations—a feature of everyday life in this era of globalization.

Globalization and Postnatural Food

Although genetic modification through breeding has been a part of food production since the first domestication of wild foodstuffs, the industrialization of agriculture and developments in science and technology has made direct modification of genetic material a standard agricultural practice. Genetically modified foodstuffs, starting with the development of a tomato that could ripen without softening so as to survive the rigors of transportation, make a global commodity chain possible. Many cash crops have become genetically modified to facilitate industrial production (such as parasite or herbicide resistance); genetically modified livestock are also being developed, but as of June 2011 have not been approved for the market. The first application for national approval for consumer consumption of a genetically modified animal, a salmon that can reach market size twice as fast as traditional fish, was submitted to the U.S. Food and Drug Administration, following the establishment of international safety standards for genetically modified animals by the United Nations Food and Agriculture Organization in 2008.

Many consumers throughout the world, especially in Europe, have been wary of genetically modified foods (and globalization in general), resulting in the formation of global organizations such as the Slow Food Movement. The Slow Food Movement emerged in 1986 in Italy as a farmer's movement led by Carlo Petrini that entered the political scene with a protest against the opening of a McDonald's near the Spanish Steps in Rome. Today, it is a leading international nongovernmental organization that promotes the use of local agriculture and the preservation of local foodways, centered on an ideology of eco-gastronomy—an emphasis on local, organic, and sustainable food. This confluence of environmental concerns and haute cuisine has resulted in the revalorization of the local, of the regional. At the same time, as globalization has matured in various modern cosmopolitan localities, national cuisines that were once exotic have become familiar. One reaction to this familiarization was the development of fusion cuisine, which blended together elements of different national cuisines into something different. Another reaction has been the renewed popularity of local, regional cuisines.

Cuisine in a Mature Globalization

Although globalization has made national cuisines possible, it has also promoted fast food anticuisine—a deterritorialized style of food that is more fuel than culinary aesthetic; it is not by accident that Barber chose the concept of McWorld to summarize his perspective on global consumer culture, nor was it merely fortuitous that Petrini chose to protest a McDonald's in Italy. Fusion cuisines are popular at the same time that authentic, regional cuisines are celebrated. In the developed cosmopolitan world, there is a myriad array of choices in the realm of food, embodying the idea that choice is the hallmark of postmodern cultures. At the same time, there are many people throughout the world who have little choice but to go hungry. In a world of plenty, we are also food insecure—whether by not having access to adequate levels of food or in potential health hazards as a result of food safety issues. However cuisine develops in the future, it will be closely tied to the workings of globalization. Although print media made possible an earlier age of globalization, reshaping the way people ate, today's globalization is mediated by information technology that compresses time and space, making the foodways of people in other cultures readily accessible through many levels of popular culture.

Eriberto Lozada

See also Agricultural Sector; Antiglobalization Movements and Critics; Cultural Hybridity; Fisheries; Food; Global Health and Nutrition; Identities in Global Societies; Social Movements; World Food Program

Further Readings

Appadurai, A. (1988). How to make a national cuisine: Cookbooks in contemporary India. *Comparative Studies in Society and History, 30*(1), 3–24.

Barber, B. (1995). *Jihad vs. McWorld: How globalism and tribalism are reshaping the world.* New York: Random House.

Bourdieu, P. (1987). *Distinctions: A social critique of the judgment of taste.* Cambridge, MA: Harvard University Press.

Counihan, C., & Van Esterik, P. (Eds.). (2008). *Food and culture: A reader.* New York: Routledge.

Goody, J. (1982). *Cooking, cuisine and class: A study in comparative sociology.* Cambridge, MA: Cambridge University Press.

Levi-Strauss, C. (1966). The culinary triangle. *Partisan Review, 33*(4), 586–595.

Mead, M. (1943, October). The problem of changing food habits. *Bulletin of the National Research Council, 108,* 20–32.

Richards, A. (1932). *Hunger and work in a savage tribe.* London: Routledge.

Watson, J. L., & Caldwell, M. (Eds.). (2005). *The cultural politics of food and eating.* Malden, UK: Blackwell.

CULINARY STYLES

See Food

CULTURAL COMMONS

Cultural commons consist of works and ideas that are available for global access because they are either in the public domain or are governed by free or open licenses that enable their reproduction, distribution, and often modification. Wikipedia is an example of a cultural commons that is created by contributors around the world and shared with a royalty-free license. Cultural commons enables legal collaboration and sharing across borders by granting permission to works that otherwise would be the exclusive property of their rights owner.

Cultural property can be sorted into three categories. First, there is the vast store of unowned ideas, inventions, and works of art we have inherited from the past that are part of *public domain.* Anyone can use them without fear of stepping on anyone else's property rights. Public domain works are part of the commons. Second, there are cultural works that are *governed by a property right.* For example, physical objects are owned by someone, and copyright protects works for certain time. The third category of cultural works is *self-made commons.* These works would otherwise fall under the copyright or some other property law, but their owners have chosen to release their works for others to enjoy and use. Typically, this is done by releasing the works into public domain or by using public and permissive licenses.

The default copyright system that is based on automatic exclusivity does not serve collaboration as such. Many have criticized the current international copyright regime for its overreaching scope and duration. Collaborative communities have had to develop alternative systems to facilitate easy sharing and collaboration. Extensive and expanding copyright spurred countermovements into existence. The founding of the Free Software Foundation (FSF) in 1985 and the Open Source Initiative (OSI) in 1998 led to the birth of the software commons movement. At the same time music, photos, and other non-software-related works were being shared more and more by amateurs, and the need for licenses designed for non-software and especially for scientific publishing grew. In 2002, Creative Commons introduced a set of licenses that have become the standard of open content licensing. Creative Commons also hosts Science commons project that designs strategies and tools for faster, more efficient web-enabled scientific research and collaboration.

Public goods are defined in terms of two characteristics: nonrivalry and nonexcludability. Digital content provides an example of the characteristic of being nonrivalrous in consumption. Cultural commons carrying capacity is endless. If you sing my song, it does not "consume" the song; it remains available for others to use. One of the relevant characteristics of commons is that no single person has exclusive control over the use and disposition of any particular resource held in common.

Commons and public goods are not synonymous. The main difference is that commons may be excludable, whereas public goods cannot be. Copyrighted work is an example of a public good. Although it is nonrivalrous in consumption, it does not always possess the quality of being nonexcludable, as copyright law enables exclusion by its very nature. Both open content and source movements use excludability to serve their causes. Goods where consumers might be excluded but the consumption by an additional consumer does not add any cost to its provisions are called *club goods.* Cultural commons share both club good and public good elements. Commons can be divided into four types: those open to anyone, those open to only a defined group, those that are regulated, and those that are unregulated.

The self-made commons movements may seem antiproperty and proanarchy, whereas the opposite is actually the case. The general property system and especially the copyright system enable licensors to maintain some control over their works. The retained control can help the licensors organize peer production and build business that takes advantage of the wide distribution of the works. The reserved rights can be withheld to keep the works and the new works built on top of them freely available (through copyleft and ShareAlike licenses) or licensed for separate compensation (through dual licensing). It is a paradox that the need for preservation of control is the reason the new commons movement is dependent on the exclusive copyright system.

Herkko Hietanen

See also Corporations, Transnational; Creativity and Innovation; Cultural Destruction; Cultural Industries; Information Age; Intellectual Property Rights; Knowledge Management Systems; Knowledge Production Systems; Power, Global Contexts of; Trade; World Trade Organization (WTO)

Further Readings

Benkler, Y. (2006). *The wealth of networks: How social production transforms markets and freedom.* New Haven, CT: Yale University Press.

Hardin, G. (1968). The tragedy of the commons. *Science, 162,* 1243–1248.

Hietanen, H. (2008). The pursuit of efficient copyright licensing: How some rights reserved attempts to solve the problems of all rights reserved. *Acta Universitatis Lappeenrantaensis, 325.*

Lessig, L. (2001). *The future of ideas: The fate of the commons in a connected world.* New York: Random House.

Rose, C. (1986). The comedy of the commons: Custom, commerce, and inherently public property. *University of Chicago Law Review, 53,* 711.

CULTURAL DESTRUCTION

In the context of globalization, *cultural destruction* can be defined in two ways. One definition refers to perceptions that globalization is having a destructive impact on local cultures, encompassing objects and sites as well as other forms of cultural expression such as traditions, beliefs, and knowledge. The other understanding of the term refers to the destruction of culture as a global phenomenon. These two definitions are examined in turn.

Destructive Impact on Local Cultures

There is no consensus on the breadth or severity of globalization's destructive impact on particular cultures; however, some mechanisms of this destruction have been identified. One way that globalization is viewed to pose a threat to cultures is through what is perceived as its homogenizing effect such that around the world, the same films, television programs, music, gastronomy, fashion, and even art exhibitions are being consumed. Tyler Cowen counters this perception by proposing that globalization has been instrumental in the development of measures for sharing information about cultural practices, and indeed engendering new ones.

The two sides of the debate came to the fore during the Uruguay rounds (1986–1993) of the General Agreement on Tariffs and Trade (GATT) during which France claimed that in questions of free market liberalization, there should be an exception made for cultural goods and services. The argument was that cultural products, the entertainment industry, and films in particular being a central element in the debate, should come under particular regulations that allowed for greater national protection and subventions. It was felt that nationally based entertainment industries were in danger of succumbing to what was perceived as an overwhelming onslaught of products from the United States, and with them not only would national creative industries suffer but the diversity of worldviews and imaginations would also decrease. The counterargument, put forth especially strongly by the United States, was that the increased movement of people and cultural products exposes individuals today to more cultures, ways of life, philosophies, and experiences than ever before, thus multiplying rather than reducing our appreciation of cultural diversity and sources of creativity. By the end of deliberations, a list of possible exceptions was added that included culture, thus giving rise to the term *l'exception culturelle*.

This debate was taken up again in 1999 by the UN Educational, Scientific and Cultural Organization (UNESCO), and in the process, the idea of safeguarding cultural diversity, as opposed to arguing for cultural goods to be treated differently, took hold. The organization's work on the topic led to the adoption of the Convention on the Protection and Promotion of the Diversity of Cultural Expressions in 2005. The creation of a normative instrument to safeguard cultural diversity was a response to the perceived threat that globalization would lead to cultural homogeneity at a world scale, a dynamic Benjamin Barber termed McWorld after the fast-food chain McDonald's. There are numerous counterarguments to this view of globalization that claim that societies do not passively consume imported products but interpret them according to ever-changing cultural frameworks and symbolic systems, ascribing to them different meanings and utility.

Linked to the homogenizing concern is the view that globalization is sweeping before it cultural diversity and turning the richness of cultural expressions into commodities to be sold on a global market. Part of the destructive impact of this dynamic, often referred to as Disneyfication, is that in trying to reach as many consumers as possible, expressions of local cultural distinctiveness and creativity are transformed into simplified and marketable goods, and, thus, denuded of their contexts, complexity, and nuances. The entertainment and tourist industries in particular are cited as examples of this destructive impact. Cultural tourism trades on the unique and authentic character of places and experiences, yet in seeking to attract and cater to increasing numbers of visitors, it is precisely this special character that it is viewed to endanger. Examples include hotel complexes destroying the natural landscape and eco-systems of coastal areas and blockbuster exhibitions demanding that fragile works of art be flown around the world with inestimable consequences to their material integrity.

An additional danger posed by this form of destruction is viewed to be the reaction against it: People respond to what they perceive as an imposed homogenization based on Western values and market interests by developing increasingly radical versions of their cultural distinctiveness: McWorld versus jihad, as proposed by Barber. This polarization and the alienating dynamic that the perceived dichotomy engenders can make communication and understanding across cultures all the more difficult. According to anthropologist Clifford Geertz, who dedicated much of his work to studying cultures, one obstacle to cross-cultural

understanding is the difficulty of interpreting the meaning of actions and the imaginative context within which they occur. The lack of understanding that results can lead to conflicts and the further destruction of culture.

An important body of writing and thinking on the topic was sparked by the publication of an article by Samuel P. Huntington titled "The Clash of Civilizations?" (*Foreign Affairs*, Summer 1993) and an ensuing book (1996). His proposal was understood by many critics to reduce the world to a handful of groups with irreconcilable worldviews. Critics of this analysis, such as Amin Maalouf and Amartya Sen, have argued that cultural identities have many facets and dimensions and that simplifying them does violence to them. Perceptions of the world as being split into dynamics of homogenization and resistance or of an inevitable clash between cultures can fuel deliberate attempts to target culture for destruction.

Destruction of Culture as a Global Phenomenon

This introduces the second definition: the destruction of culture as a global phenomenon. The practice of destroying cultures and looting cultural sites and artifacts has had a long history and has spared no continent. Wars between nations instigated an early form of globalization as soldiers, civilians fleeing the fighting, and occupying forces moved across landscapes and cultures that had previously been foreign to them. Trajan's Column (113 CE), depicting the triumphal parade after the defeat of the Dacians, testifies to the movement of people, soldiers and slaves, objects, looted trophies, and treasures. Inherent in this movement is the violence done to people and places as well as the removal of objects from their original context. Colonial conquest was another early form of a global dynamic that caused the destruction of culture on a large scale as entire societies were annihilated at the hands of the invading groups. Where they did not disappear entirely, these autochthonous communities were so violently severed from their traditions and beliefs that many were lost. The deliberate destruction of culture has not been limited to aggressions between countries. Revolutions, and the iconoclasm that they often engender, have also been motors for cultural destruction whose impact at times extended beyond national borders. Examples of revolutions include the French (1789) and Russian (1917) revolutions or the Chinese Cultural Revolution (1966), during which the Four Olds were targeted: Old Customs, Old Culture, Old Habits, and Old Ideas.

War took on an explicitly global dimension with World War I and World War II. The latter in particular observed the destruction of culture on a vast scale through a combination of weapons and methods of mass destruction. The aerial bombings of Warsaw and Dresden and the nuclear bombings of Hiroshima and Nagasaki are some of the more well-known casualties from a long list of devastated cities whose historic centers were often targeted. Art collections—private, public, and those belonging to religious institutions—were pillaged. This war also saw cultural destruction in the form of genocide: the deliberate targeting of groups in an attempt to not only destroy cultural expressions but also eradicate the individuals and communities that created them. At the end of World War II, and in an attempt to prevent war and destruction on such a scale from occurring again, the United Nations was created. Through this international organization and the negotiations between countries that it facilitated, international instruments were developed for the protection of cultural heritage: Convention for the Protection of Cultural Heritage in the Event of Armed Conflict (1954), International Charter for the Conservation and Restoration of Monuments and Sites (1964), Convention on the Means of Prohibiting and Preventing the Illicit Import, Export and Transfer of Ownership of Cultural Property (1970), and the Convention for the Protection of the World's Cultural and Natural Heritage (1972). The aftermath of World War II had other repercussions. Although attempts were being made on an international scale to prevent such destruction from occurring again, the Cold War began to wreak its own form of violence by portraying a world of opposing factions with irreconcilable differences and worldviews, depicting countries as enemies on ideological and cultural grounds.

The significance of the contexts that give rise to cultural expressions has already been alluded to; these contexts can, along with objects, extend our understanding of societies past and present. Yet these contexts are still being threatened today as a result of a demand for objects to be traded in a global market composed of dealers, collectors, auction houses, and museums with questionable scruples. The accentuation and acceleration of global movements and exchange have not caused the demand in cultural objects and artifacts to dwindle; on the contrary, the number of buyers has grown since the last decade of the 20th century as new buyers have come on the scene from countries such as Japan and China. The destruction caused by the illicit excavation of antiquities that feeds the illegal trade puts the objects at risk, but above all, it destroys the context in which they were found, making it difficult for archaeologists, or the wider public, to learn from these sites. What makes cultural objects and creations an exception, the reason their destruction provokes outrage and the reason they are targeted, is that culture is more than the sum of its material manifestations. Destroying cultural objects also destroys the possibility for cultural traditions, knowledge, and know-how to be transmitted across generations; the overemphasis that the trade in antiquities in particular places on the object fails to appreciate this.

More recent wars have impressed with their destruction of culture. The wars of the former Yugoslavia (1992–1995) in particular had a significant impact in raising awareness of this dynamic. The shelling of Dubrovnik, Sarajevo, and Mostar and the deliberate targeting of heritage sites, symbols, and monuments of the "enemy other" drew attention from the international media, intellectuals, artists, politicians, and international organizations. It also led to the first guilty verdict to be proclaimed for war crimes against culture at the International Criminal Tribunal for the former Yugoslavia for the shelling of Dubrovnik, which was a UNESCO World Heritage site. The *Review of the Convention for the Protection of Cultural Property in the Event of Armed Conflict, the Hague Convention of 1954* (Boylan, 1993) noted that the deliberate targeting of cultural sites, including monuments and collections, was becoming increasingly common in conflicts throughout the world. It has also been argued that the changed nature of conflicts is not in terms of quantitative but qualitative destruction as wars become increasingly diagnostic, revolving around group identity and involving violence over ethnic and cultural difference. Certainly, the rhetoric surrounding conflicts since the Cold War has drawn on a discourse of meaning and identity that at times seems to overshadow their realpolitik. This in turn can result in symbols of culture, religion and ethnicity increasingly becoming deliberate targets in armed conflicts. A case that incited reactions around the world was the dynamiting of the Bamiyan Buddhas in Afghanistan in 2001 by the Taliban; this act of destruction was a combination of religious iconoclasm and a defiance of the international community. Spurred by the destruction of cultural heritage in the former Yugoslavia and Afghanistan, in 2003 UNESCO adopted a Declaration Concerning the Intentional Destruction of Cultural Heritage.

Dacia Viejo Rose

See also Conflict and Conflict Resolution; Creativity and Innovation; Cultural Diversity, Convention on; Cultural Hybridity; Culture, Notions of; Hegemonic Power; Heritage; Knowledge Management Systems; Knowledge Production Systems; Power, Global Contexts of; Sites, Global

Further Readings

Appadurai, A. (2000). The new territories of culture: Globalization, cultural uncertainty and violence. In J. Bindé (Ed.), *Keys to the 21st century* (pp. 136–138). Paris: UNESCO.

Barber, B. (1995). *Jihad vs. McWorld*. New York: Ballantine Books.

Boylan, P. (1993). *Review of the Convention for the Protection of Cultural Property in the Event of Armed Conflict, the Hague Convention of 1954*. Paris: UNESCO.

Buchli, V. (Ed.). (2002). *The material culture reader*. Oxford, UK: Berg.

Cowen, T. (2002). *Creative destruction: How globalization is changing the world's cultures*. Princeton, NJ: Princeton University Press.

Geertz, C. (1973). *The interpretation of cultures*. New York: Basic Books.

Huntington, S. P. (1996). *The clash of civilizations and the remaking of world order*. New York: Simon & Schuster.

International Criminal Tribunal for the Former Yugoslavia (ICTY). (2005, January). *Prosecutor v. Pavle Strugar (Trial Judgment)*, IT-01–42-T. Retrieved October 13, 2009, from www.unhcr.org/refworld/docid/48ad42092.html

Maalouf, A. (1998). *Les identités meurtrières* [Fatal identities]. Paris: Grasset.

Saunders, F. S. (1999). *Who paid the piper? The CIA and the cultural cold war*. London: Granta.

Sen, A. (2006). *Identity and violence: The illusion of destiny*. London: Penguin Books.

CULTURAL DIVERSITY, CONVENTION ON

The UNESCO Convention on the Protection and Promotion of the Diversity of Cultural Expressions is relevant in several ways to the field of global studies since it was aimed at protecting local cultures against the forces of globalization and modernization. The convention, which is sometimes referred to as the UNESCO Convention on Cultural Diversity, was formally adopted in October 2005 and entered into force on March 27, 2007. On May 15, 2009, 98 members of UNESCO and the European Union, as a regional economic integration organization, ratified it.

The adoption of the convention was a direct answer to a perceived threat that the processes of globalization, if they afforded conditions for enhanced interaction among cultures, could also have a negative impact on the preservation of cultural identities and cultural diversity. Behind the convention also lies an issue of international governance regarding the precedence of trade agreements over cultural agreements. During the negotiations that led to the adoption of the convention, developmental issues concerning the need to cooperate to foster the emergence of a dynamic cultural sector in developing countries and the need to integrate culture in sustainable development were also considered and received attention.

The process that led to the adoption of the convention has been variously described as a debate over trade and culture, a fight in favor of cultural diversity, or a battle between free trade and cultural homogenization. Its origin goes back to the 1920s when European countries began resorting to screen quotas to protect their film industry from an influx of American films considered as a threat to their culture, a development that brought a strong reaction from the American film industry and the U.S. Department of State. From that moment until the end of the 1990s, the process was centered on the search for a cultural exception in trade agreements. At the turn of the century, however, the debate about trade and culture took a new direction: From a debate strictly about the treatment of cultural goods and services in trade agreements, it became one about the impact of globalization on cultural identities and cultural diversity. This was accompanied by a change of paradigm. The idea of a new international instrument on cultural diversity gradually emerged, an instrument that would no longer consider the protection and promotion of cultural diversity as an impediment to trade to be addressed from a trade law perspective but as a cultural problem in itself to be addressed from a cultural perspective.

A demand that UNESCO undertake the negotiation of such an instrument was formally submitted to the organization in February 2003, and the decision to move ahead with the negotiation of a convention regarding the diversity of cultural contents and artistic expression was taken by the General Assembly in October 2003. In October 2005, after three meetings of independent experts and three intergovernmental meetings of experts, with the active support of civil society, the convention was adopted by the General Assembly by a vote of 148 in favor, 2 against (the United States and Israel), and 4 abstentions.

In essence, the text in question, recognizing at the outset the distinctive nature of cultural activities, goods, and services as vehicles of identity, values, and meaning, reaffirms the sovereign right of states to maintain, adopt, and implement policies and measures that they deem appropriate for the protection and promotion of the diversity of cultural expressions on their territory and proposes a program of action designed to protect and promote the diversity of cultural expressions and to create the conditions for cultures to flourish and interact in a mutually beneficial manner. Special attention is paid to the needs of developing countries as evidenced by the insertion of provisions providing for the granting of preferential treatment to developing countries, the development of innovative partnerships, and the creation of an international fund for cultural diversity. Regarding the relationship to other treaties, the convention makes clear that if it does not prevail over other treaties, then other treaties themselves do not prevail over the convention. In other words, the convention and other international treaties stand on an equal footing. Not satisfied with this neutral position, the convention goes on to suggest ways of addressing the interface between trade and culture, demanding (among other things) that the parties take into account its relevant provision when they interpret and apply other treaties or when they enter into new international obligations.

The convention, as can be observed, is a direct outcome of globalization and can be understood only from a global studies perspective. Although it was opposed from the beginning by the United States as a disguised attempt to limit trade commitments in the field of culture and as a threat to freedom of expression, it was nonetheless signed by 148 states that were convinced of the need for such an international instrument and ratified by nearly 100 states barely 2 years after its entry into force. The future of the convention, whether it succeeds or fails, will tell something about the future of globalization.

Ivan Bernier

See also Americanization; Culture, Notions of; Economic Development; Global Governance and World Order; Heritage; Law, International; Sites, Global; Sovereignty; Trade; Trade Agreements; United Nations Educational, Scientific and Cultural Organization (UNESCO)

Further Readings

Bernier, I. (2008, May). *The UNESCO Convention on the Protection and Promotion of the Diversity of Cultural Expressions: A cultural instrument at the junction of law and politics.* Retrieved May 29, 2009, from: http://www.diversite-culturelle.qc.ca/index .php?id=133&L=1

Graber, C. B. (2006). The new UNESCO convention on cultural diversity: A counterbalance to the WTO. *Journal of International Economic Law, 9,* 553–574.

Oliver, L. (2005, October). *U.S. opposes "deeply flawed" U.N. Cultural Diversity Convention.* Retrieved May 30, 2009, from http://www.america.gov/st/washfile -english/2005/October/20051020170821GLnesnoM 3.670901e-02.html#ixzz0GyfnQqTi&A

CULTURAL HYBRIDITY

Hybridity refers to the mixture of phenomena that are held to be different or separate; on a cultural level, hybridization has become an important feature of global society. William Rowe and Vivian Schelling define hybridization as "the ways in which forms become separated from existing practices and recombine with new forms in new practices" (1991, p. 231).

Cut-and-mix experiences in consumption, lifestyles, and identities are common and everyday, for example, in food and menus. Hybridity has become ordinary and a part of everyday life in a world of intensive intercultural communication, multiculturalism, growing migration and diaspora lives, and eroding boundaries, at least in some spheres. Hence, hybridity has become a prominent theme in cultural studies. The emergence of new hybrid forms and practices indicates profound changes that are taking place as a consequence of mobility, migration, and multiculturalism. However, hybridity thinking also concerns already existing or, so to speak, old hybridity that used to be concealed under homogeneous identities. Thus, hybridity also involves different ways of looking at historical and current cultural and institutional arrangements, suggesting not only that things are no longer the way they used to be but also that they were never really the way they used to be, or, at least, the way they used to be viewed.

Hybridization as a Process

Anthropologists studying the travel of customs and foodstuffs show that our foundations are profoundly mixed, and it could not be otherwise. Mixing is intrinsic to the evolution of the species. History is a collage. Superimposed on the deep strata of mixing in evolutionary time are historical episodes of long-distance, cross-cultural trade, conquest and empire, and episodes such as transatlantic slavery and the triangular trade. Within and across these episodes, additional hybrid configurations can be distinguished. So, hybridity can be thought of as layered in history, including precolonial, colonial, and postcolonial layers. To each period belong distinct sets of hybridity because different boundaries were prominent, each with its pathos of difference.

Hybridization as a process is as old as history, but the pace of mixing accelerates and its scope widens in the wake of major structural changes, such as new technologies that enable new forms of intercultural contact. Contemporary accelerated globalization is such a new phase.

Hybridity as a Theme

If practices of mixing are as old as the hills, then the thematization of mixing as a perspective is fairly new and largely dates from the 1980s. In a wider sense, it includes the idea of bricolage in culture and art, which inspired the collage. Dada, the cultural movement involving visual arts, art theory, and graphic design, made mixing objects and perspectives its hallmark. Surrealism moved further along these lines, and so do conceptual and installation art. Psychoanalysis brought together widely diverse phenomena—such as dreams, jokes, Freudian slips, and symbols—under new headings relevant to psychological diagnosis.

Although hybridity may be ordinary and unremarkable in itself, the critical contribution of hybridity as a theme is that it questions boundaries that are taken for granted. Thus, hybridity is noteworthy from the point of view of boundaries that are considered essential or insurmountable.

Hybridity is also an important theme in that it represents one of three major approaches to globalization and culture. One is the idea that global culture is becoming increasingly standardized and uniform (as in McDonaldization); second is the idea that globalization involves a clash of civilizations; and third is globalization as hybridization or the notion that globalization produces new combinations and mixtures.

The hybridity view holds that cultural experiences past and present have not been simply moving in the direction of cultural synchronization. Cultural synchronization does take place, for instance, in relation to technological change; but countercurrents to standardization along Western lines include the impact non-Western cultures have on the West and the influence non-Western cultures exercise on one another. The cultural convergence view ignores the local reception of Western culture, the indigenization of Western elements, and the significance of crossover culture and "third cultures," such as world music. It overrates the homogeneity of Western culture and overlooks that many of the cultural traits exported by the West are themselves of culturally mixed character if one examines their lineages. Centuries of East-West cultural osmosis have resulted in intercontinental crossover culture, and European and Western culture are part of this global mélange. For a long time, Europe was on the receiving end of cultural influences from the Orient, and the dominance of the West dates only from 1800 onward.

The term *hybridity* originates in pastoralism, agriculture, and horticulture. Hybridization refers to developing new combinations by grafting one plant or fruit to another. Another application is genetics. When belief in "race" played a dominant role in culture, "race mixture" was a prominent notion. Now, hybridity also refers to cyborgs (cybernetic organisms), combinations of humans or animals with new technology (pets carrying chips for identification, biogenetic engineering).

Hybridity in the Social Sciences

Hybridity first entered social science via the anthropology of religion and the theme of syncretism. Roger Bastide defined syncretism as "uniting pieces of the mythical history of two different traditions in one that continued to be ordered by a single system" (1970, p. 101). Creole languages and creolization in linguistics were the next fields to engage social science interest. Creolization came to describe the interplay of cultures and cultural forms. In the Caribbean and North America, creolization stands for the mixture of African and European elements (as in the Creole cuisine of New Orleans), while in Latin America, *criollo* originally denotes those of European descent born in the continent. The appeal of creolization is that it goes against the grain of 19th-century racism and the accompanying abhorrence of *métissage* (mixing) as miscegenation, as in the view that race mixture leads to decadence and decay, for in every mixture the lower element would be bound to predominate. The cult of racial purity involves the fear of and disdain for the half-caste. By foregrounding the mestizo, the mixed and in-between, creolization highlights what has been hidden and values boundary crossing. The Latin American term *mestizaje* also refers to boundary-crossing mixture. Since the early 1900s, however,

this served as an elite ideology of "Whitening" or Europeanization; through the gradual "Whitening" of the population and culture, Latin America was supposed to achieve modernity. In the United States, crossover culture denotes the adoption of Black cultural characteristics by European Americans and of White elements by African Americans. A limitation of these terms is that they are confined to the experience of the post-16th-century Americas and typically focus on "racial" mixing. A different perspective is the "orientalization of the world" and Easternization, in contrast to Westernization. This concerns the influence of Japan and the rise of East Asia, China, and India and the 21st century as an "Asian century." Each of these terms—*creolization*, *mestizaje*, *crossover*, and *orientalization*—opens a different window on the global mélange and global intercultural osmosis.

Hybrid regions straddle geographic and cultural zones such as the Sudanic belt in Africa. Southeast Asia combines Indochinese and Malay features. The societies of the Malay world, Indochina, Central and South Asia, the Middle East, North Africa, and the Balkans are all ancient mélange cultures. Global cities and ethnic mélange neighborhoods within them (such as Jackson Heights in Queens, New York) are other hybrid spaces in the global landscape.

What hybridity means varies not only over time but also in different cultures. In Asia, it carries a different ring than in Latin America. In Asia, the general feeling has been upbeat, as in East-West fusion culture. Here, hybridity tends to be experienced as chosen and willed, although there are plenty sites of conflict. In Latin America, the feeling has long been one of fracture and fragmentation, and hybridity was long experienced as a fateful condition that was inflicted rather than willed. The Latin American notion of mixed times (*tiempos mixtos*) refers to the coexistence and interspersion of premodernity, modernity, and postmodernity. In recent times, Latin America's hybrid legacies are revalued as part of its cultural creativity.

Criticism

The prominence of hybridity has given rise to a debate in which hybridity is being criticized as an elite perspective. A brief account of arguments against and in favor of hybridity follows.

Critics argue that asserting that all cultures and languages are mixed is trivial; a rejoinder is that claims of purity have long been dominant. Critics hold that hybridity is meaningful only as a critique of essentialism, which is true, but there is plenty essentialism to go around. Some question whether colonial times were really so essentialist; a rejoinder is that they were essentialist enough for hybrids to be widely despised. Critics object that hybridity is a dependent notion, but so are boundaries. Some critics argue that hybridity matters only to the extent that people identify themselves as mixed, but the existing classification categories hinder hybrid self-identification. Critics claim that cultural mixing is mainly for elites, but arguably cross-border knowledge is survival knowledge also or particularly for poor migrants. Critics hold that hybridity talk is for a new cultural class of cosmopolitans, but would this justify an old cultural class policing boundaries? If critics ask what the point of hybridity is, a riposte is, what is the significance of boundaries? Boundaries and borders can be matters of life or death, and the failure to acknowledge hybridity is a political point whose ramifications can be measured in lives.

A next step is to unpack hybridity and to distinguish patterns of hybridity. The most conspicuous shortcoming of hybridity thinking is that it does not address questions of power and inequality: "Hybridity is not parity" (Shohat & Stam, 1994). This is true, but boundaries do not usually help either. In notions such as global mélange, what is missing is the acknowledgment of the actual unevenness, asymmetry, and inequality in global relations. What are not clarified are the terms under which cultural interplay and crossover take place. Relations of power and hegemony are reproduced within hybridity, for wherever one looks closely enough, one finds the traces of asymmetry in culture, place, and descent. Hence, hybridity raises, rather than erases, the question of the terms and conditions of mixing. Meanwhile, it is also important to note the ways in which relations of power are not merely reproduced but refigured in the process of hybridization.

Thus, according to the context and the relative power and status of elements in the mixture, hybridity can be asymmetric or symmetric. For instance, colonial society is asymmetric. One can think of types of hybridity along a continuum with, on one end, a hybridity that affirms the center of power, adopts the canon, and mimics hegemony and hegemonic styles, and, at the other end, mixtures that blur the lines of power, destabilize the canon, and subvert the center. The novels of V. S. Naipaul are an example of the former, and Salman Rushdie's novels often match the latter. Menus that mix cuisines and health care practices that combine diverse methods may offer examples of the symmetric end of the hybridity continuum, but completely free-floating mixtures are rare, for even at a carnival the components carry different values.

Contemporary Domains of Hybridity

The domains in which hybridity plays a part have been proliferating over time, as in the hybrid car, hybridity in organizations, and diverse cultural influences in management. Interdisciplinarity in science gives rise to new hybrids such as ecological economics. One can speak of hybridity also beyond culture, in economics, political economy, and institutions. Thus, hybridity also runs across modes of production; modes of production such as feudalism and capitalism did not simply succeed one another but coexisted in time. The combination of modes of production gives rise to mixed social formations and combinations of hunting/gathering, pastoralism and cultivation, agriculture and industry, craft and industry, and so on. Semifeudalism and feudal capitalism are other instances of mixed political economies. Forms and institutions of economic regulation are often hybrid as well. The "social market" in Europe and Scandinavia and "market socialism" in China organize economies by combining diverse principles. The mixed economy and the social economy of cooperative and nonprofit organizations are hybrid economic formations. Public-private partnership, social capital, civic entrepreneurship, and corporate citizenship—all prominent themes of our times—are also hybrid in character.

Jan Nederveen Pieterse

See also Aesthetics; Cosmopolitanism; Creativity and Innovation; Creolization; Cultural Industries; Culture, Notions of; Global Culture, Media; Globalization, Approaches to; Globalization, Phenomenon of; Heritage; Homogenization; Identities in Global Societies; McDonaldization, McWorld

Further Readings

Bastide, R. (1970). Mémoire collective et sociologie du bricolage [Collective memory and sociology of bricolage]. *L'Année Sociologique, 21,* 65–108.

Canclini, N. G. (1995). *Hybrid cultures.* Minneapolis: University of Minnesota Press.

Frank, A. G. (1998). *Re orient: Global economy in the Asian age.* Berkeley: University of California Press.

Friedman, J. (1999). The hybridization of roots and the abhorrence of the bush. In M. Featherstone & S. Lash (Eds.), *Spaces of culture: City, nation, world* (pp. 230–255). London: Sage.

Gruzinski, S. (2002). *The mestizo mind: The intellectual dynamics of colonization and globalization* (D. Dusinberre, Trans.). New York: Routledge.

Hannerz, U. (1992). *Cultural Complexity.* New York: Columbia University Press.

Nederveen Pieterse, J. P. (2009). *Globalization and culture: Global mélange* (2nd ed.). Lanham, MD: Rowman & Littlefield.

Rowe, W., & Schelling, V. (1991). *Memory and modernity: Popular culture in Latin America.* London: Verso.

Shohat, E., & Stam, R. (1994). *Unthinking Eurocentrism: Multiculturalism and the media.* New York: Routledge.

CULTURAL INDUSTRIES

Cultural industries and other aspects of the commodification of culture in the global era are important areas of investigation for global studies. At the outset, however, it is difficult to define the term *cultural industries* with any precision. Raymond Williams famously remarked that culture was one of the most complex words in the English language. And the term *cultural industries* has also had a long history, with many twists and turns. Frankfurt School theorists Max Horkheimer and Theodor Adorno, in *The Dialectic of Enlightenment* (1944), used the term *culture industry* to excoriate what they saw, in mid-20th-century American popular culture, as (in Craig Calhoun's words), "the merger of culture with big business (quintessentially the movie studios) and the abolition of the pleasure and emancipatory impulses that once characterized art in favor of palliating entertainments" (Calhoun, 2002, p. 106).

Not an auspicious start for a term that in the 1970s was resuscitated as a plural—the *cultural industries*—in recognition of the plurality of dimensions by which industrialized culture can be apprehended (conditions of production, distribution, and consumption) and by the ramified nature of Big Culture. By then, most advanced countries had significant public-sector investment through cultural policy portfolios, public broadcasting, as well as galleries, museums, and libraries, which complicated the blighted vision parlayed by Horkheimer and Adorno of duped masses being force-fed commodified cultural pap. But most importantly, cultural industries as a concept complicates the models of power, influence, and authenticity that the previous model embodied. This was an important period of theoretical, industry, and policy development in postindustrial Britain where theorists such as Nicholas Garnham argued that, for better or worse, most people's cultural needs were being met by the market and that art and the market are not inimical to each other; the market was a relatively efficient way of allocating resources and reflecting choice.

But these 1940s and 1970s ideas of cultural industries have been thrown into the mix with many other terms (the arts, creative industries, entertainment industries, copyright industries, digital content, and more), as theory and analysis tries to contend with the changes that digitization, convergence, globalization, and the rapid embedding of the Internet and web 2.0 have wrought in society, economy, and culture. Not only that, but the fact that the cultural industries exist in widely diverse states globally makes it imperative that a framework for understanding them be supple and dynamic. It is our contention that the best way to make sense of this burgeoning field is to examine the various models of the relation between culture and economy that underpin our understandings of these terms.

This is done in the spirit of Williams, who made a powerful contribution to understanding the relation between culture and economy by offering a basic typology of culture—in his foundational text *Culture*—as *residual, dominant,* or *emergent*. This is simple but powerful and emphasizes the dynamic, overlapping, and contesting nature of culture and its role in industries globally. The value of Williams's typology is that it embeds the insight that culture is always in process, always *propagating*

Table I   The Four Models

Williams's Model	Residual	Dominant	Emergent
Economic model	(1) Negative	(2) Competitive	(3) Positive (4) Emergent
Typical indicative content	Arts, crafts, material culture, heritage	"Cultural industries": film, broadcasting, music	"Creative industries": digital content, new, Internet, and mobile media
Subdiscipline/ approach	Cultural economics	Political economy/media and cultural imperialism	Innovation policy/evolutionary economics
	Keynesian	Neo-Marxist	Schumpeterian
Policy framework	Welfare subsidy	Industry policy	Investment and growth policy, innovation

(meanings, experiences, and identities) rather than merely *preserving* that which is gone.

This entry focuses on the dynamic relation between the cultural industries and the rest of the economy. This means that we must place our governing term *cultural industries* within its wider family, placing it on a continuum of the arts, cultural industries, creative industries, and digital content. We can hypothesize four models of this relation: namely, (1) negatively, (2) competitively, (3) positively, or (4) in an emergent manner. These are called, respectively, the *welfare model*, the *competitive model*, the *growth model*, and the *innovation model*. These points on the continuum also map broadly toward a specific domain of culture and industry, as Table 1 shows. They map onto Williams's residual (1), dominant (2), and emergent, crossing over (3) and (4). Each of these four hypotheses suggests different possible policy responses: In the first case, a welfare subsidy is required; in the second, standard industry policy is required; in the third, investment and growth policy is required; and in the fourth, innovation policy is best.

Four Models of the Cultural Industries

Welfare Model

Model 1—the welfare model—is the argument that the arts, broadly considered, are economically successful to the extent that they can extract rents from the rest of the economy. This is typical of what are called "public" or "merit" goods, with the economic justification for resource transfers resting on a market failure argument. Policy is then calibrated to estimates of their nonmarket value.

In model 1, cultural activities have a net negative impact on the economy, such that they consume more resources than they produce. To the extent that they exist, their value must lie fundamentally beyond market value. This model fits most accurately the (subsidized) arts end of the cultural spectrum, and the subdiscipline of cultural economics has largely been developed to address issues arising from these assumptions.

Competitive Model

Model 2—the competitive model—differs from model 1 in presuming that the cultural industries are not economic laggards or providers of special goods of higher significance but effectively are "just another industry." The term *cultural industries* has historically been used for this part of the cultural spectrum. This model might fit best the established media industry sectors that are mature, experiencing static growth, or in relative decline and that are being impacted by emergent distribution/aggregation models, as for example in some parts of publishing and print, broadcasting, and mainstream music copyright firms, and perhaps the commercial end of film.

The distinctive features of this large-scale sector—extreme levels of demand uncertainty, power-law revenue models, tendencies toward monopoly, complex labor markets and property rights, endemic hold-up problems, information asymmetries, highly strategic factor markets—are held to be addressable under competitive conditions. This is where the neo-Marxist critique concentrates its energies, analyzing how large, powerful, industrial-scale, and often multinational businesses parlay culture as commodity and behave just like the rest of the market-capitalist economy. Policy responses under model 2 are not about targeted resource reallocation but about consistent industrial treatment, or, as in the case of multinational and oligopolistic business, regulation and control of excess market power.

Growth Model

Model 3—the growth model—explicitly proposes a positive economic relation between growth in the creative industries and growth in the aggregate economy. It is for this model we deliberatively use the term *creative industries*. This is not because cultural forms, such as the established arts and media, cannot be regarded as part of the creative industries—they can be and are—but because the term *creative industries* is more an idea or proposition than a neutral descriptor of an industry sector. The creative industries are a dynamic force and not just another static sector.

The creative industries, in this view, are a growth driver by their creation of new value. In this model, culture becomes increasingly important because as economies evolve, a larger fraction of income and attention is devoted to it. In model 3, policy should properly treat the creative industries as a "special sector" not only because of its growing economic significance but also because it influences the growth of other sectors. This may plausibly lead to intervention, but unlike with model 1, the purpose is to *invest* in creative industries that yield economic growth. This model thus accommodates design as an input factor into the economy, industrial digital content and applications like games, and mobile and Internet media. It is evidenced by the positive correlation between design intensity in firms and their stock-market performance. It also is suggested by the growing proportion of creative occupations "embedded" in the broader economy. But it is perhaps best exemplified by the huge growth of mobile and Internet media use and content creation and the unexpected uses to which such activity and inventiveness has been put, such as games providing models for next generation education and learning paradigms, or for simulation and virtual reality training in industries as diverse as health and aerospace.

Innovation Model

Yet rather than thinking of the creative industries as an economic subset driving growth in the economy, as in model 3, the creative industries may not be well characterized as a sector per se, but as an element of the *innovation system* of the economy. This is model 4—the innovation model or creative economy model. The economic value of the creative industries, in this view, does not stem from their relative contribution to economic value (as in models 1–3), but from their contribution to the coordination of new ideas or technologies and thus to the process of economic and cultural change. In this view, the creative industries are mistakenly classified as an industry in the first place; they would be better modeled as a complex system that derives its "economic value" from the facilitation of economic evolution—a system that manufactures attention, complexity, identity, and adaptation though the primary resource of creativity.

If model 4 is true, this renders innovation policy a superior instrument to competition or industry policy. This justifies an "elitist" aspect to creative industries policy in the same way that traditional versions of cultural policy justified the development of culture as a public good. But unlike a heritage approach to cultural value, the value of creative industries lies in the development and adoption of new knowledge, and so it is focused on experimentation and difference rather than on conservation and equality.

The Models in Operation

Plainly, these four models exist on a continuum and, at different times and places, have been more or less appropriate. But it is true that the study of cultural industries has been dominated by models 1 and 2. This is consistent with Williams and reflects the fact that most supportive attention has been placed on the "residual" (those most vulnerable, and often most valued, parts of the cultural continuum, arts, crafts, and heritage), and most critical attention placed on the "dominant" (those large, consolidated, industrial-scale fields such as film, music, and broadcasting).

This consistency with Williams's dynamic triad also serves to highlight the difference between dominant Keynesian (focused on model 1) and neo-Marxist (focused on model 2) analysis, which are based on a static view of the economy that tends to presume no positive connection between the cultural economy and the process of economic growth and development, and emergent Schumpeterian conceptions of the cultural economy, which do recognize such a dynamic, evolutionary connection. Much can be elucidated by the dominant neo-Marxian and Keynesian frameworks, yet little of the emergent dimensions of the cultural industries and the cultural economy is captured in these approaches.

Cultural Industries in a Global Framework

In the dominant models of the cultural industries, it is usually assumed, under conditions of globalization, that there are great and worsening degrees of structural asymmetry, inequity, and exploitation. This is broadly the view of major contemporary writers on model 2 cultural industries such as David Hesmondhalgh and Toby Miller, for whom globalization has extended the reach of Western (and particularly U.S.) hegemonic interests, such that "global Hollywood" and similar global-spanning industrial powerhouses in music, broadcasting, and print now dominate the cultural landscape. It has given rise, in Miller's terms, to a "new international division of cultural labor," whereby such hegemons retain the core intellectual property rights, brand value, and high value-adding capacity while outsourcing the actual production processes to wherever wages are low, labor conditions are poor, and environmental regulation is weak.

Leading model 1 cultural economist David Throsby agrees that increased globalization and related technological change exacerbate the tension between economic and cultural value. Furthermore, for Throsby, it seems that the loss of cultural value is a *consequence* of the growth of the economic value of the cultural industries. This begs the question of whether previous eras, preglobalization, had enjoyed stable and mutually supportive relations between such values. One does not have to agree with the full thrust of Tyler Cowen's *In Praise of Commercial Culture* to admit of no automatic golden age against which the present globalizing era will seem definitively a poor

relation, or admit that the commercial domain is always opposed to the cultural.

Model 3 approaches to the cultural industries and globalization consider the rapid growth of these economic activities, in both the West and across the developing world, in "less zero-sum terms," according to Terry Flew. Global cultural flows have "a more matrix-like and mosaic structure" and have "become far more complex than was the case in the second half of the twentieth century" (Flew, 2008, p. 186). It is possible to pose, as a counterpoint to a monolithic model of Western commercial power, the ways in which contemporary technologies of potentially near-global reach and near-global popularity have thrown down the gauntlet to business-as-usual models of globalizing capital. To operate globally in capitalist cultural industries today, one must engage in a postimperialist fashion with non-Western economic and strategic power. The challenges of cross-culturalism in a globalizing world are non-negotiable, and they will consolidate with the rising power of China and India.

The major reference work *The Cultural Economy* stages some of the current ferment in the field of cultural industries and globalization, where we see, even in strong statements analyzing the realities of global asymmetry, such as that of Daniel Drache and Marc D. Froese, a dialectical acknowledgment of imminent development potential: "The global cultural economy is driven by technological change towards a global, integrated and interactive sphere of communication in which political power is inexorably moving downwards and towards the margins of international civil society because it gives a voice to those who previously did not have one" (Drache and Froese, 2008, p. 63).

This, then, leads us to consider the implications for model 4 cultural industries under conditions of globalization. The potential and current reality of the Internet and mobile media as platforms for next-generation, interactive digital cultural production and communication may present major opportunities for increased global "voice" and cultural diversity. Media production may be shifting from a closed industrial model toward a more open network in which consumers are now participatory co-creators of media culture product. To take a significant example, China is now the largest user of the Internet globally, having overtaken the United States in usage volume recently. It has the world's largest mobile phone user base. As the benefits of economic growth in China become more widely spread, there is potentially an expressive future for young people unthinkable less than a generation ago. China's versions of YouTube (Tudou and Youku) and social networking sites (Douban and QQ), in addition to the exponential growth of blogs, are driving an extraordinary bottom-up culture of communication.

Henry Jenkins is careful to remind us that this is not simply an outcome of technology but a significant cultural phenomenon in which we are seeing what happens when the means of cultural production and distribution are co-evolving among producer, aggregator, and user. He is aware that this bottom-up process plays out in the context of "an alarming concentration of the ownership of mainstream commercial media, with a small handful of multinational media conglomerates dominating all sectors of the entertainment industry" (Jenkins, 2006, p. 18); the economic value of user co-creation and social media poses a significant challenge to business-as-usual for the dominant models of the cultural industries.

Conclusion

This entry has suggested a heuristic model based on the dynamic relation of cultural industries with the rest of the economy. It has contrasted Keynesian, neo-Marxist, and Schumpeterian approaches to the cultural industries, and it has loosely aligned types of cultural industry practice and output against models that these approaches produce. All of these models are in play in contemporary practice and policy around the cultural industries, but the dominant models are being challenged by emerging evidence of changes and potential in the global disposition of the cultural industries. The kinds of growth and change in the cultural industries, and the "creative disruption" to established business practice at even, and perhaps especially, the highest levels of media capitalism, while also drawing on intensely social technologies, shows that these processes may be progressive in a social and cultural sense.

Stuart Cunningham and Jason Potts

See also Art; Cinema; Corporate Identity; Creativity and Innovation; Culture, Notions of; Global Communications and Technology; Global Culture, Media; Global Economic Issues; Knowledge Production Systems; Media, Global

Further Readings

Anheier, H. K., & Isar, Y. K. (Eds.). (2008). *The cultural economy*. Thousand Oaks, CA: Sage.

Calhoun, C. (2002). Culture industry. In C. Calhoun, J. Karaganis, & P. Price (Eds.), *Dictionary of the social sciences*. New York: Oxford University Press.

Caves, R. (2000). *Creative industries: Contracts between art and commerce*. Cambridge, MA: Harvard University Press.

Cowen, T. (1998). *In praise of commercial culture*. Cambridge, MA: Harvard University Press.

Drache, D., & Froese, M. D. (2008). The global cultural economy: Power, citizenship and dissent. In H. K. Anheier & Y. R. Isar (Eds.), *The cultural economy* (pp. 52–66). Thousand Oaks, CA: Sage.

Flew, T. (2008). *New media: An introduction* (3rd ed.). South Melbourne, Australia: Oxford University Press.

Hesmondhalgh, D. (2007). *The cultural industries* (2nd ed.). London: Sage.

Jenkins, H. (2006). *Convergence culture: Where old and new media collide*. New York: New York University Press.

Miller, T., Govil, N., McMurria, J., Maxwell, R., & Wang, T. (2005). *Global Hollywood 2*. London: BFI.

O'Connor, J. (2007). *The cultural and creative industries: A review of the literature*. London: Creative Partnerships/Arts Council England.

Potts, J., & Cunningham, S. (2008). Four models of the creative industries. *International Journal of Cultural Policy*, 14(3), 233–247.

Throsby, D. (2008). Globalization the cultural economy: A crisis of value? In H. K. Anheier & Y. R. Isar (Eds.), *The cultural economy* (pp. 29–41). Thousand Oaks, CA: Sage.

Williams, R. (1976). *Keywords: A vocabulary of culture and society*. New York: Oxford University Press.

Williams, R. (1981). *Culture*. Glasgow, UK: Fontana.

CULTURAL OBSERVATORIES

Although cultural observatories—entities that collect and monitor information on culture—are largely national and regional, there are also some efforts to develop global cultural observatories. An observatory, in the primary sense of the word, is a body that observes, measures, and monitors various categories of phenomena, for example, the stars or weather conditions (hence, astronomical or meteorological observatories). These functions were first envisaged in the late 1980s for the cultural field by a French thinker-bureaucrat, Augustin Girard, who was instrumental in the establishment of the *Observatoire des Politiques Culturelles* at Grenoble, France. His choice of term was deliberate: He wanted to indicate that the new institution was being created not to rule or control but simply to provide information to policymakers. In Girard's words, as quoted by J. Mark Schuster, "We cannot agree on a Center, but we can have an Observatory. It is a pleasant name. An Observatory is a place of negotiation, of interactivity. It does not deliver judgments" (Schuster, 2002, p. 33). The feedback function inherent in the notion, when transferred to human or social endeavor, implies not just informing the wider society about the field but advancing the field itself in its self-understanding, self-correction, and development.

The need for the functions identified by Girard was soon recognized across the cultural policy landscape and acted on steadily at the local, national, and regional levels. By the time Schuster reviewed the Euro-American research and information infrastructure for cultural policy in his pioneering 2002 volume *Informing Cultural Policy*, some 20 "cultural observatories" could be listed, plus at least an equal number of other entities performing observatory-type functions. These other models included the research divisions of governmental cultural funding agencies (the archetype here being French as well, the Ministry of Culture's *Département des études, de la prospective et des statistiques*); national statistics agencies; independent nonprofit research institutes; as well as government-designated, university-based research centers and consulting firms. By 2007, when Helmut K. Anheier and Yudhishthi Raj Isar also briefly mapped this expanding infrastructure,

several more actual observatories had come into being; and since then, the pace of establishment of observatories has accelerated still further.

Regionalization has been a key feature. As cultural flows and processes transcend the boundaries of nation-states, the collection, processing, and dissemination of cultural information needs to be organized transnationally. The rationale for such border-crossing mechanisms of knowledge management in the cultural arena echoes as well as complements a range of compelling reasons cited at the national level. These include helping the cultural sector to move from the marginal place it still occupies in the public policy landscape and affirm its own "unity in diversity"; to break down the specialized "silos" that persist within the field; to reimagine itself as a community that operates both within and beyond national boundaries; to buttress the case for culture as a central dimension of development and governance, leading public authorities, civil society, and the corporate sector alike to facilitate cultural policies that match economic and social policies in effort and resources; to build robust connections between culture on the one hand and economics, politics, and social welfare on the other, and itself take the lead in forging strategies to develop such connections; and finally, to forge better links among cultural research (whether purely academic or more action-oriented in nature), cultural policy, and cultural practice.

Regional entities have emerged that respond to such imperatives. Thus, in 2002, an Observatory of Cultural Policies in Africa was set up in Mozambique with support from the African Union, United Nations Educational, Scientific and Cultural Organization (UNESCO), and the Ford Foundation: Its mission, according to its website, is to "monitor the evolution of culture and cultural policies in the region and to enhance their development and their integration in human development strategies through advocacy and promotion of information exchange, research, capacity building and cooperation at the regional and international level." In 2003, Isar prepared for the Organization of American States a feasibility study with a view toward establishing an "Inter-American Cultural Policy Observatory" to serve the Americas as a whole, but as a result of lack of support, the project has not progressed beyond the drawing board. In 2006, at the European level and at the instigation of the European Cultural Foundation, an online platform for information, exchange, debate, and research on European cultural cooperation called LabforCulture was launched.

And what about the truly global level? UNESCO has been likened metaphorically to a worldwide observatory or "listening post." Worldwide monitoring is in fact carried out by UNESCO in several of its domains of competence, leading it to deem several of its databases or webpages observatories. In regard to cultural policy, a program was in fact devised and initiated in the year 2000 to create a platform or network to link the principal entities already carrying out observatory-type work at the city, subnational, national, or transnational levels. The project was formally discussed among a broad range of stakeholders at the Canadian Pavilion at the Hannover EXPO 2000 (the Canadian cultural authorities were at the time themselves developing a national cultural information portal). Soon afterward, however, UNESCO's priorities in this area shifted, and the project was stillborn. The plans remained, however, for a global cultural observatory to come into being.

Yudhishthir Raj Isar

See also Data Systems and Reporting, Global; Global Culture, Media; Globalization, Approaches to; Globalization, Phenomenon of; Heritage; Knowledge Management Systems; Regional Identities; United Nations Educational, Scientific and Cultural Organization (UNESCO)

Further Readings

Anheier, H. K., & Isar, Y. R. (2007). *Conflicts and tensions: The cultures and globalization series* (Vol. 1). London: Sage.

Isar, Y. R. (2003). *Towards an Inter-American Cultural Policy Observatory: A feasibility study.* Washington, DC: Organization of American States. Document OEA/Ser.W/XIII.5.1. CIDI/CIC/doc.2/03. Retrieved from http://www.oas.org/udse/cic/ingles/web_cic/estudio.htm

Schuster, J. M. (2002). *Informing cultural policy: The research and information infrastructure.* New Brunswick, NJ: Center for Urban Policy Research.

Website

Observatory of Cultural Policies in Africa: http://www.ocpanet.org

CULTURE, MEDIA, GLOBAL

See Global Culture, Media

CULTURE, NOTIONS OF

Culture became a global term in the late 20th century and thereafter was used as an organizing concept. Once a mainly scientific notion, forged in western Europe and with no equivalent in many languages on other continents, it eventually became possible to speak of culture globally, and even to consider the notion of global culture.

Culture, a Floating Signifier

The various usages of the term *culture* permeate the social realm worldwide. As Fredric Jameson observes, a vast range of phenomena—from economic value and state power to the configuration of individual psyches—are considered cultural or at least endowed with a significant cultural dimension. In the process, the term *culture* has also become a floating signifier: With no single definition generally accepted, semantic differences, overlaps, and nuances make it difficult to attain analytical rigor. Different perspectives and disciplines deploy distinct ideas of culture, each functioning as an intellectual "silo" as it were.

Both the "ways of life" understanding and the "arts and heritage" understanding of culture have given rise to global scripts that are prominent in rhetoric, policy, and practice. In many of these instances, the two meanings are conflated; out of this conflation has emerged different expectations, anxieties, and illusions. The expectations are tied to what Stuart Hall called the "centrality of culture." The anxieties develop from the large-scale use and frequent abuse of culture, both as a concept and as a reality. The illusions are the result of overblown visions, of simplifications that are reductive, and of readings that are instrumental.

Many discussions of the concept hark back to the decades-old genealogy of the British cultural historian Raymond Williams, who also observed how complicated and protean the word was. Although the terminological tangle has if anything worsened since then, Williams's three meanings, which were a simplification devised for heuristic purposes, still provide a useful starting template. These were the following: (1) a general process of intellectual, spiritual, and aesthetic development (as when one talks of a "cultured" person)—the sole usage until the late 18th century); (2) a particular way of life, whether of a people, a period or a group, or humanity in general; and (3) the works and practices of intellectual, and especially of artistic, activity, which was originally an applied form of the first sense and also the most recent understanding to emerge.

In the now globalized popular usage, the ways of life notion has become paramount; it has also become a leading term in discussions pertaining to globalization and globalism. It is followed closely by the arts and heritage understanding, which for most of the 20th century was the leading usage. This usage tends increasingly to see culture as a resource or instrumentality. In the process, it positions cultural expression as the embodiment of a particular way of life that needs to be "protected" or "promoted" in the name of that way of life. Interestingly enough, as the ways of life meaning have become dominant, people have forgotten its pre-20th-century history, so much so that cultural activists as well as international organizations such as UNESCO now take credit for having fixed this broader meaning in popular usage.

Before exploring these two understandings of culture, it is necessary to take stock briefly of where the first variant in Williams's genealogy now stands. Although equivalent to the Enlightenment notion of civilization, limited of course to those who enjoyed the light of Reason, this gloss has been universalized, so that nowadays we refer both to different civilizations and to a single world civilization. This is a globalized humanistic understanding of culture as civility. Premonitions of this came as early as Johann Wolfgang von Goethe's vision of the dawning age of *Weltliteratur*, in which writers and poets should become the first citizens of a global Republic of Letters. Or, in a different perspective, with Karl Marx in the *Communist Manifesto*, who held not only that the bourgeoisie had given a cosmopolitan character to material production and consumption but also that the intellectual creations of individual nations had become common property, that national

one-sidedness and narrow-mindedness would gradually become impossible, and that from the numerous national and local literatures, a world literature would develop. Such ideas live on in various notions of universal civilization: in the rhetoric of international diplomacy as well as in religious and/or mystical pronouncements. But these visions are largely superseded by the particularity, as opposed to the universality, that underpins the ways of life understanding of culture.

Indeed it is the contemporary destiny of the second sense of the notion—as a *particular* way of life, in other words, of culture as group identity—that has become the key global trope. Long a key term of anthropological scholarship, today it has escaped completely from academic control and has entered the quotidian vocabulary in all countries, in many different contexts, and at all levels of discourse. In the process, it has undergone a marked inflation of usages. One now speaks not just of, say, Javanese culture or Swedish culture, but also of any kind of institution, group, activity, or category as having a culture (e.g., "corporate culture," "the culture of the university," "the culture of drug addiction," "the culture of adolescence," "the culture of the Beltway," or "computer culture").

A Contested Concept

Yet in contemporary scholarship, the very concept is also under siege. Revisionist positions have emerged from the "mother discipline"—anthropology—as well as from sociology (in which the concept always had a more restricted range), cultural studies, cultural geography, political economy, and feminist writing. In anthropology itself, many variants far narrower than ways of life have emerged (while British social anthropology long shunned "culture" altogether). Thus, for Clifford Geertz, culture should be read as the webs of significance spun by humans, while other anthropolgists see it as the codes, or symbolic "software," of different human groups, to the exclusion of material manifestations. Many scholars now reject the very idea of discrete, fixed bounded wholes that the way of life notion entails, as it resulted from the local study of small non-Western societies whose cultural borders were assumed to be fixed, with only a small degree of internal differentiation and appearing homogeneous and static to the Western observer. Apart from whether such readings were accurate in the first place, the disruptions, mixings, and flows of contemporary society no longer authorize their application.

Others, such as Arjun Appadurai, challenge the substantivity that the concept implies and prefer to read it as a dimension of social phenomena related to difference, less as a property of individuals and groups and more as a heuristic device to be used in the analysis of difference. As Robert Brightman puts it, although it might have been viable in earlier historical moments, the fixity of the term is no longer relevant when social identities, practices, and ideologies are increasingly incongruent and volatile, so much so that anthropologists avoid using it altogether or use quotation marks when they do. Analogously, the field of cultural studies has theorized culture—both as ways of life and the arts—as a terrain of consent and resistance vis-à-vis the capitalist order, a site of contestation in which subordinate groups attempt to resist the imposition of meanings by dominant groups.

Yet in the 21st century, it seems that everyone must have a culture. At the same time as the scholarly critiques were beginning to be formulated, "claims of culture," in Seyla Benhabib's apposite phrasing, based on the notions they discounted were becoming current in the popular imagination. Social scientists were forced to recognize the increasingly powerful deployment of culture as a "rhetorical object," as Jane K. Cowan, Marie-Bénédicte Dembour, and Richard A. Wilson put it in their analysis of the new global discourse of cultural rights, which has recourse to the concept often in its most essentialized or essentializing forms. This discourse is shot through with "culturalism," understood here, following Appadurai, as the conscious mobilization of cultural differences in the service of some large political cause, often national or even transnational politics, and entailing struggles for recognition on the part of collectivities affirming the distinctiveness of their culture and/or identity.

Culture and Nation

Most of the conceptual discontents that scholars criticize are typical of what one might call vulgate conceptualizations that are deployed by different collectivities, principally nation-states. These usages have been globalized by organizations such as UNESCO, leading to the "one nation, one culture" way of speaking that characterizes the usages of government officials, elected officials, diplomats, and others, in international cultural diplomacy. Consider the definition adopted by the 1980 Mexico City World Conference on Cultural Policies cited here *expressis verbis* precisely because of its globally canonical status: "In its widest sense, culture may now be said to be the whole complex of distinctive spiritual, material, intellectual and emotional features that characterize a society or social group. It includes not only the arts and letters, but also modes of life, the fundamental rights of the human being, value systems, traditions and beliefs."

Similarly, when the 2005 Convention on the Protection and Promotion of the Diversity of Cultural Expressions defines cultural diversity (tautologically) as "the manifold ways in which the cultures of groups and societies find expression," there is little doubt that for each state the principal object is "its" respective and distinctive "national culture." One is reminded of Paul Gilroy's view that the idea of culture has been trivialized through being coupled with notions of identity and belonging that are overly fixed or too easily naturalized as exclusively national phenomena. What is virtue in the intergovernmental arena is in other circles the vice of methodological nationalism, in other words, the assumption that the nation-state is the right container for culture.

The global culturalism evoked here characterizes many human groups at the level of the nation-state as well as above and below that level. It is a process that began to emerge in the era of decolonization but continues to expand and diversify. As Marshall Sahlins observed, under conditions that are at once very similar and very different, peoples and communities are actually repeating in our time the late 18th-century processes that in Germany first brought the ways of life culture concept into being. Those *Kultur* theories elaborated by Johann-Gottfried Herder and others were an ideological reaction to Germany's backwardness in comparison with Enlightenment France and England. They were a typical ideological expression of societies viewed or represented as backward and resisting encroachments on their traditional culture. Later, under perceived threats of dissolution or even extinction, the values of many different ways of life have become the rallying cry of claims to a space in the planetary culture. As Sahlins put it, before, culture was just lived. Later it became a self-conscious project, as every struggle for life has become the struggle for a way of life.

Hence we observe the continuing and reinvigorated deployment and instrumentalization of the "old" notions of culture by the agents and agencies of contemporary governmentality, to use Michel Foucault's term. Collectivities *demand* to be labeled as complex wholes; they engage discursively and perfomatively with the work of producing collective identities. The symbolic images of complex wholeness they elaborate and project may well repose on the very characteristics—homogeneity, coherence, and consistency—that should no longer be the hallmarks of the concept. This is one problem with the notion of cultural diversity. The point is not to celebrate cultural diversity as an end in itself. Rather, as Verena Stolcke opines, the key question is to understand and deal with the ways in which the political meanings assigned to difference actually activate it, along with social structures and relationships, and the ways in which these in turn lead to either conflict or concord.

Indeed, as Helmut K. Anheier and Yudhishthir Raj Isar point out, strong anxieties lurk behind much of the present-day concern for culture understood in its multiple senses, particularly in the ways of life or culture as identity meaning in relation to globalization. The specter of conflict is ever-present: the cultural dimensions of conflict on the one hand, and the conflictual dimensions of culture on the other or, to put it differently, how any kind of group conflict can be culturalized and how culture itself can become a party to the confrontation between particularisms. The issue here is identity politics—including within this notion the highly reductive clash of civilizations thesis, which perceives cultural difference as the principal ground for divergences that will lead inevitably, if not addressed, to violent conflict.

In the context of globalization, a leading challenge is to understand (a) how conflicts generated by globalization in other areas come to occupy a cultural terrain and (b) how and why the cultural dimension itself may have its own inbuilt conflict and tension dynamics that might be either amplified or suppressed by globalization processes. In

other words, when is the way of life understanding of culture an agent or a pawn of conflict? When and how do economic and/or political conflicts occupy a cultural terrain? When does the cultural dimension itself have its own inbuilt conflict dynamics? How are conflicts and tensions either amplified or mitigated by globalization processes? There is increasing evidence demonstrating that cultural conflicts are not natural but constructed, not necessarily even cultural in their origins at all, but often sited at the intersection between political and economic interests and the universes of ideas, values, meanings, memories, and representations.

If in the ways of life understanding culture has become what Henrietta L. Moore calls the reified possession of a unique and bounded group, in the arts and heritage understanding (which could also be subsumed under the first), the possession has also become a resource, as George Yudice has pointed out. This idea of culture as resource, which crystallized as early as the 1970s with such slogans in the West as "preservation pays" or the close association between historic monuments and the development of income and employment in the tourism field, has grown into the formidable global discourse of the cultural industries, now more fashionably considered the creative industries or, even more ambitiously, the creative economy. This narrative has combined with that of development to form the core of "culture and development" thinking across the world, in which the cultural is considered a key ingredient of human development. As cultural goods and services are increasingly commodified and commodities themselves are increasingly aestheticized, the economic and the cultural have converged to generate a significant productive sector, whose size and rates of growth, in many industrialized nations at least, seem to be significant and impressive.

A conceptual and practical convergence has occurred between artistic practice, both individual and collective, as well as heritage resources, on the one hand, and on the other patterns of production and consumption that are industrial or belong to the newer distributive logic of the information and communication technologies. In the information and knowledge economy, the reasoning goes, the arts and heritage underpin creativity, the capacity to create new ideas and products. Hence, they are a valuable core resource. This commodification of the arts and heritage has led to their being envisioned as resources for the generation of income and employment but also in less tangible terms, for the enhancement of social and human capital; as key ingredients for better quality of life; as vectors of identity, communication, and social creativity; as tools of self-understanding and of reaching out to the Other; and as inspirations for committed citizenship and collective action, hence, essential to governance and social cohesion. In the process also, culture, economy, and place have become symbiotic with one another. Because of these new understandings, the cultural resources in question challenge policymakers in ways that they never did when perceived earlier as objects of subsidy rather than of investment: First, they have to be optimally harnessed as instruments of development, and second, development has in turn to become an engine for their ongoing flourishing.

Yet because of these new incarnations of culture, indeed precisely because of them, it would be wise, in relation to the second and third readings of the culture concept we reviewed here, to heed Terry Eagleton's warning that culture has become "too close for comfort." His idea is that these readings and their champions, buoyed up by the new economic, social, and political importance now globally acquired, have become both immodest and overweening. The idea of acknowledging culture's significance and yet putting it back "in its place" has much to commend it. The paradox is more apparent than real, for the place of culture in our time is as central as it is considerable.

Yudhishthir Raj Isar

See also Cultural Destruction; Global Culture, Media; Globalization, Phenomenon of; Hegemonic Power; Heritage; Identities in Global Societies; Knowledge Production Systems; United Nations Educational, Scientific and Cultural Organization (UNESCO)

Further Readings

Anheier, H. K., & Isar, Y. R. (2007). *Conflicts and tensions: The cultures and globalization series* (Vol. 1). London: Sage.

Benhabib, S. (2002). *The claims of culture: Equality and diversity in the global era.* Princeton, NJ: Princeton University Press.

Cowan, J. K., Dembour, M.-B., & Wilson, R. A. (2001). Introduction. In J. K. Cowan, M.-B. Dembour, & R. A. Wilson (Eds.), *Culture and rights.* Cambridge, UK: Cambridge University Press.

Eagleton, T. (2000). *The idea of culture.* Oxford, UK: Blackwell.

Jameson, F. (1984, July). Postmodernism, or the cultural logic of late capitalism. *New Left Review, 146.*

Moore, H. L. (2008). The problem of culture. In D. Held & H. Moore (Eds.), *Cultural politics in a global age* (pp. 21–28). Oxford, UK: Oneworld.

Sahlins, M. (1994). Goodbye to tristes tropes: Ethnography in the context of modern world history. In R. Borovsky (Ed.), *Assessing cultural anthropology.* New York: McGraw-Hill.

Sahlins, M. (1999). Two or three things that I know about culture. *The Journal of the Royal Anthropological Institute, 5*(3), 399–422.

Scott, A. C. (2008). Retrospect and prospect. In H. K. Anheier & Y. R. Isar (Eds.), *The cultural economy* (Vol. 2). London: Sage.

Stolcke, V. (1995). Talking culture: New boundaries, new rhetorics of exclusion in Europe [Special issue]. *Current Anthropology, 36*(1), 1–24.

Wicker, H.-R. (1997). From complex culture to cultural complexity. In P. Werbner & T. Modood (Eds.), *Debating cultural hybridity: Multi-cultural identities and the politics of anti-racism.* London: Zed Books.

Williams, R. (1976). *Keywords. A vocabulary of culture and society.* London: Fontana Press.

Yúdice, G. (2003). *The expediency of culture: Uses of culture in the global era.* Durham, NC: Duke University Press.

CURRENCIES

The history of currencies provides a useful approach to understanding how the local and the national have related to the global. In the modern world, money takes the form of currency. It can be exchanged for other things or services because people believe that it provides a reliable medium of trade, store of value, and unit of account. Since the 19th century, money has been an important symbol of national-state sovereignty. Since the 1970s, new arrangements for exchanging currencies have been an enabling force in bringing about the explosion of capital flows and trade around the world associated with globalization.

At one time people insisted on being shown the money, in the form of gold, silver, or something of equivalent value to what was being sold or purchased, for a unit of money to have more than a face value. Historically, however, there have been various types of monies. These include *commodity money*, an object that is more portable and divisible but that has value equivalent to the object in trade; *nominal money*, an accounting money for which no equivalent physical money exists; and *fiduciary money*, a money, typically a currency, that has value not directly related to the value of the material from which it is made. Fiduciary money has been around throughout much of human history, but only during the past century has it come to dominate the world completely relative to other types of monies.

In the modern era, the reputation of a currency relies on popular confidence. In particular, it relies on the confidence of investors and bankers in the backing or support the currency will receive from its issuer (almost invariably a national government), the overall strength of the national economy the currency is issued in, and the currency's utility for a variety of purposes and transactions within and between countries. From the 19th century until the 1970s, it seemed commonsensical for each country to have its own currency representing its own unique monetary sovereignty and to assume that its circulation was exclusive within the given national territory. But before that time and since, foreign currencies have had wide circulation across international borders. Currencies are not necessarily territorially exclusive and are becoming even less so. From this viewpoint, the history of currencies provides a useful perspective on the nature and historical course of globalization.

Making National Currencies

Only since the 19th century have governments come to exercise a monopoly over the issuance of currencies within their national territories. The practice of governments issuing currencies, in the form of coinage at least, goes back to ancient times. But this was hardly ever understood in exclusively territorial terms. Coins were issued by the Greek city-states of Asia Minor in the 8th and 7th centuries BCE and by Chinese authorities even earlier, around 1000 BCE. In their times and

places, these coins came to prevail over all other monies. Coins were rarely limited geographically as legal tender. In fact, foreign coins were often interchangeable with domestic ones. The distinction was irrelevant. The economic historian Carlo Cipolla (1967, p. 14) claims that currency choice was nearly unlimited:

> Monetary sovereignty is a very recent thing. As late as the nineteenth century no Western state enjoyed a complete monetary sovereignty. . . . In previous centuries, . . . the basic tenet of monetary organization [was] that foreign coins had the same rights as national coins and that they could freely come in and freely circulate without any particular limitation.

The corollary, however, was by no means true. Not every currency circulated widely. Most coins served essentially local transactions. Made of base metals such as copper and bronze, they did not travel much beyond local confines. Wider use was restricted to coins of silver and gold (so-called specie) having value as a means of exchange or store of value that could be guaranteed. Even then such coins were subject to debasement through wear and tear and to fluctuations in value as the prices of the precious metals from which they were made fluctuated. Sometimes "favorite" coins emerged to dominate long-distance transactions, reflecting their superior reputations. Such coins could dominate over large geographical areas well beyond the jurisdiction of the issuing authority. From the silver drachma of 5th century BCE Athens through the Roman denarius to the Byzantine gold solidus, international currencies were widely used in the Mediterranean region for many centuries. From the late-medieval period until the 19th century, a range of new international currencies underwritten by major trading and financial centers provided the medium for long-distance exchange. Like the drachma, the Florentine florin and somewhat later the Venetian ducat became the gold standard for other more local currencies across Europe and around the Mediterranean. With the flood of American gold and silver into Europe in the 16th century following Spanish and Portuguese colonization, coins such as the Spanish real and the Mexican peso, typically in the multiple unit "pieces of eight," became an almost universal currency. As late as 1830, it is believed, about 22% of all coins in use in the United States were pesos. The 19th century, however, was the century of the British pound sterling, and its wide use paralleled the British economy's leading role in the industrial revolution and the growth of world trade. Yet, at the same time, many other currencies managed to keep local and regional niches with often uncertain rates of exchange one-on-one and so-called ghost monies (abstract units of account that could be compared to the real values of circulating currencies) to facilitate accounting.

Only at the urging of national governments over the course of the 19th century to consolidate their power over their now territorial domains with the retreat of dynastic regimes and the slow erosion of multinational empires did governments begin to exert more control over the making and management of currency. Political economist Benjamin Cohen (1998, pp. 32–33) explains this as follows:

> Monopoly over monetary powers was a natural corollary of broader trends in global politics at the time. The nineteenth century, greatly influenced by the American and French revolutions, was a period of rising nationalism and the general centralization of political authority within state borders. Throughout the Western world, the principles embodied in the Peace of Westphalia—above all, the concept of absolute sovereignty based on exclusive territoriality—achieved a new level of tangible expression in the emergence of increasingly autonomous and homogeneous nation-states.

Controlling the supply of currency was one part of this process. Arguably, the consolidation of national currencies was a major instrument in exalting state infrastructure power and hence in giving the state relative autonomy from previously dominant social groups. The political goals of reducing transaction costs within the nation and encouraging identification with it played as large a role as did any sort of macroeconomic purpose in encouraging the nationalization of currencies. It did not come easily. Governments had to pursue two tasks simultaneously: establishing and controlling a singular national currency and limiting/prohibiting the flow of foreign currencies into the national territory. If new technologies in minting and producing high-quality banknotes, the establishment of central banks, the capacity to print money and stimulate the domestic economy, and the adoption of the gold standard were vital to the former, in providing more consistent and reliable currency, in servicing commercial banking, in facilitating monetary policy, and in managing currency convertibility, then legal-tender laws and public-receivability provisions were necessary for the latter, in restricting which currency could be used for satisfying debts and for paying taxes and other state obligations. Britain and the United States led the way, but soon full-fledged national currencies were considered an absolute requirement for a nation-state. By the 1920s, these varied economic, social, and political influences combined to produce currency areas that mapped onto the emerging national economies in which production and consumption were increasingly matched within national borders, at least for the largest and most powerful states.

Currencies and Monetary Systems

Even as this was happening, however, currencies still had to relate to one another, if only to enable trade and investment across national borders. With some national economies as much more important sources of capital flows and trade than others, an inevitable hierarchy of currencies tended to develop with some much more important than others in the denomination of trade and investment transactions. At the same time, some groups of countries either relied on some other nation's currency, simply because it was so dominant as in colonial and neo-colonial relationships, or cooperated to such an extent that they had either fixed rates of exchange between their currencies or merged their currencies completely, as in the British sterling zone and the earlier German Zollverein or currency union, respectively. Among the world's more industrialized economies from the late 19th century until the 1930s, a gold standard tended increasingly to prevail in terms of how currencies related to one another. First adopted by Britain in 1816 as a domestic standard, this eventually, because of Britain's dominant economic and geopolitical role, encouraged national-territorial standard currencies elsewhere, but it also provided the basis for currency conversion among countries that adhered to the standard. This mattered not because it was a "cosmopolitan system" as sometimes alleged; rather it was the "first 'inter-national' monetary order because it joined together countries that had begun to consolidate territorial currencies for the first time in history" (Helleiner, 2003, p. 40). As they vied for international investment, even poorer economies were attracted to a gold-based standard simply because this was the standard that prevailed among the rich, from whom they hoped to attract investment.

The need for activist monetary policies in response to the Great Depression of the 1930s led to abandonment of the gold standard as too rigid for macroeconomic management in straitened circumstances. It inevitably also led to a deepening of government control over monetary policy. Yet, this was also not complete as "local" currencies issued by merchants and town councils emerged to cope with the needs of populations facing dire circumstances and as colonial zones remained dominated by the currencies of the colonial powers. Only toward the close of World War II was there a movement toward providing a new order to the world monetary system. The Bretton Woods Agreement of 1944, negotiated mainly between the United States and Britain, served as the basis for a postwar system of semi-fixed exchange rates based on a U.S. dollar/gold standard that lasted formally from the end of the war until 1971 but that had begun to shift in many of its basic aspects from the late 1950s onward. This system prevailed among all "hard" or convertible currencies and was at the heart of the world monetary and financial systems. As with the old gold standard and its reliance on Britain as its central pillar, the Bretton Woods system (and the various international institutions, such as the International Monetary Fund, the World Bank, the General Agreement on Tariffs and Trade [later the World Trade Organization], and the Bank of International Settlements, which it spawned) was front-and-center based on the presumed centrality of the U.S. economy to that of the world as a whole. Only when that presumption began to founder in the 1960s did the system become unsustainable, and the United States unilaterally abrogated the Bretton Woods Agreement to better its own economic situation in 1971. This opened the door to a move away from fixed or semi-fixed exchange rates toward floating rates and the revolution in the world financial system that this enabled. Absent this trend, none of the world financial centers such as Wall Street and London's City would have acquired the centrality to the world economy (and the disastrous effects on it experienced since 2007) they have. A veritable explosion in capital flows followed the abrogation of the Bretton Woods Agreement, not least because capital controls as well as exchange rates were slowly liberated from the government command that had been established over them beginning in the 19th century. After the International Monetary Fund amended its charter in 1976 to allow currencies to float, governments have been free to tailor their exchange-rate arrangements, central bank role, and capital controls to their own goals.

Since the 1970s, however, no single system of exchange rates and capital controls has prevailed everywhere. If the combination of floating exchange rates and no or limited capital controls has tended to prevail ideologically, not least since the 1980s, when U.S. and British governments went heavily toward monetarist understandings of the best monetary system and away from the Keynesian emphasis on maintaining capital controls, other regimes have tended to become more and more important as the drawbacks to the open economy model lying behind floating exchange rates—investor panics, speculative attacks, capital flight—have become apparent. Many taxonomies of exchange-rate and capital-control regimes are possible. One useful approach distinguishes between currency boards and hard pegs, on the one hand, and more flexible systems, such as independent floats, managed floats, and cooperative arrangements, on the other. A continuum is apparent with the breaks between the various "types" being made more or less arbitrarily between large-scale use of foreign currency or a currency board at one extreme and an independent float at the other.

Money Games Since Bretton Woods

It is not uncommon among students of globalization to see the post–Bretton Woods era as one in which a singular model of currencies has prevailed. The most avid proponents of neoliberal globalization have been the biggest fans of floating currencies and the removal of all capital controls. The presumption is that floating currencies will better reflect the willingness of investors to "bet" on the value of a given currency as a collective, market-based judgment about the overall condition of its national economy. This also reflects the view that globalization has involved widespread adoption of a neoliberal model of open national economies in an increasingly "flat world" where all currencies float and the state retreats to make way for markets. Certainly, there has been a neoliberal political project since the 1980s to do this, but it is hardly descriptive of what has actually happened, particularly with respect to currencies. As the economic geographers Adam Tickell and Jamie Peck (2003, p. 165) argue, "globalization tendencies are very much 'real' ones in legal, material and discursive terms, but they neither produce unitary outcomes nor do they erase local and national differences in business culture, corporate strategy or government policy."

In fact, since the 1970s, the world economy has been organized into several very different "currency regimes" and the money games that each entails. This is because different governments operating in different political-economic circumstances have made different decisions about how to manage their currencies and their relationships to others. Four major ways in which currencies tend to operate with respect to any particular country and its monetary relationships with others have been suggested. These begin with the *territorial currency*, in which a national currency dominates a given country and there is limited public access to foreign currencies except through a soft pegged or carefully managed floating exchange rate controlled by the central bank. Contemporary China is a good example of this with its currency pegged against the U.S. dollar (and several other currencies) but with fairly stiff capital controls also in place limiting the ability of the Chinese public or foreigners to export Chinese capital. The second is the *transnational currency*, in which the currency issued by a powerful state circulates widely among world financial centers, floats fairly freely, and is a reserve currency in which others are denominated for many international transactions. The U.S. dollar currently serves in this role, but there is speculation that it

will increasingly come under threat from some other currency if the United States long remains a net debtor country dependent increasingly on Chinese (and other) purchases of its government bonds to finance domestic public and private debt. The third is the *shared currency*, in which a formal monetary alliance has either created a full currency union (as with a set of the European Union states and the euro) or there is an internal-managed float and external floating exchange rate for a group of countries (as in the late 1980s to 1990s European Monetary System). The crisis of the euro in 2009–2010, brought about largely because while monetary policy was centralized in the hands of the European Central Bank, fiscal and labor market policies remained in the hands of member-states, has reduced the enthusiasm for other efforts at creating currency unions. Finally, there is the *substitute currency*, in which a transnational currency either officially or unofficially substitutes for the nominal state currency within the national territory in question. This happens often as a result of a lack of faith in government economic policy, as a hedge against inflation in the national currency, or as a step on the path toward economic integration. Neither dollarization, involving use of the U.S. dollar, or euroization, involving use of the euro, may be so popular in the future given the volatility of their values against other currencies and the sense that both the United States and Europe are facing serious economic problems in the years ahead. Only currencies representing very strong economies can be expected to carry out the substitute function satisfactorily. The U.S. dollar has retained its standing so far as both a transnational and a substitute currency. Inertia in changing its use as an international medium of exchange and store of value, the large size and relative stability of the U.S. economy, and the dollar pricing of oil and other commodities will perpetuate the role of the U.S. dollar even as other economies, such as China and its currency, the renminbi, rise in importance.

Rather than a simple fourfold division of the world's countries that has remained relatively stable since the 1970s, it must be emphasized that there has been significant instability across these categories. If in the 1980s, and perhaps as a hangover from the Bretton Woods system, two thirds of all exchange-rate relationships were soft pegs, by the mid-1990s, there had been a huge expansion in the number of independent or free floats. By 2004, however, a new pattern had emerged in which managed floats and the euro expanded at the expense of both soft pegs and free floats. This dynamism reflects the continuing political and ideological struggle over the "best" fit between currency management and specific national conditions. In the aftermath of the world financial crisis of 2007–2010, brought about in part by the instantaneous transmission of financial products (such as mortgage-backed securities and credit default swaps) and the widespread geographical fallout from their failure made possible by free-floating currencies and limited capital controls, the world's governments seem likely to continue to question the costs of floating exchange rates and the absence of capital controls. These are likely to be major points of political contention in the years ahead and likely to undermine the presumably "necessary" relationship some have argued for between globalization and neoliberalism.

John Agnew

See also Bretton Woods Agreements/System; Dollar; Euro; Global Economic Issues; Gold Standard; Hegemonic Power; International Monetary Fund (IMF); Liberalism, Neoliberalism; Local Exchange and Trading Systems (LETS); Monetary Policy; Neocolonialism; Sovereignty

Further Readings

Agnew, J. A. (2009). *Globalization and sovereignty.* Lanham, MD: Rowman & Littlefield.

Cipolla, C. M. (1967). *Money, prices, and civilization in the Mediterranean world: Fifth to seventeenth century.* New York: Gordian Press.

Cohen, B. J. (1998). *The geography of money.* Ithaca, NY: Cornell University Press.

Cohen, B. J. (2008). *Global monetary governance.* London: Routledge.

Goldberg, L. S. (2010). Is the international role of the dollar changing? *Current Issues in Economics and Finance, Federal Reserve Bank of New York, 16*(1), 1–7.

Helleiner, E. (2003). *The making of national money: Territorial currencies in historical perspective.* Ithaca, NY: Cornell University Press.

Kirshner, J. (Ed.). (2003). *Monetary orders: Ambiguous economics, ubiquitous politics.* Ithaca, NY: Cornell University Press.

Tickell, A., & Peck, J. (2003). Making global rules: Globalization or neoliberalization? In J. Peck & H. Wai-chung Yeung (Eds.), *Remaking the global economy: Economic-geographical perspectives* (pp. 163–181). Thousand Oaks, CA: Sage.

CYBERCONFLICT

Cyberconflict, defined as conflict in computer-mediated environments, may be characteristic of the global age. Cyberconflict began as early as 1994 when the Zapatista guerrilla movement in Mexico transferred its mobilization online and linked with the antiglobalization movement through the Internet. In the late 1990s, John Arquilla and David Ronfeldt expressed the idea that conflicts around the world will increasingly revolve around knowledge and the use of soft power. Additionally, these RAND Corporation theorists defined *netwar* as the low, societal type of struggle, while *cyberwar* refers more to the heavy information warfare type of conflict. In this entry, the focus is on the netwar type of cyberconflicts, as historical incidents are explained and their implications for global politics and security are considered.

Cyberconflicts can act as a "barometer" of real-life conflicts and can reveal the natures and conflicts of the participating groups. Even before the advent of Internet 2.0, two types of cyberconflict were prevalent: ethnoreligious (between ethnic or religious groups fighting in cyberspace) and sociopolitical (conflicts between a social movement and its antagonistic institution).

The protagonists in sociopolitical cyberconflicts fight for participation, power, and democracy. Groups are brought together into a web of horizontal solidarities to which power might be devolved or even dissolved. The Internet encourages networked organization and mobilization, a version of the commons that is ungoverned and ungovernable, either by corporate interests or by leaders and parties. An early example of hacktivism (online activisim) was the Seattle anti-WTO (World Trade Organization) mobilization at the end of November 1999, which was the first to take full advantage of the alternative network offered by the Internet.

Also, dissidents against governments are able to use a variety of Internet-based techniques to spread alternative frames for events and to provide an online democratic public sphere. Online efforts, such as prodemocracy, activist, or antigovernment websites, point to the fact that people believe in the power of the medium enough to organize and run thousands of these types of sites. In many cases, activists are able to initiate and control events and mobilize and recruit others for their cause; examples include antigovernment sites in the Islamic world, in China, and in Latin America, as well as sites for antiglobalization and single-issue protests and mobilizations on both national and international levels.

Ethnoreligious cyberconflicts primarily include hacking enemy sites and creating sites for propaganda and mobilizational purposes. In ethnoreligious cyberconflicts, despite the fact that patriotic hackers can network, there is a greater reliance on traditional ideas, such as protecting the nation or fatherland and attacking for nationalist reasons. The Other is portrayed as the enemy, through closed, old, and primordialist ideas of belonging to an imagined community. For instance, in 2001–2003, the Israeli-Palestinian cyberconflict involved the use of national symbols, explicitly drawing attention to issues of national identity, nationalism, and ethnicity. Also, the language used by hackers relies on an "us" versus "them" mentality, where the Internet became a battleground and was used as a weapon by both sides. Full-scale action by thousands of Israeli and Palestinian youngsters involved both racist email and the circulation of instructions on how to crash the enemy's websites. Similarly, in the Indian-Pakistani cyberconflict (2001–2002), the Indian army's website was set up as a propaganda tool and was used as a weapon, as particular discourses mentioned *religion* (religious affiliation), the word *brothers* (collective identity and solidarity), and *our country* (a promised land).

The al Qaeda network and its ideology relied more on common religious affiliation and kinship networks than on strict national identity, which fits well with the borderless and network character of the Internet. The Internet has been used as a primary mobilization tool, both before 9/11 and after the breakdown of cells in Afghanistan, Saudi Arabia, and Pakistan. Al Qaeda replicates recruitment and training techniques using the Internet and is able to evade security services because it cannot be physically intercepted, as a result of the virtuality of its networks. The Internet can facilitate the dissemination of propaganda via electronic magazines, training manuals, and general recruitment sites, as well as serve as a weapon for financial disruptions aimed at financial operations or for stealing data and blueprints.

In the March 2003 Iraq conflict, the Internet's role was crucial in the conflict, the organization and spread of the movement against the war in Iraq, and its impact on war coverage and war-related cyberconflicts. The latter involved hacking between antiwar and prowar hacktivists (sociopolitical cyberconflict) but also between pro-Islamic and anti-Islamic hackers (ethnoreligious cyberconflict). Moreover, mobilization structures were greatly affected by the Internet since peace groups used it to organize demonstrations and events, to mobilize into loose coalitions of small groups that could organize very quickly, and to preserve the particularity of distinct groups in network forms of organization.

Another major incident occurred in Estonia in 2007, whereby the country was under cyberattack for a month. This incident points to the sociopolitical implications and the themes relating to cybersecurity, as NATO does not define electronic attacks as military action. Linked to the real-life protests of ethnic Russians, these cultural struggles are exacerbated by the media and propaganda, with groups defending the purity of their national space using online technologies. In the case of Georgia in 2008, the circumstances were different. A virtual war in cyberspace that accompanied the brief war in the summer of 2009 between Georgia and Russia was reported. Russia was accused of orchestrating the cyberattacks, as Estonia had been previously, and again it turned out that although coordination with the military was not deemed impossible, it was largely a result of patriotic hacking. The Georgian response involved using filters to block Russian Internet protocol addresses and moving websites elsewhere, asking Estonia and other countries for help.

In January 2010, Google reported attacks originating in China, which penetrated Google's network to steal intellectual property (source code) and hacked into gmail accounts held by human rights activists (for more, see Karatzogianni, 2010), with a declaration on changes in their China policy.

The effects are wide-reaching in the field of cyberconflict studies research, as it brings together in one discussion a complex matrix of debates: the transformations the Internet has brought to civil society, citizenship, and activism; the relationships among business, activism, censorship, and surveillance in China and beyond; and the relationship between the state and the plethora of patriotic hackers. At the same time, the Google-China incident pointed to the operation of multinationals and their ethical responsibilities, and the far-reaching activities of Google, perceived by some as a threat to privacy.

These historical incidents of cyberconflict of various types raise questions of cybersecurity as a part of global security in global politics today. Unless the precise level at which a cyberattack is considered armed conflict is defined by international law, any cyberattack could be framed as a cybercrime and prosecuted as such. This is turn would mean that any political hacking, even as a protest, could be prosecuted as a cybercrime and that patriotic hackers and cultural protesters could be convicted and/or fined for their activities. Under this logic, electronic disobedience or hacktivism, as it has been termed, despite having mostly symbolic effects, could also potentially be prosecuted.

As the effect of the role of social media on revolutions across the Arab World during 2011 will remain under discussion for some time to come, it is critical that the positions of governments in terms of digital censorship of their population; that civil society actors in terms of digital activism; and that parties in cyberconflict, in terms of regulating cyberwar, be much further studied and that policy in those areas be formulated on a global level.

Athina Karatzogianni

See also Activism, Transnational; Antiglobalization Movements and Critics; Conflict and Conflict Resolution; Cybernetics; Ethnic Identity; Global Communications and Technology; Global Conflict and Security; Information Age; Internet; Religious Identities; Social Networking; Virtual Worlds; War; Web 2.0

Further Readings

Arquilla, J., & Ronfeldt, D. (Eds.). (2001). *Networks and netwars: The future of terror, crime, and militancy.* Santa Monica, CA: RAND.

Dahlberg, L., & Siapera, E. (Eds.). (2007). *Radical democracy and the Internet.* Basingstoke, UK: Palgrave Macmillan.

Karatzogianni, A. (2006). *The politics of cyberconflict.* London: Routledge.

Karatzogianni, A. (Ed.). (2009). *Cyber conflict and global politics.* London: Routledge.

Karatzogianni, A. (2010). Blame it on the Russians: Tracking the portrayal of Russians during cyber conflict incidents. *Digital Icons: Studies in Russian, Eurasian and Central European New Media,* Issue 4: War, Conflict and Commemoration in the Age of Digital Reproduction. Available from http://www.digitalicons.org/issue04/athina-karatzogianni

Karatzogianni, A. (2010, March). The thorny triangle: Cyber conflict, business and the Sino-American relationship in the global system. *E-International Relations.* Retrieved June 15, 2010, from http://www.e-ir.info/?p=3420

McCaughey, M., & Ayers, M. (2003). *Cyberactvism: Online activism in theory and practice.* New York: Routledge.

Van de Donk, W., Loader, B., Nixon, P., & Rucht, D. (Eds.). (2004). *Cyberprotest: New media, citizens and social movements.* London: Routledge.

Yang, G. (2009). *The power of the Internet in China: Citizen activism online.* New York: Columbia University Press.

CYBERNETICS

Cybernetics has figured in global studies as a code word for global communications and media studies. Modern cybernetics began with Norbert Wiener, who defined the field with his 1948 book, *Cybernetics: Or Control and Communication in the Animal and the Machine.* In *Cybernetics,* Wiener developed the science of information feedback systems linking control and communication in an understanding of the computer as ideal "central nervous system" to an apparatus for automatic control and, therefore, referring to the automatic control of animal and machine. The term can be traced back at least to Plato, where *kybernētēs,* meaning "steersman" or "governor" (from the Latin *gubernator*)—the same root as *government*—was used to refer to governing of the city-state as an art, based on the metaphor of the art of navigation or steering a ship. Thus, from the beginning, the term was associated with politics and the art of government as well as with communication and organization.

Relationship to Systemics

Cybernetics has become a significant theoretical term in global studies, particularly with the growth of cognate terms derived from the root *cyber* as a synonym for *virtual* and emblematic of the global, such as *cyberspace, cyberculture,* and *cyberpunk.* Related to systemics and systems philosophy, the term has functioned as an approach for investigating a wide range of phenomena in information and communication theory, computer science and computer-based design environments, artificial intelligence, management, education, child-based psychology, human systems and consciousness studies, cognitive engineering and knowledge-based systems, "sociocybernetics" (i.e., sociology based on general systems theory), human development, emergence and self-regulation, ecosystems, sustainable development, database and expert systems, health and medicine, musical and theater performance, musicology, peace studies, multimedia, hypermedia and hypertext, collaborative decision-support systems, World Wide Web studies, cultural diversity, neural nets, software engineering, vision systems, global community, individual freedom and responsibility, urban revitalization, environmental design, as well as personal and spiritual development.

Governing as a major root meaning has been picked up in all major definitions, including by A. M. Ampere, a French scientist, who used it to refer to the science of government; W. Ross Ashby, who talked of the "art of steermanship"; and Stafford Beer, who talked of the science of effective organization. Other modern pioneers in the field tended to emphasize a more technical aspect of the study of systems: "systems open to energy but closed to information" (Ashby); "problems of control, recursiveness, and information" (Gregory Bateson); "feedback as purposeful behaviour in man-machines and living organisms" (Ludwig von

Bertalanffy); "the deep nature of control" (Beer); "relationship between endogenous goals and the external environment" (Peter Corning); "circularity" (Heinz von Förster); "the theory of interconnectedness of possible dynamic self-regulated systems" (G. Klaus); "the art and science of human understanding" (Umberto Maturana); and "the study of justified intervention" (James Wilk). Where one tradition emphasizes circular causality in the design of computers and automata and finds its intellectual expression in theories of computation, regulation, and control, another tradition, which emerged from human and social concerns, emphasizes epistemology—how we come to know—and explores theories of self-reference to understand such phenomena as autonomy, identity, and purpose.

Stages and Phases

Cybernetics is also broadly related to systems philosophy and theory, and as Charles François notes, both function as a metalanguage of concepts and models for cross-disciplinary use and are still evolving. François provides a detailed history of systemics and cybernetics in terms of a series of historical stages:

First, "Precursors (Before 1948): The Prehistory of Systemic-Cybernetic Language" is examined, going back to the Greeks and to Descartes in the modern world and ranging across the disciplines with important work in philosophy, mathematics, biology, psychology, linguistics, physiology, chemistry, and so on (Nicolai Hartmann, Goffried Leibnitz, Claude Bernard, André-Marie Ampère, Henri Poincaré, Denes Konig, Alfred North Whitehead, Ferdinand de Saussure, Walter Christaller, August Losch, Alexandru Dimitrie Xenopol, Bertalanffy, and Ilya Prigogine).

Second, "From Precursors to Pioneers (1948–1960)" is examined, beginning with Wiener, who aimed to address the problem of prediction and control and the importance of feedback for corrective steering and mentioning Claude E. Shannon and Warren Weaver's *Mathematical Theory of Communication,* Von Bertalanffy's 1950 paper "An Outline of General System Theory," Kenneth Boulding's "Spaceship Earth," John von Neumann's theory of automata, Von Förster's biological computer and his collaborators like Ashby,

Gordon Pask, and Maturana, who pursued questions in human learning, autopoiesis, and cognition. François rightly devotes space to Prigogine on systems and his escape from assumptions of thermodynamic models toward understanding dissipative structures in complex systems.

Third, "Innovators (After 1960)" is examined, beginning with Herbert Simon's discussion of complexity, James Miller's work on living systems, Maturana's work on autopoiesis (i.e., self-production), Benoît Mandelbrot's work on fractal forms, Lotfi Zadeh's work on fuzzy sets and fuzzy logic, René Thom's work on the theory of catastrophes, and the development of chaos theory, which François considers to be one of the most important innovations in systemics.

François also significantly details important work in ecology and economics, mentioning Howard Odum, Herman Daly on steady-state economy, and David Pimentel on the energy balance in agricultural production, among others working in the field. Fourth and finally, François examines "Some Significant Recent Contributions (After 1985)," mentioning the Hungarian Vilmos Csányi's work on the replicative model of self-organization, Christopher Langton on artificial life, H. Sabeili's theory of processes, and D. H. McNeil on the possibility of a better synthesis between physical sciences and living systems. He ends by referencing Henri Prat's work on the aura (traces that remain after the demise of the system), Pierre-Paul Grassé's work on stigmergy (indirect communication taking place among individuals in social insect societies), and Gerard de Zeeuw's work on invisibility.

In this full history, we can see cybernetics passing through several phases: the Macy conferences that focused on the new science of cybernetics; catastrophe theory; chaos theory; and complexity theory. The Macy conferences were set up by Warren McCulloch under the auspices of the Macy's Foundation from 1946 to 1953 to develop a general science of the human mind and began in the first year studying self-regulating and neural networks moving through a variety of topics covering cybernetics, systems theory, and integrative learning. Steve J. Heims provides an account of the Macy conferences as a set of dialogues that forged connections between wartime science and postwar social science, transforming it through the centrality of the notion of circular causation and feedback and its naturalization through increased quantification. Heims demonstrates how Wiener, von Neumann, Margaret Mead, Gregory Bateson, McCulloch, Kurt Lewin, Molly Harrower, and many others shaped ideas in psychology, sociology, anthropology, and psychiatry during the war period.

If modern cybernetics was a child of the 1950s, catastrophe theory developed as a branch of bifurcation theory in the study of dynamical systems originating with the work of the French mathematician René Thom in the 1960s and developed by Christopher Zeeman in the 1970s. Catastrophes are bifurcations among different equilibria, or fixed point attractors, and they have been applied to capsizing boats at sea and bridge collapses. Chaos theory also describes certain aspects of dynamical systems (i.e., systems whose state evolve over time, such as the "butterfly effect") that exhibit characteristics highly sensitive to initial conditions even though they are deterministic systems (e.g., the weather). Chaos theory goes back to Poincaré's work and was taken up mainly by mathematicians who tried to characterize reiterations in natural systems in terms of simply mathematic formulas. Both Edward Lorenz and Benoît Mandelbrot studied recurring patterns in nature—Lorenz on weather simulation and Mandelbrot on fractals (objects whose irregularity is constant over different scales). Chaos theory that deals with nonlinear deterministic systems has been applied in many disciplines but has been very successful in ecology for explaining chaotic dynamics. Complexity also relates to the theoretical foundations of computer science, being concerned with the study of the intrinsic complexity of computational tasks, and rests on understanding the central role of randomness.

Systems theory in sociology, as it was introduced through Parsonian functionalism and developed in Niklas Luhmann's system theory and Immanuel Wallerstein's world-system theory, has been largely discredited and dismissed or superseded in an attempted new synthesis. Recently, scholars have been rethinking systems theory, emphasizing mechanism and focusing on related concepts such as emergentism, self-organization, complexity theory, and evolutionary systems theory. John Urry, introducing a special issue of *Theory, Culture & Society*, commented in 2005 that the social and cultural sciences during the last few decades have experienced several incursions, including Marxism of the 1970s, the linguistic and postmodern turns of the 1980s, and the body, performative, and global culture turns of the 1990s. Without commenting on the simple metaknowledge schema he introduces, he then goes on to introduce the latest turn—*complexity*—which he traces to a shift from reductionist analyses to those involving the study of complex adaptive matter that shows ordering but remains near the "edge of chaos." The example he offers is self-assembly at the nanoscale. At this level, the laws of physics operate differently, especially in the way the molecules bind and through self-assembly can form complex structures that could be the basis of whole new products and industries.

It is, Urry says, in the 1990s that the social sciences "go complex," which he dates from the 1996 Gulbenkian Commission on the Restructuring of the Social Sciences, chaired by Wallerstein and including nonlinear scientist Prigogine, who together wanted to break down some divisions between the social and natural sciences. Complexity thought he dates from the 1990s and the global spread of "complexity practices" and its popularizations, including applications to the social and cultural sciences.

Globalization Across Disciplines

The globalization of system analyses within and across the disciplines demands a complexity approach, but more importantly, it demonstrates that these complex systems operate at the level of infrastructure, code, and content to enable certain freedoms while controlling others. Complexity as an approach to knowledge and knowledge systems now recognizes both the development of global systems architectures in (tele)communications and information with the development of open knowledge production systems that increasingly rest not only on the establishment of new and better platforms (sometimes called Web 2.0), the semantic web, new search algorithms, and processes of digitization, but also on social processes and policies that foster openness as an overriding value as evidenced in the growth of open source, open access, and open education and their convergences, which characterize global knowledge communities that transcend borders of the nation-state. This seems

to intimate new orders of global knowledge systems and cultures that portend a set of political and ethical values such as universal accessibility, rights to knowledge, and international knowledge rights to research results, especially in the biosciences and other areas that have great potential to alleviate human suffering, disease, and high infant mortality. Openness seems also to suggest political transparency and the norms of open inquiry, indeed, even democracy itself, as both the basis of the logic of inquiry and the dissemination of its results (Peters & Roberts, 2011).

Increasingly, cybernetics and its associated theories have become central in understanding the nature of networks and distributed systems in energy, politics, and knowledge and its significance in conceptualizing the knowledge-based economy. Economics itself as a discipline has come to recognize the importance of understanding systems rather than rational agents acting alone, and pure rationality models of economic behavior are being supplemented by economic theories that use complexity theory to predict and model transactions. More critical accounts of globalization emphasize a new form of global capitalism, which, according to Gary Teeple, is based on self-generating capital—that is, capital in the form of the transnational corporation, free of national loyalties, controls, and interests.

The financialization of capitalism is a process that seems to have accompanied neoliberalism and globalization. It represents a shift from production to financial services, the proliferation of monopolistic multinational corporations, and the financialization of the capital accumulation process. Richard Hudson and Benoît Mandelbrot joined forces to criticize the state of financial markets and the global economy, highlighting some key fallacies that have prevented the financial industry from correctly appreciating risk and anticipating the current crisis. These include large and unexpected changes in dynamical systems that are difficult to predict, the difficulty of predicting risk based on historical experience of defaults and losses, and the idea that consolidation and mergers of banks into larger entities makes them safer but in reality imperils the whole financial system.

Cybernetic capitalism is a system that has been shaped by the forces of formalization, mathematization, and aestheticization beginning in the early 20th century and associated with developments in mathematical theory, logic, physics, biology, and information theory. Its new instantiations now exhibit themselves in the forms of finance capitalism, informationalism, knowledge capitalism, and the learning economy with incipient nodal developments associated with the creative and open knowledge (and science) economies. The critical question in the wake of the collapse of the global finance system in 2008 and the impending ecocrisis concerns whether capitalism can promote forms of social, ecological, and economic sustainability.

Michael A. Peters

See also Capitalism; Computing; Economic Crisis; Global Communications and Technology; Globalization, Phenomenon of; Information Age; Internet; Knowledge Management Systems; Knowledge Production Systems, Web 2.0

Further Readings

Ashby, W. R. (1956). *An introduction to cybernetics.* London: Chapman & Hall.

Bailey, K. D. (1994). *Sociology and the new systems theory: Toward a theoretical synthesis.* Albany: State University of New York Press.

Bertalanffy, L. von (1950). An outline of general system theory. *British Journal for the Philosophy of Science, 1*(2), 134–165.

François, C. (1999). Systemics and cybernetics in a historical perspective. *Systems Research and Behavioral Science, 16,* 203–219.

Heims, S. J. (1993). *Constructing a social science for postwar America: The Cybernetics Group, 1946–1953.* Cambridge, UK: Cambridge University Press.

Mandelbrot, B. (1975). *The fractal geometry of nature.* New York: Freeman.

Mandelbrot, B., & Hudson, R. L. (2004). *The (Mis)behavior of markets: A fractal view of risk, ruin, and reward.* New York: Basic Books.

Maturana, H., & Varela, F. (1980). *Autopoiesis and cognition.* Boston: Reidel.

Peters, M. A., & Roberts, P. (2011). *The virtues of openness: Education, science and scholarship in the digital age.* Boulder, CO: Paradigm.

Pickel, A. (2006). *The problem of order in the global age: Systems and mechanisms.* New York: Palgrave.

Prigogine, I. (1955). *Thermodynamics of irreversible processes.* Springfield, IL: Thomas Press.

Teeple, G. (1995). *Globalization and the decline of social reform.* New York: Humanities Press.

Thom, R. (1975). *Structural stability and morphogenesis.* Reading, MA: Benjamin.

Urry, J. (2005). The complexity turn. *Theory, Culture & Society, 22*(5), 1–14.

von Förster, H. (1981). *Observing systems.* Seaside, CA: Intersystems.

von Neumann, J. (1966). *Theory of self-producing automata.* Urbana: University of Illinois Press.

Wallerstein, I. (1974). *The modern world system: Capitalist agriculture and the origins of the European world economy in the sixteenth century.* New York: Academic Press.

Wiener, N. (1948). *Cybernetics: Or control and communication in the animal and the machine.* Cambridge: MIT Press.

Darwinism and Social Darwinism

The ideas of Charles Darwin about evolutionary biology have had a global impact on fields far from narrow concerns about the evolution of species. Darwinism can be described as a pattern of evolutionary thinking about social as well as scientific matters that began soon after Darwin's time. In 1889, English naturalist Alfred Russel Wallace published a collection of essays with the title *Darwinism: An Exposition of the Theory of Natural Selection With Some of Its Applications*. Wallace's concern was with the origins of organisms, and his title paid respect to the most important figure to have written on the topic. From there, the implications of Darwinian thinking have expanded.

Evolution

Before focusing on Darwinism as such, it is perhaps better to start with the more general term *evolution*. This refers to three different, although connected, ideas. First, there is the *fact* of evolution. The claim is that all organisms—plants and animals, including humans, living and dead—are the end products of a long, slow, natural (lawbound) process of development from other organisms, probably simpler and ultimately probably from inorganic materials. Recognizing that many Christians take the early Bible stories metaphorically, if one believes in the fact of evolution, then he or she is saying that the 6-day creation story of Genesis is false.

Second, there is the *path* of evolution. It is common to use the metaphor of a tree of life, thinking that ultimately all organisms come from a few shared ancestors, although not every evolutionist in the past was committed to this metaphor. Early 19th-century French evolutionist Jean-Baptiste de Lamarck, for instance, thought that life was continually being created naturally; hence, all organisms are on a parallel series of ladder-like paths, going up to the highest point, humankind. Thus, we humans do not necessarily share common ancestors with today's tigers, for instance.

Third, there is the *mechanism* or *cause* of evolution. Here one is talking about what drives evolution. Lamarck famously (or notoriously) thought that organisms directly inherit features that were acquired or developed by ancestors. Thus, the blacksmith develops strong arms from working in the forge, and his children are born with strong arms. Contrary to the occasional newspaper reports, Lamarckism is entirely discredited today. Other mechanisms have included a kind of inborn momentum (orthogenesis) and a sort of random jumping with new forms coming spontaneously (saltationism).

Charles Darwin and Darwinism

And then there is Charles Darwin. He published his great work, *On the Origin of Species by Means of Natural Selection, or the Preservation of Favoured Races in the Struggle for Life*, in 1859. He was not the first to argue for the fact of evolution. Apart from Lamarck and many others, his own grandfather, Erasmus Darwin, pushed evolutionary ideas at the end of the 18th century. But it was Charles Darwin who made the case so strongly that from then on, it was the background position against which critics had to argue. As often remarked, Darwin never actually used the word *evolution* in his book, although the last word was *evolved*. The term was only just then coming into general use, and he used it often in later publications. Before the mid-19th century, the term used more commonly was *transmutation*. Darwin spoke of "descent with modification."

What Darwin did was to show that there are many different areas of biological inquiry that can be illuminated by the belief in (the fact of) evolution and that these insights add up to the overwhelming plausibility of the evolutionary hypothesis. For example, in support of evolution, the roughly progressive fossil record can best be given a natural explanation by supposing that those earlier in the record are the descendants of those later. Extra plausibility comes from the fact that the earlier fossils often incorporate features that are shared by otherwise different later fossils—common descent. The facts of biogeographical distribution point to evolution. Why are the inhabitants of the Galapagos archipelago—tortoises, mockingbirds, finches—similar but different? Because of descent with modification. Again, the isomorphisms between different organisms—homologies—point to shared ancestry. The forelimb of the horse, the flipper of the seal, the wing of the bird, the arm of humans: All have more or less the same bones in the same order, and this is because they all come from the same stock.

In the *Origin of Species*, Darwin said little about the details of the path of evolution, but it was he who firmly linked evolutionary thinking with the tree of life. Moreover, moving toward explanations, he showed why there would be a tree. Circumstances—challenges and opportunities—differ, and naturally different types of organisms are able to exploit different types of environment. Interestingly and significantly, Darwin said little about the ultimate origins of life, although it could be inferred that he thought them natural, that is, requiring no miracles or divine interventions.

Darwin's great triumph was in his mechanism: natural selection. He started with the fact that population numbers have a tendency to outstrip food and space supplies and that this would lead to a struggle for existence and, more importantly, a struggle for reproduction. (This was an insight expressed earlier, by Thomas Robert Malthus.) Recognizing that all populations have much variation among individual members, Darwin then argued that the success in the struggle would be a function of the differences between competitors and that overall this would lead to change, as the winners (the fit) are naturally selected over the losers (the unfit). Hence, there would be change but change of a particular kind, namely, in the direction of adaptive advantage—organisms would acquire features like hands and teeth and eyes, bark and leaves and roots, that help in the struggle for existence.

In the *Origin of Species*, Darwin showed just exactly how selection would work. For instance, the honeybee builds a comb with hexagonal chambers. Darwin showed that this is both the most efficient use of the wax and the strongest possible form. Island organisms evolve away from their mainland ancestors because they encounter very different circumstances in their new habitats. Analogously in the case of embryology, Darwin showed that the reason embryos of different species are often very similar even though the adults are very different—the human and the chick, for instance—is that selection does not work to divide the very young in the way that it works to divide the adults.

How then should we use the word *Darwinism*? Following Wallace (who, incidentally, discovered natural selection independently), we might say that the essence of Darwinism is the belief in the great importance of natural selection as the cause of change, with the consequent belief that the defining feature of life is that it is adapted to its circumstances in order to survive and reproduce. This of course implies that one accepts the fact of evolution—natural developmental origins for organisms—and that life's history was more or less tree-like. Whether the tree is a poplar or a cedar is left open for discussion.

Do today's professional biologists accept Darwinism? By and large the answer is "yes." All professional biologists are evolutionists. All accept the tree of life, although it now seems clear that bacteria can carry information directly across from one branch to another, so the picture is literally as well as metaphorically more tangled than Darwin thought. Natural selection is overwhelmingly the mechanism of choice, although subsidiary mechanisms are also thought important. At the molecular level, random "drift" is significant. What has happened since the time of the *Origin of Species* is the development of a strong theory of heredity: first Mendelian genetics and then the molecular successor (starting with the DNA double helix), something that has given Darwinian selection a firm base from which to work.

Social Darwinism

This entry turns now to social Darwinism, although few of the major so-called social Darwinians would regard themselves as such. Although one can find it used even in Darwin's lifetime, *social Darwinism* was not a term of general employ until the mid-20th century when it was used and popularized by American historian Richard Hofstadter. Nor did it have the pejorative flavor that it now has. Indeed, recognizing that we are rather stuck with the term and making the best of a bad job, defining social Darwinism as the application of evolutionary ideas to social theory with consequent prescriptions for action, it is important to recognize that we have no direct move from Darwinism proper to social Darwinism, nor do we necessarily end with a belief system that should be shunned by right-thinking people.

As soon as evolutionary ideas started to gain popularity in the mid-19th century, there were those who started to exploit them as sources for social theory and practice. The best known and most persistent was Darwin's fellow Englishman Herbert Spencer. Many of his prescriptions—and those of his followers, especially American sociologist William Graham Sumner—come across as examples of laissez-faire enthusiasm of the most unpleasant kind. There are criticisms of state interference in the workings of society and almost a delight in the fact that the weakest will go to the wall. It is therefore natural to think that what we have here is a straight transference from Darwinian struggle for existence to societal suggestions. Moreover, it all seems a classic example of self-interest when we learn that this kind of thinking was endorsed enthusiastically by late 19th century American industrialists like Andrew Carnegie and John D. Rockefeller.

The truth, as always, is somewhat more complex. For a start, little in Spencer came from Darwin. Long before the *Origin of Species* was published, Spencer was pushing his ideas, and their chief source lay more in a mix of classic liberalism and English religious dissent. Spencer saw the chief obstacles to societal reform lying in the powers of the British establishment—the aristocracy and the gentry—backed by the Church of England, and he wanted to smash its restrictions and lay the way open for the people of merit and industry rather than those simply born to power and influence. Laissez-faire grew quickly on such fertilized soil as this. If one looks at the whole of Spencer's writings, one quickly finds that his thinking is more complex and more sensitive than first impressions suggest. He was much against arms races between countries, for instance, because he thought them a waste of money and barriers in the way of free trade. His supporters were far from self-interested oafs. Carnegie, for instance, put his money into public libraries, places where poor but deserving children could go and improve themselves—very much promotion of the fit rather than elimination of the unfit.

There were others who, although not generally labeled as social Darwinians, nevertheless had the same philosophy of using biology as a guide and foundation for social policy. Wallace was a lifelong socialist, and he justified this in terms of natural selection promoting the good of individuals within groups, faced with the challenges brought on by other groups. For him, the struggle for existence spelled harmony within society and conflict outside. He combined this with a feminist agenda, arguing that in the future women will choose the best men as mates and thus raise the overall quality of the group. Similar group-based thinking can be found in the writing of Russian anarchist Prince Peter Kropotkin. He thought that there is an urge toward "mutual aid" within groups, faced as they are not so much by other groups but by the forces of nature.

What about Darwin himself? In some respects, as he made clear in his later work on the human species, *The Descent of Man*, he was keen to use biology to promote and justify social policies. For instance, he worried that modern society too readily protects the biologically unfit and that this would have catastrophic consequences in the future. In other respects, he pulled right back. For instance, although he was Victorian in thinking the White races superior to all others, he was less than enthusiastic about imperialism and was opposed to slavery. To be honest, when it came to promoting the things he thought important, his reasons were less biological than simply reflections of his class. He did argue that capitalism was a good thing because it means that some creative members of society can work unimpeded with good consequences for the group. But this was not something he felt needed a lot of biologicizing to justify.

What about others? In particular, given that this is a point that is made much of by evangelical critics of evolution, what about Hitler? Did the vile racial and military doctrines of the 20th century come straight from the *Origin of Species* or from the *Descent of Man*? It cannot be denied that sometimes Hitler sounded as though he was basing his thinking on some form of Darwinism, and this is also true of some of the German military theorists before and during World War I. However, there is no straight line connecting Hitler to Darwin. At best, it came through the distorting writings of many others like 19th-century evolutionist Ernst Haeckel, who had his own agenda about the importance of the German people and the genius of Bismarck and so forth. In any case, there were many other sources feeding into the Nazi ideology, for instance, the popular Volk movement of 19th-century Germany. There is nothing in Darwin to justify the racial policies against the Jews. Finally, balancing Hitler and his followers and fellow thinkers, there were many early evolutionists who were pacifists in the name of Darwin. They argued that wars kill the best and brightest and so go against the evolutionary mainstream. That way only leads to degeneration.

Finally, are there social Darwinians today, if not by that name? Most certainly! The best example is

Harvard student of social behavior, Edward O. Wilson. He makes direct inferences from biology to society, believing that humans have evolved in symbiotic relationship with other animals and plants. A world of plastic would be, literally, deadly. He therefore thinks that our greatest moral obligations are to preserve biodiversity and the natural world. For this reason, he has been much involved in the campaign to save the Brazilian rain forests.

Social Darwinism, whatever it was called, never lacked for critics. Most famously, Darwin's great supporter Thomas Henry Huxley gave a brilliant address attacking the soft underbelly of the whole approach. From Spencer to Wilson, the assumption has been that evolution is progressive, going from the simple to the complex, from (as used to be said) the monad to the man, from (as we might say) the worm to the woman. It is because of this progress that it is justifiable to practice laissez-faire or socialism or to preserve the rain forests. If we do not do this, progress will end and decline will set in. Huxley argued strongly to the contrary that there is little reason to think that evolution is genuinely progressive and certainly no reason to think that (even if things do get more complex) this is a value-increasing phenomenon. The adaptations of the lion and tiger serve the lion and tiger, but it is a stretch to think of them as genuinely good. Hence, the foundations of social Darwinism collapse.

Philosophers have likewise chipped in with their objections. G. E. Moore, echoing an argument made a couple of centuries before by David Hume, complained that one cannot go from matters of fact (evolution occurred) to matters of value (evolution is a good thing and we should work to keep it that way). He spoke of such inferences as committing the "naturalistic fallacy."

It should be noted that by and large social Darwinians are remarkably unperturbed by criticisms such as these. Some have suggested that social Darwinism (broadly understood) functions a little bit like a religion—a secular version, perhaps, but a religion nevertheless. It gives a world picture of origins and puts humans firmly in the favored place of creation. It gives moral imperatives. And like more familiar religions, it divides into sects with different groups promoting different things, all in the name of the same original insights—insights that go back to the same revered founding work, not the Holy Bible but the *Origin of Species*.

Michael Ruse

See also Apartheid; Biological Diversity; Environmental Change; Homogenization; Racial Supremacy

Further Readings

Darwin, C. (1859). *On the origin of species by means of natural selection, or the preservation of favoured races in the struggle for life*. London: John Murray.

Darwin, C. (1871). *The descent of man, and selection in relation to sex*. London: John Murray.

Darwin, E. (1794–1796). *Zoonomia; or, the laws of organic life*. London: J. Johnson.

Hitler, A. (1925). *Mein Kampf*. London: Secker & Warburg.

Hofstadter, R. (1944). *Social Darwinism in American thought* (Rev. ed.). Boston: Beacon Press.

Huxley, T. H. (1893). *Evolution and ethics* (M. Ruse, Ed.). Princeton, NJ: Princeton University Press.

Kropotkin, P. (1902). *Mutual aid: A factor in evolution*. Boston: Extending Horizons Books.

Ruse, M. (2005). *The evolution-creation struggle*. Cambridge, MA: Harvard University Press.

Ruse, M. (2008). *Charles Darwin*. Oxford, UK: Blackwell.

Ruse, M. (Ed.). (2009). *Philosophy after Darwin: Classic and contemporary readings*. Princeton, NJ: Princeton University Press.

Ruse, M., & Richards, R. J. (Eds.). (2008). *The Cambridge companion to* The Origin of Species. Cambridge, UK: Cambridge University Press.

Spencer, H. (1851). *Social statics; or the conditions essential to human happiness specified and the first of them developed*. London: J. Chapman.

von Berhardi, F. (1912). *Germany and the next war*. London: Edward Arnold.

Wallace, A. R. (1889). *Darwinism: An exposition of the theory of natural selection with some of its applications*. London: Macmillan.

Wilson, E. O. (1978). *On human nature*. Cambridge, MA: Harvard University Press.

Wilson, E. O. (1992). *The diversity of life*. Cambridge, MA: Harvard University Press.

Data Systems and Reporting, Global

A globalizing world requires adequate global, transnational, and international data and information systems. Monitoring and understanding intensifying international interdependencies are likely among the driving forces behind the need for more extensive data on a wide range of topics and policy fields: economic trade, employment, communications, climate, travel, finance, diseases, and security, among others.

Whereas until the 1990s, national and international statistical agencies were the lead providers of data and the developers as well as guardians of the statistical methodologies for reporting systems, this has changed in significant ways. For one, private firms such as Dun & Bradstreet, consulting firms like McKinsey, and the Economist Intelligence Unit now provide data on economic and financial performance across markets and cater to specialized demands for information and knowledge. Second, the rise of Internet-based platforms and providers such as Google has allowed for customer-oriented data mining and compilations, given the vastness of the information available. Third, the social sciences have developed international consortia of data collection and analysis and established observatories to monitor specific fields or issues such as the family, welfare, or health. Fourth, the limitations of an international statistical regime based on the nation-state as the main unit of analysis have become increasingly questioned. As a result, in the course of few decades, a greatly expanded and diverse set of international and potentially global data systems emerged, even though most existing systems are still organized on a country-by-country basis and are international rather than transnational at best.

Background and Development

Systematic international statistical reporting began in the early part of the 20th century, mostly after World War I. The main fields covered were health, peace, and security, as well as international finance and trade. Until the 1940s, the League of Nations was responsible for international reporting systems. Early examples include the following:

- *Annual Epidemiological Records* (1922–1938)
- *International Health Year Book* (1924–1932)
- *Armaments Year Book* (1924–1939/1940)
- *Statistical Yearbook of the Trade in Arms, Ammunition and Implements of War* (1924–1938)
- *Memoranda on Production and Trade* (1926–1945)
- *Money and Banking* (1913–1944)
- *Review of World Trade, Balance of Payments and International Trade Statistics* (1910–1945)
- *Statistical Yearbook of the League of Nations* (1926–1942/1944)
- *World Economic Survey* (1931/1932–1942/1944)

After World War II, the United Nations and other international organizations took up global reporting, with the European Union's Eurostat as the world's major regional statistical agency.

Major Organizations Responsible for Global Data Systems

United Nations Statistics Division

The United Nations Statistics Division (UNSD) supports the United Nations Statistical Commission in the advancement of the global statistical system, in particular the methodological and technical development, production, and distribution of statistical data and technical assistance for nations that are developing and upgrading their national statistical systems. The programmatic emphasis of the UNSD lies in economic, demographic, social, environmental, and energy statistics using international standards to make comparisons possible. The UNSD issues the UN *Statistical Yearbook*, monthly bulletins, and dedicated series on population statistics, national accounts, energy, social and gender indicators, housing, and other subjects.

The heart of the international statistical system is the System of National Accounts (SNA). The broad objective of the SNA is to provide a comprehensive conceptual and accounting framework for compiling and reporting macroeconomic statistics for analyzing and evaluating the performance of an economy. Originally developed in the late 1940s,

the SNA emphasized the need for international statistical standards for the compilation and updating of comparable statistics in support of a large array of policy needs. The SNA has been updated and improved, taking into account changes in national and international economies (e.g., rise of the service industries and communications technologies) and changing policy needs. The 2008 SNA involved a number of organizations: the Statistical Office of the European Commission (Eurostat), the International Monetary Fund (IMF), the Organisation for Economic Co-operation and Development (OECD), the UNSD, regional commissions of the UN Secretariat, and the World Bank.

Other important data systems maintained at the United Nations are population statistics and a host of social and economic data ranging from narcotic drug supplies to the Human Development Index, a composite statistic used to rank countries by level of "human development." The index combines data on life expectancy, education, and per capita gross domestic product (as an indicator of standard of living) collected at the national level. The index can also be calculated for states, cities, and communities.

All specialized UN organizations are engaged in international data reporting. Agencies with significant data and information systems include the following:

- International Labour Organization, which issues labor statistics describing the size, composition, characteristics, wages, and benefits of the workforce as well as employment and unemployment rates, labor market participation, etc., over time
- World Health Organization, which reports on vital statistics, health care and health expenditures, diseases, and public health efforts
- UNESCO, which documents information on education, science, and culture

Organisation for Economic Co-operation and Development

The OECD's Statistics Directorate offers economic statistics based on comparable standards, with a focus on developed market economies and analytic, policy-related work. Besides economic statistics, OECD offers data relating to social indicators, development, governance, innovation, and sustainability. OECD also analyzes the economic performance of member-states, presenting statistical profiles across policy fields. Areas covered include population demographics and migration, income distribution, price levels and developments, labor and wages, science and technology, environment, education, public finances, and quality of life.

The World Bank

The World Bank covers a broad range of fields and issues numerous reports on topics including agriculture and rural development, infrastructure, aid effectiveness, labor and social protection, economic policy, finance, poverty, education, energy, mining, public sector, environment, science and technology, social development, health, and urban development. The World Bank's *World Development Report* is a major annual publication analyzing and presenting key economic indicators.

The International Monetary Fund

The IMF delivers a wide range of time series data concerning exchange rates, lending, and other financial and economic indicators. Two of the main publications are the *World Economic Outlook* reports and the *International Financial Statistics* (IFS). The first is released twice a year and contains the IMF staff economists' analyses of global economic developments during the near and medium term. The World Economic Outlook Database contains selected macroeconomic data on national satellite accounts, inflation, and unemployment rates. The IFS was introduced in 1948 and covers more than 200 countries. It includes fund accounts, exchange rates, and other main country or global economic indicators.

Eurostat

Eurostat is the statistical organization of the European Union. Its mission is to deliver statistical data to the European Union, based on comparability between countries and regions. Unique among the major providers of international data, Eurostat has developed a regional system of statistical reporting, the European Statistical System. It represents a partnership between Eurostat and the national statistical organizations. Statistics focus on economy and finance, population and social conditions, industry, trade and services, agriculture and fisheries, external trade, transport, environment and energy, science and technology.

Social Science Data Systems

Since the 1980s, several international projects have resulted in an increasingly sophisticated and comprehensive data infrastructure for social science data. This includes projects like the World Values Surveys, the Eurobarometer, or the Afrobarometer, which use comparable sample designs and data collection instruments in a large number of countries and at regular intervals. In addition to data collection projects, they include data archives and retrieval systems. The leading social science data archives (e.g., University of Michigan, University of Essex, Central Archives Cologne) formed a consortium and offer training courses for analysts.

Issues and Developments

There are three major issues, despite the significant progress that has been made in recent decades. The first refers to the inherent limitations of statistical data systems that focus on the economy in a narrow sense but leave aside aspects such as environmental impact or civil society. Although the world's data systems are most developed in the field of economy, a near exclusive reliance on economic and financial data to assess the performance of countries can be misleading. Efforts to improve quality-of-life measures by adding noneconomic information such as social indicators and environmental data are increasingly important.

The second issue relates to the continued weakness of statistical agencies in developing countries and transition economies. The initiative PARIS21, or Partnership in Statistics for Development in the 21st Century, was created in response to this weakness. Founded in 1999 by the United Nations, the European Commission, the OECD, the IMF, and the World Bank, it is a partnership of national, regional, and international statisticians, analysts, policymakers, development professionals, and other users of statistics to improve statistical capacity and encourage better use of statistics.

The third issue is methodological nationalism, a conceptual and methodological tendency that was central to the development of the social sciences in the context of the nation-state. According to sociologist Andreas Wimmer, methodological nationalism is the naturalization of the global regime of nation-states by the social sciences. It takes the institution of the nation-state as a given. The major building blocks of statistical systems and social science data systems—from national accounts and labor statistics to population survey research and organizational data banks—assume that the nation-state is the primary unit of aggregation and analysis. Indeed, the nation-state remains the basic statistical context and cognitive reference point for data aggregations, analyses, and comparisons. Likewise, sampling frames for population surveys are also typically "country-bound," and even though individuals are the unit of analysis, comparisons are on a country-by-country level (see World Values Survey, Eurobarometer, or the Pew Global Attitudes Survey).

The equation of country-society-polity-economy that underlies the international statistical systems of social science data is fundamentally challenged by globalization. As many analysts have observed, globalization creates new institutions, organizations, networks, and communities and the cultures, values, behavioral patterns, or social problems that come with them. These not only cut across the nation-state and related units, but they increasingly create and reflect social realities that are sui generis and often can no longer be captured conceptually and empirically by existing social science terms and data.

Data on globalization are not simply the sum of national societies and economies. They are also more than "rest of the world accounts" and international data that relate one country or economy to others. It is something qualitatively and quantitatively different and ultimately challenges the assumed equivalence between nation-state, domestic economy, and national society. This has profound implications for the data systems in place, the terms and measures used, and the data collected.

Helmut K. Anheier

See also European Union; International Labour Organization (ILO); International Monetary Fund (IMF); Methodological Nationalism; Organisation for Economic Co-operation and Development (OECD); United Nations; World Bank; World Health Organization

Further Readings

Esty, D. C., Kim, C., Srebotnjak, T., Levy, M. A., Sherbinin, A. de, & Mara, V. (2008). *2008 Environmental performance index*. New Haven, CT: Yale Center for Environmental Law and Policy. Retrieved January 13, 2010, from http://www.yale.edu/epi/files/2008EPI_Text.pdf

International Monetary Fund. (2010). *World economic outlook reports*. Retrieved September 29, 2010, from http://www.imf.org/external/ns/cs.aspx?id=29

Office of Development Studies (Ed.). (2004). *Global reports: An overview of their evolution* (ODS Staff paper). New York: United Nations.

United Nations. (2002). *International standard industrial classification of all economic activities (ISIC)*. New York: Author.

United Nations. (2003). *Handbook on non-profit institutions in the System of National Accounts*. New York: Author.

United Nations. (2009). *System of national accounts 2008*. Retrieved September 29, 2010, from http://unstats.un.org/unsd/nationalaccount/sna2008.asp

World Bank. (2010). *Global statistical strategy*. Retrieved September 29, 2010, from http://data.worldbank.org/about/data-overview/global-statistical-strategy

DEFORESTATION

From the perspective of global studies, complex human-driven processes of environmental transformation like deforestation are seen in the light of their relationship with concurrent historical processes of global economic, cultural, and social change. Thus, the meaning that forests have to people all over the world today is seen as continually changing in association with 500 years of modernization. The most profound social and environmental effects of modernization are linked to the ongoing expansion of the world economic system, which itself is viewed through the lenses of various theoretical perspectives considered useful in understanding that process (classical, neoclassical, neoliberal, liberal, social-democratic, Marxist, feminist, green, etc.). In the current phase of this expansion—globalization—deforestation, defined as the loss of original "frontier forest" cover, emerges as a significant social problem, the dominant human causes of which include agricultural conversion, pollution (acid rain), fire, disease, pestilence, and commodification by both private and state actors, resulting in extinctions, release of carbon into the atmosphere, damage to fresh water supplies, and more.

Forest conversion for subsistence agriculture accounts for the largest source of human-caused deforestation. To understand subsistence agriculture, it is necessary to examine how the world economic system produces and maintains mass populations dependent on informal economies and subsistence lifestyles. Given that the world is significantly divided between richer, more economically developed northern countries and poorer, still developing southern countries, global analysis must take into consideration the fact that North American and Euro-Asian countries largely deforested their homelands in the process of achieving their own industrial development and now depend on forest product exports from the developing countries, thus linking the historico-political-economic pattern of colonization, imperialism, and dependency to the problem of deforestation.

Deforestation in the Brazilian Amazon forest of South America is a case in point. Colonized by Portugal, underdeveloped in the 20th century, and, until recently, dependent on northern economies, large tracts of Brazil's interior tropical forests remain intact. If tropical forest cover loss is higher on an acre-by-acre basis in Brazil than anywhere else during the first decades of the 21st century, that is because it is still 60% to 80% intact, whereas, by comparison, the original redwood forest ecosystem of the western United States was 96% cut by 1985 (3% having been preserved in parks by that time and 1% remaining in private hands, vulnerable to further deforestation), and in the eastern and midwestern United States, the original temperate deciduous and temperate coniferous forests have been nearly 100% removed (Food and

Agriculture Organization of the United Nations, 2011; Malhi et al., 2008, p. 169; Noss, 2000, p. 39). Extending this analysis around the Northern Hemisphere, if one hears little about deforestation in Europe, the Caucasus, Greece, Turkey, or the Middle East, that is because human civilization deforested these regions entirely in the centuries and indeed millennia leading up to and including the last 500 years of Western modernity.

Russia and Canada represent two unique regions within the global North that bear special consideration. Their northern boreal forests, although heavily exploited, still have significant amounts of original frontier forests. The reasons for this are complex, but they include the facts that vast acreages of evergreen and coniferous forest in these regions have been out of reach, first to traditional forestry methods and then to the early forms of mechanized logging. But now, with the spread of roadways and increasingly powerful chainsaws, tractors, railways, and helicopters, even the most remote of these forests are increasingly vulnerable to exploitation. However, logging is only one of the sources of forest cover loss associated with globalization in these regions; at least equally threatening is the spread of disease and invasive pests, much of which can be associated with global warming, which is progressively making more and more of these northern forests vulnerable to organisms previously limited by colder temperatures.

Global studies researchers and specialists thus see deforestation as associated with the tendency of all global processes of change to be increasingly determined by the dynamic expansion (globalization) of the world economic system. This fact was revealed during the protests surrounding the Fifth Ministerial Conference of the World Trade Organization, which took place in Seattle in November 1999. Forest defense activists from around the world were motivated to join the protest in part due to the inclusion in the framework agreement of a provision popularly called the Free Logging Agreement, which sought to eliminate tariffs on wood export products without including safeguards to protect indigenous communities and the world heritage of biodiversity from the increased logging that would result. The International Forum on Globalization, a San Francisco–based nongovernmental organization, conducted research on the proposed agreement and discovered that it would lead to increased deforestation in Chile, Indonesia, South America, and other places. Victor Menotti, author of the report and an official nongovernmental organization delegate to the conference, was attacked by police while reporting on negotiations over the policy to a group of reporters and activists on the street outside the meeting. Subsequently, the American Civil Liberties Union sued the City of Seattle for excessive force and political repression of speech, pursuant to which a jury awarded Menotti financial damages when it ruled in his favor. Because global studies explicitly posits the social systemic, relational, and scalable aspects of globalization as the object of study, specialists in the field are uniquely positioned to understand local events like the World Trade Organization logging agreement and the protest it spawned as emblematic of contemporary historical forces—which are encountered as conflict-ridden local compromise formations between various opposing structural forces (e.g., economic change, governance, technology, and regional and national environmental conditions), as well the various private, state, and public interests that assert themselves in resource conflicts.

State of the World's Forests

Of the world's primary forest cover, 50% has already been removed, making forest conservation a global concern. The complex problems related to the world's forests are exacerbated by the fact that every forest experiences unique forms of pressure as well as shares in the global threats associated with market-driven overexploitation, conversion for poverty-driven subsistence agriculture, and changing disease and fire profiles due to global warming.

Although the great boreal forests of Alaska, Canada, and Russia are regions of low population density and have thus historically suffered comparatively little deforestation (approximately 10% in Canada and 12% in Russia), poverty-driven exploitation has increased at such alarming rates since the fall of the USSR in 1989 that presently Russia is losing 12 million hectares of forest every year, nearly comparable to rates of Amazonian deforestation, although the country is still home to the planet's largest forested region (12 million square kilometers [km²] of forest, which is approximately

20% of the world's remaining inventory and contains 50% of the Northern Hemisphere's terrestrial carbon). In Canada and Alaska, exploitation for paper and wood products remains a significant threat, but the largest concern is increasing vulnerability to acid rain and disease and fire associated with global warming (Bryant, Nielsen, & Tangley, 1997).

Tropical forests have declined from 16 million km² to 8 million km² today; Central America has lost 40%; Asia, as well, has lost 40%. The world's largest tropical forest, the Amazon, is home to 10% of global biodiversity (species) and is located principally in Brazil, a nation that possesses about 30% of the world's remaining acreage. Thirty million people, comprising 350 ethnic groups, live in and depend on this forest (World Wildlife Foundation, 2010b, p. 9). The biome consists of 6.7 million km², stretching across Brazil, Bolivia, Peru, Ecuador, Colombia, Venezuela, Guyana, and Suriname (World Wildlife Foundation, 2010b, p. 12). Seventeen percent of the Amazon forest cover has been lost in the past 50 years alone, the leading cause of which is conversion of land for cattle ranching, agriculture, and various other forms of resource exploitation by humans. Scientists now fear it may be possible that global warming could reach a tipping point that would eliminate this biome entirely over the next century (World Wildlife Foundation, 2010b, pp. 14–64).

Indonesia, an archipelago of forested islands stretching 3,000 miles between the Indian Ocean on the west and the South Pacific on the east, possesses the world's second largest stand of tropical forest—an intense theater of deforestation, largely due to conversion of frontier forests for palm oil industrial plantations, a process that accounts for approximately 5% of world total greenhouse gas production. As recently as the 1960s, more than 80% of this forest remained pristine—but since that time, the tract has been reduced by more than 50%, contributing to the extinction of the Javan tiger and the near extinction of the orangutan.

In Africa, deforestation is driven by expansion of subsistence agriculture as well as desertification, which is increasingly being linked with global warming. In Central America, clearing for large-scale cattle ranching, state settlement plans, and dams has produced one of the highest deforestation rates in the world. In Asia, again, poverty-driven subsistence agriculture, state development plans, and increasing market pressures are the biggest threats.

Global Conservation Strategies

Moving into the 21st century, corporations, nations, and global governing institutions, led by the United Nations, have acknowledged the deep interconnection between deforestation and climate change, based on the fact that deforestation puts more carbon into the atmosphere than the entire world transportation sector. In 2007, the Conference of Parties to the United Nations Framework Convention on Climate Change adopted the Bali Action Plan, a dual strategy consisting of a market-based mitigation and offset plan called Reducing Emissions From Deforestation and Forest Degradation (REDD) and adaptation, which essentially amounts to training and preparing forest-dependent communities for the inevitable social and environmental dislocation associated with climate change, while increasing their future prospects by promoting the adoption of transformational or sustainable forestry methods that are designed to increase canopy cover, store carbon, and preserve biodiversity while at the same time providing jobs, water, and housing for forest communities as well as industrial development of forest products for the world market. The controversial mitigation and offset program (REDD) is a plan to use market mechanisms similar to the "cap and trade" approach to regulating greenhouse gasses. The basic purpose of REDD is to provide financial compensation for developing nations that reduce deforestation, but complications emerge in the process of verification, in which it has proven close to impossible to determine if any particular mitigation offset achieves anything more than mere payment to states and corporations for nominal preservation gains in the near term that in practice prove temporary, merely pushing both legal and illegal logging and forest conversion projects further down the road and out of sight. Critics suggest that, without the structural alleviation of poverty and regulation of corporate exploitation of forests, the REDD program will ultimately fail and therefore represent a waste of the world's scarce conservation resources.

Richard Widick

See also Climate Change; Environmental Change; Environmental Rights; Forests; Global Environmental and Energy Issues; Global Warming; Greenhouse Gases; Land Use

Further Readings

Bryant, D., Nielsen, D., & Tangley, L. (1997). *The last frontier forests: Ecosystems and economies on the edge.* Washington, DC: World Resources Institute. Retrieved from http://pdf.wri.org/last_frontier_forests.pdf

Davis, M. (2006). *Planet of slums.* London: Verso.

Food and Agriculture Organization of the United Nations. (2009). *State of the world's forests 2009.* Rome: Author. Retrieved from http://www.fao.org/docrep/011/i0350e/i0350e00.HTM

Food and Agriculture Organization of the United Nations. (2011). *State of the world's forests.* Rome: Author. Retrieved from http://www.fao.org/docrep/013/i2000e/i2000e00.htm

Foster, J. B. (2009). *The ecological revolution: Making peace with the planet.* New York: Monthly Review Press.

Malhi, Y., Roberts, J. T., Betts, R. A., Killeen, T. J., Li, W., & Nobre, C. A. (2008). Climate change, deforestation, and the fate of the Amazon. *Science, 319,* 169–172.

Menotti, V. (1999). *Free trade, free logging: How the World Trade Organization undermines global forest conservation.* Available from the International Forum on Globalization website: http://www.ifg.org

Noss, R. F. (2000). *The redwood forest.* Washington, DC: Island Press.

United Nations Environment Programme, United Nations Development Programme, World Bank, & World Resources Institute. (2000–2001). *People and ecosystems: The fraying web of life.* Retrieved from http://www.wri.org/publication/world-resources-2000-2001-people-and-ecosystems-fraying-web-life

Widick, R. (2009). *Trouble in the forest: California's redwood timber wars.* Minneapolis: University of Minnesota Press.

World Wildlife Foundation. (2010a). *Russia's boreal forests.* Retrieved from http://assets.panda.org/downloads/russia_forest_cc_final_13nov07.pdf

World Wildlife Foundation. (2010b, October 26). *WWF's Living Amazon Initiative: A comprehensive approach to conserving the largest rainforest and river system on Earth.* Retrieved from http://wwf.panda.org/what_we_do/where_we_work/amazon/publications/?196095

Websites

Food and Agriculture Organization of the United
    Nations: http://www.fao.org
Global Forest Watch: http://www.globalforestwatch.org
Rainforest Action Network: http://ran.org
United Nations Environment Program: http://www
    .unep.org
United Nations Forum on Forests: http://www.un.org/esa/
    forests/index.html
World Bank Forest Carbon Partnership: http://www
    .forestcarbonpartnership.org
World Wildlife Fund: http://www.wwf.org

DEMOCRACY

The last three decades of the 20th century witnessed the global spread of democratic institutions. In 1974, when the Portuguese dictatorship was overthrown, there were only 39 countries classified as democratic by Freedom House out of a total of 145 countries. By 1997, this number had increased to 117 out of a total of 191 countries. In other words, whereas roughly a quarter of the countries in the world were classified as democracies in 1974, this had increased to over 60% by the end of the century. Democratization spread from southern Europe in the 1970s to Latin America and East Asia in the 1980s, and to central and eastern Europe and Africa from 1989 to the early 1990s. Although some of these countries have moved out of the democratic category, others have joined them, especially postconflict countries, where elections are often held as an exit strategy for the international community.

The spread of democratic institutions has to be understood in the context of globalization. Common rules and procedures provide an institutional basis for the global connectedness of states. But the spread of rules and procedures is not the same as the spread of substantive democracy—that is, the possibility for ordinary people in different parts of the world to influence the decisions that affect their lives. Despite the spread of formal democracy, substantive democracy is under erosion everywhere, in the West as well as in other countries. This has something to do with globalization. If we are to renew the democratic process, then it is not just a matter of spreading the formal procedures of democracy; it also requires new fora that provide access for ordinary people to all levels of governance (local, national, global) and a new responsiveness at all levels of governance to public debate and deliberation.

Interestingly, most of the literature on what is known as democratic transition focuses on the national level. Within the globalization literature, there is a lot of discussion of the global democratic deficit, but this is rarely taken into account in the democratization literature. This is why the gap between formal and substantive democracy is usually explained in terms of the legacy of authoritarianism or the weakness of democratic culture, despite the fact that the gap characterizes older Western democracies as well as newly democratic countries.

Procedural Versus Substantive Democracy

This difference between democracy as a set of procedures or institutions and democracy as the expression or framework for a more subjective notion of freedom has been widely discussed in the literature on political thought. There have always been varying usages and definitions of the term *democracy*. Formal democracy refers to the framework of rules and institutions that provide the necessary conditions in which members of a community can shape their own lives to the extent that this does not conflict with others. These institutions encompass an inclusive citizenship; the rule of law; the separation of powers (executive, legislature, and judiciary), including an independent judiciary capable of upholding a constitution; elected power holders; free and fair elections; freedom of expression and alternative sources of information; associational autonomy; and civilian control over the security forces. Substantive democracy is a process, which has to be continually reproduced, for maximizing the opportunities for all individuals to shape their own lives and to participate in and influence debates about public decisions that affect those individuals.

This difference between formal and substantive democracy is paralleled by two other distinctions often drawn in democratic theory. One is the distinction between popular or direct democracy and liberal or representative democracy. Athens is the paradigmatic example of direct democracy, while liberal representative models emerged at the end of the 18th century in western Europe and North America. The latter was often called the republican model because it drew on the experience of republican Rome and the city-states of Italy. Until the 20th century, democracy tended to be equated with direct democracy. For this reason, political theorists were skeptical of democracy because they feared that if every citizen participated directly in decision making, it would lead to what we now call populism, decisions based on fear and prejudice rather than the public use of reason. The liberal democratic model was supposed to resolve this problem by electing representatives who would engage in rational debates about key decisions. The representatives were not supposed to express particular positions or special interests; they were supposed to debate the public good.

The other distinction that parallels that between formal and substantive democracy is that between democracy as a method and democracy as a goal. For Joseph Schumpeter (1961), democracy was viewed as a relatively efficient method of choosing a government, which he likened to a steam engine or a disinfectant. He defined this method as "that institutional arrangement for arriving at political decisions in which individuals acquire the power to decide by means of a competitive struggle for the people's vote" (p. 269). The idea that political contestation is likely to produce the best outcome in terms of decision making is the political counterpart of the economic idea that competition in the marketplace will lead to economic efficiency. This Schumpeterian view of democracy contrasts with the idea that democracy is an end in itself, a process through which individuals can realize their aspirations.

Liberal representative models of democracy and the notion of democracy as a method of choosing a government tend to emphasize procedures and institutions both as defining characteristics of democracy and as safeguards against what Immanuel Kant called "democratic despotism." But although procedures and institutions are the necessary condition for substantive democracy and although it seems true that nothing better than the liberal representative model of democracy has been invented, these are not sufficient to ensure that individuals can influence the conditions in which they live.

While substantive democracy requires formal procedures, the latter can easily be subverted or "hollowed out" without an underlying normative commitment to democracy embedded in society.

Explaining the Democratic Deficit

The "third wave" of democracy gave rise to great optimism in the 1990s, and ideas like Francis Fukayama's "end of history" expressed the conviction that the world was finally discovering that liberal representative democracy, combined with free markets, constituted the best possible system of governance.

Despite the spread of democratic institutions, there remains a big gap between formal and substantive democracy. Many of the countries classified as democracies perform poorly on Freedom House's freedom scores, which are made up of a combination of political rights and civil liberties. In many countries, democratic procedures that have been specified in laws and constitutions are only partially implemented. Thus, newly emerging democracies may be characterized, in varying combinations, by a weak rule of law, the lack of an independent judiciary, limitations on freedom of speech and association, ethnic or religious exclusion, election fraud, and presidential domination. These procedural weaknesses are often associated with substantive weaknesses, including the tendency for political parties to extend control over different spheres of social life in ways that limit political participation, especially in former communist countries; a tendency for the government to control the electronic media and restrict registration of nongovernmental organizations; a politicized and clientelistic administration; various forms of racist or xenophobic sectarianism, which may provide a basis for populism; and a widespread sense of personal insecurity that undermines the ability and readiness to debate public issues owing to inadequate law enforcement and an undeveloped judiciary. Participation is also often limited, as evidenced by low voter turnouts, low membership of political parties, and widespread apathy, disillusion, and cynicism. Indeed, the introduction of democratic procedures, especially elections, may lead to conflict, state failure, and/or elective dictatorship, and only a very few of the newly democratic countries have escaped this fate. This has resulted in the proliferation of terms like *illiberal democracy*, *pseudo democracy*, *cosmetic democracy*, *façade democracy*, *semi-democracy*, or *virtual democracy*.

The gap between formal and substantive democracy is usually explained in terms of the legacy of authoritarianism, and this is an important factor. The anomie, submissiveness, and passivity of individuals; the experience of patronage and clientelism; the suspicion of parties, politicians, and bureaucrats; the pervasiveness of exclusivist ideologies—all of these can contribute to a profoundly distorted and traumatized "societal condition." But one or two authors point out that the gap, while larger in newly emerging democracies, can be found in older democracies as well. Thus, Thomas Carothers (2004) talks about the "syndrome of postmodern fatigue with democracy and perhaps politics itself" (p. 150). So the legacy of authoritarianism cannot be the whole explanation.

What is rarely discussed in the literature on transition or newly emerging democracies is the global context. Those who write about democratization tend to analyze the process almost entirely within a national or comparative framework. Yet the spread of democratization has coincided with the speedup of the process known as *globalization*—growing interconnectedness in political, economic, or cultural spheres. Theorists of globalization point to the global democratic deficit that results from the speedup of globalization. In the context of globalization, democracy, in a substantive sense, is undermined. This is because, however perfect the formal institutions are, so many important decisions that affect people's lives are no longer taken at the level of the state. Democracy assumes congruence between the state, the people, the economy, and territory. Yet this congruence no longer exists. Increased migration means that the people cross boundaries and live in multicultural global cities. The economy is increasingly global, as it is shaped by the decisions of global companies, free-floating speculators, and international financial institutions. States have to take into account a range of international agreements, which constrain national choices.

This applies to all countries to a greater or lesser degree. What is the meaning of elections when, for example, decisions about the size of budgets or environmental regulations or war and peace are taken in Washington, D.C., Brussels, or New York? In other words, is not the gap between formal and substantive democracy that we observe in the newly emerging democracies merely a symptom of globalization that affects all democracies at a national level?

The spread of democracy, it can be argued, is both consequence and cause of globalization. The opening up of authoritarian states resulted from market pressures, increased communication (travel, radio and television, and, more recently, mobile phones and the Internet), and the extension of international law. In the 1970s and 1980s, the failure of the statist model of development, the drying up of economic aid, and the growth of indebtedness contributed to growing disaffection and to demands, often from outside donors, to introduce democratization measures to legitimize painful economic reforms. In some countries (e.g., communist countries), frustrated bureaucrats saw an opportunity to translate political positions into economic wealth. These impulses toward democratization from above were paralleled by pressure from below as communication with the outside world helped nurture nascent civil societies, especially under the rubric of human rights laws, formally adopted by nondemocratic states. But while economic, political, technological, and legal interconnectedness may have contributed to democratization, the processes of political and economic liberalization, in turn, further accelerated global integration.

Indeed, it can be argued that the spread of democratic procedures is essentially a form of global integration. It is a way in which the institutions and practices necessary for participation in the global system are established. These can range from regulations governing foreign investment and trade to the political legitimacy required to be considered a serious actor in the various fora of global governance. The Human Rights Report of the British Foreign and Commonwealth Office argues that the increased commitment to democracy promotion is driven by a twin logic "because it is the right things to do and because we have a direct interest in building the conditions for sustainable global security and prosperity while fostering reliable and responsible international partners" (quoted in Kausch, 2006, p. 212).

Strengthening Substantive Democracy

Whether global integration also leads to substantive democracy, however, depends on whether individuals are able to influence the terms of global integration. In many cases, the newly emerging democracies are offered standard recipes for transition, all of which are adopted by competing political parties. Indeed, the language of transition is often reminiscent of the language of authoritarianism, as supposedly technical solutions to social and economic problems are offered and the pain of transition is merely medicine needed to reach some promised utopia. The communists called on people to tighten their belts and work harder so that they could attain socialism; nowadays, people are told much the same things in the hopes of reaching the nirvana of capitalism. Citizens experience their rulers as distant and manipulative as in former times. Moreover, the lack of choice in the new democracies often leads to an emphasis on religious and ethnic difference as a way of winning votes in the absence of any progressive alternative to the standard transition recipe.

There are, of course, important differences among the newly emerging democracies. Some countries, especially in the Balkans and Africa, have disintegrated under the impact of liberalization. Ian Bremmer's book *The J Curve* suggests that it is during the transition from authoritarianism to democracy that the risk of instability is greatest. Other countries in southern and central Europe are considered relatively successful. Part of the explanation has to do with specific legacies and experiences in the past, and part has to do with economic factors. However, if we understand the spread of democratic institutions as a form of global integration, then these differences also have to do with the terms of global integration—the extent to which newly emerging democracies are able to shape their position in the global system. And these, in turn, depend on the various instruments through which democracy is developed. The more that democratic institutions are introduced as a result of pressure from above, the less favorable the terms are likely to be. Conversely, the more that democracy is the outcome of the actions of individuals wanting to influence the conditions of their lives, the better the terms of global integration will be and the more substantive democracy will be. Joining the European Union was very important for central and southern European countries because it strengthened significantly their ability to influence the terms of their integration into the global system.

Representative democracy is necessarily exclusive. It is territorially based, and whether citizenship is based on residency, as in civic notions of citizenship, or on race and ethnicity, as in the examples presented earlier, it necessarily excludes noncitizens, those who are not permanent residents, or those of a different ethnicity. In a world where territorial boundaries matter less and where communities are no longer congruent with territory, the exclusive character of democracy helps explain the limitations on substantive involvement in democracy. Should not Iraqis, for example, be able to vote in American elections? Should not British citizens be able to influence conditions in Pakistan since so many minority groups in the United Kingdom come from that country?

In contrast to democracy, civil society is no longer territorially bounded. Like *democracy, civil society* is one of those terms that has many definitions, and the discussion about definitions is part of what civil society is about. Civil society could be roughly described as the informal political sphere. It is the site where public issues are debated and negotiated. Civil society makes possible governance based on consent where consent is generated through politics. Substantive democracy is possible only where procedural democracy is accompanied by, and indeed constructed by, a strong and active civil society.

At a moment when democracy at a national level appears to be hollowing out, the informal political sphere is increasingly active at local and global levels. This includes nongovernmental organizations operating at local levels and those with global brand names like Oxfam, Human Rights Watch, or Greenpeace; a new wave of global social movements like the Social Forums, the antiwar movement, or Islamist and other national or religious movements; and new political forms such as political consumerism or Internet activism. Moreover, new types of informal policy making are being pioneered on big global issues like social justice, climate change, and war. These are being tackled through consumer practices (fair trade or carbon miles) or through volunteering (delivering humanitarian aid, acting as civilian monitors).

Democracy in a substantive sense depends on the possibilities for closing the gap between the political class chosen on the basis of nationally based formal democracy and a civil society that is increasingly global. Closing the gap would mean that any agreements about democratic procedures reached at local and national levels should be supplemented by debates and struggles at a global level so as to create the conditions for substantive democracy at the local and national levels. Substantive democracy is possible only if people live in a relatively secure environment, so they make decisions without fear and without coercion, and if they have some control over the allocation of resources or are able to take preventive measures in the event of environmental risks. In other words, they need to be directly involved in deliberation about the big global issues of our time—human security, social justice, or climate change.

Mary Kaldor

See also Civil Society, Global; Community; Global Conflict and Security; Globalization, Phenomenon of; Human Rights, International; Ideologies, Global; Multiculturalism; Nation-State

Further Readings

Archibugi, D., Held, D., & Kohler, M. (Eds.). (1998). *Reimagining political community.* Cambridge, UK: Polity Press.

Bremmer, I. (2006). *The J curve: A new way to understand why nations rise and fall.* New York: Simon & Schuster.

Carothers, T. (2004). *Critical mission: Essays on democracy promotion.* Washington, DC: Carnegie Endowment for Peace.

Diamond, L. (1999). *Developing democracy: Toward consolidation.* Baltimore: Johns Hopkins University Press.

Elster, J., Offe, C., & Preuss, U. K. (1998). *Institutional design in post-communist societies: Rebuilding the ship at sea.* Cambridge, UK: Cambridge University Press.

Held, D. (1995). *Democracy and the global order: From the modern state to cosmopolitan governance.* Cambridge, UK: Polity Press.

Held, D. (2006). *Models of democracy* (3rd ed.). Cambridge, UK: Polity Press.

Held, D., McGrew, A. G., Goldblatt, D., & Perraton, J. (1999). *Global transformations: Politics, economics and culture.* Cambridge, UK: Polity Press.

Kaldor, M., & Vejvoda, I. (1998). *Democratisation in east and central Europe.* London: Pinter.

Kausch, K., Mathieson, D., Menéndez, I., Youngs, R., & de Zeeuw, J. (2006). *Survey of European democracy promotion policies 2000–2006.* Retrieved from http://www.fride.org/publication/132/survey-of-european-democracy-promotion-policies-2000-2006

Rosenau, J. (1997). *Along the domestic-foreign frontier: Exploring governance in a turbulent world.* Cambridge, UK: Cambridge University Press.

Schumpeter, J. (1961). *Capitalism, socialism, and democracy.* London: Allen & Unwin.

DEMOGRAPHIC CHANGE

The dramatic demographic changes in human population beginning in the mid-20th century have had major social, economic, political, and environmental repercussions in nearly all parts of the world, and they may lead to further changes through 2050. Demographic change, as indicated by data reported by the United Nations Population Division (UNPD), is both an indicator and an instrument of development. Change has occurred at different speeds in different world regions, but there are general patterns that apply to most countries.

Demographic change matters for many reasons. First, more people in a given space put strain on the environment. Second, urbanization has changed living conditions, for both better and worse, for a large portion of humanity. Third, declining fertility rates have opened up new social and economic options for women. Fourth, an increase in the share of working-age people has allowed some countries to experience more rapid economic growth and poverty reduction. Fifth, international migration has resulted in large numbers of people living and working in new circumstances. And sixth, the rate of population growth in the developing world has been quite rapid, posing challenges for developing countries but also potentially shifting power relations among countries.

Table I   Population Growth Rates Over Time and by Region

	1950	2010	2050
World	1.8	1.1	0.3
More developed regions	1.2	0.3	−0.1
Less developed regions	2.0	1.3	0.4
Africa	2.2	2.2	1.1
Asia	1.9	1.0	0.1
Latin America and the Caribbean	2.7	1.0	0.1

Source: Data from United Nations, Department of Economic and Social Affairs, Population Division (2009).

Population Size and Growth

World population grew very slowly for many thousands of years. It is thought to have reached 8 million by 8000 BCE, and by 1800 it stood at around 1 billion. Since then, population has soared, reaching 2 billion in 1927, 4 billion in 1974, and nearly 7 billion in 2010. The UNPD projects that it will reach more than 9 billion by 2050. The annual growth rate of world population has risen and fallen dramatically over time. In the early 1950s, the rate was 1.8% per year. After rising to 2.0% per year in the late 1960s, it fell to 1.1% in 2010 and is projected to be 0.3% by mid-century.

Population growth rates have varied greatly by level of development and specific region of the world (see Table 1, which shows population growth rates in specific years). As currently categorized by the UNPD, "less developed regions" have long been growing much faster than "more developed regions." The former, which accounted for 68% of world population in 1950, represented 82% in 2010 and are projected to constitute 86% by 2050. Nearly all of the 2.2 billion population increase projected to occur between 2010 and 2050 will take place in the less developed regions, and more than one third of that will take place in what the United Nations refers to as the "least developed countries," which tend to be the economically, socially, environmentally, and politically most fragile countries of the world.

A large part of the increase in the share of world population that lives in less developed regions is attributable to population growth in Africa, which constituted 9% of world population in 1950 but is projected to make up 22% in 2050. The most rapid period of growth in Africa was the early 1980s, when the annual rate reached nearly 2.9%. Asia also grew rapidly, reaching an annual growth rate of 2.4% in the late 1960s, but its growth rate fell quickly thereafter and is projected to be nearly as low as that of the developed world by 2050. Latin America reached its peak, nearly 2.8%, in the early 1960s, but population growth there slowed even more rapidly than in Asia.

China has long been the world's most populous country. With 545 million people in 1950, it was nearly twice as large as all of Africa. India was in second place, at 372 million. In 2010, China's population had grown to 1.35 billion (less than one third larger than Africa), and India's to 1.21 billion. India is projected to overtake China by 2030, and, by 2050, it is projected to have 14% more people than China. Africa is projected to grow to 2.0 billion by 2050.

The United Nations' country-specific population projections are based on assumed fertility and mortality rates, migration rates, and historical data on the age and sex composition of the population. These projections are not static; the United Nations has made a series of downward revisions in its global population projections, based on evidence that fertility decline has proceeded faster than previously assumed and also based on the rise of AIDS mortality. For example, between 1994 and 2008, the United Nations revised its global population projection for 2050 from 10 to 9.1 billion.

Fertility

Declining fertility is another part of the major demographic upheaval the world has undergone in the past 60 years. Figure 1 plots actual and

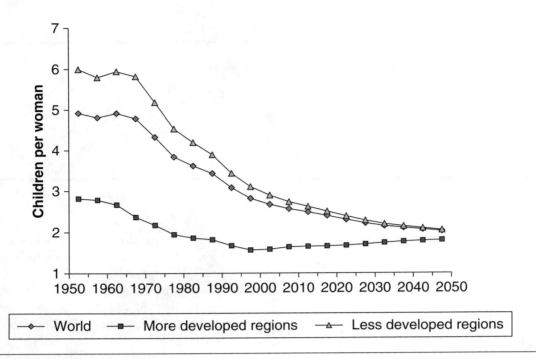

Figure 1   Declining fertility.

Source: Data from United Nations, Department of Economic and Social Affairs, Population Division (2009).

projected total fertility rates (TFR—children born per woman) over time, for the world as a whole, as well as for regions currently classified as more or less developed.

The replacement fertility rate (i.e., the rate required to maintain a steady population size in the long run) is approximately 2.1 children per woman, although a country with a high mortality rate for infants and young people would need to have a higher fertility rate to keep population constant. In 2010, TFR was 4.44 in Africa, 2.31 in Asia, 2.18 in Latin America and the Caribbean, 2.01 in North America, and 1.51 in Europe.

The world's TFR fell quite sharply from about 5 in 1950 to a little over 2.5 in 2010 and is projected to drop to about 2 by 2050. The decrease to date is largely attributable to fertility declines in the developing world and can be ascribed to a number of factors, including declines in infant mortality, greater levels of female education, increased labor market opportunities for women, and the provision of family planning services. The United Nations' TFR projections are based on a model that takes past country-specific and cross-country changes into account, and incorporates

additional assumptions needed to derive plausible figures for future years. In the case of countries that are currently below replacement fertility levels, there is little historical data on which to base assumptions about future TFR levels. For many of these countries, the United Nations assumes that fertility will increase in the coming years.

Figure 1 shows the extent of differences in TFR: Among developed countries as a whole, TFR fell to below replacement level by the 1970s. In the developing world, the fertility decline has also been striking, although average fertility remains well above replacement. In quite a few countries and some subregions, TFR has fallen far below replacement level; examples include China (1.78), Lebanon (1.86), eastern Europe (1.39), Italy (1.39), Japan (1.27), and Hong Kong (1.01). Iran saw one of the most rapid declines: from 6.63 in the early 1980s to 1.79 in 2010. In some countries, mostly in sub-Saharan Africa, TFR is still extremely high by historical and comparative standards and has only recently started to fall (from an average of 6.73 in sub-Saharan Africa in the early 1970s to 4.87 in 2010). In 2010, all of the 10 highest-TFR countries in the world are in sub-Saharan Africa.

Because high TFR is closely positively associated with poverty, population growth, ill health, low levels of education, low status of and few opportunities for women, and political fragility of countries, considerable effort has been devoted to understanding the factors that affect fertility decline. In many societies, parents traditionally choose to have large families to make sure that there will be enough surviving children to provide income for the family and to take care of the parents in old age. As infant and child mortality rates fall, parents in many parts of the world begin to have fewer children because fewer are needed to guarantee a desired number of surviving children. Rising education levels are another factor underlying fertility declines: As an increasing number of girls receive an education (and especially if they attend secondary school), TFR falls. Economists have focused on the time required to raise children and the income that parents (typically, mothers) could otherwise earn if they were not taking care of children. When wages rise, the effective cost of raising children rises, because child care limits the time that women can devote to paid work. Urbanization goes hand in hand with this effect, as the opportunities for women to earn money are generally greater in urban than in rural areas. Some cultural patterns doubtless play a role in determining fertility. Early marriage, for example, is closely linked to higher TFR.

There is strong historical evidence of populations achieving lower fertility in the absence of modern methods of contraception (i.e., prior to the advent of oral contraceptives and the intrauterine device around 1960). Nevertheless, the availability of modern contraceptive methods has been shown to lower TFR, although when fertility is highly desired the effect may be small. Countries vary greatly in the extent to which modern contraceptive methods are available and at what cost. Two hundred million women are currently estimated to have an unmet need for contraception, which refers to women of childbearing age who are married or in a consensual union and who wish to postpone or forgo childbearing but who are not using any form of traditional or modern contraception. In addition, people in some countries pay out-of-pocket for contraception while others do not. Finally, some countries have relied, to a significant extent, on abortion as a means of controlling fertility.

Mortality

Infant Mortality

The infant mortality rate (IMR) is the number of children who die prior to their first birthday in a given year, per thousand live births in that year. IMR has fallen greatly in all countries of the world since 1950, and further declines are projected. Figure 2 shows the great disparity between IMR in more developed and less developed regions.

The world IMR fell from more than 150 in 1950 to 45 in 2010, with an IMR of 23 projected for 2050. In more developed regions, it fell from about 60 in 1950 to 6 in 2010, with a further decline to 4 anticipated by 2050. By contrast, IMR in the less developed regions was about 175 in 1950, stood at about 50 in 2010, and is projected to fall to 25 in 2050. In the least developed countries, IMR in 2010 was about 79. The less developed regions as a whole took until about 2000 to reach the IMR that the more developed regions had reached in 1950; the *least* developed countries appear to be trailing the more developed regions by about 75 years. As with many demographic projections, future events, including choices made by countries and individuals, may lead to very different outcomes than those shown here.

Infant mortality rates are substantially lower (on average, 33% lower) in urban areas than rural areas, primarily because of higher income and education and better access to emergency care and skilled health personnel. However, poor urban women are much less likely than well-off urban women to deliver with a skilled birth attendant, indicating some inequities in this urban-based advantage.

Life Expectancy

Life expectancy is a well-established measure of overall population health, although it incorporates information on mortality but not morbidity. More specifically, life expectancy refers to the average age at death assuming current age-specific mortality rates remain constant.

As with other demographic indicators, life expectancy varies greatly across countries. Figure 3 shows the great disparity between life expectancy in more developed and less developed regions.

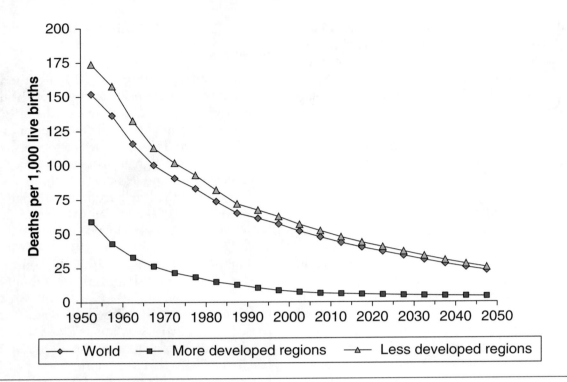

Figure 2   Declining infant mortality.

Source: Data from United Nations, Department of Economic and Social Affairs, Population Division (2009).

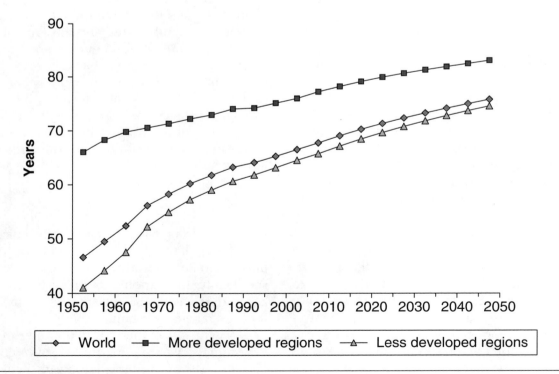

Figure 3   Increasing longevity.

Source: Data from United Nations, Department of Economic and Social Affairs, Population Division (2009).

Life expectancy at birth has risen dramatically since 1950, particularly in the less developed regions, where it rose from about 40 in 1950 to 66 in 2010. Life expectancy in the more developed regions increased during that time frame as well, but only by 12 years. In 2010, the life expectancy gap between the more and less developed regions stood at 11 years.

Longevity

Life expectancy worldwide has been increasing rapidly since 1950, and scholars working in this arena generally agree that this trend will continue. There is disagreement, however, about the magnitude of future increases. One school of thought holds that life expectancy will increase at about 2.5 years per decade, surpassing 100 by around 2100 in several wealthy industrial countries. This conclusion is supported by analyses of longitudinal data that relate people's lifestyle (vaccinations, good diet, use of seat belts, no smoking or abuse of alcohol or other drugs, a consistent exercise regimen) to health outcomes, and the assumption of perfectly healthy lifestyles. At the other end of the spectrum are those who contend that life expectancy is not likely to increase past 85. Their arguments include the view that past increases in life expectancy are due to declines in infant and child mortality that are not repeatable and that major new health threats, such as avian flu, antibiotic resistance, war, climate change, and the obesity epidemic, will hold life expectancy down.

Compression of Morbidity

Closely related to the lengthening of life is the quality of the extra years of life. A longer life span might include a longer period of good health, or it might merely mean a longer period of ill health. The former phenomenon involves the compression of the morbid years—the years in which people suffer from chronic disease and their minds and bodies break down and they lose their functional independence—into a smaller part of the life cycle, either absolutely or relatively. The "compression of morbidity" represents a clear increase in human well-being. Evidence on the compression is limited but generally consistent with this hypothesis. Presumably, it reflects a combination of improvements in

medical care and disease prevention. The extent to which continuation of the obesity epidemic offsets the benefits of these improvements remains to be seen.

Sex Differences in Mortality

In general, women live longer than men. Worldwide, life expectancy for women is 70.5, versus 66.1 for men, a difference of 4.4 years (2010 data). The disparity is greater (6.8 years) in more developed regions and is less (3.6 years) in less developed regions. It is even lower (2.6 years) in the least developed countries. The pattern was similar, although the absolute disparity was smaller, at least as far back as the early 1950s: Female life expectancy, worldwide, was 2.7 years greater than male life expectancy, with a larger difference in more developed regions.

Cross-country sex differences in infant and child mortality—and in the sex ratio at birth—are more pronounced than life expectancy differences. In the more developed regions in 2010, there were 105.4 males aged 0 to 4 for every 100 females in that age group. In less developed regions and in the least developed countries, the corresponding numbers were 107.2 and 102.4. A similar pattern prevailed in 1950. These differences may be considered relatively small, but a different situation exists in India, and even more so in China. In India in 1950, there were 104.4 males for every 100 females aged 0 to 4, a number that rose to 108.5 by 2010. In China, the corresponding 1950 and 2010 numbers were 112.2 and 121.2. The very high ratio in China has been attributed to female infanticide, neglect of female children, and sex-selective abortion.

HIV/AIDS

Between 1981 and 2010, HIV/AIDS infected nearly 60 million people, of whom 25 million have died from conditions related to the disease. There are currently approximately 33 million people living with HIV, with nearly 3 million new infections each year. Children under 15 living with HIV number approximately 2 million. In 2008, 2 million people died of the disease.

Roughly two thirds (22 million) of all infected individuals live in sub-Saharan Africa, and more than 90% of new infections among children occur there. South Asia and Southeast Asia are home to nearly 4 million infected people, followed by Latin America (2 million) and eastern Europe and central Asia (1.5 million each).

The immediate effects of the epidemic can be seen in a slowing of the rate of increase, or even decline, in life expectancy in the most heavily affected countries. Between 1950 and 1980, life expectancy in sub-Saharan Africa rose at nearly 4 years per decade. It then stagnated at around 49 years until 2000, when it began to rise again. Several countries saw declines in life expectancy in the 1990s and early 2000s, although in some cases factors other than HIV/AIDS contributed to these declines. Southern Africa was hit the hardest, with the subregion's life expectancy falling from 61.3 in the early 1990s to 51.6 in the mid-2000s.

Mortality in the Former Soviet Union

In most countries and at most times since 1950, life expectancy has been increasing. A notable exception was the mortality pattern in Russia after the dissolution of the Soviet Union. The fall in life expectancy was dramatic.

According to UN data, life expectancy in the Soviet Union rose from 64.5 in the early 1950s to around 69 a decade later, a figure that remained fairly steady (with some small deviations) through the late 1980s. In the early 1990s, at the same time that it became a country separate from the other former Soviet republics, Russia saw a precipitous drop in life expectancy—from 70 in 1989 to 64 in 1995. This decline reflected roughly 1.5 million premature deaths, which affected working-age men more than any other demographic group. Female life expectancy also dropped a small amount during this same time period.

The underlying causes of the precipitous fall in life expectancy are not certain. But the many dislocations—physical, economic, and psychological—brought about by the fall of the Soviet Union are likely a core part of the explanation. In addition, these changes may have had their effects amplified by alcohol consumption, the weakening of the health system, and deteriorating environmental conditions.

International Migration

Nearly 214 million people—roughly 50% women and constituting about 3% of world population—live in countries other than the one in which they were born. (Roughly 10% of these instantly became "migrants" when the former Soviet Union broke up.) Migrants are unevenly distributed across countries, so the importance of migration varies greatly from one country to another. Figure 4 shows the fraction of the population that was born in another country, by region of the world. Figure 5 shows that, as a proportion of population, Oceania, followed by North America, has the most immigrants. Migrant share has been rising sharply in North America and Europe. Past trends suggest that the United States will continue to be the leading destination for international migrants, attracting roughly half the flow. According to the UNPD, China, Mexico, India, the Philippines, and Indonesia will be the most significant sources of emigrants.

The motivation to emigrate reflects conditions in migrant-sending and migrant-receiving countries. Reasons for emigration include a desire to earn more, have better living conditions, obtain better education, reunite with family members, and escape persecution.

Earning more money is often closely connected to a migrant's ability to send remittances back to family in the country of origin. Remittance flows have become large enough to be a significant factor in the economies of many countries. Total remittances in 2009 were US$414 billion, of which US$316 billion went to developing countries. In absolute terms, the five countries receiving the most remittances in 2009 were India (US$49 billion), China (US$48 billion), Mexico (US$22 billion), Philippines (US$20 billion), and France (US$15 billion). As a share of gross domestic product in 2008, the top five recipient countries were Tajikistan (50%), Tonga (38%), Moldova (31%), Kyrgyz Republic (28%), and Lesotho (27%).

Many developed countries have welcomed immigrants in part because of their supply of labor. Others have experienced social problems and are seeking to limit future immigration. In some cases, countries are aware that, as their populations age, they may face the prospect of labor shortages—shortages that could be alleviated by an increased

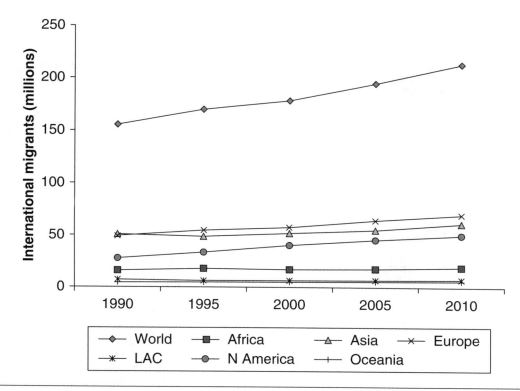

Figure 4   International migrant stock by world region, 1990–2010.

Source: Data from United Nations, Department of Economic and Social Affairs, Population Division (2009).

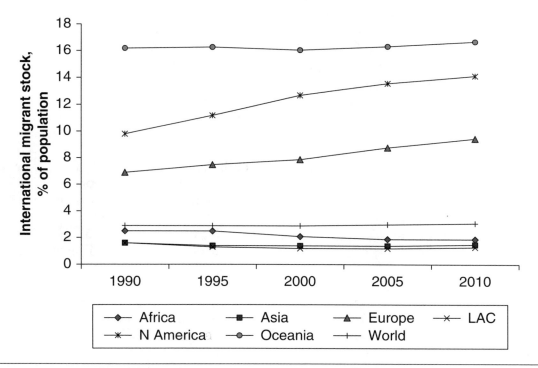

Figure 5   International migrant stock as percentage of population, 1990–2010.

Source: Data from United Nations, Department of Economic and Social Affairs, Population Division (2009).

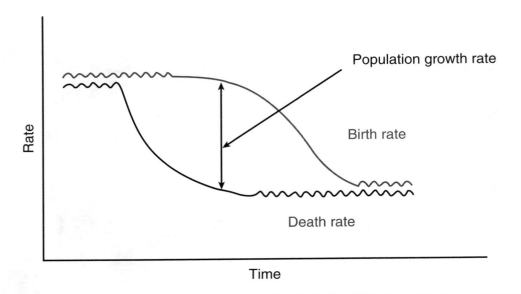

Figure 6   The demographic transition: Falling mortality precedes decline in fertility.

Source: Data from United Nations, Department of Economic and Social Affairs, Population Division (2009).

flow of immigrants, who would come from countries where unemployment or underemployment is high. This set of circumstances has drawn attention to the different but highly complementary age structures of developed and developing regions. In particular, developed regions are facing the prospect of large elderly populations and a dearth of working-age people, while some developing countries have a predominance of working-age people who need jobs. From this observation, the suggestion naturally follows that migration might serve the purposes of both sets of regions. This idea is often referred to as "replacement migration." Europe, for example, could benefit from the immigration of more Africans. Although such immigration could bring large numbers of new workers to Europe, current anti-immigrant sentiment in various European countries suggests that such levels of immigration might be unrealistic.

Age Structure

The demographic transition is among the most dominant demographic patterns since the industrial revolution (see Figure 6). This pattern, which is widely applicable, involves the transition from a regime of high fertility and mortality to one of low fertility and mortality. At first, both fertility and mortality rates are high. Due to some combination

of income and education gains, medical advances, dietary improvements, and public health measures focused on sanitation and safe drinking water, mortality rates decline, with the improvements disproportionately enjoyed by infants and children. Populations grow rapidly. Eventually, as described earlier, parents realize they need fewer children to achieve desired family size, and that size itself may change. In this situation, fertility decreases and eventually population growth slows. The initial decline in mortality defines the leading edge of a "Baby Boom" generation, while the subsequent decline in fertility defines the trailing edge. The large Baby Boom cohort initially contributes to youth dependency but later fuels growth of a relatively large working-age cohort.

The increase in the working-age share of the population is economically salient for several reasons. First, there are potentially more workers per dependent, so the level of economic output per capita can be higher than previously. Second, working-age people save more than the young and the elderly, and these increased savings can be channeled into productive investments that can spur economic growth. Third, the incentive to save may increase in expectation of longer periods of retirement that correspond to greater longevity. Fourth, the relatively low number of children, which tends to be particularly pronounced in

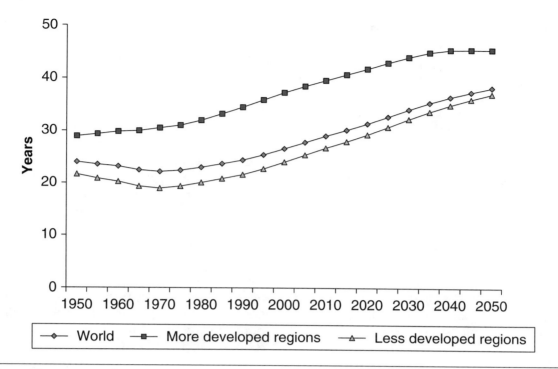

Figure 7   Changes in median age of population.

Source: Data from United Nations, Department of Economic and Social Affairs, Population Division (2009).

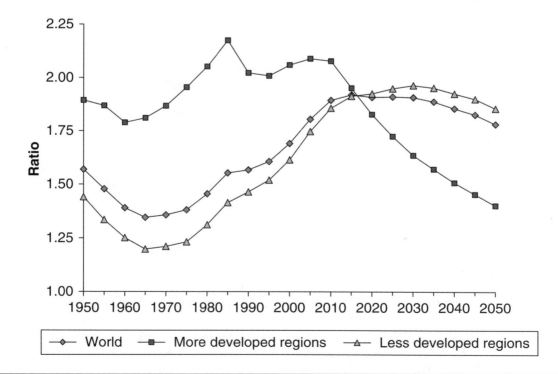

Figure 8   Trends in the ratio of working-age population to non-working-age population.

Source: Data from United Nations, Department of Economic and Social Affairs, Population Division (2009).

urban areas, frees more women to enter the labor force. And fifth, families with fewer children can afford to spend more on educating each child and keeping them healthy. These children eventually become more productive workers. The net effect of all of these changes is that a country may experience more rapid economic growth than before fertility fell, a phenomenon known as the "demographic dividend." Such a dividend is not guaranteed, however. Attaining it requires that a country have a set of policies and practices in place that allow people to be productively employed. Realization of a demographic dividend is also dependent on a country's political, economic, and military relations with other countries and, in some cases, with international financial institutions. In the absence of a favorable environment, high unemployment among working-age people can lead to economic slowdowns and political instability.

Eventually, a high share of working-age people becomes a relatively large elderly cohort. Although this group of people works and saves less than working-age people, they do not necessarily exert the same drag on economic growth that children do, because many elderly people engage in paid work or provide services (often within the family) for those who are working. In addition, unlike children, they often have savings to live on. Figure 7 shows the median age of the population in more and less developed regions. It shows that the developing world is much younger than the developed world and the median age is rising in both groups of countries.

Much demographic analysis focuses on the young (aged 0–14), working-age individuals (aged 15–64), and the elderly (aged 65 or above). The age structure of all countries has undergone major changes since 1950, with further changes certain to take place through 2050. These changes matter because they correspond to different phases of social and economic development and because different age structures may lead to different opportunities for economic growth.

Figure 8 provides a different view of the dramatic changes in population age structure that have occurred and that are projected to occur in the coming decades. It plots the ratio of the working-age to the non-working-age population (i.e., the young and the elderly) over time. In the more developed regions, the ratio has risen to high levels and is now beginning to decline, because of very low fertility rates, increasing longevity, and the aging of the post–World War II Baby Boom generation. In the less developed regions, the ratio fell to a very low level after World War II, when major public health advances throughout the world led to a large cohort of young people. When fertility rates subsequently fell, that cohort became the nucleus of what would become, several decades later, a relatively large working-age cohort. The ratio in the developing regions is now reaching a peak, and these regions will see a fall in this ratio starting around 2035.

Since 1950, developing countries have experienced a greater burden of youth dependency. The high share of young people they experienced was not predominantly caused by more children being born, but rather by health improvements that led to more newborns surviving.

As noted earlier, another aspect of changing age structure has to do with growth of the elderly population. The global number of people over the age of 60 is expected to reach 1 billion by 2020 and 2 billion by 2050. The proportion of world population aged 80 or over is projected to rise from 2% in 2010 to 4% in 2050. This rise in the elderly share of the population is taking place not only in the well-known cases of Japan and Europe but also in developing countries. By 2050, people aged 60 and older will constitute 20% of India's population and 30% of China's—roughly three fourths of a billion people in total.

In addition, there are currently 1.2 billion people aged 15 to 24—more than those aged 60 and older, although the United Nations projects that the older group will overtake the younger group in 2030.

Urbanization

In 1950, nearly 30% of the world's population lived in urban areas, a figure that reached 50% in 2008. This increase is due to three forces: migration from rural to urban areas, population growth in urban areas, and population growth in rural areas that causes those areas to be reclassified as urban. Population growth in urban areas has been rapid since 1950 (see Figure 9), with the most rapid growth occurring in Africa and Asia. Urban

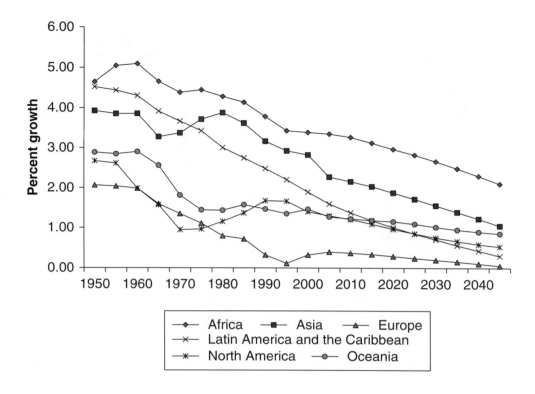

Figure 9   Population growth rate in urban areas, by region.

Source: Data from United Nations, Department of Economic and Social Affairs, Population Division (2009).

areas are projected to continue to grow, although at a declining pace, with the United Nations projecting 1.31% growth during 2035 and just 1.05% during 2045. During the next 30 years, urban population growth will account for virtually all of the world's population growth.

Urbanization is viewed as a major achievement by many, mainly because average income in urban areas is higher than in rural areas. In addition, urbanization has been accompanied by advances in waste management, provision of safe water, and economies of scale in transportation, housing, education, health services, and provision of public health information. In the other direction, urbanization has led to environmental degradation, crime, inequality, and severe congestion. In addition, the slum population stands at about 1 billion; that is, approximately 1 of every 3 city dwellers resides in a slum.

People living in cities are generally healthier than those in rural areas because of greater access to health services, the availability of skilled health personnel, better nutrition, improved sanitation,

access to clean water, and higher incomes and education levels. This positive differential is apparent both in child height and infant and child mortality rates.

Female literacy rates are considerably higher (by about 35 percentage points) among urban populations as compared with their rural counterparts, because urbanization tends to increase girls' access to education and promotes cultural acceptance of their right to education. Nevertheless, levels of literacy are dramatically different between the urban rich and the urban poor.

The growth of cities has led to a burgeoning numbers of megacities, defined by the UNPD as urban agglomerations with a population of 10 million or more. In 1975, there were only 3 megacities; today, there are 21. Together, these cities account for a little over 9.4% of the world's urban total population (in 2009) and 4.7% of the world's total population. The 10 largest urban agglomerations are, in order of descending size, Tokyo, Delhi, São Paulo, Mumbai, Mexico City, New York-Newark, Shanghai, Calcutta, Dhaka, and Buenos Aires.

Conclusion

The world is in the midst of the most dramatic demographic transformation in human history. Global population, which stood at 2.5 billion in 1950, is projected to surpass 9 billion by 2050, with a sharp increase in the share living in densely populated urban settings. Although there is considerable demographic heterogeneity across countries and regions, lower rates of mortality have been the main trigger for the increase. But the force of population growth is abating in the face of declining fertility, with population shares at the older ages increasing at an accelerating pace. These changes pose major political, social, economic, and environmental challenges, both for individual countries and for the world as a whole.

David E. Bloom

See also Aging Societies; Birth Control; Darwinism and Social Darwinism; Demographic Transition; Diseases; Family Policies; Genocides; HIV/AIDS; Hygiene; Infant Mortality; Medical Systems; Migration; Overpopulation; Population and Demographic Change; Population Growth and Population Explosion; Public Health; Viruses, Killer

Further Readings

Bloom, D. E., & Canning, D. (2006, September). Booms, busts, and echoes. *Finance & Development*, 43(3), 8–13.

Bloom, D. E., & Canning, D. (2008). Global demographic change: Dimensions and economic significance. *Population and Development Review, 33*, 17–51.

Cohen, J. E. (2005). Human population grows up. *Scientific American, 293*(3), 48–55.

Lee, R. (2003). The demographic transition: Three centuries of fundamental change. *Journal of Economic Perspectives, 17*(4), 167–190.

Livi-Bacci, M. (1992). *A concise history of world population*. Malden, MA: Blackwell.

United Nations, Department of Economic and Social Affairs, Population Division. (2009). *World population prospects: The 2008 revision* (Working Paper No. ESA/P/WP.210). Retrieved August 31, 2011, from www.un.org/esa/population/publications/wpp2008/wpp2008_highlights.pdf

DEMOGRAPHIC TRANSITION

The term *demographic transition* describes the movement of a society from a situation of high mortality and high fertility (average number of children a woman typically has over her lifetime) to one of low mortality and low fertility. It is typically characterized as a process of reductions in mortality rates followed by, after some delay, reductions in fertility. In the initial period of reductions in mortality without reductions in fertility, there is fast population growth, which is progressively slowed down as fertility starts to decline and the population momentum slows down. In the last stage, faced today by many developed and developing nations, mortality reaches low levels, and fertility stabilizes below replacement rate, leading to reductions in the size of the population in the long run.

The demographic transition is a virtually global pattern. It is probably the best documented social phenomenon in the history of modern societies, and there is a strong consensus regarding its main features. Its generality as a worldwide transformation, and its profound implications in terms of social changes, were noticed long ago by Warren S. Thompson and Adolphe Landry. In stark contrast with the post–World War II catastrophic predictions of the population explosion theorists, these first authors seemed to think of the different stages of the transition as different phases in the process of development and as a process that would eventually spread through most of the world.

Today, the demographic transition is a widespread phenomenon. Unprecedented mortality reductions have reached virtually every corner of the globe—with the exception of sub-Saharan Africa—and the vast majority of human population lives in countries where fertility has already shown significant declines and where population is expected to stabilize by mid-21st century. Major demographic changes swept the world in the course of the past hundred years. Life expectancy at birth rose from 40 years to above 70 in developing countries and to around 80 in the developed world. Total fertility rates dropped from 6 points or above to close to 2 points or below.

In various cases, this process of social change has culminated in extremely low fertility rates, with family sizes below the level necessary to keep population constant in the long run. Although this phenomenon has been associated mostly with western Europe (e.g., in Belgium, Germany, Italy, and Spain), it is not restricted to it. Today, over 70 countries, comprising more than half of the world population, have fertility rates below replacement level. Several developed and developing countries—as culturally diverse as Austria, Canada, China, Croatia, Cuba, Greece, Japan, Russia, and Spain—already face extremely low fertility rates, substantially below the cutoff level of 2.1 points.

In the demographic and economic literature, the demographic transition is also seen as marking the movement between two regimes: the Malthusian regime (or equilibrium) and the modern demographic regime. In the Malthusian regime, societies are thought to be predominantly agricultural, and fertility is supposed to respond positively to improvements in living conditions. So increases in population, with a fixed supply of land, lead to deteriorations in living conditions and, therefore, through positive and negative checks, to a halting of population growth. In this Malthusian world, living conditions cannot improve in the long run, because any gain is "consumed" by population expansion. In the modern demographic regime, on the other hand, fertility is not thought to increase with improvements in living conditions. As the theory goes, in this situation families spend resources on their children and, through a quantity-quality trade-off, increases in income lead to reductions in the size of families but increased human capital of children (investments in education and health). Investments in human capital and the negative relationship between income and fertility open up the possibility of sustained growth with stable or declining population, through increased productivity and technological innovation.

The reduction in the size of families and lengthening of individuals' life horizons imply profound social changes, which are implicit in the distinction between the Malthusian and modern demographic regimes outlined in the previous paragraph. Smaller families imply lower costs of investments in children. At the same time, lower mortality implies a more stable planning horizon in the long term and, therefore, higher returns to activities that imply current costs and future benefits, such as investments in human and physical capital and saving. For these reasons, the transition is typically followed by increased educational attainment, increased productivity, and, in some circumstances, economic development. Although other factors seem to be essential to warrant sustained long-term development, the demographic transition does appear as a necessary condition for these changes to occur.

At the aggregate level, the changes in mortality and fertility that mark the demographic transition imply radical transformations in the age structure of societies, defining a broad phenomenon that has been generally called *population aging*. The age distribution of the Malthusian society, characterized by a large fraction of young people and a relatively small fraction of older age groups, slowly shifts to a more homogeneous age distribution, with similar fractions of the population represented in each age group.

The aggregate changes implicit in the demographic transition also bring enormous challenges and opportunities. The fast population expansion during the first stage of the transition puts enormous pressure on the provision of public goods. This is in part behind the population explosion observed in the developing world during the postwar period. After substantial fertility reductions, the size of younger cohorts becomes small in comparison to the population at working ages. At that moment, it becomes cheap for societies to educate and qualify a relatively small number of children, characterizing what has been termed the *demographic dividend*. Finally, as the aging process continues, the fraction of elderly people in the population becomes relatively large, representing a burden to the working-age population and posing serious challenges to public retirement and social security systems.

Although the major importance of all these changes for the future of human societies has been widely acknowledged, there is still debate on the driving factors behind the demographic transition. Some theories have highlighted economic growth and the industrial revolution, and the way they affected the value of education, and, more generally, the return to human capital investments. Others have stressed how improvements in health and reductions in mortality, determined from developments in public health and biological sciences, affected the incentives of families in relation to number of children and investments in health and education. Some others have also analyzed the role of the relative size of cohorts and how it impacts the opportunities, ambitions, and life plans of members of a specific cohort.

It is likely that all these factors, as well as various other alternatives raised in the literature, contributed to the historical experiences of demographic transition registered around the globe. However, irrespective of its ultimate determinants, the demographic transition is undoubtedly one of the most important social phenomena in the history of humankind. Its consequences have already altered the face of human societies, and its ongoing effects will continue to be felt throughout the next century.

Rodrigo R. Soares

See also Economic Development; Fertility; Industrialization; Mortality; Population Growth and Population Explosion

Further Readings

Bloom, D. E., Canning, D., & Sevilla, J. (2003). *The demographic dividend: A new perspective on the economic consequences of population change* (Population Matters Monograph No. MR-1274). Santa Monica, CA: RAND Corporation.

Easterlin, R. A. (1976). The conflict between aspirations and resources. *Population and Development Review*, 2(3/4), 417–425.

Galasso, V. (2006). *The political future of social security in aging societies*. Cambridge: MIT Press.

Galor, O., & Weil, D. N. (2000). Population, technology, and growth: From Malthusian stagnation to the demographic transition and beyond. *American Economic Review*, 90(4), 806–828.

Hansen, G. D., & Prescott, E. C. (2002). Malthus to Solow. *American Economic Review*, 92(4), 1205–1217.

Landry, A. (1934). *La révolution démographique* [The demographic revolution]. Paris: Sirey.

Malthus, T. R. (1798). *An essay on the principle of population*. London: J. Johnson.

Meltzer, D. (1992). *Mortality decline, the demographic transition, and economic growth*. Unpublished doctoral dissertation, University of Chicago.

Soares, R. R. (2005). Mortality reductions, educational attainment, and fertility choice. *American Economic Review*, 95(3), 580–601.

Thompson, W. S. (1929). Population. *American Journal of Sociology*, 34(6), 959–975.

DEMOS

See Publics and Polis, Global

DEPENDENCY

Dependency is a term that implies an unequal relationship between societies and shapes the nature of development, especially in the global era. Dependency is both a technical term in the sociology of development and a more general proposition about the economic, cultural, or political reliance of human societies on other societies with regard to particular commodities, such as oil or the natural environment.

Dependency Theory

Dependency theory is one of the major perspectives that is employed to understand the impact of the global economy on societies around the world, especially in the "Third World" of Africa, Latin America, Asia, and the Middle East. In their classic 1979 work *Dependency and Development in Latin America*, Brazilian sociologist (and later president of Brazil) Fernando Henrique Cardoso and Chilean historian Enzo Faletto defined dependency as follows: "A system is dependent when the accumulation and expansion of capital cannot find its essential dynamic component within the system" (p. xx). For Cardoso and Faletto, the nations of Latin America, and by extension, other areas of the Third World, became dependent on the European colonial powers in the 16th and 17th centuries as they began to export raw materials such as grains and precious metals, harshly exploiting a local labor force and African workers brought to the colonies as slaves. In return, they imported virtually all of their manufactured needs.

This process of unequal trade relations, enforced politically by colonial power, gradually came to shape the social structures of Latin American nations, creating strong landholding and merchant classes that would dominate Latin American politics (often competing with each other) after independence at the turn of the 19th century. Economic dependency was reinforced in the course of the

19th century as first Great Britain and then the United States profited from a growing trade and became the owners of much mineral wealth and farmland. By 1900, the United States was intervening politically as well, sending occupation forces to much of Central America, controlling the foreign policy of Cuba, and influencing the course of events in Mexico and elsewhere.

Economic and Political Dependency

Economic and political dependency took new forms in the 20th century, especially after World War II, as massive U.S. investments gave its corporations effective control of key sectors of national economies throughout Latin America. With a near monopoly of technology and management resources, the United States had clearly made the economies of many nations dependent on it for their development. This trend intensified with the new institutions of the World Bank and International Monetary Fund, which not only made major loans to governments throughout the Third World but attached conditions to these loans that required governments to meet stringent targets in reducing their budgets for social services and providing further tax and investment incentives to First World transnational corporations.

Countries such as Cuba, Guatemala, Chile, and Nicaragua tried to reduce their dependence on the United States under revolutionary and nationalist governments between 1944 and 1990. They were successful only in Cuba, where a 1958 revolution, led by Fidel Castro, nationalized all U.S. assets and constructed a new socialist society, which withdrew from the orbit of the U.S. and world capitalist economies. Cuba received massive subsidies from the Soviet Union through 1991 and traded its primary products, such as sugar and nickel, with the Soviet bloc, prompting many social scientists to speak of a new dependence on the Soviet Union. But the economic relations between the two worked in Cuba's favor, as the Soviet Union paid high prices for Cuban sugar and in return sent oil to Cuba at a discount, reversing the unequal relations that Cuba had had with capitalist nations for several centuries. It is also true that Cuban foreign policy was somewhat beholden to Soviet interests as well, but their political relationship protected the Cuban revolution from U.S. intervention during

the Cold War. When the Soviet Union collapsed in 1991, the Cuban economy went into a severe decline known as the "Special Period." By the beginning of the 21st century, Cuba had successfully rebuilt and reoriented its economy and now trades with many countries around the world, placing strict controls on foreign capital. In this way, Cuba has shown that it is possible to break with political and economic dependency on the advanced capitalist world and achieve a socialist form of development with impressive quality of life measures for its population.

Elsewhere, the United States regained control of nationalized companies by fomenting military coups against elected governments in Iran (1953), Guatemala (1954), and Chile (1973), and helped bring about the downfall of the Sandinista government in Nicaragua in the 1990 elections by arming a counterrevolutionary army that disrupted the revolutionary development of that country. This trend of making Third World nations dependent on the United States continued into the 21st century with the invasion and occupation of Iraq, with devastating consequences for the life chances of Iraq's population. But the U.S. bid for economic and political hegemony in Iraq and throughout the Middle East has been challenged by insurgencies in Iraq, Afghanistan, and elsewhere in the region, and the same may be said for Israel's attempts to control the Palestinian populations in the West Bank and Gaza.

Cardoso and Faletto also pioneered an understanding of how development and dependency can occur together in parts of the Third World under certain conditions. "Dependent development" refers to the process whereby Third World nations industrialize, increase their exports, and raise their gross national product through inviting in transnational corporations and taking loans from the International Monetary Fund and World Bank. At the same time, the process is marked by distinctive negative trends such as the conditionality of loans, described earlier, favorable terms for the repatriation of profit back to the transnational corporations, and growing inequality and deepening poverty rates in the Third World, as well as an expanding gap between the First World and Third World as a whole.

This is not to deny that some countries have fared better than others; each country has its own historical legacy and natural resource and human capital endowments. A small handful of Third World nations such as South Korea and Taiwan have, for the past half-century, fared markedly better than the rest by using government policy to promote industrialization. Thomas Gold refers to the skillful management of dependency by Taiwanese leaders in the last three decades of the 20th century, and South Korea may even be said to have developed its way out of the Third World. China is acknowledged by all observers to be an economic powerhouse, with a hugely important economic role in the world economy as a manufacturing giant and investor in sectors of the U.S. economy. But all three countries have experienced the repression of their workforce by authoritarian governments and environmental damage along the way, and scholars have pointed out the unique advantages and timing they enjoyed to maneuver within the international system, concluding that this path is not likely to be available to the rest of the Third World.

The general trend of dependent development has intensified with the globalization of the world economy, whose rules have been set by the World Trade Organization to break down any tariff or other barriers to the operation of transnational corporations worldwide. It is a truism that the global economy is tightly linked, and political scientists have long written of the "interdependence" of nations in the international state system. But to speak of interdependence is to mask the continuing position of economic power enjoyed by the states and corporations of the advanced industrialized world of North America, Europe, Japan, and Australia vis-à-vis the rest of the world.

Leading globalization theorists such as Bill Robinson have argued that transnational capital no longer resides solely in the First World and that all nation-states now have less economic sovereignty than in previous decades. In this sense, one can speak of a new dimension of dependency in a globalized world where all nations are dependent on the world's markets, financial system, and capital investment sectors. This was illustrated by the global recession touched off in the fall of 2008 by the collapse of the U.S. banking system, triggering a dramatic drop in world stock markets and a deep recession of a magnitude not seen since the global depression of the 1930s. This shows the interconnectedness of national economies in the present era, while at the same time highlighting how all are dependent on economic forces beyond their individual control. The impact of this crisis is likely to be felt disproportionately in the Third World as their workforces depend on First World demand, investment, loans, and aid, and their governments lack the economic or political power to protect their populations from the impact of an unprecedented global downturn. The degree to which the near collapse of the world economy affected development in the First World as well suggests that the concept of dependent development, now applied to the dependence of all nations on global market forces beyond their control, may have wide applicability beyond the Third World and may help explain the limits to development being experienced even in the most "advanced" First World economies and in China as well.

Ecological Dependency

A final sense in which we may speak of dependency has to do with the ecological constraints placed on world economic development in the 21st century. The dependence of all nations on supplies of fossil fuels and petroleum products for their industry, agriculture, transportation, communications and virtually all facets of urban life is running up against the relatively rapid depletion of Earth's finite stock of fossil fuels. This process, now understood as "peak oil," has historically been driven by the disproportionate use of such supplies in the First World, particularly in the United States, and has been compounded by the increased demand for oil to fuel the economic development of rising industrial powers such as China and India. The unchecked production of greenhouse gases, such as carbon dioxide, by an industrial civilization driven by fossil fuels is now starting to raise temperatures in much of the world, the phenomenon known as *global warming*. This will in turn have severe impacts on the planet's economic and social conditions, increasing the possibility of violent conflict. In this sense, all of humankind is now dependent on the climate problems and natural resource constraints that have themselves been produced by an industrialized economy.

Twenty-first-Century Challenges

In the face of these interlinked dimensions of dependency—economic, political, and ecological—the challenge for the world's population is to fashion creative solutions, including a rapid transition to a "green," renewable energy–based economy, the reduction of the inequalities that have been imposed by five centuries of capitalist development, and the authoritarian politics that have tended to follow from dependent development in both First and Third worlds. The large network of social movements—such as the global justice movement, the wave of left-of-center governments that have come to power in Latin America, and resistance movements such as the Zapatista insurrection in Mexico—as well as the global growth of consciousness about climate change and the need for democratic solutions to the interlocking dimensions of the current crisis all form part of the solutions being sought by the world's peoples to the most pressing problems they face today and in the decades to come.

The condition of dependency thus retains a place at the center of discussions about the nature of globalization and will continue to do so as the world faces some severe challenges over the course of the 21st century.

John Foran

See also Antiglobalization Movements and Critics; Modernization; World Social Forum; World-Systems Perspective

Further Readings

Cardoso, F. H., & Faletto, E. (1979). *Dependency and development in Latin America.* Berkeley: University of California Press.
Gold, T. (1997). *State and society in the Taiwan miracle.* Armonk, NY: Sharpe.
Parker, M., Fournier, V., & Reedy, P. (2007). *The dictionary of alternatives: Utopianism and organization.* London: Zed Books.
So, A. (1990). *Social change and development: Modernization, dependency, and world-system theories.* Thousand Oaks, CA: Sage.
Starr, A. (2005). *Global revolt: A guide to the movements against globalization.* London: Zed Press.

DEPENDENCY THEORY

Dependency theory is an influential perspective from the 1960s in the sociology of development. It remains relevant in the global era for debates about the nature of economic and political change and the impact of the global economy on societies around the world, especially in the "Third World" of Africa, Latin America, Asia, and the Middle East.

The original formulation of Andre Gunder Frank argued that Third World nations could not develop economically because of the ways in which their economies were tied to more powerful First World nations and corporations, which appropriated the major part of the profits generated in the most productive sectors of the economy. A later version, elaborated by Brazilian sociologist (and later president of Brazil) Fernando Henrique Cardoso and Chilean historian Enzo Faletto, refined Frank's approach by showing how the links of Third World countries to the First World both facilitated and constrained development. The theory was recast by U.S. sociologist Immanuel Wallerstein as world-systems theory, which has been a major perspective in the sociology of development from the 1970s to the present day. This entry presents the main versions of the theory and shows how it provides important insights for the understanding of the global political economy in the 21st century.

Roots

Dependency theory was a Latin American response to North American modernization theory, a set of perspectives that had argued that all societies would eventually industrialize and develop economically to the level of the First World nations and that foreign investment and aid to the Third World would be necessary to bring this about. Partly it has roots in Marxist theories of imperialism, which extended Marx's model of a class struggle onto a worldwide scale: Just as rich and poor classes exist in a given country (Marx called these the *bourgeoisie* and the *proletariat,* or working class), so, by analogy, there are rich and poor nations in the world economy—the First and the Third worlds. Another precursor of dependency theory was a UN working group based in Latin America called the Economic Commission on Latin America (ECLA). ECLA used the terms *center* and *periphery* to characterize the dynamic economies of the advanced industrial nations (the center) and the dependent economies of the Third World (the periphery), together forming an international system in which center and periphery were linked together. They also produced historical studies of trade patterns in Latin America and concluded that, since 1870, the terms of trade had deteriorated for the Latin American economies. That is, the prices for Latin America's exports, which were mostly raw materials (food and minerals), had historically fallen, while the prices for what Latin America had to import, primarily finished manufactures, had gotten more expensive over time. This meant that Latin America had to constantly export more of its own products just to import the same amount of goods from abroad. One reason for this deterioration in the terms of trade was the low wages that Latin American workers were paid, while industrial workers in the West had seen their wages rise, as a result of union efforts and political gains, as well as higher productivity through the application of technology and machinery to industry and agriculture.

ECLA claimed further that industrial development had occurred most in Latin America when its international trade relations with the First World had been interrupted, either by world war or worldwide depressions. This is because, during such periods, the Latin American countries of necessity started to manufacture the goods they could no longer import from abroad. The development strategy advocated by ECLA in the 1950s and 1960s was for Latin America to further this process of industrialization so that it no longer needed to import so many goods from the center countries, thus retaining more jobs and wealth inside the country, a strategy referred to as *import-substitution industrialization*. The researchers of ECLA pioneered a critique of the world system by noting the structural inequalities between the center and the periphery and trying to propose some solutions to underdevelopment.

First Version

The dependency theorists of the 1960s extended this critique in several ways. The first version of the theory argued that the West had caused the underdevelopment of the Third World: By historically exploiting the resources and labor of the Third World, Europe and North America had managed to industrialize and develop. Because the Third World has no one to exploit, and indeed, was still being exploited by the West, how was it going to develop? Some theorists, such as Frank, argued that the Third World cannot develop or industrialize as long as it remains part of a world market dominated by the center, or core countries. He proposed a model of satellite and metropolis, in which the metropolis—the rich countries—controlled the trade patterns of the international system, and the poor countries—the satellites—were oriented completely toward satisfying the requirements of these rich countries. The image is of small Third World countries revolving around the rich countries like satellites orbiting a planet, held in place by the powerful gravitational force of exploitative trade relations. For Frank, the key relationship to study was the relations between countries, between center and peripheral economies. Like the economists of ECLA, he argued that Latin America truly developed only when these links were broken—during World War I, World War II, and the 1930s depression. Otherwise, the rest of the time, Latin America was being exploited, and was underdeveloping. He spoke of the development of underdevelopment as the normal condition of the Third World.

Second Version

A second, more complex strand of dependency theory was elaborated later, in the 1960s, by Cardoso and Faletto in their classic work *Dependency and Development in Latin America* (first published in Spanish in 1969, then translated into English in 1979). Unlike Frank, they did not argue that the First World completely determines development in the Third World; instead, they maintained that the historic links between the two shaped the economies of the Third World in certain directions. Thus, their definition of dependency is, in the first instance, economic: "A system is dependent when the accumulation and expansion of capital cannot find its essential dynamic component within the system" (Cardoso & Faletto, 1979, p. xx). This points to the existence of an international economic system, which they saw as capitalism, within which different nations occupy qualitatively different positions of power and influence. The advanced industrial nations control such key economic sectors as technology and finance, which the Third World nations lack and which keeps industrialization in the Third World from becoming complete. For example, a Third World country may manage to produce clothing and process food products, but heavy industry—iron and steel, chemicals, machine tools—and high technology products, such as computers, may be beyond its ability to produce on its own. Thus, the Third World often invites in multinational corporations to provide the needed technology, management skills, machinery, and capital. In so doing, the Third World nations lose some control over their own economies. In this way, development has its costs and drawbacks as well as its advantages.

A second key advance in Cardoso and Faletto's thinking was an attempt to understand not just the relations between nations but how this shapes the class structure of the Latin American societies. That is, they were interested in how external ties to the world market have shaped internal social structure over time. The key organizers of industrialization—the multinational corporations, the local capitalist (or business) classes, and the governments of the Third World, sometimes referred to as the *triple alliance* (a term popularized by U.S. sociologist Peter Evans in a 1979 study of Brazil)—are constantly bargaining over the terms of who will benefit from the industrialization process. Cardoso and Faletto also looked beyond these groups at how the peasantry, the working class, and middle classes were affected by processes of development; how they gain or lose power as the economy changes; how they react to the strategies of the multinationals and the state; and how they sometimes resist them. Thus, one insight of dependency theory is that new classes come into existence as a result of development, and this then changes the political equation, the balance of forces in society.

Cardoso and Faletto also recognized that these relationships vary across countries—that even within Latin America, there are significant differences in the situations of the small nations of Central America, which often relied on the export of a single product such as coffee or bananas, and larger, more diversified societies such as Brazil and Argentina. These differences are due in part to the fact that originally they had different economic bases and special features and also because, over the course of their histories, each was shaped in a particular direction by the outside forces of the world market.

A final innovation in their approach was the notion that, in some cases, dependency can be combined with development. That is, significant industrialization and economic growth may occur in certain Third World countries at particular moments in their history. Mexico, Argentina, Brazil, South Korea, and Taiwan, for example, are more industrialized than their neighbors. They thus acknowledged some benefits to dependency and the reality of industrialization, but they considered this a limited kind of development, which they termed *dependent development*.

Dependent development means growth, but within limits. Gross national product, exports, and other economic indicators may rise, but these gains are generally accompanied by significant negative consequences, such as inflation, unemployment, health problems, inadequate housing and education, and the like. It thus brings advances for a minority of the population and suffering for the majority. Some classes in society benefit from this process, while others do not. Positives and negatives occur together, in a pattern of overall statistical gains but individual hardship. This seminal idea, with its coequal attention to a form of "progress" and its disadvantages, stands in sharp contrast to the earlier version of the dependency thesis of Frank, who felt that no development could occur under conditions of dependency on the advanced industrial capitalist powers, unless the links were disrupted during exceptional periods of worldwide economic crisis or war. Cardoso and Faletto's interpretation of the dependency paradigm, with its attention to the interaction between external structures and patterns of internal development, constitutes a major breakthrough in the sociological literature.

Finally, Cardoso and Faletto (1979) believed that, in the long run, these trends will lead to social movements for change, whether against military dictatorships, foreign control, or unresponsive governments. As they put it, "there is room for alternatives in history" (p. xi)—people can change unequal social structures through political coalitions and social movements.

How well does this perspective account for patterns of development in a global economy? The vicissitudes of boom and bust, the deepening of inequality in many societies around the world, and the characteristic outcome of aggregate economic growth and social ills continue to plague millions of people, in both First and Third worlds, suggesting that the concept of dependent development remains vital for understanding the globalization processes of the present and future.

John Foran

See also Dependency; Modernization; Private-Public Partnerships; World Society Theory; World-Systems Perspective

Further Readings

Cardoso, F. H., & Faletto, E. (1979). *Dependency and development in Latin America.* Berkeley: University of California Press.

Evans, P. (1979). *Dependent development: The alliance of multinational, state, and local capital in Brazil.* Princeton, NJ: Princeton University Press.

Frank, A. G. (1978). *Dependent accumulation and underdevelopment.* New York: Monthly Review Press.

So, A. (1990). *Social change and development: Modernization, dependency, and world-system theories.* Newbury Park, CA: Sage.

DEPRESSION, GREAT

The Great Depression (1929–1939) was a global event, in both its causes and its effects. It was due to a global recoil of the web of credit, which landed the world in what Irving Fisher has called a "debt-deflation trap" from which it could not escape for many years. International cooperation would have been required to cope with this situation, but it did not come about because the major actors adopted their own methods to fight the depression. Protectionism was a common denominator of these various methods, and this obstructed the recovery of the world market.

The theory of cumulative causation propounded by Gunnar Myrdal indicates that the expansion of markets, technological progress, economies of scale, increasing investment, and productivity gains give rise to a virtuous circle of economic growth. However, this theory does not preclude the emergence of a vicious circle of a cumulative downturn. Factors that contribute to such a downturn include narrowing markets; a reduction of credit, investment, and production; a fall in prices; and the rise of unemployment. The crucial question is what factors may trigger the switch from a virtuous to a vicious circle. For the Great Depression, several long-term and short-term developments have been identified that contributed to the cumulative downturn.

The Gold Standard

The most important of the long-term causes was the restoration of the international gold standard in the years after World War I. The gold standard presupposed a free flow of gold, which would inflate the prices in the country that attracted it and deflate them in the country that lost gold. In due course, a reverse movement would set in, which would restore the international equilibrium. After the war, the United States experienced a massive inflow of gold, but its Federal Reserve Bank (FED) maintained price stability by sterilizing gold and issuing Reserve Bank credit. When Great Britain returned to the gold standard at the prewar parity, the FED supported this by providing ample credit worldwide. This also fueled a boom in the United States, which then led to a wave of stock market speculation that ended in the crash of October 1929.

Speculators could borrow money from the banks to buy stock and use it as collateral for further bank credits. The increasing demand for stocks led to the creation of holding companies, which did not produce anything but only owned other companies. A house of cards was built in this way. In 1925, total new investment amounted to US$3.5 billion and to US$3.2 billion in 1929, the nominal value of shares increased from US$27 to US$87 billion in this period. The FED wanted to stop this development by raising interest rates, but the speculators were not deterred by this as they expected higher returns from the stock market. It took some time before credit contraction put the brakes on speculation, and, when the crash came, the FED did not rush to provide credit. The crash by itself would not have caused the depression. The crash of 1987 was much more dramatic, but it did not cause a depression. However, in 1929, the U.S. economy was more fragile. Sales of cars and durable consumer goods dropped immediately after the crash. Even more alarming was the drop of the wheat price, which released an avalanche of wheat inundating the world market.

The Global Fall of Commodity Prices

There was a global overproduction of wheat in the 1920s, which was initially accompanied by a rise of the wheat price (Index 1913 = 100). During the war, high prices had prevailed (above 200); by 1923, they had come down to 131 but had then climbed up again although world production had reached a peak at 92 million tons (Price index 136). The United States had the largest portion of this expansion. Huge areas of the Great Plains, which were grazing land earlier, had been converted into wheat fields; farm mechanization and chemical fertilizer had increased the yield. Decades of biological innovation had ensured that the farmers could be supplied with seeds of varieties of wheat that were suitable for the new areas opened up by them. But nobody thought about the sustainability of wheat cultivation in the Great Plains. Beginning in 1930, a series of droughts turned the Great Plains into a dust bowl. Storms took away the topsoil. The government faced great difficulties in alleviating the miseries of millions of farmers. This also dampened overproduction. By 1934, total world production of wheat amounted to 73 million tons, but this did not yet lead to a recovery of the price level (Index number 66).

In the mid-1920s, farm credit had helped finance the storage of U.S. wheat. The bumper crop of 1928 had put this system under severe strain, and, when the FED raised interest rates to discourage the speculators in the stock market, it inadvertently strained farm credit. Subsequent panic sales reduced the price of wheat by half from 1929 to 1931. This affected not only American farmers but also peasants in India. Their incomes dwindled while their debts appreciated.

The debt-deflation trap showed its cruel effect. Australia had started a "Grow More Wheat Campaign" at a most inopportune time in 1929, leading to a bumper crop of 7.7 million tons in 1930. Because the country was heavily indebted, it was hoped that wheat export could earn the foreign exchange urgently needed. This export would have been impossible if Australia had not experienced a devaluation of its currency precipitated by its foreign creditors. Due to this, Australia could indulge in "exchange dumping" and export its wheat below the cost of production. The British-Indian government reacted to this by imposing a protective wheat import duty in 1931. Even earlier, in June 1930, the United States had passed the Smoot-Hawley Tariff Act, which was aimed at protecting agriculture but also included many other items. It was a signal for the global proliferation of protectionism.

The Race Toward Protectionism

Great Britain was next in the global race toward protectionism. It went off the gold standard in September 1931. This led to a devaluation of the pound sterling by about 30%. It also introduced a protective tariff on industrial products. In earlier discussions, devaluation and a protective tariff had been considered as alternative options, because devaluation also reduced imports and encouraged exports. But the new national government adopted both options. This was a protectionist "overkill," but it was very much in line with the new mercantilism spreading at that time. It was a policy of beggar-thy-neighbor, which invited retaliation by other countries. The British followed this up by introducing a regime of imperial preferences in 1932. Countries belonging to the British Empire would enjoy preferential tariffs and even free access to the British market for certain items. The British had also established a "sterling area" encompassing the empire. For this, the pound sterling, which floated since September 1931, had to be stabilized. A great flow of gold from the periphery to the center of the empire helped to achieve this.

India, which suffered from intense deflationary pressure induced by British-Indian currency policy, contributed an enormous flow of "distress gold" to this process. Moneylenders pounced on the indebted Indian peasants and snatched their savings in gold. Agrarian distress was widespread in India, because not only the price of wheat but also the prices of rice and cotton had fallen precipitously.

Rice was mostly grown in Asia and also consumed there. There was no overproduction as in the case of wheat. Moreover, only a very small fraction of the total production of rice was traded internationally. There was no reason for the rice price to follow the wheat price, as the substitution of wheat for rice was not easy for the consumers. In fact, rice prices remained high in 1930, in contrast with wheat prices. Then there was a sudden fall of the rice price in Japan by about 30% in October 1930. This was due to a good harvest and the deflationary policy of the Japanese government at that time, as it had just rejoined the gold standard and tried desperately to stick to it. Japan neither imported nor exported rice any longer. The fall of the rice price should have remained a purely domestic affair, but the rice traders in Liverpool reacted to the news in November, and the price dropped there immediately. By January 1931, when the winter rice reached the market in India, the price had dropped by about 50%. The contagion spread rapidly. The rice price remained depressed. In 1933, rice was even cheaper than wheat, a totally unprecedented event.

The cotton price had started its decline even earlier. There was no great change in the supply and demand of cotton worldwide. But the law that prices are determined by supply and demand had been invalidated in the depression years. The volume of the cotton trade did not decline much, but its value was reduced. The United States had initially a share of about 50% to 60% of cotton production, and India had about 20%. In 1929, the price for one pound of raw cotton stood at US$0.18; in 1932, it reached its lowest level, at US$0.06. This steep decline by about two thirds was worse than that of most other agricultural produce. In fact, the terms of trade went against agriculture in the depression period. Industry did not decline that much and recovered much faster. The need for colonies that supplied raw materials declined. The path toward decolonization was prepared in that way. But in the 1930s, the colonies were still debtors, and their imperial masters tightened their grip as creditors.

The World Economic Conference

By 1933, when the world had reached the bottom of the abyss, a final attempt was made to convene a World Economic Conference in London during which all governments would combine their efforts to get out of the depression. It was a complete disaster. Much has been made of U.S. president Franklin D. Roosevelt's "bombshell message" in which he informed the conference of his refusal to participate and told the Europeans to set their house in order. In fact, the British were also not interested in the conference, and Neville Chamberlain referred to it as "a miserable conference." Later on, he put the blame on Roosevelt for ruining it. Britain had put its own house in order by 1933 but was at odds with France, which stuck to the gold standard and had adopted a protectionism of its own. Germany was already controlled by Adolf Hitler. It was nominally still on the gold standard but had introduced strict exchange controls. It also introduced a sophisticated system of bilateral barter agreements with countries supplying raw materials in return for German machinery. It reflated its domestic economy and finally stimulated its industry by means of rearmament. Its future ally, Japan, had in the meantime gone off the gold standard in 1932 and strongly devalued its currency. Japanese exports boomed, and rearmament also came to play an important role in its industrial recovery.

China had the most unusual fate in the period of the depression. It was at first shielded from it because it had stuck to a silver standard, and the price of silver declined steeply. In fact, overseas Chinese living in gold-standard countries transmitted a large part of their savings to China, and there was an investment boom. Being on a silver standard was at first a saving grace, but it turned into a nightmare due to the American Silver Purchase Act of 1934. Silver was added to gold as a backing of the dollar, which had gone off the gold standard in 1933. The silver price rose steeply, and silver was sucked out of China with a vengeance. The Chinese finance minister H. H. Kung then staged a veritable financial coup. He practically nationalized all banks, demonetized silver, and introduced a currency reform. However, to gain the confidence of the people, he had to make this new currency freely convertible into foreign currencies.

This tied his hands as far as government spending was concerned. He could not indulge in Keynesian deficit spending. Nevertheless, he was successful in stabilizing the Chinese economy in the short run. The Great Depression had indeed been a global economic catastrophe.

Dietmar Rothermund

See also Depression, Recession, and Stagnation; Economics, Keynesian; Gold Standard; Monetary Policy; Protectionism

Further Readings

Boomgaard, P., & Brown, I. (Eds.). (2000). *Weathering the storm: The economies of Southeast Asia in the 1930s depression*. Leiden, Netherlands: KITLV Press.

Brown, I. (Ed.). (1989). *The economies of Africa and Asia in the inter-war depression*. London: Routledge.

James, H. (2001). *The end of globalization: Lessons from the Great Depression*. Cambridge, MA: Harvard University Press.

James, H. (Ed.). (2002). *The interwar depression in an international context*. Munich, Germany: Oldenbourg.

Kindleberger, C. P. (1986). *The world in depression, 1929–1939* (2nd ed.). Berkeley: University of California Press.

Rothermund, D. (1992). *India in the Great Depression, 1929–1939*. New Delhi, India: Manohar.

Rothermund, D. (1996). *The global impact of the Great Depression*. London: Routledge.

Shiroyama, T. (2008). *China during the Great Depression: Market, state and the world economy*. Cambridge, MA: Harvard University Press.

Thorp, R. (Ed.). (1984). *Latin America in the 1930s: The role of the periphery in world crisis*. London: Macmillan.

DEPRESSION, RECESSION, AND STAGNATION

Depressions, recessions, and stagnations usually originate in the context of a national economy but then affect the global economy as a result of their transnational spread.

Growth—an increase in gross domestic product (GDP)—is assumed to be the norm for a healthy economy. If GDP declines continuously for about half a year, this indicates a *recession*. A longer period of decline of a year or more is called a *depression*. An absence of growth without a decline is termed *stagnation*. This may occur at various levels of economic activity, for example, when a high plateau has been reached where further growth is inhibited by different constraints such as a shortage of natural resources. Stagnation may also persist because of a low-level or high-level equilibrium trap. In a low-level equilibrium trap, any increase in production leads to an equivalent growth of population; in a high-level equilibrium trap, growth is prevented by the adjustment of production to a balanced state of the respective society. The economy of Imperial China has served as the major example for this high-level equilibrium trap.

The Special Case of Stagflation

Growth has usually been associated with inflation and more or less full employment, whereas recession and depression are characterized by deflation and unemployment. Economists did not conceive of a state of affairs where inflation could coexist with unemployment and stagnation. However, the new phenomenon of stagflation upset previous economic theories. The word *stagflation* was first used by the British politician Iain Macleod in a speech in Parliament in 1965 in which he pointed out that the country was now threatened by both inflation and stagnation. The threat became more menacing in subsequent years when the oil price shock led to a general increase in prices. Workers then asked for higher wages, initiating a vicious circle of wage hikes and price increases as well as an increase in unemployment. Stagnation in this new form has rivaled recession and depression as a major impediment to economic growth.

Analyses and Theories

The experience of recurrent recessions and depressions has given rise to many attempts at analyzing the causes and effects of these phenomena. The dynamics of recovery from recessions were outlined in three curves, a V-shaped curve of sharp decline and rapid recovery, a U-shaped curve of prolonged depression, and an L-shaped curve of more or less steep decline with no recovery but a transition to stagnation. The U.S. recession of the mid-1950s serves as a demonstration of the V-curve. A peak at the end of 1952 was followed by a trough at the end of 1954. The U.S. economy then quickly climbed to a new peak in early 1955. The U-shaped curve corresponds to the experience of the Great Depression of the 1930s, and the L-shaped curve mirrors the fate of Japan, where an asset bubble burst in the late 1980s. The economy then declined steeply into a trough in the early 1990s; there was no recovery at that time but a transition to a long period of stagnation that was called Japan's "lost decade."

Economists are not satisfied with drawing such curves; they wish to explain the origins of recessions and depressions. Various theories concerning business cycles provide some explanations. However, these theories are most convincing when they deal with rather short and elementary fluctuations and become more ephemeral when they try to account for long periods and all aspects of economic activity. These theories do not help predict the points of upturns or downturns. One of the most elementary fluctuations is the so-called hog cycle of the production of pork in the United States. Farmers breeding hogs will increase their production while prices are high and reduce it when they fall. Because there is a time lag caused by the breeding period and the circulation of price information, the hog cycle takes about 4 to 5 years. A similar cycle was identified by Joseph Kitchin, who studied the behavior of producers who are faced with accumulating inventories when prices fall. The duration of the Kitchin cycle is equivalent to the hog cycle. Empirical proof of the validity of this short-term cycle can be found in the data of the U.S. National Bureau of Economic Research. It has recorded altogether 32 cycles from 1854 to 2001; the average duration of these cycles (i.e., from one peak to the next one) has been approximately 5 years.

A more sophisticated study of business cycles was conducted by Clément Juglar in the 19th century. Juglar had been almost forgotten when Joseph Schumpeter rediscovered him in the 1930s. The emphasis on the connection between credit cycles and investment cycles was Juglar's remarkable contribution to the debate on business cycles. He suggested a length of the cycle from 7 to 11 years. For Juglar and Schumpeter, recessions are

necessary corrections in the path of economic development. Schumpeter even stressed the need for "creative destruction," which removed the impediments to future growth. In this context, he paid special attention to technological change and propagated the theory of the Soviet economist Nikolai Kondratieff, who had studied the long waves of economic change from the industrial revolution to the 20th century. These waves would last for about 50 years. Basic technological innovations—such as the spread of the railways, the rise of the chemical industry, the emergence of the automobile, and, more recently, the emergence of information technology—would support such a wave but always end in a recession. Schumpeter was fascinated by Kondratieff's waves; in qualitative terms, they made sense, but it was difficult to find any quantitative proof for their actual rise and fall. Kondratieff was sentenced to death under Stalin's regime as his theory did not signal an end of capitalism but postulated its resilience due to its ability to respond to innovations.

Most theories concerning business cycles concentrated on investment and production. But Juglar had already highlighted the importance of credit cycles and thus drawn attention to the monetary aspects of economic fluctuations. A deeper evaluation of these aspects had to wait for the revolution in economic thought that was brought about by John Maynard Keynes. Before Keynes, the "real economy" of the production and exchange of goods and monetary economics were treated separately. Moreover, money was considered to be a dependent variable of the exchange of goods. The study of the real economy was dominated by supply-side economics and monetary economics by its concentration on the demand for money as a medium of exchange. Keynes changed this by stressing the relevance of the demand for goods and the vagaries of the supply of money.

The emphasis on the crucial role of money supply was reinforced by the experience of the Great Depression, which was characterized by a severe contraction of credit. This ushered in a long period of deflation, which deepened the depression. Keynes's policy recommendations concentrated on fiscal measures, as he believed that monetary policy would not be effective under the conditions prevailing at that time. He even recommended "deficit spending" by the government as it could count on increasing tax receipts after the economy recovered. Later critics of Keynes deprecated fiscal intervention and stressed the role of central banks in calibrating money supply so as to prevent monetary disturbances of the economy. This school of thought was named *monetarism*. The monetarists believed in the fundamental stability of the real economy but did not revert to earlier assumptions of the neutrality of money. Money supply was respected as an independent variable. It could seriously affect the real economy; therefore, it had to be controlled so as to protect the economy from fateful disruptions. However, monetary policy could work only in the long run and did not lend itself to measures that would quickly cure a recession or depression. As long as the growth of the economy was not seriously challenged by a depression, monetarism prevailed, but recent events have once more highlighted the need for government intervention.

Neither Keynesianism nor monetarism can explain the devastating effect of a depression and help us distinguish between different types of such effects. In the Great Depression of the 1930s, prices fell dramatically. International trade decreased in terms of value but not much in volume. Primary commodities were affected more than industrial goods. In this respect, the depression of the 1930s differs from the one that began at the end of 2007. In 2008, prices of primary commodities, such as wheat and rice but also iron ore, soared and, in subsequent years, receded. This means that the general credit contraction did not apply to these commodities. On the contrary, ample credit seems to have been available for the buying of such commodities, perhaps due to the fact that the housing market had collapsed and investment in the trade in commodities provided an alternative. The Great Depression of the 1930s was triggered by the coincidence of the overproduction of wheat and a speculative bonanza in the stock market.

The 2007 downturn of the U.S. economy was caused by the bursting of an asset bubble, which was due to the introduction of highly leveraged financial instruments, which facilitated the marketing of overvalued asset-backed securities. All this happened while funds from abroad were pouring into the United States, a country that could afford an enormous current account deficit while wallowing in a sea of ample credit. Ben Bernanke of the Federal Reserve Board attributed this in 2005 to a glut in world savings, which had to find an outlet when no opportunities for investment existed at home. He supported his argument by citing figures concerning the deficit and surplus countries, with Japan, Germany, and China taking the lead among the latter. In dealing with China, he did not comment on the nature of Chinese savings, which are, to a large extent, forced ones. Chinese wages are low, and the government appropriates export earnings, investing them in U.S. Treasury bills. This entirely new feature of global finance makes the recent financial crisis different from earlier ones. Usually the statement "this time is different" is made whenever financial advisers want to convince their clients that old expectations of financial crises are no longer valid—and this is not true, as Carmen Reinhart and Kenneth S. Rogoff have shown in their analysis of hundreds of crises over several centuries that follow more or less the same pattern. The recurrence of such crises proves to be inevitable, but their causes and effects, as well as their intensity, may nevertheless differ considerably.

Effects

Globalization has contributed to the occurrence of depressions and also to the change of their characteristic features. The Great Depression was already a global phenomenon; its long-term impact on the periphery of the world economy was severe. The depression that began in 2007 has altogether different causes and effects. Who would have expected that the enormous savings of China, a communist country, would fuel a bubble in the premier capitalist country and thus precipitate another global depression?

Whereas recessions may actually have positive effects when they lead to a shakeout and thus prepare the economy for a resurgence, depressions may lead to a paralysis of financial intermediation and thus prevent investment and reduce production for some time. Furthermore, in fighting the impact of a depression, national governments may resort to protectionism and competitive devaluation, thus damaging world trade and obstructing its revival. This was very much in evidence in the 1930s, but it seems to have been avoided so far in the depression that began at the end of 2007. In this respect, the assertion that this time is different may be correct as far as the effects of the recent depression are concerned, although it certainly would not be true for precrisis assessments indicating that the world is now safe and has overcome the dismal past of financial folly. In the global era, there is an urgent need for the creation of a new international financial infrastructure.

Dietmar Rothermund

See also Depression, Great; Economics, Keynesian; Gold Standard; Monetary Policy; Protectionism

Further Readings

Bernanke, B. (2000). *Essays on the Great Depression.* Princeton, NJ: Princeton University Press.

Bernanke, B. (2005, April 14). *The global saving glut and the U.S. current account deficit* [Remarks by Governor Ben S. Bernanke at the Homer Jones Lecture, St. Louis, MO]. Retrieved from http://www.federalreserve.gov/boarddocs/speeches/2005/20050414/default.htm

Elvin, M. (1973). *The pattern of the Chinese past.* Stanford, CA: Stanford University Press.

Hansen, A. H. (1953). *A guide to Keynes.* New York: McGraw-Hill.

Reinhart, C., & Rogoff, K. S. (2009). *This time is different: Eight centuries of financial folly.* Princeton, NJ: Princeton University Press.

Schumpeter, J. (1939). *Business cycles: A theoretical, historical and statistical analysis of the capitalist process.* New York: McGraw-Hill.

Schwartz, A. (1987). *Money in historical perspective.* Chicago: University of Chicago Press.

DESERTIFICATION

Drylands cover more than 40% of the terrestrial land surface of the globe. Climatically, with low precipitation and high evapotranspiration, drylands are classified as arid, semiarid, and dry subhumid zones. Current estimates suggest that 10% to 20% of global drylands suffer from some form of acute land degradation, or desertification, which is the reduction or loss of biological or economic productivity. The environmental and socioeconomic costs of desertification are enormous,

impacting the livelihoods of some 250 million people. This is likely to become much worse in the future, as 38% of the total human population of over 6.5 billion reside in drylands, which also have the highest human population growth of any other region of the world.

The United Nations Convention to Combat Desertification (UNCCD) defines desertification as land degradation in dryland areas resulting from various factors, including human activities (e.g., overgrazing by domestic animals, poor cultivation practices) and climatic factors (e.g., drought, increasing air temperature). The Millennium Ecosystem Assessment frames the concept of desertification in terms of decreases in the potential of the land to continue to provide the essential ecosystem goods and services needed to sustain human livelihoods (e.g., crops, woody fuels, forage for grazing animals, and sufficient water). Importantly, both the UNCCD and Millennium Ecosystem Assessment focus explicitly on the linkages between humans (H) and their environments (E) and how this affects human welfare. Desertification is intimately linked to global environmental change through human populations (food and water security, poverty, loss of biodiversity, sustainable livelihoods, and the like) and the environment (trace gas emissions to the atmosphere, dust storms, land use change, and similar matters).

In spite of its importance as a major global problem, the concept of desertification historically has been viewed quite differently by different stakeholders, which has hindered progress in finding solutions. Farmers, conservationists, social workers, ecologists, land managers, and local politicians have legitimate but different perspectives that rarely converge. Why? First, "land degradation" per se does not lend itself to easy quantification: It is usually a slow, continuous process, and the environmental (ecological, biogeochemical, hydrological) changes occurring may not result in an immediate reduction or loss of biological or economic productivity. Second, local areas have a unique set of coupled human-environment (H-E) interactions, so the drivers and consequences of land degradation vary from location to location and, importantly, change over time and spatial scales. Lastly, there are many indirect factors (national economic policies, international trade) that interact with localized direct factors (precipitation, soil fertility, cultivation practices, livestock grazing rates, culture), all of which lead to a complex suite of nonlinear interactions in H-E systems that are difficult to understand and generalize. For these reasons (and others), no focused international science program has emerged to assist the UNCCD in guiding policymakers and scientists.

As an initial step to achieving this goal, James F. Reynolds, D. Mark Stafford Smith, and others proposed the Drylands Development Paradigm (DDP), an integrated framework built around the behavior of coupled H-E systems. It draws heavily from a convergence of insights and key advances drawn from research in desertification, vulnerability, poverty alleviation, and community development. The DDP consists of five principles that, when implemented as a whole, provide a strategy for analyzing causes and consequences of desertification.

Principle 1 states that the structure, function, and interrelationships that characterize coupled H-E systems are always changing, so human and environmental factors must always be considered simultaneously. Principle 1 is especially relevant in drylands because of the close dependency of human livelihoods on the environment. However, it also presents a major challenge because H-E systems are typically subjected to high variability in both biophysical (e.g., precipitation) and socioeconomic (emigration, market volatility, etc.) factors.

Principle 2 posits that a limited suite of "slow" variables are critical determinants of H-E system dynamics. Variables such as soil fertility, household equity, and cultural traditions change very slowly (years to centuries) and, therefore, are the most useful variables for gauging long-term trends. Contrast these to "fast" variables, such as crop yields and disposable household cash, which may change very rapidly and thus are poor indicators of long-term trends. For example, crop yields (and economic profits) may be very high one year but low the next as a result of the vagaries of precipitation. Nevertheless, as Stafford Smith, Greg McKeon, and others note, human exploitation of resources is often based on fast variables, which has muddled the debate about the strategic development needs for drylands.

Principle 3 focuses on the role of thresholds. As noted in Principle 1, H-E systems are constantly changing, so if a key slow variable crosses a threshold, this can lead to a different state or condition of the land. For example, studies have shown how overgrazing can reduce grass cover to a point where overland water flow triggers soil erosion and native grasses are replaced by invasive shrubs. This new, dysfunctional state (low grass cover, patchy shrubs, increased bare soil, erosion gullies) may be potentially irreversible if management intervention is not initiated early enough.

Principle 4 concerns the hierarchical nature of H-E systems; that is, the whole is greater than the sum of its parts. Because of the many cross-scale linkages and feedbacks, adaptation, surprises, and self-organization are the norm (see Principle 3). While understanding H-E systems is difficult at local levels, it represents an even greater challenge at regional and national scales.

Principle 5 states that "solving" land degradation problems cannot be accomplished without drawing on the firsthand experience and insights (often referred to as local knowledge) of local stakeholders. Local knowledge plays an especially important role in drylands because of their remoteness, a general dearth of scientific knowledge, and the high variability of these systems.

Desertification is a complex problem that represents a major challenge to the global community of scientists and policymakers. Analytical frameworks such as the DDP are needed, not as recipes for solutions (which they are not) but rather to stimulate thinking in order to manage the complexity of coupled H-E systems so that potential solutions and opportunities can be identified and implemented. The billions of people who live in drylands globally are depending on this.

James F. Reynolds

See also Environmental Change; Global Warming; Poverty and Poverty Alleviation; Sustainability

Further Readings

Millennium Ecosystem Assessment. (2005). *Ecosystems and human well-being: Desertification synthesis.* Washington, DC: World Resources Institute.

Reynolds, J. F., Grainger, A., Stafford Smith, D. M., Bastin, G., Garcia-Barrios, L., Fernández, R. J., et al. (2011). Scientific concepts for an integrated analysis of desertification. *Land Degradation & Development,* 22(2), 166–183.

Reynolds, J. F., Stafford Smith, D. M., Lambin, E. F., Turner, B. L., II, Mortimore, M., Batterbury, S. P. J., et al. (2007). Global desertification: Building a science for dryland development. *Science, 316*(5826), 847–851.

Stafford Smith, D. M., McKeon, G. M., Watson, I. W., Henry, B. K., Stone, G. S., Hall, W. B., et al. (2007). Learning from episodes of degradation and recovery in variable Australian rangelands. *Proceedings of the National Academy of Sciences, 104*(52), 20690–20695.

United Nations, Intergovernmental Negotiating Committee for a Convention to Combat Desertification. (1994). *Elaboration of an International Convention to Combat Desertification in Countries Experiencing Serious Drought and/or Desertification, Particularly in Africa* (UN Document No. A/AC.241/27, 33 I.L.M. 1328). New York: Author.

DESKILLING

Deskilling, the transfer of a worker's dexterity and tacit knowledge to machine, is a pervasive feature of global labor. The notion of deskilling and the apprehension that it creates in the labor force have a perplexing prehistory in scientific management, the rationalization of time and motion in the premechanized 19th-century labor process called Taylorism. In the 20th century, not only was the brunt of this historical task accomplished, but also deskilling (skill redundancy) and skilling (skill formation) found their organic unity within the dynamics of labor process entwined with advanced technology. Thus, the *differentia specifica*, that is, the specificity, of skill formation relevant to present-day capitalism was born. In other words, critical understanding of the nature and meaning of skill in the contemporary world (and how it is created and destroyed) is a significant task that should be of interest across all social sciences—from public policy, industrial organization, and labor studies to political economy, sociology, and global studies.

The question is what the nature of this dexterity or skill is and how one tends to acquire or lose such a skill in a newly emerging system of skill formation. This question compels us to place the issue in a historical context and envelop the analysis with a well-defined evolutionary investigation. The traditional meaning of *skill* obtains its connotation from the immediate aftermath of the medieval era when the guild system and craft associations of the early modern premanufacturing came to flourish and dominate the sphere of production. These craft (and trade) associations were the forerunners of today's labor unions. The identity of the craft and skill has obtained an inseparable and durable unity, and then, through common usage of the language, has been similarly used in manufacturing, postmanufacturing, and modern and ultramodern production processes.

Neoclassical economists contend that, as technology advances, it correspondingly creates specialized skills that are conducive to, and useful for, further application. Thus, advances in technology are followed by gradual upgrading of education and skills within the economy as a whole. This orthodoxy is more or less replicated by conventional sociologists, as well as like-minded social scientists and education specialists in other disciplines today. In contrast, many neo-Marxian scholars argue that technological change in capitalism causes the continuous deskilling of the workforce, thus resulting in the "polarization" of workers' skills. The focus of these writers is deskilling of crafts, which pertains to the transfer of worker dexterity and skill to a machine, a task that predates the method of skill formation in capitalism proper. Harry Braverman is the quintessential protagonist of this sizable group, and his *Labor and Monopoly Capital* has turned into a source of emulation for many radical economists, heterodox sociologists, and self-proclaimed Marxists in the world. Consequently, the subject of skilling and deskilling of labor has become a contending issue between these two broad schools of thought. And, as it turns out, neither the neoclassical nor the neo-Marxian school offers a germane theory of skills for contemporary capitalism.

Neoclassical economists view skill formation axiomatically and indeed intrinsic to the person of individual worker. For a typical mainstream economist, far from being a social concept, an individual skill in capitalism is considered to be a natural extension of the worker on the job. The notion of skill is treated as an autonomous entity subject to individual choice. The problem of skilling arises only when there is a mismatch in the process, in which case it has to be overcome. This view of skill assumes the worker is in possession of something called "skill" in complete dichotomy from the labor process and whether the worker works or is out of a job. Ironically, the neo-Marxian view subscribes to similar transhistorical thinking and reckons that to begin with a skill, similar to a craft, is intrinsic to the individual worker, which is only subject to diminishing by the unremitting pace of technological change. In other words, this fetishism of skill does not allow these scholars to see that skill is a commodity and that one needs to examine how it is being formed (and destroyed) in capitalism proper. Reading Braverman carefully, such deskilling (i.e., destruction of crafts) does not even know its own limit to be methodically meaningful for modern capitalism proper.

Historically, the training and provision of skills associated with traditional crafts (and trades) were generally under the direction of guilds and subject to their inspection and certification in the preindustrial era. Prior to the industrial revolution, the acquisition of skill, the nature of apprenticeship, and the significance of institutional certification by the guilds all pointedly emphasized the intrinsic property of skills. Under the authority of the guilds, skills were certified, protected, and preserved over the lifetime of their members.

Contrary to the intrinsic view of skills, skill formation in capitalism proper requires the satisfaction of both necessary and sufficient conditions for validation. Being a commodity, skill has its twofold character, namely, use value and exchange value. The necessary condition for the formation of skill is knowledge and ability through appropriate education and training. This stands for the use value of skill, which, despite the intrinsic outlook, is not sufficient to be identified as skill with a definite exchange value; its value can be suddenly diminished to a fraction by the marketplace. Therefore, validation of the market, through mediation of the technology and compulsion of capitalist competition, is an absolute must. This evokes the exchange value of skills.

Thus, far from being an aberration, the proof of universal skill redundancy is in abundance and in growing numbers throughout the advanced capitalist countries. This observable fact is so widespread that it recently made it to the front page of the *New York Times*, where an airline captain was given a 50% pay cut for the same "skill" he had on the same job. Hence, skills in this *differentia specifica* mode of production are neither natural, hereditary, certified-proof, and immutable nor even the autonomous (personal) property of those who perceive possessing them. Here, skilling and deskilling are extrinsic to the individual worker and intrinsic to capitalist dynamics. Incessant capitalist competition and cheapening of labor power through frequent organizational restructuring and adoption of latest technology are the constant in this equation.

By virtue of further advances in technology, once newer skills replace the old ones, the workforce will become the target of skill validation/invalidation in the labor process. Newly hired workers may have a choice in acquisition of knowledge and training in order to satisfy the necessary conditions for authentication of the use value of their skills. Yet, these workers have no control over extrinsic conditions that shape the configuration of newly demanded skills. The change in technology tends to set the stage for validation (or invalidation) of these newly developed skills and, in due time, will complete yet another round of redundancy and start the creation of newer skills in the fast-paced, hypercompetitive, universally uncertain world of today. The primary consequence of all this is the tendency toward universal contingency of labor, a widespread phenomenon, despite the acquisition of quality education and training by the workers. The focal point here is the embedded ramification and universal effects of preemptive technology across the global landscape. That is why the word *overqualified* has lately found its copious usage within normal conversation of the contemporary age. This raises a critical need for never-ending education and reeducation, training and retraining in order to respond to perpetual redundancy of workers and their skills at all levels of economic activity. Similarly, it opens an ingenious and far-reaching perspective on the effect of the bulging number of unemployed and underemployed—a cautionary tale that offers a realistic approach to economic policy, crisis management, and other challenges in the field of global studies.

Cyrus Bina

See also Investments; International Labour Organization (ILO); Knowledge Management Systems; Knowledge Production Systems; Leisure; Manufacturing Sector; Work

Further Readings

Becker, G. S. (1964). *Human capital*. Chicago: University of Chicago Press.

Bina, C. (2005). Industrielle Reservearmee [The Industrial Reserve Army]. In H. von Wolfgang & F. Haug (Eds.), *Historisch-kritisches Wörterbuch des Marxismus: Band 6/II. Imperium bis Justiz* (pp. 1003–1011). Berlin, Germany: Argument-Verlag.

Bina, C., Clements, L., & Davis, C. (Eds.). (1996). *Beyond survival: Wage labor in the late twentieth century*. Armonk, NY: Sharpe.

Bina, C., & Davis, C. (1996). Wage labor and global capital: Global competition and the universalization of the labor movement. In C. Bina, L. Clements, & C. Davis (Eds.), *Beyond survival: Wage labor in the late twentieth century* (pp. 19–47). Armonk, NY: Sharpe.

Bina, C., & Davis, C. (2000). Globalization, technology, and skill formation in capitalism. In R. Baiman, H. Boushey, & D. Saunders (Eds.), *Political economy and contemporary capitalism* (pp. 193–202). Armonk, NY: Sharpe.

Bina, C., & Davis, C. (2008). Contingent labor and omnipotent capital: The open secret of political economy. *Political Economy Quarterly, 4*, 166–211.

Bina, C., & Finzel, B. D. (2005). Skill formation, outsourcing, and craft unionism in air transport. *Global Economy Journal, 5*(1). Retrieved from http://www.bepress.com/gej/vol5/iss1/4

Braverman, H. (1974). *Labor and monopoly capital*. New York: Monthly Review Press.

Griliches, Z. (1969). Capital-skill complementarity. *Review of Economics and Statistics, 51*, 465–468.

Schumpeter, J. A. (1928). The instability of capitalism. *Economic Journal, 38*, 361–386.

Uchitelle, L. (2009, October 14). Still on the job, but making only half as much. *New York Times*, pp. 1, 20.

DETERRENCE

Deterrence, the use of a punitive threat to keep someone from taking an unwanted action, is an important feature of international security matters, including security management by organizations like the UN Security Council and the North Atlantic Treaty Organization (NATO). Thus, it is an important topic in global studies. This entry defines and describes deterrence, reviews its role in the Cold War era and its importance today, outlines deterrence theory, traces the deterrence strategies that have been employed, and compares criticisms of deterrence and deterrence theory with evidence on their effects.

Description

Deterrence is part of many relationships from child-rearing to legal systems, but it is most prominent today in international politics and global studies. Some analysts see deterrence as threatening significant harm by *retaliation* to prevent an attack, and they distinguish it from *defense*, intended to physically prevent an attack from being successful. This is incorrect; a stout defense can do great harm by turning the attackers' efforts into a failure and their costs into a waste. Many analysts distinguish deterrence from *compellence*—threatening harm if an opponent continues doing something or to get it to start to do something (as opposed to avoiding something). This distinction is analytically useful, helping show that compellence is harder to achieve—the opponent must more openly give in, which is harder to accept. But it is not very useful otherwise. In serious conflicts, each party often feels it is defending itself—is practicing deterrence—while the other side is practicing compellence. Or a party will practice deterrence at one point in a conflict and compellence at another.

Deterrence is commonly employed. Its long history is reflected in the Roman adage "If you want peace, prepare for war." Its importance in global studies starts with the fact that it is at the core of the venerable balance of power approach to international politics. Whereas it is now often thought of as a strategy for avoiding war, in international politics, deterrence has regularly involved threatening a war (or starting one) to prevent some unwanted action. It is associated with threatening a military response to prevent an attack, but the harm threatened can be of other sorts, like economic sanctions.

Nuclear Deterrence

What brought deterrence to great prominence—an object of high policy and intense scrutiny—was the development of nuclear weapons in World War II. This stimulated fear of future catastrophic nuclear wars or blackmail by threats of nuclear attacks. A disturbing prospect was how nuclear weapons could inflict devastating surprise attacks. All this would mean a nuclear arms race and profound insecurity. However, a suggestion was made just after World War II that the worst of these outcomes might be prevented by using nuclear threats for deterrence—to deter wars by what Winston Churchill called a "balance of terror." In less than a decade, deterrence was thought of as a grand strategy for preventing major wars.

It was given urgent and intense study due to the Cold War; the Soviet Union's development of nuclear weapons; and fear that, as a result, East and West would soon have potent incentives to use nuclear weapons for attacks, including surprise preemptive attacks that would preclude any military response. This made World War III all too likely; the challenge was to prevent it. Peaceful East-West reconciliation, general disarmament, world government, or a highly effective United Nations seemed illusory. Nuclear deterrence was therefore seized on, starting in the 1950s, to turn capacities for war into a pillar of peace. It became the bulwark of national security for the superpowers, Britain, France, and China, and later for Israel, India, and Pakistan, as well as for the many governments protected by the superpowers. All these governments, indeed the world, bet their existence on nuclear deterrence.

Deterrence Theory

Studying deterrence, particularly nuclear deterrence, was conducted primarily by developing a theory of deterrence, and implementing deterrence was through application of various deterrence strategies. Deterrence theorists initially sought to explain how deterrence worked or failed by understanding how policymakers behaved in deterrence situations. Other studies focused on varying sorts of deterrence confrontations or on deterrence in different instances of intense rivalry to test and refine the theory.

The theory was developed by assuming that actors in (usually) a dyadic deterrence situation—one wanted, or each wanted, to deter the other—were rational, and by emphasizing that the actors were in an interdependent decision situation, the outcome would be shaped by the interactions of both of their decisions, so neither unilaterally controlled it. The theory indicated how rational governments should act in those situations: which steps would best serve deterrence stability (avoiding war) and which would pose serious risks of disaster.

The theory employed the following concepts:

Unacceptable damage—the prospective level of harm from deterrer defenses or retaliation that will make an opponent decide not to attack

Deterrence threat—promising what the attacker will consider unacceptable harm

First-strike capability—the ability to attack so effectively that the other side can do little or no harm in response, neither defend itself nor retaliate

Second-strike capability—the ability to do unacceptable damage despite suffering the opponent's most effective possible attack

General deterrence—a threat to do unacceptable harm to convince another actor to not even contemplate, and make no real preparation for, an attack

Immediate deterrence—a threat to do unacceptable harm when another government has prepared for, and is poised to launch, an attack, a crisis

Thus, deterrence involves threatening unacceptable damage in responding to an attack, thereby causing the opponent to decide not to attack. It is a psychological relationship; the opponent is persuaded to refrain from attacking. *Mutual deterrence* is when both sides threaten in this way such that both are persuaded not to attack. Deterrence is escalation control under trying conditions—preventing the escalation of a conflict into a war or a war into a larger one, when the actors are angry, suspicious, and fearful and find communication difficult.

The theory explained when a deterrence relationship exists (what the elements of the situation are), what makes deterrence work, and what can cause it to break down. Deterrence takes place when the threat of unacceptable harm is the prime reason an attack does not occur. There is no deterrence, for example, when the other side has no intent to attack—the United States never deters Canada, and vice versa.

What makes a deterrence threat work? First, the threat should be reasonably clear in stating what the opponent must not do and what the punishment will be if it does. It should be clearly delivered and clearly perceived and understood. Next, the threat must be credible—the opponent must believe the deterrer has the ability and determination to carry it out. Next, the opponent must be vulnerable to the deterrer's response. Finally, the opponent must calculate that the harm it will receive makes it not worthwhile to attack. In mutual deterrence, these things apply for both sides.

This makes it possible to figure out what can make deterrence fail. First, the threat may be ambiguous, leading to a mistaken judgment by the opponent about the consequences of an attack. Or the threat could lack credibility. Or the opponent could be irrational and therefore misread or misjudge the threat. Or the opponent might have, or believe that it has, succeeded in reducing or eliminating its vulnerability to the deterrer's threatened response. Thus, deterrence is not a simple matter of issuing fierce threats, particularly if allowance has to be made, as analysts eventually tried to do, for the effects on decision makers of the stress of a severe conflict, including feelings of hostility, suspicion, fear, and anger or a militaristic overconfidence.

The theory emphasized that nuclear weapons would be ideal for preemptive attacks and how, in a serious crisis, each side's incentive to try such an attack would be great. The closer each felt it was to a first-strike capability, the more unstable deterrence would be. This made Cold War deterrence even more complicated because technological change kept generating new kinds of possible first-strike capabilities—ballistic missiles that would arrive so fast the other side's bombers would be caught on the ground, submarine-based ballistic missiles that could be stealthily moved close to the enemy to cut warning time even further, missile accuracy improvements that made even fortified targets vulnerable, missile defense systems, ways to paralyze command and control arrangements, and others. All contributed to the *stability problem*, to

deterrence failing to prevent, even inciting, escalation of a conflict into a war or a greater war.

Analysts soon detected additional aspects of the stability problem. Of obvious concern was any proliferation of nuclear weapons, as that would generate more decision makers able to deliberately instigate a nuclear war, be irrational, display serious misperceptions, and so on. Other possibilities included accidental or other unauthorized firings of nuclear weapons due to such things as misperceived orders, nuclear war being secretly started by third parties, or by escalation of an ordinary conflict into a nuclear war. Under various conditions, a deterrence relationship, particularly nuclear deterrence, might be "delicate" rather than robust.

The stability problem was disturbing and stimulated important responses. Arms control has been the most significant. Like deterrence, arms control is an old idea that gained great prominence in the nuclear age. The basic concept involves steps, unilaterally or in cooperation with others, to limit the costs and harmful consequences stemming from the ongoing existence of arms and military forces. Several starting points in modern arms control thinking were associated with deterrence, especially nuclear deterrence. One was the assumption that disarmament was impractical—military capabilities were not about to disappear. A second was that arms and military forces developed to provide deterrence could also be quite harmful, like the costs of an arms race or when arms contributed to deterrence instability. The third assumption was that governments relying on mutual deterrence in the Cold War, as rational actors, could cooperate when necessary to restrain the costs and harmful consequences involved, in spite of their conflict, because they had a common interest in doing so. This was quite an innovative idea.

Strictly speaking, deterrence is a subset of arms control—it limits the costs and harmful consequences of arms by preventing attacks and wars. However, modern arms control emerged mainly in response to the stability problem in deterrence, as a way to make deterrence safer and less costly. Arms control became a crucial part of the superpowers' mutual deterrence and was readily extended to lesser conflicts as well. Arms control thinking was influential in promoting a wide range of activities, including the following:

- Unilateral steps to make one's nuclear weapons extremely difficult to seize and resistant to being exploded by accident or by an unauthorized party
- Unilateral steps to monitor the mental stability of people who worked with or controlled nuclear weapons
- Bilateral or multilateral agreements to limit the creation and deployment of weapons ideal for preemptive attack (offensive systems) or that could facilitate one (like defensive systems that reduced the effects of an opponent's retaliation)
- Agreement to ban new weapons that would have threatened deterrence instability or intensified the arms race at great cost but no greater security
- Agreement to ban nuclear testing everywhere but underground, to prevent damage from the radioactivity released
- Agreement to withhold assistance to others in acquiring dangerous weapon systems and to pressure them if they tried to do so
- Agreement to restrict behavior, one's own or that of friends and allies, that could provoke a crisis or war or make it more difficult to control

These measures and others were adopted during the Cold War and became part of the statesman's toolkit. They are widely employed today to deal with conflicts in international politics and inside states. Arms control concerns today provide much of the opposition to missile defense programs and some support for them as well (for offering protection against accidental missile launches).

An important aspect of the stability problem was the *credibility problem* (without credibility, deterrence would not work) and a related *stability-instability paradox*. In a mutual deterrence relationship, each side had a second-strike capability. So if one side launched a limited attack to exploit a weakness of the other side and threaten the target government with unacceptable damage if it took a major military response, given the danger of escalation to a huge war with terrible costs, why would a rational government escalate? That would only increase the damage it suffered. If so, then its threat to retaliate would not be credible, and deterrence could readily fail. This was particularly worrisome in *extended deterrence*, whereby one government threatens to harm another if it attacks a third. If the deterrer and attacker have a mutual deterrence relationship, why would either ever attack the other and possibly suffer great harm as a result in retaliation for its attack on a third party, when the harm done by the attacker had only been to the third party? Again, the deterrer's threat might therefore not be credible, and deterrence could fail. The consequences for the deterrer once deterrence failed would be unfortunate whether it responded or not.

Another possible result of the credibility problem was that if two parties could deter each other from launching huge attacks, they might feel free to conduct a lower level war because of expectations that the war would not escalate; neither party's threat to do so would be credible. But the point of deterrence is to keep from being attacked at all. Here, mutual deterrence stability at a higher level might encourage war at a low level. This is the stability-instability paradox. Sure enough, states with nuclear weapons have sometimes been attacked anyway at lower levels, not only by states with nuclear weapons but by some without any. India and Pakistan had several serious lower level clashes after they developed nuclear weapons, which some observers believe occurred because their nuclear weapons provided confidence the fighting would not escalate very far.

The credibility problem has provoked other responses that had major effects. One solution adopted by the United States and, to a lesser extent, the Soviet Union was to create numerous alliances so that extended deterrence commitments would be clear and, being public and official, would be harder, politically and psychologically, not to uphold. Unfortunately, political damage was no match for the prospective damage from a major war, particularly a nuclear war, so the credibility of extended deterrence remained questionable. Another solution was for a superpower to put its forces right in the way of any attack on an ally, making the attack a direct assault on the deterrer too. Surely the United States, for example, would fight once its own forces had been attacked. This was possible, but it was easy to see that retaliating for an attack if that meant risking a nuclear war was not rational, so alliance deterrence was still not guaranteed to be credible. Another suggested solution was to have the deterrer look irrational or be irrational, but that could lead to greater fear and greater willingness to engage.

The credibility problem has never been solved. The solution eventually used for nuclear deterrence in the Cold War provided only modest comfort. It was asserted that, if a government threatened nuclear retaliation for being attacked, it might not be rational to carry out retaliation, but the government might not be rational at that point, and if it did retaliate, the attacker would have taken a terribly risky gamble and lost. Thus, threats of retaliation from nuclear powers had inherent credibility. This is why, in theory, states like Iran or North Korea today could use small nuclear forces to deter a great power with large nuclear forces—it would be irrational for them to carry out a threat to use those weapons, but that might happen, so the great power might be deterred.

Strategies for Deterrence

Deterrence was, of course, more than a theory. It has been pursued using a variety of strategies. The main nuclear-weapons-based strategies are the following:

Minimum Deterrence—having enough second-strike capabilities to do unacceptable damage to an opponent after its attack, but little more. The simplest form is having a small number of survivable nuclear weapons targeted on an opponent's cities to do maximum harm. China, Britain, and France basically use this strategy now for any powerful opponent; so do India and Pakistan in facing each other or, for India, China.

Massive Retaliation—having a capacity to virtually destroy an opponent in retaliation. This requires more nuclear weapons than does minimum deterrence. It was used in the 1950s by the United States, USSR, Britain, and France. This is presumably Israel's ultimate strategy vis-à-vis its enemies in the Middle East.

Mutually Assured Destruction—deliberately tolerating, even helping maintain, a mutual deterrence relationship based on second-strike capabilities. This was the official strategy of the United States and the Soviet Union from the early 1970s to the end of the Cold War.

Counterforce War-Fighting—having forces and plans for defeating the opponent's forces in a nuclear war.

Of particular appeal is the ability to destroy the opponent's nuclear weapons before they are used, by a preemptive attack or combining a preemptive attack with strong defenses. The strategy can also involve launching on warning when evidence indicates the enemy attack is on the way, ensuring retaliation and in hopes of preventing any further damage after that attack has arrived. Deterrence can be sought by way of a strategy for fighting limited nuclear wars. For years during the Cold War, the superpowers had elaborate plans to destroy as many of each other's nuclear forces as soon as possible in a war, and the United States still plans this way vis-à-vis any potential enemy. Not long after the Cold War Russia adopted a partial launch on warning strategy vis-à-vis the United States.

The superpowers did not publicize their counterforce war-fighting plans to avoid indicating how poised they were to attempt preemptive attacks, which deterrence theory said was destabilizing and thus dangerous. But those plans were driven by the logic involved in adapting the classic duty of armed forces—protect the state and nation—to the nuclear age. Military logic dictated that, for a possible nuclear war, the necessary military capacity was a first-strike capability, which is what the U.S. and Soviet armed forces pursued. The public posture, affirmed in arms control agreements, was mutual assured destruction, whereas the military effort on each side was first-strike counterforce targeting oriented.

At the nonnuclear level, deterrence by effective defenses has been somewhat more feasible, and many states have maintained substantial military capabilities for defense over the years. However, defenses can be porous, so some have tried to supplement defense with retaliation. North Korea, for instance, promises a crushing defense if attacked but also promises to destroy much of Seoul by missiles and artillery barrages. However, some governments with a similar strategy end up in conflicts where deterrence is conducted by repeated retaliatory measures, low level blows, and counterblows, which is not very satisfactory. This is true of Israel's relations with some of its neighbors, the India-Pakistan relationship, and the relationship between Turkey and the Kurds in Turkey and northern Iraq.

Some states rest conventional-level deterrence on the threat to follow an attack by winning the war that results. During the Cold War, this was termed *flexible response* by the United States—being ready to fight wars successfully at all levels, including various kinds of nuclear wars. The United States remains the best example of this now. It is officially committed to maintaining more powerful forces than any possible opponent(s), and it pursues deterrence based on escalation dominance—the ability to escalate the use of force until it wins. For some years now, the United States and South Korea have threatened that a significant North Korean attack would result in invasion of the North to eliminate the regime and North Korea. During the Cold War, NATO's strategy, the opposite of flexible response (although that is what it was called) was to put up a good fight in a conventional war with the Soviet bloc and, once it was losing, escalate to nuclear weapons. This is a strategy a small country that acquires nuclear weapons might adopt against much stronger states today.

Deterrence remains important in international politics today but less so for the great powers. Deterrence relationships among them are muted because they do not expect wars or even deep crises among them, but they retain nuclear weapons and significant other forces just in case. States in serious conflicts plan on being attacked and/or attacking their opponents—Israel, Iran, India, and Pakistan, among others, work at deterrence. Certain states have felt the United States is hostile and might attack; these states include North Korea, Iran, Iraq under Saddam Hussein, Syria, and Libya until well into the 1990s. With the United States attacking Iraq and Afghanistan and making preliminary preparations for attacking North Korea in 1994, these states were concerned about deterrence.

Deterrence is also now a task for certain collective actors—organizations that can be used to uphold the general welfare via force when the members think this is necessary. They include the UN Security Council, the Organization of American States or the African Union, NATO, and others. They use deterrence to discourage aggression, get warring governments to stop fighting, halt civil wars, and get governments to cease behavior regarded as threatening international peace and security (proliferation activities, violations of human rights). The harm threatened includes economic, diplomatic, and political isolation; trial by international tribunals of leaders and others for

crimes against humanity; and the use of force. This is deterrence for international governance, and governance is of major concern in global studies.

In the second decade after the Cold War, the George W. Bush administration in the United States helped make deterrence prominent again. It asserted that important security threats (e.g., terrorists and rogue states) facing the United States and the international community could not readily be dealt with by deterrence. These opponents are too intense and risk taking, openly irrational, or so highly motivated as to be suicidal and thus impervious to threats. Numerous analyses have therefore emerged on this problem. The most influential suggestions so far are to emphasize deterrence by defense, confronting terrorists with high risks of failure, and retaliating against states and others who assist terrorists to curb their support, mobility, financing, and ability to hide. For terrorists with elaborate plans for building ideal states and societies, they might be deterred by threats to those plans. As for rogue states, the United States has tried everything from invading to deterrence to engagement and is not satisfied with the results; deterrence looks no worse, but no better, than the other options.

Another development is recent U.S. efforts to make deterrence efforts better fit the targets, often referred to as *tailored deterrence*. The idea, first broached during the Cold War, is that leaders, elites, and political systems respond differently to different threats and the combining of threats with other measures, and they respond differently depending on the issues and stakes involved, so deterrence efforts should be designed accordingly. This would require greater information for conducting what would be even more complicated deterrence efforts in the future.

Assessing Deterrence

There are numerous complaints about deterrence theory and deterrence. During the Cold War, deterrence was often called a barrier to negotiations and other steps toward peace and security because it promoted arms buildups and threats, which sustained climates of fear and hostility, and because negotiations and other conciliatory measures were then disparaged for conveying an image of being "soft" and weakening deterrence. Deterrence was also blamed for freezing conflicts—behind the shelter of deterrence, too many governments would avoid the difficult steps needed to end conflicts. It was feared that the Cold War, in particular, would go on like that indefinitely.

Although deterrence often had such an effect, it also led to a good deal of security management by the superpowers jointly and separately. The arms control agreements and elaborate negotiations to produce them contributed to the emergence of a modest regime for security management to keep the Cold War contained and keep governments from disrupting stability. That regime and the experience with it made it easier to continue and expand the management of global security after the Cold War. Deterrence also inhibited progress by other means toward peace and security at times, but in the end it did not prevent the political resolution of the Cold War or an end to the division of Europe, the Cold War, and the communist governments in Europe. Politics and political change proved more important and more potent.

Deterrence was also criticized because its ultimate manifestation, the vast superpower nuclear arsenals plus moves by other states to gain nuclear weapons, seemed to seek security by perching the world on the edge of a cliff. Governments had in hand the capacity to kill virtually everyone, and there was no guarantee they would never do so. For years the superpowers had a total of more than 50,000 nuclear weapons, most much larger than the atomic bombs that destroyed Hiroshima and Nagasaki in 1945. The financial costs of that deterrence were astronomical, many trillions of dollars, a cost U.S. president Dwight D. Eisenhower called a great "theft" from the worthy purposes on which that money could have been spent.

Over time, governments at least partially embraced this view. Thus, when the Cold War ended, the leading participants turned almost immediately to sharply reducing reliance on deterrence, particularly nuclear deterrence. Huge cuts in strategic nuclear forces of the United States, the USSR, Britain, and France were initiated and still continue. Even larger cuts in theater and battlefield nuclear weapons, including those for wars at sea, were agreed to. Whereas some of the weapons were put in storage, most have been destroyed. The world's nuclear arsenals are getting older, for the most part, with little production of new weapons and delivery vehicles, and little nuclear testing, with some concerns being expressed about whether the weapons will remain reliable. The nuclear powers' conventional military forces were also sharply cut, and the world's annual arms sales, which they dominate, shrank considerably. There are far more deterrent, and related, efforts by the international community now to contain or end internal conflicts around the world, and significant wars between states have almost disappeared.

During the Cold War, deterrence theory was repeatedly criticized as inadequate. It was said to be unreliable because it assumed rationality to model deterrence while decision making is beset by cognitive, organizational, and political barriers to it. This critique was bolstered by evidence from case studies that decision makers are affected by those barriers. This influential critique helped encourage the retreat from deterrence among the great powers described earlier. However, some analysts, using case studies, have concluded that decision makers in deterrence situations often behave as rationality dictates, that their supposed "errors" are usually caused by mistakes in the application of deterrence, such as sending inconsistent signals or not reinforcing deterrence threats with appropriate actions. So this issue is not fully resolved.

There have always been criticisms that nuclear deterrence and arms control, including nonproliferation efforts, are part of a superpower, now great-power, conspiracy. Nuclear weapons give the great powers special leverage and a special status; the nonproliferation efforts seek to preserve their monopoly and keep others from being able to deter great-power interventions in their affairs. This is why the five original nuclear powers have never lived up to their obligation under the Nuclear Non-Proliferation Treaty to move toward complete nuclear disarmament. The main opposing view is that states pursue weapons of mass destruction primarily for security, aggrandizement, and ambitions for increased status, not because of the supposed injustice of the nonproliferation regime; they would not readily abandon their weapons and related programs even if everyone else did. It is also asserted, by the United States and some others, that U.S. extended nuclear deterrence keeps many countries, like Japan, from acquiring nuclear weapons, an important contribution to global peace and security.

Serious criticisms of deterrence theory cite disturbing gaps between the theory and decision makers' behavior in the Cold War. Nuclear deterrence proponents often cited concerns about credibility and stability to disparage pursuing détente, arms control, and political settlement and that probably prevented the Cold War from dissolving sooner. Then there was the way the superpowers ignored deterrence theory in seeking first-strike capabilities, as the theory's logical approach to stabilizing nuclear deterrence ignored the logic driving the armed forces. Despite the theory and its stress on common interests across the Cold War divide, arms control arrangements were often stymied because the political climate was unaccommodating—the theory left too little room for the inevitable intrusions of politics. Meanwhile, decision makers were often intent on challenging opponents abroad even if those opponents had nuclear weapons—*existential deterrence* did not operate on everyone.

How successful was deterrence, and how successful is it today? Some analysts believe that nuclear deterrence was largely irrelevant in the Cold War; most believe that it contributed something to the long peace among the great powers after World War II, but only a few analysts believe it was so successful that it should spread, that nuclear proliferation is actually good for us. At the conventional level and lower, deterrence is often a failure, and deterrence threats frequently incite defiance and deepen conflicts. There is a well-established view that deterrence is at best a stopgap measure because in itself it does nothing to resolve a conflict. Without conflict resolution, the conflict continues, frustration about that builds, further crises inevitably erupt, there are attempts to design around the deterrence constraints, and success in deterrence becomes harder to achieve. Many analysts believe it is necessary, at minimum, to supplement deterrence with incentives, negotiations, and conflict resolution efforts, and some would like to use those things to replace deterrence entirely. Studies show that adding reassurance efforts and incentives significantly raises the chances for success in deterrence. But there is always the counterassertion that using softer measures often weakens the credibility of deterrence threats and incites further dangerous behavior by opponents, that negotiations can legitimize the opponents' claims and their violent past behavior, and that many opponents really don't want a peaceful resolution because it would require behavior—arms cuts, political reforms, concessions on the issues—that they do not like or politically cannot afford to adopt.

A classic view contrasts a deterrence perspective with a spiral model perspective in basic views about security and finds both highly durable. Proponents of the former say there are always expansionist aggressive governments and ambitious leaders who will use force to get their way unless deterred. The alternative perspective sees governments that are not necessarily aggressive often caught in spiraling suspicions and fears, which deterrence preparations just exacerbate. As deterrence remains an integral part of international politics and global studies, so do complaints that it is unreliable, dangerous, and self-defeating. The disagreement seems very likely to persist.

Patrick M. Morgan

See also Cold War; Global Conflict and Security; Global Governance and World Order; Military; Nuclear Power; War; Wars, World; Weapons

Further Readings

Betts, R. (1987). *Nuclear blackmail and nuclear balance.* Washington, DC: Brookings Institution.

Bundy, M. (1984). Existential deterrence and its consequences. In D. MacLean (Ed.), *The security gamble: Deterrence dilemmas in the nuclear age* (pp. 3–13). Totowa, NJ: Rowman & Littlefield.

Freedman, L. (1981). *The evolution of nuclear strategy.* New York: St Martin's Press.

Ganguly, S., & Haggerty, D. (2005). *Fearful symmetry: India-Pakistan crises in the shadow of nuclear weapons.* Seattle: University of Washington Press.

George, A., & Smoke, R. (1974). *Deterrence in American foreign policy: Theory and practice.* New York: Columbia University Press.

Goldblat, J. (2002). *Arms control: The new guide to negotiations and agreements.* Thousand Oaks, CA: Sage.

Goldstein, A. (2000). *Deterrence and security in the 21st century: China Britain, and France, and the enduring legacy of the nuclear revolution.* Stanford, CA: Stanford University Press.

Harvey, F., & James, P. (2009). Deterrence and compellence in Iraq, 1991–2003: Lessons for a complex paradigm. In T. V. Paul, P. Morgan, & J. Wirtz (Eds.), *Complex deterrence: Strategy in the global age*. Chicago: University of Chicago Press.

Huth, P., & Russett, B. (1990, July). Testing deterrence theory: Rigor makes a difference. *World Politics, 42*, 466–501.

Jervis, R. (1989). *The meaning of the nuclear revolution: Statecraft and the prospect of Armageddon*. Ithaca, NY: Cornell University Press.

Jervis, R., Lebow, R. N., & Stein, J. (Eds.). (1985). *Psychology and deterrence*. Baltimore: Johns Hopkins University Press.

Lebow, R., & Stein, J. (1994). *We all lost the Cold War*. Princeton, NJ: Princeton University Press.

McDonough, D. (2006). *Nuclear superiority: The "new triad" and the evolution of nuclear strategy*. London: International Institute for Strategic Studies.

Morgan, P. (2003). *Deterrence now*. Cambridge, UK: Cambridge University Press.

Sagan, S., & Waltz, K. (1995). *The spread of nuclear weapons: A debate*. New York: Norton.

Schelling, T. (1960). *The strategy of conflict*. Cambridge, MA: Harvard University Press.

Vasquez, J. (1991). The deterrence myth: Nuclear weapons and the prevention of nuclear war. In C. Kegley Jr. (Ed.), *The long postwar peace: Contending explanations and projections* (pp. 205–223). New York: HarperCollins.

DETERRITORIALIZATION AND RETERRITORIALIZATION

Territoriality is an important feature of globalization because it refers to the changing role of historically specific spatial references in social communication and of spatial framings for social interaction. Deterritorialization refers to the loss of those spatial references, and reterritorialization denotes the reclaiming of those spaces by the communities. Social communities have developed across both centuries and continents through various forms of spatial configuration as regulatory regimes for interaction and self-organization. Territoriality has become the basis for modern state building, which emerged from the attempts of multiple powers to seek zones of exclusive control over sovereignty. While the nation-state is the most prominent arrangement of territoriality, it should not be forgotten that the identification of continents with specific cultures or civilizations is also an important output of the territorialized conceptualization of the world. The concept of "territory" attempts at making congruent, to the greatest degree, the different forms of space—political, economic, cultural, and identity space—and at convincing a community with historical narratives and ethno-national arguments to imagine this space as the most applicable denominator for belonging. What makes a territory effective is the coexistence between structures of dominance—political-administrative institutions, regulation of economic activities, and social processes—and its acceptance as a framework for loyalties. As bordered and bounded political space, territory is based on a frontier that separates outside territories and the lands inside.

History of Territoriality

Territoriality is a socio-spatial formation that emerged relatively late in modern history and has changed at several historical junctures. Territoriality replaced, on the one hand, historical configurations that are often described as imperial. These forms are based on larger transitional zones between neighboring societies without clear-cut borderlines and an interwoven network of rulership, property, and loyalty regulating the relationship between different subjects, which are unaware of a universalized notion of sovereignty shared by all members of the community. On the other hand, it has been argued that territoriality is not the last spatial configuration in history, as based on the idea that post-territoriality will emerge. Whether one shares the concept of post-territoriality or not (obviously the described transformation is not yet completed), the discussion about it indicates that territoriality is a historically specific formation, slowly becoming a model for the social organization of the world from the mid-17th century onward and dominant since the mid-19th century up until the 1970s.

However, it is necessary to make two reservations. On the one hand, for a certain time, territoriality was, in the form of the modern nation-state, capable of integrating all alternative spatial configurations into a hierarchical pattern. The regional became the subnational, and border-transcending activities were interpreted as international. Remaining imperial patterns were integrated, often in contradictory ways, into new forms of national self-organization of colonial powers, with strategies of assimilation and integration being complemented by eventually granting gradual citizenship to the colonial populations. Former networks of trade and communication—which were much more instrumental between and for individual places often located within different territories—became integrated during the processes of industrialization of national economies and thus connected to their hinterlands. Nevertheless, each of these alternative spatial configurations continued to exist and act as a potential for different regimes of spatial organization. On the other hand, although territoriality has been employed as a model in all parts of the world, the emergence of well-functioning nation-states cannot be observed everywhere. Noticeably, counter-rotating tendencies have been at work, and their representatives—from inside and from outside—have remained strong enough to weaken the process of a complete territorialization.

Whereas authors who insist that globalization is a very recent phenomenon claim that territorialization and globalization are directly opposite processes, proponents of global history argue that territorialization was at times a strategy for winning back control over ongoing processes of globalization. The acceleration of speed in communication, the growing importance of emerging world markets, and the intensification of long-distance migration in the 19th century provoked the search for new sources of authority and coordination in reaction to this "global condition" (Geyer & Bright). This global condition created a new world order in which societies were condemned to integrate into these global processes while attempting to maintain as much sovereignty as possible.

In a dialectical way, the permanent challenge of deterritorializing factors at work was answered by a series of reterritorializing strategies. The increase of border-transcending mobility of people, capital, goods, and ideas—which emerged from the growing importance of the worldwide division of labor and new terms of trade—provoked attempts to better control these movements. Suitably, the concept of citizenship and the invention of the passport, for example, allowed for more efficient control of migrants and of defining who belongs directly to what territory. New regulations for border control, advanced strategies of statistical data collection, and the emergence of national banking systems allowed national elites to gain control over foreign direct investment and the influx of goods, while profiting from these instruments to fine-tune the import-export balance. The transnational circulation of new cultural patterns became an attribute of modernity; these new cultural patterns were based on the mobility of artists and scholars as well as the attention given to cultural innovation in other parts of the world. At the same time, nation-state building went hand in hand with harsh confrontations of national styles and characters. Accordingly, cultural transfers from the mid-19th to the mid-20th centuries intensified enormously but ended often in a strong national, if not nationalistic, appropriation of cultural elements whose foreign origin is carefully hidden.

The crucial relevance of space in all its forms—such as geography, social action, identity, political decision, and economic entanglement—concerns a dialectical condition that is marked by entanglements and attempts to control and regulate these entanglements. In the economic and financial domains, these can be examined through the currents of trade, investment, and circulation of technological and commercial knowledge by international corporations, transnational cartels, and governments. However, it is not only a matter of flows but rather how these flows lead to efforts of control and profit for individual market participants. With this perspective, the question of adequate space comes into play as based on economic geography, which is visible in strategies for expansion into markets that have not yet been entered or for the defense of markets that are already saturated. A similar relation of flow and control is evident in the political realm. Collaboration with international regimes for the regulation of transnational problems is confronted by attempts to find appropriate forms of government that preserve agency and guarantee sovereignty under conditions of global interconnectedness. The interplay exists on the cultural level as well, which is visible in various forms of cultural transfer and the appropriation of foreign cultural patterns. At the same time, this increasing awareness of identity problems led to the reterritorialization of cultures.

Orientation

All of these processes focus on the question of orientation in space, that is, the demarcation of a territorial core that must be balanced against entanglements with remote places. The history of territorialization calls attention to those spatial constellations that have become especially effective in producing this contradictory balance. The nation-state has indeed proven its capacity to organize power, preserve sovereignty, and enlarge and maximize profit in an entangled world market. This model, instituted in large parts of the world between 1840 and 1880, was so successful that the most influential powers of the era managed to bring important parts of the globe under colonial dominance in the form of imperial expansion. While nationalizing their societies at home, they further used the instruments of imperialistic politics. The expansion of the principle of sovereign nationalization collided, however, with the attempt of the colonial powers to hold on to their auxiliary imperial spaces during the "Wilsonian Moment" of 1918 (Manela). The universalistic formulation of the principle of self-determination of people provoked, in central and eastern Europe above all, attempts to nationalize society and economy in the newly emerging states, while conflict with the multiethnic legacy of the empires inevitably ended in the catastrophic failure of minority policies. Growing isolationism in the United States, at the same time, went hand in hand with a much more restrictive regulation of migration and indicated another strand of reterritorialization. In parts of the colonial world, national movements intensified and started to formulate a policy of autonomy and independence, which resulted later—after liberation from colonial rule—in respective economic and political strategies.

The outcome of World War II, which was provoked by the expansionist ambitions of the Axis powers, was another pattern of reterritorialization. In turn, the Cold War contained the deterritorializing tendencies both in the East and in the West within the two blocs, while separating them from one another. Although the aspect of reterritorialization became more visible over time, it was not completely dominant owing to the fact that from the 1970s onward the transcendence of political and ideological boundaries facilitated economic cooperation and vice versa. Technological innovation in the spheres of communication and production propelled deterritorialization forward. This process accelerated with the United States and China opening a new chapter of economic integration with Deng Xiaoping's turn to market mechanisms and special economic zones after 1982, and Mikhail Gorbachev's declaring disarmament a priority of the Soviet Union over the usual patterns of Cold War confrontation. The revolutions of 1989 and the subsequent global integration are the result of that ongoing deterritorialization. Recent reactions to the economic crisis of 2008 led to a new demand for state action, now coordinated and partly integrated at both regional and global levels. New regionalisms and institutions, such as the G-20, complement the existing system of international organizations within the UN system. At the same time, global commodity chains gain increasing importance in the economic sphere, while mobility and communication between cultures expand. It seems as if a new regime of spatial configurations—consisting of already approved forms and of recent and not yet fully established arrangements—emerges from the dialects of deterritorialization and reterritorialization. To conclude from the historical examples as well as from the observation of current trends, it can be observed that at all times both tendencies are at work, that various actors compete for forms of control over global flows, and that there are specific arenas and moments when the battle for a new regime of spatial configurations becomes more intense and globally synchronized. Consequently, they may be called critical junctures of globalization, indicating that they are exceptionally crucial for the further development of a globally integrated world.

Matthias Middell

See also Borders; Conquests; Diasporas; Empires; Global Terminology; Imperialism; Land Use; Landless Persons; Migration; Regional Identities; Regionalism; Tribal Identities

Further Readings

Brenner, N. (1999). Beyond state-centrism? Space, territoriality, and geographical scale in globalization studies. *Theory and Society, 28,* 39–78.

Castells, M. (1996). *The rise of the network society: Economy, society and culture.* Malden, MA: Blackwell.

Chandler, A., Jr., & Mazlish, B. (2005). *Leviathans. Multinational corporations and the new global history.* Cambridge, UK: Cambridge University Press.

Diehl, P. F. (1997). *The politics of global governance: International organizations in an interdependent world.* Boulder, CO: Lynne Rienner.

Döring, J., & Thielmann, T. (Eds.). (2008). *Spatial turn: Das Raumparadigma in den Kultur- und Sozialwissenschaften* [Spatial turn: The spatial paradigm in the cultural and social sciences]. Bielefeld, Germany: Transcript Verlag.

Geyer, M., & Bright, C. (1995). World history in a global age. *American Historical Review, 100*(4), 1034–1060.

Hoerder, D. (2002). *Cultures in contact: World migrations in the second millennium.* Durham, NC: Duke University Press.

Lewis, M. W., & Wigen, K. E. (1997). *The myth of the continents: A critique of metageography.* Berkeley: University of California Press.

Manela, E. (2007). *The Wilsonian moment: Self-determination and the international origin of anticolonial nationalism.* New York: Oxford University Press.

Middell, M., & Naumann, K. (2010). Global history and the spatial turn: From the impact of area studies to the study of critical junctures of globalisation. *Journal of Global History, 5,* 149–170.

Ó Tuathail, G., & Dalby, S. (1998). *Rethinking geopolitics.* London: Routledge.

Pries, L. (2001). *New transnational social spaces. International migration and transnational companies in the early twenty-first century.* London: Routledge.

Sassen, S. (2006). *Territory, authority, rights: From medieval to global assemblages.* Princeton, NJ: Princeton University Press.

Warf, B., & Arias, S. (2008). *The spatial turn: Interdisciplinary perspectives.* London: Routledge.

Dharma

Dharma is a central Hindu socioreligious precept that may be defined as order, the moral order, or duty, as well as both religious and customary law. It is ontologically conjoined and mutually informed by other Hindu cosmological principles such as karma (action or fate) and moksha, which is the concept of salvation or release from samsara, the cycling of existence in the phenomenal world. Dharma is related closely to these key tenets in lived social practices, which, in the era of increased globalization, global societies, and transnationalism, are continually transforming to accommodate encounters with the new without dispensing with the traditional.

In this entry, dharma will be foregrounded against and juxtaposed with some of these other precepts, in particular, karma. Dharma will be considered also in terms of the elasticity the concept has demonstrated in the past and continues to exhibit in the present in accommodating new ideas owing to the demands exerted on it through movement into either different historical epochs or transplantation into different geosocial fields. Its ancient tradition of malleability will be approached through reference to classical texts. This capacity for innovation that continues in the present will be illuminated through examples from popular culture, namely, Indian cinematic resolutions of current sociocultural dilemmas. These often arise out of the circumstances of the large Indian diaspora or are posed by effects of globalization on culture within the India of late modernity that are still being flexibly resolved within a "context" that is acceptably compliant with dharma. Conversely, dharma's conceptual permeation of, and effect on, Western popular consciousness through literature and popular culture will be considered as well. An introduction to dharma would be incomplete without mention of either the place of caste or the differing cultural emphases, respectively, between East and West of ideal-typical personhood (i.e., individual vs. collective) given that this discussion is centrally concerned with the globalized situation and transnational experience of many Hindu persons and what these circumstances might offer for such a particular understanding of dharma.

Dharma and Caste

Caste is often misunderstood as being simply the Indian social counterpart—albeit more pronounced and deplored—of class. However, as Louis Dumont has argued, caste has deeply religious and hence heavy moral and ethical dimensions that are enmeshed with concerns of purity and pollution, which are also hierarchized so that the highest caste is considered the most pure and the lowest the most polluted; those who fall outside caste categorization, such as tribal people, are considered beyond the pale altogether. In this, the proper observation of dharma formerly—in ancient times and as canonized in texts of the Veda—almost exclusively meant the proper execution of ritual karma, and this was the exclusive domain of Brahmins (the priest caste). Hence, it also had moral weight and consequences, and the relation between dharma and karma were extrapolated in the later Upanishads wherein proper or improper observation of dharma had the karmic consequence of rebirth into a high or low caste respectively, or ideally, moksha (salvation) from samsara. Thus, dharma connotes considerable moral weight regarding the caste identity that a person bears. Since early in the 20th century, when much agitation for national independence was under way, those at the lowest end, once called Untouchables and now termed *Dalit* ("oppressed"), have also been campaigning in creative ways to resolve their innumerable difficulties. As their situation pertains to the matter of dharma, conversion to Buddhism, Islam, or Christianity has been one means of resolution and one that entails total rejection of the system in which dharma is embedded. Conversely, resort has been made to a tradition called Adi Dharm, an ideology in which Dalits assert their identity as the indigenes of India and thereby carry the originary and hence more legitimate religion: the first dharma. In this philosophy, it is Vedic Aryans—Brahmins (priests), Kshatriya (warriors and kings), and Vaishyas (producers)—who are the usurpers, because they invaded India, destroyed Adi Dharm, forced caste on the inhabitants, and then codified their degradation and servitude.

Dharma as Codified Rules of Conduct

Dharma, as explicitly explicated rules of conduct, has been codified in an ancient tradition of Brahmanical erudition exemplified by the laws of Manu and reaching a zenith in the Dharmasutras, of which four survive. Their most contemporary and authoritative translator and commentator, Patrick Olivelle (2000), asserts that the Brahmin is the "implied subject of most rules" therein

(p. 11). In the Dharmasutra of Āpastamba, the four orders, or dharmas, of life are explicated: the life of the householder, living at the house of the teacher, the life of a sage, and that of a forest hermit. However, most Brahmins are not able to live out the final stages and remain enmeshed in householder dharma and karma. Conversely, the radical ascetic renouncer, who might be of any caste, performs these latter dharmas that the Brahmins claim as their own province. Furthermore, as Jonathan Parry explains, the radical ascetic achieves moksha by inverting dharma and performing acts of adharma; in this he and she aspires to transcend both, thereby realizing the ultimate unity of reality behind all appearances of multiplicity, which in this context, dharma may be seen to uphold.

Olivelle believes that the Dharmasutras' authors were part of vital and often opposing schools that engaged in passionate debate, as demonstrated, for example, by their widely divergent views on the permissibility of widow remarriage and polygyny. The documents that comprise the Dharmasutras reveal that their authors viewed dharma as having a broad range: There were many dharmas that accommodated different families, social and cultural groups, and regions. The authors hence also acknowledge that, despite the orthodox position that dharma is divinely revealed law, it is also customary. This view of different dharmas permits discussion in later Dharmasutras regarding the historical relativity of morality at different epochs; what would be adharmic conduct in present times, such as violence, could be acceptable in ancient periods because, according to Olivelle's translation of Āpastamba's Dharmasutra (2000, pp. xl–xli), "those people had extraordinary power," which corresponded to the superiority of the age (yuga) in which they lived, but to so act in a later period would incur sin. Olivelle accounts for this as a retrospective strategy for "nullifying [transgressions] that are found in the Veda." Olivelle observes that such reasoning preempted the later theory of *yugadharma*, in which each world age has its own dharma suitable for the conditions prevailing at the time. One often hears in Indian communities people bemoaning the current age—the Kaliyuga—as utterly degenerate and thus the temporal condition contributing to largely adharmic conduct, yet which is the custom and so, too, not unparadoxically, the dharma of this age.

Dharma as Customary Practice

Ruth Freed and Stanley Freed observe that in North Indian villages, conduct that contravenes custom debases dharma, and flouting dharma inextricably generates bad karma. The critical example that they give, and which will be pursued henceforth in this entry, is marriage—namely, to form an adharmic marriage alliance, which, in northern custom, means to marry a relative or to marry outside caste. In considering dharma as duty and custom, the exemplar par excellence is marriage for both traditional and diasporic contexts.

In North India, the dharma of the married woman has been and largely continues to be traditionally defined and lived out within prescriptive kinship practices, which are upheld by the principles of purdah or pardah—literally "curtain" or "veil"—expressed in dress, behavior, and seclusion. Purdah in its turn implements and protects the principles of izzat (honor) and saf (purity). Hindu moral (dharmic) values such as purity and impurity can best be understood as coefficient with material substance. Hence, dishonorable conduct or ill treatment of a wife affects the collective moral body of the family and therefore also its karma and dharma. McKim Marriott's theory of the embeddedness of enjoined substance-code in Indian existence and philosophy has been embraced by many scholars. He observed, writing in the 1970s, that only Max Weber and sometimes Louis Dumont recognize that Indian thought unites ideas that in the West are assumed to be dualistic. He stressed that there is a predominant monism in Hindu thought. Marriott (1976) develops his theory of substance-code, which stands for the absolute unity of the corporeal body with dharma, by investigating exchange practices in which transactions and transformations generate power hierarchies and social differentiation in what is no less than people's "preservation and transformation of their own natures" (p. 112). Furthermore, the identity of caste position as enjoined to dharma has to be understood in terms of the particularistic movement of Hindu thought. Hence, actors and actions, as matters of both natural and moral fact, are thought to be of vastly varied and volatile kinds, because transmissions and permutations of substance-code are endlessly occurring in numerous social transactions.

The prime example is the strength of the joint family as an ideal and an actuality as pertaining to marriage practices. This dynamism has formerly been maintained by hierarchical relationships expressed in transactions informed by the tensions of purity and pollution—kanya dan—the gift of a virgin in marriage exemplifying such a transaction.

Dharma in the Diaspora: Resolutions in Popular Culture

Present-day deviation from dharmic forms of the institution of marriage may stem, in part, from migration stemming from the pressures of industrialization, population increase that has resulted in land shortages, and the education of women. These migrations entail an unprecedented influx into cities—Indian and foreign—of large numbers of people whose ancestors had previously lived for generations in rural areas. Added to this upheaval is the growing incidence of fragmentation of traditional familial forms and, hence, the increasing difficulty of observing the appropriate prescriptions for dharmic marriage alliance—that is, alliances according to caste position. Under such stresses, as many people become alienated from their traditional patterns of living, numerous new forms of sociality are emerging in diasporic contexts.

Nevertheless, these manifold new forms of sociality that are continuously emerging often take their shape according to the pattern of preexistent social and religious structures. These new forms are driven and structured by the enduring interdependent relation of such cosmological categories as karma-dharma-moksha—action-order/law-liberation. People who are not living lives of traditional dharma are still driven to resolve their predicaments not only as they pertain to the dilemma of salvation but also in terms of basic survival in various social environments where the structures of support such as kinship are simply not present or not present in the same ways.

South Asian cinema, for which Mumbai's Bollywood is world famous, has imaginatively engaged with themes of dharmic marriage practice ambiguity that provoke worry in their audiences both in India and in its huge international diaspora. *Dilwale Dulhania Le Jayenge* (The Brave-Hearted Will Take the Bride), well known as *DDLJ*, was released in 1995 and holds the record for the longest running movie in Indian cinema's history; by 2007, it had played continuously in Mumbai for more than 600 weeks. This film poignantly and powerfully confronts the clashes of will and desire regarding arranged marriage (dharmic) and love marriage (adharmic). The heroine, Simran, and hero, Raj, are both Indians who are born and bred in London. Simran's strict father arranged her marriage to the son of his friend back in India when she was a baby, and Simran is compliant with this imminent fate until she meets Raj. Raj is "degenerately" Westernized, but employs all kinds of Hindu symbolism in his quest to win Simran from her own father's hand so that their marriage is a dharmic one. *Namaste London*, released in 2007, shows a more rebellious and worldly London-bred Indian heroine, who is also brought back into the dharmic marital fold, but through a piquant combination of trickery and the overwhelming power of her Indian-bred "rustic" husband's "traditional" dharma.

These films are exemplars of popular cultural attempts to resolve challenges posed by globalization to Hindu dharma, especially in diasporic and transnational contexts. They go far to demonstrate its enduring elastic capacity to accommodate the new and the various, observed by the sages of the Dharmasutras thousands of years ago, as well as the strong desire of Hindus that it should be able to do so.

Dharma East and West

Dharma has not only been acted on by and accommodated influences of the West but has, conversely, made an impact on Western art and culture. The precept began its circulation in Western culture via migration and the globalization of ideas. It moved into popular culture, notably in the 1950s via American Beat movement author Jack Kerouac's novel *The Dharma Bums*, a follow-up to his more famous novel *On the Road*. In the 1980s, an American band took this name, but a more famous band of this genre was Nirvana, also named for an Eastern (Buddhist) religious precept.

In the late 1990s, a situation comedy TV series *Dharma and Greg* was a long-running hit in the United States and abroad. Dharma, the central character, was constructed as an eccentric young woman, resultant from being the daughter of now-aging hippies, who has married a stuffy conservative young man, Greg, much to her parents' ongoing dismay. All three played stooge to her lovable, wacky yet ultimately wise ways—with Dharma's "way" often demonstrating the right course of action.

In the first decade of the new millennium, dharma is also made an explicit focus in the quasi sci-fi, quasi mystical/fantasy hit TV series *Lost*. "DHARMA" is an acronym for the "Dharma Initiative" or Department of Heuristics and Research on Material Applications, a fictional research project featured in the TV show. Buddhist Dharma symbolism is appropriated for a rather utopian if salvational human science experiment, that is, to develop a new "order'" of humanity at the same time as saving humanity from its worst tendencies—here the linkage between dharma and a soteriological project entailing action, albeit not one that actually names either moksha or nirvana or karma, is nevertheless explicit and obvious.

Sheleyah A. Courtney

See also Diasporas; Hinduism; Hindu-Related Movements; Immigration and Transnationalism; Migration; Multiculturalism; Nationalism, Neo-Nationalism

Further Readings

Cohen, L. (1998). *No aging in India: Alzheimer's, the bad family, and other modern things*. Berkeley: University of California Press.

Daniel, S. B. (1983). The tool box approach of the Tamil to the issues of moral responsibility and human destiny. In C. Keyes & E. V. Daniel (Eds.), *Karma: An anthropological enquiry* (pp. 27–62). Berkeley: University of California Press.

Deliege, R. (1992). Replication and consensus: Untouchability, caste and ideology in India. *Man*, 27(1), 155–173.

Dirks, N. B. (2001). *Castes of mind: Colonialism and the making of modern India*. Princeton, NJ: Princeton University Press.

Doniger, W., & Smith, B. (Trans.). (1991). *The laws of Manu*. London: Penguin Books.

Dumont, L. (1970). Homo hierarchicus: *The caste system and its implications*. London: Weidenfeld & Nicholson. (Original work published 1966)

Juergensmeyer, M. (2001). Dharma and the rights of Untouchables. In S. P. Udayakumar (Ed.), *Handcuffed to history: Narratives, pathologies, and violence in South Asia* (pp. 127–146). Westport, CT: Praeger.

Marriott, M. (1976). Hindu transactions: Diversity without dualism. In B. Kapferer (Ed.), *Transaction and meaning: Directions in the anthropology of exchange and symbolic behaviour* (pp. 109–142). Philadelphia: Institute for the Study of Human Issues.

Milner, M., Jr. (1994). *Status and sacredness: A general theory of status relations and an analysis of Indian culture.* New York: Oxford University Press.

Olivelle, P. (Trans.). (2000). *Dharmasūtras: The law codes of Āpastamba, Gautama, Baudhāyana, and Vasistha.* Delhi, India: Motilal Banarsidass.

Parry, J. (1980). Ghosts, greed and sin: The occupational identity of Brahmin funeral priests. *Man, 15*(1), 88–111.

Parry, J. (1981). Death and cosmogony in Kashi. *Contributions to Indian Sociology, 15*(1/2), 337–365.

Vertovec, S. (2000). *The Hindu diaspora: Comparative patterns.* London: Routledge.

DIASPORAS

In contemporary usage, the word *diaspora* is closely connected with migration and migrant transnationalism—two of the most visible and controversial manifestations of globalization. According to one of its most concise definitions, the term *diaspora* refers to "an imagined community living away from a professed place of origin" (Vertovec, 2009, p. 5). However, it is important to recognize that all definitions of the term are contested and therefore require a considerable amount of explanation, qualification, and contextualization. With this requirement in mind, the historical development of the term and its main current usages are outlined in this entry.

Historical Development of the Term

The word *diaspora* derives from Greek words *speiro* ("to sow") and *dia* ("over") and is related to the word *diaspeirein*: a scattering of seeds as from a bursting pod. From the Ancient Greek context, where it referred to the colonization and settlement of Asia Minor and the Mediterranean, the word found its way into the Greek translation of the Old Testament and, over the centuries, became almost inseparable from the mournful narrative of Jewish exile. Later, particularly through the 1960s and 1970s, the word was applied by extension to a handful of other victimized groups who, although forced to leave a homeland, have maintained real and symbolic ties to their homeland; these groups include Armenians, Africans, and Palestinians. Some recent scholarship insists that the term designates these specific groups rather than a more general concept.

However, the term underwent a revival during the last quarter of the 20th century, particularly in the 1980s and early 1990s, becoming an emblem of globalization and associated shifts in international migration. The term was applied much more broadly than it had been before, sparking off a prolonged definitional debate. At one extreme, some researchers began to use the term loosely to refer to any group residing outside its place of origin—and even to nonmigrant minorities such as homosexuals. Some scholars have argued that such indiscriminate usage renders the term indistinguishable from *migration* or *minority* and therefore analytically useless. As Roger Brubaker contends, if all people are in a diaspora, then no one is. Thus, at the other extreme, some traditionalists insist that the term should only be used to refer to "victim" groups dispersed through coercion, who maintain an antagonistic relationship with their host societies.

To mediate between the maximalist and minimalist definitions and to impose some kind of conceptual coherence on this flourishing literature, various scholars—notably William Safran and Robin Cohen—composed checklists of key diasporic features, which became useful analytical tools for deciding whether and in what sense particular groups "qualified" as diasporas. These definitional criteria helped focus debates around questions such as the following: Were diasporas necessarily forcibly dispersed from their homeland, and marginalized in their host countries, or could they also stem from voluntaristic migration and a sense of cosmopolitan connection to both places? What types of identity were involved—only ethnic and racial, or national and religious also? Could someone be part of a diaspora without realizing it? Did diasporas have to result from the movement of people, or could they also arise from the movement of borders? Was home a real or an imagined place?

During the 1990s, such questions fed into a more fundamental debate between social realists and constructionists, with the latter accusing the former of "essentializing" or "reifying" key diaspora concepts such as "community" and "homeland." In the social constructionist view, diasporas were not merely static, preexisting social forms or social agents to be discovered and analyzed by researchers, but products of social action. This critique of the diaspora concept was closely connected with a wider critique of *methodological nationalism* (the reification of the nation-state as the basic unit of social analysis). Coined by Herminio Martins, the term *methodological nationalism* draws an analogy with *methodological individualism* (the reduction of social analysis to the actions of individuals), a problem identified by Max Weber and named by his pupil Joseph Schumpeter. Anthony D. Smith also referred to the problem of methodological nationalism, but it has been elaborated most fully by Andreas Wimmer and Nina Glick Schiller, who see the nation-state's naturalization as a result of academic inquiry. Social constructionists and other critics of methodological nationalism have questioned earlier schools of thought for treating diasporas as homogenous groups deriving from a single point of origin in a specific nation-state, and sharing fixed essential characteristics that do or do not meet academic criteria, and not paying enough attention to questions of how diasporas coalesce and dissipate.

In the past decade, this debate over definitions has subsided somewhat into a tentative theoretical consensus on the core features of diaspora. Cohen refers to this as a "consolidation" phase in the etymology of the term, in which the strengths of earlier approaches have been augmented rather than undermined by insights from social constructionists. One feature of this consensus is an understanding and, usually, acceptance of a variety of uses and emphases, as long as individual studies specify carefully which understanding they use. Steven Vertovec makes a useful distinction between three different ways of using the word *diaspora* now in common currency, which he refers to as the "type of social form" designation, the "type of consciousness" designation, and the "type of cultural production" usage.

Diaspora as a Type of Social Form

Scholars employ the "social form" understanding of diaspora when they use the term to designate specific groups with a specific range of characteristics. According to current consensus, the essential characteristics of a diaspora group are dispersion, orientation toward a homeland, and group boundary maintenance over time—where "boundary maintenance" refers to the complementary process of internal definition (whereby groups mark out their own shared features) and external definition (whereby they are marked out by non–group members). As stated at the outset, when viewed as a type of social form, a diaspora is perhaps most succinctly defined as "an imagined community living away from a professed place of origin" (Vertovec, 2009, p. 5).

The next question that typically springs to mind when examining a specific group that has been classified in this way is how members of the diaspora can be distinguished from nonmembers. Questions of membership are simpler when they hinge on an unequivocal criterion such as territorial residence or formal membership in a particular polity. But the significance of the concept of diaspora is precisely its obvious disruption of the supposedly stable symmetry of membership and territory. In the case of ethno-national diasporas, it is important to distinguish "external citizenship" from diaspora. On one hand, not all diasporic people are citizens of their homeland: They may be former citizens or former permanent residents, kin or descendants of citizens, or people with some strong claim of affinity. As Robert Smith puts it, diasporic membership comes in different "thicknesses."

On the other hand, not all citizens abroad are diasporic: Citizenship may represent a material resource rather than an expression of national belonging; just because people share a passport does not mean they perpetually share an identity or sense of collectivity. If they feel or express diasporic identity at all, they may do so in response to specific situations, for example, when crossing a territorial border, when drawing on health or social security entitlements, or when it is expected by those around them. In this sense, being part of a diaspora is not so much a fixed status as a state or habit of mind.

Diaspora as a Type of Consciousness

As Vertovec (1997) notes, the term *diaspora* is also often used to describe "a variety of experience, a state of mind and a sense of identity" (p. 8). This type of consciousness is characterized by an awareness of attachment to multiple locations and emerges through experiences of exclusion and discrimination as well as through positive identification with a particular heritage, or with a cosmopolitan sense of "feeling global." According to James Clifford (1994),

> Diasporic consciousness "makes the best of a bad situation." Experiences of loss, marginality, and exile (differently cushioned by class) are often reinforced by systematic exploitation and blocked advancement. This constitutive suffering coexists with the skills of survival: strength in adaptive distinction, discrepant cosmopolitanism, and stubborn visions of renewal. Diaspora consciousness lives loss and hope as a defining tension. (p. 312)

Paul Gilroy argues that diaspora-consciousness has its focus in memory—a focus that, along with the contradiction of living in one place and belonging in another, is difficult to reconcile with the sociopolitical model of the nation-state, in which territory, identity, and political organization are synonymous.

When using the term *diaspora* in this way, questions that quickly come to mind include the following: What is identity? How does it come into existence? The view that group identity is an essential or unitary characteristic has been widely discredited; for example, Frederick Barth shifted emphasis from identity to identity formation and maintenance, which he saw as an iterative process in which group members define themselves in certain ways (internal definition) and are simultaneously defined by non-group members in (not necessarily compatible) ways (external definition). When looked at in this way, identities are not fixed characteristics of certain individuals but more like processes leading to situational or habitual states

of minds. This emphasis on the process of identity formation connects to a third common way of understanding diaspora—that is, as a mode of cultural production.

Diaspora as a Mode of Cultural Production

As Cohen notes, social constructionists have complained that debates in diaspora studies have focused too much on negotiation over which particular forms of social group or consciousness deserve the label "diaspora" or "diasporic," with some arguing that the term is a useful catchall and others insisting it is a "private club." From the perspective of some such critics, deciding which groups are "in" and which are "out" is more like stamp collecting than social science. For example, as Brubaker (2005) puts it,

> Diaspora can be seen as an alternative to the essentialization of belonging; but it can also represent a non-territorial form of essentialized belonging. Talk of the de-territorialization of identity is all well and good; but it still presupposes that there is "an identity" that is reconfigured, stretched in space to cross state boundaries, but on some level fundamentally the same. (p. 12)

Brubaker's point is perhaps illustrated, for example, by Gilroy's famous description of "black expressive cultures," particularly music, as manifestations of "a changing same." Nina Glick Schiller (2005) has referred to this type of reification of diasporas and transnational communities in place of nation-states as "transnational methodological nationalism" (pp. 442–443). As Arjun Appadurai and Carol Breckenridge (1989) put it, "to speak of diasporas—if by diasporas we mean phenomena involving stable points of origin, clear and final destinations and coherent group identities—seems already part of a sociology for the world we have lost" (p. i).

By contrast, social constructionist understandings of diaspora focus on constituency activities and processes of identity formation and dissolution. They move away from questions of whether or not particular groups qualify as diasporas by virtue of specific characteristics and toward questions about why diaspora communities emerge and dissipate. Certain circumstances or events—such as wars, sporting events, natural disasters, celebrations, or political campaigns, and so on—galvanize, mobilize, or produce a sense of collectivity among particular individuals. For example, Stuart Hall (1990) describes diaspora identities as "those which are constantly producing and reproducing themselves anew, through transformation and difference" (p. 235). Martin Sökefeld (2006) argues that "diaspora identity and the imagination of a diaspora community . . . [are] outcome[s] of mobilization processes. The development of diaspora identity is not simply a natural and inevitable result of migration but a historical contingency that frequently develops out of mobilization in response to specific critical events" (p. 280). Brubaker (2005) suggests that

> to overcome . . . problems of groupism, . . . we should think of diaspora not in substantialist terms as a bounded entity, but rather as an idiom, a stance, a claim. . . . In sum, rather than speak of "a diaspora" or "the diaspora" as an entity, a bounded group, an ethnodemographic or ethnocultural fact, it may be more fruitful, and certainly more precise, to speak of diasporic stances, projects, idioms, practices and so on. We can then study empirically the degree and form of support for a diasporic project among members of its putative constituency, just as we can do when studying a nationalist project. (p. 12)

This interest in the mobilization of diasporas is not new and has become increasingly important with the expansion and maturation of the field of diaspora studies. At the time of writing, the most salient manifestations of diaspora mobilization are the neoliberal "diaspora engagement" policies or strategies currently being advocated and deployed by a plethora of governmental and nongovernmental organizations at the local, national, and international levels as a way of converting "brain drain" into "brain gain" and channeling remittances so that migration contributes positively to development. These initiatives involve governments of migrant-sending states coordinating a variety of policy areas that impact on diasporas—from consular service to citizenship law, to expatriate voting regulations, to international agreements on social security portability and double taxation—in such a way that diasporic loyalties are activated and converted into concrete benefits for homelands. In this way, sending-state policies can *make* heterogeneous extra-territorial populations into members of a diaspora who share a state-centric identity, through what Robert Smith refers to as an "instituted process" leading to different "thicknesses" of diasporic membership.

Alan Gamlen

See also Communities, Transnational; Community; Identities in Global Society; Immigration; Indigenous Religions, Globalization of; Migration; Multiculturalism; National Identities

Further Readings

Appadurai, A., & Breckenridge, C. (1989). Editors' comment: On moving targets. *Public Culture, 2*(1), i–iv.

Barth, F. (1969). *Ethnic groups and boundaries: The social organization of culture difference.* Oslo, Norway: Universitetsforlaget.

Brubaker, R. (2005). The "diaspora" diaspora. *Ethnic and Racial Studies, 28*(1), 1–19.

Butler, K. (2001). Defining diaspora, refining a discourse. *Diaspora, 10*(2), 189–219.

Cohen, R. (1996). Diasporas and the nation-state: From victims to challengers. *International Affairs, 72*(3), 507–520.

Cohen, R. (2008). *Global diasporas: An introduction* (2nd ed.). London: Routledge.

Dufoix, S. (2008). *Diasporas.* Berkeley: University of California Press.

Gilroy, P. (1994). Diaspora. *Paragraph, 17*(1), 207–212.

Glick Schiller, N. (2005). Transnational social fields and imperialism: Bringing a theory of power to transnational studies. *Anthropological Theory, 5*(4), 439–461.

Hall, S. (1990). Cultural identity and diaspora. In J. Rutherford (Ed.), *Identity: Community, culture, difference* (pp. 222–237). London: Lawrence & Wishart.

Safran, W. (1999). Comparing diasporas: A review essay. *Diaspora, 8*(3), 255–291.

Sökefeld, M. (2006). Mobilizing in transnational space: A social movement approach to the formation of diaspora. *Global Networks—A Journal of Transnational Affairs, 6*(3), 265–284.

Tölölyan, K. (1996). Rethinking diaspora(s): Stateless power in the transnational moment. *Diaspora, 5*(1), 3–36.

Van Hear, N. (1998). *New diasporas: The mass exodus, dispersal and regrouping of migrant communities.* London: UCL Press.

Vertovec, S. (1997). Three meanings of "diaspora," exemplified among South Asian religions. *Diaspora,* 6(3), 277–299.

Vertovec, S. (2009). *Cosmopolitanism in attitude, practice and competence* (MMG Working Paper No. 09–08). Göttingen, Germany: Max Planck Institute for the Study of Religious and Ethnic Diversity.

Wimmer, A., & Glick Schiller, N. (2003). Methodological nationalism and the study of migration: Beyond nation-state building. *International Migration Review,* 37(3), 576–610.

DISEASES

Not only is disease a highly personal matter impacting the affected individual's daily life, but it also has social significance. Disease has become an increasingly global matter, as exemplified by, among others, the severe acute respiratory syndrome (SARS) epidemic of 2003 and the H1N1 pandemic of 2009, which proved that disease recognizes no national borders. Global trends, including the rise in population mobility and cross-border trade, climate change, and technological developments, have had marked impact—some more direct than others, some more negative than others—on the spread and control of diseases worldwide. At the same time, growing recognition of the global burden of disease has prompted enhanced international efforts to respond collaboratively and decisively.

What Are Diseases?

Simply put, a disease is an abnormal condition that impairs the normal functioning of an organism. One common differentiation is between communicable or infectious (extrinsic) diseases and noncommunicable (intrinsic) diseases. Communicable diseases, ranging from the common cold to HIV/AIDS to malaria and the H1N1 virus, are clinically evident illnesses that result from the presence of some pathogenic agent, such as viruses, bacteria, and parasites. Noncommunicable diseases include cardiovascular disease, cancer, cerebrovascular disease, and hereditary diseases.

According to the *Global Burden of Disease: 2004 Update,* published by the World Health Organization (WHO), the leading cause of death in 2004 globally was heart disease, followed by cerebrovascular disease (which may lead to, among other things, stroke) and lower respiratory infections. Among the top 12 causes of death, noncommunicable diseases, such as heart disease, cerebrovascular disease, and lung-related cancers, killed almost twice as many people worldwide as did infectious diseases, such as diarrheal diseases, HIV/AIDS, and tuberculosis.

Looking at the leading causes of death by a country's income, a different common categorization can be detected: diseases of poverty, that is, those more prevalent among the poor, versus diseases of affluence, those thought to be a result of increasing wealth in a society. Among low-income countries (by gross national product per capita), the number one killer in 2004 was lower respiratory infections, followed by heart disease, diarrheal diseases, and HIV/AIDS. Remarkably, 6 of the top 10 killers were infectious diseases. However, among high-income countries, noncommunicable diseases topped the list—heart disease, cerebrovascular disease, and lung-related cancers. The only infectious disease among the top 10 was lower respiratory infections.

The spread and control of both communicable and noncommunicable diseases are increasingly relevant to global studies because both are impacted by, and have an impact on, processes and trends related to globalization and internationalization.

The Impact of Global Trends on Disease

Increasing population mobility is considered to be one of the main drivers of the apparently broader and quicker spread of diseases, especially of the infectious sort. According to the World Tourism Organization, the number of international tourist arrivals for business, leisure, and other purposes has risen from less than 100 million in the 1950s to more than 900 million in 2009; by 2020, the number is forecast to increase to nearly 1.6 billion. As people (and the vehicles in which they travel) move around, they may either take with them or introduce pathogens that are endemic to one area or population to other places where the population may not be prepared to handle them. Given that most infectious diseases have an incubation period of more than 24 to 36 hours and that most destinations can be reached—when traveling by air—in less time, the potential for the rapid spread of disease across borders is high.

One vivid example is the SARS epidemic that broke out in early 2003. The virus became headline news globally when an American businessman, who had been in Guangdong Province in China, the virus's apparent source, fell ill on a plane from Hong Kong, which made an emergency landing in Hanoi, Vietnam. In a separate incident around the same time, a doctor from mainland China, who unwittingly carried the virus, took part in a conference in Hong Kong, infecting visitors who then returned to their homes in Canada, Singapore, Taiwan, and other countries, bringing the disease with them. Within a span of several weeks, the virus had been confirmed to have spread to 37 countries. Between November 2002 when the illness emerged in the Chinese province and July 2003 when the virus was considered to have been brought under control, more than 8,000 people spanning nearly every continent had contracted SARS, and more than 750 had died.

Like travel, cross-border trade has been seen throughout history as a contributor to the spread of disease. In recent years, with the increase of world trade, its impact seems to have intensified. Expanded trade in agricultural goods has led to an increase in foodborne diseases. Cross-border trade in something as seemingly mundane as used tires has been blamed in several instances for the emergence of various mosquito-borne diseases, for example, outbreaks of Chikungunya virus in Italy in 2007, the spread of dengue fever to cities around the globe, and the appearance of the West Nile virus in the United States; mosquitoes prefer to breed in dark, sheltered places like tires and do not seem bothered by long trips. More generally, the containerization shipping process seems to enable disease vectors to "hitchhike" from their homes to faraway places.

It could also be argued that enhanced trade raises the likelihood that appropriate vaccines and medicines would actually reach the ill or vulnerable, especially where local industry does not have the capacity to develop and produce them. In principle, this could happen. In practice, however, many factors—including faulty distribution

systems, market principles that give priority to the search for profit, and misguided health policies, among other factors—often prevent medicines from getting to where they are arguably most needed, especially to poorer countries. As described in more detail below, a number of initiatives are under way to address this.

Global climate change, especially the global warming phenomenon, is considered to exert positive or negative impact, depending on the location and disease in question. In locations where rainfall is reduced and temperatures rise to levels too high for transmission, certain vector-borne diseases are likely to decline in significance. Furthermore, shorter and milder winters in temperate zones could reduce seasonal heart and respiratory disease and death. On the other hand, climate change is likely to expand the geographical distribution of certain vector-borne infectious diseases, such as malaria, to higher altitudes and higher latitudes, to extend transmission seasons for such diseases, and to result in increased burden of diarrheal diseases. On balance, according to projections by the WHO and the Intergovernmental Panel on Climate Change, the negative effects of climate change on health in general and on infectious diseases in particular are greater—especially in developing countries and among vulnerable populations—and more strongly supported by evidence than are the positive effects.

Technological changes, especially those related to information and communication technologies, have in many senses facilitated the control of disease. Enhanced satellite and media technology combined with Internet and telecommunications technology means that information (like infectious disease) spreads more broadly and more quickly than ever. As the H1N1 influenza virus made its way across the world in 2009, the new virus made the lead story almost every day in local and international newspapers, on internationally transmitted television stations such as CNN and BBC, and on Internet news sites. The WHO posted updates and briefings on its website almost daily during the first three months of the pandemic, as did national disease control centers and other less official, and perhaps less authoritative, entities. It is likely that no other health event in history had been covered so closely and information spread so quickly as in the case of the H1N1 pandemic in 2009. On the one hand, the enhanced communications technology contributed to containing the pandemic: Disease control centers and health departments were able to share information about emerging developments rapidly and form responses based on sound intelligence, and the broader population—at least those with access to Internet and other news sources—was able to become better informed about the disease and its prevention. On the other hand, the sheer amount of information may have led to more of a sense of panic.

Certainly, advances in medical technologies and techniques to fight and prevent diseases have been hastened by changes in information and biological technologies. Whereas it took scientists 2 to 3 years to identify the HIV/AIDS virus, the SARS virus was identified in 2 to 3 months. Such advances have also been promoted through increasing collaboration among scientists and health care professionals globally. For example, the Drugs for Neglected Diseases initiative is a collaboration among a number of public sector research and health institutions (national and international) and a humanitarian organization, Médecins Sans Frontières, which devoted its 1999 Nobel Peace Prize winnings to this effort to identify, develop, and test drugs that target "orphan" infectious diseases such as African sleeping sickness, Chagas disease, and leishmaniasis.

Most of the global trends discussed above have impact either directly or indirectly on the spread and control of infectious diseases, such as influenza and malaria. Nevertheless, there is growing concern that globalization is also affecting the spread of noncommunicable diseases, such as heart-related diseases, cerebrovascular diseases that lead to stroke, and various forms of cancer. Looking back at the leading causes of death in 2004, although infectious diseases are clearly the dominant cause of death in low-income countries and noncommunicable diseases are more prevalent in high-income countries, middle-income countries also exhibit a greater tendency toward the noncommunicable diseases, with stroke, heart-related diseases, and cancer among the top ten. The trend in middle-income countries toward an increasing preponderance of noncommunicable diseases as cause of death may well be the result of improved health programs that more generally reduce the incidence of many infectious diseases. However, it is also believed that the transmission of "northern" culture to the "South"—including increasing use of tobacco products, leading to higher incidence of cancer and respiratory disease, and changes in food consumption patterns à la McDonaldization, leading to greater obesity and related heart disease and diabetes—has contributed significantly to this transition. More generally, the WHO projects that death caused by infectious diseases, including HIV/AIDS, tuberculosis, and malaria, will decline significantly by 2030 and that, with the aging of the population, especially in low- and middle-income countries, the incidence of death due to noncommunicable diseases will rise accordingly.

Disease as a Catalyst for International Cooperation

In many ways, the threat of the global spread of diseases, in particular infectious diseases, and the costs associated with them have been the catalyst for enhanced international cooperation. In the 1800s, cholera epidemics that spread throughout Europe prompted intensive diplomacy and negotiations that ultimately led to the organization of the first International Sanitary Conference in Paris in 1851. By 1951, after the establishment of the WHO, a set of International Sanitary Regulations had been adopted by WHO member-states. These were in turn revised in 1969 and renamed the International Health Regulations (IHR); these regulations covered six infectious diseases, namely, cholera, plague, yellow fever, smallpox, relapsing fever, and typhus.

Beginning in 1995, following the resurgence of some well-known diseases such as cholera in places where they were thought to have been eliminated and the emergence of new infections such as the Ebola hemorrhagic fever, several resolutions developed by the WHO's World Health Assembly (WHA) called for revision of the IHR to adapt them to the more globalized world. In the midst of the SARS epidemic, the WHA issued yet another resolution calling on the WHO and its partners to finalize the revision to address such outbreaks as they occur in the future. The WHA finally adopted the revised IHR in 2005, which entered into force in 2007. The IHR (2005) broaden the scope of the 1969 version to cover existing, reemerging, and new diseases, as well as other health emergencies such as chemical spills and nuclear meltdowns, and outline specific requirements and procedures for notifying the WHO of events that might constitute a public health emergency of international concern.

The new regulations and framework were put to the test with the outbreak of the H1N1 influenza virus in 2009. In 2010, an IHR review committee was formed to assess both the WHO's response to the H1N1 pandemic and the implementation of the IHR (2005) in general. Questions and criticisms have arisen regarding many aspects of the management of the H1N1 pandemic. Was the WHO correct to call it a pandemic in the first place? Did WHO exaggerate the threat of the disease's spread? Was the process sufficiently transparent? Were conflicts of interest at play in decisions surrounding recommendations for the use of drugs and the development and distribution of vaccines? Answers to these questions, as well as the results of the IHR review, will likely set the tone for international cooperation in response to future global outbreaks of disease.

Recognition of the global social and economic burden of disease and some sense of global social justice have also prompted greater international cooperation in the search for better understanding, prevention, and treatment of certain diseases, especially those considered "diseases of poverty" and "neglected diseases" that primarily affect populations in the poorest countries. A case in point is the Global Fund to Fight Aids, Tuberculosis and Malaria, an international financing institution established in 2002 with the support of, among others, the G-8, the United Nations, and the WHO. By October 2010, the fund had committed more than $19 billion in 144 countries to support large-scale prevention, treatment, and care programs focusing on these three diseases. At that time, the global fund's resources constituted approximately one quarter of all international financing for HIV/AIDS, two thirds of funding for tuberculosis, and three quarters of funding for malaria.

Furthermore, a sort of global public-private partnership has been established to coordinate responses to each of these diseases, including UNAIDS, the Stop TB Partnership, and the Global Malaria Partnership. These partnerships include a wide range of actors: international agencies such as the WHO and the United Nations Development Programme, national health ministries, private businesses, research centers, foundations, and other nongovernmental organizations. The primary goals of these partnerships are to reduce and ultimately eliminate their respective diseases through coordination of research, drug and vaccine development and distribution, tracking, and treatment programs. All three work with the Global Fund to Fight Aids, Tuberculosis and Malaria to help set priorities and guide resource allocation.

These are only a few of the most prominent examples. Nevertheless, they help to illustrate that, although global trends have a decided impact on the development and spread of diseases, diseases have also proven to be a catalyst for new global action through international cooperation on an unprecedented basis. With sufficient commitment on the part of all the actors, perhaps these diseases will eventually be eradicated.

Regina A. List

See also Drugs and Pharmaceuticals; Global Warming; McDonaldization, McWorld; Public Goods, Global; Public Health; Viruses and Diseases, Emerging; World Health Organization

Further Readings

Ali, S. H., & Keil, R. (Eds.). (2008). *Networked disease: Emerging infections in the global city.* West Sussex, UK: Wiley-Blackwell.

Drexler, M. (2009). *Emerging epidemics: The menace of new infections.* New York: Penguin.

Hotez, P. J. (2008). *Forgotten people, forgotten diseases: The neglected tropical diseases and their impact on global health and development.* Herndon, VA: ASM Press.

Kimball, A. M. (2006). *Risky trade: Infectious disease in the era of global trade.* Aldershot, UK: Ashgate.

Pachauri, R. K., & Reisinger, A. (Eds.). (2007). *Climate change 2007: Synthesis report.* Geneva, Switzerland: Intergovernmental Panel on Climate Change.

Saker, L., Lee, K., Cannito, B., Gilmore, A., & Campbell-Lendrum, D. (2004). *Globalization and infectious diseases: A review of the linkages* (Special Topics in Social, Economic and Behavioural Research, Report No. 3). Geneva, Switzerland: World Health Organization.

Seckinelgin, H. (2008). *International politics of HIV/ AIDS: Global disease—local pain.* Abingdon, UK: Routledge.

World Health Organization. (2008). *The global burden of disease: 2004 update.* Geneva, Switzerland: Author.

DISTRIBUTION OF WEALTH, EQUITABILITY OF

The years since the end of World War II have been marked by increasing economic interdependence. Yet, despite growing trade and investment between states and the growth of transnational corporations that straddle the globe, the benefits seem extremely inequitably shared. The global protests against corporate capitalism in 2011 were largely concerned about this inequity. Although it may be argued that there are fewer people living in absolute poverty, there is broad agreement that global inequality has grown rather than diminished. There are, of course, important exceptions to the rule. For example, millions have been lifted out of poverty in countries such as China and India. Yet, although living standards have increased for many, we are left with the paradox of a wealthier, yet more divided world than ever.

After considering measures of the global distribution of wealth, including the regions of the world where wealth is held versus those where it is not, the three main theoretical perspectives explaining this are outlined in this entry: liberal/ neoliberal, Marxist/neo-Marxist, and nationalist perspectives. While these provide different and conflicting explanations for the global distribution of wealth, as well as prescriptions for improving the equitability of it, they also have substantial and often underexplored points of commonality.

The Global Distribution of Wealth

We live in a highly unequal world. Although there is considerable debate regarding the percentage of the world's population that lives in absolute poverty, with this debate revolving around how to define it (e.g., whether it is those living below a certain threshold such as US$1 per day, or whether it should be based on the living standard

pertaining in a given country), there is considerable agreement not only that global inequality persists but that it is growing as well. For example:

- United Nations Development Programme data show that the richest 20% of the world's population accounts for over 80% of global income, while the poorest 20% accounts for less than 2%. The income gap between them has more than doubled since the 1960s.
- Gross domestic product per capita in the world's 20 richest countries is 121 times higher than in the world's 20 poorest ones.
- Average incomes in more than 50 developing countries are now lower than in the 1990s.

The disparities are staggering; just 4% of the wealth of the world's 225 richest people, whose wealth amounts to over US$1 trillion, would be enough to provide access to education and health care, sufficient food, clean water, and sanitation for all those who currently do not have access to them.

This inequality is not random. Beyond western Europe and North America, there has been a substantial reduction in poverty in some East and South Asian countries but a substantial increase in sub-Saharan Africa and either stagnation or a mixed performance in Latin American countries. Therefore, it is often said that the nations of the world are broadly divided between those in the rich Northern Hemisphere and those in the poor Southern Hemisphere. This North-South divide is reflected in patterns of global economic activity. Rich, northern countries account for 80% of world production and 70% of international trade and are the source of 70% to 90% of all foreign direct investments. In fact, nearly 90% of the world's top 500 corporations are headquartered in just 10 countries: the United States, Japan, the United Kingdom, France, Germany, Canada, the Netherlands, Switzerland, Italy, and Australia. Of these, the majority are Anglo-American. Furthermore, according to the United Nations Conference on Trade and Development, the vast majority of their foreign direct investment goes to other northern countries rather than those in the poor South, which have rarely had more than 30% of global foreign direct investment stocks.

In short, the North's share of global wealth has grown while the South's has shrunk. Global patterns of production, trade, and investment, as well as the headquarters of the largest corporations that drive them, suggest that this trend will continue.

The Free Market Conventional Wisdom

The conventional wisdom for improving the equitability of the global distribution of wealth revolves around the creation and maintenance of a global liberal (i.e., free market) economic order. At its core, liberal ideology basically promotes increased freedom for individuals and a smaller role for states. In its economic guise, at the subnational level it promotes freedom for individuals to act in their self-interest in free markets. At the international level, a world characterized by free trade between states on the basis of market forces is similarly envisaged, and this means trade on the basis of comparative advantage. The theory of comparative advantage was proposed by the classical liberal economist David Ricardo, who suggested that states should specialize in what they can produce most efficiently and trade for gains. If all states do this, the result should be a cosmopolitan world in which borders become porous to flows of goods and services, markets are no longer defined by national territories, and all the peoples of the world share in the benefits. As all nations' interests become bound together in a world of mutual interdependence, they all should enjoy prosperity and growth that would not otherwise have been possible.

It was with such free market ideals that the postwar recovery was planned by the allied nations at the end of World War II. In the context of a world ravaged by war, they met at the United Nations Monetary and Financial Conference held in 1944 at Bretton Woods, New Hampshire. Concerned about the threat of political extremism, whether in the form of Nazism or communism, and with memories of the Great Depression in the interwar period, they planned an interconnected liberal economic order for postwar reconstruction. They created the international organizations of the World Bank and International Monetary Fund (IMF) with liberal principles embedded in them. The former was intended to finance postwar reconstruction, but ultimately it became the world's multilateral lender for development assistance. The latter was intended to foster global monetary cooperation to ensure the financial stability to underpin free trade but ultimately became primarily a lender of last resort to countries facing bankruptcy. The General Agreement on Tariff and Trade was also established, which, in 1995, gave rise to the World Trade Organization to oversee agreements that ensure free trade between its member-states. Ultimately, it was hoped that the theory would become the practice: a free market global economic order in which the narrow self-interest of any one state or group of them would be avoided in favor of an increasingly interdependent world where all states and their citizens would share in the gains from free trade.

The mainstream explanation for why the outcome has been otherwise is that there simply has not been enough liberalization. The argument is that those countries that continue to "distort" global patterns of trade and investment, or put up barriers to trade via tariffs and subsidies and seek to protect their domestic interests, are missing out on the gains that will surely flow to them. They are not embracing the possibilities for globally free markets to transform their economies enthusiastically enough. It is argued that, if they did, over time, the benefits that have accrued to the few will "trickle down" to the many, if only such states would adhere to a liberal agenda.

This view came to dominate liberal free market thought, as a more strident version of liberalism, known as neoliberalism, came to take hold. Promoted in the 1980s by British prime minister Margaret Thatcher and U.S. president Ronald Reagan, the version of free market liberalism they espoused was not one in which states had to create a liberal world order but one in which their role was to get out of the way. In this context, the free market principles embedded in the World Bank and IMF had led, by the 1980s, to what John Williamson called a "Washington Consensus." He used this phrase as a reflection of where these organizations are located and of the neoliberal free market ideology that was embraced by policymakers there. His point was that this ideology was reflected in the conditions that came with IMF and World Bank loans and development programs to developing countries, particularly those in Latin America, which involved privatization, deregulation, market-determined exchange and interest rates, minimal government spending, and the opening of borders to trade, investment, and financial flows.

The upshot of neoliberal ideology, therefore, was that if globalization is a recipe for development, then radically and rapidly exposing all nations' economies to global market forces is a way of ensuring the development and wealth of all. Although this was the conventional wisdom, it has been critiqued by many.

The Marxist/Neo-Marxist Challenge

Although Karl Marx had very little to say about international affairs, he did say that capitalism has a tendency to reproduce itself and create a world in its own image: one in which capitalist relations of production involve those who control the means of production (the bourgeoisie) exploiting those who do not (the proletariat). Marxist scholars who have come since, known as neo-Marxists, have taken up the idea of capitalist relations of production writ large on the world. There is no single neo-Marxist theory of international relations, but what neo-Marxists share is a lack of surprise at the inequitable global distribution of wealth, seeing it as the inevitable outcome of the spread of (liberal) capitalist relations of production.

One influential strand of neo-Marxist thought is world-systems theory. Adherents, such as Immanuel Wallerstein, see a world comprised of countries in the industrialized "core," where the means of production is controlled (i.e., the North), versus the exploited "periphery," where it is not (i.e., the South). Countries in the periphery are exploited for their raw materials and cheap labor, in much the same way that the bourgeoisie exploits the proletariat on the factory floor. This allows the proletariat in the counties of the core to be "bought off" with cheaper goods and services while exploitation is shifted offshore. The prosperity of the few in the core, therefore, depends on exploiting the many in the periphery.

Over time, this implies that greater exposure to global market forces leads developing countries to become further underdeveloped, the exact opposite of what liberals would suggest. In other words, globalization produces underdevelopment rather than development, and neoliberal globalization accelerates the trend. There is evidence for this.

Historically, it has been observed that certain states and regions have actually done better when their links to global economic forces were weaker, as was the case for Latin American countries during World War II. And it is notable that poorer countries grew at around 3% per annum on average over the 1960s and 1970s, by comparison to around half this rate after the 1980s, when they adopted the neoliberal policies of the Washington Consensus.

Neo-Marxists' prescription for poorer countries is that they should withdraw from the global capitalist system if they do not wish to be further impoverished and forced to the periphery by it. After all, a world in which capitalist relations of production dominate will only serve to increase wealth for states in the core, which benefit from a liberal economic world order, versus those on the periphery, which can only have their underdevelopment entrenched and poverty deepened as a result of it.

The Nationalist "Reality"

For neo-Marxists, the benefits of an economically interdependent world are seen more in terms of a periphery that becomes dependent on the core for whatever economic "crumbs" are left on the table. Indeed, Latin American neo-Marxists' dependency theory is based on the premise that exposure to global economic forces produces dependence on the core nations' demand for raw materials and cheap labor to support their drive for increased profits, so that what they are exporting to periphery countries is exploitation as much as goods, services, and foreign direct investment.

However, neo-Marxists are not the only voices to attack what has become the neoliberal orthodoxy. Those with a nationalist perspective note that the state is crucial in ensuring the benefits of globalization are more equitably shared. For example, in his book *Bad Samaritans*, Ha-Joon Chang points out that the neoliberal prescription for poorer countries does not reflect the reality of how industrialized countries became wealthy. They all went through protracted periods of protectionism, in which they closed their economies to global competition, favored and supported the development of domestic industry, and discriminated against foreign goods, services, and investment. Chang refers to the World Bank, IMF, and WTO as the "Unholy

Trinity," claiming that their neoliberal policies—and the dominant ideology of the world's powerful nations that support them—have resulted in the "ladder" to development being kicked away from states in the global South. This is because the conditionality they impose on developing states, not to mention simply their "expert" advice, does not equate with the path followed by rich northern states in the process of their development.

There is evidence that this is not just a historical argument but a contemporary fact. The newly industrialized states of the postwar era, such as Japan, South Korea, and the territory of Taiwan, are often said to have succeeded because they followed a similar path. The result was that they experienced development with increased equitability of the distribution of wealth. Furthermore, developed countries continue to subsidize their agricultural production to the extent that their protection of whatever they do not have a comparative advantage in producing far outweighs the overseas development aid they provide with neoliberal conditions. It is no exaggeration to say that some cows in Europe receive more "aid" than many sub-Saharan Africans. At the same time, tariffs on manufactured goods from developing countries are 4 times higher than those from member countries of the Organisation for Economic Co-operation and Development. Therefore, the inequitable distribution of wealth may, in large part, be a result of states with the ability to do so acting in their own interest to liberalize their gains and socialize their losses. Indeed, in the aftermath of the 2008 global financial meltdown, governments in the North have stepped in to stimulate their economies and to bail out their key corporations and financial sectors, including taking over entire companies and financial institutions. The lesson seems to be that neoliberal economic globalization is a recipe for greater wealth for industrialized countries in times of growth and stability, but when a country is developing or threatened, an economic nationalist stance is the default policy position.

Common Ground

Each of the previously described perspectives offers different explanations and prescriptions for the equitable distribution of wealth, but their differences are often overemphasized by comparison to their points of commonality. For example, the dangers of a polarized world where poor states become dependent on, rather than interdependent with, rich states is a concern shared by those with neo-Marxist and nationalist perspectives. The former desire a revolution that overthrows capitalism altogether, whereas the latter see a role for national governments in ensuring the benefits of economic openness are realized, but both reject the neoliberal ideal that economic openness alone will result in benefits for all.

Yet, it is important to recognize that the "father" of liberalism, Adam Smith, was aware of, and cautioned against, the potential inequities and instability produced by what is now known as neoliberalism. He saw it as a legitimate role of government to moderate the exposure of domestic industry to foreign competition so as not to cause dramatic economic, political, and social dislocation. He also saw it as reasonable that governments impose tariffs and subsidies to balance the effect of these in other countries, while for strategic reasons certain industrial sectors should not be open to global market forces at all. It is doubtful that he would have approved of the policies of the Washington Consensus, and in something of a case of "back to the future," the states that previously embraced neoliberal policies are increasingly questioning them since the 2008 financial crisis. At the 2009 G-20 summit to address the crisis, its host, British prime minister Gordon Brown, declared that "the old Washington Consensus is over." Therefore, while it may be hoped that global markets will recover so that the long-term benefits of a global liberal economic order may be realized, it may also be that greater acceptance is emerging that there is a role for states as well as markets in realizing the benefits for all. As Dany Rodrik (2001) notes, "[global] integration is the result, not the cause, of economic and social development" (p. 59). To this, he could also have added the equitability of the distribution of wealth.

John Mikler

See also Bretton Woods Agreements/System; Capitalism; Economics, Keynesian; Global Economic Issues; Inequality, Global Economic; Liberalism, Neoliberalism; Poverty and Poverty Alleviation; Trade Agreements

Further Readings

Bhagwati, J. (2004). *In defense of globalization.* New York: Oxford University Press.

Chang, H. (2008). *Bad Samaritans: The myth of free trade and the secret history of capitalism.* New York: Bloomsbury Press.

Dollar, D., & Kraay, A. (2002). Spreading the wealth. *Foreign Affairs, 81*(1), 120–133.

Glenn, J. (2007). *Globalization: North-South perspectives.* London: Routledge.

Helleiner, E., & Pickel, A. (Eds.). (2005). *Economic nationalism in a globalizing world.* Ithaca, NY: Cornell University Press.

Rodrik, D. (2001, March/April). Trading in illusions. *Foreign Policy, 123,* 54–62.

Wallerstein, I. (2004). *World-systems analysis: An introduction.* Durham, NC: Duke University Press.

Willamson, J. (2003, September). From reform agenda to damaged brand name: A short history of the Washington Consensus and suggestions for what to do next. *Finance and Development, 40*(3), 10–13.

Wolf, M. (2004). *Why globalization works.* New Haven, CT: Yale University Press.

DOLLAR

The U.S. dollar is considered much more than just another national monetary unit, and many regard it as the world's global currency. It is considered an international currency because it has been the world's foremost monetary vehicle for invoicing and international transactions since the mid-20th century.

Legally, the U.S. dollar (USD, US$) is the official currency primarily of the United States and the U.S. territories of Puerto Rico, Northern Mariana Islands, U.S. Virgin Islands, American Samoa, Guam, and the United States Minor Outlying Islands. It is also the official currency of a number of other countries, such as Panama since 1904, Ecuador since 2000, and El Salvador since 2001. The U.S. dollar was born with the Coinage Act of 1792, which established the dollar as the basic unit of account for the United States. The first U.S. dollar coin was minted in 1794. The origin of the U.S. dollar is the Spanish dollar, or piece of eight.

On January 1, 1999, the introduction of the euro (€, ISO 4217 code EUR) as the common currency of the eurozone with a flexible or floating exchange rate regime challenged the hegemony of the U.S. dollar as the world international currency. Because the foreign exchange market is a zero-sum game, it was believed that the euro would be able to end the preeminence of the U.S. dollar, particularly after 2002 (Figure 1), when the U.S. dollar began to steadily depreciate in value against the euro. Many predicted that this would mark the end of the "Pax Americana" (the peace and prosperity period established at the end of World War II resulting from the hegemony of the United States).

The Federal Reserve has created the Trade Weighted U.S. Dollar Index (commercial U.S. dollar) to measure and reflect the strength of the U.S. dollar relative to the currencies of other countries with which the United States enjoys close and important trading ties. Figure 2 plots the commercial U.S. dollar and the Brazilian real. It illustrates that, since June 2004, the commercial U.S. dollar has been suffering a dramatic depreciation, which means that currencies included in the index have been appreciating against the U.S. dollar. For instance, this figure also shows that the Brazilian real has been appreciating against the U.S. dollar. Nevertheless, since 2010, the commercial U.S. dollar has been gaining strength and beginning a period of appreciation, which means that the Brazilian real has experienced a depreciation period by almost the same amount.

The prominence of the U.S. dollar as an international currency has helped it become the world's primary reserve currency. A reserve currency is a currency other than the national currency that is held by governments and institutions as part of their foreign exchange reserves. Further, a reserve currency is accumulated because of its capacity to act as a store of value, which helps a country reduce, or offset, the risk of its own economy and currency. The greater the importance of a particular currency is, the larger the held amount will be. In 2009, the amount of U.S. dollars held as reserve currency worldwide stood at historic record highs, despite economic problems in the United States, while the second most widely held currency was the euro.

The U.S. dollar has been considered as good as gold for many years. The U.S. dollar's run as the world's safe haven has been questioned as a result of criticism by Chinese authorities, who have placed in doubt the hegemony of the U.S. dollar as a reserve currency. Chinese authorities claim that the

Figure 1   The euro.

Source: Provided courtesy of eSignal, a division of Interactive Data Corporation (NYSE: IDC).

Figure 2   The Brazilian real and the commercial U.S. dollar.

Source: Provided courtesy of eSignal, a division of Interactive Data Corporation (NYSE: IDC).

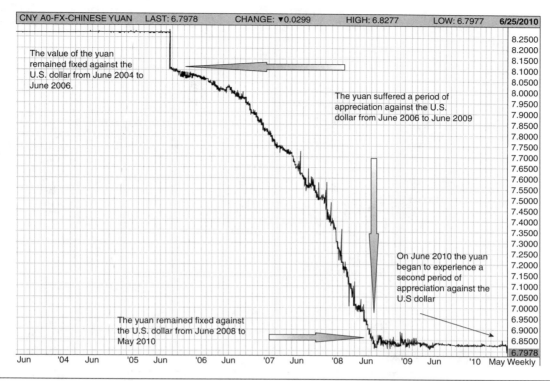

Figure 3 The Chinese yuan.

Source: Provided courtesy of eSignal, a division of Interactive Data Corporation (NYSE: IDC).

Figure 4 The British pound.

Source: Provided courtesy of eSignal, a division of Interactive Data Corporation (NYSE: IDC).

Figure 5   The U.S. Dollar Index.

Source: Provided courtesy of eSignal, a division of Interactive Data Corporation (NYSE: IDC).

U.S. economy has been facing a difficult economic and financial situation since 2007 and that countries with a large share of U.S. dollar reserve currency are accumulating the United States' risk. A weak dollar combined with a downgrade of the U.S. economy undermines the international purchasing power of these countries. Thus, Chinese monetary authorities, represented by the president of the People's Bank of China, have argued that the world needs a stable international reserve currency.

Further, there is a debate between U.S. and Chinese authorities regarding the value of the Chinese yuan (or renminbi). China has received criticism from the United States and the European Union for not allowing the yuan to fluctuate freely in the foreign exchange market in order for it to reach a value based on demand and supply. On the contrary, Chinese monetary authorities are intervening in the market to maintain a "fixed" value with respect to the U.S. dollar. To maintain this fixed value, Chinese authorities must buy up dollars. This has led to China's accumulation of U.S. dollars, which are pairing up with a large trade surplus mainly denominated in U.S. dollars because of the competitive trading advantage obtained by a

"devalued" currency. As a consequence, Chinese authorities are investing all those billions of U.S. dollars—close to US$2 trillion—in U.S. Treasury bills. This is what has been defined as a "dollar trap." Ever since the U.S. dollar began to decrease in value, Chinese investments in U.S. treasuries have been losing value as well. This has negatively affected the value of the Chinese foreign investment portfolio in U.S. dollars. Figure 3 shows that the yuan has appreciated from 8 yuan per U.S. dollar in June 2006 to 6.8 yuan per U.S. dollar in June 2009, remaining flat ever since. This appreciation of the yuan has helped boost Chinese exports and has received a rapid response from the U.S. government, pressuring China to revalue its currency.

Nonetheless, the different political and economic events in the United States, as well as the first truly global economic recession, have not been able to end the prestige of the U.S. dollar. In fact, Figure 4 demonstrates that since the beginning of 2010, the U.S. dollar has begun to regain its strength against the British pound as a result of its being considered the best alternative not only to the euro but also to most other currencies.

Therefore, the U.S. dollar remains the only world currency that is considered both an international and global currency. In addition, the value of the U.S. Dollar Index, which measures the value of U.S. currency against the currency of major countries (the euro, Japanese yen, British pound, Canadian dollar, Swedish krona, and Swiss franc), remains a leading economic index, as is represented in Figure 5.

Maria Lorca-Susino

See also Banks; Economic Crises; Euro; Gold Standard; Markets; Mercantilism

Further Readings

Baker, A. (2006). American power and the dollar: The constraints of technical authority and declaratory policy in the 1990s. *New Political Economy, 11*(1), 23–45.

Bergsten, C. F. (1997, July/August). The dollar and the euro. *Foreign Affairs, 76*(4), 83–95.

Cline, W. R. (2005). The case for a New Plaza agreement. *Policy Briefs in International Economics,* No. PB05-4. Washington, DC: Institute for International Economics.

Dieter, H. (2005). The US economy and the sustainability of Bretton Woods II. *Journal of Australian Political Economy, 55,* 48–76.

Klein, M., Mizrach, B., & Murphy, R. G. (1991). Managing the dollar: Has the Plaza Agreement mattered? *Journal of Money, Credit and Banking, 23*(4), 742–751.

Mann, C. L. (1999). *Is the U.S. trade deficit sustainable?* Washington, DC: Institute for International Economics.

McKinnon, R. (2001). The international dollar standard and the sustainability of the U.S. current account deficit. *Brookings Papers on Economic Activity, 1,* 227–237.

Ruckriegel, K., & Seitz, F. (2002). *The Eurosystem and the Federal Reserve System compared: Facts and challenges* (ZEI Working Paper No. B 02-2002). Bonn, Germany: Center for European Integration Studies.

Zimmermann, H. (2004). Ever challenging the buck? The euro and the question of power in international monetary governance. In F. Torres, A. Verdum, C. Zilioli, & H. Zimmermann (Eds.), *Governing EMU: Economic, political, legal and historical perspective* (pp. 233–247). Badia Fiesolana, Italy: European University Institute.

DRUGS AND PHARMACEUTICALS

Among the most rapidly advancing global technologies, pharmaceuticals are at the center of global struggles for human rights, health, trade, and human connectivity. Drugs and pharmaceuticals are important in two significant ways for global studies: (1) The development, production, and regulation of legal drugs and pharmaceuticals are producing new global forms of quality assurance and protection for intellectual property, and (2) drugs and pharmaceuticals have been the catalyst for the mobilization of a transnational social movement around issues of global access.

Globalization processes have been linked to increasing epidemics of diet or lifestyle diseases (e.g., diabetes, heart disease, lung disease, and asthma) in rich countries and infectious diseases (e.g., HIV/AIDS, tuberculosis, and malaria, often referred to simply as "the three diseases" as a statement of their impact on global health) in poor countries. The causal links between global processes and disease vectors are complex and not unidirectional (proving that the links between globalization and disease remain more ideological than empirical). Still, given the progress in drug development, nutrition, and hygiene, levels of morbidity (sickness) and mortality remain much higher than expected. Understanding why this is the case is important for understanding global processes.

Spending on pharmaceuticals alone accounts for more than 15% of measured total global spending on health. The development of new drugs, including testing in clinical trials, and distribution of existing ones are genuinely global in scope. Struggles over access to good quality drugs have mobilized political action in countries as diverse as Brazil, South Africa, and the United States. Yet, most significantly for global studies, these movements have not drawn support primarily from national citizens but from transnational linkages between citizens who communicate and act using new media and global communications.

Understanding the economics and politics of how pharmaceuticals is linked to how drugs, or the lack of them, influence people's everyday lives. João Biehl's work on Brazil documents how what he calls the "pharmaceuticalization" of governance and citizenship creates new forms of inequality between those who have access to drugs and those who do not. In the process, this pharmaceuticalization highlights the deficiencies in the national health care structures as well as the poverty and inequality among citizens. Today, drugs and pharmaceuticals are technologies with implications for individual health and for social, economic, and political well-being.

Drug Development and Production

The modern pharmaceutical industry can be traced to the 19th-century isolation and mass production of powerful compounds such as cocaine, morphine, nicotine, quinine, and strychnine. Around the time of World War II, scientific breakthroughs made penicillin and other antibiotics available to treat devastating and previously untreatable diseases such as tuberculosis. By the mid-20th century, thousands of drugs had been patented. At this time, pharmaceutical companies were already operating internationally for licensing and marketing agreements, subsidiaries, and joint ventures. Today, medicine production is highly concentrated in the industrialized countries, where just five countries—the United States, Japan, Germany, France, and the United Kingdom—account for two thirds of the value of all medicines produced. They dominate by value largely because they produce expensive, branded drugs to treat diseases that occur in populations of customers who can pay for them. However, large-volume markets of lower priced medicines also exist in the highly competitive domestic markets of countries such as Brazil, Thailand, China, and India. In these countries, a growing number of producers manufacture the bulk of generic drugs in global distribution, but they are also beginning to compete in high-value pharmaceutical production through exports. Still, a small number of transnational companies dominate the global production, trade, and sales of medicines. Ten of these companies now account for almost half of all sales. This concentration has increased considerably since a rapid boom began in 1987. Overall, the global pharmaceutical trade has experienced unprecedented growth since around 1985 and continues to grow. The market value of global pharmaceuticals had a compound annual growth rate from 2002 to 2006 of 6.6%, and it remains one of the highest profit industries in the world, according to the global pharmaceutical industry.

As documented by Adriana Petryna, drug development has become increasingly globalized. There are central debates in the literature over whether the globalization of clinical drug trials is contributing to a social good and thus providing an integral part of health care delivery in poor countries where patients receive better treatment than is available outside of the research setting, or whether drug development outsourcing is exploiting the weakness of dysfunctional health systems and sick, disadvantaged people. However, clinical trials involving human subjects are increasingly taking place outside the western European or North American countries that house the major pharmaceutical companies. Yet whether trials are conducted in the United States or Brazil, the pharmaceutical industry is most likely the sponsor of clinical research taking place globally. This is an important shift, as the percentage of industry-sponsored clinical trials nearly doubled between 1980 and 2000 alone (from 32% to 62% of all clinical research endeavors sponsored by the pharmaceutical industry). Petryna argues that individual governments have limited control over experimental research, and the global public has little information regarding the conditions under which drug trials are carried out, the design or content of research protocols, or the dependability of the evidence that comes from global trials.

Regulation and Quality

One response to the boom in pharmaceutical experimentation has been an ongoing attempt to control experiments and regulate drug safety through global standards. In the late 1990s, the International Conference on Harmonisation of Technical Requirements for Registration of Pharmaceuticals for Human Use brought industry experts and regulatory authorities from the United States, the European Union, and Japan together to develop global guidelines. These included an international ethical and scientific quality control standard for ensuring the protection of human subjects and credibility of data.

Still, there are vast inequalities surrounding the quality of the pharmaceuticals that are available throughout the world. For example, the World

Health Organization (WHO) estimates that less than one third of the contraceptives used globally are of the quality required in industrialized countries. The proportion of pharmaceuticals that are actually counterfeit is estimated to be approximately 1% of drugs in developed countries and up to 50% of those in developing countries. The growing percentage of fake drugs can be linked to the globalization of production, which has created more steps between the manufacture of drugs and their consumption by patients. Counterfeiters have easily duplicated medicines with look-alikes. The rise of Internet pharmacies has also made counterfeit trade easier, and the WHO estimates that approximately half of all drugs sold over the Internet are fake. This booming global trade in counterfeit drugs is estimated by the United Nations to be worth over US$75 billion, and it hits consumers in poor countries hardest. Although data on illegal trade are highly suspect, the increasing trends in counterfeit drugs suggest that transnational producers and consumers are operating in ways that profit most from states' inability to enforce quality standards. Organizations like WHO have been working to develop global norms and quality standards for pharmaceuticals. Simultaneously, new consortia, such as the ACT Consortium working on malaria drugs in Africa and Asia, are trying to develop quality testing procedures to prevent the use of fake drugs, particularly in developing countries.

Access

Tropical diseases in poor countries do not offer the same economic incentives for drug development and distribution that drive the proliferation of noninfectious and chronic diseases in rich countries. Approximately 15% of the world's population who live in high-income countries purchase and consume about 90% of the world's pharmaceuticals, by value, as reported by the WHO. Yet we continue to experience the growing division between populations that have access to lifesaving drugs and the ability to pay for them, and populations that lack such access and must depend on other mechanisms for distribution, such as international aid. Partly in response to global social movements, new initiatives such as the Global Fund to Fight AIDS, Tuberculosis and Malaria;

the International AIDS Vaccine Initiative; private foundations; and public-private partnerships for pharmaceutical research and development have evolved to promote technology development and transfer in countries and diseases that are unprofitable. Drugs and pharmaceuticals are the focus of much of the new philanthropy initiatives by organizations like the Bill & Melinda Gates Foundation. These are considered to be transformative technologies that, according to the foundation, can find "big solutions for big problems."

New drug technologies are brought quickly to global markets, and their rapid spread across rich countries and to the rich citizens of poor countries brings issues of unequal access to the forefront. The WHO estimates that nearly 30,000 children are dying every day from diseases that could be easily treated if they had access to a basic range of essential drugs. There are four key factors that influence access to pharmaceuticals: rational use (drugs selected on the basis of essential drugs lists and treatment guidelines), affordable prices (for governments, health care providers, and consumers), sustainable financing (to ensure access for the poor as well as those who can pay), and reliable health and supply systems (including public and private providers). Failure in any of these areas can jeopardize people's access to pharmaceuticals.

Access to drugs can be improved through three differing but complementary strategies on the producer side: more flexible rules on intellectual property rights, differential pricing policies to lower drug prices in poor countries, and public-private partnerships like the Global Fund to pay the costs that exceed governments' health budgets. In some cases, public pressure has pushed the development and distribution of innovative drugs for specific diseases like cancer or AIDS. For example, at the beginning of 2000, the price of antiretroviral drugs to treat one patient for 1 year was typically between $10,000 and $12,000. By the end of 2001, generic combinations were available for as low as $350. The dramatic reductions in price in only 1 year were brought about by activist organizations, but changes were also linked to dialogue between national governments, international organizations, and pharmaceutical companies; competition from generic drug manufacturers; and legal and diplomatic action (UNAIDS, 2002, p. 147). Local modalities of pharmaceutical use in health care and treatment of illness are governed by global trade rules, including the implementation of patents on medicines in the World Trade Organization (WTO), and within the context of global aid through development assistance by multilateral AIDS initiatives and bilateral agencies. It has been argued that although industrialized countries set aside donations to fight AIDS in developing countries, the same countries use the WTO to prevent developing countries from accessing cheap medicines.

There has been increasing debate over the rights for producing and distributing pharmaceuticals globally. In 1994, when the WTO was established, the Agreement on Trade-Related Aspects of Intellectual Property Rights (TRIPS Agreement) was ratified to protect a range of intellectual rights through patents on new products and processes lasting for a minimum of 20 years. Although these patents are not granted globally—the inventor must file for a patent individually in each country or region—they are in fact globalized, as holding a patent in one state gives the holder the right to file for the same protection in all others. Granting 20-year patents on drugs has been seen as constraining national health priorities in poor countries with a high disease burden. Thus, during the 1990s, global concern grew about how countries could protect intellectual property rights without denying developing countries access to pharmaceutical inputs necessary for individual health and national development.

The Doha Declaration of 2001 on the TRIPS Agreement and Public Health was formulated to restate and clarify provisions for granting compulsory licenses to deal with the treatment of the diseases most devastating to the majority of the world's population, most of whom live in developing countries: HIV/AIDS, malaria, and tuberculosis. These compulsory licenses on drugs would allow other parties to produce essential pharmaceuticals for a limited time in situations of national emergency or extreme urgency and thus subject global regulation to national needs.

Countries with advanced pharmaceutical industries and large populations, such as Thailand, Brazil, and India, have been able to use compulsory license provisions. However, most developing countries have thus far not been able to take advantage of the more recent provisions in global trade that should have allowed them greater flexibility and autonomy regarding necessary drugs; this is due to political pressures in their relations with donor countries and limited domestic capacity to negotiate the international legal terrain or the local production of affordable pharmaceuticals. The WTO TRIPS Agreement should govern global trade to allow developing countries to disregard the most strident property-rights protections for essential medicines, but this did not lead to large-scale increased access in poor countries. Very few countries have made use of provisions to grant compulsory licenses and import cheaper generic medicines. Debates over drug access in poor countries led to immense civil society mobilization that linked citizens across national, cultural, and economic boundaries in a movement around global pharmaceuticals.

Activism

In March 2001, 39 transnational pharmaceutical companies initiated a legal case against South Africa for overruling national patents on antiretroviral drugs. The drug companies wanted to stop the government from adopting various measures to lower drug prices, but when the court judge allowed participation by an AIDS activist group as amicus curiae (friend of the court), the case was portrayed as putting profits before lives, and irreparable damage was caused to the global pharmaceutical industry. The activist group Treatment Action Campaign was credited with forcing the eventual withdrawal of the case, a notable victory for activist groups over global drug companies. Initially, the South African government was determined not to allow the Treatment Action Campaign to participate in the trial, but when the case was taken up by global activist groups, such as Médecins Sans Frontières and Oxfam, public opinion prevented the government from negotiating with the pharmaceutical companies before the case came to court. As the parties battled inside the South African court, Cipla, a large Indian pharmaceutical company that produces a variety of generic drugs, decided to use South Africa's patent laws to apply for a compulsory license to supply generic antiretroviral drugs to South Africa. At the same time, Merck, one of the 39 companies involved in the court case, agreed to cut prices of their branded antiretroviral drugs. This legal case became the symbol for the conflict between private companies' intellectual property rights and national governments' room for maneuver. It also placed drugs at the center of new forms of activism across borders.

Conclusion

Globalization is an economic and technological process with a pervasive, if irregular, impact. It has brought pharmaceutical access to the forefront of political debates over global inequality. Drugs and pharmaceuticals are important for understanding the formation of new global institutions, networks, and transnational activism. These processes of pharmaceuticalization, as well as the drugs that are its products, are central to global studies.

Lisa Ann Richey

See also Crime, Transnational; Health Care Access; HIV/ AIDS; World Trade Organization (WTO)

Further Readings

Barnard, D. (2002, June). In the high court of South Africa, case no. 4138/98: The global politics of access to low-cost AIDS drugs in poor countries. *Kennedy Institute of Ethics Journal, 12*(2), 159–174.

Biehl, J. (2008). Drugs for all: The future of global AIDS treatment. *Medical Anthropology, 27*(2), 99–105.

Castner, M., Hayes, J., & Shankle, D. (2007, April 15). *The global pharmaceutical industry: International trade and contemporary trends.* Durham, NC: Duke University. Retrieved from http://www.duke.edu/web/soc142/team2/trade.html

Epstein, S. (1996). *Impure science: AIDS, activism, and the politics of knowledge.* Berkeley: University of California Press.

Haakonsson, S. J., & Richey, L. A. (2007). TRIPS and public health: The Doha Declaration and Africa. *Development Policy Review, 25*(1), 71–90.

Petryna, A. (2009). *When experiments travel: Clinical trials and the global search for human subjects.* Princeton, NJ: Princeton University Press.

Petryna, A., Lakoff, A., & Kleinman, A. (Eds.). (2006). *Global pharmaceuticals: Ethics, markets, practices.* Durham, NC: Duke University Press.

Reich, M. (2000, March). The global drug gap. *Science, 17,* 1979–1981.

UNAIDS. (2002). *Report on the global HIV/AIDS epidemic 2002.* Barcelona, Spain: Author.

World Health Organization. (2004). *The world medicines situation.* Retrieved from http://apps.who.int/medicinedocs/pdf/s6160e/s6160e.pdf

Websites

ACT Consortium: http://www.actconsortium.org

International Conference on Harmonisation of Technical Requirements for Registration of Pharmaceuticals for Human Use: http://www.ich.org

DUBAI

In the first decade of the 21st century, the dramatic economic development of Dubai was touted as one of the great successes of the global economy. The multicultural society of Dubai and the global reach of its business relationships made it an exemplar of a newly emerging global society. In 2006, roughly midway through Dubai's 6-year economic boom, an account by the journalist Adam Nicolson posed these questions about the wider global significance of the city-state's recent development: Is Dubai, in fact, the fulcrum of the future global trading and financial system? Is it, in embryo, what London was to the 19th century and Manhattan to the 20th? Not the modern center of the Arab world but, more than that, the Arab center of the modern world?

At the time, Dubai's extraordinary construction and real estate–led growth was receiving worldwide press and had garnered academic attention and seized the public imagination. The emirate, one of the seven states of the United Arab Emirates (UAE), was growing at an average annual rate of over 8% and was said to be adding between 100,000 and 150,000 new people to its estimated population of 1.4 million every year. This population was global in its origins: Expatriates and migrants from allegedly over 200 countries accounted for some 85% of this total. Some 350,000 people alone were construction workers, largely from South Asia, living in poor conditions in labor camps in the desert. Residential, hotel, retail, and office space all saw huge increases as the city expanded upward and outward.

The boom was neither novel, as it is often presented, nor accidental. Real estate development was, rather, central to the growth strategy of the ruling al-Maktoum family, under Sheikh Mohammed bin Rachid al-Maktoum. This strategy was directed at the realization of the family's long-run ambition for the city-state: to rise to global city status and become the acknowledged trading, commercial, financial, and tourism hub of the Middle East, and a key entrepôt for a region spanning Asia, sub-Saharan Africa, and Europe. This realization was to be built on a half-century-long tradition of infrastructure development promoted by the family, notably the large-scale port, airport, free zone, airline, highway, and telecommunications projects constructed from the 1960s onward in service of Dubai's regional trading hub role.

With government as principal strategist, organizer, and actor, the boom saw an acceleration in the pace and intensity of urban and infrastructure development. New economic opportunities, especially in construction and real estate, business services, and tourism and leisure, were simultaneously created and housed. Learning particularly from Singapore's experience, Dubai, like Shanghai at the time, explicitly followed a global city strategy.

Although this is often overlooked, Dubai's traditional economic strengths of shipping, aviation, and trade were also expanded. New port, airport, and related facilities were located on or adjacent to the coastline. This stimulated the further development of advanced business service and technology-based firms housed in purpose-built, incentive-laden business zones, or "cities," as they are called, as well as export-based heavy and, increasingly, light industrial enterprises, located in nearby free trade zones.

A small number of state-owned or state-backed real estate firms—Dubai Investment Corporation's listed Emaar, Dubai World's Nakheel, and property entities within the Sheikh Mohammed–owned Dubai Holding—controlled up to an estimated 70% of the market. Excess global liquidity from 2002 onward and the petrodollar surpluses of the Gulf States from mid-decade played a crucial underpinning role, as did the availability of a cheap and super-exploitable migrant construction workforce.

The firms were strongly encouraged to compete in outdoing one another in developing large-scale, expensive "iconic" projects, of which the best known were Nakheel's offshore developments, the three Palm Islands and the World, and Emaar's 828-meter tower, which opened as the world's tallest building in early 2010. To deliver development on this scale, real estate development firms large and small were driven to borrow massively from capital markets.

Well into 2008, Dubai's real estate–led growth strategy seemed to have been hugely successful. After the global economic crisis hit in September 2008, however, the real estate market crashed as spectacularly as it had risen. Housing prices and rents fell, reportedly by an average of 50%, the following year, and construction projects were put on hold or canceled all over the city. Out-migration rather than population growth started to occur. The indebtedness of Dubai's government and government-owned companies was soon revealed to be as high as $80 billion, some $25 billion of it due by the end of 2010.

Initially, Dubai's ruling family appeared to be in denial at the scale of the bust, despite an initial bailout of $10 billion in February 2009 by oil-rich Abu Dhabi, which dominates the federal government, through the UAE central bank. This posture became far more difficult to maintain after a descent into well-documented crisis late the same year, when Dubai World acknowledged its inability to meet a scheduled $4 billion debt repayment.

The period since then has seen a further $10 billion bailout from Abu Dhabi, and significant restructuring of the state's real estate companies. In total, these companies face annual debt repayments of $15 to $20 billion in the period to 2013. The road ahead for the city-state's economy is difficult and uncertain.

In this respect, Dubai can be seen as a national exemplar of how a real estate- and construction-driven growth strategy reached its real limits as it faced and responded to global economic crisis. Nonetheless, the question posed earlier—about Dubai's global role and significance—remains wholly relevant. The wider response to economic crisis by Dubai's rulers has been, in fact, a kind of "back to the future" move: to revisit, rethink, and revalidate the city-state's core business, its regional hub role—if not as the Arab center of the modern world, then certainly as the modern world's Arab center.

Throughout the global economic crisis, aviation, logistics, and tourism all performed better than real estate. Trade and shipping have largely recovered. Investment in these sectors continues in Dubai. Despite excesses, the boom has left Dubai with unparalleled infrastructure assets and overall endowment. Dubai is still the hub for a large region and a key point for conducting business. The necessary physical and economic infrastructure is unequaled in the Middle East and North Africa, if not more widely. Dubai stands to benefit from a sustained recovery in the global economy and will then attempt to capitalize—again—on that.

Robin Bloch

See also Natural Gas; Oil; Organization of Petroleum Exporting Countries (OPEC); Petroleum Geopolitics; Regional Identities; Tourism Sector

Further Readings

Bloch, R. (2010). Dubai's long goodbye. *International Journal of Urban and Regional Research, 34*(4), 943–951.

Davidson, C. M. (2008). *Dubai: The vulnerability of success*. London: Hurst.

Davis, M. (2006). Fear and money in Dubai. *New Left Review, 41,* 47–68.

Elsheshtawy, Y. (2004). Redrawing boundaries: Dubai, an emerging global city. In Y. Elsheshtawy (Ed.), *Planning Middle Eastern cities: An urban kaleidoscope in a globalizing world* (pp. 169–199). London: Routledge.

Krane, J. (2009). *Dubai: The story of the world's fastest city*. London: Atlantic Books.

Nicolson, A. (2006, February 13). Boom town. *The Guardian.* Retrieved from http://www.guardian.co.uk/business/2006/feb/13/unitedarabemirates.travel

Pacione, M. (2005). City profile: Dubai. *Cities, 22*(3), 255–265.

Parker, I. (2005, October 17). The mirage: In Dubai, a building boom unlike any other. *New Yorker,* pp. 128–143.

DYNASTIES

The term *dynasty* refers to a succession of leaders from the same family who exert extraordinary political and/or economic influence across generations. Dynasties that are most relevant to global politics are the political elites of states whose political systems are monarchies (as opposed to republics).

The Role of Dynasties in Global Politics and Economics

Almost all contemporary monarchies are based on what can be called the *dynastic principle*: The rule is handed over from one member of the ruling family to another, mostly from the father to the son. Yet, two qualifications have to be taken into account. First, nonaristocratic dynasties, such as the Rockefellers or Kennedys, have played a role in global politics and economics. Second, not all dynasties that nominally head a state exert real political power. For instance, the British royal family no longer holds much influence or authority.

Nonaristocratic dynasties play only a limited role in global politics, although in the United States, some dynasties such as the Kennedys have indeed exerted political influence over the course of generations. The Bush family managed to send two descendants to the White House. Yet, in general, nonaristocratic dynasties play a much bigger role in economics than in politics because capitalism encourages the intergenerational transfer of material values, whereas in politics the republican principle promotes nonfamilial patterns of elite recruitment. Thus, while running a state like a family enterprise has become the exception in modern politics, despite the trend to stock corporations, dynasties are still common in economic systems dominated by private actors.

Nonaristocratic dynasties often owe their eminence not only to their wealth but also to their donations and sometimes their lifestyle. Many of the most prominent, globally renowned dynasties are among the richest in the present day; at the same time, many of them, such as the Rothschilds (and, to a lesser degree, the Rockefellers), have undergone a process of rapid rise and relative fall whose pronounced historical model appears to have also been the fate of the Fuggers, who rose from a small tanner family in 14th-century Swabia to one of the first global merchant dynasties in the 15th and 16th centuries. Although to date the Fuggers play an economic role in their headquarters in the German city of Augsburg and surrounding regions, their impact on the global economy has been insignificant for centuries.

In politics, aristocratic dynasties exist on most continents: in Africa, Asia, Europe, and Oceania. However, it is striking that the Arab world hosts comparatively more dynastic rules than other regions. Indeed, 8 of the 21 members of the Arab League—the membership of Libya was suspended in February 2011—are ruled on the basis of the dynastic principle. Moreover, Arab dynasties are also set apart by the facts that all of them, in essence, control internal politics, and some of them, such as Saudi Arabia, exert much higher influence on global politics than most monarchies in other parts of the world, such as Tonga.

Most dynastic rules became extinguished in the 20th century; others survived as toothless tigers in the form of constitutional monarchies. Dynastical rules could not keep up with the expectations of enlightened citizens in terms of participation rights and services to be provided by the state. Thus, they were replaced by republics whose recruitment pattern of political elites is much more inclusive. One of the interesting questions for global politics is why some dynastic regimes survived and others did not.

It is striking that many of the surviving dynasties that exert real political power—such as the Gulf monarchies—have a comparatively small population. In fact, it is plausible that smallness makes governing less complex and thereby easier for a dynasty to internally meet the challenges of modernization. Still, many other small dynasties disappeared. Why did those remaining survive? Moreover, why were these small monarchies—weak as they are vis-à-vis external enemies—not swallowed by a bigger neighboring country as was the case with many mini-dynasties in 19th-century Germany?

Oil Monarchies

The first reason why so many Arab dynasties remained in power is that—the exceptional cases of Morocco and Jordan notwithstanding—high income was at their disposal. When Gamal Abdel Nasser seized power in Egypt in 1952 and abolished the Egyptian monarchy, he also claimed hegemonic power over the Arab world, thereby threatening the dynastic rules in the Gulf countries. In the critical period of the 1950s and 1960s, however, major Gulf monarchies such as Saudi Arabia and Kuwait, ranked among the least developed and poorest countries worldwide at the end of World War II, transformed into oil economies.

The making of strong monarchies buttressed by high oil exports was mainly a result of U.S. determination rather than of local actors. When the defeat of Nazi Germany became conceivable, the United States decided to base its future hegemony over the capitalist system on oil as its dominant source of energy, thereby taking advantage of the discovery of incommensurably cheap oil fields in the Gulf area. Thus, on the one hand, the U.S. administration challenged the supremacy of British Petroleum in the Gulf and invested great efforts to pave the way for the U.S. oil industry into this area, particularly in Saudi Arabia. On the other hand, U.S. oil majors became involved in a consortia system: To stabilize the then weak Saudi dynasty, the government in Washington impelled "their" companies to pay royalties to the Saudi kingdom; in free negotiations, the weak Saudi government would not have been able to produce such a favorable outcome. Although the oil companies were compensated through exemptions from the U.S. Treasury, the design of the system was political rather than economic, thereby enabling the emergence of real statehood in the Gulf area.

Exporting oil empowered the Gulf monarchies to establish a strong state-centered rule vis-à-vis a weakened society. An essential prerequisite for that development was the rent character of oil income. A rent is an earning that is not balanced by investment or labor. As a result of geological particularities on the Arab peninsula, the production costs of Gulf oil are much lower than elsewhere in the world. Therefore, Gulf oil achieves a price that exceeds its production costs several times over. At the same time, due to complex conveying conditions, the appropriation of the oil rent requires a minimum of centrality, which is why it goes into the pockets of the state bureaucracy rather than to private actors. Contrary to entrepreneurs, rentiers such as state bureaucracies in the Gulf are not forced to reinvest the bulk of their income in order to accrue one in the future. Rather, the rent is to the free disposal of the rentier. Therefore, since the 1950s, state bureaucracies of the Gulf have been in the position to depoliticize their societies.

In comparison to many other monarchies, dynasties of the Gulf enjoyed two major advantages when they became exposed to republican challengers. First, they had at their disposal a fairly high rent income generated from abroad; second, the societies were very poor. Therefore, rather than taxing their societies and thereby provoking participation ambitions according to the principle of the American War of Independence "No Taxation Without Representation," the regimes legitimized their rules by distributing financial means in various forms, such as providing subsidies, offering career opportunities, and donating social services. Thus, the regular relationship between the state and the society was reversed: Rather than receiving taxes, the state alimented the society. Thereby, threats to overthrow the dynastic rule from within were significantly reduced.

A second reason to help explain why the Gulf monarchies survived is military protection from Western states (i.e., Great Britain and the United States). In the period commencing after the takeover of Egypt by Nasser and concluding with the devastating Arab defeat in the Six-Day War in 1967, which Malcolm H. Kerr has labeled the "Arab Cold War," the conflict between republics and monarchies was indeed systemic. The republics, which came into being as the results of what Ellen K. Trimberger has called "revolutions from above," launched a decided modernization program; they had two incentives to threaten the monarchies to which purpose the ideology of Pan-Arabism was perfectly suited. From a political point of view, they were interested in "harmonizing" their political environment, that is, in exporting their then revolutionary principle of Arab republicanism to the whole of the Arab world (and to finally "reunite" it to one strong entity). Furthermore, from an economic standpoint, the monarchies appeared as an attractive prey because of their oil richness.

Despite their control of significant resources, the small and low-population states of the Gulf were vulnerable as a result of their weak military capabilities. During the Arab Cold War, military dependence of the Gulf States on Western actors was obvious, in some cases still executed in imperialist raiment. Thus, Kuwait gained its independence only in 1961. The only strong foothold the Mashriq republics could get hold of in the Gulf was in oil-poor Yemen, where Egypt and Saudi Arabia fought a proxy war from 1962 to 1967. Moreover, following the end of the Arab Cold War and the 1981 establishment of the Gulf Cooperation Council, designed as a security alliance, the Gulf monarchies continued to remain dependent on Western protection. Thus, Kuwait proved to be incapable of countering Iraq's invasion in 1990 without U.S. interference in 1991, which was crucial to maintaining the city-state's independence.

The monarchies had been on the defensive vis-à-vis the republics in the 1950s and 1960s, but around 1970 the tide turned. As a result of Egypt's and Syria's defeat in the 1967 June War and the oil revolution of the early 1970s, the Gulf monarchies gained power in relation to the republics of the Mashriq. The Gulf States, particularly Saudi Arabia and Kuwait, used their gains in financial strength to establish the regional system of "Petrolism," as Bahgat Korany has called it, which, apart from labor flows from the capital-poor to the oil-rich countries, mainly consisted of budget support and other financial transactions in favor of the Mashriq.

Yet, the conflict between republics and monarchies left its mark on the dynastic rules. To survive the Arab Cold War, the dynasties had to adapt to their new political environment by copying major measures promoted by their republic enemies such as establishing modern bureaucracies. However, as a result of possessing high financial capabilities, they managed to avoid falling victim to the "king's dilemma." According to Samuel Huntington, a king perishes either because he fails to modernize or, if he does, because he is unable to meet the expectations of actors created by modernization. In contemporary Arab politics in general, the degree of modernization does not appear to be higher among republics than monarchies. The crisis the Arab world has been experiencing for the past few decades is in fact mainly a crisis of the Arab republics. Some of them even diluted the republican principle of elite recruitment: For instance, in Syria, the presidential chair was passed from father to son in 2000.

The development of the Arab uprising of 2011 (which is an ongoing process during the production of this entry) so far confirms major findings presented earlier. With the exception of Bahrain, all other monarchies of the Gulf have managed to maintain stable rules, whereas the regimes of most republics have been shattered. Oil wealth and size indeed appear to be a major explanatory factor since—with the significant exception of Libya—the comparatively stable monarchies tend to be both oil-wealthier and smaller in size than the relatively destabilized Arab republics.

Conclusion: Causes for the Survival of Arab Monarchies

It must be emphasized that oil abundance is neither a sufficient nor a necessary condition for the survival of monarchies. In Iraq (1958), Libya (1969), and Iran (1979), monarchies were toppled that were major recipients of oil revenues. These examples show that some(times) monarchies (as also sometimes republics) are overstrained with using financial resources in a functional way to strengthen their (authoritarian) rule. Yet, oil richness is also not a necessary condition for the survival of (Arab) dynastic rules. For example, Morocco and Jordan survived without oil, and some regimes, such as the Omani, benefited from oil rents only fairly late. In these cases, other factors offer plausible explanations. For instance, the Hashemite Kingdom of Jordan owes its survival to the interest of both Israel and the West in having an island of conservatism and stability in the middle of one of the most turbulent world areas. As a result of this strategic setting, the Jordanian regime enjoys political rents, that is, external budget support, whose political feature is similar to oil rent in that it goes to the free disposal of the recipient. To conclude, ceteris paribus, oil abundance and, often related to that, Western interest in stability appear to be strong factors in explaining that the Arab world stands out for the survival of comparatively many regimes based on the dynastic principle.

Martin Beck

See also Imperialism; Legitimacy; Oil; Organization of Petroleum Exporting Countries (OPEC); Petroleum Economy; Petroleum Geopolitics; State–Civil Society Relations; Taxation

Further Readings

Beblawi, H., & Luciani, G. (Eds.). (1987). *The rentier state*. London: Croom Helm.

Fähndrich, H. (Ed.). (2005). *Vererbte Macht: Monarchien und Dynastien in der arabischen Welt* [Inherited power: Monarchies and dynasties in the Arab World]. Frankfurt, Germany: Campus.

Nahas, M. (1985). State-systems and revolutionary challenge: Nasser, Khomeini, and the Middle East. *International Journal of Middle East Studies, 17*, 507–527.